THE BEST LIGHT RECIPE

A BEST RECIPE CLASSIC

THE
BEST
LIGHT
RECIPE

A BEST RECIPE CLASSIC

BY THE EDITORS OF

COOK'S ILLUSTRATED

PHOTOGRAPHY

CARL TREMBLAY

DANIEL J. VAN ACKERE

ILLUSTRATIONS

JOHN BURGOYNE

AMERICA'S TEST KITCHEN

BROOKLINE, MASSACHUSETTS

America's Test Kitchen
17 Station Street
Brookline, MA 02445

ISBN 0-936184-97-3
Library of Congress Cataloging-in-Publication Data
The Editors of *Cook's Illustrated*

The Best Light Recipe
Would you make 28 light cheesecakes to find one you'd actually want to eat? We did. Here are 300 lower fat recipes that put flavor first.

1st Edition

ISBN 0-936184-97-3 (hardcover): $35
I. Cooking. I. Title
2006

Manufactured in the United States of America

10 9 8 7 6 5 4 3 2 1

Distributed by America's Test Kitchen, 17 Station Street, Brookline, MA 02445

Senior Editor: Lori Galvin
Senior Food Editor: Julia Collin Davison
Associate Editor: Keith Dresser
Assistant Editor: Charles Kelsey
Editorial Assistant: Elizabeth Wray Emery
Test Cooks: Rachel Toomey; Diane Unger
Nutrition Consultant: Randi Beranbaum MS, RD
Series Designer: Amy Klee
Jacket Designer: Richard Oriolo
Book Production Specialist: Ronald Bilodeau
Interior and back cover photographers: Carl Tremblay and Daniel J. van Ackere
Front cover photographer: Keller + Keller
Front cover food styling: Mary Jane Sawyer
Interior and back cover food styling: Marie Piraino; Mary Jane Sawyer
Illustrator: John Burgoyne
Senior Production Manager: Jessica Lindheimer Quirk
Copyeditor: Cheryl Redmond
Proofreader: Debra Hudak
Indexer: Elizabeth Parson

Note: The nutritional values for the recipes in this book were calculated using The Food Processor, Version 7.5 (ESHA Research).

Pictured on back of jacket: Guacamole (page 18), Meat and Cheese Lasagna (page 180),
Chicken Parmesan (page 201), Brownies (page 333), and New York Cheesecake (page 351).

CONTENTS

PREFACE

FOR YEARS, I HAVE PREACHED THE BENEFITS of ignoring fat and calories. (I admit that I am blessed with a rapid metabolism that precludes weight gain.) I have even suggested that the individual who invented low-fat cheesecake ought to be exiled to a small island in the Pacific. Who needs low-fat brownies? Why would anyone want to reduce fat? If you eat a varied diet, use common sense, and stay away from processed foods, you can avoid the tyranny of calorie and cholesterol counting. After all, that is what Julia Child preached for the duration of her very long career.

So why am I writing the preface to a book entitled *The Best Light Recipe?* Good question.

The answer is to be found in a test kitchen tasting of cheesecakes conducted two years ago. I told our culinary staff that if they could produce a low-fat cheesecake that was almost as good as the high-fat version, I would have to agree that the notion of a "light" cookbook made sense. I tasted three recipes that day: our own regular cheesecake from *The Best Recipe,* a new lower fat recipe that the kitchen had just developed, and a third recipe from someone else's low-fat cookbook. This last recipe, from a well-known cookbook author, turned out just as I had expected: pasty, gummy, and unsatisfying. No surprise, I loved the cheesecake from *The Best Recipe,* but our new lower fat version was substantially creamier. That made the case for this book: Perhaps our test kitchen could make lighter recipes taste better.

Sure, I still believe that a good helping of common sense is the key ingredient in healthy eating. We serve our kids fruit for dessert most nights of the week, we often eat produce from our own root cellar (potatoes, carrots, beets, and apples), in the summers our cooking is centered on whatever is in the garden, and we don't eat between meals. (OK, maybe the kids do.) But, as we discovered in working on this book, our test kitchen could make "light" recipes taste much better. (How about removing the grated beets from the low-fat chocolate cake recipe, for example?) And we found plenty of naturally healthy recipes in need of improvement, which our kitchen accomplished through the rigorous application of better cooking technique. All in all, not a bad contribution to the world of home cooking.

I often think that I should have been born around 1800. I still believe that hay should be mowed with a team of horses, that milk ought to be served up warm and frothy from the cow out back, that a wood cookstove is the ultimate kitchen appliance, that radio is vastly preferable to television, and that a New England boiled dinner is equivalent to culinary heaven. Still, despite my personal motto, "Always wrong but never in doubt," I have grown open to change.

But I do insist that if the culinary world is going to demand new recipes and new approaches to food, then our test kitchen still has to be committed to excellence, or, as we often say around here, "If we wouldn't eat it, why should you?"

For my part, I am happy to have a second helping of our light cheesecake just because it tastes so good. After all, I could use the calories!

Christopher Kimball
Founder and Editor
Cook's Illustrated Magazine

INTRODUCTION

LET'S FACE IT. IN THE TEST KITCHEN, OUR GOAL has always been clear: Develop the best recipe possible. Only rarely have we stopped to consider the fat or calorie content of the food we make. *The Best Light Recipe* is different. In response to the steadily increasing clamor from you, our readers, for "lighter" food, we decided to create a book that does take fat and calories into account—but without abandoning our quest for quality.

We've eaten our share of misguided light recipes, so the sheer challenge of coming up with something better—much better—really intrigued us. Could we discover a whole host of techniques that would lower the fat and the calories without sacrificing the flavor? What about all those low-fat and nonfat products on the market—which ones are worth using, and what's the best way to use them? In short, we were curious. We wanted to see if we could find a way to make "light" recipes just as good as every other recipe we make here in the test kitchen.

We also wanted to come up with recipes for "real" food—food that most people eat for dinner on a typical weeknight: cheesy chicken enchiladas, fluffy mashed potatoes, and fudgy brownies. At the heart of this book are our lighter versions of this classic, high-fat American fare. And while all the recipes in the book have accompanying nutritional analyses, for these particular recipes we have given you nutritional information about the classic version, too (the numbers shown are the average of several published recipes), so you can see how our lightened version stacks up.

And what about that food we all eat when our doctors (or our waistlines) are telling us we need to cut back? We'd be lying if we said we enjoyed broiled chicken breasts or plain brown rice with steamed veggies night after night, so we decided to take a hard look at "naturally" light recipes, too, dishes we know we should eat more of (if only they tasted better).

With flavor as our ultimate goal, we tested just about every low-fat and nonfat product on the market as well as every odd fat substitute imaginable. Our special "Testing Notes" feature runs throughout the book and tells this story—what worked, what didn't—and additional boxes on ingredients give you the lowdown on everything from low-fat peanut butter and vegetable oil sprays to nonfat dairy and sugar substitutes.

Often the key to success was not as simple as substituting a low-fat (or nonfat) ingredient for a full-fat one. Sometimes a different technique was the key (like toasting crumbs for chicken Parmesan to give it that pan-fried flavor or using just a teaspoon of oil and covering the pot when sweating vegetables for a soup or stew, which saves lots of calories at the outset). Every technique we discovered is highlighted as a "Core Technique" so you can put it to work in your own recipes—time and time again.

But some of the recipes we tried to remake simply didn't pass muster (see, for example, "Low-Fat Pie Crust: Is it Possible?" on page 354). In those cases, we opted not to include the recipe. Nor did we include any recipe that relied on smoke and mirrors to reduce fat and calories, like beef stew with only one forkful of beef and a preponderance of vegetables or cookies about the size of quarter.

It is our hope that as you read through this book, you'll find many tips and techniques that will serve you in all of your cooking, helping you to prepare more food that is both healthful and satisfying. Whether you're using milk and cornstarch instead of cream and butter to make a simple pan sauce (this really works) or reserving the good olive oil to drizzle on your pasta before serving (when you can use less and it will add the most flavor), you'll find that the tips and techniques in this book will last over a lifetime of cooking.

A Note on Conversions

SOME SAY COOKING IS A SCIENCE AND AN art. We would say that geography has a hand in it, too. Flour milled in the United Kingdom and elsewhere will feel and taste different from flour milled in the United States. So we cannot promise that the loaf of bread you bake in Canada or England will taste the same as a loaf baked in the States, but we can offer guidelines for converting weights and measures. We also recommend that you rely on your instincts when making our recipes. Refer to the visual cues provided. If the bread dough hasn't "come together in a ball," as described, you may need to add more flour—even if the recipe doesn't tell you so. You be the judge. For more information on conversions and ingredient equivalents, visit our Web site at www.cooksillustrated.com and type "conversion chart" in the search box.

The recipes in this book were developed using standard U.S. measures following U.S. government guidelines. The charts below offer equivalents for U.S., metric, and Imperial (U.K.) measures. All conversions are approximate and have been rounded up or down to the nearest whole number. For example:

1 teaspoon = 4.9292 milliliters, rounded up to 5 milliliters

1 ounce = 28.3495 grams, rounded down to 28 grams

Volume Conversions

U.S.	METRIC
1 teaspoon	5 milliliters
2 teaspoons	10 milliliters
1 tablespoon	15 milliliters
2 tablespoons	30 milliliters
¼ cup	59 milliliters
⅓ cup	79 milliliters
½ cup	118 milliliters
¾ cup	177 milliliters
1 cup	237 milliliters
1¼ cups	296 milliliters
1½ cups	355 milliliters
2 cups	473 milliliters
2½ cups	592 milliliters
3 cups	710 milliliters
4 cups (1 quart)	0.946 liter
1.06 quarts	1 liter
4 quarts (1 gallon)	3.8 liters

Weight Conversions

OUNCES	GRAMS
½	14
¾	21
1	28
1½	43
2	57
2½	71
3	85
3½	99
4	113
4½	128
5	142
6	170
7	198
8	227
9	255
10	283
12	340
16 (1 pound)	454

Conversions for Ingredients Commonly Used in Baking

Baking is an exacting science. Because measuring by weight is far more accurate than measuring by volume, and thus more likely to achieve reliable results, in our recipes we provide ounce measures in addition to cup measures for many ingredients. Refer to the chart below to convert these measures into grams.

INGREDIENT	OUNCES	GRAMS
1 cup all-purpose flour*	5	142
1 cup whole-wheat flour	5½	156
1 cup granulated (white) sugar	7	198
1 cup packed brown sugar (light or dark)	7	198
1 cup confectioners' sugar	4	113
1 cup cocoa powder	3	85
Butter†		
4 tablespoons (½ stick, or ¼ cup)	2	57
8 tablespoons (1 stick, or ½ cup)	4	113
16 tablespoons (2 sticks, or 1 cup)	8	227

*U.S. all-purpose flour, the most frequently used flour in this book, does not contain leaveners, as some European flours do. These leavened flours are called self-rising or self-raising. If you are using self-rising flour, take this into consideration before adding leavening to a recipe.

† In the United States, butter is sold both salted and unsalted. We generally recommend unsalted butter. If you are using salted butter, take this into consideration before adding salt to a recipe.

Oven Temperatures

FAHRENHEIT	CELSIUS	GAS MARK (IMPERIAL)
225	105	¼
250	120	½
275	130	1
300	150	2
325	165	3
350	180	4
375	190	5
400	200	6
425	220	7
450	230	8
475	245	9

Converting Temperatures from an Instant-Read Thermometer

We include doneness temperatures in many of our recipes, such as those for poultry, meat, and bread. We recommend an instant-read thermometer for the job. Refer to the table at left to convert Fahrenheit degrees to Celsius. Or, for temperatures not represented in the chart, use this simple formula:

Subtract 32 degrees from the Fahrenheit reading, then divide the result by 1.8 to find the Celsius reading.

EXAMPLE:
"Roast until the juices run clear when the chicken is cut with a paring knife or the thickest part of the breast registers 160 degrees on an instant-read thermometer." To convert:

$160°\ F - 32 = 128°$
$128° \div 1.8 = 71°\ C$ (rounded down from 71.11)

WELCOME TO AMERICA'S TEST KITCHEN

THIS BOOK HAS BEEN TESTED, WRITTEN, AND edited by the folks at America's Test Kitchen, a very real 2,500-square-foot kitchen located just outside of Boston. It is the home of *Cook's Illustrated* magazine and is the Monday through Friday destination for close to two dozen test cooks, editors, food scientists, tasters, and cookware specialists. Our mission is to test recipes over and over again until we understand how and why they work and until we arrive at the "best" version.

We start the process of testing a recipe with a complete lack of conviction, which means that we accept no claim, no theory, no technique, and no recipe at face value. We simply assemble as many variations as possible, test a half dozen of the most promising, and taste the results blind. We then construct our own hybrid recipe and continue to test it, varying ingredients, techniques, and cooking times until we reach a consensus. The result, we hope, is the best version of a particular recipe, but we realize that only you can be the final judge of our success (or failure). As we like to say in the test kitchen, "We make the mistakes, so you don't have to."

All of this would not be possible without a belief that good cooking, much like good music, is indeed based on a foundation of objective technique. Some people like spicy foods and others don't, but there is a right way to sauté, there is a best way to cook a pot roast, and there are measurable scientific principles involved in producing perfectly beaten, stable egg whites. This is our ultimate goal: to investigate the fundamental principles of cooking so that you become a better cook. It is as simple as that.

You can watch us work (in our actual test kitchen) by tuning in to *America's Test Kitchen* (www.americastestkitchen.com) on public television or by subscribing to *Cook's Illustrated* magazine (www.cooksillustrated.com), which is published every other month. We welcome you into our kitchen, where you can stand by our side as we test our way to the "best" recipes in America.

1

APPETIZERS

PARTY FOODS ARE FUN, FESTIVE, TASTY, AND, unfortunately, often so rich that they fill us up before we even sit down to dinner. We're talking creamy dips, crispy chips, fried finger foods, and bacon-wrapped everything. We wanted to come up with lighter hors d'oeuvres without resorting to serving our guests rice cakes and celery sticks; after all, parties are for festive occasions. And we also wanted to avoid the same pitfalls other cookbooks fall into in developing lighter fare, such as relying on odd substitutions. (Tofu guacamole, anyone?) In short, we aimed to develop lighter versions of our favorite party foods that are tasty enough to complement a cocktail or glass of wine and light enough to leave room for dinner.

We had our work cut out for us, but some decisions were easy. Right off the bat, we nixed any fried foods. As alluring as buffalo wings and popcorn shrimp are, the reality is, they fill you up fast—not to mention the greasy finger factor. And, as much as we love a nice cheese board, we know that it is far too easy to spoil dinner indulging in this classic cocktail party centerpiece. Some may argue that low-fat cheeses are an option, but we find they work better in recipes such as lasagna, macaroni and cheese, and the like. We did, however, find a tasty alternative to the usual cream cheese spread—one made with yogurt cheese. (Read more about yogurt cheese on page 8.) We also found ways to use boldly flavored cheeses that are naturally lower in fat, such as Parmesan, in recipes such as Roasted Artichoke Dip (page 13) and Crostini with Spinach and Parmesan (page 21).

No party would be complete without dips, but we knew this would be a particular challenge. A couple swipes of a carrot stick through a traditional onion dip can easily spin the calorie count out of control. We tried recipes for low-fat dips from other cookbooks, many of which rely on nonfat dairy products such as sour cream, yogurt, and mayonnaise, but couldn't get past their off flavors and odd chalky textures. Still, we aimed to put great tasting dips on our buffet table. And by combining a few key low-fat dairy products with the judicious use of highly flavored ingredients—such as chipotle peppers, caramelized onions, and roasted garlic—we were able to replicate the creamy consistency and bold flavors of our favorite full-fat dips such as Green Goddess Dip (page 4) and Caramelized Onion Dip (page 4). We also offer a number of quick-to-prepare low-fat dips, many of which rely on pantry staples you probably already have on hand.

Some of the recipes we included might surprise you, like Stuffed Mushrooms (page 23) and Roasted Artichoke Dip (page 13). Most think of mushroom caps simply as vehicles for cheesy, buttery breaded stuffings, but we worked to punch up the mushroom flavor by roasting the caps and incorporating the stems into the stuffing for an extra hit of mushroom in every bite. And when we revisited hot artichoke dip, a longtime favorite, we discovered that this '70s relic, albeit tasty, was in desperate need of a makeover. We not only cut out a lot of the fat, but entirely reinvented this dip by tossing the canned artichokes in favor of the fresher tasting, but just as convenient, frozen variety.

We also aimed to emphasize convenience in our recipes. Because entertaining poses its own challenges—answering the door, pouring drinks, catching up with friends—we wanted to minimize the recipe preparation. Most of our recipes can be prepared ahead and a few of our hot appetizers can be assembled and baked just before serving.

Lastly, the question we hear most often about party foods concerns quantity. How many types of hors d'oeuvres and how many pieces are required? The answer depends on how long you plan to be serving the appetizers and what follows. Some examples: If you plan a short cocktail hour (let's say 45 minutes to an hour, while you wait for all of your guests to arrive) followed by a multicourse meal, you may want to serve just one or two appetizers. (If you are expecting a larger crowd, you might consider making three.) Provide three or four pieces per person if you plan on one hour or less for cocktails. For more than one hour, make at least two appetizers and plan on four to six pieces per person. Take into account how rich and filling the appetizers you have chosen are. Guests are likely to be satisfied by one or two slices of topped crostini, or might only want a few veggies with dip from a crudités platter. Don't knock yourself out; you want to enjoy the party, too.

TEST KITCHEN MAKEOVER

CREAMY PARTY DIPS

ALTHOUGH WE ENJOY MODERN-STYLE DIPS such as salsas, hummus, and bean dips for their eclectic flavors, tasty ingredients, and lighter, healthier nature, there is still something very satisfying about dipping a crisp carrot stick or salty pita chip into a cool, savory, creamy dip. With this in mind, we set out to develop recipes for low-fat creamy dips that pack as much flavor-punch as their full-fat counterparts, and are as low in fat as the modern-style dips out there.

We first tackled the creamy dip base. Most dips rely on sour cream or mayonnaise or a combination of both (as the test kitchen does in our recipe for full-fat creamy party dips). For our lower fat dip, we logically turned to nonfat and low-fat versions. After testing them, we came to some firm conclusions.

Tasters disliked the nonfat mayonnaise because of its overwhelming sweetness and gluey, gloppy texture, but liked the creamy texture and mild flavor of the reduced-fat mayonnaise, though some tasters did notice an off "sweet" flavor. Nonfat sour cream was thrown out for tasting "too thin" and "flat," and for having a "persistently tart flavor," but tasters were pleased with the low-fat sour cream.

Our traditional full-fat dip base uses equal parts mayo and sour cream, but in using the low-fat varieties, we found that the sweetness of the reduced-fat mayo was overtaking the tang of the sour cream. This shortfall was easily corrected by reducing the amount of mayonnaise and increasing the amount of sour cream. Tasters liked a combination of 1½ cups low-fat sour cream and ¾ cup reduced-fat mayonnaise best because it was "richer, with a creamier texture and a more well-balanced flavor." However, some commented that it still lacked brightness and was a bit too thick. A tablespoon of fresh lemon juice solved the brightness issue and we used ⅓ cup of water to thin out our dip to an ideal consistency—perfect for dipping and scooping. With our dip base in hand, it was time to tackle flavorings.

Throughout our testing we realized that these dips needed to be seasoned with gusto; however, we had to keep a check on the calorie count and fat content. That meant using generous amounts of ingredients such as fresh herbs, and smaller amounts of boldly flavored ingredients such as caramelized onions, roasted garlic, blue cheese, and sun-dried tomatoes, where a little goes a long way. Mincing them also helps distribute their flavor more evenly. These dips might not be as convenient as ripping open a pack of soup mix, but they taste a whole lot better and our use of lower fat dairy products makes them a better option when you're watching calories and fat.

MAKEOVER AT A GLANCE

–Classic–
Green Goddess Dip
(per serving)

Calories: 180	Cholesterol: 20 mg
Fat: 18 g	Saturated Fat: 4.5 g

–Light–
Green Goddess Dip
(per serving)

Calories: 60	Cholesterol: 10 mg
Fat: 4 g	Saturated Fat: 2 g

How We Did It

- Used a combination of low-fat sour cream and reduced-fat mayonnaise for a creamy base with a well-rounded flavor
- Added water to the base to make it less stiff and more dip-able
- Used generous amounts of seasonings such as garlic, minced anchovies, tarragon, parsley, and chives to compensate for the lack of fat

Green Goddess Dip
MAKES ABOUT 2 ½ CUPS

Be sure to mince the garlic cloves and the anchovies before adding them to the food processor or they won't break into fine enough pieces in the dip.

1 ¼	cups low-fat sour cream
¾	cup reduced-fat mayonnaise
⅓	cup water
¼	cup packed fresh parsley leaves
1	tablespoon fresh tarragon leaves
1	tablespoon juice from 1 lemon
2	anchovy fillets, rinsed, patted dry, and minced
2	medium garlic cloves, minced or pressed through a garlic press (about 2 teaspoons)
¼	cup minced fresh chives
	Salt and ground black pepper

1. Process the sour cream, mayonnaise, water, parsley, tarragon, lemon juice, anchovies, and garlic together in a food processor until smooth and creamy, stopping to scrape down the sides of the bowl with a rubber spatula as needed.

2. Transfer the mixture to a serving bowl; stir in the chives and season with salt and pepper to taste. Cover with plastic wrap and refrigerate until the flavors meld, about 1 hour. (The dip, covered, can be refrigerated for up to 2 days. Season with additional lemon juice, salt, and pepper as needed before serving.)

PER 3-TABLESPOON SERVING: Cal 60; Fat 4 g; Sat Fat 2 g; Chol 10 mg; Carb 4 g; Protein 2 g; Fiber 0 g; Sodium 170 mg

Caramelized Onion Dip
MAKES A GENEROUS 2 ½ CUPS

Caramelizing the onion brings out its natural sweetness and adds a complex flavor to this classic party dip.

1	tablespoon vegetable oil
1	large onion, minced (about 1 ¼ cups)
½	teaspoon light brown sugar
	Salt
1 ¼	cups low-fat sour cream
¾	cup reduced-fat mayonnaise
⅓	cup water
1	tablespoon cider vinegar
2	scallions, sliced thin
	Dash Worcestershire sauce (optional)
	Ground black pepper

1. Heat the oil in a 10-inch nonstick skillet over high heat until shimmering. Add the onion, brown sugar, and ¼ teaspoon salt; cook until the onion begins to soften, about 5 minutes. Reduce the heat to medium-low and continue to cook, stirring frequently, until the onion is golden brown, 20 to 25 minutes. Transfer the caramelized onion to a large plate and let cool.

2. Mix the caramelized onion, sour cream, mayonnaise, water, vinegar, scallions, and Worcestershire (if using) together in a serving bowl; season with salt and pepper to taste. Cover with plastic wrap and refrigerate until the flavors meld, about 1 hour. (The dip, covered, can be refrigerated for up to 2 days. Season with additional vinegar, salt, and pepper as needed before serving.)

PER 3-TABLESPOON SERVING: Cal 80; Fat 5 g; Sat Fat 2.5 g; Chol 10 mg; Carb 6 g; Protein 2 g; Fiber 0 g; Sodium 150 mg

HUMMUS

HUMMUS IS A TRADITIONAL COMBINATION of chickpeas and tahini (sesame seeds ground into a rich paste) seasoned with olive oil. The addition of tahini along with fruity olive oil gives hummus its characteristically rich nuttiness and creamy consistency, but also can make this dip high in fat and calories. We wanted to create a lower fat hummus—a dip mixed to a smooth, stiff, scoopable texture that would be perfect as a snack with pita chips or crudités, or as a sandwich spread.

Testing canned chickpeas against dried ones, we were impressed by the results obtained with canned chickpeas. Typically, the beans are packed in a slippery, water-based liquid, and we found that the hummus tasted cleaner when we rinsed the chickpeas before pureeing them. A 15-ounce can of chickpeas made a good-sized batch of hummus.

Tahini adds the toasted nutty flavor typical of hummus. In our research, many hummus recipes called for ¼ cup or more of tahini. With nine grams of fat per tablespoon, this amount sent our dip off the calorie charts. We tried a few batches of hummus without any tahini at all, which resulted in weak-flavored dips that just didn't taste anything like hummus. Trying various amounts of tahini, we found that 2 tablespoons yielded a rich and creamy dip with just enough of a distinct nutty flavor. Half a small clove of garlic along with a pinch of cayenne added just the right bite, and 3 tablespoons of lemon juice contributed citrusy brightness.

Last but not least, we needed to address the texture, as our dip was a bit stiff. Traditionally, hummus is thinned with generous amounts of olive oil (sometimes as much as ½ cup) which also serves to season the dip. We aimed to thin our dip without so much oil and without compromising the flavor. We tried replacing the olive oil with chicken broth (found in some recipes) and even water, but these substitutions made our dip taste insipid. Tasters found that the broth flavor was off and muddied, while the water washed out the dip's flavors. However, tasters did comment that the water had a nice clean taste, one that went well with the chickpeas. Our answer was found in a combination of olive oil and water—just 2 teaspoons of oil to bring all the flavors together and 6 tablespoons of water to make a smooth puree. Refrigerating the hummus for at least 30 minutes allowed the flavors to meld.

Just before serving, hummus is traditionally finished with a drizzle of olive oil. We opted for just a teaspoon across the top. It made for a nice presentation and was just enough to boost the taste of every bite. At last, we had reached our goal of creating a great-tasting hummus that was lighter too.

Hummus

MAKES ABOUT 1¾ CUPS

Serve hummus with Easy Homemade Pita Chips (page 12) or fresh pita breads, cut into wedges, or with crudités. Hummus also makes a great vegetarian sandwich spread—try some in a wrap. Tahini can be purchased in Middle Eastern markets as well as in the international foods aisle of many supermarkets. Be sure to use just half of a small clove of garlic or its flavor will be overwhelming.

- 1 (15-ounce) can chickpeas, drained and rinsed
- 6 tablespoons water
- 3 tablespoons juice from 1 large lemon
- 2 tablespoons tahini (see note)
- 1 tablespoon extra-virgin olive oil
- ¾ teaspoon salt
- ½ small garlic clove, minced or pressed through a garlic press (about ¼ teaspoon)
  Pinch cayenne pepper

1. Process the chickpeas, water, lemon juice, tahini, 2 teaspoons of the oil, salt, garlic, and cayenne together in a food processor until very smooth, 1 to 1½ minutes, stopping to scrape down the sides of the bowl with a rubber spatula as needed.

2. Transfer the hummus to a serving bowl; cover with plastic wrap and refrigerate until the flavors meld, about 30 minutes. (The hummus, covered, can be refrigerated for up to 2 days. Bring to room temperature and season with additional lemon juice, salt, and cayenne as needed before serving.) To serve, make a well in the center of the hummus, and drizzle the remaining teaspoon of olive oil in the well.

PER ¼-CUP SERVING: Cal 100; Fat 5 g; Sat Fat .5 g; Chol 0 mg; Carb 10 g; Protein 4 g; Fiber 3 g; Sodium 320 mg

➤ VARIATION
Roasted Red Pepper Hummus
MAKES ABOUT 2 CUPS
Roasted red peppers lend this variation a slightly sweet flavor and vivid color.

Follow the recipe for Hummus, reducing the amount of lemon juice to 2 tablespoons and the water to 2 tablespoons. Add ¾ cup jarred roasted red peppers, drained, rinsed, and thoroughly patted dry with paper towels, to the food processor with the chickpeas in step 1.

PER ¼-CUP SERVING: Cal 100; Fat 5 g; Sat Fat .5 g; Chol 0 mg; Carb 12 g; Protein 4 g; Fiber 3 g; Sodium 360 mg

FAST CREAMY DIPS

SUPERMARKET CRUDITÉ PLATTERS SEEM LIKE A HEALTHY IDEA, BUT LOOKS CAN BE DECEIVING. At the center of all those carefully arranged vegetables, there's a tub of dip, chock-full of calories, fat, and sodium. We suggest you toss this wayward dip and make your own healthy version. With our Light and Creamy Dip Base, you can whip up any number of fresh-flavored dips by stirring in one of our flavor add-ins, depending on your mood, the season, or the contents of your pantry. Better yet, cut up your own vegetables for crudités—they'll taste considerably better than the precut ones you can buy at the store.

Light and Creamy Dip Base

MAKES ABOUT 2 ½ CUPS

1 ¼ cups low-fat sour cream
¾ cup reduced-fat mayonnaise
⅓ cup water
1 tablespoon juice from 1 lemon
Salt and ground black pepper

Stir the sour cream, mayonnaise, water, and lemon juice together with a flavor add-in (see our favorites below for inspiration); season with salt and pepper to taste. Cover with plastic wrap and refrigerate until the flavors meld, about 1 hour. (The dip, covered, can be refrigerated for up to 2 days. Season with additional lemon juice, salt, and pepper as needed before serving.)

PER 3-TABLESPOON SERVING: Cal 50; Fat 4 g; Sat Fat 2 g; Chol 10 mg; Carb 3 g; Protein 2 g; Fiber 0 g; Sodium 135 mg

Flavor Add-Ins

Sun-Dried Tomato and Basil Dip

Add ¼ cup finely chopped oil-cured sun-dried tomatoes and 2 tablespoons minced fresh basil leaves.

PER 3-TABLESPOON SERVING: Cal 60; Fat 4 g; Sat Fat 2 g; Chol 10 mg; Carb 4 g; Protein 2 g; Fiber 0 g; Sodium 140 mg

Chipotle-Cilantro Dip

Use lime juice instead of lemon juice, add 2 to 4 tablespoons minced chipotle chiles plus 1 teaspoon adobo sauce, ½ cup minced fresh cilantro leaves, and 2 thinly sliced scallions.

PER 3-TABLESPOON SERVING: Cal 60; Fat 4 g; Sat Fat 2 g; Chol 10 mg; Carb 4 g; Protein 2 g; Fiber 0 g; Sodium 135 mg

Tapenade Dip

Add ¼ cup minced Kalamata olives, 1 medium garlic clove, minced, and 1 tablespoon minced fresh parsley leaves.

PER 3-TABLESPOON SERVING: Cal 70; Fat 5 g; Sat Fat 2 g; Chol 10 mg; Carb 4 g; Protein 2 g; Fiber 0 g; Sodium 210 mg

Lemon-Caper Dip

Add an additional tablespoon lemon juice, ½ teaspoon grated lemon zest, ¼ cup minced capers, and 2 tablespoons minced fresh chives.

PER 3-TABLESPOON SERVING: Cal 60; Fat 4 g; Sat Fat 2 g; Chol 10 mg; Carb 4 g; Protein 2 g; Fiber 0 g; Sodium 210 mg

Pesto Dip

Add ¼ cup chopped fresh basil leaves, ¼ cup grated Parmesan cheese, and 1 medium garlic clove, minced.

PER 3-TABLESPOON SERVING: Cal 60; Fat 4.5 g; Sat Fat 2.5 g; Chol 10 mg; Carb 4 g; Protein 3 g; Fiber 0 g; Sodium 170 mg

Blue Cheese, Scallion, and Black Pepper Dip

Add 2 tablespoons crumbled blue cheese, 2 thinly sliced scallions, and 1 teaspoon freshly cracked black pepper.

PER 3-TABLESPOON SERVING: Cal 60; Fat 4 g; Sat Fat 2 g; Chol 10 mg; Carb 4 g; Protein 2 g; Fiber 0 g; Sodium 150 mg

ROASTED RED PEPPER SPREAD

MUHAMMARA, MADE FROM ROASTED RED peppers, walnuts, and pomegranate molasses, is a popular spread made throughout the eastern Mediterranean. We wanted to develop an easy-to-prepare, lower fat version, based on pantry staples, without losing the sweet, smoky, savory flavors that make this spread so popular.

The first hurdle was the roasted peppers. Although roasting red peppers is fairly easy, we found that good-quality jarred peppers could be used (see our tasting below). The trick is to rinse them of their brine before using them, and to make sure that they are thoroughly patted dry.

Our next challenge was to find a replacement for the pomegranate molasses, which is difficult to locate in typical American supermarkets. Seeking its thick, syrupy texture and sweet-and-sour flavor, we tested a variety of pantry ingredients before coming up with a substitute. In the end, we found that a combination of lemon juice and mild molasses worked well.

Typically, the primary source of fat in this recipe comes from walnuts—most recipes call for a cup or more. Crucial to the spread's flavor and texture, walnuts were a must. We knew we couldn't do without them. The key, it turned out, lay in doing more with less. We started with just ¼ cup of nuts, but their flavor was easily diluted by the other ingredients in the spread, and the spread's texture suffered. We solved the flavor issue by toasting the nuts before incorporating them into the spread. Toasting heightened their flavor, making just a little go a long way.

Crumbled wheat crackers are another traditional ingredient in muhammara; they lend the dip flavor and texture, and help bind the dip together. Although our dip tasted great, the texture was still lacking. Since our dip was so lean, the cracker crumbs weren't binding and giving it the body we were after. We wondered if soft sandwich bread would make a better binder. It did, giving the spread a smooth, cohesive texture. When seasoned with cayenne, ground cumin, and salt, the spread required only a minimal amount of olive oil (thanks to the moisture in the bread) to bring together the dip's flavors and add finesse to its consistency.

INGREDIENTS: Roasted Red Peppers

Jarred peppers are convenient, but are all brands created equal? To find out, we collected six brands from local supermarkets. The top two brands, Divina and Greek Gourmet, were preferred for their "soft and tender texture" (Divina) and "refreshing," "piquant," "smoky" flavor (Greek Gourmet). The other brands were marked down for their lack of "roasty flavor" and for the unpleasantly overpowering flavor of the brines. These peppers tasted as if they'd been "buried under brine and acid" or were thought to have a "sweet and acidic aftertaste." The conclusion? Tasters preferred peppers with a full, smoky, roasted flavor, a brine that was spicy but not too sweet, and a tender texture.

THE BEST JARRED ROASTED RED PEPPERS
Divina peppers (left) were the top choice of tasters. Greek Gourmet peppers (right) came in a close second.

Roasted Red Pepper Spread

MAKES ABOUT 2 CUPS

Serve this dip with Easy Homemade Pita Chips (page 12), fresh pitas cut into wedges, or baguette slices. Also, try it spread in a sandwich wrap.

¼	cup walnuts
1 ⅔	cups jarred roasted red peppers, drained, rinsed, and thoroughly patted dry with paper towels
2	slices wheat or white sandwich bread, torn into quarters
3	tablespoons juice from 1 large lemon
2	tablespoons extra-virgin olive oil
1	tablespoon mild molasses
¾	teaspoon salt
¼	teaspoon ground cumin
⅛	teaspoon cayenne pepper

1. Toast the walnuts in a dry skillet over medium heat, shaking the pan occasionally, until they are fragrant, about 5 minutes. Transfer the nuts to a plate to cool.

2. Process the toasted walnuts with the remaining ingredients in a food processor until smooth, about 10 pulses. Transfer the mixture to a serving bowl; cover with plastic wrap and refrigerate until the flavors meld, about 1 hour. (The dip, covered, can be refrigerated for up to 2 days. Season with additional lemon juice, salt, and cayenne as needed before serving.) Serve the dip either cold or at room temperature.

PER 3-TABLESPOON SERVING: Cal 70; Fat 4.5 g; Sat Fat .5 g; Chol 0 mg; Carb 8 g; Protein 1; Fiber 0 g; Sodium 270 mg

YOGURT CHEESE

YOGURT CHEESE IS A TASTY LOWER CALORIE (and lower fat) alternative to both cream cheese and light cream cheese. Two tablespoons of plain low-fat yogurt cheese contain just 25 calories and .5 gram of fat (an equal amount of cream cheese contains 100 calories and 10 grams of fat and light cream cheese contains 70 calories and 5 grams of fat). Available in health food stores and Middle Eastern markets (where it's called laban or labana), yogurt cheese can also be made at home—without any special equipment. All you need is a wire mesh strainer lined with a couple of basket-style coffee filters or cheesecloth. Draining the yogurt of its liquid (the whey) results in a soft, spreadable cheese that's just a bit tangier than cream cheese. Serve yogurt cheese as is, or flavor it (see recipe variations). Spread yogurt cheese on a bagel or on a cracker—or on anything you'd serve with cream cheese. You can bake with yogurt cheese too—check out our New York Cheesecake (page 351). Yogurt cheese can also be thinned out with a little water or lemon or lime juice to make a reasonable stand-in for sour cream—try a spoonful stirred into black bean soup or dolloped onto a baked potato.

Yogurt Cheese
MAKES 1 CUP

Check the label on your yogurt since you'll want to avoid using yogurt containing modified food starch, gelatin, or gums—they prevent the yogurt from draining. You can use either regular, low-fat, or nonfat yogurt to make the cheese; however, if you're watching calories we found that low-fat yogurt offered the best balance of fat and flavor.

16   ounces (2 cups) plain low-fat yogurt (see note)

1. Following the illustrations on page 9, line a fine-mesh strainer with 3 basket-style paper coffee filters or a double layer of cheesecloth. Set the strainer over a deep container (there should be enough room for a generous 1 cup liquid to drain without touching the strainer). Spoon the yogurt into the strainer, cover tightly with plastic wrap, and refrigerate until the yogurt has released about 1 cup liquid and has a creamy, cream cheese–like texture, 10 to 12 hours (it can stay in the strainer for up to 2 days).

2. Transfer the yogurt cheese to a clean container, discarding the drained liquid, and cover with plastic wrap. (The cheese, covered, can be refrigerated for up to 1 week in the refrigerator.)

PER 2-TABLESPOON SERVING: Cal 25; Fat .5 g; Sat Fat 0 g; Chol 5 mg; Carb 3 g; Protein 2 g; Fiber 0 g; Sodium 30 mg

➤ VARIATIONS
Chipotle-Cilantro Yogurt Cheese Spread
MAKES ABOUT 1 CUP
Spread a thin layer of this yogurt cheese in a wrap with turkey, lettuce, and thinly sliced onion.

1   recipe Yogurt Cheese (see above)
1/2   canned chipotle chile in adobo, minced, plus 1 teaspoon adobo sauce
1/2   teaspoon ground cumin
1/8   teaspoon garlic powder
2   tablespoons minced fresh cilantro leaves
       Salt and ground black pepper

Stir the yogurt cheese, chipotle chile and adobo sauce, cumin, garlic powder, and cilantro together in a serving bowl; season with salt and pepper to taste. Cover with plastic wrap and refrigerate until the flavors meld, about 1 hour. (The spread, covered, can be refrigerated for up to 2 days. Bring to room temperature and season with additional salt and pepper as needed before serving.)

PER 2-TABLESPOON SERVING: Cal 25; Fat .5 g; Sat Fat 0 g; Chol 5 mg; Carb 3 g; Protein 2 g; Fiber 0 g; Sodium 30 mg

Smoked Salmon Yogurt Cheese Spread
MAKES ABOUT 1 1/4 CUPS
Serve this spread the same day it's prepared.

1	recipe Yogurt Cheese (page 8)
4	ounces smoked salmon, chopped fine
2	tablespoons minced red onion
2	tablespoons capers, drained and minced
1	tablespoon minced fresh dill
	Ground black pepper

Stir the yogurt cheese, salmon, onion, capers, and dill together in a serving bowl; season with pepper to taste. Cover with plastic wrap and refrigerate until the flavors meld, about 1 hour. Bring to room temperature and season with additional pepper as needed before serving.

PER 2-TABLESPOON SERVING: Cal 45; Fat 1.5 g; Sat Fat 0.5 g; Chol 10 mg; Carb 3 g; Protein 5 g; Fiber 0 g; Sodium 200 mg

MAKING YOGURT CHEESE

Line a fine-mesh strainer set over a deep container with 3 paper coffee filters or a double layer of cheesecloth. Spoon the yogurt into the lined strainer, cover, and refrigerate. After 10 to 12 hours, about 1 cup of the liquid will have drained out of the yogurt, and the yogurt will have a creamy, cream cheese–like consistency. Transfer the yogurt cheese to a covered container and refrigerate—it will keep for about 1 week.

Garlic and Herb Yogurt Cheese Spread
MAKES ABOUT 1 CUP
Serve this spread in a crock, accompanied by crackers, thin slices of baguette, or Crostini (page 20).

1	recipe Yogurt Cheese (page 8)
3	tablespoons minced fresh parsley leaves
1	tablespoon minced fresh tarragon leaves
1/8	teaspoon garlic powder
	Salt and ground black pepper

Stir the yogurt cheese, parsley, tarragon, and garlic powder together in a serving bowl; season with salt and pepper to taste. Cover with plastic wrap and refrigerate until the flavors meld, about 1 hour. (The spread, covered, can be refrigerated for up to 2 days. Bring to room temperature and season with additional salt and pepper as needed before serving.)

PER 2-TABLESPOON SERVING: Cal 25; Fat .5 g; Sat Fat 0 g; Chol 5 mg; Carb 3 g; Protein 2 g; Fiber 0 g; Sodium 30 mg

Red Pepper Jelly–Almond Yogurt Cheese Spread
MAKES ABOUT 1 1/4 CUPS
Finely chopped mango chutney can be used in place of the red pepper jelly.

1	recipe Yogurt Cheese (page 8)
1/4	cup hot red pepper jelly
2	tablespoons chopped toasted almonds
1	tablespoon minced fresh parsley leaves
1/2	teaspoon hot pepper sauce, or more to taste
	Salt and ground black pepper

Stir the yogurt cheese, jelly, almonds, parsley, and hot pepper sauce together in a serving bowl; season with salt and pepper to taste. Cover with plastic wrap and refrigerate until the flavors meld, about 1 hour. (The spread, covered, can be refrigerated for up to 2 days. Bring to room temperature and season with additional salt and pepper as needed before serving.)

PER 2-TABLESPOON SERVING: Cal 60; Fat 1.5 g; Sat Fat 0 g; Chol 5 mg; Carb 10 g; Protein 2 g; Fiber 0 g; Sodium 35 mg

Pimiento Yogurt Cheese Spread

MAKES ABOUT 1 1/4 CUPS

Because the olives lend the spread saltiness, you may not need to season it with additional salt.

1	recipe Yogurt Cheese (page 8)
1/4	cup pimiento-stuffed green olives, chopped
	Salt and ground black pepper

Stir the yogurt cheese and olives together in a serving bowl; season with salt and pepper to taste. Cover with plastic wrap and refrigerate until the flavors meld, about 1 hour. (The spread, covered, can be refrigerated for up to 2 days. Bring to room temperature and season with additional salt and pepper as needed before serving.)

PER 2-TABLESPOON SERVING: Cal 40; Fat 1.5 g; Sat Fat 0 g; Chol 5 mg; Carb 3 g; Protein 2 g; Fiber 0 g; Sodium 150 mg

HOT ARTICHOKE DIP

A STAPLE OF PARTY BUFFETS IN THE '70S, hot artichoke dip is an ode to convenience cooking. There are various permutations of this recipe, but most involve a simple concoction of canned artichokes, mayonnaise, and Parmesan cheese all combined in the food processor. The mixture is then poured into a baking dish, topped with buttery bread crumbs, and baked into a creamy, cheesy mass ready to be scooped up with crackers, bread-sticks, or crudités. There was some snickering going on in the test kitchen when discussing this guilty-pleasure dish, though it can't be denied that this dish disappears almost as fast as it is served. But with 240 calories and 21 grams of fat per 1/4-cup serving, there's no disputing that hot artichoke dip is out of reach for anyone intent on watching their weight. Therefore our goal was to lighten this dip substantially. In the process, we also wanted to dust off what has become something of a relic and give the flavors a fresher, less dated spin.

Right off the bat, we knew we'd need to find a replacement for the tinny-tasting canned artichoke hearts this recipe typically relies on. Fresh artichokes were too expensive and too much effort for the return (not to mention the fact that we would need to use up to six pounds). First, we turned to jarred marinated artichokes (packed in oil with herbs and spices), but they made our dip over-seasoned and greasy. Even when the artichokes were well rinsed, our dip still tasted of the marinade. We had much better success with frozen artichokes. Following the directions on the package, we cooked the artichokes in boiling water until just tender. They had a fresh, clean artichoke flavor, much preferred to that of the marinated and acrid canned varieties. Certainly this was an improvement, but their flavor was a bit muted. We turned to roasting the artichokes with olive oil, salt, and pepper until just tender and browned on

---

MAKEOVER AT A GLANCE

–Classic–
Hot Artichoke Dip
(per serving)

Calories: 240	Cholesterol: 15 mg
Fat: 21 g	Saturated Fat: 4 g

–Light–
Roasted Artichoke Dip
(per serving)

Calories: 140	Cholesterol: 10 mg
Fat: 8 g	Saturated Fat: 3 g

How We Did It

- Replaced bland, watery canned artichokes with frozen artichokes, roasted to intensify their flavor
- Used a combination of reduced-fat mayonnaise and light cream cheese for a dip base that remained creamy even after baking
- Sprayed the bread-crumb topping lightly with vegetable oil spray to encourage browning in the oven, rather than tossing the topping with butter or oil

the edges. This simple technique was a revelation, deepening and intensifying their flavor.

With the artichokes settled, we turned to the dip's other key ingredients: mayonnaise and Parmesan cheese. Choosing low-fat mayo (see page 19) was a no-brainer given our success with it in other dips. But the Parmesan was a different matter. Typical recipes for this dip use a 1-1 ratio of mayo to cheese. Did we really need all that cheese? After all, we reasoned, we'd be using real Parmesan—not the dusty stuff in the green container. We reduced the Parmesan by half, but now the dip lacked richness. In our research, we noticed that some lightened artichoke dip recipes included nonfat or low-fat sour cream or cream cheese (in addition to the mayonnaise). We gave it a try. Both nonfat and low-fat sour cream were too tangy and thinned the dip too much. Fat-free cream cheese was a big loser—it separated during baking and resulted in an unattractively curdled dip. Light cream cheese, on the other hand, was just the breakthrough we needed, and just a small amount gave the dip the creamy body and richness it lacked.

Our lightened dip was coming together, but it still needed some tweaking. We wanted to keep the simplicity of the artichoke dip intact, so we looked to flavors that would complement, not obscure, the existing flavors. Sautéed onion and garlic were a natural with the artichokes and cheese. Lemon juice lent the dip a fresh brightness and zing missing from the original dip. After trying a variety of herbs, the woodsy flavor of fresh thyme won tasters over and a pinch of cayenne gave the dip a welcome bit of heat.

We now had a well-balanced, complex dip with bright flavors, but we still needed to address the bread-crumb topping—typically a mixture of butter and bread crumbs. The butter binds the bread crumbs, adds flavor, and promotes browning. But from prior testing, we knew that we could omit the butter altogether and simply spray the bread-crumb topping with a fine mist of vegetable oil spray (olive oil spray works fine too). With the savings in fat and calories from omitting the butter, we were able to add a little Parmesan in with the bread crumbs giving the topping an extra hit of flavor (the cheese also helps bind the bread crumbs a bit). With all these steps, we were able to cut the calories by half to just 140 calories per ¼-cup serving and the fat grams to 8 grams, down from 21 per serving. And, to boot, we had a dip with fresh, sophisticated flavors that was anything but a relic.

MAKING FRESH BREAD CRUMBS

Fresh bread crumbs are far superior to bland, overly fine commercial crumbs. Any stray hunk of good-quality bread (preferably made without sweetener, seeds, or other extraneous ingredients) can be turned into fresh crumbs. Country white bread, plain Italian bread, and baguettes are ideal. Slightly stale bread is easier to cut, but crumbs can be made from fresh bread. You can use the crumbs as is or toast them in a dry skillet over medium heat until golden brown.

1. Slice off and discard the bottom crust of the bread if it is tough and overbaked.

2. Slice the bread into ⅜-inch-thick pieces. Cut these slices into ⅜-inch strips, then cut these into cubes and chop until you have small pieces about the size of lemon seeds.

3. To make the crumbs in a food processor, cut the trimmed loaf into 1-inch cubes, then pulse the cubes in a food processor to the desired crumb size.

EASY HOMEMADE PITA CHIPS

HOMEMADE PITA CHIPS ARE A GREAT ALTERNATIVE TO HIGH-FAT STORE-BOUGHT CRACKERS and chips. And if you choose whole-wheat pita bread, you'll get the maximum health benefits since it delivers much more fiber than pita bread made with white flour. Although these addictively crunchy snacks are ripe for dipping, they are also good on their own and can be jazzed up with a range of herb and spice variations, a few of which are listed below. To control the amount of olive oil on the chips, use an olive oil mister, which will give the chips a light, even sheen of oil. Brushing will work too, but we don't recommend it because you'll end up using more oil than is needed.

Basic Pita Chips

MAKES 48 CHIPS, SERVING 8

An olive oil mister or olive oil spray is a quick and easy way to evenly coat the chips with a fine spray of oil. In addition to dipping, try the chips crumbled crouton-style over soup or salad.

4   (8-inch) pita breads, cut into wedges
     (see illustrations below)
     Olive oil mister or olive oil spray
I   teaspoon salt

1. Adjust the oven racks to the upper-middle and lower-middle positions and heat the oven to 350 degrees. Spread the pita wedges, smooth-side down, over 2 rimmed baking sheets. Spray the top of each wedge with oil and then sprinkle with the salt.

2. Bake the wedges until they begin to crisp and brown lightly, 8 to 10 minutes. Remove the baking sheets from the oven and flip the wedges so their smooth side is up. Return the baking sheets to the oven, reversing their positions from top to bottom, and continue to bake until the chips are fully toasted, 8 to 10 minutes longer. Remove the baking sheets from the oven and cool the chips before serving. (The chips can be held in an airtight container for up to 3 days. If necessary, briefly re-crisp in a 350-degree oven for a few minutes before serving.)

PER SERVING: Cal 80; Fat 0 g; Sat Fat 0 g; Chol 0 mg; Carb 17 g; Protein 3 g; Fiber 1 g; Sodium 450 mg

VARIATIONS
Garlic-Herb Pita Chips

Follow the recipe for Basic Pita Chips, mixing 1½ teaspoons garlic powder and 2 tablespoons fresh minced thyme, basil, or oregano with the salt before sprinkling it over the chips in step 1.

PER SERVING: Cal 80; Fat 0 g; Sat Fat 0 g; Chol 0 mg; Carb 17 g; Protein 3 g; Fiber 1 g; Sodium 450 mg

Chili-Spiced Pita Chips
Try these in lieu of cornbread with chili.

Follow the recipe for Basic Pita Chips, mixing 1 tablespoon chili powder, ½ teaspoon garlic powder, and a pinch of cayenne with the salt before sprinkling it over the chips in step 1.

PER SERVING: Cal 90; Fat .5 g; Sat Fat 0 g; Chol 0 mg; Carb 17 g; Protein 3 g; Fiber 1 g; Sodium 460 mg

CUTTING PITA BREAD

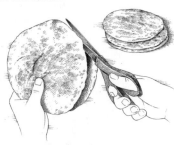

1. Using kitchen shears, cut around the perimeter of each pita bread to yield 2 thin rounds.

2. Stack the pita rounds and, using a chef's knife, cut them into 6 wedges each.

Choosing the Right Choke

We found that the type of artichokes you use in the Roasted Artichoke Dip can make all the difference.

FRESH ARTICHOKES
Too much work

Fresh artichokes taste great; however, they simply take too much time to prep and cook for this dip (and they aren't cheap either). We wanted something simpler.

CANNED ARTICHOKES
No flavor

The canning process and the watery packing liquid robs canned artichokes of any flavor. When made into a dip, tasters said it "tasted like nothing" and "if it didn't say 'Artichoke Dip' on the top of the tasting sheet, I wouldn't know what I was eating."

JARRED MARINATED ARTICHOKES
Not a shortcut

These artichokes are usually marinated in an Italian-style vinaigrette. When we used them straight out of the jar tasters said the dip took on a "nasty flavor" that was "all over the place." When we rinsed them, tasters thought the dip still tasted of the marinade.

THE WINNER

FROZEN ARTICHOKES

In our first test, frozen artichokes tasted a bit watery when cooked following the package instructions but we discovered that roasting them in the oven for 20 minutes not only helped to evaporate the excess water, but intensified their flavor resulting in a dip that was the hands-down favorite. Tasters remarked, "This is what artichoke dip is supposed to taste like!"

Roasted Artichoke Dip

SERVES 10 TO 12

It's important that the cream cheese be at room temperature, otherwise it will not mix well and distribute evenly. Also, this dip is best served warm, so make sure it comes out of the oven just as your guests are starting to arrive. Serve with crackers, thin slices of baguette, or Crostini (page 20). The dip can be prepared (without the bread crumb topping) and refrigerated, covered tightly with plastic wrap, for up to 3 days. To bake, sprinkle the breadcrumb mixture over the dip, spray with vegetable oil, and bake, as directed in the recipe. You do not need to increase the baking time.

DIP
- 2 (9-ounce) boxes frozen artichokes (do not thaw)
- 2 teaspoons olive oil
- Salt and ground black pepper
- 1 medium onion, minced (about 1 cup)
- 2 medium garlic cloves, minced or pressed through a garlic press (about 2 teaspoons)
- 1 cup reduced-fat mayonnaise
- 1/2 cup light cream cheese, at room temperature
- 1 ounce Parmesan cheese, grated (about 1/2 cup)
- 1 tablespoon juice from 1 lemon
- 1 tablespoon minced fresh thyme leaves
- Pinch cayenne pepper

TOPPING
- 1 cup fresh bread crumbs (see page 11)
- 2 tablespoons grated Parmesan cheese
- Vegetable or olive oil spray

1. FOR THE DIP: Adjust an oven rack to the middle position and heat the oven to 450 degrees. Line a rimmed baking sheet with foil. Toss the artichokes with 1 teaspoon of the oil, 1/2 teaspoon salt, and 1/4 teaspoon pepper until evenly coated, and spread over the prepared baking sheet. Roast, rotating the baking sheet from front to back halfway through, until the artichokes are browned at the edges, 20 to 25 minutes. Let the artichokes cool and then chop coarse. Reduce the oven temperature to 400 degrees.

2. Meanwhile, combine the onion, garlic, the remaining 1 teaspoon oil, and ½ teaspoon salt in a 10-inch nonstick skillet. Cover and cook over medium-low heat, stirring occasionally to prevent burning, until softened, 8 to 10 minutes. Scrape the onion mixture into a large bowl.

3. Add the mayonnaise, cream cheese, Parmesan, lemon juice, thyme, and cayenne to the onion mixture and stir to combine, smearing any lumps of cream cheese against the side of the bowl to break them up. Gently fold in the chopped artichokes; season with salt and pepper to taste. Scrape the mixture into an ungreased 8-inch-square baking dish.

4. FOR THE TOPPING: Toss the bread crumbs and Parmesan together in a medium bowl until combined, then sprinkle evenly over the top of the dip; spray the bread crumbs lightly with vegetable oil. Bake until browned, 20 to 25 minutes. Serve immediately.

PER ¼-CUP SERVING: Cal 140; Fat 8 g; Sat Fat 3 g; Chol 10 mg; Carb 13 g; Protein 5 g; Fiber 3 g; Sodium 630 mg

FRESH TOMATO SALSA

SALSA IS A STAR CONDIMENT IN THE HEALTHY cook's repertoire. Sure, you can dip chips in salsa, but you can also use it to add flavor to foods without adding fat and adding only a very few calories. Some of our favorite uses for salsa include spooning it over a split baked potato, folding it into chicken or tuna salad, and serving it alongside grilled seafood or meats. Store-bought salsas just don't compare to one you can easily make fresh at home. Those packed in jars are just plain awful and the ones sold in plastic tubs in the refrigerated section, though more palatable, are lackluster. We wanted a fresh-tasting, juicy salsa with true tomato flavor.

Backyard, farm-stand, and supermarket summertime tomatoes alike should be sweet, juicy, and ready for top billing before you use them in a fresh tomato salsa. But even in the midst of tomato season, some can be less than stellar. Complicating matters, salsa's popularity has opened the door to versions employing ingredients that are extravagant (smoked paprika) and extraneous (canned tomato juice), relegating fresh tomatoes to a minor role. One such recipe had us fishing around in water for minuscule pieces of tomato, while another used four different chiles but only one measly tomato. We wanted a fresh, chunky Mexican-style salsa, or salsa cruda, that would emphasize the tomatoes; the other traditional flavors—lime, garlic, onion, chile, and cilantro—would have supporting roles. We also wanted to get the texture just right for scooping up and balancing on a tortilla chip.

Simply combining salsa ingredients in one bowl for mixing and serving turned out to be a bad idea. The tomatoes exuded so much juice that the other

CUTTING TOMATOES FOR SALSA

1. Cut each cored tomato in half through the equator.

2. Cut each half into ⅜-inch-thick slices.

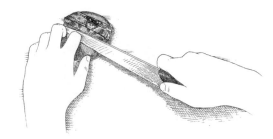

3. Stack two slices, cut them into ⅜-inch strips, and then cut them into ⅜-inch dice.

ingredients were submerged in liquid within minutes. The first step, then, was to solve the problem of watery salsa. Peeling and seeding the tomatoes seemed like the logical way to remove excess moisture from the tomatoes. Peeling, however, removed the structure that kept the diced pieces intact, resulting in a salsa that was too mushy. And seeding diminished the tomatoes' flavor (and tasters did not mind the presence of seeds). So much for peeling and seeding. We recalled that here in the test kitchen we often salt tomatoes to concentrate flavor and exude liquid. This technique was promising, but because much more surface area was exposed when the tomatoes were diced, the salt penetrated too deeply and broke them down too much. We were left with mealy, mushy tomatoes, and the salsa was just as watery as before. Dicing the tomatoes larger to expose less surface area was out of the question; the tomato pieces would be too large to balance on a tortilla chip. Taking round slices of tomatoes, salting them, and then dicing them after they had drained was just too much work.

Frustrated, we diced a few whole tomatoes (skin, seeds, and all), threw them into a colander, and walked away. Thirty minutes later, to our surprise, a few tablespoons of liquid had drained out; after a few shakes of the colander, the tomatoes were chunky and relatively dry. We found that in fewer than 30 minutes not enough liquid drained out, whereas more time didn't produce enough additional juice to justify the wait. Overall, we found that really ripe tomatoes exude more juice than less ripe supermarket tomatoes. This simple technique, with minimal tomato prep, had accomplished a major feat: It put all tomatoes, regardless of origin, ripeness, or juiciness, on a level—and dry—playing field.

With the main technique established, we fixed the spotlight on the supporting ingredients. Red onions were preferred over white, yellow, and sweet onions for color and flavor. Jalapeño chiles were chosen over serrano, habanero, and poblano chiles because of their wide availability, slight vegetal flavor, and moderate heat. Lime juice tasted more authentic (and better) than red wine vinegar, rice vinegar, or lemon juice.

We also investigated the best way to combine the ingredients and rejected all but the simplest technique. Marinating the tomatoes, onion, garlic, and chile in lime juice resulted in dull, washed-out flavors and involved extra bowls and work. We tried letting the drained tomatoes, onion, chile, garlic, and cilantro sit for a bit before adding the lime juice, sugar, and salt. Now the flavors of the chile and onion stole the show. It was much more efficient to chop the chile, onion, garlic, and cilantro and layer each ingredient on top of the tomatoes while they drained in the colander.

Once the tomatoes were finished draining, the chile, onion, garlic, cilantro, and tomatoes needed just a few stirs immediately before the salsa was finished with the lime juice, sugar, and salt, and then served.

Fresh Tomato Salsa
MAKES ABOUT 3 CUPS

Heat varies from jalapeño to jalapeño, and because much of the heat resides in the ribs, or pale-colored interior flesh, we suggest mincing the ribs (along with the seeds) separately from the dark green exterior flesh, then adding the minced ribs and seeds to taste. The amount of sugar and lime juice needed varies depending on the ripeness of the tomatoes. The salsa can be made 2 to 3 hours in advance, but hold off adding the salt, fresh lime juice, and sugar until just before serving. This salsa is perfect for tortilla chips, but it's also a nice accompaniment to grilled steaks, chicken, and fish.

1 1/2 pounds firm, ripe tomatoes, cored and cut into 3/8-inch dice (about 3 cups) (see the illustrations on page 14)

1 large jalapeño chile, seeds and ribs minced and reserved (see note), flesh minced (about 2 tablespoons)

1/2 cup minced red onion

1 small garlic clove, minced or pressed through a garlic press (about 1/2 teaspoon)

1/4 cup minced fresh cilantro leaves

1/2 teaspoon salt
     Pinch ground black pepper

2–6 teaspoons juice from 1 to 2 limes
     Sugar to taste (up to 1 teaspoon)

1. Place the tomatoes in a large colander set inside a large bowl and set aside to drain for 30 minutes. As the tomatoes drain, layer the jalapeño, onion, garlic, and cilantro on top. Shake the colander to drain off the excess tomato juice; discard juice.

2. Transfer the drained tomatoes and vegetables to a serving bowl. Add the salt, pepper, and 2 teaspoons of the lime juice; toss to combine. Taste and add the minced jalapeño ribs and seeds, sugar, and additional lime juice to taste.

PER ¼-CUP SERVING: Cal 15; Fat 0 g; Sat Fat 0 g; Chol 0 mg; Carb 3 g; Protein 1 g; Fiber 1 g; Sodium 100 mg

TEST KITCHEN MAKEOVER

GUACAMOLE

GUACAMOLE IS A SIMPLE DIP. TYPICALLY IT'S made by mashing avocados until creamy, forming a smooth base, and then folding in diced avocado, minced onion, minced jalapeño, lime juice, and cilantro. Some versions also contain chopped tomato, garlic, and cumin, Full-fat guacamole has a chunky, scoopable consistency, and without a doubt it's addictively delicious, making it hard not to mound heaping portions on every chip. But with 100 calories and 9 grams of fat per serving (about ¼ cup), it is anything but light.

We'd seen recipes for low-fat guacamole over the years and some of us had even prepared them, with varying degrees of success. Most low-fat guacamole recipes rely on some sort of vegetable puree as a replacement for the high-fat avocado. But we were skeptical. How could a dip of pureed peas, asparagus, or zucchini ever taste as good as the Mexican classic—a creamy, rich homage to its main ingredient? It seemed like quite a challenge, but we set out to develop a lighter, velvety dip made chunky by bits of buttery avocado in every bite—a dip that wouldn't make a party guest think twice about going back for second helpings.

After making a few recipes replacing the avocado with green peas, asparagus, zucchini, and the like, we realized we just couldn't let go of all the avocado. Some recipes we consulted replaced just some of the avocado with another vegetable. We gave them all a try and we were surprised by the results. Some of the dips were not as terrible as we thought they might be, although they still didn't quite mimic the flavor and texture of guacamole made with 100 percent avocado. Peas had an overwhelming earthy flavor and unwanted sweetness; zucchini made the dip watery and hollow tasting; and asparagus, also watery, had a fibrous texture and an unappetizing army green color. Edamame (green soybeans), which have a

PITTING AN AVOCADO

Digging out the pit of an avocado with a spoon can mar the soft flesh and is generally a messy proposition. This method avoids that problem.

1. Start by slicing the avocado around the pit and through both ends with a chef's knife. With your hands, twist the avocado to separate the two halves.

2. Stick the blade of the chef's knife sharply into the pit. Lift the knife, twisting the blade to loosen and remove the pit.

3. Don't pull the pit off the knife with your hands. Instead, use a large wooden spoon to pry the pit off the knife safely.

DICING AN AVOCADO

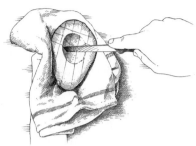

1. Use a dish towel to hold the avocado steady. Make ½-inch cross-hatch incisions in the flesh of each avocado half with a dinner knife, cutting down to but not through the skin.

2. Separate the diced flesh from the skin using a spoon inserted between the skin and the flesh and gently scoop out the avocado cubes.

fairly subtle, buttery flavor, worked well to carry the flavor of the diced avocado folded into the dip. Unfortunately, the soybeans also gave our dip a grainy texture, which remained, even after a long spin in the food processor. But the use of the soybeans certainly got our wheels turning, and we surmised that other types of beans might work.

Looking for a bean variety with a subtle flavor that would lend creaminess to our puree, we narrowed our choices down to canned white beans and frozen lima beans. The white beans were less than impressive, leaving behind too many skins in the puree, and giving our guacamole an off-putting dirty color. Tasters, however, were astonished by the lima beans, and how much they complemented the avocado in taste and texture. Boiling the lima beans muted their distinct beany flavor and proved to be the best way to cook them to a perfect creaminess. And after a quick rinse under cold water, our beans were cool enough to use right away.

With this obstacle overcome, we felt we were close to matching the classic texture and flavor of traditional guacamole, but tasters thought that the pureed lima bean base should taste more like avocado. Tasters also thought the flavors of the base and diced avocado were too discrete. Looking for a way to bring the taste of the base together with the diced avocado, we pureed a quarter of the avocado with the lima beans. Eureka—the puree now had great avocado flavor, tasting very much like guacamole!

We then diced the remaining three-quarters of the avocado into substantial ½-inch cubes and mixed them into the base using a very light hand. The mixing action broke down the cubes somewhat, resulting in a chunky, cohesive dip. A chopped tomato, which some recipes include, added a pleasant sweet acidity to the dip. The texture, however, still needed to be a bit creamier.

Taking cues from a number of recipes we found in our research, we added 2 tablespoons of low-fat varieties of cottage cheese, sour cream, and mayonnaise. We found that cottage cheese made our guacamole too thick. Sour cream added a pleasant creaminess, but made the dip too tangy. The reduced-fat mayonnaise, however, was subtle enough flavorwise and provided just the right amount of silky creaminess. Once we rounded out our guacamole with the usual flavor suspects—lime juice, jalapeño, garlic, onion, cumin, and cilantro—tasters were hard-pressed to find much difference between our lighter version and the full-fat traditional. But with less than half the fat, there's no disputing that we'd developed a dip far kinder to our waistlines, which makes a big difference all around.

MAKEOVER AT A GLANCE

–Classic–
Guacamole
(per serving)

Calories: 100	Cholesterol: 0 mg
Fat: 9 g	Saturated Fat: 1.5 g

–Light–
Guacamole
(per serving)

Calories: 70	Cholesterol: 0 mg
Fat: 4 g	Saturated Fat: 0.5 g

How We Did It

- Replaced 2 (out of 3) avocados with 1 cup of cooked, pureed, and peeled lima beans
- Added reduced-fat mayonnaise to the lima bean puree to make it smoother and creamier
- Extended the dip by folding in 1 chopped tomato, which also gives the dip some necessary acidity to balance the flavors

Guacamole
MAKES 2 CUPS

We prefer to use mature lima beans rather than baby lima beans because their skins are easier to remove after cooking, resulting in a smoother dip. If using baby limas, you can opt to leave the skins on after cooking because they are more delicate and more time consuming to remove. (The puree will be slightly less smooth.) If you like your guacamole with more heat, include the seeds and ribs of the jalapeño.

1	medium tomato (about 5 ounces), cored, seeded, and chopped fine (about 1 cup)
1	cup frozen lima beans (about 5 ounces)
1	medium ripe avocado, preferably pebbly-skinned Hass (about 7 ounces)
3	tablespoons juice from 2 limes
2	tablespoons reduced-fat mayonnaise
	Salt
¼	cup minced fresh cilantro leaves
1	medium jalapeño chile, stemmed, seeded, and minced
1	tablespoon minced red onion or shallot
1	medium garlic clove, minced or pressed through a garlic press (about 1 teaspoon)
½	teaspoon ground cumin
	Ground black pepper

1. Place the tomato in a small colander set inside a bowl and set aside to drain while preparing the rest of the guacamole.

2. Bring 4 cups of water to a boil in a small saucepan over high heat. Add the frozen lima beans and cook until tender and creamy, about 5 minutes. Drain the beans and rinse under cold water until cool. Pat the beans dry with paper towels then remove the skins by pinching the beans so the skins slide off.

3. Halve the avocado, remove the pit, and scoop out a quarter of the flesh. Puree a quarter of the avocado, skinned lima beans, lime juice, mayonnaise, and ½ teaspoon salt together in a food processor until smooth, 1 to 1½ minutes, stopping to scrape down the sides of the bowl with a rubber spatula as needed.

4. Cube the remaining three-quarters of the avocado into ½-inch pieces, following the illustrations on page 17, and scrape into a medium bowl. Add the pureed lima mixture, drained tomato, cilantro, jalapeño, onion, garlic, and cumin; stir gently to combine. Season to taste with salt and pepper. Transfer the guacamole to a serving bowl; cover with plastic wrap and let stand at room temperature until the flavors meld, about 1 hour. (The guacamole, covered with plastic wrap pressed flush against the surface of the dip, can be refrigerated for up to 1 day. Bring to room temperature and season with additional lime juice, salt, and pepper as needed before serving.)

PER ¼-CUP SERVING: Cal 70; Fat 4 g; Sat Fat .5 g; Chol 0 mg; Carb 8 g; Protein 2 g; Fiber 3 g; Sodium 210 mg

---

THE LOWDOWN ON LOW-FAT MAYONNAISE

Because mayonnaise is fatty by definition (it's mostly oil and egg yolks), low-fat mayonnaise is a popular product among the diet-conscious.

In the past, Hellmann's Light Mayonnaise has been the winner of taste tests here in the test kitchen, among leading brands of low-fat mayonnaise. (And among leading brands of full-fat mayos, Hellmann's full-fat mayo has also come in first.) But in developing recipes for this book, we discovered Hellmann's now makes another, even lighter, mayonnaise called Hellmann's Reduced Fat Mayonnaise, which only has 2 fat grams per tablespoon compared to Hellmann's Light, which has 4.5 grams of fat per tablespoon. (Regular mayonnaise has about 11 grams of fat per tablespoon.) We thought a little testing was in order to see if there would be a significant difference between these two light mayos.

Because mayonnaise is a key ingredient in both Green Goddess Dip (page 4) and Caramelized Onion Dip (page 4), we prepared a batch of each using each low-fat mayonnaise. Tasters found little difference between the dip made with Hellmann's Light versus Hellmann's Reduced Fat. As we already knew, there is a significant difference in fat grams between the two: ¾ cup of Hellmann's Reduced Fat Mayonnaise has 24 grams of fat compared to Hellmann's Light's, which has more than twice as much—54 grams.

Pushing on, we also ran tests with the two mayos tasted on their own and spread on bread. This time the Hellmann's Light won out. Tasters complained that on its own Hellmann's Reduced Fat has an off sweet flavor.

Our conclusion: Hellmann's Light is great for spreading on a sandwich, especially when you're using a modest amount, but in recipes where significant amounts of mayo are called for (and fat grams are a concern), Hellmann's Reduced Fat Mayonnaise is your best bet.

THE BEST LOW-FAT MAYONNAISES

HELLMANN'S LIGHT
Hellmann's Light Mayonnaise earned the highest scores with its bright balanced flavors, but its fat grams can add up quickly if you're using it for more than a sandwich spread.

HELLMANN'S REDUCED FAT
"Just 2 Good" Hellmann's Reduced Fat Mayonnaise worked just as well as Hellmann's Light in dips and dressings and saved us a substantial amount of fat and calories.

CROSTINI

SMALL TOASTS, CALLED *CROSTINI* IN ITALY, are the vehicle for a variety of spreads and toppings. A perfect two-bite cocktail party appetizer, crostini are crusty, rustic pieces of toast lightly flavored with garlic and olive oil. There wasn't much we wanted to change about this already light nibble. The toppings, however, would be another story.

Most Italian cookbooks offer similar directions for crostini, wherein the bread is toasted and then rubbed lightly with a clove of raw garlic. The crisp texture of the toast acts like sandpaper against the garlic, releasing flavorful, perfumed oil. The dry, garlic-infused toast is then allowed to soak up a bit of olive oil, turning an otherwise ordinary piece of bread into a tasty morsel.

We discovered that the toasting technique is the most important part of the crostini process. It is best to toast the bread for about 10 minutes in a 400-degree oven. Although this may seem like a slow way to make toast, it dries the interior of the bread so that the crostini are crunchy throughout.

The amount of olive oil to administer was an issue with tasters. Although traditionally the toasts are brushed with olive oil, we found it was difficult to control the amount of oil we were using, so we turned to an oil mister. The mister evenly disperses a light sheet of olive oil, just enough to season the toasts, without making them greasy.

When it came to deciding on the toppings for crostini, we focused on classic Italian-inspired flavored combinations, like tomato and basil, and white bean and arugula. Spinach and Parmesan are natural partners, giving us another topping. Ricotta is traditional on crostini, but we found that part-skim ricotta was just too bland and full-fat ricotta upped the calorie count too much. Instead we turned to pureed low-fat cottage cheese, which is saltier and a bit tangier. Yogurt cheese, a cream cheese–like product that is low in fat and calories, also works well. (For more information on yogurt cheese, see page 8.) In Crostini with Roasted Red Pepper and Olives, a thin spread of this cheese helps anchor toppings to the crostini and provides a rich and creamy counterpoint to the zesty toppings.

The crostini are best when toasted at the last possible moment, and it's a huge bonus if you can serve them slightly warm. It doesn't take much to turn a crostini into a flavorful appetizer since they make a great foil for all manner of flavorful ingredients. These recipes will get you started but feel free to check out your own pantry or crisper drawer for inspiration.

Crostini

MAKES ABOUT 30 CROSTINI, SERVING 10

You want small slices for crostini, so try to find a loaf with a diameter of 2½ to 3 inches. An oil mister filled with olive oil works great here but you can also use olive oil spray.

I   large baguette, cut on the bias into
     ½-inch-thick slices (about 30 slices)
I   large garlic clove, peeled
     Olive oil mister or olive oil spray
     Salt and ground black pepper

1. Adjust an oven rack to the middle position and heat the oven to 400 degrees. Arrange the bread slices in a single layer on a baking sheet. Bake until the bread is dry and crisp, 8 to 10 minutes, turning over the slices halfway through baking.

2. Remove the toasts from the oven and, while still hot, rub one side of each toast with the raw garlic clove. Spray with the oil and sprinkle liberally with salt and pepper. (The toasts are best topped and served shortly after they come out of the oven, but you can set the toasts themselves aside for several hours and then top them just before serving.)

PER SERVING: Cal 260; Fat 3 g; Sat Fat .5 g; Chol 0 mg; Carb 50 g; Protein 8 g; Fiber 3 g; Sodium 640 mg

Crostini with White Beans and Arugula

MAKES ABOUT 30 CROSTINI, SERVING 10

We found that thoroughly pureeing the beans until smooth and using a high-quality extra-virgin olive oil make all the difference here.

2   (15-ounce) cans cannellini beans, drained
    and rinsed

2   tablespoons extra-virgin olive oil

2   tablespoons juice from 1 lemon

2   medium garlic cloves, minced or pressed
    through a garlic press (about 2 teaspoons)

1   medium shallot, minced (about
    3 tablespoons)
    Pinch cayenne
    Salt and ground black pepper

1   recipe Crostini (page 20)

1   ounce arugula, chopped (about ½ cup)

1. Puree the beans, oil, lemon juice, and garlic together in a food processor until smooth, about 1 to 1 ½ minutes, stopping to scrape down the sides of the bowl with a rubber spatula as needed. Transfer the mixture to a medium bowl and stir in the shallot and cayenne; season with salt and pepper to taste.

2. Cover with plastic wrap and let stand at room temperature until the flavors meld, about 1 hour. (The spread, covered, can be refrigerated for up to 2 days. Bring to room temperature and season with additional lemon juice, salt, and pepper as needed before serving.) When ready to serve, spread about 1 tablespoon of the bean puree over each crostini, and sprinkle with the arugula.

PER SERVING: Cal 360; Fat 6 g; Sat Fat 1 g; Chol 0 mg; Carb 63 g; Protein 12 g; Fiber 6 g; Sodium 820 mg

Crostini with Tomato and Basil

MAKES ABOUT 30 CROSTINI, SERVING 10

4   medium ripe tomatoes, cored, seeded, and cut
    into ¼-inch dice

⅓ cup shredded fresh basil leaves

1   tablespoon extra-virgin olive oil
    Salt and ground black pepper

1   recipe Crostini (page 20)

Place the tomatoes in a small colander set inside a bowl and set aside to drain for 30 minutes. When drained, transfer the tomatoes to a small bowl and

toss with the basil and oil; season with salt and pepper to taste. Spoon about 1 tablespoon of the topping over each crostini before serving.

PER SERVING: Cal 290; Fat 4.5 g; Sat Fat 1 g; Chol 0 mg; Carb 52 g; Protein 9 g; Fiber 4 g; Sodium 650 mg

Crostini with Spinach and Parmesan

MAKES ABOUT 30 CROSTINI, SERVING 10

Be sure to squeeze the spinach dry so it doesn't make the crostini soggy.

1   (10-ounce) box frozen chopped spinach,
    thawed and squeezed dry

1 ½ cups low-fat cottage cheese (12 ounces)

1   ounce Parmesan cheese, grated
    (about ½ cup)

¼ cup packed fresh basil leaves

1   tablespoon juice from 1 lemon

1   tablespoon olive oil

1   large garlic clove, sliced thin
    Pinch cayenne
    Salt and ground black pepper

1   recipe Crostini (page 20)

1. Process the spinach, cottage cheese, half of the Parmesan, basil, lemon juice, oil, garlic, and cayenne together in a food processor until smooth, 1 to 1 ½ minutes, scraping down the sides of the bowl with a rubber spatula as needed. Transfer the mixture to a medium bowl and season with salt and pepper to taste.

2. Cover with plastic wrap and let stand at room temperature until the flavors meld, about 1 hour. (The spread, covered, can be refrigerated for up to 2 days. Bring to room temperature and season with additional lemon juice, salt, and pepper as needed before serving.) When ready to serve, spread about 1 tablespoon of the mixture over each crostini and sprinkle with the remaining Parmesan before serving.

PER SERVING: Cal 320; Fat 6 g; Sat Fat 1.5 g; Chol 5 mg; Carb 52 g; Protein 15 g; Fiber 3 g; Sodium 860 mg

Crostini with Roasted Red Pepper and Olives

MAKES ABOUT 30 CROSTINI, SERVING 10

You can also roast your own peppers for this recipe (see page 108). If roasting your own peppers, you will need about 4 large peppers.

1	(17-ounce) jar roasted red peppers, drained, rinsed, and thoroughly patted dry with paper towels, chopped fine (about 2 cups)
12	oil-cured sun-dried tomatoes, rinsed, patted dry, and minced
2	ounces pitted Kalamata olives (about 20 olives), minced
1	tablespoon sherry vinegar
1	teaspoon olive oil
1	medium garlic clove, minced or pressed through a garlic press (about 1 teaspoon)
	Salt and ground black pepper
¾	cup Yogurt Cheese (page 8)
1	recipe Crostini (page 20)

1. Stir the peppers, sun-dried tomatoes, olives, vinegar, oil, and garlic together in a medium bowl and season with salt and pepper to taste.

2. Cover with plastic wrap and let stand at room temperature until the flavors meld, about 1 hour. (The mixture, covered, can be refrigerated for up to 2 days. Bring to room temperature and season with additional sherry vinegar, salt, and pepper as needed before serving.) When ready to serve, spread a thin layer of yogurt cheese over each crostini, top with about 1 tablespoon of the pepper mixture, and serve.

PER SERVING: Cal 320; Fat 6 g; Sat Fat 1 g; Chol 5 mg; Carb 26 g; Protein 10 g; Fiber 3 g; Sodium 860 mg

TEST KITCHEN MAKEOVER

STUFFED MUSHROOMS

MORE THAN A COCKTAIL PARTY THROWBACK, stuffed mushrooms make a welcome, hot hors d'oeuvre. Small enough to eat in one bite, stuffed mushrooms are meant to be potently flavored with the earthy, robust flavors of the forest. More often than not, though, the mushroom flavor is weighed down by the buttery bread-crumb filling, which is usually loaded with cheese, bacon, or sausage—not exactly light fare. And did we need to forage our own fungi, or could we tease flavor out of simple cultivated white mushrooms found at the supermarket?

We began by trying a few stuffed mushroom recipes and immediately realized that we would first have to tackle exactly how to prepare the mushroom caps. Testing revealed that as the stuffed mushrooms cooked in the oven, they released their moisture, becoming watery and turning the whole hors d'oeuvre, filling and all, terribly soggy. We realized that the mushrooms had to be cooked before they were stuffed and knew that roasting was the answer. The dry heat would allow the released moisture to evaporate while the roasting would intensify the mushroom flavor. By roasting the mushroom caps upside-down first, we were able to drain much of their natural moisture before flipping them over and roasting the other side. Although this technique produced better flavor, the mushrooms still tasted too bland. In an effort to add more flavor to the mushrooms as they cooked, we tossed them with olive oil, garlic, salt, and pepper before roasting. This last-minute boost worked wonders, and the mushroom caps emerged from their roast dry, full of flavor, and ready for the stuffing.

In our research, we found that the biggest problems with mushroom fillings are that they lack any true mushroom flavor, and that they are most often greasy, mushy, and just too wet. Wanting to pack the stuffing with lots of mushroom flavor, we naturally thought we'd use mushrooms in the filling. We based our stuffing on a classic French duxelles, a cooked mixture composed of finely chopped mushrooms and shallots seasoned with herbs. Traditionally, the mixture is added to stuffings for meats, vegetables, and fish; it is also used to fortify soups and sauces with mushroom flavor.

Since we knew we would want a drier filling base than a classic duxelles, which is a relatively wet mixture, we cooked our chopped mushrooms quickly over moderately high heat. And to save a bit on fat we found that only a small amount of oil coupled with a nonstick skillet did the trick. The higher heat helped the mushrooms quickly release their liquid, which evaporated instantly upon contact with the hot pan, thus leaving behind the concentrated essence of the mushrooms. In order to ensure we had all of that essence in our filling we deglazed the pan with dry sherry, which not only lifted that dried essence off of the pan's surface, but also gave us the classic flavor combination of mushrooms and sherry as a backbone for our filling. Minced garlic and shallots rounded out the savory mushroom flavor.

With the cooking method under control, tasters found that the filling needed a bit more cohesion. We tried a number of cheeses and found that grated Parmesan added the best flavor—a nice sharp contrast to the woodsiness of the mushrooms—and the perfect amount of richness. And because of its sharp, concentrated tangy flavor, we didn't need to use very much Parmesan. Lastly, we added fresh bread crumbs to our filling to bind the mixture together, but it took a few tries to figure out the amount. Most recipes we looked at use as much as 1 cup of bread crumbs, but because our filling was enriched with mushroom stems, we thought we could get away with less. After testing various amounts, we settled on ½ cup, which gave us the appropriate amount of binding, without making our filling bland or gluey—the bane of many a stuffed mushroom.

Now that we had an intensely flavored mushroom filling, we just needed to make a few last adjustments. Fresh thyme—a classic complementary partner for mushrooms—was the tasters' herb of choice. And just to give our filling some brightness and oomph, we stirred in a tablespoon of white wine vinegar, which added the zip we were after.

Once stuffed and topped with a pinch of grated Parmesan, the mushrooms took only 10 minutes to heat through. Far from being bogged down by a heavy filling, our stuffed mushrooms emerged from the oven with the unmistakable, earthy aroma and flavor of mushrooms cooked to perfection.

MAKEOVER AT A GLANCE

–Classic–
Stuffed Mushrooms
(per serving)

Calories: 170	Cholesterol: 10 mg
Fat: 14 g	Saturated Fat: 3.5 g

–Light–
Stuffed Mushrooms
(per serving)

Calories: 60	Cholesterol: 0 mg
Fat: 3 g	Saturated Fat: 0.5 g

How We Did It

- Roasted the mushroom caps before stuffing them to intensify their flavor
- Used chopped mushrooms in the filling, instead of sausage or bacon
- Reduced bread crumbs by half to emphasize mushroom flavor
- Used a small amount of potent Parmesan for big, bold flavor
- Sautéed the filling in a nonstick pan with very little oil before stuffing the mushrooms to concentrate its mushroomy flavor

---

Stuffed Mushrooms

MAKES 30 MUSHROOMS, SERVING 10

The mushroom caps shrink significantly as they cook, so be sure to buy ones that are 1½ to 2 inches wide. To prepare the mushrooms up to 2 days ahead, roast the caps and stuff them, but do not top with the reserved Parmesan. Arrange the unbaked stuffed mushrooms on a plate, wrap tightly with plastic wrap, and refrigerate. To bake, transfer to a foil-lined rimmed baking sheet, sprinkle with the Parmesan, and bake as directed in the recipe. You do not need to increase the cooking time.

MUSHROOMS

30	(1½- to 2-inch wide) white mushroom caps, wiped clean
1	tablespoon olive oil
3	medium garlic cloves, minced or pressed through a garlic press (about 1 tablespoon)
¼	teaspoon salt
	Pinch ground black pepper

FILLING

1	teaspoon olive oil
2	large shallots, minced (about ½ cup)
1	medium garlic clove, minced or pressed through a garlic press (about 1 teaspoon)
12	ounces white mushrooms, wiped clean and chopped fine (about 2 cups)
1	tablespoon fresh minced thyme leaves
	Salt
2	tablespoons dry sherry
1	tablespoon white wine vinegar
½	cup fresh bread crumbs (see page 11)
1	ounce Parmesan cheese, grated (about ½ cup)
	Ground black pepper

1. FOR THE MUSHROOMS: Adjust an oven rack to the middle position and heat the oven to 450 degrees. Line a large rimmed baking sheet with foil. Toss the mushroom caps with the oil, garlic, salt, and pepper, then lay gill-side down on the prepared baking sheet. Roast the mushrooms until they release their juices, about 20 minutes. Flip the caps over and continue to roast until the liquid has evaporated completely and the mushrooms are brown all over, about 10 minutes longer. Remove the mushrooms from the oven, flip gill-side down, and set aside to drain any excess moisture while preparing the filling. (Do not turn off the oven.)

2. FOR THE FILLING: Heat the oil in a 12-inch nonstick skillet over medium-high heat until shimmering. Add the shallots and cook, stirring often, until softened, about 2 minutes. Stir in the garlic and cook until fragrant, about 30 seconds. Add the chopped mushrooms, thyme, and ½ teaspoon salt and cook, stirring often, until the mushroom mixture is dry, about 6 minutes. Stir in the sherry and cook until it is absorbed, about 1 minute. Off the heat, gently stir in the vinegar, bread crumbs, and 6 tablespoons of the Parmesan; season with salt and pepper to taste.

3. TO ASSEMBLE: Flip the roasted mushroom caps gill-side up and spoon about 1 teaspoon of the filling into each cap. Top each mushroom with a pinch of the remaining 2 tablespoons Parmesan. Bake the mushrooms at 450 degrees until the cheese has melted and the filling is warm, 10 to 15 minutes. Serve immediately.

PER SERVING: Cal 60; Fat 3 g; Sat Fat .5 g; Chol 0 mg; Carb 6 g; Protein 3 g; Fiber 0 g; Sodium 240 mg

PARTY CHICKEN SKEWERS

CHICKEN SKEWERS ARE PERFECT COCKTAIL party fare. Because they're packed with flavor, you can eat them without feeling full, getting your hands messy, or even putting your beverage down. And as an added bonus, they are naturally low in fat.

Chicken breasts, a relatively blank canvas flavorwise, call for a zesty marinade or highly spiced glaze. We wanted our chicken to brown, but not dry out, so we turned to marinade ingredients with a high sugar content. The sugar promotes browning, giving the chicken a lacquered look in a brief amount of time under the broiler. And, in turn, the marinade's glazy consistency helps the fresh herbs and spices stick to the chicken—a big plus.

We wanted to make enough skewers to feed a crowd, so we needed a cooking method that could produce a lot of food in little time. Grilling was an option, but the problems of hot spots, charred skewers, and sprints out to the backyard while guests are arriving nixed that idea. Broiling was a better option—it allowed us to prepare about 30 skewers at a time, keeping our guests satisfied and our sanity intact.

Because these hors d'oeuvres would be eaten out of hand, tasters preferred bamboo to metal skewers; the bamboo skewers are disposable and easier to handle straight from the oven. The only downside to bamboo skewers is that they run the risk of smoldering, or even catching fire, under the broiler. To combat this issue, we lined up the meat side of the skewers on the same side of the broiler pan and protected the exposed bamboo with a strip of aluminum foil. Arranged about 6 inches below the broiler element, the chicken cooked through in five to six minutes and the skewers remained unharmed.

Skewered chicken is often served with a dipping sauce and any dipping sauce worth its salt complements and enhances its partner. Wanting to avoid the potential mess a thin sauce could make, we knew we needed a thick sauce that wouldn't run down our arms or drip on our shirts. Tasters really liked the creamy richness of a dipping sauce made from low-fat sour cream and low-fat mayo, which is finished with fresh cilantro and scallions. And everyone enjoyed a sweet-and-sour sauce featuring apricot preserves.

At last we had easy-to-prepare tender party skewers (and dips to boot) that were guaranteed to disappear at our next cocktail party.

PROTECTING CHICKEN SKEWERS

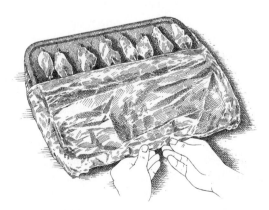

To keep the exposed portions of the skewers (the portion people will use as a handle) from burning, cover the ends of the skewers (but not the chicken) with foil.

Spicy Orange Chicken Skewers with Apricot-Orange Dipping Sauce

MAKES ABOUT 30 SKEWERS, SERVING 10

You will need thirty 6- or 8-inch bamboo (or wooden) skewers for this recipe. The cooking time will depend on the strength and type of your broiler. Under-the-oven drawer-style broilers tend to take a few minutes longer than in-oven-style broilers.

CHICKEN

2	pounds boneless, skinless chicken breasts (about 5 medium breasts), trimmed
2	tablespoons minced fresh parsley leaves
1 1/2	teaspoons salt
1/2	teaspoon grated zest from 1 orange
1/2	teaspoon red pepper flakes
1/2	teaspoon paprika
1/4	teaspoon garlic powder
1/4	teaspoon ground black pepper
1/4	cup apricot preserves
	Nonstick cooking spray

DIPPING SAUCE

1	cup apricot preserves
2	tablespoons red wine vinegar
1	tablespoon minced fresh parsley leaves
1/2	teaspoon grated zest from 1 orange
1/2	teaspoon salt
1/4	teaspoon red pepper flakes
1/8	teaspoon ground black pepper

1. FOR THE CHICKEN: Slice the chicken breasts across the grain into ½-inch-thick strips (you should have about 30 strips). In a large bowl, toss the chicken with the parsley, salt, orange zest, red pepper flakes, paprika, garlic powder, and pepper. Add the apricot preserves and toss to coat. Cover tightly with plastic wrap and refrigerate until the flavors meld, about 30 minutes. (The chicken, covered, can be refrigerated for up to 1 day before cooking.)

2. FOR THE DIPPING SAUCE: Puree the apricot preserves and vinegar together in a blender or food processor until smooth, about 1 minute. Transfer to a small serving bowl and stir in the parsley, orange zest, salt, red pepper flakes, and pepper. Cover with

plastic wrap and let stand at room temperature until the flavors meld, about 30 minutes. (The dipping sauce can be covered and refrigerated for up to 2 days. Season with additional vinegar, salt, and pepper before serving.)

3. Meanwhile, adjust an oven rack to the top position and heat the broiler. Line a broiler pan bottom with foil and top with a slotted broiler pan top; spray the broiler pan top with nonstick cooking spray. Weave each piece of chicken onto individual bamboo skewers; lay half of the skewers on the broiler pan top and cover the skewer ends with foil, making sure not to cover the chicken. Broil until the meat is lightly browned and cooked through, 5 to 8 minutes, flipping the skewers over halfway through. Transfer the skewers to a serving platter and serve immediately with half the apricot sauce. Repeat, broiling the remaining skewers and serving with the remaining dipping sauce.

PER SERVING: Cal 200; Fat 1.5 g; Sat Fat 0 g; Chol 55 mg; Carb 26 g; Protein 21 g; Fiber 0 g; Sodium 540 mg

Chipotle Chicken Skewers with Creamy Cilantro Dipping Sauce

MAKES ABOUT 30 SKEWERS, SERVING 10

You will need thirty 6- or 8-inch bamboo (or wooden) skewers for this recipe. The cooking time will depend on the strength and type of your broiler. Under-the-oven drawer-style broilers tend to take a few minutes longer than in-oven-style broilers. A small clove of minced garlic (about ½ teaspoon) can be substituted for the garlic powder in the sauce, if desired.

CHICKEN

2	pounds boneless, skinless chicken breasts (about 5 medium breasts), trimmed
¼	cup packed light brown sugar
2	tablespoons minced fresh cilantro leaves
I	chipotle chile in adobo, minced, plus 2 teaspoons adobo sauce
1 ½	teaspoons salt
½	teaspoon chili powder
¼	teaspoon garlic powder

¼	teaspoon ground black pepper
	Nonstick cooking spray

DIPPING SAUCE

¾	cup low-fat sour cream
¼	cup reduced-fat mayonnaise
¼	cup juice from 2 to 3 limes
⅛	teaspoon garlic powder
2	tablespoons fresh minced cilantro leaves
2	scallions, minced
½	teaspoon salt
⅛	teaspoon ground black pepper

1. FOR THE CHICKEN: Slice the chicken breasts across the grain into ½-inch-thick strips (you should have about 30 strips). In a large bowl, toss the chicken with the brown sugar, cilantro, chipotle, adobo sauce, salt, chili powder, garlic powder, and pepper. Cover tightly with plastic wrap and refrigerate until the flavors meld, about 30 minutes. (The chicken, covered, can be refrigerated for up to 1 day before cooking.)

2. FOR THE DIPPING SAUCE: In a bowl, stir all the ingredients together. Cover with plastic wrap and let stand at room temperature until the flavors meld, about 30 minutes. (The dipping sauce can be covered and refrigerated for up to 2 days. Season with additional lime juice, salt, and pepper to taste before serving.)

3. Meanwhile, adjust an oven rack to the top position and heat the broiler. Line a broiler pan bottom with foil and top with a slotted broiler pan top; spray the broiler pan top with nonstick cooking spray. Weave each piece of chicken onto individual bamboo skewers; lay half of the skewers on the broiler pan top and cover the skewer ends with foil, making sure not to cover the chicken. Broil until the meat is lightly browned and cooked through, 5 to 8 minutes, flipping the skewers over halfway through. Transfer the skewers to a serving platter and serve immediately with half the dipping sauce. Repeat, broiling the remaining skewers and serving with the remaining dipping sauce.

PER SERVING: Cal 160; Fat 3.5 g; Sat Fat 1.5 g; Chol 60 mg; Carb 8 g; Protein 22 g; Fiber 0 g; Sodium 590 mg

2

SALADS

SALADS ARE A DELICIOUS WAY TO ENJOY FRESH greens and vegetables; however, it's a common misconception that eating salads always equals eating healthy. This is partially true; after all, salads are made up of things that are good for you, like lettuce, fresh vegetables, hearty grains, and beans. However, after running a few traditional salad recipes and dressings—such as chicken Caesar salad and blue cheese dressing—through our nutritional analysis, we were surprised by the high amounts of fat and calories that lurked within them. In fact, some side salads had enough fat and calories to qualify as an entire meal. Dressings, be they vinaigrettes or creamy, were the biggest culprits, although popular salad add-ins such as olives, cheese, bacon, nuts, and croutons didn't help matters much. We wanted to create lighter versions of our favorite dressings and salads but were committed to keeping our new recipes both substantial and satisfying.

The recipes in this chapter fall into three basic categories: salad dressings, side salads, and main course salads. For the salad dressings category we shook things up a bit by making over classic salad dressings like Basic Vinaigrette (page 29) and creamy dressings (pages 38–39). Tasters were impressed by the authenticity and richness of our new lightened versions of these classics. For the vinaigrette, we managed to replace a large portion of the oil with water, and for the creamy dressings we made use of the low-fat dairy products on the market. Buttermilk, reduced-fat mayonnaise, and low-fat sour cream were central to the success of our creamy dressings and even our Caesar Dressing (page 41).

And for side salads, we focused on creating full-flavored recipes, light enough to pair with lean main course fare such as grilled fish or sautéed chicken breasts. For example, to make French Potato Salad (page 55) lighter (and tastier) we replaced some of the oil in the vinaigrette with the potato-cooking liquid to add flavor and viscosity. We also include legume and bean salads—but not what you remember from the school cafeteria— these are salads inspired by the Mediterranean.

And for the times when you just want a salad for lunch or dinner, we developed recipes for more substantial main course salads. We're not talking taco or chef's salad here—we brought new, tasty ideas for dinner salads to the table. Our idea for these supper salads involves fresh greens and/or vegetables combined with a lean protein, all drizzled or tossed with a light, fragrant dressing. The refreshing flavors of Salmon Salad with Red Potatoes and Green Beans (page 47), for example, are perfect for a healthy springtime or summer dinner, while Wilted Spinach and Apple Salad with Sausage (page 46) is hearty enough for an autumn supper. Tasters complimented our use of leaner proteins, lots of fresh vegetables and greens, as well as lighter vinaigrette-style dressings.

In the end, we are much happier knowing that these recipes are tasty without unnecessarily high amounts of fat and calories. We're now convinced and truly believe that eating salads can equal eating healthy.

BASIC VINAIGRETTE

MANY PEOPLE WHO ARE WATCHING FAT AND calories typically reach for a vinaigrette rather than a creamy dressing, assuming it's a better option. Not so fast. Most vinaigrettes typically contain 11 grams of fat and 100 calories per serving. We aimed to make a vinaigrette that really would be a better option, healthwise.

We began by reviewing recipes for lower fat vinaigrettes. Many replace all or part of the oil with broth or water. Those that completely replace the oil with broth or water were either insipid or so acidic they made our mouths pucker. Even worse, these dressings didn't cling to the salad greens but instead, simply slipped off them, puddling in the bottom of the bowl. Eliminating the oil altogether, then, just wasn't an option.

We next explored reducing the amount of oil. We began with a recipe for a basic full-fat vinaigrette: ¾ cup extra-virgin olive oil and 3 tablespoons vinegar (either red or white wine). Some vinaigrette recipes also include mustard for flavor and to help emulsify the dressing. Because we would be reducing the amount of oil, we'd definitely need the mustard to give the dressing some body. We moved on to supplementing a portion of the oil with the three liquids most often used in lower fat vinaigrettes: low-sodium vegetable broth, low-sodium chicken broth, and water. We were surprised to find that both broths came up short. The vegetable broth gave the vinaigrette a distracting sweetness and off-putting aroma. The chicken broth, which we assumed would have the most promise since we'd seen it used so frequently in our research, did have more body but still imparted off flavors to the vinaigrette. Water's neutral flavor made it the winner. It maintained the balance of the vinaigrette's flavors without obscuring it with off tastes and aromas.

Our next task was to finesse the amounts of oil, water, and vinegar to give the vinaigrette the right balance of body (viscosity) and flavor. In our tests, the vinaigrettes made with higher amounts of water were much too thin, while those made with too little had good body but tasted too acidic. After much measuring and mixing, tasters were

pleased with the following combination: ¼ cup extra-virgin olive oil, 6 tablespoons water, and 3 tablespoons vinegar. (For a few of our flavor variations, we substituted peanut or vegetable oil for the olive oil.)

Now that we had the basics down, it was just a matter of choosing other flavor elements to enrich our dressing. Some vinaigrettes include garlic or shallots, but our tasters liked both. As for herbs, fresh thyme gave our vinaigrette an aromatic kick and a bit of salt and pepper brought all the flavors into line.

You can whisk all the ingredients together in a bowl or shake them in a tightly covered jar. Leftover dressing can then be stored in the same container and refrigerated. Most vinaigrettes last about 1 week in the refrigerator. Before serving, bring the vinaigrette to room temperature and shake the jar vigorously to recombine the ingredients. To make a salad for four, use ¼ cup of the vinaigrette to dress 8 cups of loosely packed greens.

MAKEOVER AT A GLANCE

—Classic—
Vinaigrette
(per serving)

Calories: 100	Cholesterol: 0 mg
Fat: 11 g	Saturated Fat: 1.5 g

—Light—
Vinaigrette
(per serving)

Calories: 35	Cholesterol: 0 mg
Fat: 3.5 g	Saturated Fat: 0 g

How We Did It

- Replaced ½ cup of the oil with 6 tablespoons water
- Boosted the flavor with shallot, garlic, and fresh thyme
- Increased the amount of mustard to add flavor and body

Basic Vinaigrette

MAKES ABOUT 1 CUP

This vinaigrette is a great alternative to bottled dressings and it will last for up to a week in the refrigerator.

6	tablespoons water
¼	cup extra-virgin olive oil
3	tablespoons red or white wine vinegar
2	teaspoons minced shallot or red onion
2	teaspoons Dijon mustard
1	medium garlic clove, minced or pressed through a garlic press (about 1 teaspoon)
1	teaspoon minced fresh thyme leaves
½	teaspoon salt
¼	teaspoon ground black pepper

Shake all of the ingredients together in a jar with a tight-fitting lid. The dressing can be refrigerated for up to 7 days; bring to room temperature, then shake vigorously to recombine before using.

PER 1-TABLESPOON SERVING: Cal 35; Fat 3.5 g; Sat fat 0 g; Chol 0 mg; Carb 0 g; Protein 0 g; Fiber 0 g; Sodium 90 mg

➤ VARIATIONS

Carrot-Ginger Vinaigrette

This vinaigrette is our take on the Japanese restaurant favorite. Do not substitute dried ground ginger for the fresh ginger.

6	tablespoons water
1/4	cup peanut or vegetable oil
3	tablespoons rice vinegar
2	teaspoons low-sodium soy sauce
1 1/2	teaspoons toasted sesame oil
1	carrot, peeled and shredded
2	teaspoons minced shallot or red onion
1 1/2	teaspoons grated fresh ginger
1/2	teaspoon salt
1/2	teaspoon sugar
1/4	teaspoon ground black pepper

Shake all of the ingredients together in a jar with a tight-fitting lid. The dressing can be refrigerated for up to 7 days; bring to room temperature, then shake vigorously to recombine before using.

PER 1-TABLESPOON SERVING: Cal 40; Fat 4 g; Sat fat 0 g; Chol 0 mg; Carb 1 g; Protein 0 g; Fiber 0 g; Sodium 100 mg

Balsamic Vinaigrette

Follow the recipe for Basic Vinaigrette substituting balsamic vinegar for the wine vinegar and oregano for the thyme.

PER 1-TABLESPOON SERVING: Cal 35; Fat 3.5 g; Sat fat 0 g; Chol 0 mg; Carb 0 g; Protein 0 g; Fiber 0 g; Sodium 90 mg

Raspberry Vinaigrette

Raspberry vinegar can be found with other vinegars in well-stocked supermarkets or gourmet shops.

Follow the recipe for Basic Vinaigrette, substituting raspberry vinegar for the wine vinegar. Omit the garlic and mustard and increase the amount of minced shallot or red onion to 4 teaspoons.

PER 1-TABLESPOON SERVING: Cal 30; Fat 3.5 g; Sat fat 0 g; Chol 0 mg; Carb 0 g; Protein 0 g; Fiber 0 g; Sodium 75 mg

Honey-Dijon Vinaigrette

This sweet-and-sour dressing is a bit thicker than the other vinaigrettes and yields about 1¼ cups. Poppy seeds are optional in this recipe; we like them because they add a nutty flavor and crunchy texture to the vinaigrette.

Follow the recipe for Basic Vinaigrette, substituting vegetable oil for the extra-virgin olive oil, cider vinegar for the wine vinegar, and increasing the mustard to 2 tablespoons. Omit the shallot and the thyme and add 2 tablespoons honey and, if desired, 1 tablespoon poppy seeds.

PER 1-TABLESPOON SERVING: Cal 35; Fat 3 g; Sat fat 0 g; Chol 0 mg; Carb 2 g; Protein 0 g; Fiber 0 g; Sodium 95 mg

---

TESTING NOTES

Time for an Oil Change

In our research, we found numerous recipes that replace some of the oil in a basic vinaigrette with other lower fat ingredients, such as chicken broth, vegetable broth, and water. After trying them, we found one substitution that worked well. And, for vinaigrettes with an intense, complex flavor, fruit juices are an excellent substitution for oil (see page 32).

CHICKEN BROTH
When the oil was replaced with chicken broth, tasters found that although the dressing's body was okay, the flavors were off.

VEGETABLE BROTH
Substituting vegetable broth for the oil in our basic vinaigrette made it taste "much too sweet" and "vegetal—in a bad way."

THE WINNER

WATER
By replacing some, but not all, of the oil with water and punching up the flavorings substantially, we were able to make simple, full-flavored vinaigrettes with a lot less fat.

Salad 101

CLEANING GREENS

Nothing ruins a salad faster than gritty leaves, so the first step in making any salad is cleaning the greens. (Unwashed greens should be carefully stowed away in the crisper with the rubber band or twist tie removed, as the constriction encourages rotting.) Our favorite way to wash small amounts of greens is in the bowl of a salad spinner; larger amounts require a sink. Make sure there is ample room to swish the leaves about and rid them of sand and dirt. The dirt will sink to the bottom. Exceptionally dirty greens (spinach and arugula often fall into this category) may take at least two changes of water. Do not run water directly from the faucet onto the greens as the force of the water can bruise them. When you are satisfied that the leaves are grit-free, lift them out of the water, leaving the dirt behind, and spin them dry in a salad spinner. Greens must be quite dry; otherwise, the vinaigrette will slide off and taste diluted. Here are some guidelines for washing and drying greens:

1. Using your hands, gently move the greens about under water to loosen grit, which should fall to the bottom of the salad spinner bowl. Lift the greens out of the water rather than pouring the water out of the bowl with the greens still inside.

2. If you own a crank-style salad spinner, place it in the corner of your sink. This increases your leverage by pushing the spinner into the floor and walls of the sink, thereby stabilizing it.

3. Line the salad spinner with paper towels, then layer in the greens, covering each layer with additional towels. In this manner, the greens will keep for at least 2 days.

4. To store greens for up to a week, loosely roll the greens in paper towels and then place the rolled greens inside a large zipper-lock bag and place in the refrigerator.

THE BEST SALAD SPINNERS

After testing eight salad spinners, we ended up with a two-way tie between spinners made by Zyliss and Oxo Good Grips. They both excelled at drying greens, though they had minor trade-offs: The Zyliss finished the task nominally faster, but the Oxo had a more ergonomic handle and a nonskid bottom, a big bonus. The design enhancements lifted the Oxo's price to $26, $5 more than the Zyliss.

ZYLISS   OXO

DRESSING AND TOSSING GREENS

We found that an ideal salad bowl is wide-mouthed and relatively shallow, so that the greens become evenly coated with vinaigrette quickly. A wide bowl also facilitates gentle handling of the greens. The bowl should be roughly 50 percent larger than the amount of greens to make sure there is adequate room for tossing. Whatever utensils you choose to toss the salad—wooden spoons, hands (our favorite method), or tongs—a light touch is crucial. A roughly tossed salad will wilt much faster than a lightly tossed salad. Here's how we dress and toss greens:

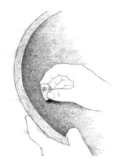 

1. Add mild garlic flavor: Peel and cut a clove of garlic. With the cut side down, rub the interior of your salad bowl.

2. Measure the greens: Loosely pack the greens into a large measuring cup, figuring on 2 cups per serving.

3. Tear the greens: If the greens are too large, tear them gently into manageable pieces with your hands just before serving the salad. If torn ahead of time, they will discolor and wilt.

4. Shake the dressing: Just before adding the dressing, give it a quick shake to make sure that it is fully combined and that the solid ingredients, such as shallots, are evenly dispersed.

 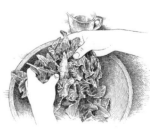

5. Drizzle the dressing: To prevent overdressed greens, add the dressing in small increments, 1 tablespoon per serving, as you toss the salad.

6. Toss the salad: Coat the greens by gently "fluffing" them, adding more vinaigrette only when you are certain the greens need it.

FRUIT JUICE VINAIGRETTES

IN OUR QUEST FOR DEVELOPING LOWER FAT vinaigrettes, we came across a flavorful technique for making bold, fruit-flavored dressings. The technique involves simmering fruit juice until it has reduced to a syrup, which is then mixed with the other vinaigrette ingredients. The viscous nature of the finished vinaigrette causes the dressing to cling to pieces of lettuce, without needing much oil. And by replacing most of the oil with a thick and syrupy reduced fruit juice, we were able to retain a rich fruit flavor. Testing a few approaches, we found that nearly any fruit juice will work. In addition to the standard vinaigrette ingredients of herbs, shallots, and vinegar, a small dash of good extra-virgin olive oil is still necessary for well-rounded flavor.

Orange-Lime Vinaigrette

MAKES ABOUT 1 CUP

Any type of orange juice will work here; however, the flavor of fresh squeezed juice really sparkles. These fruit juice dressings work best on sturdy or flavorful greens, such as endive or arugula, but will overwhelm more delicate greens, such as Bibb lettuce.

2	cups orange juice
3	tablespoons juice from 2 limes
2	tablespoons extra-virgin olive oil
1	tablespoon honey
1	tablespoon minced shallot
1/2	teaspoon salt
1/2	teaspoon ground black pepper

1. Bring the orange juice to a boil in a small saucepan over medium-high heat. Reduce the heat to medium and simmer briskly until the juice is thick, syrupy, and measures ⅔ cup, 25 to 35 minutes. Transfer the orange juice syrup to a small bowl and refrigerate until cool, about 15 minutes. (The syrup can be refrigerated in a covered container for up to 2 days.)

2. Transfer the cooled orange juice to a jar and add the lime juice, oil, honey, shallot, salt, and pepper. Seal the lid and shake the mixture vigorously until emulsified, about 20 seconds. The dressing can be refrigerated for up to 7 days; bring to room temperature, then shake vigorously to recombine before using.

PER 1-TABLESPOON SERVING: Cal 35; Fat 2 g; Sat fat 0 g; Chol 0 mg; Carb 5 g; Protein 0 g; Fiber 0 g; Sodium 75 mg

➤ VARIATIONS

Pomegranate and Honey Vinaigrette
Pomegranate juice, which is high in antioxidants, is available at most supermarkets and natural food stores. Be sure to purchase straight pomegranate juice, which is sweet and slightly tart, not a flavored variety.

Follow the recipe for Orange-Lime Vinaigrette, substituting pomegranate juice for the orange juice in step 1. In step 2, substitute red wine vinegar for the lime juice.

PER 1-TABLESPOON SERVING: Cal 40; Fat 2 g; Sat fat 0 g; Chol 0 mg; Carb 6 g; Protein 0 g; Fiber 0 g; Sodium 75 mg

---

CORE TECHNIQUE

GIVE IT SOME JUICE, AND REDUCE

We tested a number of methods for making low-fat vinaigrettes and dressings (see "Time for an Oil Change," page 30), and discovered that using fruit juice worked well. But you can't just replace the oil with juice, or the dressing turns out thin with diluted flavor. The fruit juice needs to be cooked to a syrupy consistency, a technique known as "reducing." This not only concentrates the fruit flavor, but also gives the low-fat dressing body tantamount to that of a full-fat version. And by using reduced fruit juice in the place of oil, we were able to work with flavors that are otherwise difficult to get into a dressing, such as pomegranate, apple, and pear.

Ruby Red Grapefruit and Sesame Vinaigrette

Any type of grapefruit juice will work here, however, the flavor and color of fresh squeezed juice from ruby red grapefruit is our favorite. Keep a close eye on the sesame seeds as they toast, since they can burn quickly.

Follow the recipe for Orange-Lime Vinaigrette, substituting ruby red grapefruit juice for the orange juice in step 1. In step 2, substitute rice vinegar for the lime juice and peanut or vegetable oil for the olive oil. Add 1 tablespoon minced fresh cilantro leaves and 1 teaspoon sesame seeds, toasted in a dry skillet over medium heat until golden (about 2 minutes), to the remaining ingredients.

PER 1-TABLESPOON SERVING: Cal 40; Fat 2 g; Sat fat 0 g; Chol 0 mg; Carb 6 g; Protein 0 g; Fiber 0 g; Sodium 75 mg

Apple Cider–Sage Vinaigrette

Apple juice can be substituted for the apple cider—simply omit the honey.

Follow the recipe for Orange-Lime Vinaigrette, substituting apple cider for the orange juice in step 1. In step 2, substitute cider vinegar for the lime juice, and add ½ teaspoon minced fresh sage leaves to the remaining ingredients.

PER 1-TABLESPOON SERVING: Cal 35; Fat 2 g; Sat fat 0 g; Chol 0 mg; Carb 5 g; Protein 0 g; Fiber 0 g; Sodium 75 mg

Pear-Rosemary Vinaigrette

Pear juice is available at your local natural food store or Italian market.

Follow the recipe for Orange-Lime Vinaigrette, substituting pear juice for the orange juice in step 1. In step 2, substitute lemon juice for the lime juice, and add ¼ teaspoon minced fresh rosemary to the remaining ingredients.

PER 1-TABLESPOON SERVING: Cal 35; Fat 2 g; Sat fat 0 g; Chol 0 mg; Carb 5 g; Protein 0 g; Fiber 0 g; Sodium 75 mg

Cranberry-Balsamic Vinaigrette

The flavors in this vinaigrette make it a great choice to dress salad greens during the holidays.

Follow the recipe for Orange-Lime Vinaigrette, substituting cranberry juice for the orange juice in step 1. In step 2, substitute balsamic vinegar for the lime juice and add 1 small garlic clove, minced or pressed through a garlic press (about ½ teaspoon), and 1 teaspoon fresh thyme leaves to the remaining ingredients.

PER 1-TABLESPOON SERVING: Cal 40; Fat 2 g; Sat fat 0 g; Chol 0 mg; Carb 6 g; Protein 0 g; Fiber 0 g; Sodium 75 mg

ROASTED GARLIC DRESSING

GARLIC PACKS A FLAVORFUL PUNCH—TOO strong for some. But when roasted, garlic mellows, becomes slightly sweet, and even people who normally shy away from it won't be able to resist its allure. For those new to using roasted garlic in recipes, a creamy dressing is a great place to start.

In our research we came across a number of low-fat recipes for this velvety dressing, and many of them omit a large portion, or all, of the oil. The result is an oddly sweet dressing lacking in balance, body, and any notion of roasted garlic flavor. We were puzzled that there wasn't an existing recipe that better exploited an ingredient as flavorful

---

CORE TECHNIQUE

TAMING THE BEAST WITHIN

Roasting garlic is one way to pack a dressing, sauce, dip, or most any dish with flavor, without adding any fat. The spicy sharpness of the garlic becomes mellow and subtly sweet when roasted. And roasting garlic is easy (see our method on page 35). Roasted heads of garlic will hold in the refrigerator about 1 week.

as roasted garlic. We set out to develop a low-fat roasted garlic dressing recipe that would showcase the subtle caramelized sweetness and mellow flavor of garlic, one with the perfect amount of body for clinging to salad greens.

We started our testing by roasting garlic using a no-fat method that we developed (see page 35), in which heads of garlic are wrapped in foil packets, sprinkled with a bit of water, and roasted in the oven for about 40 minutes. With soft, lightly caramelized heads of garlic out of the oven our first task was to adjust the amount of oil in the dressing. Knowing that roasted garlic has a creamy consistency of its own, we figured we could use this to our advantage in replacing most of the oil. First, we made

a few dressings using no oil at all. Tasters reacted negatively to the absence of oil, commenting that the final products were an off mix of harsh flavors, with obscured roasted garlic flavor, not unlike many of the bottled fat-free dressings out there. It was clear that we would need to include some oil in our dressing.

In our next run of tests we used various minimal amounts of olive oil. Out of all the amounts tried, we discovered that tasters most preferred 2 tablespoons of oil in the dressing. The general consensus was that the oil enhanced the other flavors in the dressing and allowed the earthy sweetness of the garlic to become the star of the show. To round out the flavor of the dressing, we used some cider

---

INGREDIENTS: Supermarket Extra-Virgin Olive Oils

When you purchase an artisanal oil in a high-end shop, certain informational perks are expected (and paid for). These typically include written explanations of the character and nuances of the particular oil as well as the assistance of knowledgeable staff. But in a supermarket, it's just you and a price tag (usually $8 to $10 per liter). How do you know which supermarket extra-virgin olive oil best suits your needs? To provide some guidance, we decided to hold a blind tasting of the nine best-selling extra virgin olive oils typically available in American supermarkets.

Tasting extra-virgin olive oil is much like tasting wine. The flavors of these oils range from citrusy to herbal, musty to floral, with every possibility in between. And what one taster finds particularly attractive—a slight briny flavor, for example—another might find unappealing. Also like wine, the flavor of a particular brand of olive oil can change from year to year, depending on the quality of the harvest and the olives' place of origin.

We chose to taste extra-virgin olive oil in its most pure and unadulterated state: raw. Tasters were given the option of sampling the oil from a spoon or on neutral-flavored French bread and were asked to eat a slice of green apple—for its acidity—to cleanse the palate between oils. The olive oils were evaluated for color, clarity, viscosity, bouquet, depth of flavor, and lingering of flavor.

Whereas in a typical tasting we are able to identify a clear winner and loser, in this case we could not. In fact, the panel seemed to quickly divide itself into those who liked a gutsy olive oil with bold flavor and those who preferred a milder, mellower approach. Nonetheless, in both camps one oil clearly had more of a following than any other—the all-Italian-olive Da Vinci

brand. Praised for its rounded and buttery flavor, it was the only olive oil we tasted that seemed to garner across-the-board approval with olive oil experts and in-house staff alike. Tasters in the mild and delicate camp gave high scores to Pompeian and Whole Foods oils. Among tasters who preferred full-bodied, bold oils, Colavita and Filippo Berio earned high marks.

THE BEST ALL-PURPOSE OLIVE OIL
Da Vinci Extra-Virgin Olive Oil was the favorite in our tasting of leading supermarket brands. It was described as "very ripe," "buttery," and "complex."

THE BEST MILD OLIVE OIL
Pompeian Extra-Virgin Olive Oil was the favorite among tasters who preferred a milder, more delicate oil. It was described as "clean," "round," and "sunny."

THE BEST FULL-BODIED OLIVE OIL
Colavita Extra-Virgin Olive Oil was the favorite among tasters who preferred a bolder, more full-bodied oil. It was described as "heavy," "complex," and "briny."

vinegar, Dijon mustard, and fresh thyme, resulting in a potent but nicely balanced roasted garlic flavor. This low-fat dressing is a great change of pace from the simpler flavors of a basic vinaigrette.

Roasted Garlic Dressing

MAKES ABOUT 1 CUP

Pureed roasted garlic gives this flavorful dressing a thick and creamy consistency.

ROASTED GARLIC

2	large garlic heads
2	tablespoons water
	Salt

2	tablespoons extra-virgin olive oil
4	teaspoons cider vinegar
1	tablespoon Dijon mustard
½	teaspoon minced fresh thyme leaves
⅛	teaspoon ground black pepper

1. Adjust an oven rack to the upper-middle position and heat the oven to 400 degrees. Following the illustrations below, cut ½ inch off the top of each garlic head to expose the tops of the cloves. Set the garlic heads cut-side up on a small sheet of aluminum foil and sprinkle with the water and a pinch of salt. Gather the foil up around the garlic tightly to form a packet, place it directly on the oven rack, and roast for 45 minutes.

2. Carefully open just the top of the foil to expose the garlic and continue to roast until the garlic is soft and golden brown, about 20 minutes longer. Allow the roasted garlic to cool for 20 minutes, reserving any juices in the foil packet.

3. Squeeze the garlic cloves from the skins, following the illustration below. Process the roasted garlic, reserved garlic juices, ½ teaspoon salt, and the remaining ingredients together in a blender (or food processor) until thick and smooth, about 1 minute. The dressing can be refrigerated for up to 4 days in a lidded jar; bring to room temperature, then shake vigorously to recombine before using.

PER 1-TABLESPOON SERVING: Cal 25; Fat 2 g; Sat fat 0 g; Chol 0 mg; Carb 2 g; Protein 0 g; Fiber 0 g; Sodium 100 mg

CREAMY SALAD DRESSINGS

IT'S NO SECRET THAT CREAMY DRESSINGS pack a caloric wallop. Made from rich, heavy ingredients like mayonnaise, sour cream, and sometimes heavy cream, the average creamy dressing contains about 8 grams of fat and 100 calories in a 2-tablespoon serving.

Does that mean that creamy dressings are off limits for those watching fat and calories? Too many of us in the test kitchen are fans of creamy dressings to throw in the towel. Having had previous success with our creamy party dips (see page 3), we

ROASTING GARLIC

1. Cut ½ inch from the tip end of the head of garlic so that the clove interiors are exposed.

2. Place the garlic, cut-side up, in the center of a 10-inch square of aluminum foil. Sprinkle with water and seal.

3. After the garlic has roasted, open the foil package and cool. With your hand or the flat edge of a chef's knife, squeeze the garlic cloves from the skins, starting from the root end and working up.

speculated that we could develop a creamy dressing along the same lines—a standard creamy dressing base to which pungent flavorings like garlic, fresh herbs, and mustard could be added. And we aimed to use the base as a jumping off point to capture some classic creamy dressing flavors such as blue cheese and ranch.

We first tackled the creamy base for the dressing. Typically, full-fat creamy dressings have a mayonnaise base, which is thinned out or enriched with one or a combination of the following: sour cream, milk, buttermilk, heavy cream, yogurt, and water. Low-fat recipes usually make substitutions for the more fattening ingredients like mayonnaise, sour cream, and heavy cream. However, we found that some of these substitutions included oddball ingredients, which made lean, sharp-tasting dressings. Ingredients like soft tofu and cottage cheese were added to give the illusion of "creamy." These recipes made use of the blender to puree lumpy ingredients smooth, but it didn't always work so well. Soft tofu put on a mediocre performance, giving the dressing a pleasant creamy texture but making it watery and thin tasting. Tasters complained that the tofu just didn't have the creamy quality of dairy they wanted. And even after minutes on the blender's "liquefy" setting, the dressing made with cottage cheese still had an unpleasant texture. We observed that the cottage cheese worked well to thicken the dressing; however, it was bland, and a few tasters complained that they detected a slightly grainy texture. In the end, we concluded that these lower calorie ingredients merely add bulk rather than body.

Other low-fat creamy dressing recipes make use of ingredients such as low-fat yogurt, reduced-fat mayonnaise, and light sour cream. And from previous tests of full-fat creamy dressing, we discovered that the key to a well rounded dressing—one that didn't taste dull or overly tangy—is to use a trio of dairy ingredients: buttermilk, sour cream, and mayonnaise. We used this as a platform for our tests, plugging low-fat varieties of these dairy products into the equation. We bypassed trying versions of nonfat mayonnaise and sour cream because of their dismal performances in previous tests (nonfat mayo

has an unavoidable pasty-sweet character and fat-free sour cream a lip-puckering tartness). And to keep things simple, we tested the base using equal parts of each ingredient. Tasters were impressed with the performance of low-fat versions of mayonnaise and sour cream when combined with the buttermilk (which is already a low-fat ingredient). All gave the dressing a nice balance of flavors and a pleasing consistency. The mayonnaise contributed a creamy, round sweetness; the sour cream acted as a rich thickener, giving the dressing some great body and brightness; and the buttermilk added its signature tangy kick.

Now we were ready to finesse our creamy dressing base's taste, and add some zesty flavors. For a bit more depth and body we added mustard, and minced shallot contributed a great, round allium flavor. And tasters were pleased with the addition of white wine vinegar, commenting that it accentuated the buttermilk tang while balancing

---

MAKEOVER AT A GLANCE

—Classic—
Blue Cheese Dressing
(per serving)

Calories: 100	Cholesterol: 20 mg
Fat: 8 g	Saturated Fat: 3.5 g

—Light—
Blue Cheese Dressing
(per serving)

Calories: 40	Cholesterol: 5 mg
Fat: 2.5 g	Saturated Fat: 1.5 g

How We Did It

- Replaced the sour cream and mayonnaise with reduced-fat products
- Used a strongly flavored blue cheese to get maximum flavor from a smaller amount (and thus used less fat)
- Built up the flavor with garlic powder, vinegar, and a pinch of sugar

the creaminess of the mayonnaise–sour cream combination. Sticking with pungent ingredients like Parmesan cheese, garlic, and peppercorns, we were able to flavor our dressing without adding significant amounts of fat and calories. Our low-fat creamy dressings were a success, and tasters were amazed at the new numbers—only 2–3 grams of fat and 30–45 calories per serving. However, we weren't quite done flavoring our dressing, as we had our sights set on recreating the classic ranch and blue cheese flavors.

We tackled blue cheese first. The ideal version of this steakhouse classic is creamy and tangy, with a hint of sweetness and a few crumbles of blue cheese. We were focused on achieving something just like this, and started by exploring the type of blue cheese to use. Typically, blue cheese dressing recipes call for about ¾ cup of blue cheese but this doesn't necessarily account for the intensity of the cheese variety. Stella and Danish blues are much milder than, say, Stiltons and Roqueforts. We reasoned that if we used a stronger flavored blue cheese we might be able to get away with using less of it. The result: tasters were amazed that it took as little as ¼ cup of strong blue cheese to flavor our dressing. And although our dressing lacked the thick viscosity of a traditional blue cheese dressing, we found that our thinner dressing coated the greens more evenly.

So with the type of cheese nailed down, we looked to balancing and livening up the dressing a bit. We added a smidge of sugar for sweetness and garlic powder, which worked better than fresh garlic. Tasters complained that fresh garlic was too spicy, and no matter how little we used, the flavor was always too overpowering. Ordinarily, in a full-fat dressing, the garlic flavor is softened by the fat, but in our leaner dressing the garlic was just too prominent. Once we added a splash of white wine vinegar for zing, our dressing now had high and low notes that titillated the taste buds. It was also jam-packed with blue cheese flavor, and delicious when tossed with greens.

With blue cheese dressing under our belt, we focused on pinning down classic ranch flavor. In essence, ranch is a zesty mix of spices and alliums such as minced shallot and garlic, punctuated by

the full flavor of fresh herbs like dill and cilantro. And with our new creamy base, we had just the right amount of buttermilk tang and creaminess to accommodate ranch flavors. To season our creamy dressing base, we tried a number of ingredients called for in other recipes, including Worcestershire sauce, Dijon mustard, lime juice, red wine vinegar, celery seeds, and a host of dried herbs. In the end, we found that fresh herbs were the key. Fresh dill and cilantro, accompanied by minced shallot and garlic powder, along with a splash of lemon juice (in place of the white wine vinegar in our base), worked in unison to give the dressing a bright, zippy, authentic flavor.

On a final note, we discovered that creamy dressings worked best over sturdy greens, such

TESTING NOTES

Choose Your Cheese Wisely

STELLA BLUE CHEESE   DANISH BLUE CHEESE

Milder blue cheeses like Stella or Danish blue worked in our dressing, but we had to use a large quantity, which meant more fat and calories.

THE WINNERS

STILTON   ROQUEFORT

We found that strong blues like Stilton and Roquefort helped us pack our dressing with great blue cheese flavor without adding large amounts of fat and calories.

as romaine, iceberg, and green leaf lettuce. Some tasters preferred softer lettuces, such as Boston or Bibb; however, it should be noted that these varieties wilted quickly under the weight of the creamy mixture. And when it came to more assertively flavored greens, several tasters liked the way the tartness of the buttermilk accented the spiciness of arugula and the bitterness of radicchio.

While many of the recipes we have encountered recommend dousing 8 cups of loosely packed greens with as much as 1 cup of creamy dressing, we noted that ½ cup of dressing is all it takes to sufficiently coat 8 cups of loosely packed greens, which serves about four people as a side salad. Also, we found that these dressings can be stored for up to four days.

Blue Cheese Dressing
MAKES ABOUT 1 CUP

If you like a dressing with milder blue cheese flavor, use a less pungent cheese, such as Stella or Danish blue.

1	ounce strongly flavored blue cheese, such as Roquefort or Stilton, crumbled (about ¼ cup)
¼	cup buttermilk
¼	cup reduced-fat mayonnaise
¼	cup low-fat sour cream
1	tablespoon water
2	teaspoons white wine vinegar
¼	teaspoon salt
¼	teaspoon garlic powder
⅛	teaspoon ground black pepper

Mash the blue cheese and buttermilk in a small bowl with a fork until the mixture resembles cottage cheese with small curds. Stir in the remaining ingredients. The dressing can be refrigerated in an airtight container for up to 4 days.

PER 2-TABLESPOON SERVING: Cal 40; Fat 2.5 g; Sat fat 1.5 g; Chol 5 mg; Carb 2 g; Protein 2 g; Fiber 0 g; Sodium 200 mg

Parmesan–Peppercorn Dressing
MAKES ABOUT 1 CUP

If you like the dressing with more peppercorn flavor, season with additional ground black pepper to taste.

¼	cup buttermilk
¼	cup reduced-fat mayonnaise
¼	cup low-fat sour cream
¼	cup grated Parmesan cheese
1	tablespoon water
1	tablespoon juice from 1 lemon
1	teaspoon Dijon mustard
1	teaspoon minced shallot
½	teaspoon ground black pepper
¼	teaspoon salt

Stir all of the ingredients together until smooth. The dressing can be refrigerated in an airtight container for up to 4 days.

PER 2-TABLESPOON SERVING: Cal 45; Fat 3 g; Sat fat 1.5 g; Chol 5 mg; Carb 2 g; Protein 2 g; Fiber 0 g; Sodium 230 mg

Tarragon–Mustard Dressing
MAKES ABOUT 1 CUP

This classic combination of mustard and tarragon is excellent drizzled over sliced tomatoes or cucumbers.

¼	cup buttermilk
¼	cup reduced-fat mayonnaise
¼	cup low-fat sour cream
1	tablespoon water
1	tablespoon whole-grain mustard
1	teaspoon white wine vinegar
1	teaspoon minced shallot
1	teaspoon minced fresh tarragon leaves
¼	teaspoon salt
⅛	teaspoon ground black pepper

Stir all of the ingredients together until smooth. The dressing can be refrigerated in an airtight container for up to 4 days.

PER 2-TABLESPOON SERVING: Cal 30; Fat 2 g; Sat fat 1 g; Chol 5 mg; Carb 2 g; Protein 1 g; Fiber 0 g; Sodium 190 mg

Creamy Cucumber-Dill Dressing

MAKES ABOUT I CUP

The trio of buttermilk, reduced-fat mayonnaise, and low-fat sour cream gives this dressing its rich and creamy texture, the perfect backdrop for cool cucumber and dill.

- ¼ cup buttermilk
- ¼ cup reduced-fat mayonnaise
- ¼ cup low-fat sour cream
- I cucumber, peeled, seeded (see page 50), and grated
- I teaspoon water
- I teaspoon white wine vinegar
- I teaspoon Dijon mustard
- I teaspoon minced shallot
- I teaspoon minced fresh dill
- ¼ teaspoon salt
- ⅛ teaspoon ground black pepper

Stir all of the ingredients together until smooth. The dressing can be refrigerated in an airtight container for up to 4 days.

PER 2-TABLESPOON SERVING: Cal 35; Fat 2 g; Sat fat 1 g; Chol 5 mg; Carb 3 g; Protein 1 g; Fiber 0 g; Sodium 170 mg

Ranch Dressing

MAKES ABOUT I CUP

Fresh herbs are essential for the flavor of this dressing; do not use dried herbs.

- ¼ cup buttermilk
- ¼ cup reduced-fat mayonnaise
- ¼ cup low-fat sour cream
- I tablespoon water
- I tablespoon minced shallot or red onion
- I tablespoon minced fresh cilantro leaves
- I tablespoon juice from I lemon
- 2 teaspoons minced fresh dill
- ½ teaspoon garlic powder
- ¼ teaspoon salt
- ¼ teaspoon ground black pepper
   Pinch cayenne

Stir all of the ingredients together until smooth. The dressing can be refrigerated in an airtight container for up to 4 days.

PER 2-TABLESPOON SERVING: Cal 30; Fat 1.5 g; Sat fat 1 g; Chol 5 mg; Carb 2 g; Protein 1 g; Fiber 0 g; Sodium 150 mg

CHICKEN CAESAR SALAD

CHICKEN CAESAR SALAD APPEARS ON MANY restaurant menus. And because it's a salad, many assume it's a safe bet when watching fat and calories. Think again. The dressing, the cheese, the croutons, and depending on how the chicken is prepared—well, it all adds up. In fact, some chicken Caesar salads can be more fattening than a bacon cheeseburger.

We love a great Caesar salad here in the test kitchen. The ideal version includes crisp romaine lettuce sprinkled with grated Parmesan cheese, tossed with toasty garlic croutons, the whole coated with a dressing containing garlic, anchovy, and lemon juice, boosted by the zip of Worcestershire sauce and bound together by a rich emulsion of egg yolks and olive oil. The downside, however, is that this classic salad is rich, weighing in with 660 calories and 40 grams of fat per serving. We knew we could do better than this. But, having tasted existing recipes for low-fat Caesar salads, we also knew it wouldn't be easy.

When it comes to Caesar, the dressing is one of the most crucial components, so you can only imagine the importance of developing a tasty, light dressing recipe. It's been our experience that many low-fat Caesar dressings omit the egg yolk and most of the oil, thus removing the creamy character of the dressing without replacing it. What you're left with is a wildly out-of-balance dressing, without enough body to cling to the sturdy pieces of romaine. We were determined to create a Caesar dressing with a creamy body and the classic amalgam of zesty flavors that was lower in fat and calories than the original.

We set out to find a way to omit the fattening

egg and oil emulsion in traditional Caesar dressing without compromising taste and richness. Before getting started, though, we analyzed the function of the egg and oil in the dressing. In our experience making full-fat Caesar dressing, we've observed that the egg emulsion not only adds richness, but also works to smooth out the other intense flavors in the dressing. We concluded that we would need to find a creamy replacement for the emulsion.

Some low-fat recipes emulsify with ingredients like sour cream, yogurt, tofu, and buttermilk. We found that sour cream was too tart and dairy rich; yogurt gave us similar results and just didn't blend well; and soft tofu added a nice creamy texture but was just too bland. Tasters, however, were impressed with buttermilk's pleasant tang and its silkiness, almost identical to egg yolks. But some complained that the dressing was still missing a bit of richness. To correct this, we added 2 tablespoons of reduced-fat mayonnaise. This technique worked well, and helped us knock the amount of extra-virgin olive oil from the ⅓ cup called for in the classic recipe down to 2 tablespoons. Tasters praised the dressing with this new oil amount for its balance of richness and seasoning.

Now that we had the basics of our light Caesar dressing figured out, we looked to finesse the balance of flavors. Tasters favored 2 tablespoons of lemon juice, a modest teaspoon of Worcestershire sauce, and 1½ teaspoons of minced garlic. Three anchovy fillets contributed a classic flavor dimension to the dressing, while Dijon mustard—an untraditional ingredient—added a bit more depth and helped emulsify the dressing. Instead of tossing the romaine with grated Parmesan before dressing the salad—a classic technique—we decided to stir the Parmesan into the dressing itself. (When we added the Parmesan with all the other ingredients in the blender, tasters complained that the cheese developed an unfavorable grainy character.) This technique helped spread the flavor of the cheese even further, and added an intensity to the dressing that had a cohesive effect on all its flavors.

As for the lettuce, romaine is the standard choice. Its fresh crunch is a welcome contrast to the intensity of Caesar dressing. Some Caesar salads sport whole leaves of romaine, but tasters found these unwieldy on the plate, so instead we tore the lettuce into easy-to-fork, ½-inch pieces.

We wanted the chicken in our salad to be fresh and moist, so leftover roast or grilled chicken were not an option. At the same time, we also didn't want to make a big production out of preparing the chicken. We found our answer in a half sautéing and half poaching method using very little fat. Using a nonstick skillet, we brown the chicken breast, on just one side, in 1 teaspoon of vegetable oil, which takes about 5 minutes. Next we flip the chicken over, add water to the skillet, reduce the heat, and cover the skillet until the breast is cooked through, which takes only about 5 minutes more. This method yielded just what we were looking for: moist, well-seasoned chicken breast. (Feel free to use this method whenever you need chicken for salad.)

Caesar salad wouldn't be complete without the crunch of croutons—and we found a way to make our croutons lighter than store-bought varieties (and most traditional methods) by using olive oil spray and garlic powder (see page 42) rather than the traditional garlic oil. At last, we had a zesty main-course salad we could really dig into.

TRIMMING BONELESS, SKINLESS CHICKEN BREASTS

Most boneless, skinless chicken breasts have a little yellow or white fat still attached to the breast meat. Lay each cutlet smooth side facing up, and smooth the top with your fingers. Any fat will slide to the edge of the cutlet, where it can be easily trimmed away with a knife.

Chicken Caesar Salad

SERVES 4

Note that you'll only use half the dressing in the salad—leftovers, which will keep refrigerated for up to 1 day, make a great dip for crudités.

CAESAR DRESSING

¼	cup buttermilk
2	tablespoons juice from 1 lemon
2	tablespoons reduced-fat mayonnaise
2	teaspoons Dijon mustard
1	teaspoon Worcestershire sauce
1–2	medium garlic cloves, minced or pressed through a garlic press (1 to 2 teaspoons)
3	anchovy fillets, rinsed and patted dry
½	teaspoon salt
½	teaspoon ground black pepper
2	tablespoons extra-virgin olive oil
1	ounce Parmesan cheese, grated (½ cup)

CHICKEN

4	boneless, skinless chicken breast halves (about 6 ounces each), trimmed of excess fat
	Salt and ground black pepper
1	teaspoon vegetable oil

SALAD

2	medium heads romaine lettuce (larger outer leaves removed) or 2 large romaine hearts, washed, dried, and torn into ½-inch pieces (about 10 cups loosely packed)
1⅓	cups Garlic Croutons (page 42)

1. FOR THE DRESSING: Puree all of the dressing ingredients except the oil and Parmesan in a blender (or food processor) until smooth, about 30 seconds, scraping down the sides as needed. With the motor running, add the oil in a steady stream. Stir in the cheese. Set aside ½ cup of the dressing for the salad and refrigerate the remaining ½ cup for another use (see note).

2. FOR THE CHICKEN: Pat the chicken dry with paper towels, then season generously with salt and pepper. Heat the oil in a large nonstick skillet over medium-high heat until just smoking. Add the chicken and cook until browned on the first side, about 5 minutes. Flip the chicken over, add ½ cup water, and reduce the heat to medium-low. Cover and continue to cook until the thickest part of the breast is no longer pink and registers about 165 degrees on an instant-read thermometer, about 5 minutes. Transfer the chicken to a plate and set aside to cool; slice the chicken breasts crosswise into ½-inch-thick slices.

3. TO ASSEMBLE THE SALAD: In a large bowl, toss the lettuce with all but 1 tablespoon of the dressing to coat; divide evenly among individual plates. Add the chicken to the bowl used to dress the lettuce and toss with the remaining 1 tablespoon dressing to coat. Arrange the chicken evenly among the plates, on top of the lettuce. Sprinkle each plate with a portion of the croutons.

PER SERVING: Cal 330; Fat 10 g; Sat fat 2 g; Chol 105 mg; Carb 14 g; Protein 45 g; Fiber 3 g; Sodium 740 mg

---

MAKEOVER AT A GLANCE

–Classic–
Chicken Caesar Salad
(per serving)

Calories: 660	Cholesterol: 215 mg
Fat: 40 g	Saturated Fat: 7 g

–Light–
Chicken Caesar Salad
(per serving)

Calories: 330	Cholesterol: 105 mg
Fat: 10 g	Saturated Fat: 2 g

How We Did It

- Replaced most of the fat in the dressing with buttermilk and reduced-fat mayonnaise
- Cooked the chicken in just 1 teaspoon oil, first browning the chicken, then poaching it
- Replaced traditional high-fat croutons with our recipe for low-fat croutons

SUPERMARKET SHELVES ARE LOADED WITH bags and boxes of croutons in all sizes, shapes, and flavors. We were surprised at the relatively low number of calories and fat grams that most of these products claimed. Taking a closer look, however, we realized that "one serving" amounts to what you snacked on while you were preparing your salad, about eight wimpy croutons. And while homemade croutons taste far superior to any you can purchase at the supermarket, they usually require significant amounts of oil or butter to toast to a tasty golden brown. In fact, one serving (about 1/3 cup) of traditional homemade croutons contains 70 calories and 4 fat grams.

Determined to reduce the calories and fat grams, we developed a technique for making croutons with a generous coating of vegetable or olive oil spray. This proved to be a great way to evenly distribute a small amount of oil, which allows for even browning. For flavor, we relied on various herbs, spices, cheese, and, of course, salt. Nearly any type of bread will make decent croutons, from stale pieces of baguette to end slices of a sandwich loaf. These croutons are so tasty that we guarantee you will want to snack on them while you make your salad.

❧

Croutons

MAKES 4 CUPS

Leftover croutons will keep in an airtight container or zipper-lock bag for about one week.

    4   cups 1/2-inch bread cubes
         Vegetable or olive oil spray
    1/4 teaspoon salt

Adjust an oven rack to the middle position and heat the oven to 350 degrees. Generously coat the bread cubes with the vegetable oil spray. Sprinkle with salt and toss to combine. Spread the bread onto a baking sheet and bake until golden brown, 20 to 25 minutes, tossing halfway through to promote even browning. Allow the croutons to cool to room temperature before serving.

PER 1/3-CUP SERVING: Cal 40; Fat .5 g; Sat fat 0 g; Chol 0 mg; Carb 8 g; Protein 1 g; Fiber 0 g; Sodium 130 mg

➤ VARIATIONS

Garlic Croutons
Sprinkle 1 teaspoon garlic powder onto the bread cubes with the salt.

PER 1/3-CUP SERVING: Cal 40; Fat .5 g; Sat fat 0 g; Chol 0 mg; Carb 8 g; Protein 1 g; Fiber 0 g; Sodium 130 mg

Chili Croutons
Sprinkle 1 teaspoon garlic powder, 1 teaspoon chili powder, 1/4 teaspoon pepper, and 1/8 teaspoon cayenne onto the bread with the salt.

PER 1/3-CUP SERVING: Cal 45; Fat .5 g; Sat fat 0 g; Chol 0 mg; Carb 8 g; Protein 1 g; Fiber 0 g; Sodium 135 mg

Spiced Croutons
These croutons are not only good in salad, they're also terrific in soup, such as Cream of Roasted Butternut Squash Soup (page 78) or Cream of Roasted Carrot Soup (page 77).

Sprinkle 1/2 teaspoon ground cumin, 1/2 teaspoon ground coriander, 1/4 teaspoon paprika, and 1/8 teaspoon cayenne pepper onto the bread with the salt.

PER 1/3-CUP SERVING: Cal 40; Fat .5 g; Sat fat 0 g; Chol 0 mg; Carb 8 g; Protein 1 g; Fiber 0 g; Sodium 130 mg

Herbed Croutons
Sprinkle 1/4 teaspoon pepper, 2 teaspoons fresh rosemary or 1/2 teaspoon dried, and 2 teaspoons minced fresh thyme leaves, sage, or dill (or 1/2 teaspoon dried) onto the bread with the salt.

PER 1/3-CUP SERVING: Cal 40; Fat .5 g; Sat fat 0 g; Chol 0 mg; Carb 8 g; Protein 1 g; Fiber 0 g; Sodium 130 mg

Parmesan Croutons
Sprinkle 1 ounce grated Parmesan cheese (1/2 cup) onto the bread with the salt.

PER 1/3-CUP SERVING: Cal 50; Fat .5 g; Sat fat 0 g; Chol 0 mg; Carb 8 g; Protein 2 g; Fiber 0 g; Sodium 170 mg

INGREDIENTS: Salad Greens

The following glossary starts with the four main varieties of lettuce and then covers the most commonly available specialty greens (called mesclun or mesclun mix when sold in combination). When substituting one green for another, try to choose greens with a similar intensity. For example, peppery arugula could be used as a substitute for watercress or dandelion greens, but not for red leaf lettuce, at least not without significantly altering the flavor of the salad.

Main Varieties of Lettuce

BUTTERHEAD LETTUCES Boston and Bibb are among the most common varieties of these very mild-tasting lettuces. A head of butterhead lettuce has a nice round shape and loose outer leaves. The color of the leaves is light to medium green (except, of course, in red-tinged varieties), and the leaves are extremely tender.

ICEBERG LETTUCE Iceberg is the best-known variety of crisphead lettuce. Its shape is perfectly round, and the leaves are tightly packed. A high water content makes iceberg especially crisp and crunchy but also robs it of flavor.

LOOSELEAF LETTUCES Red leaf, green leaf, red oakleaf, and lolla rossa are the most common varieties. These lettuces grow in a loose rosette shape, not a tight head. The ruffled leaves are perhaps the most versatile because their texture is soft yet still crunchy and their flavor is mild but not bland.

ROMAINE LETTUCE The leaves on this lettuce are long and broad at the top. The color shades from dark green in the outer leaves (which are often tough and should be discarded) to pale green in the thick, crisp heart. Also called Cos lettuce, this variety has more crunch than either butterhead or looseleaf lettuces and a more pronounced earthy flavor. Romaine lettuce is essential in Caesar salad, where the greens must stand up to a thick, creamy dressing.

Specialty Greens

ARUGULA Also called rocket, these tender, dark green leaves can be faintly peppery or downright spicy. Larger, older leaves tend to be hotter than small, young leaves, but the flavor is variable, so taste arugula before adding it to a salad. Try to buy arugula in bunches with the stems and roots still attached—they help keep the leaves fresh. Arugula bruises and discolors quite easily. If possible, keep stemmed leaves whole. Very large leaves can be torn just before they are needed.

BELGIAN ENDIVE With its characteristic bitter chicory flavor, endive is generally used sparingly in salads. Endive is crisp and crunchy, not tender and leafy. The yellow leaf tips are usually mild in flavor, while the white, thick leaf bases are more bitter. Endive is the one salad green we routinely cut rather than tear. Remove whole leaves from the head and then slice them crosswise into bite-size pieces.

CHICORY Also known as curly endive, chicory has curly, jagged leaves that form a loose head. The leaves are bright green, and their flavor is usually fairly bitter. The outer leaves can be tough, especially at the base. Inner leaves are generally more tender.

DANDELION GREENS Dandelion greens are tender and pleasantly bitter. The leaves are long and have ragged edges. The flavor is similar to that of arugula or watercress, both of which can be used interchangeably with dandelion greens. Tougher, older leaves that are more than several inches long should be cooked, not eaten raw.

ESCAROLE The smooth, broad leaves of escarole are bunched together in a loose head. With its long ribs and softly ruffled leaves, it looks a bit like leaf lettuce. As a member of the chicory family, escarole can have an intense flavor, although not nearly as strong as that of endive or chicory.

MIZUNA This Japanese spider mustard has long, thin, dark green leaves with deeply cut, jagged edges. Sturdier than arugula, watercress, or dandelion greens, it can nonetheless be used interchangeably with these slightly milder greens in salads when a strong peppery punch is desired. Note that larger, older leaves are better cooked, so choose small "baby" mizuna for salads.

RADICCHIO This most familiar chicory was almost unknown in this country two decades ago. The tight heads of purple leaves streaked with prominent white ribs are now a supermarket staple. Radicchio has a decent punch but is not nearly as bitter as other chicories, especially Belgian endive.

SPINACH Of all the cooking greens, spinach is the most versatile in salads because it can be used in its miniature or full-grown form. Flat-leaf spinach is better than curly spinach in salads because the stems are usually less fibrous and the spade-shaped leaves are thinner, more tender, and sweeter. Curly spinach is often dry and chewy, while flat-leaf, sold in bundles rather than in cellophane bags, is usually tender and moist, more like lettuce than a cooking green.

TATSOI This Asian green has thin white stalks and round, dark green leaves. A member of the cruciferous family of vegetables that includes broccoli and cabbage, tatsoi tastes like a mild Chinese cabbage, such as bok choy. However, the texture of these miniature leaves is always delicate.

WATERCRESS With its small leaves and long stalks, watercress is easy to spot. It requires some patience in the kitchen because the stalks are really quite tough and must be removed one at a time. Like arugula, watercress usually has a mildly spicy flavor.

WILTED SPINACH SALADS

DARK GREEN LEAFY VEGETABLES, SUCH AS spinach, supply us with more nutrients per calorie than most any other food. It only made sense for us to develop a recipe utilizing this healthful green. And what better way to get our essentials than in wilted spinach salads, a great alternative to their cold-dressed cousins?

Although it's mostly thought of as a first course salad, we aimed to create warm spinach salad hearty enough to qualify as a main course by bulking the dish up with a protein and other ingredients. However, we've found that wilted salads are the victims of unfair stereotyping. Thought of as complicated and difficult to execute, they are somehow perceived as an item you can enjoy only in a restaurant. This isn't true; warm spinach salads are easy enough to be a mid-week dinner, as they require little time and effort. But that's not to say there aren't pitfalls you must avoid when preparing them.

Warm spinach salad at its finest is a pleasant dish of tender spinach leaves lightly wilted by a warm aromatic dressing. But after several tests in the kitchen, we found this ideal is not automatically achieved. The salads we tried ran the gamut from tough leaves covered with bland, insipid dressing to overdressed piles of mushy greens standing in puddles of greasy vinaigrette. Thus, in our testing we knew we had to address two major factors: the type of spinach to use and how to dress it. As for making the salad into a main course, we decided on quick-cooking proteins like rich, briny scallops and piquant poultry-based sausage—ingredients we favored for their combination of hearty character and minimal fat/calorie content.

We tackled spinach type first. There are two categories of spinach: curly leaf and flat leaf. Curly-leaf spinach is probably the variety most people are familiar with; it is usually packaged in cellophane bags and sold at the local supermarket. This type of spinach didn't do well in our tests. Tasters felt the leaves were too dry and chewy, and the remaining stems were fibrous. The leaves also didn't wilt with the addition of the warm vinaigrette, so we decided to reserve this type for recipes in which the spinach is cooked.

When we tried flat-leaf spinach, our results were more encouraging. We found two types of flat-leaf spinach commonly available at the market. The larger leaf spinach, which was sold in bundles, worked fine in our salad; its tender leaves were moist and wilted well. But the bunches we bought were full of dirt and required several washings to rid them of all the grit. Discouraged by the amount of time it took to wash and prepare the spinach, we bought a bag of the baby spinach sold in the supermarket in the same aisle as the prepared salads-in-a-bag. Baby spinach worked perfectly. The small, tender leaves came washed and trimmed, and all we had to do was open the bag and place the spinach in a bowl. You can't get much quicker than that.

With the base of our salad tested, we could focus on how to make a flavorful dressing that didn't overpower the greens or make them greasy. We knew that the flavor of the acidic component in the warm dressing should be varied based on the accompanying salad ingredients. The scallop salad vinaigrette would need to be light, bright, and citrusy, because scallops have a delicate flavor. We found that a mixture of orange juice and sherry vinegar was most preferred by tasters, especially when combined with the sweet burst of orange segments, savory crispness of thinly sliced red onion, and crunch of toasted almonds.

Because poultry sausage is richer, with more assertive flavors than scallops, we settled on a stronger dressing that combined apple cider and cider vinegar, punctuated with a tablespoon of whole-grain mustard for depth. This vinaigrette went well with the sliced apple and walnuts we had added to the dish, and tasters liked its autumnal theme.

As for the oil component of the dressing, we concluded that we didn't need to add much. Tasters thought that vinaigrettes made with 1 tablespoon of oil tasted most balanced. Too much olive oil in the vinaigrette bogged down the spinach, making it wet and slick. And too little made for an overly sharp vinaigrette, which overpowered all of the other elements of the salad. Also, during our testing, we found that if we added the acidic component of the dressing in the early stages of the cooking process, the flavors were muted. Swirling in the acid at the end, after the pan had been removed from the heat, restored some of the punch. Our new vinaigrettes wilted the spinach perfectly; the leaves retained a satisfying crunch without becoming cooked and slimy. We now had bright, fresh-tasting spinach salads that weren't too greasy, and were hearty enough to serve as a main course.

Wilted Spinach and Orange Salad with Pan-Seared Scallops

SERVES 4

8	ounces baby spinach (about 8 cups loosely packed)
1/4	cup sliced almonds, toasted (see box)
24	large sea scallops (about 1 1/2 pounds), patted dry, and tendons removed (see the illustration on page 252)
	Salt and ground black pepper
2	tablespoons vegetable oil
1	tablespoon extra-virgin olive oil
1/2	medium red onion, sliced thin
1	tablespoon orange juice
1	teaspoon minced fresh thyme leaves
2	large oranges, peel and pith removed, quartered, and sliced crosswise into 1/2-inch-thick pieces
2	tablespoons sherry vinegar

1. Place the spinach and almonds in a large bowl. Lay the scallops out over a paper towel–lined plate or baking sheet; season the scallops with salt and pepper. Lay a single layer of paper towels over the scallops; set aside.

2. Heat 1 tablespoon of the vegetable oil in a large nonstick skillet over high heat until just smoking. Meanwhile, press the paper towel flush to the scallops to dry. Add half of the scallops to the skillet and cook until evenly golden on one side, 1 to 2 minutes. Using tongs, transfer the scallops, golden side facing up, to large plate; set aside. Wipe out the skillet using a wad of paper towels. Add the remaining 1 tablespoon vegetable oil to the empty skillet and return to high heat until just smoking.

Add the remaining scallops and cook until evenly golden, 1 to 2 minutes. Turn the heat to medium, flip the scallops over, and return the first batch to the pan, golden side facing up. Cook until the sides have firmed up and all but the middle third of the scallop is opaque, 30 to 60 seconds longer. Transfer all the scallops to a large plate; set aside. Wipe out the skillet using a wad of paper towels.

3. Add the olive oil, onion, orange juice, thyme, and 1/2 teaspoon salt to the skillet and return to medium-high heat until the onion is slightly softened, about 1 minute. Remove the pan from the heat, add the oranges and vinegar, and swirl to incorporate. Pour the warm dressing over the spinach mixture and gently toss to wilt. Divide the spinach salad among four plates and arrange the scallops on top.

PER SERVING: Cal 340; Fat 15 g; Sat fat 1.5 g; Chol 55 mg; Carb 22 g; Protein 32 g; Fiber 5 g; Sodium 800 mg

TOASTING NUTS

IT'S NO SURPRISE THAT NUTS AND SEEDS contain a substantial amount of fat and calories. But this doesn't mean they don't fit into a lighter, healthier diet. Nuts are nutrient dense, a good source of fiber, and we find that a small amount goes a long way in the flavor department. The best way to maximize the flavor of nuts and seeds is to toast them, whether you are sprinkling them on a salad, adding them to pie filling, or tossing them into a dish of pasta.

To toast a small amount (less than 1 cup) of nuts or seeds, put them in a dry skillet over medium heat. Shake the skillet occasionally to prevent scorching and toast until they are lightly browned and fragrant, 3 to 8 minutes. Watch the nuts closely because they can go from golden to burnt very quickly. To toast a large quantity of nuts, spread the nuts in a single layer on a rimmed baking sheet and toast in a 350-degree oven. To promote even toasting, shake the baking sheet every few minutes, and toast until the nuts are lightly browned and fragrant, 5 to 10 minutes.

Wilted Spinach and Apple Salad with Sausage

SERVES 4

We found lots of different chicken and turkey sausage flavors at our supermarket. Try to choose those with flavors that will complement this salad, such as apple, herb, or garlic. Make sure that you slice the apple just before serving to prevent it from turning brown.

8	ounces baby spinach (about 8 cups loosely packed)
1/4	cup walnuts, toasted and chopped coarse (see page 45)
1	teaspoon vegetable oil
1	pound chicken or turkey sausages
1/4	cup plus 1 tablespoon apple cider or apple juice
1	tablespoon extra-virgin olive oil
1/2	medium red onion, sliced thin
1	teaspoon minced fresh thyme leaves
	Salt and ground black pepper
2	tablespoons cider vinegar
1	tablespoon whole-grain mustard
1	large apple, cored, halved, and sliced thin

1. Place the spinach and walnuts in a large bowl. Heat the vegetable oil in a large nonstick skillet over high heat until just smoking. Add the sausages and cook until evenly golden, about 8 minutes. Add ¼ cup of the apple cider to the skillet; bring to a simmer, then cover, reduce the heat to medium-low, and cook until the sausages are cooked through, about 8 minutes. Transfer the sausages to a plate. When cool enough to handle, slice the sausages on the bias into ½-inch-thick pieces. Wipe out the skillet using a wad of paper towels.

2. Add the olive oil, remaining tablespoon of apple cider, onion, thyme, ½ teaspoon salt, and ¼ teaspoon pepper to the skillet and return to medium-high heat until the onion is slightly softened, about 1 minute. Remove the pan from the heat, add the cider vinegar and mustard to the skillet, and swirl to incorporate. Pour the warm dressing over the spinach mixture and gently toss to wilt. Add the apple and toss to combine. Divide the spinach salad among four plates and arrange the pieces of sausage on top.

PER SERVING: Cal 340; Fat 19 g; Sat fat 3.5 g; Chol 85 mg; Carb 20 g; Protein 24 g; Fiber 5 g; Sodium 1130 mg

POACHED SEAFOOD SALADS

POACHED SEAFOOD SALAD IS A SPA CUISINE staple, since seafood is a lean protein, and poaching is one of the leanest cooking techniques out there. Typically, salmon or shrimp is gently poached in an aromatic liquid, cooled, and then tossed with a light vinaigrette and tender vegetables. Too many of the modern renditions have gone overboard with this classic's signature "lightness," leaving us hungry for more. And all too often, this salad consists of dry, overcooked fish or tough, tiny shrimp plopped onto lifeless lettuce leaves. We wanted to develop a salad featuring properly cooked seafood in a bright, flavorful dressing, complemented by fresh vegetables.

Our poaching method entails bringing a mixture of water, lemon juice, bay leaf, and whole black peppercorns to a bare simmer, adding the seafood, and cooking for several minutes. This classic technique worked well for our salmon fillets, but we needed to make adjustments to our method to poach the shrimp, which are smaller and more delicate than salmon. Our solution was to bring the poaching liquid to a boil, turn off the heat, add the shrimp, and cover the pot. With this method, the shrimp poach in the water for about eight minutes, enough time to pick up flavor from the poaching liquid, and because there is no direct heat, the danger of overcooking is eliminated.

With the cooking methods for our seafood settled, we moved on to the salad's other components. We homed in on the salmon salad first. We used classic salade niçoise as a model and added green beans and sliced boiled potatoes to the plate. The potatoes were sprinkled with a vinaigrette right after coming out of the cooking liquid—a technique we came upon when developing French Potato Salad (page 55). The hot potato slices soak up the dressing more thoroughly than if they were cool. To the subtly sweet vinaigrette we added whole-grain mustard; it provided a sharp contrast to the full flavor of the salmon and the creaminess of earthy potatoes. And finally, dill seemed like a natural pairing with salmon; tasters also liked how its summery green flavor meshed with the vegetal quality of the green beans.

Next we worked on the shrimp salad, choosing to combine our perfectly poached crustaceans with avocado, snow peas, and grapefruit segments. We found it best to puree a quarter of the avocado in the dressing to help evenly distribute its mellow, buttery flavor. And because we were using the fatty avocado, we didn't need to add any extra oil to the vinaigrette, keeping our salad that much lighter. Lime juice was favored over lemon juice in the dressing for its brightness, and it was a nice match with the avocado. We also added ginger for its floral bite and honey to balance the lime's acidity. The remaining avocado was diced and gently folded into the salad, along with the crisp strips of snow peas and juicy grapefruit segments.

The salads were a success in the test kitchen, as many tasters commented on how light, flavorful, and easy these new classics were to prepare.

Salmon Salad with Red Potatoes and Green Beans

SERVES 4

Do not drain the green beans in a colander; instead use a slotted spoon to remove them from the water. Note that you will use the same cooking water to poach the salmon.

	Salt
8	ounces green beans, cut into 2-inch lengths (a generous 2 cups)
1	lemon, halved
1	bay leaf
1/2	teaspoon black peppercorns

4	salmon fillets (4 to 6 ounces each), pin bones removed (see page 231) Ground black pepper
6	tablespoons whole-grain mustard
6	tablespoons juice from 3 lemons
1	small shallot, minced (2 tablespoons)
3	tablespoons extra-virgin olive oil
2	tablespoons minced fresh dill
1	pound red potatoes (2 to 3 medium potatoes), halved and sliced 1/4 inch thick
16	Bibb lettuce leaves, washed and dried

1. Bring 2 quarts water and 1 tablespoon salt to a boil in a large Dutch oven; have ready a medium bowl filled with ice water. Add the green beans to the boiling water and cook until tender, about 5 minutes. Using a slotted spoon, transfer the green beans to the ice water to stop the cooking and chill, about 3 minutes (do not drain the boiling water from the Dutch oven). Drain the green beans from the ice water; set aside.

2. Squeeze the juice of both lemon halves into the water; add the squeezed halves to the pot of water and add the bay leaf and peppercorns. Return to a boil over high heat and boil for 2 minutes. Pat the salmon dry with paper towels and season with salt and pepper. Reduce the heat to a light simmer and slip the salmon fillets into the water. Cover and cook until the fish is still slightly pink in the middle, 4 to 6 minutes. Using a slotted spoon, gently transfer the salmon fillets to a large plate; let cool to room temperature. Refrigerate until needed, removing the skin before serving.

3. Meanwhile, shake the mustard, lemon juice, shallot, oil, and dill together in a jar with a tight-fitting lid. Season with salt and pepper to taste. Toss 1/4 cup of the dressing with the green beans; set aside.

4. Place the potatoes, 6 cups cold water, and 2 tablespoons salt in a large saucepan; bring to a boil over high heat, then reduce the heat to a simmer and cook, uncovered, until the potatoes are tender but still firm (a thin-bladed paring knife can be slipped into and out of the center of a potato slice with no resistance), about 5 minutes. Drain the potatoes; arrange them close together in a single

layer on a rimmed baking sheet. Sprinkle with ¼ cup of the dressing; set aside to cool.

5. To serve, arrange the lettuce leaves on four plates and top with a portion of the potatoes and a portion of the green beans. Place a salmon fillet on top of each plate of vegetables and drizzle with the remaining dressing.

PER SERVING: Cal 550; Fat 31 g; Sat fat 5 g; Chol 100 mg; Carb 30 g; Protein 39 g; Fiber 5 g; Sodium 720 mg

Shrimp Salad with Avocado and Grapefruit

SERVES 4

Taste the grapefruit; if it is especially tart you can add an additional ½ teaspoon honey to the dressing.

SHRIMP

1	lemon, halved
1	bay leaf
½	teaspoon black peppercorns
1	pound extra-large shrimp (21 to 25 per pound), peeled and deveined (see below)

SALAD AND VINAIGRETTE

2	medium ruby red grapefruits, segmented and juice reserved
1	large avocado, pitted, peeled, and cut into ½-inch dice (see page 17)
2	tablespoons juice from 1 lime
½	teaspoon honey
1 ½	teaspoons grated fresh ginger
½	teaspoon salt
¼	teaspoon ground black pepper
1	tablespoon chopped fresh mint leaves
2	ounces snow peas (about 24), strings removed and cut lengthwise into ⅛-inch strips
16	Bibb lettuce leaves, washed and dried

1. TO POACH THE SHRIMP: Place 3 cups water in a medium saucepan. Squeeze the juice of both lemon halves into the water; add the squeezed halves to the water, and add the bay leaf and peppercorns. Bring to a boil over high heat and boil for 2 minutes. Remove the pan from the heat and add the shrimp. Cover and let stand off the heat for 8 minutes. Have ready a medium bowl filled with ice water.

2. Drain the shrimp into a colander, discarding the lemon halves, bay leaf, and peppercorns. Immediately transfer the shrimp to the ice water to stop the cooking and chill, about 3 minutes. Drain the shrimp and transfer them to a large dry bowl; refrigerate until needed. (The shrimp can be refrigerated for up to 2 days.)

3. TO PREPARE THE VINAIGRETTE: Place the reserved grapefruit juice in a ¼-cup measure. If necessary, add enough water to equal ¼ cup. Puree the juice, one-quarter of the avocado, lime juice, honey, ginger, salt, and pepper together in a blender until smooth.

4. To serve, remove the bowl of chilled shrimp from the refrigerator and add the grapefruit, mint, snow peas, and remaining avocado. Pour the dressing over the mixture and toss gently to coat. Arrange the lettuce leaves on four plates and top with the shrimp mixture. Drizzle each salad with any dressing left in the bowl.

PER SERVING: Cal 280; Fat 9 g; Sat fat 1.5 g; Chol 170 mg; Carb 25 g; Protein 26 g; Fiber 10 g; Sodium 460 mg

DEVEINING SHRIMP

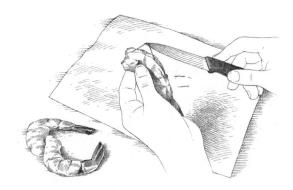

Hold the shelled shrimp between thumb and forefinger and cut down the length of its back, about ⅛ to ¼ inch deep, with a sharp paring knife. If the shrimp has a vein, it will be exposed and can be pulled out easily. Once you have freed the vein with the tip of a paring knife, just touch the knife to a paper towel and the vein will slip off the knife and stick to the towel.

THAI-STYLE BEEF SALAD

THAI CUISINE IS ALL ABOUT THE BALANCE and contrast of big, bold fresh flavors. The elements of sweet, sour, salty, and spicy heat work together in harmony. Thai salads offer an enticing variety of tastes, textures, and colors. Traditionally composed of crunchy raw vegetables and the simple addition of a single protein—in this case, beef—these salads are quick to prepare and require little cooking. In addition, they are healthy, typically relying on the fresh flavors of pungent ingredients like lime juice, garlic, cilantro, mint, and chiles, with a judicious amount of meat. And dressings for many Thai salads contain no oil, so they are naturally low fat.

Thai salads are normally dressed with a fish sauce–based dressing, which is sometimes mixed with ginger, garlic, chiles, sugar, and lime juice. The question we faced when creating a new recipe was whether we could achieve a balanced and traditional-tasting dressing. Even before we began, we knew we would use fish sauce. A salty, briny liquid made from fermented fish, fish sauce is, culinarily, the Thai equivalent of Chinese soy sauce. Lime juice provided the sour component in our dressing, and we found that an equal amount of lime juice and fish sauce struck the right balance. We tried several sweeteners, including granulated sugar, honey, and brown sugar. The granulated sugar gave the dressing a slightly artificial flavor, and even small amounts of honey were too strong, accenting the dressing with unwanted floral notes. Brown sugar, however, provided a subtle, pleasant sweetness, complementing the sour and the salty flavors. For spiciness, we considered fresh chiles, such as jalapeños and serranos, because traditional Thai bird chiles are difficult to find. But it was hard to control the heat level from one salad to another because fresh chiles vary in spiciness from one to the next. So we settled on a small amount of red pepper flakes. While this approach is not authentic, it allowed us to achieve a consistent heat level every time.

We tested a number of lean beef cuts to add to our Thai salad and found that flank steak was the one that best met our criteria. We cooked the steak to medium rare, which tasters preferred, and sliced it thin across the grain to keep this ordinarily tough cut of meat tender. Slicing the steak thin also ensured that there was plenty of steak to go around. Finally, when we tossed the sliced flank steak with the dressing, it took on the flavors better than any other cut tested.

With our dressing done and flank steak as our cut of choice, we turned to the vegetables. We looked for vegetables that would cut the richness of the beef, which we felt would benefit the salad. Cucumber was a good choice, due to its crispness and mild flavor. Thinly sliced red onion also worked well, adding crunch and a sweet allium flavor, and Bibb lettuce lightened the salad. And it wouldn't be a Thai salad without a hefty amount of fresh herbs; this job was filled by a duo of cilantro and mint, both of which added a bright, clean flavor. Topped with a little bit of chopped peanuts, our Thai-style salad was now complete.

Thai-Style Beef Salad
SERVES 4

If you prefer, omit the oil and grill the steak. Look for fish sauce in Asian markets or the international aisle of most well-stocked supermarkets.

1 ¼	pounds flank steak, trimmed of excess fat
	Salt and ground black pepper
1	teaspoon peanut or vegetable oil
¼	cup fish sauce
¼	cup juice from 3 limes
4	teaspoons brown sugar
¼	teaspoon red pepper flakes
½	medium cucumber, peeled, seeded (see page 50), and sliced thin
½	small red onion, sliced thin
2	tablespoons packed fresh cilantro leaves, torn
2	tablespoons packed fresh mint leaves, torn
1	head Bibb or Boston lettuce, washed, dried, and torn into pieces (4 cups lightly packed)
¼	cup unsalted dry-roasted peanuts, chopped coarse

1. Pat the steak dry with paper towels, then season generously with salt and pepper. Heat the oil in a large nonstick skillet over medium-high heat until just smoking. Add the steak and cook until well browned on both sides, about 10 minutes, reducing the heat to medium if the pan begins to scorch or smoke. Transfer the steak to a plate and let rest for 10 minutes.

2. Meanwhile, whisk the fish sauce, lime juice, brown sugar, and pepper flakes together in a small bowl until the sugar is dissolved. Pour half of the dressing into a large bowl and set aside.

3. Slice the steak crosswise on the bias into ⅛-inch-thick slices. Cut the longer slices in half, into roughly 3-inch lengths. Add the steak to the small bowl of dressing, toss to coat, and let marinate for 5 minutes.

4. Remove the steak from the dressing and discard the marinade. Toss the steak, cucumber, onion, cilantro, and mint with the reserved dressing in the large bowl. Arrange the lettuce on a large serving platter or individual plates. Spoon the steak and vegetables over the lettuce. Drizzle the salad with any dressing left in the bowl and sprinkle with the peanuts before serving.

PER SERVING: Cal 300; Fat 13 g; Sat fat 4 g; Chol 50 mg; Carb 12 g; Protein 35 g; Fiber 2 g; Sodium 1540 mg

SEEDING CUCUMBERS

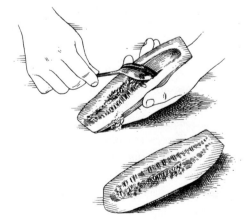

Peel each cucumber and halve lengthwise. Use a small spoon to remove the seeds and surrounding liquid from each cucumber half.

CHINESE CHICKEN SALAD

WHEN SERVED ON TOP OF TENDER FIELD greens or accompanied by a few leaves of crunchy iceberg lettuce, Chinese chicken salad becomes a satisfying summer supper. The major problem, however, with most Chinese chicken is that the dressing is too oily and the salad itself is completely overwhelmed by too many ingredients. A number of recipes we found call for more than one oil; usually a combination of a neutral salad oil, like canola, and an overbearing amount of toasted sesame oil. These recipes yield a salad with ingredients coated by a dull sheen of oil, which deadens any fresh flavor in the dish. And the poorest, most caloric renditions of Chinese chicken salad top an already greasy salad with more fattening ingredients, like cashews, peanuts, and sesame seeds. And we were shocked to discover that some recipes for this Asian-inspired salad call for upwards of 20 ingredients (one had 50!). We had had enough and headed to the test kitchen to create a simple Chinese chicken salad that was light; one with a mix of crisp vegetables and moist chicken, all tossed in a bright, well-balanced vinaigrette.

Setting our sights on the dressing component of the salad, we made several vinaigrettes from recipes we had found; our goal was to knock down the amount of oil. Some recipes called for as much as ½ cup of oil, which made the salad insipid. Our inclination was to next try the dressing only using ¼ cup of oil, a reasonably low amount of oil for a light-style dressing. This new amount of oil worked well, however tasters were convinced that we could lessen the amount even still. Surprisingly, we settled on only 1 tablespoon of oil in the dressing. Tasters commented that the minimal addition of oil added the perfect richness, and still allowed the brighter flavors of the salad to ring through. Our next task was to balance those flavors.

We found that rice vinegar was the most commonly used acid in existing recipes, and it turned out to be the best option. The dressing recipes calling for other vinegars, such as white wine vinegar, were harsh, and the vinegar fought with other flavors. Tasters commented on how the mild acidity and slight sweetness of the rice vinegar matched well with the scallion, red bell pepper, carrot, and napa cabbage in the salad. Minced ginger seemed a natural addition to our dressing, as did soy sauce. But the dressing still lacked depth, so we rummaged through our Asian pantry items and settled on hoisin sauce. Hoisin added both sweetness and a hint of spiciness, which contrasted well with the flavors of the soy sauce and the rice vinegar.

With the dressing developed, all we had left to do was to decide which vegetables we wanted in our salad. Thinly sliced Napa cabbage, or Chinese cabbage was a perfect fit. Crisp and tasty, its slight mustard flavor wasn't overpowering, and it worked well with the sweetness of the red peppers and carrot. Tasters favored bean sprouts for their fresh, crisp bite and subtle earthy flavor. And thinly sliced scallions, plus the addition of minced cilantro added a superb fresh green quality to the salad. And one last touch: a sprinkle of crisp chow mein noodles topped off our salad with welcome crunch.

Chinese Chicken Salad with Hoisin Vinaigrette

SERVES 6

Chow mein noodles, often sold in 5-ounce canisters, can be found in most supermarkets with other Asian ingredients; La Choy is the most widely available brand. These Americanized noodles add a welcome crunch to this salad.

4	boneless, skinless chicken breast halves (about 6 ounces each), trimmed of excess fat
	Salt and ground black pepper
4	teaspoons peanut or vegetable oil
1/3	cup rice vinegar
3	tablespoons hoisin sauce
1 1/2	tablespoons low-sodium soy sauce
1	tablespoon grated fresh ginger
1	carrot, peeled and shredded
1/2	medium head napa cabbage, sliced thin crosswise (about 4 cups)
1/2	large red bell pepper, stemmed, seeded, and sliced thin (about 1 cup)
1	cup bean sprouts
2	scallions, sliced thin
1	tablespoon minced fresh cilantro leaves
1	cup chow mein noodles

1. Pat the chicken dry with paper towels, then season generously with salt and pepper. Heat 1 teaspoon of the oil in a large nonstick skillet over medium-high heat until just smoking. Add the chicken and cook until browned on the first side, about 5 minutes. Flip the chicken over, add 1/2 cup water, and reduce the heat to medium-low. Cover and continue to cook until the thickest part of the breast is no longer pink and registers about 165 degrees on an instant-read thermometer, about 5 minutes. Transfer the chicken to a plate and cover with plastic wrap. Poke a few vent holes in the plastic wrap and refrigerate the chicken while preparing the other ingredients. When the chicken is cold, shred it into bite-sized pieces.

2. Meanwhile, shake the vinegar, remaining 1 tablespoon oil, hoisin, soy sauce, and ginger together in a jar with a tight-fitting lid; set aside.

3. Toss the shredded chicken, carrot, cabbage, red pepper, sprouts, scallions, and cilantro in a large serving bowl. Shake the dressing to recombine, pour it over the chicken salad, and toss to coat. Sprinkle with the chow mein noodles before serving.

PER SERVING: Cal 250; Fat 7 g; Sat fat 1 g; Chol 65 mg; Carb 18 g; Protein 29 g; Fiber 2 g; Sodium 670 mg

PASTA SALAD

ALMOST EVERY DELI IN AMERICA SELLS A PASTA salad dressed with vinaigrette. Often made with fusilli, this salad invariably looks unappetizing. The pasta is so mushy you can see it falling apart through the glass deli case. And the vegetables are tired and sad. Any green vegetable included in the salad is an drab olive green, and the shredded carrots that most markets add have wilted. And as for the flavor—these unattractive salads usually look better than they taste. We wanted to develop a light, vinaigrette-dressed, vegetable-loaded pasta salad that looked good and tasted even better.

We started by making salads with very simple vinaigrettes. Balsamic vinegar, white wine vinegar, lemon juice, and red wine vinegar seemed like the best choices to test in our vinaigrettes. The balsamic gave a lackluster performance; tasters disliked it for its sweetness, lack of bite, and the beige color it added to the pasta. And white wine vinegar was just too acidic, and lacked dimension. Red wine vinegar stole the show with its great bite, and tasters agreed that it had a cohesive effect in the salad—it brought all the flavors together. We settled on 3 tablespoons of red wine vinegar, which really came alive when combined with 1 small clove of garlic, 2 teaspoons of Dijon mustard, and a bit of red pepper flakes. Our next task was to see what vegetables we could agree on for our salad.

Our goal was to add more vegetables to our salad than the norm. Cherry tomatoes were a good choice, as they have a perky tomato flavor, even out of season. And lightly cooked fresh green beans had a subtle vegetal sweetness that we liked. Minced red onion was a welcome addition and shredded carrot not only added its sweet earthiness, but its small size and rough texture helped our vinaigrette cling to all the components of the salad.

However, tasters complained that the vegetables tasted bland. To correct this, we tried tossing the vegetables with the vinaigrette first and letting them stand for 30 minutes to marinate. This didn't work as well as we'd hoped—the veggies still weren't soaking up any of the vinaigrette. Pressing on, we tried tossing the tomatoes, green beans, onion, and carrot with a smidgen of salt and 1 tablespoon of the vinegar slated to go into the vinaigrette. Eureka—this worked great! And when tossed with the pasta and vinaigrette, the vegetables became a lively, cohesive component of the salad.

At this point, we had a master recipe that we liked well enough, but it still needed further flavors to really stand out. For herbs, we chose basil and parsley to perk things up (although other herbs work well, too). And tasters raved about the subtle, nutty richness and piquancy of real Parmigiano-Reggiano. In one variation, we chose smoked mozzarella for its hearty richness and in another variation, provolone was the cheese of choice. With a couple of turns of the pepper mill, we had created a perfect, light pasta salad, thousands of times better than anything found in a grocer's deli case.

Pasta Salad with Summer Vegetables
SERVES 6

We like the assertive flavor of red wine vinegar in this recipe. Instead of penne, other short, bite-size pasta such as fusilli, farfalle, or orecchiette can be used in this salad. This recipe can easily be doubled to serve a crowd.

	Salt
4	ounces green beans, cut into 2-inch lengths (a generous 1 cup)
4	ounces cherry tomatoes, halved (about 1 cup)
1	carrot, peeled and shredded
2	tablespoons minced red onion
3	tablespoons red wine vinegar
8	ounces penne (about 2 1/2 cups)
1/4	cup minced fresh basil leaves
2	teaspoons minced fresh parsley leaves
2	tablespoons extra-virgin olive oil
2	teaspoons Dijon mustard
1	small garlic clove, minced or pressed through a garlic press (about 1/2 teaspoon)
1/8	teaspoon red pepper flakes
1	ounce grated good-quality Parmesan cheese, such as Parmigiano-Reggiano (about 1/2 cup)
	Ground black pepper

1. Bring 4 quarts of water to a boil in a large Dutch oven, and fill a medium bowl with ice water. Add 1 tablespoon salt and the green beans to the boiling water; cook until the green beans are tender, about 3 minutes. Using a slotted spoon, transfer the green beans to the ice water; let the beans chill for 3 minutes. (Do not drain the boiling water from the Dutch oven.) Remove the beans from the ice water, pat them dry with paper towels, and transfer them to a large bowl. Toss the tomatoes, carrot, onion, 1 tablespoon of the vinegar, and 1/4 teaspoon salt with the beans; set aside.

2. Return the water to a boil and add the pasta; cook until the pasta is al dente. Drain the pasta and rinse under cold water until cool. Drain the pasta well and transfer it to the bowl with the vegetables. Add the basil and parsley, and toss to combine.

3. Whisk the remaining 2 tablespoons vinegar, oil, mustard, garlic, and pepper flakes together in a small bowl, then toss with pasta and vegetables until combined. Stir in the Parmesan and season with salt and pepper to taste.

PER SERVING: Cal 220; Fat 7 g; Sat fat 1.5 g; Chol 5 mg; Carb 32 g; Protein 8 g; Fiber 3 g; Sodium 330 mg

➤ VARIATIONS

Pasta Salad with Asparagus and Smoked Mozzarella
If smoked mozzarella is not available, substitute aged or smoked Gouda.

	Salt
4	ounces asparagus, tough ends removed (see page 97) and cut into 1-inch lengths
1/2	large red bell pepper, stemmed, seeded, and chopped (about 1 cup)
2	tablespoons minced red onion
3	tablespoons red wine vinegar
8	ounces penne (about 2 1/2 cups)
1	teaspoon minced fresh oregano leaves
2	tablespoons extra-virgin olive oil
2	teaspoons Dijon mustard
1	small garlic clove, minced or pressed through a garlic press (about 1/2 teaspoon)
1/8	teaspoon red pepper flakes
1	ounce smoked mozzarella, shredded (about 1/3 cup)
	Ground black pepper

1. Bring 4 quarts of water to a boil in a large Dutch oven, and fill a medium bowl with ice water. Add 1 tablespoon salt and the asparagus to the boiling water; cook until the asparagus is tender, about 3 minutes. Using a slotted spoon, transfer the asparagus to the ice water; let the asparagus chill for 3 minutes. (Do not drain the boiling water from the Dutch oven.) Remove the asparagus pieces from the ice water, pat them dry with paper towels, and transfer them to a large bowl. Toss the bell pepper, onion, 1 tablespoon of the vinegar, and ¼ teaspoon salt with the asparagus; set aside.

2. Return the water to a boil and add the pasta; cook until the pasta is al dente. Drain the pasta and rinse under cold water until cool. Drain the pasta well and transfer it to the bowl with the vegetables. Add the oregano and toss to combine.

3. Whisk the remaining 2 tablespoons vinegar, oil, mustard, garlic, and pepper flakes together in a small bowl, then toss with pasta and vegetables until combined. Stir in the mozzarella and season with salt and pepper to taste.

PER SERVING: Cal 210; Fat 6 g; Sat fat 1.5 g; Chol 5 mg; Carb 31 g; Protein 7 g; Fiber 2 g; Sodium 250 mg

Pasta Salad with Arugula and Sun-Dried Tomatoes
We like the sweet flavor and pliable texture of oil-cured sun-dried tomatoes. Rinse them well to remove any excess oil.

1/4	cup oil-cured sun-dried tomatoes, rinsed, patted dry, and minced
2	tablespoons minced red onion
3	tablespoons red wine vinegar
	Salt
8	ounces penne (about 2 1/2 cups)
2	cups lightly packed arugula
1	tablespoon minced fresh parsley leaves
2	tablespoons extra-virgin olive oil
2	teaspoons Dijon mustard
1	small garlic clove, minced or pressed through a garlic press (about 1/2 teaspoon)
1/8	teaspoon red pepper flakes
1	ounce provolone cheese, grated (about 1/3 cup)
	Ground black pepper

1. Toss the sun-dried tomatoes, onion, 1 tablespoon of the vinegar, and ¼ teaspoon salt together; set aside. Bring 4 quarts of water to a boil in a large Dutch oven. Stir in 1 tablespoon salt and the pasta; cook until the pasta is al dente. Drain the pasta and rinse under cold water until cool. Drain the pasta well and transfer it to the bowl with the vegetables. Add the arugula and parsley; toss to combine.

2. Whisk the remaining 2 tablespoons vinegar, the oil, mustard, garlic, and pepper flakes together in a small bowl, then toss with the pasta and vegetables until combined. Stir in the provolone and season with salt and pepper to taste.

PER SERVING: Cal 210; Fat 7 g; Sat fat 1.5 g; Chol 5 mg; Carb 30 g; Protein 7 g; Fiber 2 g; Sodium 290 mg

FRENCH POTATO SALAD

HAVING LITTLE IN COMMON WITH ITS American counterpart, French potato salad is a lighter dish which is served warm or at room temperature. This classic side dish is composed of creamy slices of potatoes tossed with olive oil, white wine vinegar, and plenty of fresh herbs. Refined and elegant, French potato salad truly is a far cry from its mayo-based, pickle-studded, chunky cousin.

We expected quick success with this seemingly simple recipe—how hard could it be to boil a few potatoes and toss them in vinaigrette? We sliced the potatoes, dressed them while they were still warm (warm potatoes are more absorbent than cool ones), and then served them up to our tasters. The salad looked mangled, because the warm potatoes consistently broke apart when we tried to slice them, and our dressing was insipid. We determined that we would need to work on the potato preparation and develop a well-balanced, boldly flavored dressing that accented the potatoes without dominating the dish.

Our first task was to put a stop to the jagged, broken potatoes and ripped skins. We tried shocking the whole potatoes after cooking (reasoning that the ice-cold water might somehow set the skin—it didn't) and slicing the potatoes with a serrated knife (this helped a little bit, but the results were inconsistent). It was proving impossible to slice a just-cooked potato without having it fall apart.

On a whim, we sliced some potatoes before boiling them. This, surprisingly, did the trick. The potato slices emerged from the water unbroken and with their skins intact. They had a clean (not starchy) taste, were evenly cooked, and held together perfectly, unlike those that had been cooked whole before slicing.

This one simple change in technique offered multiple benefits. First, the frustrating (and sometimes painful) task of slicing hot potatoes was eliminated. Second, we now had no need to find uniformly sized potatoes to ensure even cooking. We just needed to cut the potatoes into slices of uniform thickness. Third, we found we could perfectly season the cut potatoes while they cooked by adding a hefty 2 tablespoons of salt to the cooking water.

We now shifted our focus to the vinaigrette and its usual ingredients: olive oil, white wine vinegar, herbs, mustard, minced onion, chicken broth, and white wine. Because our initial tests had produced relatively dull salads, we decided to experiment with each component until we found a surefire way to pump up the flavor. The first improvement came by using 1½ tablespoons of vinegar combined with 2 teaspoons of Dijon mustard. Tasters commented that the bland potatoes could handle extra acid, and the mustard really elevated

CORE TECHNIQUE

TURNING WATER INTO FLAVOR

For potato and lentil salads tossed with vinaigrette instead of mayonnaise, the oil in the vinaigrette plays an important role. Not only does it coat the salad and keep it from drying out, but it also acts as a binding agent that holds the various components of a salad together. Substituting plain water for some of the oil (as we did in our Basic Vinaigrette, page 29) didn't work well—it simply produced wet salads with diluted flavor. Our solution to this problem, after several unsuccessful batches, was to use the potato or lentil cooking water. The water had good flavor from the potatoes and lentils, and the starch released by those ingredients performed as a light thickening agent—not unlike a cornstarch slurry—to bind the salads together.

the salad's flavors. We loved the sharp floral notes added by champagne vinegar but found that white wine vinegar worked just as well. As for the olive oil, we searched for the minimum amount that would lend maximum seasoning without making our potatoes oily. Tasters settled on 2 tablespoons, which added the perfect amount of richness; however, our salad was still a tad dry. Not wanting to add more oil to solve the moisture issue, we looked into some other classic ingredients.

We liked the extra moisture and layer of complexity that chicken broth and wine added, but it seemed wasteful to uncork a bottle or open a can only to use a few tablespoons. We found a solution to this problem and a revelation when we consulted Julia Child's *The Way to Cook* (Knopf, 1989). She suggests adding some of the potato cooking water to the vinaigrette, a quick and frugal solution to our moisture problem that also added great potato flavor, a nice touch of saltiness, and saved us from having to add more olive oil.

Some final touches to our vinaigrette included a sprinkle of freshly ground black pepper, which perked things up, while the gentle assertiveness of minced shallots and a blanched garlic clove (raw garlic was too harsh) added depth. As for the fresh herbs, we made salads with all manner of them. But an inherently French fines herbes mixture seemed appropriate in theory and was heavenly

in reality. Chives, parsley, tarragon, and chervil make up this classic quartet.

Our last challenge: How to toss the cooked, warm potatoes with the vinaigrette without damaging the slices? The solution was simple. We carefully laid the potatoes in a single layer on a rimmed baking sheet, and then poured the vinaigrette over them. Spreading out the potatoes in this way also allowed them to cool off a bit, preventing residual cooking and potential mushiness. While we let the vinaigrette soak into the potatoes, we had just enough time to chop the herbs and shallot before sprinkling them on the finished salad. Adding the herbs just before serving guards against wilting and darkening.

French Potato Salad

SERVES 6

If fresh chervil isn't available, substitute an additional 1 ½ teaspoons of minced parsley and an additional ½ teaspoon of minced tarragon. For best flavor, serve the salad warm, but to make it ahead, follow the recipe through step 2, cover with plastic wrap, and refrigerate. Before serving, bring the salad to room temperature, and then add the shallot and herbs. Remember to reserve ⅓ cup of the potato cooking water to make the dressing.

2	pounds red potatoes (about 6 medium), scrubbed and sliced ¼ inch thick
2	tablespoons salt
1	medium garlic clove, peeled and threaded on a skewer
1 ½	tablespoons white wine or champagne vinegar
2	teaspoons Dijon mustard
2	tablespoons extra-virgin olive oil
½	teaspoon ground black pepper
1	small shallot, minced (about 2 tablespoons)
1	tablespoon minced fresh chervil leaves
1	tablespoon minced fresh parsley leaves
1	tablespoon minced fresh chives
1	teaspoon minced fresh tarragon leaves

1. Bring the potatoes, 6 cups water, and salt to a boil in a large saucepan, then reduce to a simmer. Lower the skewered garlic into the simmering water and partially blanch, about 45 seconds.

DRESSING THE POTATOES

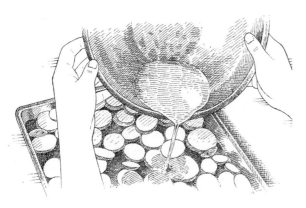

After the potatoes have been thoroughly drained, spread them out on a rimmed baking sheet and drizzle evenly with the vinaigrette.

Immediately run the garlic under cold tap water to stop the cooking; remove the garlic from the skewer and set aside. Continue to simmer the potatoes, uncovered, until tender but still firm (a thin-bladed paring knife can be slipped into and out of the center of a potato slice with no resistance), about 5 minutes. Drain the potatoes, reserving ⅓ cup cooking water. Arrange the hot potatoes close together in a single layer on a rimmed baking sheet.

2. Press the garlic through a garlic press or mince by hand. Whisk the garlic, reserved potato cooking water, vinegar, mustard, oil, and pepper together in a small bowl until combined. Drizzle the dressing evenly over the warm potato slices; let stand 10 minutes.

3. Meanwhile, toss the shallot and herbs gently together in a small bowl. Transfer the potatoes to a large serving bowl. Add the shallot-herb mixture and mix lightly with a rubber spatula to combine.

PER SERVING: Cal 160; Fat 5 g; Sat fat .5 g; Chol 0 g; Carb 25 g; Protein 3 g; Fiber 3 g; Sodium 250 mg

➤ VARIATION

French Potato Salad with Radishes, Cornichons, and Capers
Follow the recipe for French Potato Salad, omitting the herbs and substituting 2 tablespoons minced red onion for the shallot. Toss the dressed potatoes with 2 medium red radishes, sliced thin, ¼ cup capers, rinsed, and ¼ cup cornichons, sliced thin, along with the red onion in step 3.

PER SERVING: Cal 160; Fat 5 g; Sat fat .5 g; Chol 0 g; Carb 26 g; Protein 3 g; Fiber 3 g; Sodium 490 mg

BEAN SALADS
SORRY TO SAY, OUR COLLECTIVE MEMORIES OF bean salads involve overly sweet and soupy mixtures of canned green, yellow, and red kidney beans, a relic from the 1950s. We were looking for a modern day bean salad, one with fresh flavors unified by a dressing that did not overpower the beans' subtle flavor, so we decided on a Greek-themed bean salad (feta cheese, Kalamata olives, and red onion).

Focusing first on the type of bean, our initial task was to determine which one was best suited for a cold salad. While we generally prefer dried beans to canned, it made more sense to use canned in a salad, where the beans would be bathed in a zesty vinaigrette.

Determining which canned beans were best in a cold salad proved challenging. We tried many varieties of canned beans, starting with cannellini beans, but we found that an entire salad of cannellini beans or kidney beans was bland, because the beans did not absorb the flavors of the vinaigrette. And black beans, which tasters thought were better suited for a salsa rather than a salad, were quickly ruled out for lack of versatility. Tasters' favorite beans were chickpeas because of their great buttery bean flavor and their porousness, which allowed them to take on the flavors of a vinaigrette without breaking down or getting mushy. Even when eaten cold, they had a pleasant creamy texture.

Now that we had the type of bean settled, we started building the dressing. Lemon juice, olive oil, and garlic were obvious choices in our Greek-themed salad, but because we wanted to reduce the amount of oil in the salad, we needed something to provide depth. We tried both reduced-fat mayonnaise and low-fat yogurt, but tasters didn't like the creamy coating on the beans. Taking a cue from our basic vinaigrette recipe, we added Dijon mustard, which provided the depth we were after, without adding fat.

Minced Kalamata olives made sense in our salad, and even though olives are high in fat, they are strongly flavored, so we only needed to use 2 tablespoons for maximum effect. And by mincing them fine and adding them to the dressing, we were able to better distribute (stretch) their flavor. We used the same technique with feta cheese, another strong-flavored ingredient—a little goes a long way, so we only needed a minimal amount. To finish our salad, we added minced red onion and a heavy dose of mint (¼ cup) along with a bit of parsley. Something was still missing; tasters commented that they wanted something crunchy in the salad, something with a mellow flavor to break up and tame some of the strong flavors. Chopped cucumber seemed logical, and the combination of creamy chickpeas and crisp cucumber worked to our advantage, providing exactly what we were looking for in a refreshing salad.

Greek-Style Chickpea Salad

SERVES 6

This refreshing salad is excellent served over a bed of greens with Garlic-Herb Pita Chips (page 12).

2 (15.5-ounce) cans chickpeas, drained and rinsed
1/2 small red onion, minced
1/2 large cucumber, peeled, seeded, and chopped (about 3/4 cup)
1/4 cup minced fresh mint leaves
1 ounce feta cheese, crumbled (about 1/4 cup)
1 tablespoon minced fresh parsley leaves
3 tablespoons juice from 1 lemon
2 tablespoons minced pitted Kalamata olives
1 tablespoon Dijon mustard
1 tablespoon extra-virgin olive oil
1 small garlic clove, minced or pressed through a garlic press (about 1/2 teaspoon)
Salt and ground black pepper

Toss the chickpeas, onion, cucumber, mint, feta, and parsley together in a large bowl. Whisk the lemon juice, olives, mustard, oil, and garlic together in a small bowl, then toss with the chickpeas and vegetables until combined. Season with salt and pepper to taste. (The salad can be refrigerated in an airtight container for up to 3 days. Season with additional lemon juice, salt, pepper, and oil as needed before serving.)

PER SERVING: Cal 170; Fat 6 g; Sat fat 1 g; Chol 5 mg; Carb 22 g; Protein 8 g; Fiber 6 g; Sodium 300 mg

VARIATION
North African–Style Chickpea Salad
To turn this salad into a main course, serve it alongside Couscous with Tomato, Scallions, and Lemon (page 144).

2 (15.5-ounce) cans chickpeas, drained and rinsed
1 carrot, peeled and shredded
1/2 cup raisins
2 tablespoons minced fresh mint leaves
2 tablespoons extra-virgin olive oil
1 1/2 tablespoons juice from 1 lemon
1 small garlic clove, minced or pressed through a garlic press (about 1/2 teaspoon)
1/2 teaspoon cumin
1/2 teaspoon paprika
Salt and ground black pepper

Toss the chickpeas, carrot, raisins, and mint together in a large bowl. Whisk the oil, lemon juice, garlic, cumin, and paprika together in a small bowl, then toss with the chickpeas and vegetables until combined. Season with salt and pepper to taste. (The salad can be refrigerated in an airtight container for up to 3 days. Season with additional lemon juice, salt, pepper, and oil as needed before serving.)

PER SERVING: Cal 200; Fat 7 g; Sat fat .5 g; Chol 0 mg; Carb 30 g; Protein 7 g; Fiber 6 g; Sodium 150 mg

LENTIL SALAD

LENTIL SALAD IS A SIMPLE COMPOSITION OF tender, fiber-rich lentils tossed with a light vinaigrette. It's one of our favorites for eating light because it's a dish rich in flavor and texture rather than fat and calories. In its poorest form, lentil salad is bland and greasy with no interplay between the flavors of the lentils and vinaigrette. We wanted to develop a recipe with great harmony between the vinaigrette and lentils.

We began our research with the main ingredient, the lentil, of which there are several varieties. Not surprisingly, lentilles du Puy (French green lentils) turned out to be the best legume for this salad. Fully cooked and tossed with dressing, they held their shape nicely compared to common brown lentils, which turned mushy after being tossed with dressing, and red split lentils, which disintegrated before we could even pour on the dressing.

We next focused on developing the seasonings for the recipe. Given that we were using French lentils, we narrowed our search to primarily French cookbooks. Many of the recipes we found employed similar cooking methods and flavorings. Most called for simmering the lentils, draining them, and then tossing them, still warm, with vinaigrette. More often than not, the vinaigrette contained walnut oil, wine vinegar, and other aromatics. Armed with this information, we made several batches of lentil salad. Generally, these salads were good, but there was room for improvement.

Tasters raised several issues about the vinaigrette; some felt it lacked punch, and others disliked the walnut oil. Figuring that the vinegar (everyone liked sherry vinegar best in this recipe) in the dressing lost potency when mixed with the warm lentils, we decreased the ratio of oil to vinegar. Minimizing the oil to 2 tablespoons gave us the perfect amount of seasoning and body, but while this improved the brightness of the salad, it didn't improve it enough to meet our standards. By doubling the amount of Dijon mustard in the vinaigrette to 1 tablespoon, we gave the dressing a little more bite, which in turn solved the problem of dull flavors.

Another change we made to the vinaigrette was to omit the walnut oil, which tended to overpower the salad. Even in small amounts, its slight bitterness muted the other flavors. But we needed to replace that dimension of flavor with another ingredient. Remembering a technique we discovered while testing French Potato Salad (page 55), we added some reserved lentil cooking water to the salad. This worked well, and tasters liked that the cooking liquid gave the dish even more lentil richness. We moved to one final issue—texture.

Many of the salads we made tasted fine but were rather one-dimensional. They needed crunch. Topping the salad with a sprinkling of toasted walnuts improved the salad greatly, both adding texture and accentuating the earthiness of the lentils. And we found that a minimal amount of nuts (only ¼ cup) was able to impart walnut flavor and crunch. Introducing scallions to the mix also improved the overall texture and provided pungency. The final ingredient, roasted red peppers, sweetened the salad and rounded out the other flavors.

Lentil Salad with Walnuts and Scallions
SERVES 4

This salad is a natural with grilled chicken or turkey sausages; with the addition of lettuce leaves or other greens, it also can be served as a light vegetarian entrée.

1	cup Puy lentils, rinsed and picked over
½	medium onion, halved
2	bay leaves
1	large sprig fresh thyme
	Salt
2	tablespoons sherry vinegar
2	tablespoons extra-virgin olive oil
1	tablespoon Dijon mustard
	Ground black pepper
¼	cup walnuts, toasted and chopped coarse (see page 45)
2	scallions, sliced thin
½	cup jarred roasted red peppers (about 2 medium peppers), rinsed, patted dry, and minced

1. Bring the lentils, onion, bay leaves, thyme, ½ teaspoon salt, and 4 cups water to a boil in a medium saucepan. Reduce to a simmer and cook until the lentils are tender but still hold their shape, 25 to 30 minutes.

2. Meanwhile, whisk the vinegar, oil, mustard, ⅛ teaspoon pepper, and ¼ teaspoon salt together in a small bowl; set aside.

3. Drain the lentils through a fine-mesh strainer, reserving ¼ cup of the cooking liquid, and discard the onion, bay leaves, and thyme. Transfer the lentils to a medium bowl. Toss the warm lentils with the vinaigrette and cool to room temperature, about 15 minutes. Add the reserved cooking liquid, 1 tablespoon at a time as needed, until the lentils are well coated. Stir in the walnuts, scallions, and roasted red peppers. Season with salt and pepper to taste; serve immediately.

PER SERVING: Cal 290; Fat 12 g; Sat fat 1.5 g; Chol 0 mg; Carb 33 g; Protein 13 g; Fiber 8 g; Sodium 400 mg

3

SOUPS, STEWS, AND CHILIS

HOMEMADE SOUP IS JUST WHAT THE DOCTOR ordered for those looking to incorporate more vegetables, legumes, and lean meats into their diet. Canned soups may be fine in a pinch, but with their high sodium content, mushy vegetables, and generally lackluster flavor, their shortcomings outweigh their convenience.

For this chapter, we took a look at our favorite broth-based soups and looked for ways to enrich their natural healthfulness without compromising their flavor. We also looked at a number of cream-based soups and examined how we could achieve their trademark richness and velvety texture without relying on the copious amounts of cream and butter these soups traditionally contain. In addition to soups, we also turned our attention to meaty chilis and chunky stews, where we aimed to emphasize lean meats such as chicken and turkey as well as vegetables. Through all of our testing (and there was a lot), we learned that by following a few basic techniques, flavorful and satisfying healthful soups are easy to prepare.

In developing these soups, we found that it was crucial to eke out as much flavor as possible from key ingredients. One technique we came to rely on involved sweating aromatic vegetables such as onion, garlic, and celery, with a small amount of oil and salt in a heavy-bottomed pot set over medium-low heat. The oil prevents the vegetables from burning. The salt draws the moisture from the vegetables, allowing them to sweat in their own juices, all resulting in a deep concentration of flavor (with little fat required), the perfect start for creating flavorful and healthy soups.

As for cream-style soups, many healthy cookbooks reduce the fat by simply relying on skim milk thickened with flour or another starch, which leads to unpleasantly starchy-tasting soups. We chose a multilevel approach that yielded superior results. First, we found that replacing the butter in which the aromatics were sautéed with vegetable oil, and using less of it, was the first key to cutting back on fat. We also found that by increasing the amount of vegetables found in classic recipes, and adding a little wine, we were able to intensify the vegetable flavor and increase the soup's nutritional value. We finished these soups with half-and-half instead of heavy cream and still ended up with the creamy flavor and velvety texture we desired.

And in our chilis, we replaced the traditional ground beef with leaner ground turkey and chicken. To make up for the loss of fat (and flavor), we increased the amount of vegetables and used a generous hand with fresh herbs and spices, as well as bright flavors from citrus and hot peppers. Long, slow simmering allowed the spices and other ingredients to meld and the flavors to concentrate, resulting in a richly flavored chili.

Lastly, one of the beauties of soup is the fact that it holds up so well. Many of the recipes in this chapter can be made on the weekend and enjoyed during the week. We offer tips for storing and reheating soup on page 68.

CHICKEN STOCK

THERE ISN'T TOO MUCH ABOUT CHICKEN stock that isn't already healthy. It's the basis for countless soups and is the most important stock in any cook's repertoire. The problem is that most recipes for chicken stock require that it be simmered anywhere from four to six hours and be religiously skimmed every fifteen minutes, making it a day-long commitment—especially if you plan on making soup after the stock is made. While this tried-and-true method yields the absolute best stock, we know that there are times when you need stock in a hurry or don't want to hang around the house for five hours. Here in the test kitchen, our goal was simple: Create a chicken stock with as much unadulterated chicken flavor as possible. We also wanted to streamline and speed up the process as much as we could.

We tried blanching a whole chicken, on the theory that blanching keeps the chicken from releasing foam during cooking. The blanched chicken was then partially covered with water and placed in a heatproof bowl over a pan of simmering water. Cooked this way, the chicken never simmered, and the resulting stock was remarkably clear, refined, and full flavored. The only problem: It took four hours to develop sufficient flavor.

A number of recipes promote roasting chicken bones or parts and then using them to make stock. The theory, at least, is that roasted parts will flavor stock in minutes, not hours. We tried this several times, roasting chicken backs, necks, and bones—with and without vegetables. We preferred the roasted stock with vegetables. The resulting stock was dark in color and had a nice caramelized onion flavor, but it still wasn't the full-flavored stock we were looking for. While the roasted flavor was quite strong, the actual chicken flavor was too tame.

Last, we tried sautéing a chicken, hacked into small pieces, until the chicken was slightly browned. We then covered the pot and cooked the chicken over low heat until it released its rich, flavorful juices, which took about 20 minutes. Only at this point did we add water, and the stock was simmered for just 20 minutes more. We knew we were onto something when we smelled the chicken sautéing, and the finished stock confirmed what our noses had detected. It tasted pleasantly sautéed, not boiled. We had some refining to do; for once, we had too much flavor.

We tried substituting inexpensive chicken backs and wing tips and whole legs for the whole chicken and used more water. This stock was less intense, but just the right strength to serve as a base for some of the best chicken soup we've ever tasted. Just don't try to salvage the meat from the legs. After five minutes of sautéing, 20 minutes of sweating, and another 20 minutes of simmering, the meat is void of flavor.

If you are making a soup that needs some chicken meat, use a whole chicken as directed in Quick Chicken Stock with Sautéed Breast Meat (page 62). The breast is removed, cut in two pieces, sautéed briefly, and then added with the water to finish cooking. The rest of the bird—the legs, back, wings, and giblets—is sweated with the onions and discarded when the stock is done. The breast meat, however, is perfectly cooked, ready to be skinned and shredded when cool. We particularly liked the tidiness of this method: One chicken yields one pot of soup.

Now that we had the method down, we tested a tremendous number of ingredients—everything from thyme and parsley to carrots, celery, and parsnips—and found that we preferred stock with fewer ingredients. Onions, salt, and bay leaves complemented the flavor of the chicken; everything else was a distraction.

After much trial and error, we had a master recipe that delivered liquid gold in just one hour. While this recipe requires more hands-on work (hacking up parts, browning an onion, then chicken parts), it is ready in a fraction of the time required to make a traditional, long-cooking stock.

One note about our recipe for quick stock: We found it necessary to cut the chicken into pieces small enough to release their flavorful juices in a short period of time (see "Hacking Up Chicken for Stock" on page 62). A cleaver or poultry shears

TWO WAYS TO DEFAT STOCK

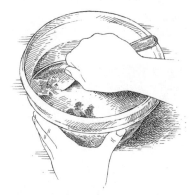

Stock should be defatted before being used. The easiest way to do this is to refrigerate it until the fat rises to the surface and congeals. Use a spoon to scrape the fat off the surface of the stock.

If you don't have time to refrigerate the stock and allow the fat to congeal, use a gravy skimmer, then pour it out through the spout attached to the bottom of the skimmer. The fat floating on top of the liquid will remain behind.

speeds up this process. Don't try to cut through chicken bones with a chef's knife. The blade isn't strong enough to cut through bone, and you may hurt yourself as the knife slips and slides. Even if you do manage to cut through the bone, your knife may become nicked in the process.

Quick Chicken Stock

MAKES ABOUT 2 QUARTS

Chicken pieces are sautéed and then sweated before being cooked in water for a rich but very quick stock. This is our favorite all-purpose stock. It takes about an hour to prepare.

1	medium onion, chopped medium
1	teaspoon vegetable oil
2 ½	teaspoons salt
4	pounds whole chicken legs or backs and wing tips, cut into 2-inch pieces
2	quarts boiling water
2	bay leaves

1. Combine the onion, oil, and ½ teaspoon of the salt in a large stockpot or Dutch oven. Cover and cook over medium-low heat, stirring often, until softened, 8 to 10 minutes. Transfer the onion to a large bowl.

HACKING UP CHICKEN FOR STOCK

To hack through bone, place your hand near the far end of the meat cleaver's handle, curling your fingers securely around it in a fist. Handle the meat cleaver the way you would a hammer, with the motion in your arm rather than your wrist and the weight of the blade's front tip leading the force of the chop. If you cannot chop through the bone in one strike, place the cleaver in the groove of the first chop, then strike the blade's blunt edge with a heavy mallet.

2. Add half of the chicken pieces to the pot; cook over medium-high heat until no longer pink, about 5 minutes. Transfer the cooked chicken to the bowl with the onion. Cook the remaining chicken pieces. Return the onion and chicken pieces to the pot. Reduce the heat to low, cover, and cook until the chicken releases its juices, about 20 minutes.

3. Add the boiling water, the remaining 2 teaspoons salt, and bay leaves. Bring to a boil over medium-high heat; partially cover, reduce the heat to medium-low, and simmer until the stock is flavorful, about 20 minutes.

4. Strain the stock; discard the solids. Before using, defat the stock. (The stock can be refrigerated in an airtight container for up to 2 days or frozen for several months.)

PER 1½-CUP SERVING: Cal 25; Fat 1 g; Sat fat 0 g; Chol 0 mg; Carb 2 g; Protein 2 g; Fiber 0 g; Sodium 910 mg

VARIATION

Quick Chicken Stock with Sautéed Breast Meat

Make this stock when you want to have some breast meat to add to soup, as in Hearty Chicken Noodle Soup (page 64). This recipe starts with a whole chicken.

Substitute 1 whole chicken (about 4 pounds) for the whole legs. Remove the breast from the bone, split, and reserve. Cut the remaining chicken into 2-inch pieces. In step 1, heat the oil until just smoking and add the chicken breast halves; cook both sides until lightly browned, about 5 minutes. Remove the chicken breasts from the pot and cook the onions and chicken pieces, following the recipe. Return the breasts to the pot with the boiling water in step 3. Before straining the stock in step 4, remove the breasts from the pot; when cool enough to handle, remove the skin and shred the meat into bite-sized pieces. (The shredded chicken and stock can be refrigerated separately in airtight containers for up to 2 days.)

PER 1½-CUP SERVING: Cal 70; Fat 1.5 g; Sat fat 0 g; Chol 25 mg; Carb 2 g; Protein 12 g; Fiber 0 g; Sodium 940 mg

CHICKEN NOODLE SOUP

WITH HOMEMADE CHICKEN STOCK ON HAND, making chicken noodle soup is a relatively easy proposition. Add some vegetables, herbs, and noodles and you've got a great-tasting bowl of soup that is good for you, too. We did have several questions, though. Which vegetables (and how much) should be added to this soup? As for the pasta, which kind of noodles work best, and should they be cooked in the soup or in a separate pot of boiling water? We wanted to answer these questions, develop a basic master recipe, then create a tasty variation.

We tackled the vegetable issue first. We tested a wide range of vegetables, including onions, carrots, celery, peas, leeks, potatoes, zucchini, tomatoes, and mushrooms. We concluded that the classic mirepoix ingredients (onions, carrots, and celery) should be part of a basic chicken noodle soup. Peas, although welcome for their sweetness and the bright green color they contributed, didn't seem traditional for our classic soup, so we decided to make them optional. Other vegetables did work well, but we decided that they should be candidates for our variations. For instance, tomatoes and zucchini give chicken noodle soup an Italian character, and shiitake mushrooms and napa cabbage are a natural choice for an Asian noodle soup.

As for the amount of vegetables added to the soup, we found that in most published recipes you are lucky if you get a vegetable in every bite. Most recipes for chicken noodle soup contain just one measly carrot and one celery rib. If you're sick in bed or nursing a cold, broth and a few pieces of shredded chicken may suffice, but we wanted a hearty soup that would satisfy even the hungriest among us at mealtime.

We started by increasing the vegetables found in traditional recipes by half, but tasters still wanted more. Throwing caution to the wind, we tripled the number of carrots and celery called for in most recipes, and found that there was still an excellent ratio of broth to vegetables. Tasters were pleased, but felt that something was still missing. This soup needed something green. We decided to revisit peas, which we'd previously thought of as option. They now won tasters over—no longer just an option, peas would be essential.

To settle the issue of how to cook the vegetables, we prepared two batches of soup. For the first batch, we sautéed the onions, carrots, and celery in a little vegetable oil until softened and then added the chicken stock. For the second batch, we simply simmered the sliced vegetables in the stock. As might be expected, we found that sautéing brought out flavors in the vegetables and made a big difference in the finished soup.

The noodles were the next element to address. Dried egg noodles are the most common choice here, so we decided to stick with what we knew would work. Dried thyme perfumed the soup and fresh parsley lent vibrant color and freshness.

While the recipes that follow can be altered to your own tastes in terms of seasoning, we have carefully timed the addition of vegetables, noodles,

CORE TECHNIQUE

SWEAT VEGETABLES AND SLASH FAT

When making soups, stews, chilis, and sauces, the first step is to sauté some aromatic vegetables such as onions, carrots, celery, and garlic to build a base of flavor. But this technique usually employs a tablespoon or more of oil, and since we are cognizant of every gram of fat in these recipes, every drop of oil has to be worth it. Wondering if we could find a method to cook these aromatic vegetables using less fat, we found our answer after just a few batches. Rather than use a higher level of heat to sauté the vegetables in oil, we turned the heat down to medium-low, tossed the vegetables with just 1 teaspoon of oil and some salt, and put the lid on. The relatively low heat and the oil prevent the vegetables from burning, the salt draws the moisture from the vegetables, and the cover traps the moisture in the pan, allowing the vegetables to sweat in their own juices, all resulting in a deep concentration of flavor.

and other ingredients to make sure that each item is perfectly cooked—not overcooked. With generous amounts of lean chicken, tender noodles, and lots of tasty vegetables, this is a chicken soup that definitely earns its hearty name.

Hearty Chicken Noodle Soup

SERVES 6

Because so much of the flavor in this recipe is dependent on the broth, do not substitute store-bought broth for homemade stock.

3	large carrots, peeled and sliced 1/4 inch thick
3	medium celery ribs, sliced 1/4 inch thick
1	medium onion, chopped fine
1	teaspoon vegetable oil
	Salt
1	recipe Quick Chicken Stock with Sautéed Breast Meat (page 62)
1	teaspoon minced fresh thyme leaves, or 1/2 teaspoon dried thyme
2	cups (3 ounces) wide egg noodles
2/3	cup frozen peas, thawed
1/4	cup minced fresh parsley leaves
	Ground black pepper

1. Combine the carrots, celery, onion, oil and 1/2 teaspoon salt in a large Dutch oven. Cover and cook over medium-low heat, stirring often, until the vegetables have softened, 8 to 10 minutes.

2. Stir in the broth, shredded chicken meat, and thyme. Bring to a boil over medium-high heat; reduce the heat to medium-low and simmer until the vegetables are tender and the soup is flavorful, 10 to 15 minutes.

3. Stir in the noodles; continue to simmer until the noodles are just tender, about 5 minutes. Off the heat, stir in the peas; cover and let stand until the peas are hot, about 4 minutes. Stir in the parsley and season with salt and pepper to taste. Serve immediately.

PER 1 1/2-CUP SERVING: Cal 170; Fat 2.5 g; Sat fat 0 g; Chol 35 mg; Carb 21 g; Protein 14 g; Fiber 3 g; Sodium 1050 mg

VARIATIONS

Chicken Soup with Shells, Tomatoes, and Zucchini

Serve this Italian-inspired soup with a dusting of freshly grated Parmesan, if desired.

Follow the recipe for Hearty Chicken Noodle Soup, omitting the peas and adding 1 medium zucchini, diced medium, with the carrots, celery, and onion in step 1. Add 1/2 cup chopped tomatoes (fresh or canned) with the broth in step 2. Substitute 1 cup small shells or macaroni for the egg noodles and simmer until the pasta is just tender, about 10 minutes. Substitute 1/4 cup minced fresh basil leaves for the parsley.

PER 1 1/2-CUP SERVING: Cal 160; Fat 2.5 g; Sat fat 0 g; Chol 20 mg; Carb 21 g; Protein 14 g; Fiber 3 g; Sodium 1030 mg

Asian Chicken Noodle Soup

This soup is excellent served with Asian chili sauce. Note that we soak our rice noodles in boiling water until tender, and then add them to the soup just before serving; boiled rice noodles have a tendency to get mushy and, if left in the soup for any length of time, to break apart.

3	ounces dried wide rice noodles
4	ounces shiitake mushrooms, cleaned and sliced (about 2 cups)
2	large celery ribs, sliced 1/4 inch thick
1	medium onion, chopped fine
1	teaspoon vegetable oil
	Salt
2	teaspoons grated fresh ginger
2	medium garlic cloves, minced or pressed through a garlic press (about 2 teaspoons)
1	recipe Quick Chicken Stock with Sautéed Breast Meat (page 62)
1/2	small head napa cabbage, sliced thin (2 cups)
1/4	cup minced fresh cilantro leaves

GARNISHES
Sliced scallions (optional)
Mung beans (optional)

1. Bring 2 quarts of water to a boil in a medium saucepan. Off the heat, add the rice noodles and let stand, stirring occasionally, until tender, 10 to 15

minutes. Drain and distribute the noodles among four large soup bowls.

2. Combine the mushrooms, celery, onion, oil, and ½ teaspoon salt in a large Dutch oven. Cover and cook over medium-low heat, stirring often, until the mushrooms have released their liquid and the vegetables have softened, 8 to 10 minutes. Stir in the ginger and garlic; cook until fragrant, about 1 minute. Stir in the broth and shredded chicken meat. Bring to a boil over medium-high heat; reduce the heat to medium-low, and simmer until the vegetables are tender and the soup is flavorful, 10 to 15 minutes.

3. Just before serving, stir in the cabbage and cilantro. Pour the hot soup over the noodles in each bowl. Garnish with sliced scallions and mung beans if desired. Serve immediately.

PER 1½-CUP SERVING: Cal 150; Fat 2 g; Sat fat 0 g; Chol 20 mg; Carbs 20 g; Protein 11 g; Fiber 2 g; Sodium 1000 mg

Tortilla Soup

IF YOU'RE MINDFUL OF FAT AND CALORIES, you might dismiss Mexican food as an option. And if you're thinking of the kind of Mexican food that has become popular in fast-food joints and mall food courts you'd be absolutely right. However, authentic Mexican cuisine can be quite healthful. Case in point—tortilla soup.

Chances are that any food lover who has been to Mexico has eaten *sopa de tortilla*. A meal in a bowl, this heady chicken-tomato broth overflowing with garnishes (tortilla strips, sour cream, diced avocado, and lime wedges) always satisfies with intensely rich flavors and contrasting textures. In essence, it's a turbocharged, south-of-the-border chicken soup. The problem is that authentic recipes call for a few uniquely Mexican ingredients such as cotija and epazote. And as for garnishes, the tortilla strips, which are usually fried, aren't as light as we'd like, and the shredded cheese and sour cream also contribute a significant amount of calories and fat. We wanted to create a version of this Mexican classic that was not only lighter, but would also rely on ingredients easily

found in American supermarkets.

Just to get our bearings, we did make a few of these authentic recipes (after a long hunt for ingredients). They tasted great, but the preparation was arduous at best. Yet when we cooked a few "Americanized" recipes, we ended up with watery brews of store-bought chicken broth and canned tomatoes topped with stodgy, off-the-shelf tortilla chips. Quick, but definitely not what we would call great-tasting—or particularly healthy.

We broke the soup down into its three classic components: a flavor base made with fresh tomatoes, garlic, onion, and chiles; chicken stock; and an array of garnishes. We zeroed in on the flavor base first, recalling that the best of the soups we had made called for a basic Mexican cooking technique in which the vegetables are charred in a cast-iron skillet, then pureed and fried to create a concentrated paste that flavors the soup.

We charred our tomatoes and the results were superb, even with mediocre supermarket tomatoes. The downside was that it took 25 attentive minutes to complete the task. We wondered if we could skip charring altogether by adding chipotle chiles (smoked jalapeños) to the mix. Canned in a vinegary tomato mixture called adobo sauce, chipotles pack heat, roasted smoky flavor, and, more important, convenience. We also found that aggressively frying the raw tomatoes, onion, and chipotle puree over high heat forced all of the water out of the mixture and further concentrated its flavor.

With the vegetable-charring step eliminated, we moved on to the chicken stock. Yes, the test kitchen does have an excellent recipe for quick homemade stock (see page 62), but we were hoping to move this recipe into the express lane. The obvious alternative was to "doctor" store-bought low-sodium chicken broth, especially since this soup is awash with so many other vibrant flavors. We tried cooking chicken in broth bolstered with onion and garlic, reasoning that the chicken would both release and take on flavor while it poached. We chose bone-in chicken breasts, since they have more flavor than boneless, and are naturally lean. Split chicken breasts poached in just 20 minutes and could then be shredded and stirred back into the soup before serving. Cooked this way, the chicken retained its juiciness and tender texture and the broth was nicely flavored.

Every authentic recipe for tortilla soup calls for fresh epazote, a common Mexican herb that imparts a heady, distinctive flavor and fragrance to the broth. Unfortunately, while epazote is

INGREDIENTS: Chicken Broth

What chicken broth product should you reach for you when you haven't got time for homemade? We recommend choosing a mass-produced, lower-sodium brand and checking the label for evidence of mirepoix ingredients, such as carrots, celery, and onions. Swanson Certified Organic was our clear favorite, but the less expensive, third-place Swanson Natural Goodness was solid as well. And if you don't mind adding water, Better Than Bouillon chicken base came in a very close second and was the favorite of several tasters.

THE BEST CHICKEN BROTH

SWANSON CERTIFIED ORGANIC CHICKEN BROTH
Swanson's newest broth won tasters over with "very chickeny, straightforward, and honest flavors," a hearty aroma, and restrained "hints of roastiness."

BETTER THAN BOUILLON CHICKEN BASE
We're not ready to switch to a concentrated base for all our broth needs (you have to add water), but the 18-month refrigerator shelf life means it's a good replacement for dehydrated bouillon.

SWANSON "NATURAL GOODNESS" CHICKEN BROTH
Swanson's standard low-sodium broth was full of chicken flavor, but several tasters noted an out-of-place tartness reminiscent of lemon.

IMAGINE ORGANIC FREE RANGE CHICKEN BROTH
This broth had very prominent onion notes, which some tasters loved and others disliked. Some panelists weren't fond of the pale yellow color.

widely available in the Southwest, it is virtually nonexistent in other parts of the country. Still, we managed to track some down for testing purposes. Its wild, pungent flavor is difficult to describe, but after careful tasting we decided that it most closely resembles fresh cilantro, mint, and oregano. Using a broth steeped with epazote as a control, we sampled broths made with each of these herbs. The winner was a pairing of strong, warm oregano with pungent cilantro. It was not identical to the flavor of epazote, but it scored highly for its intensity and complexity. We now had deeply-flavored broth that, when stirred together with the tomato mixture, made for a soup that was starting to taste like the real thing.

Flour tortillas, whether fried or oven-baked, tasted fine on their own but quickly disintegrated in the hot soup. That left us with corn tortillas. The classic preparation is frying, but cooking up two or three batches of corn tortilla strips added unnecessary fat to the soup, and took more time and attention than we wanted to muster. Tasters flatly rejected the use of raw corn tortillas—a recommendation we found in more than one recipe—as they rapidly turned gummy and unpalatable when added to the hot soup. Corn tortillas require some sort of crisping. After much testing, we came up with a technique that was quick, easy, and didn't involve copious amounts of oil: lightly coating tortilla strips with vegetable cooking spray and toasting them in the oven. The result? Chips that are just as crisp, not greasy, and much less trouble to prepare than their fried cousins.

As for the garnishes, we worked through the list one ingredient at a time. Lime added sharp, fresh notes to an already complex bowl, as did cilantro leaves and minced jalapeño. Finely diced avocado was another no-brainer, the perfect finishing touch. Most tasters didn't miss the other traditional garnishes of crumbled cotija, a Mexican cheese, or crema, a sour cream–like product. But a spoonful of low-fat sour cream and a sprinkle of shredded reduced-fat Monterey Jack can be added, if desired.

Tortilla Soup

SERVES 6

If you prefer a soup with mild spiciness, trim the ribs and seeds from the jalapeño (or omit the jalapeño altogether). If desired, serve this soup with a dollop of low-fat sour cream and a sprinkling of shredded reduced-fat Monterey Jack.

TORTILLA STRIPS

8	(6-inch) corn tortillas, cut into ¹/₂-inch-wide strips
	Vegetable oil spray
	Salt

SOUP

8	cups low-sodium chicken broth
2	bone-in, skin-on split chicken breasts (about 1¹/₂ pounds), skin removed
1	very large white onion (about 1 pound), trimmed of root end, peeled, and quartered
4	medium garlic cloves, peeled
8–10	sprigs fresh cilantro
1	sprig fresh oregano
	Salt
2	medium tomatoes (about 12 ounces), cored and quartered
¹/₂	medium jalapeño chile (see note)
1	canned chipotle chile in adobo, plus 1 teaspoon adobo sauce
1	teaspoon vegetable oil
1	Hass avocado, peeled, pitted, and chopped
2	tablespoons fresh cilantro leaves
	Minced jalapeño (optional)
1	lime, cut into wedges

1. FOR THE TORTILLA STRIPS: Adjust an oven rack to the middle position and heat the oven to 425 degrees. Spread the tortilla strips on a rimmed baking sheet and spray both sides evenly with vegetable oil. Bake until the strips are deep golden brown and crisp, about 10 minutes, rotating the pan and shaking the strips (to redistribute) halfway through. Season the strips lightly with salt and transfer to a plate lined with several layers of paper towels.

2. FOR THE SOUP: Combine the broth, chicken breasts, 2 of the onion quarters, 2 of the garlic cloves, cilantro, oregano, and ½ teaspoon of the salt in a large saucepan. Bring to a boil over high heat; cover, reduce the heat to medium-low, and simmer until the chicken is just cooked through, about 20 minutes. Transfer the chicken to a large plate; when cool enough to handle, shred the chicken into bite-sized pieces, discarding the bones. Meanwhile, pour the broth through a fine-mesh strainer; discard the solids in the strainer. (The shredded chicken and broth can be covered and refrigerated separately for up to 2 days.)

3. Process the 2 remaining onion quarters, 2 remaining garlic cloves, tomatoes, jalapeño, chipotle chile, and adobo sauce together in a food processor until smooth, 15 to 20 seconds. Heat the oil in a large Dutch oven over high heat until smoking. Add the onion-tomato mixture and ⅛ teaspoon salt; cook, stirring often to prevent burning, until the mixture has darkened in color, about 10 minutes.

4. Stir the strained broth into the Dutch oven with the onion-tomato mixture. Bring to a boil over medium-high heat; reduce the heat to medium-low and simmer until the flavors have blended, about 15 minutes. (The soup can be made up to this point and refrigerated for up to 2 days; return to a simmer over medium-high heat before proceeding. The tortilla strips and garnishes are best prepared the day of serving.)

5. Add the shredded chicken and continue to simmer until heated through, about 5 minutes. To serve, place portions of the tortilla strips in bottom of individual bowls and ladle the soup into bowls. Top each serving with a portion of the avocado, cilantro, and, if desired, jalapeño, passing the lime wedges separately.

PER 1¹/₂-CUP SERVING: Cal 280; Fat 9 g; Sat fat 1.5 g; Chol 55 mg; Carb 25 g; Protein 26 g; Fiber 6 g; Sodium 1130 mg

SPRING VEGETABLE SOUP

SPRING VEGETABLE SOUP HAS SEVERAL interpretations. Some consider it to be inherently vegetarian, while others use beef bones and meat for flavor. Many recipes go for something clear and brothy, while others aspire to a thickened puree. Some even note the importance of taking the time to cut the vegetables into tiny, perfect cubes for the ultimate presentation. We wanted a spring vegetable soup that would be simple and clean tasting, and would make use of the tender, green vegetables of the new season. Moreover, it should be light and fresh, yet substantial enough to serve as supper with a crusty roll or a slice of whole-grain bread.

As we began to research and cook some of these recipes, one obvious problem arose. None of them had a truly spring-like character and they tasted too rich, seeming more along the lines of a stew than a light spring soup. In other recipes we tried, the purees turned out too heavy, and the lighter soups had the tinny taste of the canned broth we used to make them. As for the vegetables, most recipes simply packed in the standard, year-round varieties without paying much attention to the spring season.

Our first tentative steps quickly taught us something about the inherent nature of a soup based on spring vegetables. While most other soups rely on their main ingredients for flavor, character, and overall heft, we soon found that spring vegetables are simply too delicate to carry this load. They are easily overcooked if simmered too long, and their flavors can be overpowered at the drop of a hat. To make a good spring soup, these tender vegetables would need the support of a broth that was rich and multidimensional, not characterized by any single, distinctive flavor. So we threw aside the idea of a heavy puree and focused on building a flavorful liquid base.

One solution to this problem would be to make a rich, savory vegetable stock, but we felt its hearty flavors would eclipse the delicate vegetables in this spring-style soup. We tried using store-bought vegetable broths but they, too, were too strong for the delicate broth we wanted. Homemade chicken stock was delicious, but the soup was too chickeny, more like chicken vegetable soup. We wanted the broth to have more vegetable notes, and it seemed silly to start tinkering with good homemade stock.

We then tried using store-bought chicken broth, which, while not perfect, was promising, with a mellow and sturdy character. On its own it wasn't nearly balanced or flavorful enough, but we figured it would work well with a little doctoring.

We tried simmering some onion in store-bought chicken broth. The resulting broth was

TIPS ON STORING AND REHEATING SOUPS

Unless otherwise specified, all the soups in this book can be refrigerated for several days or frozen for several months. Store soup that has been cooled to lukewarm in an airtight container. When ready to serve, reheat only as much soup as you need at that time. You can reheat soup in a microwave oven or in a covered saucepan set over medium-low heat. Because microwave ovens tend to heat unevenly, this method is best for single servings. Just heat the soup right in the serving bowl or mug. Larger quantities of soup are best reheated on the stovetop.

You may find that the soup has thickened in the refrigerator or freezer. (As soups cool, liquid evaporates in the form of steam.) Simply thin out the soup with a little water to achieve the proper texture.

While most soups can be cooled, then reheated without harm, some will suffer, especially in terms of texture. Soups with rice and pasta are best eaten immediately; when refrigerated,

rice and pasta become mushy and bloated as they absorb the liquid in the soup. If you plan on having leftovers, cool the soup before adding the rice or pasta, which is often the last step in most recipes. Add a portion of the rice or pasta to the soup you plan on eating immediately, then add the rest when you reheat the remaining soup.

Typically, soups with seafood also fail to hold up well when stored. For instance, clams will almost always overcook and become tough when reheated. Anticipate serving seafood soups as soon as they are done.

Lastly, pureed soups made from green vegetables will look their best if served immediately upon completion as well. Reheating breaks down the chlorophyll in some green vegetables (asparagus is especially prone to this problem). A soup that is bright green can turn drab army green if stored for several hours and then reheated. These soups will still taste delicious, but their visual appeal will be greatly diminished.

better, but still not there. We began to realize that it would take more than just onions to turn this broth around. Not wanting to cut or cook anything unnecessary, we worked our way stingily through a variety of other vegetables, from carrots and celery to dried mushrooms and cauliflower. In the end, we found a core group of vegetables was key. The hallowed trio of carrot, celery, and onion, with some extra help from fennel, leek, and garlic, turned the broth into something rich and satisfying. Parsley stems, a sprig of thyme, and a bay leaf also helped to reinforce the overall flavor change from store-bought to fresh. One by one we tried omitting each of the vegetables and herbs for the sake of simplicity, but we found that each made its own important contribution to the stock.

Now that we had decided on the vegetables for the stock, we wanted to streamline the process of making it. We tried using a food processor to prepare the vegetables, but it produced an inferior result. The processed vegetables had a harsher edge and rougher flavor than those cut by hand. As it turns out, the blades of the food processor actually batter and tear the vegetables, eliciting an off, acidic flavor from the onions, leek, and fennel. Chopping the vegetables by hand, we realized how important it is to cut them into small pieces so they can cook and release their flavors more quickly. It may take a couple of minutes more to cut the vegetables into petite pieces, but the resulting flavor and speedy cooking time are worth the extra effort.

Taking a cue from our other stock recipes, we tried sweating the vegetables lightly on their own first, before covering them with the broth. When the stock made from the sweated vegetables was compared with one in which the vegetables and stock were simply simmered together, the difference in flavor was dramatic. Once strained, the sweated stock had a full, round flavor, while the simmered stock tasted thin and one-dimensional. Sweating allows the vegetable cells to break down and release their flavor into the pot before the broth is added. This process is a good way to get flavor into the stock without taking the time for a long simmer. Finally, we had a quick stock that was chock-full of flavor without being overly sweet or meaty. Now we could focus on the main characters of this soup: spring vegetables.

Not wanting to clutter the soup with any vegetables that weren't essential, we steered toward a simple, clean soup filled only with vegetables of the season. Leeks, green peas, asparagus, and baby spinach all made the cut quickly. Their tender flavors, different shapes, and varying shades of green made for a balanced and elegant spring lineup. Tomatoes, on the other hand, added unwelcome acidity, while fava beans involved too much work—both were out. Although chard and arugula were brightly colored and flavorful, their spicy, overpowering flavors were too strong a presence in the otherwise delicate soup. Small, new red potatoes were a nice addition, giving the soup some body and a little variety in color. Scallions, celery, and carrots did little but crowd and distract.

Cooking the five finalists—leeks, peas, baby spinach, asparagus, and red potatoes—was easy enough. The stock, still warm after being doctored and strained, was at the near-perfect temperature to poach this somewhat fragile combination. The leeks and potatoes went in first; then the asparagus, and finally spinach, and peas just before serving. The vegetables took well to this gentle cooking process, as the simmering stock brought out and reinforced the flavor of each. Garnished only with some chopped tarragon, the soup has an unmistakable spring flavor. It's a spring vegetable soup that lives up to its name.

Spring Vegetable Soup
SERVES 6

This soup uses store-bought low-sodium chicken broth doctored with vegetables and herbs to brighten its flavor. Once completed, the soup is best served immediately.

BROTH

2	medium onions, minced
1	medium carrot, peeled and minced
1	celery rib, minced
1	medium leek, washed well, white and light green parts only, minced
1	fennel bulb, minced
3	medium garlic cloves, unpeeled and crushed
1	teaspoon vegetable oil

½   teaspoon salt
7   cups low-sodium chicken broth
2   black peppercorns, crushed
I   sprig fresh thyme
5   sprigs fresh parsley

SOUP
12 ounces red potatoes (about 2 medium),
     scrubbed and cut into ¾-inch dice
2   medium leeks, washed well, white and light
     green parts only, halved lengthwise, cut into
     1-inch lengths
½   bunch medium asparagus (about 8 ounces),
     tough ends removed and cut on the bias into
     1-inch lengths
3   ounces baby spinach (about 2 packed cups)
I   cup frozen peas
2   tablespoons minced fresh tarragon leaves
     Salt and ground black pepper

1. FOR THE BROTH: Combine the onions, carrot, celery, leek, fennel, garlic, oil, and salt in a large Dutch oven. Cover and cook over low heat, stirring often, until the vegetables have softened, 8 to 10 minutes. Stir in the broth, peppercorns, thyme, and parsley. Bring to a boil over medium-high heat; reduce the heat to medium-low and simmer until the broth is flavorful, about 15 minutes. Strain the broth through a fine-mesh strainer; discard the solids. (The broth can be refrigerated for up to 3 days or frozen in an airtight container for up to 2 months.)

2. FOR THE SOUP: Bring the broth to a simmer in a large saucepan over medium heat. Add the potatoes and leeks and simmer for about 5 minutes. Add the asparagus and cook until all the vegetables are just tender, about 5 minutes. Off the heat, stir in the spinach, peas, and tarragon, cover, and let sit until heated through, about 4 minutes. Season with salt and pepper to taste. Serve immediately.

PER 1½-CUP SERVING: Cal 120; Fat 1.5 g; Sat fat 0 g; Chol 0 mg; Carb 22 g; Protein 6 g; Fiber 5 g; Sodium 930 mg

GAZPACHO

POPULAR ON BOTH SIDES OF THE ATLANTIC, gazpacho is an ice-cold, uncooked vegetable soup, made principally of tomatoes (whole and juice), cucumbers, bell peppers, and onions and seasoned with olive oil and vinegar. From a nutritional standpoint, this soup, sometimes referred to as "liquid salad" in its native Spain, required no tinkering at all. It is inherently low in fat and calories. The problem we did find, however, is the way many American recipes treat gazpacho, which is to instruct the cook to simply puree all the vegetables together in the blender. The resulting mixture is a thin vegetable porridge with an anonymous vegetal flavor, whereas we were looking for a soup with clearly flavored, distinct pieces of vegetables in a bracing tomato broth.

With our preference for a chunky-style soup established, we had to figure out the best method for preparing the vegetables. Although it was a breeze to use, the blender broke the vegetables down beyond recognition, which was not at all what we wanted. The food processor fared

CORING AND DICING TOMATOES

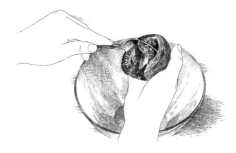

1. Core the tomatoes, halve them pole to pole, and, working over a bowl to catch all the juices, scoop out the inner pulp and seeds. Chop the tomato pulp into ¼-inch cubes.

2. Cut the tomato halves into ¼-inch slices, then cut again into ¼-inch cubes.

somewhat better, especially when we processed each vegetable separately. This method had distinct pros and cons. On the pro side were ease and the fact that the vegetables released some juice as they broke down, which helped flavor the soup. The cons were that no matter how we finessed the pulse feature, the vegetable pieces were neither neatly chopped nor a consistent size. This was especially true of the tomatoes, which broke down to a pulp. The texture of the resulting soup was more along the lines of vegetable slush, which might be acceptable given the ease of preparation, but still not ideal. On balance, the food processor is a decent option, especially if you favor speed and convenience, so we've included a variation that uses this machine.

For our main recipe, though, we settled on the old-fashioned, purist method of hand chopping the vegetables. It does involve some extra work, but it went much more swiftly than we'd imagined, and the benefits to the gazpacho's texture were dazzling. Because the pieces were consistent in size and shape, they not only retained their individual flavors but also set off the tomato broth beautifully, adding immeasurably to the whole.

One last procedural issue we investigated was the resting time. Gazpacho is best served ice-cold, and the chilling time also allows the flavors to develop and meld. We found that four hours was the minimum time required for the soup to chill and the flavors to blossom.

Several of the key ingredients and seasonings also bore some exploration. Tomatoes are a star player here, and we preferred beefsteak over plum because they were larger, juicier, and easier to chop. Gazpacho is truly a dish to make only when local tomatoes are plentiful. We made several batches using handsome supermarket tomatoes, but the flavor paled in comparison to those batches made with perfectly ripe, local, farm-stand tomatoes.

When it came to peppers, we preferred red over green for their sweeter flavor. Tasters favored sweet onions, such as Vidalia or Maui, and shallots equally. We did note, however, that any onion was overpowering if used in the quantities recommended in most recipes (especially in leftovers), and the same was true of garlic, so we dramatically reduced the quantity of both. To ensure thorough seasoning of the whole mixture, we marinated the vegetables briefly in the garlic, salt, pepper, and vinegar before adding the bulk of the liquid. These batches had more balanced flavors than the batches that were seasoned after all the ingredients were combined.

The liquid component was also critical. Most recipes called for tomato juice, which we sampled both straight and mixed in various amounts with water and canned low-sodium chicken broth. The winning combination was 5 cups of tomato juice thinned with 1 cup of water. Given our preference for ice-cold gazpacho, we decided to add ice cubes instead of straight water. The ice cubes helped chill the soup while providing water as they melted. We also conducted a blind tasting of tomato juices in which Welch's showed very well.

Finally, a word about the two primary seasonings, vinegar and olive oil. Spain is a noted producer of sherry, so it follows that sherry vinegar is a popular choice for gazpacho. When we tasted it, along with champagne, red wine, and white wine vinegars, the sherry vinegar was our favorite by far, adding not only acidity but also richness and depth. If you find that your stock of sherry vinegar has run dry, you can substitute white wine vinegar, our runner-up. A drizzle of olive oil just before serving contributes both flavor and a lush mouthfeel to this simple soup, and just a small amount of extra-virgin will do.

Gazpacho
SERVES 8

This recipe makes a large quantity because the leftovers are so good, but it can be halved if you prefer. For the tomato juice in our gazpacho, we prefer Welch's. Traditionally, diners garnish their own bowls with more of the same diced vegetables that are in the soup. If that appeals to you, cut some extra vegetables while you prepare those called for in the recipe. Additional garnish possibilities include Croutons (page 42), finely diced avocado, and a drizzle of extra-virgin olive oil.

3   medium ripe beefsteak tomatoes
     (about 1½ pounds), cored and cut into
     ¼-inch dice (see the illustrations on page 70)

2   medium red bell peppers (about 1 pound), stemmed, seeded, and cut into 1/4-inch dice

2   small cucumbers (about 1 pound), one peeled and the other with skin on, both seeded and cut into 1/4-inch dice

1/2 small sweet onion, such as Vidalia, Maui, or Walla Walla, or 2 large shallots, minced (about 1/2 cup)

2   medium garlic cloves, minced or pressed through a garlic press (about 2 teaspoons)

1/3 cup sherry vinegar
    Salt and ground black pepper

5   cups (40 ounces) tomato juice (see note)

1   teaspoon hot pepper sauce (optional)

8   ice cubes

1. Combine the tomatoes, bell peppers, cucumbers, onion, garlic, vinegar, 2 teaspoons salt, and 1/8 teaspoon pepper in a large (at least 4-quart) nonreactive bowl. Let stand until the vegetables just begin to release their juices, about 5 minutes. Stir in the tomato juice, hot sauce (if using), and ice cubes. Cover tightly and refrigerate to blend the flavors, at least 4 hours and up to 2 days.

2. Season with salt and pepper to taste and remove and discard any unmelted ice cubes. Serve cold, topping with the desired garnishes (see note).

PER 1 1/2-CUP SERVING: Cal 80; Fat 0 g; Sat fat 0 g; Chol 0 mg; Carb 17 g; Protein 3 g; Fiber 4 g; Sodium 890 mg

➤ VARIATIONS
Quick Food Processor Gazpacho
This is a speedy, but equally tasty variation of the original. This recipe can also be halved if you prefer, but it is great leftover so we recommend making the entire batch.

Using the same ingredients and quantities as for Gazpacho, core and quarter the tomatoes and process them in a food processor until broken down into 1/2- to 1-inch pieces, about twelve 1-second pulses; transfer to a large bowl. Cut the stemmed and seeded peppers and seeded cucumbers into rough 1-inch pieces and process them separately until broken down into 1/2-inch pieces, about twelve 1-second pulses; add to the bowl with the tomatoes. Add the onion, garlic, vinegar, salt, and

black pepper to taste; proceed with the recipe as directed.

PER 1 1/2-CUP SERVING: Cal 80; Fat 0 g; Sat fat 0 g; Chol 0 mg; Carb 17 g; Protein 3 g; Fiber 4 g; Sodium 890 mg

Spicy Gazpacho with Chipotle Chiles and Lime
With hot pepper sauce and chipotle chiles giving this version some heat, a sprinkle of finely diced ripe avocado is a must with this variation.

Follow the recipe for Gazpacho or Quick Food Processor Gazpacho, omitting the optional hot pepper sauce and adding 2½ tablespoons minced canned chipotle chiles in adobo sauce, ¼ cup minced fresh cilantro leaves, 6 tablespoons fresh lime juice, and 2 teaspoons grated lime zest along with the tomato juice and ice cubes.

PER 1 1/2-CUP SERVING: Cal 80; Fat 0 g; Sat fat 0 g; Chol 0 mg; Carb 19 g; Protein 3 g; Fiber 4 g; Sodium 890 mg

TEST KITCHEN MAKEOVER

CREAM OF VEGETABLE SOUPS

CLASSIC CREAM OF VEGETABLE SOUP SHOULD be bursting with vegetable flavor, flawlessly smooth and silky, with a colorful representation of the vegetable itself. Too often these soups are overly rich from a heavy hand with cream and/or butter, which dilutes the vegetable's flavor and dulls its color. Amounts of butter are often in the range of 4 tablespoons, and we haven't come across a recipe calling for any less than 1 cup of heavy cream—no wonder eating just a few bites is enough to fill us up fast!

Our challenge, therefore, would lie in developing a lighter cream of vegetable soup in which the richness of the cream wouldn't overtake the flavor of the vegetables. We also wanted a master recipe that we could use to apply the same proportions and core technique to a host of different vegetables—a one-size-fits-all approach to cream of vegetable soup, if you will.

Typically, cream soups start out by sautéing aromatics, such as onion and garlic, in as much as half a stick of butter. Once the aromatics are softened, flour is added and cooked to make a roux, which aids in thickening the soup and creating its velvety texture. Next, broth (usually chicken) is whisked in and simmered in order for the liquid to thicken and the flavors to meld. The vegetables are then added and simmered until tender, at which point the soup is pureed and finished with heavy cream, which gives the soup a rich and creamy texture, provides body, and rounds out its flavors. Following this basic technique, we made a batch of soup with broccoli.

We replaced the butter traditionally used to sauté the aromatics with just one teaspoon of vegetable oil, as we've done in other soups to cut the fat. We added the stock and broccoli and simmered until the broccoli was tender. Next we figured that we would substitute an equal amount of low-fat milk for the heavy cream. Much to our dismay, the soup lacked body, was drab in color, and scant in flavor. Without a doubt, it tasted unpalatably lean and low-fat. (This soup also tasted too much like other low-fat cream of vegetable soups, which typically rely on skim milk for the dairy.) As for the vegetable flavor, it was meager at best. This was not going to be as easy as we had thought.

First, we determined it was best to start at the top—with the aromatics. Which ones were best suited to cream of vegetable soups? Tasters didn't seem to have a preference between soups made with onion, shallot, or leek, but they felt strongly about the inclusion of garlic. Also, since we dramatically reduced the amount of fat that the aromatics were sautéed in, we had to make adjustments to our technique in order to prevent them from burning and to bring out their maximum flavor. By combining the onion with just 1 teaspoon oil and ½ teaspoon salt, then cooking the mixture, covered, over low heat for a lengthy amount of time (about 10 minutes), we were successful. The oil coated the onion and prevented it from burning, while the salt and covered pan

---

TESTING NOTES

The Skinny on Dairy

After testing several substitutions for heavy cream in our soups and chowders, we finally found one that has less fat and calories and makes a better-tasting soup.

MILK (SKIM, LOW-FAT, WHOLE)
Watery
Most recipes substitute milk for the cream in soups and chowders, but we found that milk, whether skim, low-fat, or whole, made the soup taste watery and hollow.

EVAPORATED MILK (FAT-FREE, 2 PERCENT, WHOLE)
Creamy, but stale
We liked the creamy texture that evaporated milk added to our soups, but we needed to use more of it to achieve the same effect as heavy cream—and this resulted in excessive calories.

THE WINNER

HALF-AND-HALF
Just ½ cup of half-and-half added the luxurious texture and creamy, sweet flavor of heavy cream. And because half-and-half contains less than half the fat of heavy cream and one-third as many fat grams, it's a wiser choice when going light.

further helped the cause. The onion released its moisture and sweated in its own flavorful juices. We also chose to add the broccoli stems at this point in with the onion, hoping to extract more flavor from the vegetable (the tender florets, which don't require as much cooking, would be added later in the process).

As for the stock used in the soup, we tested chicken and vegetable broths, both homemade and store-bought low-sodium versions. Both of the homemade broths were perfect in these recipes, but honestly, the store-bought broths fared just as well. Chicken broth added more depth, but the vegetable broth was light and pleasant. We decided to use half chicken broth and half vegetable broth for balance, but you could certainly use all one or the other if you prefer.

Next we moved on to the dairy. Instead of skim milk, some lower fat cream soup recipes call for evaporated milk as a low-fat alternative—we thought we'd give it a shot. Evaporated milk is whole milk that has been cooked to evaporate as much as half of its water content; the result is a creamier product with, cup for cup, higher

amounts of sugar, protein, and calcium. Though many tasters like the flavor and texture evaporated milk imparted, others complained that it was "too sweet" with an "off flavor." Running out of dairy alternatives, we had one choice left: half-and-half.

We tried substituting an equal amount (1 cup) of half-and-half for the heavy cream, but the soup was too rich and the dairy flavor masked the vegetable flavor. We reduced the amount to ¾ cup, but the dairy was still overpowering. We settled on ½ cup—it provided the right amount of dairy flavor and fat, giving the soup a smooth and creamy mouthfeel without eclipsing the vegetable. Fattier than whole milk, but leaner than heavy cream, half-and-half proved a good compromise.

We were pretty pleased at how our tests were proceeding. We started swapping in other vegetables for the broccoli, first asparagus, then peas. Both were great. But trouble started when we tried vegetables like carrots, butternut squash, mushrooms, and tomatoes. None of them worked in our one-size-fits-all soup. We realized that if we wanted to showcase each vegetable in its best

THE LOWDOWN ON FAT-FREE HALF-AND-HALF

The term half-and-half refers to a mixture of half milk and half cream, which, according to the United States Food and Drug Administration, must contain between 10.5 and 18 percent butterfat, putting it at about 1.5 grams of fat and 20 calories per tablespoon. Recently, however, fat-free half-and-half has appeared on supermarket shelves. We wondered: What exactly is fat-free half-and-half?

A little research led us to find out that fat-free half-and-half is made from fat-free milk, corn syrup, and a whole slew of natural and artificial additives, giving it the viscosity and color of the real stuff. Curious about this oxymoron of an ingredient, containing no fat and just 10 calories per tablespoon, we decided to put it to through some test-kitchen tests.

We gathered several brands of fat-free half-and-half from our local supermarkets and made a pot of cream of broccoli soup with each one, as well as a batch with true half-and-half. As it turns out, fat-free half-and-half varies tremendously

by brand. Among national brands, tasters preferred Land O Lakes Fat-Free Half-and-Half. Some brands, though not as rich and creamy tasting, were decent substitutes for regular half-and-half, while others produced batches of soup that were virtually inedible, leaving curdled white specks in the soup and tasting like the cleaning products stored under our kitchen sinks.

We also tasted fat-free half-and-half in coffee. While some tasters complained of a chemical aftertaste and little dairy flavor, others couldn't detect a difference from regular half-and-half and were happy to save the fat grams and still have a rich and creamy cup of coffee.

When it comes down to it, we do not recommend using fat-free half-and-half for cooking; it only saves about 6 grams of fat and 80 calories per entire batch of soup and it just isn't as dairy-rich or creamy. That said, if you like your coffee creamy, and you are looking to save fat and calories, give it a try.

light, we would have to tailor the recipe around each type of vegetable. Accordingly, we divided them into three groups: broccoli, asparagus, and sweet peas in group 1, carrots and butternut squash in group 2, and tomatoes and mushrooms in group 3.

Since we had the green vegetables covered we moved on to group 2. Our initial batches of carrot and butternut squash soups made following our working recipe tasted bland. Instead of simmering the vegetables until tender in the stock, we tried sautéing them with the aromatics. This was an improvement, but we thought the vegetable flavor could still be improved. Starchy vegetables are often roasted to concentrate their sweet flavor, so we tried roasting them prior to adding them to the soup. This method worked well, turning out soups with deep and complex flavors. We were able to further boost flavor by then sweating the roasted vegetables with the garlic, which coaxed out any

remaining moisture and concentrated the flavors. The starchy vegetables provided enough thickness to the soup, so we were able to omit the flour. We did need to add an additional teaspoon of oil, both to roast the vegetables and to sweat them, but this amount of fat was still small.

Lastly, we were on to group 3, tomatoes and mushrooms. Both these vegetables are very high in moisture, resulting in soups that were watery in flavor and texture. We found that sautéing the tomatoes and mushrooms with the aromatics before simmering them in the broth cooked out much of their moisture and heightened their flavor.

Our tests were proceeding nicely. Now that all of our cream of vegetable soups tasted creamy and

PREPARING BROCCOLI

1. Place the head of broccoli upside down on a cutting board and, using a large knife, trim off the florets very close to their heads and cut into 1-inch pieces.

2. Stand each stalk up on the cutting board and square it off with a large knife, to remove the outer ⅛ inch, which is quite tough. Cut the stalk in half lengthwise and chop fine.

MAKEOVER AT A GLANCE

–Classic–
Cream of Broccoli Soup
(per serving)

Calories: 300	**Cholesterol:** 70 mg
Fat: 23 g	**Saturated Fat:** 15 g

–Light–
Cream of Broccoli Soup
(per serving)

Calories: 120	**Cholesterol:** 10 mg
Fat: 5 g	**Saturated Fat:** 2.5 g

How We Did It

- Replaced 4–6 tablespoons butter with just 1–2 teaspoons oil
- Sweated the aromatics over medium-low heat, with the cover on, to draw out their moisture and concentrate their flavors
- Finished the soup with half-and-half instead of heavy cream and used half as much
- Boosted the flavor with white wine, a generous amount of garlic, and a bay leaf

were bursting with vegetable flavor, we needed to complement their flavors. Some cream soups require a hint of acidity. In most cases, it took only a little white wine, though there were a few exceptions. We chose to pair Madeira with the mushroom soup and brandy with the tomato soup simply because they are classic combinations.

Though it wasn't as easy as we had thought it would be, we finally achieved success with seven lower fat rich and creamy soups with great vegetable flavor. On average, we were able to cut half of the calories and three-quarters of the fat from traditional versions of creamy vegetable soups.

Cream of Broccoli Soup
SERVES 4

We found that this soup tastes best when made with part chicken broth and part vegetable broth; however, for a vegetarian soup, you can use all vegetable broth (the soup will taste sweeter). To preserve the delicate flavor and green color of the broccoli, this soup is best when served immediately.

1½	pounds broccoli (about 1 large bunch), florets cut into 1-inch pieces, enough stalks peeled and chopped fine to make ¾ cup (discard any remaining stalks)
1	medium onion, 3 medium shallots, or 1 medium leek, washed well, white and light green parts only, chopped fine
1	teaspoon vegetable oil
	Salt
3	garlic cloves, minced or pressed through a garlic press (about 1 tablespoon)
1	tablespoon unbleached all-purpose flour
¼	cup dry white wine
1	bay leaf
1½	cups low-sodium chicken broth
1½	cups low-sodium vegetable broth
½	cup half-and-half
	Ground black pepper

1. Combine the chopped broccoli stalks, onion, oil, and ½ teaspoon salt in a large saucepan. Cover and cook over medium-low heat, stirring often, until softened, 8 to 10 minutes. Stir in the garlic

and cook until fragrant, about 30 seconds.

2. Stir in the flour and cook for 1 minute. Whisk in the wine and bay leaf; cook until the wine is absorbed, about 1 minute. Whisking constantly, gradually add the broths. Bring to a boil over medium-high heat; cover, reduce the heat to medium-low, and simmer until slightly thickened and the broth no longer tastes of flour, about 5 minutes. Add the florets and continue to simmer, uncovered, until tender, 7 to 10 minutes. Remove the bay leaf.

3. Puree the mixture in a blender (or food processor) until smooth, and return to a clean saucepan. Stir in the half-and-half and cook over low heat until just hot (do not boil), about 3 minutes. Season with salt and pepper to taste. Serve immediately.

PER 1½-CUP SERVING: Cal 120; Fat 5 g; Sat fat 2.5 g; Chol 10 mg; Carb 13 g; Protein 5 g; Fiber 3 g; Sodium 760 mg

Cream of Asparagus Soup
SERVES 4

We found that this soup tastes best when made with part chicken broth and part vegetable broth, however for a vegetarian soup, you can use all vegetable broth (the soup will taste a bit sweeter). To preserve its delicate flavor and green color, this soup is best when served immediately.

1	medium onion, 3 medium shallots, or 1 medium leek, washed well, white and light green parts only, chopped fine
1	teaspoon vegetable oil
	Salt
3	garlic cloves, minced or pressed through a garlic press (about 1 tablespoon)
1	tablespoon unbleached all-purpose flour
¼	cup dry white wine
1	bay leaf
1½	cups low-sodium chicken broth
1½	cups low-sodium vegetable broth
1½	pounds asparagus (1½ bunches), tough ends removed (see page 97) and cut into ½-inch lengths
½	cup half-and-half
	Ground black pepper

1. Combine the onion, oil, and ½ teaspoon salt in a large saucepan. Cover and cook over medium-low heat, stirring often, until softened, 8 to 10 minutes. Stir in the garlic and cook until fragrant, about 30 seconds.

2. Stir in the flour and cook for 1 minute. Whisk in the wine and bay leaf; cook until the wine is absorbed, about 1 minute. Whisking constantly, gradually add the broths. Bring to a boil over medium-high heat; cover, reduce the heat to medium-low, and simmer until the broth is slightly thickened and no longer tastes of flour, about 5 minutes. Add the asparagus and continue to simmer, uncovered, until tender, 7 to 10 minutes. Remove the bay leaf.

3. Puree the mixture in a blender (or food processor) until smooth, and return to a clean saucepan. Stir in the half-and-half and cook over low heat until just hot (do not boil), about 3 minutes. Season with salt and pepper to taste. Serve immediately.

PER 1½-CUP SERVING: Cal 140; Fat 5 g; Sat fat 2.5 g; Chol 10 mg; Carb 15 g; Protein 6 g; Fiber 5 g; Sodium 730 mg

Cream of Sweet Pea Soup
SERVES 4

Remove the peas from the freezer before starting the soup so that when you are ready to add them, they will be only partially thawed. We found that adding lettuce leaves cuts the sweetness of the peas and contributes a rounded flavor. A few Croutons (page 42) or chopped fresh mint or tarragon leaves are the perfect embellishment.

I	medium onion, 3 medium shallots, or I medium leek, washed well, white and light green parts only, chopped fine
I	teaspoon vegetable oil
	Salt
3	garlic cloves, minced or pressed through a garlic press (about I tablespoon)
I	tablespoon unbleached all-purpose flour
¼	cup dry white wine
I	bay leaf
1½	cups low-sodium chicken broth
1½	cups low-sodium vegetable broth
4	cups frozen peas
12	leaves Boston lettuce (about 3 ounces), washed and dried
½	cup half-and-half
	Ground black pepper

1. Combine the onion, oil, and ½ teaspoon salt in a large saucepan. Cover and cook over medium-low heat, stirring often, until softened, 8 to 10 minutes. Stir in the garlic and cook until fragrant, about 30 seconds.

2. Stir in the flour and cook for 1 minute. Whisk in the wine and bay leaf; cook until the wine is absorbed, about 1 minute. Whisking constantly, gradually add the broths. Bring to a boil over medium-high heat; cover, reduce the heat to medium-low, and simmer until the broth no longer tastes of flour, about 5 minutes. Add the peas and lettuce and continue to simmer, uncovered, until the peas no longer taste starchy, 7 to 10 minutes. Remove the bay leaf.

3. Puree the mixture in a blender (or food processor) until smooth, and return to a clean saucepan. Stir in the half-and-half and cook over low heat until just hot (do not boil), about 3 minutes. Season with salt and pepper to taste. Serve immediately.

PER 1½-CUP SERVING: Cal 240; Fat 6 g; Sat fat 2.5 g; Chol 10 mg; Carb 33 g; Protein 13 g; Fiber 11 g; Sodium 980 mg

Cream of Roasted Carrot Soup
SERVES 4

Roasting the carrots brings out their natural sweetness and concentrates their flavor. If desired, add 1 tablespoon grated fresh ginger with the garlic in step 2. This soup can also be served chilled.

1½	pounds carrots (about 8 medium), peeled and sliced ½ inch thick
I	medium onion, halved and sliced ½ inch thick
2	teaspoons vegetable oil
	Salt
3	garlic cloves, minced or pressed through a garlic press (about I tablespoon)

¼ cup dry white wine

I bay leaf

I ½ cups low-sodium chicken broth

I ½ cups low-sodium vegetable broth

½ cup half-and-half

Ground black pepper

1. Adjust an oven rack to the middle position and heat the oven to 450 degrees. Toss the carrots, onion, 1 teaspoon of the oil, and ½ teaspoon salt on a rimmed baking sheet and then spread in an even layer. Roast until the vegetables are well browned and softened, stirring occasionally, 25 to 30 minutes.

2. Transfer the roasted vegetables to a large saucepan. Add the remaining 1 teaspoon oil, cover, and cook over medium-low heat, stirring often, until the carrots soften further, 3 to 5 minutes. Add the garlic and cook until fragrant, about 30 seconds. Stir in the wine and bay leaf; cook until the wine has reduced by half, about 1 minute. Add the broths. Bring to a boil over medium-high heat; cover, reduce the heat to medium-low, and simmer until the soup is flavorful, about 5 minutes. Remove the bay leaf.

3. Puree the mixture in a blender (or food processor) until smooth, and return to a clean saucepan. Add the half-and-half and warm over low heat until hot, about 3 minutes. Season with salt and pepper to taste. (The soup can be refrigerated in an airtight container for up to 4 days. Warm over low heat until hot; do not boil.)

PER 1½-CUP SERVING: Cal 170; Fat 7 g; Sat fat 2.5 g; Chol 10 mg; Carb 23 g; Protein 4 g; Fiber 6 g; Sodium 850 mg

Cream of Roasted Butternut Squash Soup

SERVES 4

Some nice accompaniments to this soup are lightly toasted pumpkin seeds, a drizzle of aged balsamic vinegar, or a sprinkle of paprika.

3 pounds butternut squash (about I large), peeled, seeded, and cut into ½-inch chunks

I medium onion, halved and sliced ½ inch thick

2 teaspoons vegetable oil

Salt

3 garlic cloves, minced or pressed through a garlic press (about I tablespoon)

¼ cup dry white wine

I bay leaf

I ½ cups low-sodium chicken broth

I ½ cups low-sodium vegetable broth

½ cup half-and-half

Ground black pepper

1. Adjust an oven rack to the middle position and heat the oven to 450 degrees. Toss the squash, onion, 1 teaspoon of the oil, and ½ teaspoon salt on a rimmed baking sheet and then spread in an even layer. Roast until the vegetables are well browned and softened, stirring occasionally, 25 to 30 minutes.

2. Transfer the roasted vegetables to a large saucepan. Add the remaining 1 teaspoon oil, cover, and cook over medium-low heat, stirring often, until the squash is softened further, 3 to 5 minutes. Add the garlic and cook until fragrant, about 30 seconds. Stir in the wine and bay leaf; cook until the wine has reduced by half, about 1 minute. Add the broths. Bring to a boil over medium-high heat; cover, reduce the heat to medium-low, and simmer until the soup is flavorful, about 5 minutes. Remove the bay leaf.

PUREEING SOUP SAFELY

Many vegetable soups are best pureed in a blender to create a smooth texture. Blending hot soup can be dangerous, though. To prevent mishaps, don't fill the blender jar past the halfway point, and hold the lid in place with a folded kitchen towel.

3. Puree the mixture in a blender (or food processor) until smooth, and return to a clean saucepan. Add the half-and-half and warm over low heat until hot, about 3 minutes. Season with salt and pepper to taste. (The soup can be refrigerated in an airtight container for up to 4 days. Warm over low heat until hot; do not boil.)

PER 1½-CUP SERVING: Cal 170; Fat 6 g; Sat fat 2.5 g; Chol 10 mg; Carb 24 g; Protein 5 g; Fiber 6 g; Sodium 740 mg

Cream of Mushroom Soup
SERVES 4

A splash of Madeira or sherry added at the end rounds out the flavors and adds just the right touch of sweetness—you may need to add a little more or less depending on the brand. Garnish with Croutons (page 42) and snipped chives.

3   large shallots, minced (about ¾ cup)
2   teaspoons vegetable oil
     Salt
2   medium garlic cloves, minced or pressed through a garlic press (about 2 teaspoons)
¼   teaspoon freshly grated nutmeg
I   pound white mushrooms, wiped clean and sliced ¼ inch thick (about 3 cups)
I ½   cups low-sodium chicken broth
2   cups hot water
¼   ounce dried porcini mushrooms, rinsed well
½   cup half-and-half
2–3   tablespoons Madeira or dry sherry
I   teaspoon juice from I lemon
     Ground black pepper

1. Combine the shallots, 1 teaspoon of the oil, and ½ teaspoon salt in a large saucepan. Cover and cook over medium-low heat, stirring often, until softened, 8 to 10 minutes. Stir in the garlic and nutmeg and cook until fragrant, about 30 seconds.

2. Stir in the remaining 1 teaspoon oil and white mushrooms. Increase the heat to medium and cook, stirring occasionally, until the mushrooms begin to release their liquid, about 7 minutes. Cover, reduce the heat to medium-low, and continue to cook, stirring occasionally, until the mushrooms have released all their liquid, about 20 minutes.

3. Stir in the broth, water, and porcini mushrooms. Bring to a boil over medium-high heat; cover, reduce the heat to medium-low, and simmer until the mushrooms are tender, about 20 minutes.

4. Puree the mixture in a blender (or food processor) until smooth and return to a clean saucepan. Add the half-and-half and cook over low heat until hot, about 3 minutes. Off the heat, stir in the Madeira and lemon juice and season with salt and pepper to taste. (The soup can be refrigerated in an airtight container for up to 4 days. Warm over low heat until hot; do not boil.) If desired, garnish with croutons and chives.

PER 1½-CUP SERVING: Cal 130; Fat 6 g; Sat fat 2.5 g; Chol 10 mg; Carb 12 g; Protein 5 g; Fiber 1 g; Sodium 530 mg

Cream of Tomato Soup
SERVES 4

Carrot and brown sugar tame the acidity of the tomatoes in this soup. For information on specific brands of canned whole tomatoes, see page 000. Croutons (page 42) make a nice accompaniment.

3   large shallots, minced (about ¾ cup)
I   carrot, peeled and minced
I   tablespoon tomato paste
I   teaspoon vegetable oil

SEEDING AND DRAINING CANNED WHOLE TOMATOES

With your fingers, carefully open the whole tomatoes over a strainer set in a bowl and push out the seeds, allowing the juices to fall through the strainer and into the bowl.

Salt

Pinch ground allspice

2   (28-ounce) cans whole tomatoes, drained and
seeded (see the illustration on page 79)

4 ½   teaspoons dark brown sugar

1   tablespoon unbleached all-purpose flour

1 ½   cups low-sodium chicken broth

1 ½   cups low-sodium vegetable broth

½   cup half-and-half

1–2   tablespoons brandy or dry sherry (optional)
Cayenne

1. Combine the shallots, carrot, tomato paste, oil, ½ teaspoon salt, and allspice in a large saucepan. Cover and cook over medium-low heat, stirring often, until the carrot is tender, 8 to 10 minutes. Stir in the tomatoes and sugar; continue to cook, uncovered and stirring often, until the mixture is dry, about 10 minutes. Stir in the flour and cook for 1 minute.

2. Whisking constantly, gradually add the broths. Bring to a boil over medium-high heat; cover, reduce the heat to medium-low, and simmer until the flavors blend, about 10 minutes.

3. Puree the mixture in a blender (or food processor) until smooth and return to a clean saucepan. Add the half-and-half and cook over low heat until hot, about 3 minutes. Off the heat, stir in the brandy (if desired) and season with salt and cayenne to taste. (The soup can be refrigerated in an airtight container for up to 4 days. Warm over low heat until hot; do not boil.)

PER 1½-CUP SERVING: Cal 150; Fat 5 g; Sat fat 2.5 g; Chol 10 mg; Carb 23 g; Protein 4 g; Fiber 2 g; Sodium 1080 mg

BLACK BEAN SOUP

EATING BLACK BEAN SOUP IS A TASTY WAY to incorporate beans into your diet. High in fiber and protein, rich in iron, and with virtually no fat, black beans have been a staple in Mexican, Cuban, and Caribbean diets for years. But in the 1960s when black bean soup hit American shores, it became a popular restaurant offering, particularly at New York City's Coach House Restaurant. Other restaurants went on to imitate the Coach House's recipe, which called for soaked dried beans that needed to be simmered for hours, with, among other ingredients, parsnips, carrots, beef bones, and smoked ham hocks. The pureed soup was finished with a splash of Madeira, chopped hard-cooked eggs, and thinly sliced lemon. Is this recipe realistic for the modern cook? No. We wanted to bring this soup back to its healthier and authentic Latin-American roots minus the restaurant fanfare.

When beans are the star ingredient, it's preferable to use the dried variety, not canned; although there are no nutritional differences between the two, the former release valuable flavor into the broth as they cook, while the latter generally make vapid soup. (We simmered five brands of dried beans, including an organic variety and beans from the bulk bin of a natural food store, and there were only minor variations in flavor. In short, brand doesn't seem to matter.) We've also learned that there's no reason to soak dried beans overnight—doing so only marginally reduces the cooking time and requires too much forethought. Similarly, the "quick-soak" method, in which the beans are brought to a boil and then soaked off the heat for an hour, is disappointing in that it causes many of the beans to explode during cooking.

As for seasoning, a teaspoon of salt added at the outset of cooking provided tastier beans than salt added at the end of cooking. We've found that salting early does not toughen the skins of beans, as some cooks claim. In addition to salt, we threw a couple of aromatic bay leaves into the pot.

We knew we didn't want to make from-scratch beef stock, so we focused on more time-efficient flavor builders. While tasters liked the meaty flavor offered by the ham hock and beef bones, it wasn't the healthiest approach. We turned to untraditional (for black bean soup) ham steak. Ham steak is lean, but nevertheless, it contributed a good amount of smoky pork flavor and as a bonus, offered up nice bits of tender ham.

We found full flavor using a sofrito, a Spanish or Italian preparation in which aromatic vegetables and herbs (we used green pepper, onion, garlic, and oregano) are sautéed until softened and lightly browned. But our sofrito needed refinement.

We replaced the oregano with cumin, which had a warmer, more likable taste. We slowly incorporated the ground spice, working our way up to 4½ teaspoons. Sound like a lot? It is, but we were after big flavor, and when we sautéed the cumin along with the aromatics, it was able to "bloom" and its pungency was tempered. We also replaced the bitter green pepper with minced carrot and celery for a sweeter, fresher flavor.

Tasters wanted more minced garlic and hot red pepper flakes: We added six cloves and ½ teaspoon, respectively. The soup was now a hit, layered with sweet, spicy, smoky, and fresh vegetable flavors. While the Coach House recipe called for homemade beef stock, our aggressive seasonings meant that a mixture of water and store-bought broth was all that was needed.

Here in the test kitchen, tasters were united in their request for a partially pureed soup, refusing both ultrasmooth mixtures and chunky, brothy ones. By pureeing only some of the black beans and cooking liquid, we were able to achieve the perfect texture.

We were finally satisfied, save for the soup's unappealing gray color. As often happens, the solution came to us in a roundabout way. While our food scientist was looking into remedies for the gas-causing effects of beans in digestion, we noticed that a side effect of cooking beans with baking soda is that the beans retain their dark color. The coating of the black beans contains anthocyanins (colored pigments) that change color with changes in pH: A more alkaline broth makes them darker, and a more acidic broth makes them lighter. We experimented by adding various amounts of baking soda to the beans both during and after cooking. The winning quantity was a mere ⅛ teaspoon, which produced a great-tasting soup (there was no soapy aftertaste, as was the case with larger quantities) with a darker, more appetizing color than unadulterated beans. Problem solved.

Classic additions to black bean soup include Madeira, rum, sherry, or Scotch from the liquor cabinet and lemon, lime, or orange juice from the citrus bin. Given the other flavors in the soup, lime juice seemed the best fit. Because it is acidic, too much lime juice can push the color of the soup toward pink. Two tablespoons added flavor without marring the color.

Without an array of colorful garnishes, even the best black bean soup might be dull. Sour cream (reduced fat) and diced avocado offset the soup's heat, while red onion and minced cilantro contribute freshness and color. Finally, wedges of lime accentuate the bright flavor of the juice that's already in the soup.

Black Bean Soup

SERVES 6

Dried beans tend to cook unevenly, so be sure to taste several beans to determine their doneness in step 1. For efficiency, you can prepare the soup ingredients while the beans simmer and prepare the garnishes while the soup simmers. Though you do not need to offer all of the garnishes listed below, do choose at least a couple; garnishes are essential for this soup as they add not only flavor but texture and color as well.

BEANS

6	cups water
1	pound (2 cups) dried black beans, rinsed and picked over
2	bay leaves
⅛	teaspoon baking soda
1	teaspoon salt

SOUP

4	ounces ham steak, trimmed of rind and cut into ¼-inch cubes
3	medium celery ribs, chopped fine
2	large onions, chopped fine
1	large carrot, peeled and chopped fine
6	medium garlic cloves, minced or pressed through a garlic press (about 2 tablespoons)
4½	teaspoons ground cumin
1	tablespoon vegetable oil
½	teaspoon red pepper flakes
	Salt
4½	cups low-sodium chicken broth
2	tablespoons juice from 1 to 2 limes

GARNISHES
Lime wedges
Minced fresh cilantro leaves
Finely diced red onion
Diced avocado
Low-fat sour cream

1. FOR THE BEANS: Bring 5 cups of the water, the beans, bay leaves, and baking soda to a boil in a large saucepan with a tight-fitting lid over medium-high heat; using a large spoon, skim off any scum that rises to surface. Stir in the salt; reduce the heat to low, cover, and simmer briskly until the beans are tender, 1¼ to 1½ hours (if necessary, add the remaining 1 cup water and continue to simmer until beans are tender); do not drain the beans. Discard the bay leaves.

2. FOR THE SOUP: Combine the ham steak, celery, onions, carrot, garlic, cumin, oil, pepper flakes, and ½ teaspoon salt in a large Dutch oven. Cover and cook over medium-low heat, stirring often, until the vegetables are lightly browned, about 15 minutes. Stir in the cooked black beans with their cooking liquid and 4 cups of the chicken broth. Bring to a boil over medium-high heat; partially cover, reduce the heat to medium-low, and simmer, stirring occasionally, until the soup is flavorful, about 30 minutes.

3. Puree 1½ cups of the beans with 2 cups of the cooking liquid in a blender (or food processor) until smooth; return to the pot. (If the soup is too thick, add the remaining ½ cup of chicken broth as needed.) Off the heat, stir in the lime juice. Serve immediately, passing the garnishes separately. (The soup can be refrigerated in an airtight container for 3 or 4 days.)

PER 1½-CUP SERVING: Cal 350; Fat 4 g; Sat fat .5 g; Chol 10 mg; Carb 56 g; Protein 20 g; Fiber 8 g; Sodium 1290 mg

➤ VARIATION
Black Bean Soup with Chipotle Chiles
The addition of chipotle chiles in adobo—smoked jalapeños packed in a seasoned tomato-vinegar sauce—makes this a spicier, smokier variation of our original Black Bean Soup. The same garnishes will work equally well with this version.

Follow the recipe for Black Bean Soup, omitting the red pepper flakes and adding 1 tablespoon minced canned chipotle chiles plus 2 teaspoons adobo sauce to the soup with the chicken broth in step 2.

PER 1½-CUP SERVING: Cal 350; Fat 4 g; Sat fat .5 g; Chol 10 mg; Carb 56 g; Protein 21 g; Fiber 9 g; Sodium 1290 mg

TEST KITCHEN MAKEOVER

CREAM CHOWDERS

MANY HEALTHY COOKBOOKS AVOID CREAM chowders, for obvious reasons—the fat from butter, bacon or salt pork, and heavy cream. We wanted to see if we could lighten up two classic American chowders, corn chowder and New England clam chowder, without compromising their rich flavor.

We knew that in a recipe that traditionally relies on three fats, we would have to step back and take a look at which fats were absolutely essential to the flavor and texture. For both chowders, we would need pork flavor so, taking a cue from prior testing, we started out by slowly sautéing just one slice of bacon, minced fine to distribute the pork flavor (see "Just One Slice" on page 85 for more information). Then we used the rendered fat to cook our onion. This way we were able to eliminate the butter altogether. As for the cream, we would explore this issue later. First, we needed to zero in on each chowder, starting with corn.

We knew from the outset that we were looking first for a chowder base infused with fresh corn flavor. Corn stock, corn puree, corn juice, and corn pulp were all possibilities.

First, we made two quick stocks with corn cobs and husks, using water in one and chicken broth in the other. Although both had some corn flavor, their overall effect on the chowder was minimal; making corn stock was clearly not worth the effort. We did learn, though, that water diluted the flavor of the chowder while chicken broth improved it. Chicken broth would be our liquid of choice for the base.

Still looking to attain great fresh corn flavor, we next tried pureeing the corn kernels and dumping them into the chowder. This wasn't going to work. The hulls made for an unpleasantly rough texture.

In our research, we identified "milking" (grating and scraping) as a good means of extracting flavor from corn to be used for chowder. This approach is time-consuming and messy, but the result convinced us that it was worth the effort. Here was one of the secrets to great corn chowder. The pulp was thick, lush, smooth-textured, and full of corn flavor. When added to the chowder, it improved both flavor and texture dramatically.

Our next concern was the dairy and, as it turned out, the thickener. A problem with the dairy component of chowder is its tendency to curdle when heated, with lower fat products more likely to curdle than high-fat products such as heavy cream. It's the protein component of dairy that causes curdling, and heavy cream is not as susceptible because it has so much fat (about 40 percent); the protein molecules are thus completely surrounded by fat molecules, which keep the proteins from breaking down. We were determined to create a richly flavored chowder without the use of heavy cream.

While some dairy was needed to give the base depth of character, low-fat milk (we liked 2 percent), which is wonderfully neutral and therefore capable of being infused with corn flavor, would make up the larger part of the dairy. This composition gave us some concern about curdling, which is where the thickening factor came in. We realized that the most practical thickener to use would be flour, which is known to help stabilize dairy proteins and thereby prevent curdling. Having a dual objective of both thickening the base and stabilizing the dairy made our work easier. To prevent curdling, the flour has to be added to the soup before the dairy. The logical choice of technique, then, would be to make a roux, stirring the flour into the onions at the beginning of the cooking process.

Determining the vegetables for the chowder was a relatively simple matter. Onions, potatoes, and corn kernels were a given; the questions were what variety of onion and potato and how much of each? All-purpose onions and leeks were serviceable, but Spanish onions proved best, adding flavor without dominating the other ingredients. Our favorite potatoes were red potatoes, which remained firm and looked great with their skins left on. For added richness we stirred a little half-and-half into the chowder toward the end of simmering. Some chowders rely on heavy cream, but as we'd found in our creamy vegetable soups (see page 73), half-and-half works very well.

Now that we had our lighter corn chowder

MAKEOVER AT A GLANCE

–Classic–
Corn Chowder
(per serving)

Calories: 530	Cholesterol: 85 mg
Fat: 32 g	Saturated Fat: 16 g

–Light–
Corn Chowder
(per serving)

Calories: 320	Cholesterol: 20 mg
Fat: 6 g	Saturated Fat: 2.5 g

How We Did It

- Replaced 3 ounces salt pork with 1 slice of bacon, minced and sautéed over low heat to release its flavorful fat
- Omitted the butter
- "Milked" some of the corn to extract its flavorful juices, giving the chowder a rich backbone of flavor
- Replaced the whole milk with low-fat milk
- Replaced the heavy cream with half-and-half and used less of it
- Added whole kernels close to the end of the cooking time for textural contrast and more fresh corn flavor

down, we moved on to a lighter clam chowder. We wanted our clam chowder to be an easily prepared weeknight chowder that relied on pantry ingredients so we decided to use canned minced clams rather than fresh. (Fresh clams are only available from late summer through winter and can often be expensive, depending on what area of the country you're purchasing them from.)

A combination of clam broth and milk or cream is the traditional base for clam chowder, but since we'd be using minced clams, we'd be missing the broth. Instead, we replaced the broth with clam juice, a reasonable substitution. We hit a stumbling block, however, when we turned to the dairy. In our tests, we found that so much low-fat and even whole milk was required to make the clam chowder look and taste creamy that it diluted the clam flavor and became more like a mild bisque or the clam equivalent of oyster stew. Instead, we found that making the clam chowder with almost all clam broth, skipping the milk altogether, then finishing the stew with ½ cup of half-and-half, gave us what we were looking for—a rich, creamy chowder that tasted distinctly of clams.

Corn Chowder

SERVES 6

We prefer Spanish onions for their sweet, mild flavor, but all-purpose yellow onions will work fine too. Do not substitute skim milk for the 2 percent milk in this recipe, or the chowder will taste watery.

10	medium ears fresh yellow corn, husks and silk removed
1	slice bacon (about 1 ounce), minced
1	large onion, preferably Spanish, minced
	Salt
2	medium garlic cloves, minced or pressed through a garlic press (about 2 teaspoons)
3	tablespoons unbleached all-purpose flour
3	cups low-sodium chicken broth
12	ounces red potatoes (about 2 medium), scrubbed and cut into ¼-inch pieces
1	bay leaf
1	teaspoon minced fresh thyme leaves, or ¼ teaspoon dried thyme
1	cup low-fat milk
½	cup half-and-half
2	tablespoons minced fresh parsley leaves
	Ground black pepper

1. One at a time, stand 4 ears of corn on end in a bowl and, following the illustration below, use a paring knife to remove the kernels (you should have about 3 cups). Reserve the cobs and kernels separately and set aside. Grate the kernels from the remaining 6 ears of corn on the large holes of a box grater into a separate bowl. Firmly scrape the pulp from all of the cobs with the back of a butter knife into the bowl with the grated corn (you should have 2 generous cups of kernels and pulp).

2. Cook the bacon in a large Dutch oven over medium-low heat, stirring occasionally, until the fat is rendered and the bacon is crisp, about 8 minutes. Add the onion and ½ teaspoon salt; cover and cook until the onion has softened, 8 to 10 minutes. Stir in the garlic and cook until fragrant, about 30 seconds. Stir in the flour and cook, stirring constantly, about 2 minutes. Whisking constantly, gradually add the chicken broth. Add the potatoes, bay leaf, thyme, milk, and grated corn mixture. Bring to a boil over medium-high heat; reduce the heat to medium-low and simmer until the potatoes are almost tender, about 10 minutes.

3. Stir in the reserved corn kernels and half-and-half; continue to simmer until the corn kernels are tender yet still slightly crunchy, about 5 minutes longer. Discard the bay leaf. Stir in the

REMOVING KERNELS FROM THE COB

Hold the cob on its end inside a large, wide bowl and cut off the kernels use a paring knife.

parsley, and season with salt and pepper to taste. (The chowder can be refrigerated in an airtight container for up to 2 days. Warm over low heat until hot; do not boil.)

PER 1¹/₂-CUP SERVING: Cal 320; Fat 6 g; Sat fat 2.5 g; Chol 20 mg; Carbs 49 g; Protein 12 g; Fiber 5 g; Sodium 950 mg

New England Clam Chowder

SERVES 6

We tested seven brands of minced and small whole canned clams and preferred Doxsee Minced Clams teamed with Doxsee brand clam juice as well as Snow's Minced Clams and Snow's clam juice. These clams were neither too tough nor too soft, and they had a natural clam flavor.

4	(6.5-ounce) cans minced clams
2	(8-ounce) bottles clam juice
	Water
I	slice bacon (about I ounce), minced
I	large Spanish onion, chopped medium
	Salt
¹/₄	cup unbleached all-purpose flour
I¹/₂	pounds red potatoes (about 4 medium), scrubbed and cut into ¹/₂-inch pieces
I	bay leaf
I	teaspoon fresh thyme leaves, or ¹/₄ teaspoon dried thyme
¹/₂	cup half-and-half
2	tablespoons minced fresh parsley leaves
	Ground black pepper

CORE TECHNIQUE

JUST ONE SLICE

Some soups and chowders really need that smoky bacon flavor, or they just don't taste like the real deal. Mindful of the fat, we found we could eke a lot of flavor out of just one bacon slice if we minced it up very fine and let it render in the pot first. The tiny pieces of bacon all but disappear into the soup, but leave behind that telltale bacon flavor that a good soup or chowder depends on.

1. Drain the clams, reserving the juice, and set the clams aside. Combine the reserved juice and bottled clam juice in a large liquid measuring cup; add water until the mixture measures 5 cups and set aside. Cook the bacon in a large Dutch oven over medium-low heat, stirring occasionally, until the fat is rendered and the bacon is crisp, about 8 minutes. Add the onion and ¹/₂ teaspoon salt; cover and cook until the onion has softened, 8 to 10 minutes.

2. Stir in the flour and cook, stirring constantly, about 2 minutes. Whisking constantly, gradually add the clam juice mixture. Add the potatoes, bay leaf, and thyme. Bring to a boil over medium-high heat; reduce the heat to medium-low and simmer until the potatoes are almost tender, about 10 minutes.

MILKING CORN

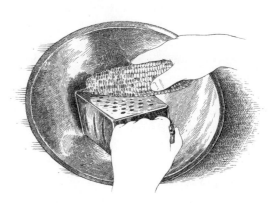

1. Start by grating the corn ears on a box grater.

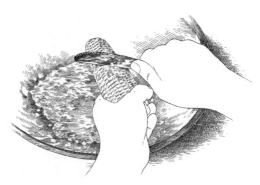

2. Finish by firmly scraping any remaining kernels off the cob with the back of a butter knife.

3. Add the clams, half-and-half, and parsley. Bring to a brief simmer and then remove from the heat. Remove the bay leaf, season with salt and pepper to taste, and serve immediately.

PER 1¹/₂-CUP SERVING: Cal 210; Fat 4.5 g; Sat fat 2 g; Chol 35 mg; Carb 29 g; Protein 13 g; Fiber 2 g; Sodium 920 mg

HEARTY VEGETABLE STEW

OUR GOAL HERE WAS SIMPLE: WE WANTED TO create a classic vegetable stew recipe that would be as hearty and satisfying as a traditional meat stew (which would be impossible to make low-fat).

We started our testing by preparing a number of basic vegetable stews to get a feel for what tasters liked. Early in our testing we learned that we preferred stews that started with onions, carrots, and celery. For maximum flavor, we found it best to mince these vegetables and let them sweat following our core technique for using less fat when sautéing (see "Sweat Vegetables and Slash Fat" on page 63).

The addition of garlic and strong herbs, such as rosemary and thyme, added further depth to this base. Next we deglazed the pot with a little white wine (red wine overpowered the flavor of the vegetables) to add a little flavor and some acidity. Half a cup was the perfect amount of wine, since batches of stew made with any more tasted boozy. Once the wine had reduced, it was time to add the other liquids. We experimented with various liquids and liked the combination of vegetable broth, water, and the juice from the canned tomatoes the best. Vegetable stews tend to be on the sweet side because of the sugars in the vegetables, so it's best to avoid broths that are more sweet than savory. You can almost tell by looking at the broth how it will taste. If the color is bright orange, the broth was made with a lot of carrots and will be achingly sweet.

For the other vegetables, we first turned to mushrooms. Tasters like halved and sliced portobellos for their earthy flavor and meaty texture. We did find that it was necessary to remove the gills from the mushrooms—otherwise they gave the stew a sludgy appearance. We also included halved white mushrooms—though not as meaty as portobellos, white mushrooms gave the stew a contrasting mushroom flavor that tasters appreciated. Some stews contain dried beans, but tasters felt stews made with beans were too reminiscent of chili. Chickpeas are another common ingredient in vegetable stews, but tasters wanted something more familiar. Potatoes filled the bill and their earthy character added a necessary heft to the mixture. Because they retain their shape, red potatoes were chosen over starchier baking potatoes. Tomatoes were another good addition to our vegetable stew, both for flavor and color. Their acidity helped balance some of the sweetness of the vegetables, and the red color kept the stew from looking dull or brown.

We found it best to cut these vegetables quite large. Stews made with small diced vegetables did not feel hearty enough. One-inch pieces of potatoes and carrots gave the stew a heartier texture and appearance.

When the stew was almost done, we added delicate green peas. We used thawed frozen peas, turned off the heat, and let the residual heat in the covered pot warm the peas through. Frozen peas overcook if they actually simmer in this stew.

Because different vegetables must go into the

REMOVING GILLS FROM PORTOBELLO MUSHROOMS

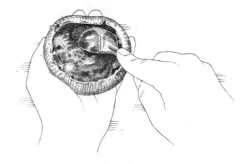

We found that it was necessary to remove the black gills from the portobello mushrooms because they made the stew muddy in appearance. Using a soup spoon, scrape and discard the dark-colored gills from the underside of the mushroom.

pot at different times, we prefer to cook vegetable stews on the stovetop rather than in the oven like meat stews. Vegetable stews can be simmered (not boiled—you don't want the veggies to fall apart) rather quickly, just until the vegetables are tender.

Vegetable stews taste watered down when the vegetables are cooked in too much liquid. It's best to cook the vegetables in just as much liquid as is necessary. Some sources suggest thickening vegetable stews with flour (like meat stews) or a cornstarch slurry (cornstarch diluted in cold water). We tested both options and found that flour sometimes stuck inside tiny crevices in the vegetables (especially mushrooms) and imparted a raw floury taste to the stew. The slurry gave the stew a gluey mouthfeel. We found that the stew was best thickened naturally by reduction, which concentrated the flavor and did not detract from the vegetables. Cooking the stew without the cover also allowed the liquid to thicken to a nice consistency.

Just before serving the stew, we added a little acid (we tested both lemon juice and balsamic vinegar and preferred the latter for its complexity and depth) to balance the sweetness of the vegetables. Parsley finished things off nicely. Reviewing the nutritional information, we were pleased to find that this delicious stew contained just 180 calories and 1 gram of fat per 1½ cup serving

Unlike other stews, vegetable stews are best eaten immediately. The texture of the vegetables will suffer if the stews are held and reheated, and the flavors will become muddled. Choose crusty bread for an accompaniment—it nicely soaks up the flavorful broth.

Hearty Vegetable Stew

SERVES 8

Portobello mushrooms give this all-purpose stew a deep, meaty flavor, however, it is necessary to remove the gills on the underside of each cap, or else the flavor and color of the stew will turn muddy.

2	medium onions, minced
1	medium celery rib, minced
1	medium carrot, peeled and minced, plus 4 large carrots (about 1 pound), peeled, halved lengthwise, and cut into 1-inch lengths
1	teaspoon olive oil
	Salt
9	medium portobello mushrooms (about 1¼ pounds), stems discarded, gills removed (see page 86), caps halved and then sliced ½ inch thick
10	ounces white mushrooms, wiped clean, stems trimmed and mushrooms halved
2	medium garlic cloves, minced or pressed through a garlic press (about 2 teaspoons)
1	teaspoon minced fresh rosemary, or ½ teaspoon dried rosemary
1	teaspoon fresh minced thyme leaves, or ½ teaspoon dried thyme
½	cup dry white wine
4	cups low-sodium vegetable broth
1½–2	cups water
1	(14.5-ounce) can diced tomatoes
2	bay leaves
1½	pounds red potatoes (about 4 medium), peeled and cut into 1-inch pieces
1	cup frozen peas, thawed
¼	cup minced fresh parsley leaves
1	tablespoon balsamic vinegar
	Ground black pepper

1. Combine the onions, celery, carrot, oil, and ½ teaspoon salt in a large Dutch oven. Cover and cook over medium-low heat, stirring often, until the vegetables are softened, 8 to 10 minutes.

2. Add the portobello and white mushrooms. Increase the heat to medium-high and cook until all the liquid they release has evaporated, about 10 minutes. Stir in the garlic, rosemary, and thyme and cook until fragrant, about 30 seconds. Stir in the wine, scraping up any browned bits; cook until the wine has reduced by half, about 2 minutes.

3. Add the broth, 1½ cups of the water, tomatoes with their juices, bay leaves, and potatoes. Bring to a boil over medium-high heat; partially cover, reduce the heat to medium-low, and simmer until the stew is thickened and flavorful, about 1 hour. If the stew seems too thick, add the remaining ½ cup water.

4. Off the heat, stir in the peas; cover let stand until the peas are hot, about 4 minutes. Stir in the parsley and vinegar, and discard the bay leaf. Season with salt and pepper to taste. Serve immediately.

PER 1¹/₂-CUP SERVING: Cal 180; Fat 1 g; Sat fat 0 g; Chol 0 mg; Carb 34 g; Protein 7 g; Fiber 5 g; Sodium 620 mg

WHITE CHICKEN CHILI

A LIGHTER COUNTERPART TO TRADITIONAL red meat chili, white chicken chili contains a chicken and white bean base, simmered in chicken broth and, depending on the recipe, a wide range of ingredients, including diced tomatoes, green salsa, pickled chiles, and chili powder. White chili is a fairly recent creation, which is good news because it allowed us free rein in somewhat new territory, without any risk of breaking the rules.

White chicken chili is typically made with either diced chicken or ground chicken. We started with ground chicken. Tasters were not sold; they wanted more substance and a meatier texture. We then prepared a batch with diced breast meat chicken that we simmered in the chicken broth. This was certainly an improvement, but the cubed meat was reminiscent of the tasteless, dry meat floating in canned chicken soup. Instead, we browned bone-in, skin-on chicken breasts, simmered them in chicken broth just until they were cooked through, and then shredded the meat and returned it to the mix at the end. Tasters raved about the flavor the meat contributed to the chili, and the shredded meat was hearty and moist.

Obstacles still remained. The first few batches we made contained the obvious onions and garlic, but also red bell peppers, tomato paste, diced tomatoes, and chili powder, ingredients found in several of the recipes we researched. The flavor these ingredients contributed was welcomed, but some of our tasters rejected all things red from the start, under the premise that white chili should have nothing in common with red chili. This left us with no flavor base.

We thought about adding green bell peppers, but wanted something that packed a little more punch. We settled on a combination of poblano, Anaheim, and jalapeño chiles. The dark blackish-green poblanos and the long green Anaheims provided sweetness and depth, while the jalapeños imparted richness and heat. Sautéing the chiles before simmering them in the chili contributed an excellent green chile flavor, but tasters complained that it was still a little dull. We decided to sauté the chiles, remove half, continue to cook the chili, and stir in the reserved chiles at the end, along with a little raw minced jalapeño. The chiles that remained in the chili continued to simmer, melding with the other ingredients in terms of flavor and texture. The chiles that were stirred in at the end added a bright flavor and a nice contrast in texture, since they were still slightly firm.

The backbone was in place, but we still needed to iron out the details of seasonings. We knew that we would need to add some spices at the beginning of the cooking process in order to build flavor, but the chili would also benefit from some bright, fresh flavors added just before serving. Using a generous hand with cumin and dried oregano produced a mellow yet complex effect on the chili, while scallions, cilantro, and lime juice provided the perfect finish.

This white chili pleased even the skeptics and self-proclaimed chili aficionados in the test kitchen. Certain individuals still refused to categorize it as "chili," preferring to refer to it as a chicken stew, but they gobbled it up nevertheless.

White Chicken Chili
SERVES 8

Most of a chile's heat resides in the ribs. If you prefer more heat, we suggest mincing the ribs along with the seeds and adding them to the recipe to taste. If you prefer less heat, discard the seeds and ribs. For chili reminiscent of posole, substitute two (15-ounce) cans white or yellow hominy, drained and rinsed, for the beans. This chili is excellent with a dollop of low-fat sour cream.

3   pounds bone-in, skin-on chicken breasts (2 whole breasts, split)
    Salt and ground black pepper

<table>
<tr><td>I</td><td>teaspoon vegetable oil</td></tr>
</table>

I   teaspoon vegetable oil

3   medium poblano chiles, stemmed, seeded, and
     chopped medium

3   medium Anaheim chiles, stemmed, seeded,
     and chopped medium

I   medium jalapeño chile, plus I small jalapeño
     chile, seeds and ribs removed and set aside
     (see note), flesh minced

2   medium onions, minced

6   medium garlic cloves, minced or pressed
     through a garlic press (about 2 tablespoons)

2   tablespoons ground cumin

2   tablespoons dried oregano

8   cups low-sodium chicken broth

2   (15-ounce) cans cannellini beans, drained and
     rinsed

1/4 cup juice from 2 to 3 limes

1/4 cup minced fresh cilantro leaves

4   scallions, sliced thin

1. Season the chicken breasts with salt and pepper. Heat the oil in a Dutch oven over medium-high heat until just smoking. Sear the chicken, skin side down, until browned, about 4 minutes. Flip the chicken and sear on the second side until browned, about 4 minutes. Transfer the chicken to a plate and remove and discard the skin.

2. Add all of the chiles except the small jalapeño, onions, garlic, cumin, oregano, and 1 teaspoon salt in a large Dutch oven. Cover and cook over medium-low heat, stirring often, until the vegetables are softened, 12 to 15 minutes. Transfer half of the chile mixture to a clean plate; set aside.

3. Stir in the broth, chicken, and beans. Bring to a boil over medium-high heat; reduce the heat to medium-low and simmer, stirring occasionally, until the chicken is fully cooked, about 20 minutes. Using tongs, transfer the chicken to a large plate. Continue to simmer the chili, uncovered, until it has thickened, 35 to 40 minutes.

4. When the chicken is cool enough to handle, shred the chicken into bite-sized pieces, discarding the bones. Stir the shredded chicken, reserved chile mixture, lime juice, cilantro, scallions, and small jalapeño into the chili. Season with salt and pepper to taste. If the chili is too thick, stir in additional water to thin it out. (The chili can be refrigerated in an airtight container for up to 3 days.)

PER 1¹/₂-CUP SERVING: Cal 320; Fat 4.5 g; Sat fat .5 g; Chol 80 mg; Carb 28 g; Protein 39 g; Fiber 9 g; Sodium 1240 mg

TURKEY CHILI

MANY LOW-FAT TURKEY CHILI RECIPES YIELD a pot of raw-tasting spices, dry meat, and under-flavored chili. Our goal was to develop a no-fuss chili that would rival its beef counterpart—rich, meaty, and thick, with just the right amount of spices.

Most of the recipes for this plainspoken chili begin by sautéing onions and garlic. We used our sweating method (see "Sweat Vegetables and Slash Fat" on page 63), which allows us to use less oil. Tasters liked red bell peppers added to these aromatics but rejected other options, including green bell peppers, celery, and carrots. After this first step, things became less clear. The most pressing concerns were the spices and the meat (how much and what kind). There were also the cooking liquid (what kind, if any) and the proportions of tomatoes and beans to consider.

Our first experiments with these ingredients followed a formula we had seen in lots of recipes: 2 pounds ground turkey, 3 tablespoons chili powder, 2 teaspoons ground cumin, and 1 teaspoon each red pepper flakes and dried oregano. Many recipes add the spices after the turkey has been browned, but we knew from our Black Bean Soup (page 81) that with such a small amount of fat in the recipe, the ground spices needed to have direct contact with the cooking oil, and have plenty of time in the pot to "bloom."

To see if these results would apply to chili, we set up a test with three pots of chili—one with the ground spices added before the turkey, one with the spices added after the turkey, and a third in which we toasted the spices in a separate skillet and added them to the pot after the turkey. The batch made with untoasted spices added after the turkey tasted raw and harsh. The batch made with spices toasted in a separate pan was better, but the clear favorite was the batch made with spices added directly to the pot before the meat. In fact, subsequent testing revealed that the spices should be added at the outset—along with the aromatics—to develop their flavors fully.

Although we didn't want a chili with killer heat, we did want real warmth and depth of flavor. Commercial chili powder is typically 80 percent ground dried red chiles, with the rest a mix of garlic powder, onion powder, oregano, ground cumin, and salt. To boost the flavor, we increased the amount of chili powder from 3 to 4 tablespoons, added more coriander, cumin, and oregano, and tossed in some cayenne for heat.

It was now time to consider the meat. Two pounds seemed ideal when paired with two 15-ounce cans of beans. We made pots of chili with every brand of lean ground turkey we could get our hands on, including 99 percent fat-free and 93 percent lean ground turkey. The results showed that the brand of meat didn't matter nearly as much as the fat percentage; there is such a thing as too lean. The 99 percent fat-free meat was dry and stringy when cooked, and contributed nothing to the flavor of the chili. The 93 percent lean ground turkey added excellent flavor to the chili, and the meat remained moist and juicy.

Tasters did complain, however, that the chili was visually unappealing. Since the meat is stirred into the pot with the cooked vegetables and then simmered for over an hour, it breaks down dramatically—looking more along the lines of a fine meat sauce, like Bolognese, than thick meat chili. We tried adding the meat at a later stage, which helped visually, but the chili then lacked a cohesive flavor. By adding half of the meat to the cooked vegetables and the other half after the chili had

---

EQUIPMENT: Dutch Ovens

We find that a Dutch oven (also called a lidded casserole) is almost always essential to making soups, stews, and chilis. To make recommendations about buying a Dutch oven, we tested 12 models from leading makers of cookware.

We found that a Dutch oven should have a capacity of at least 6 quarts to be useful. Eight quarts is even better. As we cooked in the pots, we came to prefer wider, shallower Dutch ovens because it's easier to see and reach inside them and they offer more bottom surface area to accommodate larger batches of meat for browning. This reduces the number of batches required to brown a given quantity of meat and, with it, the chances of burning the flavorful pan drippings. Ideally, the diameter of a Dutch oven is twice as great as its height.

We also preferred pots with a light-colored interior finish, such as enameled cast iron or stainless steel. It is easier to judge the caramelization of the drippings at a glance in these pots. Dark finishes can mask the color of the drippings, which may burn before you realize it. Our favorite pot is the 7 ¼ -quart Le Creuset Round French Oven. Because it's made of cast iron the Le Creuset retains heat beautifully, so it's a natural for simmering soups and stews or maintaining hot oil at the perfect temperature for frying. The 8-quart All-Clad Stockpot (also called a Dutch oven), made of stainless steel, also performs well in a variety of tasks, from making stew to boiling water for pasta. These pots are quite expensive, costing at least $150 even on sale. If you're looking for a less expensive alternative you might want to try the 7-Quart Tramontina Sterling II Dutch Oven at about $57. With a heavy "tri-ply" base of aluminum sandwiched between stainless steel, this pot takes a little extra time to heat up, but maintains very even heat over the large cooking area. The lightweight lid sputters over a pot of boiling water, but that's a small price to pay for an otherwise solid performer at a reasonable price.

THE BEST DUTCH OVENS

Our favorite pot is the 7¼-quart Le Creuset Round French Oven (left). Expect to spend nearly $200 for this sturdy piece of cookware. It performed excellently in all our tests and the cast-iron construction conducts and retains heat beautifully. A less expensive alternative is the Tramontina Sterling II Dutch Oven at about $57 (right), and it is our best buy.

simmered for 1 hour, we were able to create the perfect balance of flavor, while at the same time keeping some of the meat in larger pieces. We did find that when adding the second pound of meat to the chili, it is important to mash the meat into a ball, and then break off pieces to add it to the simmering chili. This prevents the meat from cooking in long strands (see the illustration below).

As for the type of liquid to add to our chili, we tried batches made with water (too watery), wine (too acidic), chicken broth (too chickeny and dull), and no liquid at all except for that in the tomatoes (too vegetal, but by far the best). By adding a little chicken broth (2 cups) to the chili made with only the liquid from the tomatoes, we were able to get the perfect amount of flavor, rich and rounded.

Tomatoes were definitely going into the pot, but we had yet to decide on the type and amount. We first tried two small (14.5-ounce) cans of diced tomatoes. Clearly not enough tomatoes. What's more, the tomatoes were floating in a thin sauce. We tried two 28-ounce cans of diced tomatoes, pureeing the contents of one can in the blender to thicken the sauce. Although the chunkiness was reduced, the sauce was still watery. Next we paired one can of crushed tomatoes with one can of diced tomatoes and, without exception, tasters preferred the thicker consistency and combination of tomato products.

GETTING THE RIGHT TEXTURE FROM GROUND POULTRY

Pack the meat together into a ball, then pinch off teaspoon-sized pieces of meat and stir them into the chili. This technique makes the ground turkey appear crumbled, like ground beef, rather than stringy.

Most recipes add the beans toward the end of cooking, the idea being to let them heat through without causing them to fall apart. But this method often makes for very bland beans floating in a sea of highly flavorful chili. After testing several options, we found it best to add the beans with the tomatoes. The more time the beans spent in the pot, the better they tasted. In the end, we preferred dark red kidney beans because they keep their shape better than light red kidney beans, the other common choice.

One hour and 40 minutes of gentle simmering was sufficient to meld the flavors. Our chili, basically complete, required little more than lime wedges, passed separately at the table, which both brightened the flavor of the chili and accentuated the heat of the spices.

Turkey Chili with Kidney Beans
SERVES 8

If you like your chili spicy, use the higher amount of red pepper flakes and cayenne listed. You can also substitute lean ground chicken for the turkey if desired. Garnishes, such as diced tomato, diced avocado, sliced scallions, shredded low-fat cheddar cheese, low-fat sour cream, and chopped cilantro, are a nice addition.

2	medium onions, minced
I	medium red bell pepper, stemmed, seeded, and cut into $1/2$-inch pieces
6	medium garlic cloves, minced or pressed through a garlic press (about 2 tablespoons)
$1/4$	cup chili powder
I	tablespoon ground cumin
2	teaspoons ground coriander
$1/2$-I	teaspoon red pepper flakes
I	teaspoon dried oregano
$1/4$-$1/2$	teaspoon cayenne
I	tablespoon vegetable oil
	Salt
2	pounds 93 percent lean ground turkey
2	(15-ounce) cans dark red kidney beans, drained and rinsed
I	(28-ounce) can diced tomatoes

1   (28-ounce) can crushed tomatoes
2   cups low-sodium chicken broth
2   limes, cut into wedges (for serving)

1. Combine the onions, bell pepper, garlic, chili powder, cumin, coriander, pepper flakes, oregano, cayenne, oil, and ½ teaspoon salt in a large Dutch oven. Cover and cook over medium-low heat, stirring often, until the vegetables are softened, 8 to 10 minutes.

2. Add half the turkey and increase the heat to medium-high; cook, breaking up the meat with a wooden spoon, until no longer pink and just beginning to brown, about 4 minutes. Stir in the beans, diced tomatoes with their juices, crushed tomatoes, broth, and 1 teaspoon salt. Bring to a boil over medium-high heat; reduce the heat to medium-low and simmer, uncovered, until the chili has begun to thicken, about 1 hour.

3. Following the illustration on page 91, pat the remaining 1 pound of turkey together into a ball, then pinch off teaspoon-size pieces of meat and stir them into the chili. Continue to simmer, stirring occasionally, until the turkey is tender and the chili is rich and slightly thickened, about 40 minutes longer (if the chili begins to stick to the bottom of the pot, stir in ½ cup water). Season with salt to taste. Serve with the lime wedges and garnishes (see note), if desired. (The chili can be refrigerated in an airtight container for up to 3 days, or frozen for up to a month.)

PER 1½-CUP SERVING: Cal 340; Fat 10 g; Sat fat 2.5 g; Chol 65 mg; Carb 34 g; Protein 32 g; Fiber 9 g; Sodium 1380 mg

---

CORE TECHNIQUE

DON'T SQUAWK AT GROUND POULTRY

Substituting ground turkey or chicken for ground beef in a chili or tomato sauces is a well-known way to reduce fat and calories. The problem is that after a few hours of simmering, the texture and flavor of ground poultry don't compare to that of beef. Ground poultry doesn't brown as well as beef nor does it impart the same meaty flavor. The texture of ground poultry can also be soft and unappetizing. We tried reducing the simmering time of the ground poultry, which helped preserve the texture, but then the flavor suffered. (The ground poultry must simmer for an hour to draw out its flavor.) After many tests we discovered a few solutions. First, we sauté just half of the ground poultry at the start, breaking it up into little pieces with a spoon, to really distribute the flavor while it simmers. Then we increase the dish's meatiness by adding chicken broth to the chili. As it simmers, it thickens and lends a meatier flavor to the chili. And for improved texture and moisture, we add the remaining ground poultry toward the end of the simmering time. We pinch the poultry into small pieces before stirring them in to mimic the crumbled appearance of ground beef (see the illustration on page 91).

VEGETARIAN BEAN CHILI

WHAT EXACTLY IS VEGETARIAN CHILI? AFTER researching the subject thoroughly, we identified three basic styles of vegetarian chili—those that rely on a mixture of vegetables; those that rely on a soy product to replicate the texture of meat; and those that rely on beans.

We decided to make a couple of versions of each style to narrow the field. The vegetable-heavy chilis were the first to go. While we love vegetables, the recipes we had gathered were chock-full of zucchini, eggplant, tomatoes, and mushrooms, and all we could think was "ratatouille," the classic French dish of stewed vegetables.

Next, we attacked the soy-based chilis. We went down the list of soy products and, based on their textures and flavors, started to rule some out. Even though tofu comes in a range of textures, none of them seemed right for chili. Silken and soft tofu disintegrated (as expected), but even extra-firm tofu crumbled into unappealing bits. Textured vegetable protein, or TVP, won no one over, but some tasters were intrigued by tempeh.

Tempeh is a tender but firm soybean cake made with fermented whole soybeans, sometimes mixed with other grains such as rice or millet. The texture certainly had potential, although the flavor was a bit bland. We decided to put the tempeh on hold and focus on the bean chilis, which were the real standouts in this first round of testing.

Most people, even nonvegetarians, expect to find at least one kind of bean in chili. When we prepared a vegetarian chili with several kinds of beans, tasters were impressed. We narrowed down a list of eight initial contenders to just three beans—red kidney, pinto, and black. All three have an earthy flavor and firm texture that work well in chili.

We also took a moment to consider whether or not to use canned beans. Dried beans are usually thought to have superior flavor, but we all agreed that in the case of chili, a dish packed with seasonings and aromatics, canned beans would be just fine. Our only worry, then, was the canned beans' tendency to fall apart when simmered, so in order for the beans to hold their shape and lend body to the chili, we did not let the beans cook for more than half an hour.

We moved on to consider the spice base. Most of our research recipes called for a host of dried herbs, including commercial chili powder, ground cumin, and dried oregano. But we wondered if a homemade chili powder would add more depth.

After conducting a dozen tests using toasted and pulverized dried ancho and New Mexico chiles, we concluded that this technique was not suited to vegetarian bean chili. Homemade chili powder has too much kick and simply overwhelms the flavor of the beans and vegetables. Without a strong meat presence, our homemade chili powder tasted hot and bitter. It seemed silly to add more oil to bean chili just to mellow the flavor of the chili powder.

We went back to the drawing board and decided to test commercial chili powder. Hoping to mellow the heat and bitterness of the chili powder, we decided to add a sweet red pepper to our base of onions and garlic. This worked nicely. We also wondered if some frozen sweet corn, added with the beans, would help tip the balance away from the bitter components. Tasters responded well to a chili made with three kinds of beans and corn. The flavor of the corn was great and it had visual appeal, too.

Although the commercial chili powder was fine, the flavor of the final dish was a bit flat. We thought adding some whole cumin seeds would give the chili depth, and they did. A little cayenne provided some heat, and brown sugar rounded out the other flavors.

We focused next on the liquid. Several recipes suggested using beer to build complexity in bean chili. Although beans and beer would seem to have a natural affinity, we found that beer added a sour note. We decided to stick with water and the customary tomatoes. Crushed tomatoes, rather than diced, were preferred for their smooth texture and body.

A sprinkle of cilantro and a squeeze of lime just before serving brightened the flavors. Everyone agreed that this bean chili was good. It was rich and highly flavorful, and it had a nice, sharp heat as well as some gentle sweetness.

It was time to return to the issue of the tempeh. We wondered if we could add some to the bean chili. It made sense to brown the tempeh (much as you might brown meat) before adding it to the pot. Tempeh soaks up flavors like a sponge, so it is usually marinated before cooking. We soaked the tempeh in a mixture of oil, garlic, smoky chipotle chiles, cumin, and salt. After broiling it for a few minutes on each side, the tempeh was crisp, spicy, and well seasoned. Tasters loved it—even plain, out of hand. But having to turn the broiler on bothered us. We wanted to keep the chili and its components in one place—on the stove. We browned the tempeh in a nonstick skillet and found it to be just as tasty as the broiled version. We also tried marinated and plain tempeh and decided that because the tempeh absorbs the flavors from the chili, marinating was unnecessary.

But adding the tempeh to the chili as it was—with 3 cups of mix-and-match beans and 1 cup of corn—made it too thick and chunky. So we took out 2 cups of beans to alleviate the crowding. Everyone was happy, and the chili—with tempeh or without—was good enough even for the die-hard meat eaters in the test kitchen. Recognizing that everyone might not want to include tempeh in their chili, we made this a variation of the master recipe.

Vegetarian Bean Chili

SERVES 4

We recommend a mix of pinto, black, and red kidney beans. If you like your chili spicier, you can increase the amount of cayenne. Serve this chili over rice.

1	tablespoon cumin seeds
1	medium onion, minced
1	large red bell pepper, stemmed, seeded, and chopped fine
9	medium garlic cloves, minced or pressed through a garlic press (about 3 tablespoons)
3	tablespoons chili powder
1	tablespoon vegetable oil
1/4	teaspoon cayenne
	Salt
3	cups canned beans (see note), drained and rinsed
2	cups water
1	(28-ounce) can crushed tomatoes
1	teaspoon dried oregano
1	tablespoon brown sugar
1	cup frozen corn kernels
1/4	cup coarsely chopped fresh cilantro leaves
1	tablespoon juice from 1 lime

1. Toast the cumin seeds in a large Dutch oven over medium-low heat, stirring constantly, until fragrant, 1 minute. Stir in the onion, bell pepper, garlic, chili powder, oil, cayenne, and ½ teaspoon salt. Cover and cook, stirring often, until the vegetables are softened, about 8 to 10 minutes.

2. Stir in the beans, water, tomatoes, oregano, and brown sugar, scraping up any browned bits. Bring to a boil over medium-high heat; reduce the heat to medium-low and simmer until the chili is slightly thickened, about 25 minutes.

3. Stir in the corn and continue to simmer until heated through, 5 to 10 minutes. Off the heat, stir in the cilantro and lime juice, and season with salt to taste. (The chili can be refrigerated in an airtight container for up to 3 days.)

PER 1¹/₂-CUP SERVING: Cal 360; Fat 6 g; Sat fat .5 g; Chol 0 mg; Carb 66 g; Protein 18 g; Fiber 18 g; Sodium 1190 mg

➤ VARIATION

Vegetarian Bean and Tempeh Chili

Tempeh gives this chili a meaty texture.

Heat 1 teaspoon oil in a Dutch oven over medium-high heat until shimmering. Add 1 (8-ounce) package tempeh, crumbled into small pieces, and cook until browned, about 5 minutes. Transfer the browned tempeh to a plate and set aside. Follow the recipe for Vegetarian Bean Chili, reducing the amount of beans to 1 cup, and adding the browned tempeh with the beans in step 2.

PER 1¹/₂-CUP SERVING: Cal 380; Fat 13 g; Sat fat 2 g; Chol 0 mg; Carb 51 g; Protein 21 g; Fiber 12 g; Sodium 800 mg

4

VEGETABLES

WE ALL KNOW THAT SIMPLE, PERFECTLY steamed vegetables with just a squeeze of lemon juice are healthiest, but if you eat them that way every day they can be rather ho-hum. Same goes for many of the vegetable dishes you might rely on day after day, such as baked potatoes and boiled corn. But what about those times when you want something more complex or have a craving, say, for a dish of cheesy scalloped potatoes? Is there a place for them at the light and healthy table? Our goal for this chapter was two-fold. First, we aimed to put a fresher spin on a few of our favorite everyday vegetable dishes. Second, we wanted to transform those richer vegetable dishes we find so tempting into lighter, more healthful fare.

For our workaday recipes, we have included a great way to cook green beans quickly and simply—in a skillet. And we offer two distinctly different flavor variations: Skillet Green Beans with Garlic and Lemon (page 99) is an Italian-inspired dish and Skillet Green Bean Casserole (page 99) is a tasty yet healthful take on the classic green bean casserole. We did the same with asparagus, using a pan-roasting technique that relies on very little oil. Butternut squash requires little enhancement, beyond a bit of oil, salt, and pepper, and we provide a fuss-free roasting technique that works with either squash pieces or halves.

Potatoes were a given in this chapter and allowed the test kitchen to focus its resources on making healthful versions of potato favorites. We started with makeovers of classics like mashed potatoes and scalloped potatoes. For our Mashed Potatoes (page 111) we found that with the addition of low-fat sour cream we were able to cut out most of the butter and replace the cream with 2 percent milk. Likewise, we turned to 2 percent milk thickened with cornstarch and light cream cheese for rich and creamy Scalloped Potatoes (page 116). A little Parmesan cheese sprinkled on top promotes browning and gives the dish a nice hit of cheesy flavor. And since everybody loves french fries, we developed a recipe for Oven Fries (page 120), which don't have nearly the fat and calories of their french-fried cousins, but are certainly as golden, crisp, and tasty.

For the times when you want a vegetarian entrée, see our Veggie Burgers (page 124). A hearty mix of lentils, bulgur, mushrooms, and vegetables, these burgers are a far tastier alternative to the familiar frozen versions. We also made over the Italian classic, Eggplant Parmesan (page 101). Using a technique in which we coated only one side of each eggplant slice with toasted panko (crispy, Japanese-style bread crumbs) and "fried" the breaded eggplant on a hot sheet pan in the oven, we were able to create crispy eggplant that wasn't greasy or overly fatty. Toasted panko also adds a crunchy texture and toasty flavor to Zucchini Stuffed with Corn and Basil (page 104), which is terrific as part of a light lunch. We cover grilled vegetables, too, for those warm summer nights when your garden is overflowing.

So for those times when your everyday standbys won't do, you'll have a host of vegetable dishes to make your meals healthier, tastier, and anything but dull.

PAN-ROASTED ASPARAGUS

ALTHOUGH WE CONSIDER GRILLING TO BE the ultimate method for cooking asparagus, there are plenty of rainy nights when we feel like celebrating this sign of spring, but don't feel like breaking out the charcoal. Rather than waste time heating a finicky broiler, we wanted to figure out a simple stovetop method that would deliver crisp, nicely browned spears. Pan-roasting is a technique that is often used for firm vegetables such as winter squash or potatoes. We wondered if we could adapt this method, which produces a great caramelized exterior, to a tender vegetable like asparagus.

In many of the recipes we tried, the spears were indeed browned but also limp, greasy, and shriveled. Equally daunting were the logistics of cooking enough asparagus to feed a hungry group of asparagus lovers. All of the recipes suggested laying the spears out in a single layer, then individually rotating them to ensure even browning. This seemed like a lot of meticulous fuss for one small bunch of asparagus, which, with these restrictions, was all we could fit into a 12-inch pan.

After testing different-sized spears, heat levels, pan types, and cooking fats, a few things became clear right away. As in grilling, the thinner spears would have to be eliminated. They overcooked so quickly that there was no way to get a proper sear. Selecting thicker spears helped solved this problem, but we were still a long way from getting them to brown properly. Over moderate heat, the spears took so long to develop a crisp, browned exterior that they overcooked. But cranking up the burner did not solve the problem; the spears skipped brown altogether and went straight to spotty and blackened.

We knew that in professional restaurant kitchens, line cooks blanch pounds of asparagus in boiling water and then shock them in an ice bath before service. Then, they are tossed, to order, into a smoking hot skillet for a quick sear. Restaurants cook asparagus (and other vegetables) this way primarily to save time, but we wondered if par cooking would also enhance browning. We tried searing some asparagus spears that had first been quickly blanched in boiling water. Sure enough, they quickly developed a crispy, golden brown crust.

It turns out that the exterior of raw asparagus is dry and waxy, and all of the sugars necessary for browning reactions are locked up inside the plant's tough cell walls. Some initial cooking is required to release these sugars, just as it is in sliced onions, which need to sweat for a time before they caramelize. Always on the lookout for tricks to save time in the kitchen, we wondered if our pan-roasted asparagus would benefit from the same sort of technique we had used for another green vegetable, green beans (see Skillet Green Beans, page 98). While we didn't want to steam asparagus, we figured that if we added the asparagus to a skillet with a mere teaspoon of oil, then covered it for an initial steam, we might be able to skip the blanching process all together.

This method worked great. The teaspoon of oil coated the asparagus evenly, and the spears began to steam from the moisture trapped in the hot skillet, without our having to fuss with the blanch-and-shock rigmarole. However, while they were nicely steamed and barely tender after about 5 minutes, they lacked the brown crispiness that we associate with pan-roasting. To help the browning process along, we cranked the heat up to high and cooked the asparagus for another 5 to 7 minutes (depending on the size of the spears), until they were golden brown. We found that it wasn't necessary to get them brown on all sides, in fact tasters preferred some of the surface to be left bright green to let the true flavor of this spring favorite shine through. A squeeze of fresh lemon juice was all that was needed to adorn the golden spears. They were sweet, tender, and beautifully flavored.

For a variation, tasters liked the simple addition of garlic combined with the distinctive flavor of a high-quality Parmesan cheese. Served family style, on your favorite platter, there could be no easier or lighter way to showcase this harbinger of spring.

TRIMMING THE TOUGH ENDS FROM ASPARAGUS

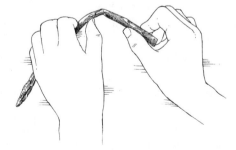

In our tests, we found that the tough, woody part of the stem will break off in just the right place if you hold the spear the right way. With one hand, hold the asparagus about halfway down the stalk; with the thumb and index finger of the other hand, hold the spear about an inch from the bottom. Bend the stem until it snaps.

Pan-Roasted Asparagus
SERVES 6

This recipe works best with asparagus that is at least ½ inch thick near the base. If using thinner spears, reduce the covered cooking time to 3 minutes and the uncovered cooking time to 5 minutes. Do not use pencil-thin asparagus spears because they simply cannot withstand the heat and will overcook too easily.

I   teaspoon olive oil
2   pounds (2 bunches) asparagus, tough ends
    removed
    Salt and ground black pepper
I   tablespoon juice from I lemon (optional)

1. Heat the oil in a 12-inch nonstick skillet over medium-high heat until shimmering. Add half of the asparagus to the skillet with tips pointed in one direction; add the remaining asparagus with tips pointed in the opposite direction. Using tongs, distribute the asparagus in an even layer so that as many spears as possible make contact with the surface of the pan (not all will fit into single layer). Cover and cook until the asparagus is bright green and still crisp, about 5 minutes.

2. Uncover and season with salt and pepper. Increase heat to high and continue to cook until the spears are tender and well browned along one side, 5 to 7 minutes, occasionally moving the spears from the center of the pan to the edge of the pan to ensure all are browned. Off the heat, season with additional salt and pepper to taste, and sprinkle with the lemon juice (if using).

PER SERVING: Cal 50; Fat 1 g; Sat fat 0 g; Chol 0 mg; Carb 7 g; Protein 3 g; Fiber 3 g; Sodium 95 mg

➤   VARIATION
Pan-Roasted Asparagus with Garlic and Parmesan

Don't step away from the skillet once you've added the garlic—it cooks quickly and can easily burn.

Follow the recipe for Pan-Roasted Asparagus, pushing the asparagus spears to one side of the skillet after they have browned in step 2. Add 3 medium garlic cloves, minced (about 1 tablespoon), mixed with 1 teaspoon olive oil to the empty side of the skillet and cook until fragrant, about 30 seconds. Toss the asparagus with the garlic. Sprinkle with 2 tablespoons grated Parmesan cheese before serving.

PER SERVING: Cal 70; Fat 2 g; Sat fat .5 g; Chol 0 mg; Carb 7 g; Protein 4 g; Fiber 3 g; Sodium 140 mg

SKILLET GREEN BEANS

FOR US ELEVENTH-HOUR COOKS, THE CONventional method for cooking green beans—boiling in salted water, then shocking in ice water, drying with paper towels, and finishing in a separately made sauce—simply takes too long and dirties too many dishes. We wanted a streamlined technique that would yield tender beans, and a flavorful sauce that would be speedy enough for a last-minute supper, but rich enough in taste and texture, and low enough in calories, to warrant a place on the dinner table on a regular basis.

We began by using a stovetop steaming technique originally developed in the test kitchen for stir-frying tough vegetables. Steaming the beans in a covered skillet with a little water, our plan was to remove the lid part way through to evaporate the water, and then build a quick pan sauce around the beans as they finished cooking. The beans, however, steamed in only 10 minutes, leaving little time to make a decent sauce after the water had evaporated. We decided to partially steam the beans (for about seven minutes) in a garlic and herb infused broth instead of water. In doing so, we had essentially already started the sauce while the green beans were going through their initial steam.

The garlic, cayenne pepper, and thyme we had added to the green beans lent great flavor, but the liquid definitely needed some sort of thickener to qualify it as a "sauce." To that end, we tried adding a small amount of flour, but that created a more gravy-like consistency than we were hoping for. A small amount of cornstarch achieved the perfect texture; just enough to coat the beans in a translucent glaze of flavorful sauce. Up to this point, we had been partially steaming the beans, and then removing them while we finished the sauce. After several tests, we realized that the beans could easily stay in the skillet, while the sauce simmered, and the beans finished cooking. A simple squeeze of lemon juice and a dusting of Parmesan cheese and we finally had a one-skillet side dish that was satisfying, healthy, and a snap to make.

With this method under our belts, we decided to try to create a variation that would mimic the tried-and-true "green bean casserole" made popular in the '50s when condensed soups were all the rage.

Traditionally loaded with fat, typically in the form of condensed cream of mushroom soup or heavy cream, and topped with canned french-fried onion strings, this dish would definitely be a challenge for us. We started out with fresh mushrooms, but found that the sauce tasted rather bland. To bump up the flavor we turned to dried porcini mushrooms, which gave an intense woodsy, earthy flavor to the skillet with a mere ¼ ounce. We thickened the sauce with cornstarch as we had in the master recipe, and put the "casserole" to the test kitchen taste test. Unfortunately, while it was deemed tasty, it still did not have the creamy consistency that tasters liked in the holiday favorite.

To replicate the creaminess that was eluding us, we tried half-and-half, low-fat sour cream, and even a stingy amount of heavy cream. None produced the creamy, silky sauce we were looking for. Necessity being the mother of invention, we made a last ditch effort that proved to be a winner. We turned to light cream cheese, a trick that we had found when making pan sauces in our poultry chapter, as a viable full-fat cream substitute. The result was a comforting, creamy mushroom-infused sauce that blanketed the beans like the 1950s favorite, without resorting to the red and white can. As for the crispy onion strings that typically adorn the top of this casserole, we found that we didn't mind forgoing their calories and saturated fat. Our casserole tasted great just the way it was, with all fresh ingredients, and a fraction of the fat.

Skillet Green Beans with Garlic and Lemon

SERVES 6

Low-sodium vegetable broth can be substituted for the chicken broth here.

- 1 teaspoon olive oil
- 3 medium garlic cloves, minced or pressed through a garlic press (about 1 tablespoon)
- 1 teaspoon minced fresh thyme leaves
  Pinch cayenne
- 1 cup low-sodium chicken broth
- 1 ½ pounds green beans, ends trimmed

- 1 teaspoon cornstarch
- 1 tablespoon water
- 1 tablespoon juice from 1 lemon
  Salt and ground black pepper
- 2 tablespoons grated Parmesan cheese

1. Combine the oil, garlic, thyme, and cayenne together in a 12-inch nonstick skillet and cook over medium heat until fragrant, about 30 seconds. Stir in the broth and add the green beans. Increase the heat to medium-high, cover, and cook until the beans are tender with a light crunch in the center, 6 to 9 minutes.

2. Push the green beans to one side of the skillet. Whisk the cornstarch and water together, then pour into the empty side of the skillet and bring to a simmer, about 30 seconds. Toss the sauce with the green beans and continue to cook, uncovered, until the green beans are tender and the sauce has thickened, 1 to 3 minutes. Off the heat, stir in the lemon juice and season with salt and pepper to taste. Sprinkle with the Parmesan before serving.

PER SERVING: Cal 60; Fat 1.5 g; Sat fat 0 g; Chol 0 mg; Carb 9 g; Protein 3 g; Fiber 4 g.; Sodium 140 mg

Skillet Green Bean Casserole

SERVES 6

Dried porcinis are available in most supermarkets in small packets. Low-sodium vegetable broth can be substituted for the chicken broth here.

- 1 teaspoon olive oil
- 8 ounces white mushrooms, wiped clean and sliced ¼ inch thick
- 1 medium onion, minced
  Salt
- 3 medium garlic cloves, minced or pressed through a garlic press (about 1 tablespoon)
- 1 teaspoon minced fresh thyme leaves
  Pinch cayenne
- 1 cup low-sodium chicken broth
- ¼ ounce dried porcini mushrooms, rehydrated, mushrooms minced and rehydrating liquid strained (see page 139)
- 1½ pounds green beans, ends trimmed

1   teaspoon cornstarch
1   tablespoon water
3   tablespoons light cream cheese
     Ground black pepper
2   tablespoons grated Parmesan cheese

1. Combine the oil, white mushrooms, onion, and ¼ teaspoon salt in a 12-inch nonstick skillet. Cover and cook over medium-low heat, stirring occasionally, until the mushrooms release their liquid, 5 to 10 minutes. Uncover, increase the heat to medium-high, and continue to cook, stirring often, until the liquid released by the mushrooms has evaporated and the mushrooms are browned, 2 to 5 minutes.

2. Stir in the garlic, thyme, and cayenne, and cook until fragrant, about 30 seconds. Stir in the broth, porcini mushrooms, and strained mushroom liquid and add the green beans. Increase the heat to medium-high, cover, and cook until the beans are tender with a light crunch in the center, 6 to 9 minutes.

3. Push the green beans to one side of the skillet. Whisk the cornstarch and water together, then pour into the empty side of the skillet and bring to a simmer, about 30 seconds. Whisk the cream cheese into the sauce until smooth. Toss the sauce with the green beans and continue to cook, uncovered, until the green beans are tender and the sauce has thickened, 1 to 3 minutes. Season with salt and pepper to taste. Sprinkle with the Parmesan before serving.

PER SERVING: Cal 100; Fat 3 g; Sat fat 1.5 g; Chol 5 mg; Carb 14 g; Protein 5 g; Fiber 5 g; Sodium 280 mg

TEST KITCHEN MAKEOVER

EGGPLANT PARMESAN

EGGPLANT PARMESAN IS CLASSIC ITALIAN comfort food, sharing a place in our hearts with meat and cheese lasagna and fettuccine Alfredo. Although eggplant Parmesan tastes awfully good, we suspected it's not something we should eat on

a regular basis. To find out exactly where it stood, we started by running a nutritional analysis of a classic recipe, and things were even worse than we thought. This recipe not only tipped the scale, it broke the scale altogether, with 760 calories, 59 grams of fat, and 140 milligrams of cholesterol.

The reasons were obvious. In most recipes, slices of eggplant are coated with a standard breading of flour, egg, and bread crumbs, and then shallow fried, an innocuous term that means frying in a couple of inches of oil. Given the porous nature of eggplant, even after salting and pressing, oil gets absorbed into the thirsty eggplant and the surrounding crumbs. The fried eggplant is then layered with shredded mozzarella cheese (about 7 grams of fat per ounce), and topped with tomato sauce that includes more oil and grated Parmesan cheese. We needed a fresh take on this classic Italian dish, and we started our testing with a hard-line goal in mind: We wanted to cut the calories and fat in half at the very least, ideally by more, if it was possible without sacrificing taste.

In our first effort to sidestep frying, we dispensed with the breading altogether, baking naked, salted eggplant slices on a baking sheet coated with cooking spray. (This method is often employed in low-calorie recipes for eggplant Parmesan.) The resulting eggplant earned negative comments from tasters. We concluded that although baking the eggplant showed promise, breading was essential and we ticked off a list of possibilities. Flour alone wasn't substantial enough. Eggplant swathed in reduced-fat mayonnaise then coated with bread crumbs turned slimy. Eggplant coated in a flour and egg batter and then bread crumbs was thick and tough. A standard single breading (dipping the eggplant first in egg, then in bread crumbs) was too messy—the egg slid right off the eggplant, leaving the crumbs with nothing to adhere to.

We decided to try a method that had been successful with our Chicken Parmesan recipe (page 201). We dipped the eggplant in beaten egg whites (instead of whole eggs), then in crispy, pre-toasted and seasoned panko (Japanese bread crumbs). After a quick mist with vegetable oil spray we baked the eggplant in a hot oven until the eggplant was tender. Initial tastings were promising; the eggplant was tender on the inside and crisp on the outside, without a greasy morsel in the bunch. Hoping that we were onto something, we layered the eggplant with quick tomato sauce containing just 1 teaspoon of oil and, forgoing the whole-fat mozzarella cheese, we substituted shredded reduced-fat mozzarella and grated Parmesan cheese.

Our hopes were soon dashed when we retrieved the eggplant from the oven. The once-crisp exterior had turned the texture of wet cardboard, and all tasters felt that the breading was overwhelming, especially on the underside of the eggplant that hadn't had the benefit of the heat. This layer had dramatically absorbed moisture from the sauce

and fat from the cheese. Add to that a follow-up nutritional analysis, and we were sent back to the drawing board. One taster suggested breading the eggplant on just one side. The idea was that after the eggplant had been prebaked, we could then layer it, naked side down, in the casserole. There would be less breading to absorb any moisture from the tomato sauce, and less to interfere with the delicate eggplant flavor.

Another colleague suggested that in addition to the one-sided breading technique, we might want to consider using less tomato sauce in the casserole, and save a large portion of it to serve on the side. We were willing to give this unconventional method a try. To our delight, the offbeat idea worked well. The eggplant was no longer blanketed in a dull coating of bread crumbs, and our judicious use of tomato sauce was a success. With a skinny 330 calories and only 9 grams of fat per serving, we had more than met our expectations. This was still comfort food. But with numbers like this, it was comfort without a catch.

MAKEOVER AT A GLANCE

—Classic—
Eggplant Parmesan
(per serving)

Calories: 760   Cholesterol: 140 mg
Fat: 59 g   Saturated Fat: 13 g

—Light—
Eggplant Parmesan
(per serving)

Calories: 330   Cholesterol: 15 mg
Fat: 9 g   Saturated Fat: 4 g

How We Did It

- Replaced whole eggs with egg whites for the breading
- Used toasted panko (Japanese bread crumbs) for an extra crispy exterior
- Breaded the eggplant on only one side of each piece
- Misted the eggplant with vegetable oil spray
- Baked the eggplant in a hot oven instead of frying
- Replaced whole milk mozzarella with reduced-fat mozzarella

Eggplant Parmesan
SERVES 6

We like to use kosher salt when salting the eggplant because the coarse grains don't dissolve as readily and any excess can be easily wiped away. It's necessary to toss the eggplant with the salt in two batches. To be time-efficient, use the 30 to 40 minutes during which the salted eggplant sits to prepare the breading, cheeses, and sauce. Take care not to let the eggplant sit salted for more than the time given.

2   medium globe eggplants (1 pound each), ends trimmed, cut crosswise into 1/3-inch-thick rounds
Kosher salt
1 1/2   cups panko (Japanese-style bread crumbs)
1   tablespoon olive oil
1   ounce Parmesan cheese, grated (about 1/2 cup), plus extra for serving
1/2   cup unbleached all-purpose flour
1 1/2   teaspoons garlic powder
Ground black pepper
3   large egg whites
1   tablespoon water

Vegetable oil spray

5   cups Quick Tomato Sauce for Eggplant
    Parmesan (recipe follows), warmed

8   ounces reduced-fat mozzarella cheese,
    shredded (about 2 cups)

2   tablespoons minced fresh basil leaves

1. Toss half of the eggplant with 1 teaspoon kosher salt, then place in a large colander set over a bowl. Repeat with the remaining eggplant and 1 more teaspoon kosher salt, and transfer to the colander with the first batch. Let sit until the eggplant releases about 2 tablespoons liquid, 30 to 40 minutes. Spread the eggplant slices on a triple thickness of paper towels and cover with another triple thickness of paper towels. Press firmly on each slice to remove as much liquid as possible, and wipe off the excess salt.

2. Adjust the oven racks to the lower-middle and upper-middle positions and heat the oven to 475 degrees. Combine the bread crumbs and oil in a 12-inch nonstick skillet and toast over medium heat, stirring often, until golden, about 10 minutes. Spread the bread crumbs into a shallow dish and let cool slightly; when cool, stir in the ½ cup Parmesan. Combine the flour, garlic powder, and ½ teaspoon pepper together into a second shallow dish. In a third shallow dish, whisk the egg whites and water together.

3. Line 2 rimmed baking sheets with foil and coat with vegetable oil spray. Season the eggplant with pepper. Lightly dredge one side of each eggplant slice in the seasoned flour, shaking off the excess. Dip the floured side of the eggplant into the egg whites, and then coat the same side with the bread crumbs. Press on the crumbs to make sure they adhere. Lay the eggplant, breaded side up, on the baking sheets in a single layer.

4. Lightly spray the top of the eggplant slices with vegetable oil spray. Bake until the top of the eggplant slices are crisp and golden, about 30 minutes, rotating and switching the baking sheets halfway through baking.

5. Spread 1 cup of the tomato sauce in the bottom of a 13 by 9-inch baking dish. Layer in half of the eggplant slices, breaded side up, overlapping the slices to fit. Distribute ½ cup of the sauce over the eggplant; sprinkle with half of the mozzarella. Layer in the remaining eggplant, breaded side up, and dot with 1 cup of the sauce, leaving the majority of the eggplant exposed so it will remain crisp; sprinkle with the remaining mozzarella. Bake until bubbling and the cheese is browned, about 10 minutes. Cool for 5 minutes, then sprinkle with the basil and serve, passing the remaining sauce and extra Parmesan separately.

PER SERVING: Cal 330; Fat 9 g; Sat fat 4 g; Chol 15 mg; Carb 40 g; Protein 22 g; Fiber 6 g; Sodium 1520 mg

❥
Quick Tomato Sauce for Eggplant Parmesan
MAKES ABOUT 5 CUPS

This easily prepared tomato sauce goes well with Eggplant Parmesan, but it can also be served with pasta. The sauce can be prepared up to 3 days ahead of time and stored, covered, in the refrigerator.

2   (28-ounce) cans diced tomatoes

4   medium garlic cloves, minced or
    pressed through a garlic press (about
    4 teaspoons)

1   tablespoon tomato paste

1   teaspoon extra-virgin olive oil

⅛   teaspoon red pepper flakes

½   cup minced fresh basil leaves
    Salt and ground black pepper

Process the tomatoes with their juices in a food processor until mostly smooth, fifteen to twenty 1-second pulses; set aside. Cook the garlic, tomato paste, oil, and pepper flakes in a medium saucepan over medium heat until the tomato paste begins to brown, about 2 minutes. Stir in the pureed tomatoes and cook until the sauce is thickened, about 25 minutes. Off the heat, stir in the basil and season with salt and pepper to taste. Cover and set aside until needed.

PER ¼-CUP SERVING: Cal 15; Fat 0 g; Sat fat 0 g; Chol 0 mg; Carb 4 g; Protein 1 g; Fiber 0 g; Sodium 220 mg

STUFFED ZUCCHINI

ZUCCHINI (AND ITS YELLOW COUNTERPART, summer squash) is extremely versatile and can be cooked by many different methods, with vastly different results. Halving and stuffing zucchini is a method that often gets overlooked, condemned for being too time-consuming and fussy, but it's a great way to make the most of a late summer bumper crop and incorporate the vegetable into your repertoire.

The problem with many stuffed zucchini recipes is that they are often overly bready, filled with a "stuffing" better suited for a turkey than a squash. Some that we tried were filled with cubed bread that quickly disintegrated into a pudding-like mush when cooked in the moisture-packed squash. Other recipes bind rice and vegetables with cheese and egg, rendering the once healthy vegetable much less so. Still others gave the impression that the zucchini was merely a vessel to hold myriad combinations of leftover grains and ground meat.

In many cases, the zucchini itself is either overcooked, watery, and limp, or undercooked, hard, and flavorless, and is not an integral part of the dish. We wanted to make a filling for zucchini that would be substantial, yet not bogged down with excess starch and fat. We wanted the zucchini to be cooked through, yet firm and flavorful in its own right. The logical place to start in our testing was at the bottom, with the zucchini, and figure out the best way to cook it.

The moisture in the zucchini was the biggest problem. Roasting, with its hot, dry heat, seemed a promising way to lose this moisture while simultaneously precooking the squash. We tested roasting zucchini whole, roasting it halved, and roasting it halved and seeded. The whole zucchini took too long to cook, and steamed itself soggy. Although the halved squash cooked in less time, the seeds still held onto some moisture, leaving behind a soggy shell. The seeded squash, on the other hand, retained just the texture we were looking for and also developed a more concentrated flavor. With the heat of the oven able to hit the flesh of the zucchini directly, more moisture evaporated, intensifying the squash flavor.

Next, we did side-by-side roasting tests. When the zucchini was roasted cut-side up, the moisture that did not evaporate pooled in the hollow space once occupied by the seeds and later seeped into the stuffing, making it watery. When roasted cut-side down, however, the squash dripped moisture onto the hot roasting pan, where it turned to steam. Some of this steam got trapped underneath the overturned squash, speeding up the cooking process. Using a preheated pan further reduced the roasting time while creating a flavorful, golden brown crust along the edges of the squash. Salt and pepper brought out the subtle flavor, while a quick hit with vegetable oil spray prevented sticking. With its lightly browned edges and toothsome texture, the seeded squash roasted cut-side down on a preheated pan was by far the best of the lot. Now we could turn our attention to the problematic filling.

Right off the bat, we set up a few guidelines. We wanted to use ingredients that we would likely have on hand, and we wanted to prepare the filling while the squash roasted. We also wanted a filling that would transform the squash into an elegant side dish. To start, we tried simple combinations of sautéed vegetables and low-fat cheese (light cheddar and reduced-fat mozzarella), but tasters wanted something more substantial. We then tested fillings made with white and brown rice, couscous, and bulgur. They each tasted fine, but tasters wanted a lighter, less starchy filling with a more pronounced vegetable presence. We decided to pair the zucchini with other seasonal summer vegetables, such as corn and tomatoes.

After sweating an onion in just 1 teaspoon of olive oil, we added garlic and canned diced tomatoes (we tried fresh tomatoes, but found the juice from the canned tomatoes added a more intense tomato flavor), and reduced the liquid. To add bulk and reinforce the zucchini flavor, we diced a couple of the roasted squashes and stirred them, along with sweet corn and fresh basil, into our filling. The mixture tasted great, but we could tell even before an attempt at stuffing the zucchini that excess moisture was going to be our downfall. It became clear that we were going to need something absorbent to add to our filling.

To bind our vegetable filling together, we added tomato paste and panko (Japanese bread crumbs), which did the trick. To give the bread crumbs flavor (and a legitimate reason for taking up real estate in our filling), we browned them in a skillet with olive oil and garlic, then added Parmesan cheese. Just 2 tablespoons of bread crumbs bound the filling sufficiently, without being obtrusive. We stuffed the zucchini and then baked them until the filling had heated through. The filling was firm enough to mound into the zucchini, and the flavors were fantastic.

Often in the test kitchen, tasters become divided into two (or more) camps. Some tasters felt that the zucchini needed to have a golden topping, so that it looked and tasted like a finished dish. We tested low-fat cheeses, but combined with the filling, they tasted more like a pizza topping than a light vegetable side dish. By utilizing the crispy, golden, garlicky Parmesan crumbs that were already in the filling, we were able to make the perfect topping for the zucchini, without added kitchen time or effort: We simply had to toast a few extra bread crumbs. The crumbs stayed crisp, added great flavor and texture to the zucchini, and gave the finished appearance we were searching for. This recipe can easily be made with summer squash or try using a mixture of green and yellow squashes for an attractive presentation.

Zucchini Stuffed with Corn and Basil

SERVES 6

Buy firm zucchini with tiny prickly hairs around the stem end; the hairs indicate freshness. If possible, try to pick zucchini that are the same size, with smooth bright green skin. If you cannot find panko, you can substitute fresh bread crumbs (see page 11).

- 4 medium zucchini (about 6 ounces each), stem end removed
  Salt and ground black pepper
  Vegetable oil spray
- 1/2 cup panko (Japanese-style bread crumbs)
- 4 teaspoons extra-virgin olive oil
- 6 medium garlic cloves, minced or pressed through a garlic press (about 2 tablespoons)
- 2 ounces Parmesan cheese, grated (about 1 cup)
- 1 medium onion, minced
- 2 teaspoons tomato paste
- 1 (14.5-ounce) can diced tomatoes
- 3/4 cup frozen corn, thawed
- 1/4 cup minced fresh basil leaves

1. Adjust an oven rack to the lowest position, place a rimmed baking sheet on the rack, and heat the oven to 450 degrees. Slice the zucchini in half lengthwise, then use a spoon to scoop out the sides and inner flesh of the zucchini until the thickness of the zucchini measures 1/4 inch.

2. Season the cut sides of the zucchini with salt and pepper and spray with vegetable oil spray. Lay the zucchini halves, cut-side down, on the hot baking sheet. Roast the zucchini until slightly softened and the skins are wrinkled, about 10 minutes. Remove the zucchini from the oven and flip cut-side up on the baking sheet; set aside. When cool enough to handle, dice 2 of the roasted zucchini halves into 1/4-inch pieces.

3. Meanwhile, combine the bread crumbs and 1 teaspoon of the oil in a 12-inch nonstick skillet and toast over medium heat, stirring often, until golden, about 10 minutes. Stir in 1 teaspoon of the garlic and cook until fragrant, about 30 seconds. Transfer the bread crumbs to a small bowl and let cool slightly; when cool, stir in 6 tablespoons of the Parmesan.

4. Add the onion and 1 teaspoon more oil to the skillet. Cover, return to medium heat, and cook until the onion is softened, 8 to 10 minutes. Stir in the remaining 5 teaspoons garlic and the tomato paste and cook, stirring constantly, until fragrant, about 30 seconds. Stir in the tomatoes, increase the heat to medium-high, and simmer, uncovered, until the tomato juices have evaporated, about 5 minutes. Transfer the mixture to a large bowl.

5. Stir the corn, diced zucchini, 2 tablespoons of the toasted bread crumbs, remaining 2 teaspoons oil, and remaining 10 tablespoons Parmesan into the cooked tomato mixture. Season with salt and pepper to taste. Divide the mixture

evenly between the 6 squash halves on the baking sheet, and pack the filling lightly. Sprinkle evenly with the remaining toasted bread crumbs. Bake until the zucchini halves are heated through and the topping is crisp, 6 to 10 minutes. Serve hot.

PER SERVING: Cal 150; Fat 6 g; Sat fat 2 g; Chol 5 mg; Carb 18 g; Protein 8 g; Fiber 3 g; Sodium 480 mg

TEST KITCHEN MAKEOVER

STUFFED BELL PEPPERS

MENTION STUFFED PEPPERS TO MOST PEOPLE and either bad diner food or the elementary school cafeteria comes to mind. Served up from a steam table, many old-school recipes for stuffed peppers contain rice (and lots of it) and ground beef, bound together with cheese, and little else save the ubiquitous bottle of ketchup served alongside to enhance (or cover up) the flavor. Even worse, the forlorn army green shell often bursts before it even makes it to your plate, at which point the filling spews forth, leaving a greasy, orange puddle in its wake. Since a typical stuffed pepper has 550 calories, and 36 grams of fat per serving, we couldn't find a good excuse for eating one of these at all.

Diner versions aside, stuffed peppers had their fans in the test kitchen, but most of us were eagerly anticipating a healthier version of the 1950s favorite. We began our testing by sampling a few classic recipes. Although these trial runs produced nothing as bad as what we remembered, they were far from perfect. First off, the peppers themselves varied greatly in degree of doneness. Some were so thoroughly cooked that they slumped onto their sides, unable to support their stuffed weight. On the other end of the spectrum, barely cooked peppers added an unfriendly crunch and bitter flavor to the mix. To be a success, the stuffed peppers would have to yield a tender bite yet retain enough structural integrity to stand up proudly on the plate.

None of the fillings hit home, either. One recipe called for small amounts of so many varied ingredients that it made us think its creator just wanted to clean out the refrigerator. An all-rice version was uninteresting, while another stuffed with just meat was leaden and greasy. Perhaps we could explore a combination of the two, just like the diner classic? First, however, we'd need to turn to the peppers themselves.

To support the filling, we needed a solid pepper foundation with minimal crunch. So we steamed, roasted, and blanched a round of peppers and lined them up for everyone in the test kitchen to examine. The steamed peppers were bland in both color and flavor. The roasted peppers were cooked in an uncovered dish filled with a little water, an uncovered dish with no water, and a covered dish. Each procedure produced a bitter, subpar pepper. We knew that if we allowed the peppers to roast a little longer, their sugars would caramelize and the peppers would turn sweet. But at that point their texture would also have disintegrated into that of an Italian sandwich ingredient. Tasters unanimously preferred the vibrant color, sturdiness, and overall sweeter flavor of the blanched peppers; the hot water actually seemed to have washed away some of their bitterness.

Usually, a freshly blanched vegetable is plunged immediately into an ice-cold water bath in a process known as shocking. The point is to halt the cooking process at just the right moment while stabilizing the vegetable's brightened color. We find water baths to be a real pain, especially in a kitchen where counter space is prime property. Although the shocked peppers had a slightly brighter hue than those that had been blanched but not shocked, they took much longer to heat through in the oven. So we abandoned shocking and instead fussed with blanching times, being careful to remove the peppers a little early and then allow the residual heat to finish their cooking. We found that a three-minute dip in boiling water followed by a cooling period on the countertop yielded the perfect balance of structure and tenderness.

While we were at it, we tested green, red, yellow, and orange peppers to determine if color mattered. While all four proved equally functional, tasters preferred the sweetness of the red, yellow, and orange peppers. (Red peppers are simply green bell peppers that have been allowed to ripen longer, thus making them sweeter.) They also kept a more vibrant color than their less mature counterparts.

Even with a pepper that's cooked to perfection, everyone knows that in this dish the filling is the real star of the show. Our earlier testing revealed that we didn't want a filling with an everything-but-the-kitchen-sink approach. Instead we focused on a combination of rice and meat—we wanted stuffed peppers hearty enough to serve as a meal. First, we started with the rice. Many recipes simply call for leftover rice; not at all convenient if you haven't planned ahead. We started with raw rice and discovered that we could use the water that we had blanched the peppers in to cook the rice. While the peppers cooled and the rice cooked, we could work on some of the other elements.

As we have in other lightened recipes, we turned to ground turkey (93 percent lean) as a leaner replacement for ground beef. We also included sautéed onion and garlic and then rounded out the flavors with canned diced tomatoes and some parsley. We tried replacing Monterey Jack with the more strongly flavored Parmesan; it imparted great flavor to the filling and we found that 2 ounces was all we needed.

The only thing missing was a topping to give the peppers a more finished look. In an attempt to stay away from incorporating more cheese into the dish, we gave a nod to the universal condiment, ketchup. On its own, it was too thick to top our peppers with. During baking it dried out and formed an unappealing skin. We found that by mixing the ketchup with a small amount of the juice that we had drained from our tomatoes, the resulting "sauce" ran attractively over the edge of the pepper as it baked, and it tasted great. The filling was lean, well seasoned, and flavorful. And the peppers were tender yet toothsome, and firm enough to support our efforts.

We also decided to develop a vegetarian alternative, and turned to Tex-Mex inspired flavors. This time we enriched our rice and tomato filling with hearty black beans, corn, and jalapeño chile. Light Monterey Jack cheese stood in for the Parmesan and fresh cilantro was the obvious herb of choice.

MAKEOVER AT A GLANCE

–Classic–
Stuffed Bell Peppers
(per serving)

Calories: 550	Cholesterol: 100 mg
Fat: 36 g	Saturated Fat: 14 g

–Light–
Stuffed Bell Peppers
(per serving)

Calories: 340	Cholesterol: 60 mg
Fat: 10 g	Saturated Fat: 3.5 g

How We Did It

- Replaced ground beef with leaner ground turkey
- Reduced the oil from 1½ tablespoons to 1 teaspoon
- Replaced 5 ounces cheddar cheese with 2 ounces stronger-flavored Parmesan cheese

---

Stuffed Bell Peppers
SERVES 4

When shopping for bell peppers to stuff, it's best to choose those with broad bases that will allow the peppers to stand up on their own. It's easier to fill the peppers after they have been placed in the baking dish because the sides of the dish will hold the peppers steady. In testing, we found it best to drain the peppers cut-side up. When we drained them cut-side down, the hot water draining from the peppers continued to steam them, making the peppers soggy.

¼   cup ketchup
1   (14.5-ounce) can diced tomatoes, drained,
      ¼ cup juice reserved
      Salt

4   medium red, yellow, or orange bell peppers
     (6 ounces each), 1/2 inch trimmed off tops,
     stemmed, and seeded
1/2   cup long-grain white rice
1   teaspoon olive oil
1   medium onion, minced
12   ounces 93 percent lean ground turkey or
     chicken
3   medium garlic cloves, minced or pressed
     through a garlic press (about 1 tablespoon)
2   ounces Parmesan cheese, grated (about 1 cup)
1/4   cup minced fresh parsley leaves
     Ground black pepper

1. Adjust an oven rack to the middle position and heat the oven to 350 degrees. Stir the ketchup and reserved tomato juice together in a small bowl; set aside.

2. Bring 4 quarts water to a boil in a large pot. Add 1 tablespoon salt and the bell peppers. Cook until the peppers just begin to soften, about 3 minutes. Using a slotted spoon, remove the peppers from the pot, drain off the excess water, and place the peppers cut-side up on paper towels. Return the water to a boil, stir in the rice, and boil until tender, about 13 minutes. Drain the rice and transfer it to a large bowl; set aside.

3. Meanwhile, combine the oil, onion, and 1/2 teaspoon salt in a 12-inch nonstick skillet. Cover and cook over medium-low heat until the onion is softened, 8 to 10 minutes. Stir in the ground turkey and cook, breaking the meat into small pieces with a spoon, until no longer pink, about 4 minutes. Stir in the garlic and cook until fragrant, about 30 seconds. Stir in the tomatoes and cook until warmed through, about 2 minutes. Transfer the mixture to the bowl with the rice. Stir in the Parmesan and parsley and season with salt and pepper to taste.

4. Place the peppers cut-side up in a 9-inch-square baking dish. Divide the filling evenly among the peppers, packing the filling lightly. Spoon 2 tablespoons of the ketchup mixture over the top of each pepper. Bake until the filling is heated through, 25 to 30 minutes. Serve hot.

PER SERVING: Cal 340; Fat 11 g; Sat fat 4 g; Chol 60 mg; Carb 37 g; Protein 27 g; Fiber 3 g; Sodium 1200 mg

Stuffed Bell Peppers with Black Beans and Corn

SERVES 4

Feel free to substitute pinto or kidney beans for the black beans. If fresh corn is in season, substitute 1 cup cooked fresh corn for the frozen. Most of a chile's heat resides in the ribs; if you prefer more heat, we suggest mincing the ribs along with the seeds and adding them to the recipe to taste; if you prefer less heat, discard the seeds and ribs.

     Salt
4   medium red, yellow, or orange bell peppers
     (6 ounces each), 1/2 inch trimmed off tops,
     stemmed, and seeded
1   cup long-grain white rice
1   teaspoon olive oil
1   medium onion, minced
1   medium jalapeño chile, seeds and ribs
     removed and set aside (see note), flesh minced
3   medium garlic cloves, minced or pressed
     through a garlic press (about 1 tablespoon)
1   (14.5-ounce) can diced tomatoes, drained
1   (15.5-ounce) can black beans, drained
     and rinsed
1   cup frozen corn, thawed
4   ounces 50 percent light cheddar or pepper
     Jack cheese, shredded (about 1 cup)
1/4   cup minced fresh cilantro leaves
     Ground black pepper

1. Adjust an oven rack to the middle position and heat the oven to 350 degrees.

2. Bring 4 quarts water to a boil in a large pot. Add 1 tablespoon salt and the bell peppers. Cook until the peppers just begin to soften, about 3 minutes. Using a slotted spoon, remove the peppers from the pot, drain off the excess water, and place the peppers cut-side up on paper towels. Return the water to a boil, stir in the rice, and boil until tender, about 13 minutes. Drain the rice and transfer it to a large bowl; set aside.

3. Meanwhile, combine the oil, onion, jalapeño, and 1/2 teaspoon salt together in a 12-inch nonstick skillet. Cover and cook over medium-low heat until the onion is softened, 8 to 10 minutes. Stir in the garlic and cook until fragrant, about 30

ROASTED BELL PEPPERS

WHEN ROASTED, SWEET RED BELL PEPPERS
assume a whole new layer of complex, smoky flavor. They are a great way to boost flavor in salads,
sandwiches, and dips without adding fat. Roasted
peppers can also be served on their own, sprinkled
with salt, pepper, and a drizzle of extra-virgin
olive oil. We admit, it is easy to reach for the
jarred variety (see page 7 for our tasting of jarred
roasted red peppers), but with a little effort, great
roasted red peppers can be made at home.

Roasted Red Bell Peppers

MAKES 4 ROASTED PEPPERS

*Cooking times vary, depending on the broiler, so watch
the peppers carefully as they roast. You will need to
increase the cooking time slightly if your peppers are just
out of the refrigerator instead of at room temperature.
Yellow and orange peppers roast faster than red ones, so
decrease their cooking time by 2 to 4 minutes. Do not
roast green or purple peppers—their flavor is bitter and
not worth the effort.*

> 4   medium-to-large red bell peppers (6 to
>   9 ounces each), prepared according to
>   illustrations 1 through 3

1. Adjust an oven rack to the top position. The
oven rack should be 2½ to 3½ inches from the heating element. If it is not, set a rimmed baking sheet,
turned upside down, on the oven rack to elevate the
pan (see illustration 4). Turn the broiler on and heat
for 5 minutes. Broil the peppers until spotty brown,
about 5 minutes. Reverse the pan in the oven and
roast until the skin is charred and puffed but the
flesh is still firm, 3 to 5 minutes longer.

2. Transfer the peppers straight from the oven
to a large heat-resistant bowl, cover it with plastic
wrap, and steam for 15 minutes. (You may also
allow the peppers to cool directly on the baking
sheet.) Peel and discard the skin from each piece
(see illustration 5). Use immediately or transfer
to an airtight container and refrigerate for up to
2 days.

PREPARING BELL PEPPERS FOR ROASTING

1. Slice ¼ inch from the top and bottom of the bell pepper, then
gently remove the stem from the top lobe. Pull the core out of the
pepper.

2. Make a slit down one side of the pepper, then lay it flat, skin-side
down, in one long strip. Slide a sharp knife along the inside of the
pepper to remove all ribs and seeds.

3. Arrange the strips of pepper and the top and bottom lobes skin-
side up on a foil-lined baking sheet. Flatten the strips with the palm
of your hand.

4. Adjust an oven rack to the top position. If the rack is more than
3½ inches from the heating element, set another rimmed baking
sheet, bottom up, on the rack under the baking sheet with the peppers. Roast until the skin of the peppers is charred and puffed up like
a balloon but the flesh is still firm.

5. Remove the baking sheet from the oven. You may steam the
peppers at this point or not, as you wish. When the peppers are
cool enough to handle, start peeling where the skin has charred and
bubbled the most. The skin will come off in large strips.

seconds. Stir in the tomatoes, black beans, and corn and cook until warmed through, about 2 minutes. Transfer the mixture to the bowl with the rice. Stir in the cheese and cilantro, and season with salt and pepper to taste.

4. Place the peppers cut-side up in a 9-inch baking dish. Divide the filling evenly among the peppers, packing the filling lightly. Bake until the filling is heated through, 25 to 30 minutes. Serve hot.

PER SERVING: Cal 420; Fat 7 g; Sat fat 3.5 g; Chol 15 mg; Carb 77 g; Protein 21 g; Fiber 10 g; Sodium 1280 mg

TEST KITCHEN MAKEOVER

MASHED POTATOES

FOR US, THE CONSUMMATE MASHED POTATOES are creamy, soft, and supple, yet with enough body to stand up to the sauce or gravy from an accompanying dish. As for flavor, the sweet, earthy, humble potato comes first, then the buttery richness that keeps you coming back for more. Mashed potatoes are often made by adding chunks of butter and copious amounts of half-and-half or cream. Not surprisingly, a typical recipe of mashed potatoes can contain upwards of 470 calories and 29 grams of fat (20 grams of them saturated) per serving. And to think this is just a side dish! Flavor and richness notwithstanding, we wanted to shave some fat grams and calories off this classic comfort food.

Looking through some other healthy cookbooks, we noticed that many recipes for mashed potatoes used Yukon Gold potatoes for their buttery flavor. We thought we'd give them a try. After making batches of mashed potatoes with both russet potatoes and Yukon Golds, we quickly determined that high-starch potatoes, such as russets, are best for mashing. Yukon Golds, though praised for their buttery flavor, did not have the light and fluffy texture that the russets had. We then needed to

address the simple matter of cooking the potatoes. We started by peeling and cutting some potatoes into chunks to expedite their cooking. Tasters were happy with the results, so we moved forward.

Next were the matters of butter and dairy. We knew right off the bat that we couldn't forgo the butter altogether, since its flavor is integral to the mashed potatoes, but we did have to reduce the amount significantly. In our lightened recipe we wanted just enough butter to impart its flavor, unlike classic mashed potatoes, where the butter also adds a creamy texture and rich mouthfeel. Working with 2 pounds of potatoes, which serves four, we added only 1 tablespoon of butter for flavor, and then moved on to the dairy to give our potatoes a smooth and creamy texture.

When considering dairy, we investigated both the type and the quantity. We tried the lowest fat

---

MAKEOVER AT A GLANCE

–Classic–
Mashed Potatoes
(per serving)

Calories: 470	Cholesterol: 80 mg
Fat: 29 g	Saturated Fat: 20 g

–Light–
Mashed Potatoes
(per serving)

Calories: 260	Cholesterol: 15 mg
Fat: 5 g	Saturated Fat: 3.5 g

How We Did It

- Reduced the amount of butter from 8 tablespoons to just 1 tablespoon and melted it for better distribution
- Replaced 1 cup of half-and-half with ¾ cup of 2 percent milk
- Added ¼ cup of low-fat sour cream to create a creamy texture and a rich dairy flavor

products first. Mashed potatoes made with skim milk were watery, wimpy, and washed-out, and batches made with fat-free evaporated milk had an off-sweetness that competed with the flavor of the potatoes and butter. On the other hand, both whole and 2 percent milk were just what was needed, and 1 cup was just the right amount. Since there wasn't a discernable difference between the two (aside from 30 calories and 4 grams of fat), and we had already used the 2 percent milk in other light recipes, we decided to stick with it.

Overall, the mashed potatoes were good. They had a buttery flavor and a smooth, creamy texture, though tasters complained that something was missing; the potatoes tasted lean. Without the stick of butter or richness from the half-and-half, we needed an ingredient that would enrich the potatoes, giving them the illusion of butter and cream, without the fat and calories. After trying the likes of cottage cheese (too chunky), low-fat yogurt (too liquid and tangy), light cream cheese (too thick and gluey), and buttermilk (too tangy for traditional mashed potatoes, but we liked its flavor, so we made it a variation), we settled on low-fat sour cream, since it is a natural pairing with potatoes (think latkes and baked potatoes). Although the sour cream added a just-barely detectable tanginess to the potatoes, it was welcomed, as opposed to the tanginess of the yogurt, which was harsh and detracted from the potato flavor. We added only ¼ cup of low-fat sour cream to the potatoes, but with 1 cup of milk, the potatoes were on the soupy side. We found it necessary to reduce the amount of milk to ¾ cup. The mashed potatoes now had a lovely, light suppleness and a full, rich flavor.

EQUIPMENT: Food Mills

A food mill is no longer a fixture in American kitchens, but it is a terrific tool to have on hand. Think of it as part food processor, because it refines soft foods to a puree, and part sieve, because it separates waste such as peels, seeds, cores, and fiber from the puree. And it accomplishes all of this with the simple turn of a crank, which rotates a gently angled, curved blade. The blade catches the food and forces it down through the holes of a perforated disk at the bottom of the mill. The separation of unwanted material from the puree is the food mill's raison d'être, but another benefit is that it does not aerate the food as it purees, as do food processors and blenders, so you are able to avoid an overly whipped, lightened texture. (In the case of mashed potatoes, a food processor or blender creates a gummy texture.)

Because you can spend as little as $15 and as much as $100 on a food mill (some really huge mills cost as much as $200), we wondered if some were better than others. We gathered five different models and used them to make mashed potatoes and applesauce. Honestly, there was very little difference in the resulting purees—they were all fine, smooth, and free of unwanted material. Thus, we evaluated the mills more on design factors, such as how easy it was to turn the crank, how efficiently the food was processed, and how snugly it fit over a pot or bowl

set beneath. One feature we found to be very important was interchangeable disks (fine, medium, and coarse) to adjust the fineness of the puree. The models with a fixed disk not only performed less favorably than their multidisk counterparts, but were significantly more difficult to clean.

The best mill of the group was the beautiful stainless steel Cuisipro. It was easy to crank, efficient, and came with fine, medium, and coarse disks.

At $75, it is also the most expensive mill we tested, but its durable design makes it ideal for frequent use.

THE BEST FOOD MILL

In our test of five food mills, the Cuisipro took top honors.

TESTING NOTES

Choosing the Right Dairy

Since we couldn't rely on a stick of butter and a cup of half-and-half to make our mashed potatoes fluffy and creamy, we tried a whole host of alternatives.

LOW-FAT COTTAGE CHEESE *Chunky*

Cottage cheese did not incorporate into the potatoes and left white curds throughout.

LOW-FAT YOGURT
Too Liquid and Tangy

Low-fat yogurt made the potatoes soupy and harsh in flavor.

LIGHT CREAM CHEESE
Thick and Gluey

It was difficult to incorporate the light cream cheese into the potatoes, and by the time it was mixed in, the potatoes were thick and gluey.

BUTTERMILK *Too Tangy*

Tasters liked the rich tanginess that buttermilk imparted, though they thought it was too much for traditional mashed potatoes. Instead, we made it into a variation (see page 112).

SKIM MILK *Watery and Wimpy*
Skim milk did not add any richness or dairy flavor to the potatoes.

LOW-FAT EVAPORATED MILK *Off Flavor*
Low-fat evaporated milk made for potatoes that had an off-sweetness and strange flavor.

THE WINNERS

LOW-FAT SOUR CREAM AND 2 PERCENT MILK

When used in combination, low-fat sour cream and 2 percent milk gave the mashed potatoes a light suppleness and a rich, full flavor.

As for the order in which to incorporate the butter and dairy, we found it essential to add the butter and milk first to the mashed potatoes, before adding the sour cream. When the melted butter and warmed milk go in before the room-temperature sour cream, the result is a silkier, creamier, smoother texture than when the sour cream goes in first (by comparison, the sour cream-first potatoes were pasty and thick). Also, using melted rather than softened butter made the potatoes even more creamy, smooth, and light.

After one taster asked in disbelief: "These are low fat?" we knew we really had developed the best light recipe for mashed potatoes. At just 260 calories and 5 grams of fat per serving, these are good enough to serve your family for Thanksgiving dinner.

Mashed Potatoes

SERVES 4

This recipe yields smooth mashed potatoes. If you don't mind (or prefer) lumps, use a potato masher. Mashed potatoes stiffen and become gluey as they cool, so they are best served piping hot. If you must hold mashed potatoes before serving, place them in a heatproof bowl, cover the bowl tightly with plastic wrap, and set the bowl over a pot of simmering water. Be sure to occasionally check the water level in the pan. The potatoes will remain hot and soft-textured for 1 hour.

2 pounds russet potatoes (about 4 medium), scrubbed, peeled, and cut into 1-inch chunks
Salt
3/4 cup 2 percent milk, warmed
1 tablespoon unsalted butter, melted
1/4 cup low-fat sour cream
Ground black pepper

1. Place the potatoes and 1 tablespoon salt in a large saucepan and add enough water to cover the potatoes by 1 inch. Bring to a boil over high heat, then reduce the heat to medium-low and simmer until a fork can be slipped easily into the center of the potatoes, about 18 minutes. Drain the potatoes.

2. Set a food mill or ricer over the now-empty but still-warm saucepan. Working in batches, drop

the potatoes into the hopper of the food mill or ricer and process into the saucepan.

3. Stir in the milk and melted butter with a wooden spoon until incorporated. Gently fold in the sour cream. Season with salt and pepper to taste and serve immediately.

PER SERVING: Cal 260; Fat 5 g; Sat fat 3.5 g; Chol 15 mg; Carb 49 g; Protein 6 g; Fiber 4 g; Sodium 190 mg

➤ VARIATIONS

Buttermilk Mashed Potatoes with Tarragon

It is important to bring the buttermilk to room temperature before adding it to the potatoes.

Follow the recipe for Mashed Potatoes, substituting 1 cup room-temperature buttermilk for the milk and omitting the sour cream in step 3. Just before serving, stir in 1 teaspoon minced fresh tarragon leaves.

PER SERVING: Cal 250; Fat 3.5 g; Sat fat 2.5 g; Chol 10 mg; Carb 49 g; Protein 6 g; Fiber 4 g; Sodium 220 mg

Mashed Potatoes with Garlic and Chives

The garlic can be peeled after toasting, when the skins will slip right off. Just make sure to keep the heat low and to let the garlic stand off the heat until fully softened. This may sound like a lot of garlic, but toasting the cloves brings out the garlic's sweetness and mellows its harsh bite.

Toast 20 to 25 small to medium garlic cloves (about ⅔ cup), skins left on, in a small covered skillet over the lowest possible heat, shaking the pan frequently, until the cloves are spotty dark brown and slightly softened, about 22 minutes. Remove the pan from the heat and let stand, covered, until the cloves are fully softened, 15 to 20 minutes. Peel the cloves and, using a paring knife, cut off the woody root ends. Follow the recipe for Mashed Potatoes, adding the peeled garlic cloves to the food mill or ricer with the potatoes in step 2. Stir in 2 tablespoons minced chives before serving.

PER SERVING: Cal 290; Fat 5 g; Sat fat 3.5 g; Chol 15 mg; Carb 55 g; Protein 8 g; Fiber 5 g; Sodium 190 mg

MASHED SWEET POTATOES

THE SWEET POTATO HAS TO BE ONE OF NATURE'S most perfect foods, and it contains a natural sweetness that is hard to improve upon. Sadly, many recipes for this simple mash are often overdressed with candy-like ingredients that make it an appealing side dish for kids, but not for grownups. Honey, maple syrup, brown sugar, and even molasses were among the sweeteners we spotted. Not to mention the ubiquitous marshmallow that rears its ugly head at many a Thanksgiving gathering. With a deep, natural sweetness that requires little assistance, the humble sweet potato, we thought, would taste far better if prepared simply.

Yet even with a simple recipe, mashed sweet potatoes can pose problems. Nailing a fork-friendly puree every time is a form of cooking roulette. Mashed sweet potatoes often turn out thick and gluey or, at the other extreme, sloppy and loose. We also found that most recipes overload the dish with pumpkin pie seasonings that obscure the potato's natural flavor. We wanted a recipe that pushed that deep, earthy sweetness to the fore and that reliably produced a silky puree with enough body to hold its shape on a fork. We decided to focus first on the cooking method, then test the remaining ingredients, and, finally, fiddle with the seasonings.

To determine the best cooking method, we tested a variety of techniques: baking potatoes unpeeled, boiling them whole and unpeeled, boiling them peeled and diced, steaming them peeled and diced, and microwaving them whole and unpeeled.

The baked sweet potatoes produced a mash with a deep flavor and bright color, but the potatoes took more than an hour to bake through, and handling them hot from the oven was risky business. Boiling whole sweet potatoes in their skins yielded a wet puree with a mild flavor. When we used a fork to monitor the potatoes as they cooked, we made holes that apparently let the flavor seep out and excess water seep in. Boiling pieces of peeled potato produced the worst purees, with zero flavor and a loose, applesauce-like texture.

The microwave, although fast and easy, was also a disappointment. The rate of cooking was difficult to control, and the difference between undercooked and overdone was only about 30 seconds. Over-microwaving the potatoes, even slightly, produced a pasty mouthfeel and an odd plastic flavor.

By all accounts, this first round of testing bombed. Yet, it did end up pointing us in a promising direction. We had certainly learned a few facts about cooking sweet potatoes. First, their deep, hearty flavor is surprisingly fleeting and easily washed out. Second, the tough, dense flesh reacts much like winter squash when it's cooked, turning wet and sloppy. We also found it safer to peel the sweet potatoes when raw and cold rather than cooked and hot. Taking all of this into account, we wondered if braising the sweet potatoes might work. If cut into uniform pieces and cooked over low heat in a covered pan, the sweet

---

EQUIPMENT: Mandolines and V-Slicers

What's cheaper than a food processor and faster (if not also sharper) than a chef's knife? A mandoline. This hand-operated slicing machine comes in two basic styles—the classic stainless steel model, supported by legs, and the plastic handheld model, often called a V-slicer. We put both types of machines—ranging in price from $8.99 to $169—to the test. To determine the winners, we sliced melons, cut carrots into julienne (matchstick pieces), cut potatoes into batonettes (long, skinny french-fry pieces), and sliced potatoes into thin rounds. Then we evaluated three aspects of the mandolines: ease of use, including degree of effort, adjustment ease, grip/handle comfort, and safety; quality, including sturdiness and uniformity/cleanliness of slices; and cleanup.

The Progressive Mandoline Multi Slicer ($8.99) and the Target Mandoline Slicer ($9.99) are plastic V-slicers with similar designs. Testers gave these models high marks for safety, handle comfort, and blade sharpness, which helped them whip through melon and potato slices. Interchangeable blade platforms cut respectable batonettes and julienne, though these cuts required more effort on the part of testers.

The two other V-slicers tested were the Börner V-Slicer Plus ($34.95) and the Joyce Chen Asian Mandoline Plus ($49.95). The latter produced flawless melon slices, carrot julienne, and potato batonettes but got low marks for its small, ineffective safety mechanism and tricky blade adjustment. Testers also downgraded the poorly designed and not very sturdy base. The Börner unit sliced melons and carrots with little effort, but the potato slices were inconsistent and required more effort to produce. The Börner's well-designed safety guard, however, kept hands away from blades, and its adjustments were quick and easy to make. In the end, testers preferred the cheaper V-slicers made by Progressive and Target to either of these more expensive options.

We also tested two classic stainless steel mandolines. The deBuyer mandoline from Williams-Sonoma ($169) was controversial. Shorter testers had difficulty gaining leverage to cut consistently; some melon slices were 1/8 inch thicker on one side. However, the safety mechanism, sturdiness, and adjustment mechanism were lauded by taller testers. With some practice, all testers were able to produce perfect slices, julienne, and batonettes with the Bron Coucke mandoline ($99). This machine has fewer parts to clean and switch out than its plastic counterparts and requires less effort to operate once the user becomes familiar with it. Still, the quality comes at an awfully high price.

THE BEST V-SLICERS
Plastic mandolines (also called V-slicers) may not be as sturdy as stainless steel versions, but their quality far exceeds the minimal dollar investment. Among the four models tested, we liked the Progressive and Target slicers, which are similar in design.

THE BEST CLASSIC MANDOLINE
Of the two stainless steel mandolines tested, we preferred this model made by Bron Coucke. Note, however, that it costs 10 times more than a good V-slicer.

potatoes might release their own moisture slowly and braise themselves.

Adding a little water to the pan to get the process going, we found the sweet potatoes were tender in about 40 minutes. We then simply removed the lid and mashed them right in the pot. To our delight, they were full of flavor because they cooked, essentially, in their own liquid. We tried various pots and heat levels and found that a medium-size pot (accommodating two or three layers of potatoes) in combination with low heat worked best. The sweet potatoes steam-braised to a perfect consistency, absorbed the water in the pot without becoming soupy, and retained all of their natural flavor goodness.

To season the sweet potatoes, we made four batches side by side, using whole milk, half-and-half, 2 percent milk, and a combination batch with 2 percent milk and light cream cheese. To all of the batches we added 2 tablespoons of unsalted butter. Tasters unanimously preferred the texture that the half-and-half lent to the pot, so we decided to use it in moderation. The potatoes had a hearty flavor and full body that the 2 percent milk just couldn't match. The light cream cheese, a favorite in many of our recipes, gave the potatoes an unpleasant gumminess.

With the dairy component decided on, we wondered if we could take out some of the butter (a big fat contributor) without sacrificing flavor. Side by side, tasters were satisfied with just one tablespoon of butter. The puree stood up on a fork, with a luxurious texture that was neither loose nor gluey, nor overly rich.

For a change of pace, we cooked up some variations that would please more sophisticated tastes. We found that the addition of fresh ginger, combined with a judicious amount of brown sugar won tasters over. The combination of maple and orange also worked well to complement the natural sweetness of the mash. The sweet potato flavor was more intense than ever, with just enough dairy to make it taste special enough for the holiday table, and waistline-friendly for any night of the week.

Mashed Sweet Potatoes
SERVES 4

Cutting the sweet potatoes into evenly sized pieces is important so that they cook at the same rate. This recipe can be doubled and prepared in a Dutch oven; the cooking time must be doubled as well. If you prefer smoother mashed sweet potatoes, use a food mill (see page 110).

2	pounds sweet potatoes (2 large or 3 medium), peeled, quartered lengthwise, and cut crosswise into 1/4-inch-thick slices
	Salt
1	teaspoon sugar
3/4	cup water
1	tablespoon unsalted butter, melted
6	tablespoons half-and-half, warmed
	Ground black pepper

1. Combine the sweet potatoes, 1/2 teaspoon salt, sugar, and water in a 3- to 4-quart saucepan. Cover and cook over low heat, stirring occasionally, until the potatoes fall apart when poked with a fork, 35 to 45 minutes.

2. Off the heat, mash the sweet potatoes in the saucepan with a potato masher. Stir in the melted butter and half-and-half with a wooden spoon until incorporated. Season with salt and pepper to taste.

PER SERVING: Cal 230; Fat 6 g; Sat fat 3.5 g; Chol 15 mg; Carb 42 g; Protein 4 g; Fiber 6 g; Sodium 360 mg

VARIATIONS

Mashed Sweet Potatoes with Ginger and Brown Sugar
Fresh ginger gives this variation a pleasantly spicy bite.

Follow the recipe for Mashed Sweet Potatoes, replacing the sugar with 1 tablespoon light or dark brown sugar, and adding 2 teaspoons minced or grated fresh ginger along with the sweet potatoes in step 1.

PER SERVING: Cal 240; Fat 6 g; Sat Fat 3.5 g; Chol 15 mg; Carb 44 g; Protein 4 g; Fiber 6 g; Sodium 360 mg

Mashed Sweet Potatoes with Maple and Orange

Follow the recipe for Mashed Sweet Potatoes, replacing the sugar with 2 tablespoons maple syrup, and adding ½ teaspoon grated orange zest to the butter and half-and-half in step 1.

PER SERVING: Cal 250; Fat 6 g; Sat fat 3.5 g; Chol 15 mg; Carb 48 g; Protein 4 g; Fiber 6 g; Sodium 360 mg

TEST KITCHEN MAKEOVER

SCALLOPED POTATOES

SCALLOPED POTATOES ARE THE KIND OF comforting dish that you could easily make into an entrée if fat and calories were of no concern. But because it usually weighs in at 410 calories, 28 grams of fat (18 of them saturated), and 100 mg of cholesterol per serving, we were afraid that one of our perennial favorites was destined for extinction, appearing only on holidays, and even then with reservations. Our goal was to develop a recipe for scalloped potatoes that you could feel good about eating on more than just a special occasion. We wanted it to be as rich as the original, without all the fat. We had our work cut out for us.

Most of the recipes for low-fat scalloped potatoes left a lot to be desired, and none came close to the real deal. Many of the recipes replaced high-fat dairy, such as heavy cream, with chicken broth. Leaner, to be sure, but the potatoes tasted like . . . chicken. After testing combinations of chicken broth and other lower fat dairy products, tasters came to the conclusion that without the predominant flavor of sharp cheddar cheese to mask the flavor, we didn't care for any amount of chicken broth. We wanted honest potato, not chicken, flavor in this recipe.

To knock down the fat right off the bat, we tried to find a substitute for the heavy cream and whole milk combination. From evaporated milk to skim milk and everywhere in between, we tried

all variety of dairy. Evaporated milk was too sweet for our tastes; all whole milk with no heavy cream worked, but did not fall within the range of fat grams that we had set as our goal (we were shooting for 5 grams or less per serving). Skim milk broke into a nasty, curdled mess, while 2 percent milk fared better but still curdled. We thought if we could find a stabilizer that also worked to give body to the sauce, we might be able to stick with 2 percent milk.

Two teaspoons of cornstarch helped immensely in stabilizing and thickening our sauce, but it still lacked the creamy richness that tasters were hoping for. We then turned to an ingredient that had saved the day on many occasions when we needed the feel of high fat without the calories—light cream cheese. We tested two batches of potatoes

---

MAKEOVER AT A GLANCE

–Classic–
Scalloped Potatoes
(per serving)

Calories: 410   Cholesterol: 100 mg

Fat: 28 g   Saturated Fat: 18 g

–Light–
Scalloped Potatoes
(per serving)

Calories: 210   Cholesterol: 15 mg

Fat: 5 g   Saturated Fat: 2.5 g

How We Did It

- Sautéed the onion in 1 teaspoon oil rather than 2 tablespoons of butter
- Replaced heavy cream and whole milk with 2 percent milk, cornstarch, and light cream cheese
- Replaced 4 ounces cheddar cheese with 2 ounces stronger-flavored Parmesan cheese, using some in the casserole and the remainder on top for a browned and flavorful crust

side by side, one made with just our thickened 2 percent milk, and one made the same way, but with 3 tablespoons of light cream cheese stirred in. The cream cheese won, hands down. It added just the right amount of silkiness to the sauce to give the illusion of creaminess without all of the calories. To add flavor to the potatoes, we added onion and garlic, along with fresh thyme.

Up until this point, russets had been our potato of choice, but we were curious to see if other varieties might elevate our recipe even further. Tasters suggested buttery Yukon Gold potatoes and red skinned potatoes, and we pitted both against our working recipe with russets. Tasters unanimously preferred the scalloped potatoes made with russets. While the Yukon Golds added a slight "buttery" flavor, they also lent a slight sweetness, and a yellow tinge that we didn't care for. The red potatoes didn't thicken the casserole properly due to their lower starch content, and they lacked the clean potato flavor that we desired. We were satisfied that we had selected the right spud, and the dish had great flavor throughout. The only thing that was missing from our lightened-up potatoes was that elusive brown, crispy cheese topping that many of us in the test kitchen consider the best part of scalloped potatoes.

Full-fat cheddar cheese was clearly not an option for this recipe. Our first inclination was to substitute reduced-fat cheddar, which we had used successfully in other recipes. Unfortunately, the cheese added little flavor to the casserole and lacked the browning capabilities we were looking for in the topping. We turned to the potent flavor of Parmesan cheese, and were pleased with the results. Using only 2 ounces (about 1 cup), we were able to add flavor to the casserole itself with just 2 tablespoons, and reserved the remaining cheese to sprinkle on top. In a hot oven, the Parmesan created the golden brown crust we had been striving for, and had great flavor to boot. In short, we finally had everything the test kitchen expected from great scalloped potatoes.

We were so satisfied with our new scalloped potatoes that we decided some variations were in order. We tested combinations of root vegetables that would work well with potatoes. Sweet

potatoes, fennel, and parsnips were our favorites, but feel free to pair the potatoes with whatever root vegetables suit your preference. The master recipe calls for 2½ pounds of potatoes. You will need 1½ pounds of white potato to provide the starch needed to bind the casserole together, but the remaining pound can be a combination of your favorite root vegetables.

Scalloped Potatoes

SERVES 8

The quickest way to slice the potatoes is in a food processor fitted with a ⅛-inch-thick slicing blade. Halve the potatoes crosswise and put them in the feed tube cut-side down so that they sit flat on the surface of the slicing disk. A mandoline or V-slicer is the other option. Don't try to slice the potatoes with a knife; you won't get them thin enough. It is best to assemble all of your ingredients before slicing the potatoes. If the potato slices discolor as they stand, put them in a bowl and cover with the milk in the recipe. Don't be tempted to slice the potatoes and store them in water—this will remove some of the starch that is necessary to thicken the milk.

1	medium onion, minced
1	teaspoon vegetable oil
½	teaspoon salt
1	medium garlic clove, minced or pressed through a garlic press (about 1 teaspoon)
1	teaspoon minced fresh thyme leaves
¼	teaspoon ground black pepper
2 ½	pounds russet potatoes (about 5 medium), peeled and sliced ⅛ inch thick
2	cups 2 percent milk
2	bay leaves
2	teaspoons cornstarch
1	tablespoon water
3	tablespoons light cream cheese
2	ounces Parmesan cheese, grated (about 1 cup)

1. Adjust an oven rack to the middle position and heat the oven to 450 degrees.

2. Combine the onion, oil, and salt in a Dutch oven. Cover and cook over medium-low heat, stirring occasionally, until the onion is softened, 8

to 10 minutes. Stir in the garlic, thyme, and pepper and cook until fragrant, about 30 seconds.

3. Add the potatoes, milk, and bay leaves and bring to a simmer. Cover, reduce the heat to low, and simmer until partially tender and a fork can be slipped into a potato slice with some resistance, about 10 minutes. Discard the bay leaves. Whisk the cornstarch and water together, then add to the pot and bring to a simmer. Off the heat, stir in the cream cheese and 2 tablespoons of the Parmesan, being careful not to break up the potatoes.

4. Transfer the mixture to an 8-inch-square baking dish and sprinkle with the remaining

Parmesan. Cover the dish with foil and bake for 20 minutes. Uncover and continue to bake until the potatoes are completely tender, a fork can be slipped into the center of the dish without resistance, and the top is golden brown, 10 to 15 minutes longer. Let cool for 10 minutes before serving.

PER SERVING: Cal 210; Fat 5 g; Sat fat 2.5 g; Chol 15 mg; Carb 35 g; Protein 8 g; Fiber 3 g; Sodium 340 mg

➤ VARIATIONS

Scalloped Potatoes with Celery Root and Parsnip
Follow the recipe for Scalloped Potatoes, substituting 8 ounces celery root, peeled and sliced ⅛ inch thick, and 8 ounces parsnips (2 medium), peeled and sliced ⅛ inch thick, for 1 pound of the potatoes.

PER SERVING: Cal 200; Fat 5 g; Sat fat 2.5 g; Chol 15 mg; Carb 31 g; Protein 8 g; Fiber 4 g; Sodium 370 mg

Scalloped Potatoes with Leek and Turnip
Follow the recipe for Scalloped Potatoes, substituting 1 medium leek, white part only, sliced ⅛ inch thick, for the onion. Substitute 1 small turnip (8 ounces), peeled and sliced ⅛ inch thick, for 8 ounces of the potatoes.

PER SERVING: Cal 200; Fat 5 g; Sat fat 2.5 g; Chol 15 mg; Carb 31 g; Protein 8 g; Fiber 3 g; Sodium 360 mg

Scalloped Potatoes with Sweet Potato, Fennel, and Leek
Follow the recipe for Scalloped Potatoes, substituting 1 medium leek, white part only, sliced ⅛ inch thick, for the onion. Add ¼ teaspoon fennel seeds, crushed, along with the thyme in step 2. Substitute 1 pound sweet potatoes, peeled and sliced ⅛ inch thick, for 1 pound of the white potatoes. Add 1 small fennel bulb (8 ounces), cored and sliced ⅛ inch thick, along with the potatoes in step 2.

PER SERVING: Cal 220; Fat 5 g; Sat fat 2.5 g; Chol 15 g; Carb 35 g; Protein 8 g; Fiber 4 g; Sodium 370 mg

---

TESTING NOTES

The Proper Potato

Since potatoes vary in their moisture and starch content, we thought we would put a few varieties to the test. We wanted a potato that had a great flavor of its own and was smooth and creamy, but didn't fall apart completely in the baking dish.

YUKON GOLD POTATOES
Sweet and Yellow

Yukon Gold potatoes added a nice, buttery flavor, but they were too sweet and yellow in color.

RED POTATOES
Too Much Moisture, Not Enough Flavor

Red potatoes lacked the starch content to properly thicken the casserole, and they didn't have a pronounced potato flavor.

THE WINNER

RUSSET POTATOES
Russet potatoes were just right. Their high starch content helped to thicken the casserole, and their hearty flavor won over tasters.

OVEN FRIES

LOW FAT IS NEVER A GOOD EXCUSE FOR LOUSY food, and oven fries should be no exception. Abysmal flavor and texture just aren't worth the savings in calories, especially when these light fries taste like over-roasted potatoes with thick, leathery crusts and hollow interiors. In other cases, they are limp, pale, mealy, and bland—a complete failure in all respects. Yet because the method is easy and clean, oven frying is such an engaging proposition that we decided to see if we could make an oven fry worth eating on its own terms. If it didn't have a golden, crisp crust and a richly creamy interior, we simply wouldn't bother.

First off, we tested russet, Yukon Gold, and boiling potatoes. Tasting wimpy and sporting spotty crusts, both the Yukon Gold and boiling potatoes couldn't hold a candle to the russets, with their hearty flavor and facility for turning golden brown. Less obvious were the results of the peeled-versus-unpeeled-potato test. The unpeeled fries tasted more distinctly of potato, whereas the peeled fries had a slightly cleaner flavor. The tasters didn't have a preference. Since the potato peel is packed with fiber, and peeling the potatoes added an extra step, we decided to leave it on. Tasters liked the ample size and easy preparation of unpeeled potatoes cut into wedges, as opposed to the fussy and wasteful option of peeling and trimming the potatoes down into squared, fast-food-fry wannabes.

Next we baked the fries at 400, 425, 450, 475, and 500 degrees. At lower temperatures, the fries didn't brown sufficiently. The 500-degree oven was a bit too hot and burned the fries at the edges. Baking at 475 degrees was best, but the fries still needed a deeper golden color and a crispier texture. Adjusting the oven rack to the lower-middle position was only moderately helpful, but moving it to the lowest position made for a significant improvement in the fries. The intense heat from the bottom of the oven browned them quickly and evenly, which, in turn, prevented the interiors from overcooking and melding into the crust (thereby becoming the unlikable hollow fry). Lightweight baking sheets can't handle this extreme temperature, so a heavy pan is a must;

even better is a nonstick baking sheet, which, because of its dark surface, encourages deep and even browning.

Up until now, we had been simply tossing the potatoes with oil, salt, and pepper before spreading them out on the baking sheet. Turning our attention to the amount of oil, we found the differences between 1 and 5 tablespoons to be astounding. Any fewer than 4 tablespoons left some of the fries uncoated and caused them to bake up dry and tough; any more than 5 tablespoons made them disagreeably greasy. Using exactly 4 tablespoons, however, ensured that each wedge was evenly coated with oil as it baked. To guarantee even distribution of oil, however, we found it best to spread 4 tablespoons on the baking sheet and to toss the raw fries with just 1 teaspoon more oil. Glistening slightly as they emerge from the oven, the fries require a brief drain on paper towels to blot away excess fat, and keep them from tasting oily.

As for the type of oil, olive oil tasted slightly bitter and out of place, while the mild flavor of vegetable oil and the slight nuttiness of peanut oil (which we prefer to use when deep-frying) both worked well. Although the fries were now sticking to the pan far less than before, we were still plagued by the occasional stuck-on fry until we discovered one last trick. Rather than tossing the potatoes with salt and pepper, we sprinkled the seasonings over the oiled baking sheet. Acting like little ball bearings, the grains of salt and pepper

---

SCIENCE: The Power of Soaking

Experts agree that russet potatoes are the best variety for oven-frying. Unlike other potato varieties, russets produce oven fries with light, ethereal centers. But they are not perfect.

Russets can produce excessively thick crusts and somewhat dry interiors. The thick crust is caused by the browning of simple sugars in the russet, and the best way to remove some of the surface sugar is to soak the potatoes in water. The water has an added benefit. Potato starches gelatinize completely during cooking. The water introduced during soaking improves the creaminess and smoothness by working its way between the strands of gelled starch. The final result is an oven fry that has a good surface crunch married to a smooth interior.

---

kept the potatoes from sticking to the pan without getting in the way of browning.

Even though we had nailed down the basic method for cooking the fries, they were still beset with crusts that were too thick and interiors that were unappealingly mealy. Wondering what would happen if we steamed the fries before baking them (a technique we'd seen in a few other recipes), we steamed one batch on top of the stove in a steamer basket and another in the oven by covering the baking sheet tightly with foil. This seemingly odd method delivered just the thing we had been after: an oven fry with the creamy, smooth core of an authentic french fry. Steaming on the stovetop had been a counter-clogging, time-consuming affair, but wrapping a baking sheet with foil was easy. The foil trapped the potatoes' natural moisture as they steamed themselves in the oven, and we then took it off so the crusts could crisp for the balance of cooking. Five minutes of steaming was just

right, turning the dry, starchy centers of the fries to a soft, creamy consistency without interfering with browning.

Now the only problem remaining was the crust. Steaming, although beneficial for the interior, turned the already thick crust even tougher; this was a far cry from the thin, brittle crust of a good french fry. To solve this problem, we decided to try the techniques of rinsing and soaking, which are often employed when making french fries. Rinsing the raw fries under running water made for a slightly more delicate crust, but soaking them for about an hour in cold tap water was pure magic. Slowly turning the water cloudy as they soaked, the fries emerged from the oven with thin, shatteringly crisp crusts and interiors more velvety than any oven fry we had tasted. But perhaps the biggest surprise came when we tried soaking the fries in water at different temperatures: ice-cold, cold from the tap, and hot

NUTRITION 101
What Does the Organic Label Really Mean?

Now that more and more traditional supermarkets are carrying organic varieties of many fruits and vegetables, some organic meats, and perhaps even a section devoted to natural or whole foods, it's important to understand what these labels really mean, especially since you pay such a premium for these products. Are the terms "organic" and "natural" interchangeable? Why do some products feature the U. S. Department of Agriculture (USDA) organic seal while others do not?

The USDA has standards to regulate the term "organic," while "natural" is not regulated in a similar manner. Therefore, if you see "natural" on a label, know that it does not mean the food is organic. The organic symbol you see on labels means that these foods were produced meeting standards set by the USDA. In other words, it is food produced by farmers who do not use synthetic fertilizers or pesticides when growing their food and do not feed additives to the animals they raise. And before a product can be labeled organic, a government-approved certifier must inspect the farm where the food

is grown to ensure the farmer is following all of the USDA standards. Here's a quick guide to help you understand different organic labels:

- **100 percent Organic**—The product contains ONLY organic ingredients and may display the "USDA Organic" seal.

- **Organic**—The product has 95 percent to 100 percent organic ingredients and may display the "USDA Organic" seal.

- **Made with organic ingredients**—The product has 70 percent to 95 percent organic ingredients. The label may include the words "Made with these organic ingredients" with up to three organic ingredients listed, on the front panel or main label. The label may not display the "USDA Organic" seal.

from the tap. The ice water took hours to become cloudy, the cold tap water took about 1 hour, and the hot tap water took a convenient 10 minutes, which meant that we could scrub, cut, and soak the potatoes in roughly the same time it took to heat up the oven.

These fries might be low in fat and calories, but they are not at all reminiscent of any other lame attempts at healthy french fries we have tried. They have a crisp, golden brown exterior, a moist and creamy interior, and great potato flavor.

EQUIPMENT: Vegetable Peelers

For years, the Oxo Good Grips peeler has been a standard in our test kitchen. But two new peelers on the market led us back into the kitchen for another look. Oxo's new I-Series line includes a redesigned vegetable peeler that we found to be exceptionally sharp. The blades are replaceable (much like razor blades that click on and pop off). I-Series vegetable peelers have a more slender handle, which solves the only problem we had with the original Good Grips peeler: it was a bit bulky. Nonetheless, the I-Series peeler is heavier, tipping the scale at nearly a quarter pound. The balance of extra weight falls to the blade end, which seems to allow the peeler to do some of the work for you.

Similar in appearance to Oxo's Good Grips peeler is the Messermeister serrated blade peeler. We were surprised that what we thought would be a novelty peeler could rival and even replace a Good Grips at the usual peeling tasks. What makes this peeler exceptional is its ability to peel ripe peaches and tomatoes, which even the noticeably sharper I-Series peeler was reluctant to do effectively. The Messermeister's narrow black rubber handle, however, makes it difficult to get a good grip.

So what peeler should you reach for? We'll be reaching for the Oxo I-Series. With replaceable blades and solid construction, this peeler will have a home in our kitchen for many years to come. That is, until Oxo introduces a new peeler.

THE BEST VEGETABLE PEELER

The Oxo I-Series peeler ($10) is our new favorite.

Oven Fries

SERVES 4

Take care to cut the potatoes into even wedges so that all of the pieces will cook at about the same rate. We prefer the texture and ease of unpeeled potatoes; however, feel free to peel the potatoes if desired. Although it isn't required, a nonstick baking sheet works particularly well for this recipe. It not only keeps the fries from sticking, but because of its dark color, it encourages deep and even browning. Whether you choose a nonstick baking sheet or a regular baking sheet, make sure that it is heavy-duty. The intense heat of the oven may cause lighter pans to warp.

3   russet potatoes (8 ounces each), scrubbed, each potato cut lengthwise into 10 to 12 even wedges

¼   cup plus 1 teaspoon vegetable or peanut oil
    Salt and ground black pepper

1. Adjust an oven rack to the lowest position and heat the oven to 475 degrees. Place the potatoes in a large bowl, cover them with hot tap water, and let soak for 10 minutes. Meanwhile, coat an 18 by 12-inch heavy-duty rimmed baking sheet (preferably nonstick) with ¼ cup of the oil and sprinkle evenly with 1 teaspoon salt and ¼ teaspoon pepper; set aside.

2. Drain the potatoes. Spread the potatoes out on a triple thickness of paper towels and pat dry thoroughly with additional paper towels. In a bowl, toss the dried potatoes with the remaining 1 teaspoon oil.

3. Arrange the potatoes in a single layer on the prepared baking sheet and cover tightly with foil. Bake for 5 minutes, then remove the foil and continue to bake until the bottoms of the potatoes are spotty golden brown, 15 to 20 minutes, rotating the baking sheet after 10 minutes.

4. Scrape the potatoes loose from the pan with a metal spatula, then flip over each wedge using tongs, keeping the potatoes in a single layer. Continue to bake until the fries are golden and crisp, 7 to 10 minutes longer, rotating the pan as needed if the fries are browning unevenly. Spread the potatoes out over paper towels to drain briefly, discarding the oil left on the baking

sheet. Season with additional salt and pepper to taste. Serve hot.

PER SERVING: Cal 230; Fat 12 g; Sat fat 1.5 g; Chol 0 mg; Carb 31 g; Protein 4 g; Fiber 2 g; Sodium 590 mg

Winter Squash

THERE ARE MANY WAYS TO COOK WINTER squash, but the ideal method for one kind may not necessarily be the best for another. We quickly discovered this when we set out to find the optimum way to cook the two most common winter squash, acorn and butternut. After only a few tests, we found that they responded very differently. We figured that we should develop a couple of basic cooking methods, then recommend the best kinds of squash for each method.

One thing that all winter squash have in common is that, counter to the current fashion for al dente vegetables, they must be cooked until well done to develop the sweetest flavor and smoothest texture. With this as the only given, we tried cooking various kinds of squash by baking, roasting, steaming, boiling, and even microwaving.

After some experimentation, we found that baking unpeeled and seeded squash halves cut-side down produced a slightly better texture than baking them cut-side up. We found it best to cook the squash on a foil-lined baking sheet that had been oiled. The oil promoted browning and reduced the risk of sticking, and the foil made cleanup easy.

Although this method was a success, when we began thinking about serving the squash, we realized that a baked squash half was fine if you could find relatively small squash, but what about those times when the market has only 3-pound butternut squashes? Roasting chunks of peeled squash proved to be a much more successful way to cook such big squash. We peeled the squash and cut it into 1-inch cubes, then roasted it uncovered at varying oven temperatures. The squash became quite caramelized, with a good chewy texture and a much sweeter and more pronounced flavor. The ideal temperature turned out to be 450 degrees (a bit higher than the 400 degrees at which we like to roast squash halves). At lower temperatures, the squash was no better and took much longer to cook, and at higher temperatures it burned on the outside before it was fully cooked inside.

Whichever approach you choose, roasting chunks or halves, winter squash is so flavorful that it needs little in terms of seasoning, making it a

CUTTING WINTER SQUASH

Cutting butternut squash needn't be an arduous chore. A cleaver, mallet, and damp kitchen towel will make the task easier. This method works for both butternut and acorn squash.

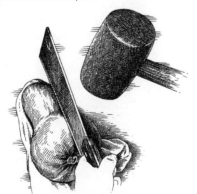

1. Set the squash on a damp kitchen towel to hold it in place. Position the cleaver on the skin of the squash.

2. Strike the back of the cleaver with a mallet to drive the cleaver deep into the squash. Continue to hit the cleaver with the mallet until the cleaver cuts completely through the squash. Use an ice cream scoop with a curved bowl to remove all the seeds and strings without damaging the flesh.

healthy choice to include in your repertoire any day of the week.

Roasted Winter Squash
SERVES 6

This recipe is best with sweet and naturally buttery butternut, buttercup, or hubbard squash. One whole 2-pound squash yields about 1 pound of trimmed pieces. Peeled and cut squash pieces (usually butternut) are available in the produce section of most grocery stores; however, for best flavor and texture, it is preferable to peel and cut your own. If peeling the squash yourself, use a heavy-duty vegetable peeler that will remove a thick layer of the skin and the tough greenish flesh right below the skin (see page 120 for details on our test of peelers).

- 2   pounds winter squash, peeled, seeded, and cut into 1-inch cubes
- 1   medium shallot, minced (about 3 tablespoons)
- 1   tablespoon extra-virgin olive oil
- 2   teaspoons minced fresh thyme leaves
       Salt and ground black pepper

CORE TECHNIQUE

MAXIMIZING THE OIL

Usually, before vegetables are roasted they are tossed in a bowl with a generous amount of oil, salt, pepper, and other seasonings, and then spread out on a baking sheet to go into the oven. The oil coats the vegetables and prevents them from sticking to the baking sheet, and also helps them to develop a tasty golden brown exterior. We knew the oil was an essential ingredient here, but mindful of every fat gram, we needed to use it sparingly. We found that by tossing the vegetables with just 1 tablespoon of oil and the seasonings on the baking sheet, rather than in a bowl, we were able to coat the baking sheet and the vegetables. This kept all the oil In one place, without leaving any behind in the bowl—and we had one less dish to wash.

Adjust an oven rack to the lower-middle position and heat the oven to 450 degrees. Line a rimmed baking sheet with foil. Toss the squash, shallot, oil, thyme, ¼ teaspoon salt, and ⅛ teaspoon pepper together on the prepared baking sheet. Spread the squash pieces into an even layer. Roast, shaking the pan after 15 minutes, until the squash is tender and evenly browned, 25 to 35 minutes. Season with salt and pepper to taste before serving.

PER SERVING: Cal 80; Fat 2.5 g; Sat fat 0 g; Chol 0 mg; Carb 16 g; Protein 1 g; Fiber 3 g; Sodium 105 mg

Roasted Winter Squash Halves
SERVES 6

This recipe can be made with acorn, buttercup, butternut, or delicata squash. The cooking time will vary depending on the kind of squash you use. Start checking for doneness after the first 30 minutes.

- 1   tablespoon extra-virgin olive oil
- 1   medium or 2 small winter squash (2 pounds), halved lengthwise and seeded (see the illustrations on page 121)
       Salt and ground black pepper

1. Adjust an oven rack to the lower-middle position and heat the oven to 400 degrees. Line a rimmed baking sheet with foil and brush with half of the oil. Brush the cut sides of the squash with the remaining oil and sprinkle with salt and pepper. Place the squash cut-side down on the foil. Roast until a fork can be slipped easily into the center of the squash, 40 to 50 minutes.

2. Remove the squash from the oven and turn it cut-side up. Season the squash with salt and pepper to taste, cut into smaller serving sizes if desired.

PER SERVING: Cal 80; Fat 2.5 g; Sat fat 0 g; Chol 0 mg; Carb 16 g; Protein 1 g; Fiber 3 g; Sodium 100 mg

VEGGIE BURGERS

VEGGIE BURGERS HAVE BECOME INCREASINGLY popular in recent years. And while the concept is a good one—backyard barbecue offerings are rarely vegetarian and are even less frequently healthy—most of us in the test kitchen have not yet tasted a veggie burger worth eating.

To explore what was available on the market, we enlisted a few of our fellow test cooks and sampled box after box of frozen commercial brands. Comments such as "dreadful" and "smells like dog biscuits" (see "Frozen Veggie Burgers" on page 124) quickly motivated us to make our own.

Guided by a variety of vegetarian cookbooks, we stepped into the test kitchen to try our hand with a number of recipes. What we learned after making a dozen or so was pretty clear. Homemade veggie burgers are much more work than their beefy brethren. They are truthfully a labor of love, so they'd better taste great. And no veggie burger tastes like a hamburger; that's a foolish goal. But tasters wanted these burgers to "act" like hamburgers. They wanted a patty with a modicum of chew, a combination of savory ingredients that would not taste specifically of any one thing (nobody wanted a "black bean" burger, for example), and the ability to go from grill to bun without falling apart.

Many supermarket veggie burgers start with soy-based products to boost the protein content and achieve a meaty texture. It didn't take long, however, for the meat substitutes we tested to disappoint, even when used as only one of several ingredients. Tofu, made from the curds of soymilk, was up first but all varieties of tofu (extra-firm to silken) produced veggie burgers that were wet and mushy. Textured vegetable protein, or TVP, has the appearance and texture of ground beef but little flavor of its own. It produced bland burgers. We also tried tempeh, a soybean cake made by fermenting cooked soybeans. Although tempeh also has a rich, meaty texture, its sour flavor made for terrible burgers. We even tried seitan, a wheat gluten product. This resulted in overly soft patties that tasters described as "gummy" and "fishy."

Next on our list were legumes. During our first round of recipe testing, tasters had rated lentil burgers best in terms of flavor but not texture; they were soggy and hard to cook. To get rid of some of this moisture, we drained the cooked lentils thoroughly in a sieve and then laid them out on a thick layer of paper towels. Because many recipes for veggie burgers pair legumes with a grain, we decided to follow suit. Rice was too soft and pasty, whereas barley was too hard. The grains of bulgur wheat, however, were small enough to incorporate easily into the mix and married well with the lentils in terms of flavor. Just like the lentils, the rehydrated bulgur had to be drained thoroughly.

With a base of lentils and bulgur, it was time to turn to vegetables. Onions, garlic, celery, and leeks proved the best choices, delivering depth of flavor without being overwhelming. As with the other ingredients, excess moisture was an issue. We found it necessary to cook all four of these vegetables long enough to remove residual moisture. Using our core technique for sweating vegetables (see page 63), we first cooked the vegetables (tossed with a little oil and salt) in a covered pan over medium-low heat until they were softened. We then uncovered the pan and increased the heat to cook out the moisture and brown the vegetables, which also boosted flavor.

So far so good, but tasters kept telling us that the burgers needed some "meat." We immediately thought of mushrooms, a vegetable known for having a meaty texture and rich flavor. We were happy with the performance of cremini mushrooms, but white mushrooms were nice as well. Because uncooked mushrooms are more than 80 percent water, we had to be sure to cook them until all their moisture had evaporated. Borrowing the technique we used for the onion mixture, we were able to cook the mushrooms until the moisture evaporated and they browned, in just 1 teaspoon of oil. The addition of cashews, though relatively high in fat (the good, unsaturated kind), also provided meaty texture and a tremendous amount of flavor to the burgers.

A remaining issue was texture: tasters wanted a burger without big chunks of vegetables. Pulsing everything together in the food processor made for a more cohesive and even-textured mix, but the burgers still didn't hold together as well as we would have liked. We tried various binders including

INGREDIENTS: Frozen Veggie Burgers

Chopping, simmering, draining, shaping, chilling—are homemade veggie burgers really worth the effort? Not if there was something decent to be had at the supermarket, we reasoned. So we tasted seven products, all fully cooked frozen patties that required just two kitchen skills: heating and plopping onto a bun.

All brands won high marks for convenience, but that's about it. Veggie-burger veterans and first-timers alike agreed that the flavors and textures were not very good across the board. Even more perplexing, hardly any of these burgers tasted of vegetables. The problem is that most seemed to be trying to replicate an all-beef burger in texture and taste, but no combination of soy protein, wheat gluten, or smoke flavor pulled that off convincingly.

FOR TIME-PRESSED VEGETARIANS ONLY

Our "winner," Gardenburger Original Burgers, boasted strong mushroom and grain flavors, but the dehydrated-vegetable texture was reminiscent of "stuffing mix." The best of the lot, but that's not saying much.

low-fat sour cream, cheese, egg, and reduced-fat mayonnaise, and finally settled on the mayonnaise. It provided the necessary fat and binding qualities along with good flavor. (If you want vegan burgers, Nayonaise also worked as a binder, but every test cook gave it poor reviews for its flavor.)

While these burgers had come a long way, we were still bothered by the fact that tasters referred to them as "soggy," hardly the adjective we were looking for. To soak up excess moisture, we tried flour and bread crumbs. Flour made the burgers taste pasty. Plain bread crumbs worked reasonably well, but some tasters complained that these "heavy" burgers reminded them of "meatloaf." The solution was to reduce the amount of bread crumbs and to use panko, Japanese bread crumbs that are especially flaky, light, and crunchy. While they did not remain crunchy in the veggie burger mix for long, they did absorb residual moisture and remained virtually undetectable in terms of flavor.

Finally, we were ready to cook. Because the ingredients in these veggie burgers are already cooked, our goal was to achieve a golden crust while just heating them through. A large nonstick skillet and medium-high heat did the trick. Paired with buns and all the fixins' or on their own with a simple green salad, this labor of love was much appreciated not only by our vegetarian friends but also by the meat eaters in the test kitchen. Although they're not a replacement for the real thing, these nutritious "change-of-pace" burgers are a healthy and satisfying meal in their own right.

Veggie Burgers
MAKES TWELVE 4-INCH BURGERS

For the sake of convenience, you can use canned lentils, though some flavor will be sacrificed. Thoroughly rinse a 15-ounce can of lentils in a mesh strainer, then spread them out over paper towels and dry them before using them in step 2 below (skip step 1). If you cannot find panko, use 1 cup of plain bread crumbs. To make these veggie burgers suitable for vegans, Nayonaise can be used in place of the mayonnaise.

5	cups water
¾	cup brown lentils, rinsed and picked over
	Salt
¾	cup bulgur wheat
1	pound cremini or white mushrooms, wiped cleaned and sliced ¼ inch thick
2	medium onions, minced
1	large celery rib, chopped fine
1	large leek, white and light green parts only, chopped fine, and rinsed thoroughly
2	medium garlic cloves, minced or pressed through a garlic press (about 2 teaspoons)
3	tablespoons plus 1 teaspoon vegetable oil
1	cup raw unsalted cashews
⅓	cup reduced-fat mayonnaise
2	cups panko (Japanese-style bread crumbs)
	Ground black pepper

1. Bring 3 cups of the water, lentils, and ¼ teaspoon salt to a boil in a medium saucepan over high heat. Reduce the heat to medium-low and continue to simmer, stirring occasionally, until the lentils are just beginning to fall apart, about 25 minutes. Drain the lentils, then spread out over a

124

paper towel–lined baking sheet and gently pat dry with additional paper towels; cool.

2. Meanwhile, prepare the bulgur. Bring the remaining 2 cups water and ¼ teaspoon salt to a boil in a small saucepan. Stir in the bulgur, cover, and let stand off the heat until the water is absorbed, 15 to 20 minutes. Drain in a fine-mesh strainer, using a rubber spatula to press out any excess moisture. Transfer the bulgur to a large bowl and set aside.

3. Combine the mushrooms, onions, celery, leek, garlic, 1 teaspoon of the oil, and ½ teaspoon salt in a 12-inch nonstick skillet. Cover and cook over medium-low heat, stirring often, until the vegetables are softened and have released their moisture, 10 to 15 minutes. Uncover, increase the heat to medium-high, and continue to cook, stirring occasionally, until the liquid has evaporated and the vegetables have browned, 15 to 20 minutes longer. Spread the vegetables on the paper towel–lined baking sheet with the lentils to cool.

4. Process the cashews in a food processor until finely chopped, about fifteen 1-second pulses (do not wash the food processor blade or bowl). Stir the processed cashews, cooled lentils, vegetables, and mayonnaise into the bulgur until well combined. Transfer half of mixture to the food processor, and pulse until the mixture is coarsely chopped and cohesive, 15 to 20 pulses, scraping down the bowl with a rubber spatula as needed. Transfer the processed mixture to a large bowl. Repeat with the remaining mixture and combine with the first batch.

5. Stir in the panko and season with salt and pepper to taste. Stir the mixture until uniformly combined. Line a baking sheet with a double layer of paper towels. Form the mixture into 12 patties, about ½ cup each, shaping each into tightly packed patties, about 4 inches around and about ½ inch thick. Set the patties on the prepared baking sheet until ready to cook (the paper towels will absorb excess moisture). (If not using immediately, the patties can be covered with plastic wrap and refrigerated up to 3 days. For freezing instructions, see page 126.)

6. To cook the burgers: Heat 1 tablespoon of the oil in a 12-inch nonstick skillet over medium-

---

TESTING NOTES

Finding the Best Burger Base

We found that the base you use in veggie burgers can make all the difference in flavor and texture.

TOFU
Soggy and Wet Burgers
No matter what type of tofu we tried (extra-firm, firm, soft, silken), the burgers had way too much moisture and lacked flavor.

TEXTURED VEGETABLE PROTEIN (TVP)
Bland Burgers
TVP has the appearance and texture of ground beef; however, it has very little flavor of its own.

TEMPEH
Sour Flavor
Tempeh, a cake made from fermented soybeans, has a rich and meaty texture, but its sour flavor made for awful burgers.

SEITAN
Soft and Gluey Patties
Seitan, a wheat gluten product, produced burgers that were overly soft and gluey. Tasters described these burgers as "gummy" and "fishy."

THE WINNER

LENTILS AND BULGUR WHEAT
Lentils, when cooked and drained properly, had a nice mild flavor and firm texture. The small grains of rehydrated bulgur wheat were easy to incorporate, and the flavors complemented that of the lentils. We now had the perfect base for our burgers.

Grilling Vegetables 101

Grilled vegetables are the perfect accompaniment to grilled meat and fish: Simply cook the veggies while the main course rests. Vegetables are best cooked over a medium-hot single-level fire (see pages 221–222), so adjust the grill as necessary. If using a charcoal grill, spread the hot coals in an even layer and, if necessary, add more briquettes to increase the heat of the fire. All vegetables should be sprayed lightly with vegetable oil spray (except for corn on the cob) and sprinkled with salt and pepper. Vegetables can be served hot off the grill or at room temperature.

PREP AND YIELD	GRILLING INSTRUCTIONS
ASPARAGUS Tough ends snapped off 1 pound serves 4	Grill 5 to 7 minutes, turning once.
BELL PEPPERS Stemmed, seeded, and flattened 4 medium serve 4	Grill 8 to 10 minutes, turning once.
CORN ON THE COB All but inner layer of husk removed and silk snipped 8 ears serve 8	Grill 8 to 10 minutes, turning every 2 minutes.
EGGPLANT Ends trimmed and cut crosswise into ¾-inch-thick rounds 1 large (1½ pounds) serves 4	Grill 8 to 10 minutes, turning once.
FENNEL Fronds removed, base trimmed, and sliced vertically into ¼-inch-thick planks 2 bulbs serve 4	Grill 8 to 10 minutes, turning once.
PORTOBELLO MUSHROOMS Stems removed and discarded, caps wiped clean 4 (5- to 6-inch) caps serve 4	Grill 8 to 12 minutes, turning once.
WHITE OR CREMINI MUSHROOMS Wiped clean and skewered 1 pound serves 4	Grill 8 to 12 minutes, turning every 3 minutes.
ONIONS Peeled, cut crosswise into ½-inch-thick rounds, and skewered 2 large serve 4	Grill 10 to 12 minutes, turning once.
ZUCCHINI OR SUMMER SQUASH Trimmed and sliced lengthwise into ½-inch-thick strips 2 pounds (4 medium) serves 4	Grill 8 to 10 minutes, turning once.

high heat until shimmering. Gently lay 4 of the burgers in the skillet and cook until well browned and heated through, about 4 minutes per side, lowering the heat if the burgers are browning too quickly. Repeat with the remaining oil and burgers as needed. (If cooking multiple batches, the burgers can be kept warm in a 250-degree oven for up to 30 minutes.)

PER BURGER: Cal 240; Fat 10 g; Sat fat 1.5 g; Chol 0 mg; Carb 31 g; Protein 9 g; Fiber 5 g; Sodium 250 mg

FREEZING VEGGIE BURGERS

THIS RECIPE YIELDS A GENEROUS NUMBER of burgers, and extras can be frozen before cooking. With freezing and defrosting, however, the patties increase in moisture content; it is therefore necessary to add more bread crumbs before freezing. For each burger to be frozen, add 1 teaspoon panko or ½ teaspoon plain bread crumbs to the mixture before shaping. Thaw frozen patties overnight in the refrigerator on a triple layer of paper towels covered loosely with plastic wrap. Before cooking, pat the patties dry with paper towels and reshape to make sure they are tightly packed and cohesive.

5

RICE, GRAINS, AND BEANS

NUTRITION EXPERTS TELL US THAT IF WE WANT to include more complex carbohydrates in our daily diet, and achieve that ever-looming quota of fiber, whole grains and beans are the ticket. Doing this, they say, will pave the way to a healthier, more nutrient-dense diet. This advice sounded good to us: trade in a few portions of potatoes and pasta for servings of whole grains and/or beans. In reality, though, we found that most of us don't manage to make the trade, and we wondered why.

More often than not, unfamiliarity turned out to be the culprit. Sometimes it's with the grain itself, like quinoa—we might not know how to pronounce it (it's keen-wa), never mind have any idea what it tastes like. And sometimes it's with the preparation and serving options. Whole grains and beans have a reputation for being bland and boring, and even some of us in the test kitchen think of them more as "health food" than a tasty side dish. Our goals, then, were to demystify some of these lesser-known grains and to develop low-fat, foolproof techniques for preparing the more familiar ones, like risotto, pilafs, and refried beans.

We started with grains. One of the first things we learned is that the "pilaf" method we often use for preparing rice also works with more unusual grains such as bulgur and quinoa. It's a simple technique: you start the pilaf method by sautéing aromatics, such as onions, then you toast the grains until fragrant (bulgur is an exception—we just didn't find that toasting made a difference). Next, broth or water (or a mix of the two) is added to the pot and the grains are simmered until they absorb the liquid. The pot is taken off the heat to sit for 10 minutes, whereby the grains steam. Finally, the grains are fluffed and seasoned. We found this technique produced light, pillowy pilafs every time.

Our biggest discovery, however, was that you don't have to use much fat to make a stellar pilaf. Too much fat just bogs down the grains in a pilaf and makes them greasy. The true tastiness in a pilaf comes from a layering of flavor. The mellow sweetness of sautéed aromatics, toasting of the grains until nutty, and the addition of intensely flavored ingredients—like lemon zest, fresh herbs, and dried fruits—all work together to form a low-fat, healthy side dish. Dishes such as Quinoa Pilaf with Corn and Jalapeños (page 149) and Bulgur Pilaf with Shiitakes and Asian Flavors (page 148) have become new favorites in the test kitchen.

Following this lead, we then found we could take the basic recipe for our reduced-fat Parmesan Risotto (page 136) and adapt it to another grain—barley. We also developed a foolproof method for making perfect brown rice, a notoriously finicky grain to cook. Our oven-baked method yields a fluffy, springy brown rice every time, a much different picture from the usual train wreck: a bland, mishmash of over- and under-cooked grains of rice. We've included flavor variations, too, like Brown Rice with Parmesan, Lemon, and Herbs (page 142), a versatile side dish and perfect platform for a light dinner alongside roast chicken or grilled fish.

Beans, like grains, are another commonly overlooked nutrient-dense food. Most recipes we've seen have you start from scratch with dried beans, which are usually presoaked for hours, then take even longer to cook. But who wants to spend hours cooking dinner on a weeknight after a long day at work? Utilizing the convenience of canned beans and relying on quick-cooking legumes such as lentils, we were able to create great bean recipes with minimal effort, perfect for any night of the week.

Many bean side dishes are laden with pork fat (used to boost flavor and richness), an ingredient that doesn't really lend itself to eating light. However, we were able to make over a classic—Refried Beans (page 152)—and found that we could cut out an astounding amount of fat without losing all the flavor. We discovered that canned red kidney beans (not the traditional pinto bean) worked best for this recipe. Their deep, nutty flavor and creamy pureed consistency were big bonuses, as was the convenience factor. But the key to success for making these beans so tasty was using judicious amounts of fresh jalapeño, onion, cumin, garlic, cilantro, and a tiny bit of olive oil.

An exciting discovery came when we figured out that we could apply the refried bean technique to create other types of bean purees. By substituting a different type of canned bean and changing the flavor combination, we uncovered a side dish that makes a stellar alternative to the usual mashed potatoes. We enthusiastically recommend trying the White Bean Puree with Rosemary (page 153).

Not all of the dishes in this chapter are meant to be accompaniments. Butternut Squash Risotto with Sage and Toasted Almonds (page 137) and Curried Brown Rice with Tomatoes and Peas (page 142) are intended to be one-pot meals, perfect for a healthy, satisfying weeknight supper. In addition, we've supplemented our specific recipes with helpful charts such as "Cooking Grains 101" and "Cooking Beans 101" to provide the home cook with a base of knowledge upon which to build and experiment with a variety of ingredients and flavor combinations. With these recipes in hand, grains and beans have become new favorites at our dinner tables, and we hope they will at yours, too.

NUTRITION 101
Demystifying Fiber

So what exactly is fiber and why all the fuss about getting enough of it into your daily diet? Fiber is an indigestible carbohydrate found in plants. Our bodies do not absorb fiber and therefore it has no calories. There are two kinds of fiber, soluble and insoluble. Soluble fibers (found in many fruits like apples, oranges, and peaches and in oat bran and oatmeal) dissolve in water, forming a sticky gel, while insoluble fibers (found in celery, carrots, cucumbers, seeds, dried beans, and whole grains) do not. All fiber passes through the digestive tract fairly quickly but also help make you feel full for longer because they take up more space in the stomach.

We all know that fiber aids in the digestion of other foods, preventing constipation, but there are even more benefits. Some soluble fibers help keep cholesterol levels low by helping pass it though the digestive tract instead of into the bloodstream. Fiber also helps keep blood sugar levels in check by coating the lining of the gut, which slows the absorption of sugars after a meal. Its effect on cholesterol and blood sugar levels helps fiber play a role in reducing the risk of heart disease and diabetes.

The Surgeon General and most professional health organizations in the United States recommend 20–35 grams of fiber a day. Most Americans fall short of this goal, taking in only 10–15 grams per day. Increasing your intake of fruits, vegetables, and whole grains at each meal is an easy way to get more fiber in your diet. The best way to do this is to gradually increase intake over time (intestinal problems may occur if too much fiber is consumed suddenly) and drink at least eight 8-ounce glasses of water a day.

AN OVERVIEW OF GOOD SOURCES OF FIBER*

SOURCE	AMOUNT OF FIBER	SOURCE	AMOUNT OF FIBER
Apple (1 medium)	4 g	Plain bagel (½ bagel)	1 g
Blueberries (½ cup)	4 g	Whole-wheat bread (1 slice)	2 g
Pear (1 medium)	4.5 g	Brown rice, cooked (½ cup)	2 g
Broccoli, cooked (½ cup)	2 g	Whole-wheat spaghetti, cooked (½ cup)	3 g
Carrots, cooked (½ cup)	3 g	Oatmeal, cooked (¾ cup)	3 g
Potato with skin, baked (1 medium)	6 g	Chunky peanut butter (2 tablespoons)	1.5 g
Hummus (½ cup)	5 g	Popcorn, popped (1 cup)	1 g
Lentils, cooked (½ cup)	8 g		

* Values derived from 2005 USDA National Nutrient Database for Standard Reference, Release 18.

Cooking Grains 101

From amaranth to wheat berries, types of grains and the best methods for cooking them can vary tremendously. Some grains, such as bulgur, cook in minutes, while others, such as barley, must be simmered for close to an hour. We homed in on three basic methods for cooking grains, and then determined which ones are best for each type of grain. While one method may be ideal for cooking quinoa, it may not work well for millet. Grains in their simplest form, cooked in the pilaf style, have a light and fluffy texture and are more flavorful than their simmered or microwaved counterparts. Toasting the grains in oil is the source of much of that flavor, while cooking the grains covered over low heat and letting them stand before fluffing with a fork contributes to their fluffy texture. Follow the chart below; each recipe makes enough to serve 3 to 4.

STOVETOP DIRECTIONS

Bring the water to a boil in a large saucepan. Stir in the grain and 2½ teaspoons salt. Return to a boil, then reduce to a simmer and cook until the grain is tender, following the cooking time given in the chart. Drain the grain through a fine-mesh strainer.

PILAF DIRECTIONS

Rinse the grain in a fine-mesh strainer until the water runs clear. Heat 1 teaspoon oil in a small saucepan over medium-high heat. Add the grain and toast it until it turns light golden and smells toasted, about 3 minutes. Stir in the water and ¼ teaspoon salt. Bring the mixture to a boil, then reduce the heat to low, cover, and cook until the grain is tender and has absorbed all the water, following the cooking time given in the chart. Off the heat, let the grain stand for 5 minutes. Fluff the grain with a fork.

MICROWAVE DIRECTIONS

Rinse the grain in a fine-mesh strainer until the water runs clear. Combine the water, grain, 1 teaspoon oil, and ¼ teaspoon salt in a large microwave-safe bowl and cover tightly with plastic wrap. Microwave the grain, following the time and temperature given in the chart. Remove the grain from the microwave and fluff with a fork. Re-cover with plastic wrap and poke several vent holes in the plastic wrap with the tip of a paring knife. Let the grain sit until completely tender, about 5 minutes.

TYPE OF GRAIN	COOKING METHOD	AMOUNT OF GRAIN	AMOUNT OF WATER	COOKING TIME
AMARANTH*	Stovetop	X	X	X
	Microwave	1 cup	2 cups	5 to 10 minutes on high, then 15 to 20 minutes on medium
	Pilaf-style	1 cup	1½ cups	20 to 25 minutes
PEARL BARLEY	Stovetop	1 cup	4 quarts	20 to 25 minutes
	Microwave	X	X	X
	Pilaf-style	X	X	X
BUCKWHEAT (KASHA)	Stovetop	1 cup	4 quarts	5 minutes
	Microwave	X	X	X
	Pilaf-style	X	X	X
BULGUR**	Stovetop	1 cup	4 quarts	5 minutes
	Microwave	1 cup	1 cup	5 to 10 minutes on high
	Pilaf-style	1 cup	1 cup	10 to 15 minutes
MILLET***	Stovetop	X	X	X
	Microwave	X	X	X
	Pilaf-style	1 cup	2¼ cups	25 to 30 minutes
QUINOA	Stovetop	1 cup	4 quarts	10 to 15 minutes
	Microwave	1 cup	1 cup	5 minutes on medium, then 5 minutes on high
	Pilaf-style	1 cup	1 cup	10 to 15 minutes
WHEAT BERRIES	Stovetop	1 cup	4 quarts	1 hour
	Microwave	X	X	X
	Pilaf-style	X	X	X

*   Do not rinse.

**   For pilaf, skip rinsing and toasting steps.

***   For pilaf, increase the toasting time until the grains begin to pop, about 12 minutes.

X = not recommended

RICE PILAF

AT ITS MOST BASIC, RICE PILAF IS A LIGHT, simple dish, made rich and flavorful by sautéed aromatics and toasted rice. Classic pilaf technique hinges on sautéing long-grain rice in oil or butter until lightly browned and fragrant, before simmering it in—typically—either water or stock. The toasting teases out the rice's nuttiness and builds a deep flavor. More importantly though, it helps to create a light and fluffy pilaf with evenly cooked, discrete grains of rice (we should point out that this differs from regular steamed rice, which is usually starchy and more compact). When too much fat is used in making a pilaf (some classic recipes call for 1 cup of butter to cook 1 cup of rice!) it makes the finished dish greasy and dense. We were aware that we could not simply omit the fat, but we hoped to trim back the amount many recipes call for and find the perfect balance of fat and rice.

From previous testing of rice pilafs, we already had the basics of the perfect pilaf in place. We knew that long-grain rice— preferably basmati— was the best choice, as medium and short-grain rice, inherently starchy varieties, made sticky pilafs. Onion was chosen for its mellow flavor over piquant garlic. And as for cooking liquids, tasters preferred the simple, clean taste of water to chicken stock. Most important, we already had our ratio of rice to liquid down. Most sources indicate that the proper ratio of rice to liquid for long-grain white rice is 1 to 2, but many cooks use less water. After testing every possibility, from 1:1 to 1:2, we found that we made the best rice using 1⅔ cups of water for every 1 cup of rice. To

RINSING RICE OR GRAINS

Before cooking rice or grains, it's best to rinse them. This washes away any excess starch and prevents the final dish from turning out sticky or gummy. Simply place the rice or grain in a fine-mesh strainer and rinse under cool water until the water runs clear, occasionally stirring the rice or grains around lightly with your hand. Set the strainer of rinsed rice or grain over a bowl and let drain until needed.

INGREDIENTS: Long-Grain Rice

The beauty of white rice resides in its neutral flavor, which makes it good at carrying other flavors. But is all long-grain white rice created equal? We set up a taste test to find out.

We rounded up a converted rice, three standard supermarket options, and an organic white rice available in bulk from a natural food store. The most noticeable difference was an unpredictable variance in cooking time. According to the U.S. Rice Producers Association, the age of the rice, its moisture content, and the variety used can affect the rate of water uptake. Inconsistent cooking times are barely noticeable in plain rice, but they can become more apparent when other ingredients—such as aromatics and vegetables—are added to the pot.

All rices but one were noted for being "clean" and "like rice should be." The exception was Uncle Ben's, a converted rice that failed to meet our standards on all fronts. Converted rice is processed in a way that ensures separate grains, a firm texture, and more pronounced flavor. Those "round," "rubbery"

grains and the telltale yellowish tint immediately brought back not-so-fond memories of "dining hall rice." Tasters agreed that some "stickiness" and minor "clumping" make for more natural-looking and better-tasting rice. The recommended brands were universally liked.

THE BEST LONG-GRAIN RICE

The flavor of Canilla Extra Long (left) was likened to that of jasmine rice, and tasters found Carolina Extra Long Grain Enriched Rice (center) to have a good, clean slate on which to add flavor. Sem-Chi Organically Grown Florida Long Grain Rice (right) was rated the chewiest, with roasted and nutty flavors.

make this easier to remember, as well as easier to measure, we simply increased the rice by half to 1½ cups and the liquid to 2½ cups.

In previous testing, we had learned a few classic tricks to help create a perfectly fluffy pilaf. The first is to thoroughly rinse the rice in four to five changes of cold water, or until the water runs clear enough to see the grains distinctly. We believe this step to be essential for producing rice with separate, light, and fluffy grains. Second, we discovered that allowing the rice to steam for 10 minutes after being removed from the heat ensures that the moisture gets evenly distributed throughout. In addition, we found that placing a clean kitchen towel

EQUIPMENT: Large Saucepans

In the test kitchen (and at home), most of us reach for a 3- to 4-quart saucepan more than any other because its uses go beyond boiling water. This begs an obvious question: Does the brand of pan matter? With prices for these large saucepans ranging from $24.99 for a Revere stainless steel model with thin copper cladding at the base up to $140 for an All-Clad pan with a complete aluminum core and stainless steel interior and exterior cladding, a lot of money is riding on the answer. We tested eight models, all between 3 and 4 quarts in size, from well-known cookware manufacturers.

The tests we performed were based on common cooking tasks and designed to highlight specific characteristics of the pans' performance. Sautéing minced onions illustrated the pace at which the pan heats up and sautés. Cooking white rice provided a good indication of the pan's ability to heat evenly as well as how tightly the lid sealed. Making pastry cream let us know how user-friendly the pan was—was it shaped such that a whisk could reach into the corners without trouble, was it comfortable to pick up, and could we pour liquid from it neatly? These traits can make a real difference when you use a pan day in and day out.

Of the tests we performed, sautéing onions was the most telling. In our view, onions should soften reliably and evenly (and with minimal attention and stirring) when sautéed over medium heat. In this regard, the All-Clad, Calphalon, KitchenAid, and Sitram pans all delivered. The Chantal and Cuisinart pans sautéed slightly faster, necessitating a little more attention from the cook, but still well within acceptable bounds. Only the Revere and Farberware Millennium sautéed so fast that we considered them problematic.

Incidentally, the Revere and Farberware pans that sautéed onions too fast for us were the lightest pans of the bunch, weighing only 1 pound 10 ounces and 2 pounds 6 ounces, respectively. This indicates that they were made from thinner metal, which is one reason they heat up quickly. On the flip side of the weight issue, however, we found that too heavy a pan, such as the 4-pound Calphalon, could be uncomfortable to lift when full. The ideal was about 3½ pounds; pans near this weight, including the All-Clad, KitchenAid, Chantal, Sitram, and Cuisinart, balanced good heft with easy maneuverability.

While none of the pans failed the rice test outright, there were performance differences. In the Sitram, Revere, and Farberware pans, the rice stuck and dried out at the bottom, if only a little bit. Although this did not greatly affect the texture, the flavor, or the cleanup, we'd still choose a pan for which this was not an issue.

Every pan in the group turned out perfect pastry cream. During this test, we did observe one design element that made it easy to pour liquid from the pan neatly, without dribbles and spills. A rolled lip that flares slightly at the top of the pan helped control the pour. Only two pans in the group did not have a rolled lip: the All-Clad and the Calphalon.

So which pan should you buy? That depends largely on two things: your budget and your attention span. Based on our tests, we'd advise against really inexpensive pans—those that cost less than $50. For between $50 and $100, you can get a competent pan such as the Chantal, Sitram, or Cuisinart. The only caveat is that you may have to watch them carefully; they offer less room for error than our favorite pans, made by All-Clad, Calphalon, and KitchenAid.

THE BEST LARGE SAUCEPAN

The All-Clad (left), Calphalon (center), and KitchenAid (right) saucepans are our favorites, but they are not flawless. The Calphalon ($110) is heavy, both it and the All-Clad pan ($140) lack rolled lips, and the KitchenAid pan ($119) has a relatively short curved handle. However, these three pans provide moderate, steady heat, which guards against food scorching or burning if you turn your back for a moment.

(or two layers of paper towels) between the pan and the lid, right after removing the rice from the heat, prevents condensation from forming. The towel absorbs the excess condensation, preventing water from dripping back into the pan during steaming, which in turn produces drier, fluffier rice.

With our pilaf basics in place, we were ready to test the traditional rice toasting method using less fat. We made four separate pilafs, each with a different amount of fat—1 teaspoon, 2 teaspoons, 1 tablespoon, and 2 tablespoons—and lined up the finished products for a side-by-side tasting. Right off the bat tasters complained that the pilaf made with 1 teaspoon of fat was too dry and sticky; one participant commented that it tasted like reheated Chinese take-out rice. Two teaspoons proved a bit more promising; however, it produced a pilaf that was a bit clumpy and dry, as if the rice grains didn't get coated with enough fat. Overall though, we agreed that 2 teaspoons made a pilaf with a good lightness—a step in the right direction. The winner wound up being 1 tablespoon of fat, which beat out 2 tablespoons, an amount that tasters complained was a tad too heavy. One tablespoon of fat perfectly coated the rice, making the grains separate and tender, and giving the pilaf a good balance of flavor and moisture.

Up until this point in the process we performed our tests using olive oil. Some tasters wondered if butter would give the rice a nuttier toasted flavor than olive oil. This made sense to

us in theory; however, when we pitted the two fats against one another we found that tasters detected nary a difference. We settled on olive oil because of its health benefits and absence of saturated fat, but either fat would be acceptable in this recipe.

The addition of flavorings, seasonings, and other ingredients is what gives a pilaf its distinctive character. Because we wanted to keep our pilafs light, we looked to lighter ingredients with bold flavors, such as citrus zest, scallions, and tomato paste. We found that dried spices, chiles, and onion and garlic are best sautéed in the fat before the raw rice is added to the pan. Saffron is best added to the liquid as it heats up, while fresh herbs and toasted nuts should be added to the pilaf just before serving to maximize freshness, texture (in the case of nuts), and flavor. Frozen peas and dried fruits such as raisins, currants, or figs can be incorporated just before steaming the rice, which gives them enough time to heat through and plump up.

Basic Pilaf-Style Rice
SERVES 6

In Middle Eastern cuisines, the term "pilaf" also refers to a more substantial dish in which the rice is cooked using the pilaf method and then flavored with other ingredients like spices, nuts, dried fruits, and sometimes chicken or other meat. To avoid confusion, we decided to call the simple master recipe for our dish "pilaf-style" rice, designating the flavored versions as rice pilaf. A wide-bottomed saucepan with a tight-fitting lid works best for evenly cooked rice. We prefer olive oil for this dish, but butter can be used as well.

2½ cups water
    Salt and ground black pepper
1 small onion, chopped fine
1 tablespoon olive oil
1½ cups basmati or plain long-grain rice, rinsed (see the illustration on page 131)

1. Bring the water to a boil, covered, in a small saucepan. Add 1 teaspoon salt and season with pepper to taste; cover to keep hot.

STEAMING RICE

After the rice is cooked, cover the pan with a clean kitchen towel, replace the lid, and allow the pan to sit for 10 minutes.

2. Meanwhile, combine the onion, oil, and ½ teaspoon salt in a large saucepan. Cover and cook over medium-low heat, stirring occasionally, until the onion is softened, 8 to 10 minutes.

3. Increase the heat to medium, add the rice, and stir to coat the grains with oil. Cook until the edges of the grains begin to turn translucent, about 3 minutes. Stir in the hot seasoned water and bring to a boil. Reduce the heat to low, cover, and simmer until all the water is absorbed, 16 to 18 minutes.

4. Remove the pot from the heat and lay a clean, folded kitchen towel underneath the lid (see the illustration on page 133). Let stand for 10 minutes, then fluff the rice with a fork and season with salt and pepper to taste.

PER SERVING: Cal 180; Fat 2.5 g; Sat Fat 0 g; Chol 0 mg; Carb 37 g; Protein 3 g; Fiber 0 g; Sodium 200 mg

➤ VARIATIONS

Rice Pilaf with Peas, Scallions, and Lemon

The simple flavors of this pilaf pair well with roast chicken or grilled fish.

Follow the recipe for Basic Pilaf-Style Rice, adding ⅛ teaspoon red pepper flakes, 2 medium garlic cloves, minced or pressed through a garlic press, and 1 teaspoon grated zest from 1 lemon to the pot with the onion. Before covering the rice with the kitchen towel in step 4, sprinkle ½ cup frozen peas over the top (do not mix in). Let stand as directed, then add 1 tablespoon lemon juice and 2 scallions, sliced thin, when fluffing the rice.

PER SERVING: Cal 200; Fat 2.5 g; Sat Fat 0 g; Chol 0 mg; Carb 40 g; Protein 4 g; Fiber 1 g; Sodium 220 mg

Rice Pilaf with Currants and Toasted Almonds

The combination of dried fruits and nuts in a pilaf is classic. When toasting the almonds, note that they can go from toasted to burnt and inedible very quickly (see page 45).

Follow the recipe for Basic Pilaf-Style Rice, adding ½ teaspoon turmeric, ¼ teaspoon ground cinnamon, and 2 garlic cloves, minced or pressed through a garlic press, to the pot with the onion.

Before covering the rice with the kitchen towel in step 4, sprinkle ¼ cup currants over the top (do not mix in). Let stand as directed, then add ¼ cup toasted sliced almonds when fluffing the rice.

PER SERVING: Cal 220; Fat 4.5 g; Sat Fat 0 g; Chol 0 mg; Carb 43 g; Protein 4 g; Fiber 1 g; Sodium 200 mg

Rice Pilaf with Mexican Flavors

This variation is based on authentic Mexican rice; however, our version is much quicker to prepare.

Follow the recipe for Basic Pilaf-Style Rice, adding 2 jalapeño chiles, stemmed, seeded, and minced, to the pot with the onion. Before adding the rice in step 3, stir in 1 tablespoon tomato paste and 2 garlic cloves, minced or pressed through a garlic press, and cook until fragrant, about 30 seconds. Before covering the rice with the kitchen towel in step 4, add ¼ cup minced fresh cilantro leaves and 1 medium tomato, halved, seeded, and diced small (about ½ cup)—but do not mix in. When fluffing the rice with a fork, add 1 tablespoon juice from 1 lime.

PER SERVING: Cal 190; Fat 2.5 g; Sat Fat 0 g; Chol 0 mg; Carb 39 g; Protein 4 g; Fiber 1 g; Sodium 200 mg

TEST KITCHEN MAKEOVER

RISOTTO

RISOTTO IS A SIMPLE DISH ELEVATED TO ambrosia by the presence of a simple starchy sauce. Teased out and enriched by judicious additions of wine and stock, the starch in the rice creates a velvety, creamy sauce that clings to the "al dente" cooked grains. Classically, lots of butter and cheese are added to boost the richness and silkiness of the sauce in this Italian rice dish. Could we make a somewhat leaner risotto that didn't taste so, well, lean?

From previous testing, we already knew a lot about the perfect risotto. Starting with the rice, we knew Italian medium-grain rice was a must and that tasters preferred the widely available Arborio variety to the hard-to-find, esoteric Carnaroli and Vialone Nano varieties. In our testing, Arborio worked double duty to create the characteristic supple sauce as well as the firm bite we were looking for. The other varieties yielded a nice creamy sauce but produced soft grains that lacked the slightly resistant texture we were after.

But having good-quality rice was only half the battle; cooking was the rest. After making countless batches with minute variations, we became certain about a few points. First, slowly cooking diced onion until it yielded its juices and softened was imperative to the final flavor and texture of the dish. And using a healthier technique we developed (see page 63)—in which we traded in the butter for just 1 teaspoon of oil, covered the pot, and allowed the whole to sweat—cut significant fat from our dish.

Second, toasting the rice until aromatic and translucent at the edges was crucial for avoiding a mushy and chalky risotto, and it also gave us a good visual cue for when to start adding liquid. We learned that the order in which the liquids are added to the rice is also important. The wine must be added before the broth so that any harsh alcohol flavor has a chance to cook off, and we discovered that virtually all risottos are made with a light, dry white wine (although there are some regional Italian specialties made with red wine). Risotto made without wine lacks dimension and tastes bland, so don't skip this ingredient.

As far as what type of broth to use, the recipes we researched offered a wide range of options, from plain water to veal stock. Water did little for us, and veal stock is rare in all but the best-provisioned professional kitchens. Straight beef broth and chicken broth proved too intense, but diluting chicken broth with some water was just right.

Our next discovery was quite surprising and ran contrary to conventional wisdom and most cookbook instructions: Constant stirring of the risotto is unnecessary. We added half the broth once the wine had cooked off and allowed the rice to simmer for about 10 minutes, or half the cooking time, with little attention. During this period, we stirred the rice infrequently—about every three minutes—to ensure that it was not sticking to the bottom of the pan. Once the rice absorbed the broth, we added more, a half cup at a time. For this period, stirring every minute or so was important; if we did not, the rice stuck to the bottom of the pan.

Finally, we looked at our findings on risotto doneness, a controversial topic to say the least. Some insist that perfectly cooked risotto should have a chalky, solid bite, while others feel it should be soft to the core. We concluded that doneness is a matter of individual preference, and found the best way to test for it is to begin tasting the rice near the completion of cooking (after about 20 minutes).

With the basics of making our risotto all lined up, we were ready to tackle the butter and cheese issue. Our goal, obviously, was to create a lighter risotto that contained the least amount of butter and cheese possible, without compromising taste and texture. Aware that the starch in the rice is responsible for the velvety texture of the sauce, we determined that the rich dairy element of the dish should complement the sauce rather than overwhelm it. We started our tests by cooking four risottos, each made with a different amount of butter: one with 3 tablespoons, another with 2 tablespoons, one with 1 tablespoon, and lastly a risotto with no butter at all. We finished each risotto by stirring the butter in at the end of cooking when the pan was off the heat. A traditional risotto technique, its purpose is to enrich the dish—the Italians call it *mantecato,* or "the beating."

The usual 3 tablespoons of butter tasted great, but added too much fat to our light risotto. Nobody cared much for the risotto with no butter. We observed that a proper risotto really needs some butter, as the creamy fat diminishes the subtle tacky character of the starchy sauce. All tasting participants, however, had trouble choosing a favorite between the risotto made with 2 tablespoons of butter and the one made with 1 tablespoon. In the end, tasters settled on 1 tablespoon of butter, rationalizing that, by omitting the 11 grams of fat and 100 calories that an extra tablespoon of butter would add, they could afford to splurge and sprinkle the finished risotto with a little extra Parmesan cheese.

We finally turned our attention to the Parmesan cheese. Traditionally, the Parmesan goes in at the very end to preserve its distinctive flavor and aroma. Grated cheese proved best, as it melted almost instantaneously. We tried to reduce the amount of cheese typically called for in risotto recipes, but our tasters spoke loud and clear— nothing but the full 2 ounces (about 1 cup of grated cheese) would do. We weren't too concerned about this amount of cheese, as Parmesan packs a lot of flavor without adding too many calories and fat grams. And with only 6 grams of fat and 220 calories per generous 1-cup serving of risotto, we could afford to pass a little extra grated cheese at the table.

One last note: the quality of the cheese is paramount, as its taste is so prominent. This is the

perfect occasion for buying authentic Parmigiano-Reggiano freshly cut from the wheel, with its branded trademark boldly displayed on the rind.

Parmesan Risotto

SERVES 6

This is risotto at its simplest. It can accompany a variety of meals, from grilled or braised meats to a mélange of roasted vegetables. Parmesan risotto is also appropriate as a first course. Don't fret if you have broth left over once the rice is finished cooking; different brands of rice all cook differently, and we prefer to err on the side of slightly too much broth rather than too little.

4	cups low-sodium chicken broth
3	cups water
1	medium onion, chopped fine
1	teaspoon olive oil
	Salt
2	cups Arborio rice
1	cup dry white wine
2	ounces grated Parmesan cheese (about 1 cup)
1	tablespoon unsalted butter
	Ground black pepper

1. Bring the broth and water to a simmer in a medium saucepan; reduce the heat to the lowest possible setting and cover to keep warm.

2. Meanwhile, combine the onion, oil, and ½ teaspoon salt in a large saucepan. Cover and cook over medium-low heat, stirring occasionally, until the onion is softened, 8 to 10 minutes. Increase the heat to medium, add the rice, and cook, stirring frequently, until the edges of the grains are transparent, about 4 minutes. Stir in the wine and continue to cook, stirring frequently, until the wine has been completely absorbed, about 2 minutes.

3. Stir in 3 cups of the warm broth and simmer, stirring occasionally, until the liquid is absorbed and the bottom of the pan is dry, 10 to 12 minutes.

4. Continue to cook the risotto, stirring frequently and adding ½ cup of the remaining broth at a time as needed to keep the pan bottom from becoming dry (about every 4 minutes), until the grains of rice are cooked through but still somewhat firm in the center, 10 to 12 minutes. Off

---

MAKEOVER AT A GLANCE

–Classic–
Parmesan Risotto
(per serving)

Calories: 300	Cholesterol: 35 mg
Fat: 15 g	Saturated Fat: 9 g

–Light–
Parmesan Risotto
(per serving)

Calories: 220	Cholesterol: 10 mg
Fat: 6 g	Saturated Fat: 3 g

How We Did It

- Sweat the onion in a covered saucepan using only 1 teaspoon of oil to draw out moisture and concentrate flavors
- Limited the butter to 1 tablespoon stirred in at the end of cooking, just enough fat to add richness and balance
- Used the highest-quality Parmesan cheese for the greatest depth of flavor

the heat, stir in the cheese and butter, and season with salt and pepper to taste. Serve immediately in warmed shallow bowls.

PER SERVING: Cal 220; Fat 6 g; Sat fat 3 g; Chol 10 mg; Carb 27 g; Protein 7 g; Fiber 1 g; Sodium 750 mg

➤ VARIATIONS

Saffron Risotto with Peas

Also known as risotto alla Milanese in honor of the city of Milan, saffron risotto is one of the simplest and best variations on basic risotto. We like to toss in a nontraditional handful of frozen peas at the end of cooking. See below for more information on buying saffron.

Follow the recipe for Parmesan Risotto, adding ⅛ teaspoon crumbled saffron threads to the pot with the rice. Before stirring in the Parmesan and butter in step 4, stir in ½ cup frozen peas and allow them to warm through, about 3 minutes.

PER SERVING: Cal 230; Fat 6 g; Sat fat 3 g; Chol 10 mg; Carb 29 g; Protein 8 g; Fiber 2 g; Sodium 760 mg

INGREDIENTS: Saffron

While many people know that saffron is the most expensive spice in the world, few are aware that it is grown in a variety of locations and that its price and quality can vary considerably. Though the bulk of commercially produced saffron comes from Spain and Iran, it is also harvested on a small scale in India, Greece, France, and, closer to home, in Lancaster County, Pennsylvania. We decided to toss saffron from different places purchased at different prices into a few pots and set up a test. We prepared three batches of Saffron Risotto—the purest way to taste the subtle differences and discern the different shades of orange—and flavored one with Spanish saffron, one with Indian, and one with American.

The finished risottos were similar in hue, though the Indian "Kashmir" saffron threads were darkest prior to cooking. In a blind tasting, we overwhelmingly chose the Pennsylvania-grown saffron over both the Spanish and Indian, judging it the "most potent" and "most perfumed" of the three. Surprisingly, no one cared much for the Indian saffron, which is almost twice as costly as the other two and is generally regarded as one of the best in the world. Greider's Saffron is exclusively available from the Pennsylvania General store (www.pageneralstore.com).

Butternut Squash Risotto with Sage and Toasted Almonds

Squash that's in season really makes this dish, and when combined with sage and a touch of nutmeg—two classic flavors with squash—it creates more than just a side dish.

Follow the recipe for Parmesan Risotto, adding a pinch of nutmeg and 3 cups butternut squash (about 1 pound) cut into ½-inch cubes, with the broth in step 3. Stir in 2 teaspoons minced fresh sage leaves with the Parmesan and butter, and sprinkle with ¼ cup toasted sliced almonds (see page 45) before serving.

PER SERVING: Cal 270; Fat 8 g; Sat fat 3 g; Chol 10 mg; Carb 37 g; Protein 9 g; Fiber 3 g; Sodium 750 mg

Asparagus Risotto with Lemon

The flavors in this dish are light, making it a suitable accompaniment to broiled or poached salmon or a simple roast chicken. It is essential to use thin asparagus for this recipe, so that it cooks through by the time the rice is done.

Follow the recipe for Parmesan Risotto, adding 1 pound thin asparagus spears, tough ends removed and cut on the bias into ½-inch lengths, to the pot after the first addition of broth has simmered for just 6 minutes in step 4. Stir in ½ teaspoon grated zest from 1 lemon with the Parmesan and butter, and serve with lemon wedges.

PER SERVING: Cal 240; Fat 6 g; Sat fat 3 g; Chol 10 mg; Carb 31 g; Protein 9 g; Fiber 2 g; Sodium 750 mg

BARLEY RISOTTO

BARLEY HAS BEEN AROUND FOR THOUSANDS of years as a staple for a number of ancient civilizations. Today, in this country, it is mostly used in beer and whiskey production or in soups such as beef barley or mushroom barley. In an effort to find other ways to incorporate this wholesome grain into our diet, we decided to approach it as a side dish. Our research turned up a number of barley dishes with a recurring theme: the barley is prepared using a risotto cooking method. This technique piqued our curiosity and seemed like a great way to enjoy this ancient grain. We headed into the test kitchen to see if barley would work using our existing low-fat risotto method.

First we decided to learn more about the grain itself. Barley is sold in numerous forms—hulled, pearl, Scotch, and flake to name a few—however, we were most concerned with hulled and pearl, the two whole forms of the grain. (The other forms are crushed or flattened; not really the consistencies we were after.) Hulled barley is the most nutritious form of barley on the market, although it is not that easy to find. It is sold with the hull removed and the fiber-rich bran still intact, which causes long cooking times and an unavoidable chewy texture. For these reasons it did not strike us as a feasible option, so we turned our attention to the widely available pearl barley.

Basically, pearl barley is hulled barley that has been polished until the bran is gone. With the bran removed, the cooking time is substantially reduced and the texture of the grain becomes springy when cooked (a texture similar to that of perfectly cooked Arborio rice). Also, because the bran is removed, the grain's starchy interior is exposed, which creates a supple, velvety sauce when simmered (much the same as the sauce in risotto). While not quite as nutritious as hulled barley, pearl barley is still fairly nutrient rich and has a decent amount of fiber.

With our choice of barley nailed down, we decided to use our existing risotto method to cook the pearl barley. We started by sautéing onions until soft, and then we added the barley, which we sautéed until it was nutty and aromatic. Next, we added the wine and cooked the mixture until the pan turned dry. At this point we ladled hot broth into the pot in stages, until the grains were cooked al dente (meaning the grains were cooked through but still somewhat firm in the center). We finished the dish with a handful of grated Parmesan cheese and a small amount of butter (1 tablespoon) for richness and to subdue the tackiness of the starchy sauce. We determined that this method worked well, but we needed to make one minor adjustment: Because pearl barley takes longer to cook than Arborio rice, we needed to have a bit more hot liquid on hand to allow the barley more time to cook through. We upped the water amount by 1 cup, which worked great.

With the cooking technique under control, all we had to do now was boost the flavor of the risotto just a bit with the addition of a few new ingredients. For our basic recipe, we turned to simple flavors that would elevate and complement the barley's subtle earthy flavor. Chopped carrot, sautéed along with the onion, added a bit of welcome sweetness and depth, and a small amount of minced fresh thyme lent a woodsy flavor that tasters liked.

In creating a variation, we also found success with stronger flavors like mushrooms, red wine, and rosemary. We discovered that a combination of fresh, earthy-flavored cremini mushrooms and intense, dried porcini mushrooms added much flavor. And the addition of red wine complemented the mushrooms. Omitting the carrot in our variation made sense, as its sweetness clashed with the fruity notes of the red wine. Finally, we traded in the thyme for some minced fresh rosemary (a classic pairing with mushrooms), which tasters preferred for its assertive perfume. They found that the rosemary stood up well to the other strong flavors in the risotto. While no one will mistake barley risotto for traditional risotto, it is a unique and flavorful alternative and pairs well with dishes like roast chicken, beef tenderloin, or grilled vegetables.

Barley Risotto
SERVES 6

Pearl barley is crucial for this risotto and is widely available in supermarkets. We find that this dish is best when garnished with minced fresh parsley and lemon wedges. You may not need to use all of the broth when finishing this risotto (we prefer to err on the side of having a little extra).

4	cups low-sodium chicken broth
4	cups water
1	medium onion, chopped fine
1	medium carrot, peeled and chopped fine
1	teaspoon olive oil
	Salt

1½ cups pearl barley, rinsed (see the illustration on page 131)

1 cup dry white wine

1 teaspoon minced fresh thyme leaves

2 ounces grated Parmesan cheese (about 1 cup)

1 tablespoon unsalted butter

Ground black pepper

1. Bring the broth and water to a simmer in a medium saucepan; reduce the heat to the lowest

REHYDRATING DRIED PORCINI MUSHROOMS

We find that the microwave cuts soaking time for dried porcini from 20 to 30 minutes at room temperature to just 5 minutes. Place the dried porcini in a small strainer and rinse under cool running water. Transfer the porcini to a microwave-safe bowl, add ½ cup hot tap water, and cover with plastic wrap. Cut several steam vents in the plastic wrap and microwave on high power for 30 seconds. Remove the bowl from the microwave and let stand, covered, until the mushrooms soften, about 5 minutes. Here's how to remove the softened mushrooms from the liquid and leave the sand behind.

1. When soaking dried porcini mushrooms, most of the sand and dirt will fall to the bottom of the bowl. Use a fork to lift the rehydrated mushrooms from the liquid without stirring up the sand. If the mushrooms still feel gritty, rinse them briefly under cool running water.

2. The soaking liquid is quite flavorful and should be reserved. To remove the grit, pour the liquid through a small strainer lined with a coffee filter or a single sheet of paper towel and set over a measuring cup.

possible setting and cover to keep warm.

2. Meanwhile, combine the onion, carrot, oil, and ½ teaspoon salt in a large saucepan. Cover and cook over medium-low heat, stirring occasionally, until the vegetables are softened, 8 to 10 minutes. Increase the heat to medium, add the barley, and cook, stirring frequently, until lightly browned and aromatic, about 4 minutes. Stir in the wine and continue to cook, stirring frequently, until the wine has been completely absorbed by the barley, about 2 minutes.

3. Stir in the thyme and 3 cups of the warm broth and simmer, stirring occasionally, until the liquid is absorbed and the bottom of the pan is dry, 10 to 12 minutes. Stir in 2 more cups of the warm broth and continue to simmer, stirring occasionally, until the liquid is absorbed and the bottom of the pan is dry, 10 to 12 minutes longer.

4. Continue to cook the risotto, stirring frequently and adding ½ cup of the remaining broth at a time as needed to keep the pan bottom from becoming dry (about every 4 minutes), until the grains of barley are cooked through but still somewhat firm in the center, about 20 minutes. Off the heat, stir in the Parmesan and butter, and season with salt and pepper to taste. Serve immediately in warmed shallow bowls.

PER SERVING: Cal 290; Fat 6 g; Sat Fat 3 g; Chol 10 mg; Carb 43 g; Protein 10 g; Fiber 9 g; Sodium 760 mg

➤ VARIATION

Barley Risotto with Mushrooms and Red Wine

We found that a medium bodied, dry red wine, such as Merlot, worked perfectly in this dish. This full-flavored risotto is best garnished with a little extra grated Parmesan cheese.

4 cups low-sodium chicken broth

4 cups water

1 medium onion, chopped fine

2 teaspoons olive oil
Salt

8 ounces cremini (preferably) or white mushrooms, wiped clean, trimmed, and quartered (or cut into 6 pieces if large)

½ ounce dried porcini mushrooms, rehydrated, mushrooms minced and rehydrating liquid strained (see the illustrations on page 139)

1½ cups pearl barley, rinsed (see the illustration on page 131)

1 cup dry red wine

1 teaspoon minced fresh rosemary

2 ounces grated Parmesan cheese (about 1 cup)

1 tablespoon unsalted butter

Ground black pepper

1. Bring the broth and water to a simmer in a medium saucepan; reduce the heat to the lowest possible setting and cover to keep warm.

2. Meanwhile, combine the onion, 1 teaspoon of the oil, and ½ teaspoon salt in a large saucepan. Cover and cook, stirring occasionally, until the onion is softened, 8 to 10 minutes. Stir in the remaining teaspoon oil, cremini mushrooms, and porcini mushrooms. Increase the heat to medium-high and continue to cook, uncovered, until the cremini begin to brown, about 4 minutes.

3. Add the barley, reduce the heat to medium, and cook, stirring frequently, until the barley is lightly browned and aromatic, about 4 minutes. Stir in the wine and continue to cook, stirring frequently, until the wine has been completely absorbed, about 2 minutes.

4. Stir in the rosemary, strained porcini liquid, and 3 cups of the warm broth. Simmer, stirring occasionally, until the liquid is absorbed and the bottom of the pan is dry, 10 to 12 minutes. Stir in 2 more cups of the warm broth and continue to simmer, stirring occasionally, until the liquid is absorbed and the bottom of the pan is dry, 10 to 12 minutes longer.

5. Continue to cook the risotto, stirring frequently and adding ½ cup of the remaining broth at a time as needed to keep the pan bottom from becoming dry (about every 4 minutes), until the grains of barley are cooked through but still somewhat firm in the center, about 20 minutes. Off the heat, stir in the Parmesan and butter, and season with salt and pepper to taste. Serve immediately in warmed shallow bowls.

PER SERVING: Cal 310; Fat 7 g; Sat fat 3 g; Chol 10 mg; Carb 45 g; Protein 11 g; Fiber 9 g; Sodium 760 mg

BROWN RICE

BROWN RICE AND WHITE RICE ARE CUT from the same cloth so to speak—white rice being a permutation of processed brown rice. The difference is that each grain of brown rice still has the bran attached, a nutrient-rich coating, brown in color. Healthy by design, brown rice is a good source of fiber and is considered a whole grain. (See page 129 for more information on fiber.) We wondered why brown rice wasn't on our dinner plate nearly as much as white rice, so we headed into the kitchen to find out.

The first thing we learned is that the bran, while dense with nutrients, also complicates the cooking of brown rice. The tough bran makes it difficult for liquid to permeate the grain, which in turn causes unevenly cooked rice. At its worst, brown rice can be a wet, dense, sticky mess of unevenly cooked grains—a totally inedible disaster. Yet, when done right, perfectly cooked brown rice results in a fluffy pillow of nutty grains that have a slightly sticky texture with a hint of chew. We wanted the ideal brown rice every time, and we knew that the right cooking technique would be crucial in achieving this goal.

An ideal version of white rice is easy to come by: Just throw rice and water in a pot and set the timer. Yet cooks who have attempted to prepare brown rice know it isn't that simple. Most cooks make the mistake (born of impatience) of cranking up the flame in an effort to hurry along the slow-cooking grains (brown rice takes roughly twice as long to cook as white), which inevitably leads to a burnt pot and crunchy rice. Adding plenty of water isn't the remedy, either; excess liquid swells the rice into a gelatinous, wet mass.

We used an expensive, heavy-bottomed pot with a tight-fitting lid (many recipes caution against using inadequate cookware), fiddled with the traditional absorption method (cooking the rice with just enough water), and eventually landed on a workable recipe. Yet when we tested the recipe with less-than-ideal equipment—namely, a flimsy pan with an ill-fitting lid—we were back to burnt, underdone rice. With the very best pot and a top-notch stove, it is possible to cook brown rice properly, but we wanted a surefire method that would work for every cook, no matter the equipment.

Although we rarely use the microwave, we thought it might work well in this instance, given that it cooks food indirectly, without a burner. Sadly, it delivered inconsistent results, with one batch turning brittle and another, prepared in a different microwave, too sticky. A rice cooker yielded flawless brown rice on the first try, but many cooks don't own one.

We set out to construct a homemade cooker that would approximate the controlled, indirect heat of a rice cooker. We started with an everyday collapsible vegetable steamer and lined the steamer basket successively with cheesecloth, a coffee filter, and a thin kitchen towel. In each case, it was impossible to stir neatly and consistently during cooking, and the result was irregularly cooked rice. A long-handled fine-mesh strainer used in place of the steamer also failed; the strainer's handle precluded a tight seal between pot rim and lid, and the rice was still raw after two hours.

We then began to consider the merits of cooking the rice in the oven. We'd have more precise temperature control, and we figured that the oven's encircling heat would eliminate the risk of scorching. Our first try yielded extremely promising results: With the pan tightly covered in aluminum foil, the rice steamed to near perfection. Fine-tuning the amount of water, we settled on a ratio similar to that used for our white rice recipe: 2⅓ cups of water to 1½ cups of rice, falling well short of the 2:1 water-to-rice ratio advised by most rice producers and nearly every recipe we consulted. Perhaps that is why brown rice often turns out sodden and overcooked.

Our next task was to spruce up the recipe by bringing out the nutty flavor of the rice. Adding a small amount (1 tablespoon) of oil to the cooking liquid added mild flavor while keeping the rice fluffy. To reduce what was a long baking time of 90 minutes at 350 degrees, we tried starting with boiling water instead of cold tap water and raising the oven temperature to 375 degrees. These steps reduced the baking time to a reasonable one hour. (A hotter oven caused some of the fragile grains to explode.)

We were successful in clearing brown rice's bad reputation for being sticky, wet, and dense by creating a recipe that yielded light and fluffy grains. And everyone was pleased that we had developed a foolproof cooking method that didn't take up extra space on the stovetop. Our final objective, however, was to jazz things up a bit by creating a couple of bold flavor variations. We turned to flavorful low-fat ingredients that pair well with the subtle nuttiness of the rice. Tasters favored a combination of Parmesan, lemon, and fresh herbs, commenting that the dish's flavor seemed versatile enough to serve alongside almost any main course. And for a more assertively flavored rice, we settled on a mix of curry, tomatoes, and peas—easily a meal in itself.

Oven-Baked Brown Rice
SERVES 6
To minimize any loss of water through evaporation, cover the saucepan as the water is heating, and use the water as soon as it reaches a boil. If you own an 8-inch ceramic baking dish with a lid, use it instead of the glass baking dish and foil. To double the recipe, use a 13 by 9-inch baking dish; the baking time need not be increased.

1½	cups long-, medium-, or short-grain brown rice
2⅓	cups water
1	tablespoon olive oil
	Salt

1. Adjust an oven rack to the middle position and heat the oven to 375 degrees. Spread the rice in an 8-inch-square glass baking dish.

2. Bring the water and oil to a boil, covered, in a medium saucepan. Once the water is boiling, immediately stir in ½ teaspoon salt and pour the water over the rice. Cover the baking dish tightly with a double layer of foil and bake until the rice is tender, about 1 hour.

3. Remove the baking dish from the oven, uncover, and fluff the rice with a fork. Cover the dish with a clean kitchen towel and let stand for 5 minutes. Uncover and let the rice stand for 5 minutes longer before serving.

PER SERVING: Cal 190; Fat 3.5 g; Sat fat .5 g; Chol 0 mg; Carb 36 g; Protein 4 g; Fiber 2 g; Sodium 200 mg

➤ VARIATIONS

Brown Rice with Parmesan, Lemon, and Herbs

We strongly suggest avoiding dried herbs here, as fresh herbs really make this dish.

1½	cups long-, medium-, or short-grain brown rice
1	small onion, chopped fine
1	tablespoon olive oil
½	teaspoon salt
2⅓	cups low-sodium chicken broth
1	ounce Parmesan cheese, grated (about ½ cup)
¼	cup minced fresh parsley leaves
¼	cup minced fresh basil leaves
½	teaspoon juice and 1 teaspoon grated zest from 1 lemon
⅛	teaspoon ground black pepper

1. Adjust an oven rack to the middle position and heat the oven to 375 degrees. Spread the rice in an 8-inch-square glass baking dish.

2. Combine the onion, oil, and salt in a medium saucepan. Cover and cook over medium-low heat, stirring occasionally, until the onion is softened, 8 to 10 minutes. Stir in the chicken broth and bring to a boil, covered. Once the broth is boiling, immediately pour it over the rice. Cover the baking dish tightly with a double layer of foil and bake until the rice is tender, about 1 hour and 10 minutes.

3. Remove the baking dish from the oven, uncover, and fluff the rice with a fork. Stir in the Parmesan, parsley, basil, lemon juice, lemon zest, and pepper. Cover the dish with a clean kitchen towel and let stand for 5 minutes. Uncover and let the rice stand for 5 minutes longer before serving.

PER SERVING: Cal 220; Fat 5 g; Sat fat 1.5 g; Chol 5 mg; Carb 38 g; Protein 6 g; Fiber 2 g; Sodium 500 mg

Curried Brown Rice with Tomatoes and Peas

This is a hearty dish and makes for a nice light main course. If hot curry powder is too spicy, regular works just fine.

1½	cups long-, medium-, or short-grain brown rice
1	small onion, chopped medium
1	tablespoon grated fresh ginger
1	garlic clove, minced or pressed through a garlic press (about 1 teaspoon)
1	tablespoon olive oil
1½	teaspoons hot curry powder
½	teaspoon salt
1	(14.5-ounce) can diced tomatoes, drained
2⅓	cups low-sodium vegetable broth
½	cup frozen peas, thawed

1. Adjust an oven rack to the middle position and heat the oven to 375 degrees. Spread the rice in an 8-inch-square glass baking dish.

GETTING THE TEXTURE RIGHT

PROBLEM:
WET & SOUPY

PROBLEM:
BURNT & CRUNCHY

PERFECT:
FLUFFY & CHEWY

We found that following the directions on the back of the bag usually results in wet, porridge-like rice (left). Many recipes call for too much heat, and, unless you use a very heavy pot, the rice will scorch (center). By using less water than is typical and taking advantage of the even heat of the oven, you can turn out perfectly cooked brown rice every time (right).

2. Combine the onion, ginger, garlic, oil, curry powder, and salt in a medium saucepan. Cover and cook over medium-low heat, stirring occasionally, until the onion is softened, 8 to 10 minutes. Stir in the tomatoes and cook until heated through, about 2 minutes. Stir in the vegetable broth and bring to a boil, covered. Once the broth is boiling, immediately pour it over the rice and cover the baking dish tightly with a double layer of foil. Bake the rice until tender, about 1 hour and 10 minutes.

3. Remove the baking dish from the oven, uncover, and fluff the rice with a fork. Stir in the peas, cover the dish with a clean kitchen towel, and let stand for 5 minutes. Uncover and let the rice stand for 5 minutes longer before serving.

PER SERVING: Cal 230; Fat 4 g; Sat fat .5 g; Chol 0 mg; Carb 43 g; Protein 6 g; Fiber 3 g; Sodium 620 mg

COUSCOUS

A STAPLE IN NORTH AFRICA, COUSCOUS IS, technically, pasta. It is made from semolina flour "rolled" with lightly salted water until minute balls form; these are then steamed and dried for long-term storage. When it comes to cooking, couscous is treated more like a grain than pasta. Traditionally, it's cooked in a special pot called a couscoussier, which is essentially a stockpot fitted with a small-holed colander. The couscous sits in the colander and plumps in the steam produced by the pot's contents—stock, soup, or stew.

Because it's known for being a light and fluffy grain side dish, we were surprised by the amounts of oil and butter found in some of the couscous recipes we came across in our research. And after making and sampling some of them, we came to the conclusion that the extra fat usually made for a couscous dish that was dense and greasy. Tasters also agreed that the overabundance of fat also obscured any other flavors added to the couscous, rendering the entire dish bland. We knew that we could cut back on the fat and calories, but we were determined to create a couscous that was not only lighter, but also fluffy and packed with fresh, bright flavors.

When it comes to flavor, couscous is a relatively blank slate. This distinguishes it from other grains such as brown rice and quinoa, which have more pronounced aromatic flavors on their own. Therefore, we knew that if we were trimming back on the fat, we would have to rely on cooking technique and flavorful low-fat ingredients like fresh herbs, lemon, and onion to build bold layers of flavor in our couscous.

We first looked to earlier tests, where we had established the basics for making the perfect couscous. We had uncovered a simple method for making the dish, which we found to be the best. The first step is to toast the couscous in a bit of fat and then remove it from the pan, reserving it in a big bowl (the bowl is what we end up hydrating the couscous in). Next, more oil is added to the hot empty pan and then the aromatics (for example, onion and garlic) are sautéed. After they turn tender and golden and release their mellow sweetness, the liquid and spices are added to the pot. The mixture is brought to a boil and poured over the toasted couscous. The bowl is then tightly sealed with plastic wrap and the couscous sits for exactly 12 minutes. We found this amount of time to be optimum for yielding tender grains. Finally, the couscous is finished with a generous handful of minced fresh herbs and then fluffed before serving.

Hoping to cut some fat out right from the start, we turned our attention to the toasting technique. From previous tests, we knew that toasting the couscous helps the grains stay discrete in the finished dish and, more important, it adds a nice base of nutty flavor and depth. We made three separate pots of couscous, each using a different amount of oil—1 tablespoon, 2 teaspoons, and 1 teaspoon—in which to sauté the grains. Tasters had a hard time detecting differences between the three, which gave us the idea that we might be able to toast the couscous in a dry pan, with no oil at all. We were successful, and tasters agreed that the grains stayed just as separate and the flavor just as nutty as if the grains had been sautéed in oil.

Now that we had a base, we sought to further pump up flavor without bumping up the fat and calories. Tasters agreed that sautéed onion with a few cloves of minced garlic created a nice contrast to our toasty, nutty couscous. Sautéing onion and garlic usually involves a considerable amount of fat, but we knew from previous testing that we could actually use a mere teaspoon of oil to sauté aromatics and vegetables with good results (see page 63). We applied this simple technique to the aromatics for our couscous and it worked perfectly.

For liquid, water seemed like the obvious choice, but it made for a bland couscous, even with the onion and garlic. We then tried chicken broth, but it was too strong; the chicken flavor overpowered the mild couscous. A combination of chicken broth and water, however, worked best, giving the couscous body and a pleasant richness.

With the basics of our couscous lined up, we were ready to add other flavors. We wanted to first develop a basic couscous recipe with simple flavors that could accompany almost any meal. The perfumed intensity of lemon zest, which tasters hailed for its fresh citrus essence, gave us the simplicity we were after. And when paired with the sharp bursts of acid from diced tomato and the subtly sweet, round allium flavor of sliced scallions, it completed our basic recipe.

Next, we wanted to develop a heartier variation. Chickpeas and carrots proved to be a flavorful way of adding bulk, and as a bonus introduced vegetables and legumes to our side dish. Because of its full flavor, we felt this version could also handle an abundance of fresh herbs. We tried the typical couscous additions—parsley, cilantro, and mint—and couldn't reach a consensus. Some tasters favored the clean, bright flavor of parsley, while others liked the sharpness of cilantro, and a few held out for the exotically aromatic mint. In the end, we decided not to decide, as they all work equally well. We leave the choice to you.

In our third version of the recipe we looked to some authentic couscous flavor combinations. Raisins—a classic North African couscous ingredient—matched well with toasted almonds (we used just a small amount for crunch and flavor) and saffron. The alluring golden hue from the saffron, as well as its distinct aroma, added great depth to the couscous.

We now had three distinctly different recipes, but we felt they could all benefit from one final touch. We decided to finish them with a small amount of extra-virgin olive oil right before serving—a fitting ingredient, considering our couscous dishes are all Mediterranean in spirit. This minor adjustment had a great impact on the flavors in our couscous, giving them a greater, more complex role in the dish. One last addition was a little bit of lemon juice, which brightened all the flavors of the dish, accentuating the toasty quality of the couscous itself, and amplifying the high tones of the aromatics and the flavorings.

Couscous with Tomato, Scallions, and Lemon
SERVES 6

For the fluffiest texture, use a large fork to fluff the grains; a spoon or spatula can destroy the light texture. The simple flavors of this couscous pair well with a wide variety of meat, poultry, and vegetable dishes. Do not use Israeli couscous for this recipe, as its larger size requires a different cooking method.

1½	cups couscous
1	medium onion, chopped fine
4	teaspoons extra-virgin olive oil
	Salt
2	medium garlic cloves, minced or pressed through a garlic press (about 2 teaspoons)
1	teaspoon grated zest from 1 lemon
⅛	teaspoon cayenne
2	cups water
¾	cup low-sodium chicken broth
1½	teaspoons juice from 1 lemon
1	medium tomato, halved, cored, seeded, and diced small (about ½ cup)
2	scallions, sliced thin
	Ground black pepper

1. Toast the couscous in a medium saucepan over medium-high heat, stirring frequently, until some grains are just beginning to brown, about 3 minutes. Transfer the grains to a large bowl; set aside.

2. Combine the onion, 1 teaspoon of the oil, and ½ teaspoon salt in the saucepan. Cover and

cook over medium-low heat, stirring occasionally, until the onion is softened, 8 to 10 minutes. Stir in the garlic, lemon zest, and cayenne and cook until fragrant, about 30 seconds. Stir in the water and broth and bring to a boil.

3. Stir the boiling liquid into the couscous, cover the bowl tightly with plastic wrap, and let sit until the grains are tender, about 12 minutes. Uncover and fluff the grains with a fork. Stir in the remaining 1 tablespoon oil, lemon juice, tomato, and scallions and season with salt and pepper to taste.

PER SERVING: Cal 210; Fat 3.5 g; Sat fat 0 g; Chol 0 mg; Carb 38 g; Protein 6 g; Fiber 3 g; Sodium 270 mg

➤ VARIATIONS

Couscous with Carrots, Chickpeas, and Herbs

Sprinkled with additional lemon juice, this dish is also good cold as a salad. Harissa, a fiery Algerian hot sauce flavored with chiles, caraway, garlic, and cumin, is an authentic accompaniment and worth seeking out in the spice aisle of a well-stocked supermarket or specialty store. You can substitute vegetable broth or water for the chicken broth if you'd like to make a vegetarian version of this dish.

1½	cups couscous
2	medium carrots, chopped fine
1	medium onion, chopped fine
4	teaspoons extra-virgin olive oil
	Salt
4	medium garlic cloves, minced or pressed through a garlic press (about 4 teaspoons)
½	teaspoon ground coriander
½	teaspoon ground ginger
2	cups water
¾	cup low-sodium chicken broth
1	(15.5-ounce) can chickpeas, drained and rinsed
¼	cup minced fresh parsley, cilantro, and/or mint leaves
1½	teaspoons juice from 1 lemon
	Ground black pepper

1. Toast the couscous in a medium saucepan over medium-high heat, stirring frequently, until some grains are just beginning to brown, about 3 minutes. Transfer the grains to a large bowl; set aside.

2. Combine the carrots, onion, 1 teaspoon of the oil, and ½ teaspoon salt in the saucepan. Cover and cook over medium-low heat, stirring occasionally, until the vegetables are softened, 8 to 10 minutes. Remove the lid, increase the heat to medium-high, and continue to cook, stirring frequently, until the vegetables are lightly browned, about 4 minutes. Stir in the garlic, coriander, and ginger and cook until fragrant, about 30 seconds. Stir in the water, broth, and chickpeas and bring to a boil.

3. Stir the boiling liquid into the couscous, cover the bowl tightly with plastic wrap, and let sit until the grains are tender, about 12 minutes. Uncover and fluff the grains with a fork. Stir in the remaining 1 tablespoon oil, herbs, and lemon juice and season with salt and pepper to taste.

PER SERVING: Cal 280; Fat 4.5 g; Sat fat .5 g; Chol 0 mg; Carb 49 g; Protein 10 g; Fiber 6 g; Sodium 370 mg

Couscous with Saffron, Raisins, and Toasted Almonds

If you don't have saffron or dislike its potent flavor, don't skip this dish. Simply omit the saffron and ground cinnamon and substitute a couple of cinnamon sticks for a pleasant flavor and aroma. Add them with the onion so that they are exposed to dry heat, which intensifies their flavor.

1½	cups couscous
1	medium onion, chopped fine
4	teaspoons extra-virgin olive oil
	Salt
⅛	teaspoon saffron threads, crumbled with your fingertips
⅛	teaspoon ground cinnamon
⅛	teaspoon cayenne
2	cups water
¾	cup low-sodium chicken broth
¾	cup raisins
1½	teaspoons juice from 1 lemon
¼	cup toasted sliced almonds (see page 45)
	Ground black pepper

1. Toast the couscous in a medium saucepan over medium-high heat, stirring frequently, until some grains are just beginning to brown, about 3 minutes. Transfer the grains to a large bowl; set aside.

2. Combine the onion, 1 teaspoon of the oil, and ½ teaspoon salt in the saucepan. Cover and cook over medium-low heat, stirring occasionally, until the onion is softened, 8 to 10 minutes. Stir in the saffron, cinnamon, and cayenne and cook until fragrant, about 30 seconds. Stir in the water, broth, and raisins and bring to a boil.

3. Stir the boiling liquid into the couscous, cover the bowl tightly with plastic wrap, and let sit until the grains are tender, about 12 minutes. Uncover and fluff the grains with a fork. Stir in the remaining 1 tablespoon oil, lemon juice, and almonds and season with salt and pepper to taste.

PER SERVING: Cal 290; Fat 5 g; Sat fat .5 g; Chol 0 mg; Carb 52 g; Protein 7 g; Fiber 4 g; Sodium 280 mg

BULGUR AND MUSHROOM PILAF

THROUGHOUT THE COUNTRIES OF THE eastern Mediterranean, including Turkey and Greece, bulgur is a staple grain. Produced from whole wheat kernels, it is vitamin rich and a great way to add fiber to your diet. Packed with an earthy, nutty flavor that is quite distinctive, bulgur is used in everything from tabbouleh (most famously) to meatballs (called kibbeh) and—our top choice—pilaf.

An ideal canvas for any number of assertive flavors, bulgur teams up with mushrooms in one of our favorite pairings. We find that the deep, complex essence, and forest notes of the mushrooms match well with the earthy nuttiness of the bulgur. And because mushrooms are naturally low in calories and fat, they add a ton of intense flavor without adding too much around the waistline.

In terms of how much fat we'd be adding to our pilaf, we have found that grains really don't require all that much oil for cooking. In fact, we've observed that too much fat often deadens flavors and prohibits a light and fluffy consistency. For our bulgur pilaf, we would need a bit of oil to sauté the aromatics, and a little bit more to brown the mushrooms, but we knew from previous testing that it wouldn't take much (see page 63). Therefore, the focus of our testing would be on how to best prepare bulgur pilaf with the goal of creating a one-pan, quick-cooking, nutritious grain dish.

When bulgur is made, the whole wheat kernels are steamed, dried, and crushed into one of three grades—coarse, medium, or fine—each of which requires a different cooking method. Fine-grain bulgur, the variety most often seen in Middle Eastern dishes, must be rehydrated in hot liquid, not unlike couscous. Larger-grain bulgur, which we prefer for pilafs, must be simmered until tender, usually about 15 minutes.

Based on our work developing other pilaf recipes, we already had a cooking method in mind. We would use a large saucepan from start to finish, the aromatics would be sautéed using our low-fat method (see page 63), the mushrooms would be lightly browned, and then the bulgur and cooking liquid would be added and simmered until tender. Testing, then, was a matter of developing the fullest mushroom flavor and discovering how long and at what temperature to simmer the bulgur for the best texture.

To get intense mushroom flavor without resorting to pricey exotics, we frequently combine standard cultivated mushrooms—white or cremini—with dried porcini mushrooms. Relatively inexpensive and packed with flavor, the dried mushrooms impart an intensely earthy flavor and pungent aroma to the most mild-mannered fresh mushrooms. After rehydrating in hot water, the dried mushrooms are ready to cook, and the leftover soaking water can be used as a portion of the cooking liquid. To further boost the mushroom flavor, we added both onion and garlic (pressed through a garlic press for the biggest impact) as well as soy sauce—odd in a Mediterranean dish but welcome nonetheless for its dramatic impact on mushroom flavor. Not identifiable as soy sauce once added to the dish, it deepened the mushrooms' flavor and color.

For the liquid, we tried both chicken broth and water. Independently, chicken broth was too strong and muddied the dish's flavors, but water made the pilaf too lean tasting. A combination of the two gave the pilaf body without calling attention to the chicken flavor. Roughly 2 parts broth to 1 part water was just right. And as we explored the best way to cook the bulgur, we tried every approach from a full boil to a quiet simmer. Rapid simmering cooked the bulgur unevenly and gave it an unpleasant chewiness. Very low heat cooked the bulgur more evenly, but it was not perfect. Some of the bulgur grains were still a bit chewier, and overall tasters found the pilaf to be too dense and moist. But as we discovered in our rice pilaf, allowing the pilaf to steam for 10 minutes after being removed from the heat ensures that the moisture gets distributed throughout.

And while almost all recipes for pilaf call for toasting the grain before adding liquid, we found this step unnecessary with bulgur. Herbs were, however, necessary to enliven the monotonous palette of browns as well as for flavor. Thyme reinforced the pilaf's earthy edge but lacked visual presence. Parsley brightened both flavor and color, so we chose it over the thyme and opted for a fairly generous amount: ¼ cup. One last final adjustment was made, in reaction to a taster's comment that we had minimized the amount of oil too much. The taster complained that the flavors of the pilaf were too discrete and that, overall, the grains were lacking richness. To correct this, we stirred a little bit of olive oil into the finished pilaf. This worked perfectly to fuse all of the flavors in the dish, and it added great body and mouthfeel to the grains. And by stirring the oil in at the end of cooking, we ensured maximum olive oil flavor, because the potency and complexity of olive oil dulls when cooked.

Bulgur Pilaf with Mushrooms

SERVES 6

Watch for the term "cracked wheat" when purchasing bulgur; while it looks like bulgur, the two are not the same. Cracked wheat is uncooked, whereas bulgur is par cooked, and the two require different cooking methods. We prefer moderately coarse bulgur, which has a texture like that of kosher salt, to finer, sandy bulgur. Cremini mushrooms, also sold as "baby bellas," are juvenile portobellos.

Water
½ ounce dried porcini mushrooms, rehydrated, mushrooms minced and rehydrating liquid strained (see the illustrations on page 139)
1 medium onion, chopped fine
5 teaspoons olive oil
Salt
8 ounces cremini (preferably) or white mushrooms, wiped clean, trimmed, and quartered (or cut into 6 pieces if large)
2 medium garlic cloves, minced or pressed through a garlic press (about 2 teaspoons)
1½ cups bulgur, preferably medium-grain
1¾ cups low-sodium chicken broth
1½ teaspoons soy sauce
¼ cup minced fresh parsley leaves
Ground black pepper

1. Add enough water to the strained porcini liquid to measure 1 cup; set aside.

2. Combine the onion, 1 teaspoon of the oil, and ½ teaspoon salt in a large saucepan. Cover and cook over medium-low heat, stirring occasionally, until the onion is softened, 8 to 10 minutes. Stir in 1 more teaspoon oil, cremini mushrooms, and porcini mushrooms. Increase the heat to medium-high and continue to cook, uncovered, until the cremini begin to brown, about 4 minutes. Stir in the garlic and cook until fragrant, about 30 seconds.

3. Stir in the bulgur, broth, soy sauce, and reserved porcini soaking liquid and bring to a boil. Cover, reduce the heat to low, and simmer until the bulgur is tender, 16 to 18 minutes.

4. Remove the pot from the heat and lay a clean, folded kitchen towel underneath the lid (see the illustration on page 133). Let stand for 10 minutes, then fluff the bulgur with a fork. Stir in the parsley and the remaining 1 tablespoon oil, and season with salt and pepper to taste.

PER SERVING: Cal 190; Fat 4.5 g; Sat fat .5 g; Chol 0 mg; Carb 33 g; Protein 7 g; Fiber 8 g; Sodium 490 mg

➤ VARIATION

Bulgur Pilaf with Shiitakes and Asian Flavors

Despite its bold flavors, this pilaf is at home with a wide variety of main courses, including roast chicken, pork, and firm-fleshed fish such as halibut, swordfish, and salmon.

Follow the recipe for Bulgur Pilaf with Mushrooms, substituting 8 ounces shiitake mushrooms, stemmed and sliced ¼ inch thick, for the cremini mushrooms. Add 1 tablespoon grated fresh ginger to the pot with the garlic in step 2. Substitute 2 scallions, sliced thin, for the parsley.

PER SERVING: Cal 200; Fat 4.5 g; Sat fat .5 g; Chol 0 mg; Carb 37 g; Protein 7 g; Fiber 8 g; Sodium 490 mg

QUINOA PILAF

QUINOA HAS BEEN CULTIVATED AND consumed for thousands of years throughout South America. It was a staple of the Inca civilization and is still a staple food of Peru. Generally treated as a grain, quinoa is actually the seed of the goosefoot plant. It contains significantly more protein than most grains, and its protein is complete—that is, quinoa possesses all of the amino acids necessary for protein metabolism, unlike grains that must be consumed in conjunction with other foodstuffs, such as beans, to unlock their nutritional contribution. Quinoa possesses a wholesome, hearty taste with a texture that is addictively crunchy—the individual seeds pop when chewed, not unlike caviar.

Given all these miraculous nutritional properties, we expected the wonders of quinoa to be balanced with some significant drawback, like intensive preparation or finicky cooking requirements. We were wrong. Quinoa couldn't be easier to prepare. Almost every recipe we found employed the same method for cooking. Rinse the quinoa well to rid the grains of a mildly toxic protective layer (called saponin), which is unpleasantly bitter, bring it to a boil in stock or water, and simmer over low heat, covered, for 15 minutes. This basic method worked well; however, it made for a wet, dense side dish, so we decided to focus our attention on making a pilaf, which we hoped would be lighter, drier, and fluffier.

Using our standard pilaf method we first sautéed an onion in a minimal amount of oil (1 teaspoon) until it became soft and released its juices. Next, we added the quinoa to the pan, increased the heat, and sautéed it. Tasters were surprised by the degree to which quinoa's flavor improved after toasting. Although toasting grains before adding liquid is standard pilaf procedure because it ensures plumped, individual grains, this step had an unexpectedly substantial impact on quinoa, whose otherwise subtle flavor undertones were greatly intensified.

We added chicken broth next, which was a clear winner when tested side by side with pilafs made with water (which tasters thought were too bland). In previous testing, we found that a mixture of broth and water typically works best in grain dishes, as straight broth tends to muddy the grain's flavor. However, with quinoa, straight broth worked best to give our pilaf excellent body and fortified the other flavors in the dish. Finally, after the quinoa had simmered, we pulled the pan off the heat and let it sit, covered, for an extra 10 minutes. The grains steam during this stage, soaking up extra moisture, which is evenly distributed. Our conclusion: Quinoa takes very well to the pilaf method of cooking, which produces flawlessly and evenly cooked, slightly crunchy grains every time.

We moved on to flavoring our quinoa pilaf. It was decided that quinoa's earthy nuttiness would pair well with lighter ingredients. Tasters preferred the subtle sweetness of onion to the slight pungency of garlic. Lemon zest lent a nice hit of citrusy perfume to the quinoa and the earthiness of thyme provided good balance. As a final adjustment, tasters requested that a small amount of citrus juice be stirred in at the end, which added brightness and helped finish the dish. For a bolder variation, tasters thought corn, jalapeño, and cilantro worked well together, and those ingredients are a nod to flavors commonly found in South American cuisines. The sweetness of the corn brought out the nuttiness of the quinoa, while the jalapeño added zip and worked well with the cilantro.

Quinoa Pilaf

SERVES 6

If your market does not carry quinoa, try the local natural food store, which will certainly sell it. Quinoa must be thoroughly rinsed before cooking to remove the bitter exterior coating, called saponin. The seeds are washed before packaging, but a bit of the compound may remain; it is worth the precaution, as a small amount of saponin can ruin a dish. It's easy to tell when quinoa is done, as the brown seeds turn translucent.

1	medium onion, chopped fine
1	teaspoon olive oil
	Salt
2	cups quinoa, rinsed (see the illustration on page 131)
1 ¾	cups low-sodium chicken broth
1	teaspoon grated zest from 1 lemon
2	teaspoons minced fresh thyme leaves
2	teaspoons juice from 1 lemon
	Ground black pepper

1. Combine the onion, oil, and ½ teaspoon of salt in a large saucepan. Cover and cook over medium-low heat, stirring occasionally, until the onion is softened, 8 to 10 minutes.

2. Add the quinoa, increase the heat to medium, and cook, stirring frequently, until the quinoa lightly browns and becomes aromatic, about 5 minutes. Stir in the broth and lemon zest and bring to a boil. Reduce the heat to low, cover, and simmer until the quinoa is transparent and tender, 16 to 18 minutes.

3. Remove the pot from the heat and lay a clean, folded kitchen towel underneath the lid (see the illustration on page 133). Let stand for 10 minutes, then fluff the quinoa with a fork. Stir in the thyme and lemon juice and season with salt and pepper to taste.

PER SERVING: Cal 230; Fat 4 g; Sat fat 0 g; Chol 0 mg; Carb 42 g; Protein 8 g; Fiber 4 g; Sodium 380 mg

> VARIATION

Quinoa Pilaf with Corn and Jalapeños

Fresh corn really makes this dish but when it's not available you can substitute 1½ cups of thawed, frozen corn. If you like spicy food, don't bother removing the seeds and the ribs from the chiles.

2	teaspoons olive oil
2	medium ears of corn, kernels removed from cob (see the illustration on page 84)
1	medium onion, chopped fine
	Salt
2	cups quinoa, rinsed (see the illustration on page 131)
1 ¾	cups low-sodium chicken broth
2	medium jalapeño chiles, seeds and ribs removed (see note), then minced
¼	cup minced fresh cilantro leaves
2	teaspoons juice from 1 lime
	Ground black pepper

1. Heat 1 teaspoon of the oil in a large saucepan over medium-high heat until shimmering. Add the corn and cook, stirring frequently, until corn starts to brown, about 5 minutes. Transfer the corn to a bowl; set aside.

2. Add the onion, remaining teaspoon oil, and ½ teaspoon salt to the saucepan. Cover and cook over medium-low heat, stirring occasionally, until the onion is softened, 8 to 10 minutes. Add the quinoa, increase the heat to medium, and cook, stirring frequently, until the quinoa lightly browns and becomes aromatic, about 5 minutes. Stir in the broth and jalapeños and bring to a boil. Reduce the heat to low, cover, and simmer until the quinoa is transparent and tender, 16 to 18 minutes.

3. Remove the pot from the heat and lay a clean, folded kitchen towel underneath the lid (see the illustration on page 133). Let stand for 10 minutes, then fluff the quinoa with a fork. Stir in the cilantro, lime juice, and reserved corn and season with salt and pepper to taste.

PER SERVING: Cal 270; Fat 5 g; Sat fat .5 g; Chol 0 mg; Carb 48 g; Protein 9 g; Fiber 5 g; Sodium 380 mg

Cooking Beans 101

Here in the test kitchen, we were under the impression that beans had to be soaked before cooking to expedite the time on the stove. Sometimes, though, we either don't plan far enough ahead or we forget to soak our beans. When faced with a glitch of this kind, do we resort to canned beans or forgo the intended meal completely? The answer is no to both possibilities. We decided to simmer dried beans that had not been soaked and see what transpired. Much to our surprise, the unsoaked beans only took an average of about 30 minutes longer to cook than soaked beans did. Our unsoaked beans also required more cooking liquid and, admittedly, weren't as evenly cooked, but they were an acceptable alternative, especially when the beans were going to be pureed or mashed. Each recipe makes enough to serve 4 to 6.

OVERNIGHT-SOAKING METHOD
Pick through and rinse 1 pound beans. Cover the beans with 5 cups water and soak overnight. Drain.

QUICK-SOAKING METHOD
Pick through and rinse 1 pound beans. Cover the beans by 1 inch with water in a large saucepan. Bring the beans to a boil and cook for 2 minutes. Remove the saucepan from the heat, cover, and let the beans sit for 1 hour. Drain.

COOKING DIRECTIONS
Bring the beans, 2½ teaspoons salt, and the water to a boil. Reduce to a gentle simmer and cook until the beans are tender, following the time given in the chart. Stir the beans occasionally to prevent them from sticking to the bottom of the pan, and adjust the heat as needed to maintain a gentle simmer. Drain.

JAZZING UP BEANS
Cooked beans can be used in soups, stews, and chilis or in salads and salsas. To serve them as a side dish, try drizzling them with a bit of olive oil, lemon juice, and chopped fresh herbs, or simply toss the beans with a light vinaigrette (see pages 29–30). Alternatively, chopped roasted red peppers or sun-dried tomatoes often help to spruce up the flavor of a bean side dish.

TYPE OF BEANS		AMOUNT OF BEANS	AMOUNT OF WATER	COOKING TIME
BLACK BEANS	Soaked	1 pound	4 quarts	1½ to 2 hours
	Unsoaked	1 pound	5 quarts	2¼ to 2½ hours
BLACK-EYED PEAS	Soaked	1 pound	4 quarts	1 to 1¼ hours
	Unsoaked	1 pound	5 quarts	1½ to 1¾ hours
CANNELLINI BEANS	Soaked	1 pound	4 quarts	1 to 1¼ hours
	Unsoaked	1 pound	5 quarts	1½ to 1¾ hours
CHICKPEAS	Soaked	1 pound	4 quarts	1½ to 2 hours
	Unsoaked	1 pound	5 quarts	2¼ to 2½ hours
GREAT NORTHERN BEANS	Soaked	1 pound	4 quarts	1 to 1¼ hours
	Unsoaked	1 pound	5 quarts	1½ to 1¾ hours
NAVY BEANS	Soaked	1 pound	4 quarts	1 to 1¼ hours
	Unsoaked	1 pound	5 quarts	1½ to 1¾ hours
PINTO BEANS	Soaked	1 pound	4 quarts	1 to 1¼ hours
	Unsoaked	1 pound	5 quarts	1½ to 1¾ hours
RED KIDNEY BEANS	Soaked	1 pound	4 quarts	1 to 1¼ hours
	Unsoaked	1 pound	5 quarts	1½ to 1¾ hours
LENTILS: BROWN, GREEN, OR FRENCH DU PUY*	Unsoaked	1 pound	4 quarts	20 to 30 minutes

*Red or yellow lentils should be used only in soups as they will disintegrate during cooking.

BEAN PUREES

WHEN WE THINK OF BEAN PUREES, WE USUALLY think of refried beans. However, in our research for developing a lighter refried bean recipe, we came across a number of recipes for bean purees made with other types of legumes, such as cannellini and lima beans. Making a flavorful puree from beans seemed like great new way to enjoy them. And the idea of using a bean puree in place of pasta, mashed potatoes, or the typical supper side dish appealed greatly to us.

After trying some of these existing puree recipes, we found them to be a great pairing with grilled meats or, even better, as a tasty landing for a ladleful of hearty stew. Yet, the recipes with which we did our tests definitely needed some revision. Much like refried beans, these other bean purees used an abundance of fat. With 12 grams of fat and 310 calories in a typical ⅔-cup serving, we were a bit leery about making this type of side dish a regular on our dinner plate. We decided our goal would be to develop a simple, lightened refried bean recipe and then apply the technique to different types of beans, making flavor adjustments where appropriate.

Most of the recipes we researched employed the time-consuming step of soaking dried beans, but we were hoping to keep the process as streamlined as possible. Fortunately, we already knew from previous refried bean testing that we could skip the hours of waiting for a pot of beans to cook, because canned beans, when pureed with a bit of water, created the smooth consistency we were looking for.

This made our refried beans quick and easy, taking less than 15 minutes to prepare. Our first step was to process rinsed and drained canned beans in a food processor with a little water until smooth. Next, we slowly sautéed onion—which acts as the foundation of flavor—until it softened and released its sweet, mellow essence. We tossed in a bit of garlic and cumin, then added the pureed bean mixture to the saucepan and simmered everything until it was thickened and the flavors had fused. Finally, we finished the puree with a handful of minced fresh cilantro to give the beans a fresh, authentic flavor.

With the framework of our bean puree in place, we turned our attention to minimizing the amount of oil in the recipe. From previous testing, we knew that tasters liked olive oil for its full flavor and rich mouthfeel; we decided to start with 2 tablespoons and then see if we could reduce this amount without sacrificing quality. While all the tasters liked this amount of fat in the beans, they also felt that we could go lower. We tried subsequent batches of beans, taking out a teaspoon of oil at a time until tasters complained that the puree tasted too lean with only 1 tablespoon of oil.

In the end, we agreed on 4 teaspoons of oil. In an effort to maximize the oil's flavor, we found it best to use just 1 teaspoon of the oil to sauté the onion and fry the beans, and then stir in the remaining 1 tablespoon to finish the beans. By adding a portion of the oil at the end, we were assured maximum flavor and complexity, which is typically diminished when olive oil is cooked. Our beans now only had 3 grams of fat and 230 calories per ⅔-cup serving, and they were still well-seasoned, creamy, and rich.

Now that we had a core technique for our low-fat bean purees, we moved on to bean choices and flavorings. Starting with our refried beans, we quickly determined that we preferred red kidney beans to the more traditional pinto bean: Pinto beans are bland and make a lean-textured puree compared to the red kidney beans, which have a deep, nutty flavor and give the puree a velvety consistency. For additional ingredients, onion, jalapeño, garlic, cumin, and cilantro were the winners. We found that this flavor profile also complements black beans, which won the affection of many tasters.

With a lighter refried bean recipe under our belt, we started to experiment with other types of beans. We cleared the slate, flavor-wise, and set up new tests using only simple flavors like onion, olive oil, salt, and pepper. We started with lima beans, a legume used in their fresh form in a number of existing bean puree recipes. Since they are only available a few weeks out of the year, we ruled out fresh lima beans for practical reasons (although if they are available, you can certainly use them). Instead we turned to using frozen lima beans, a product we had found success with in past recipes (much more so than canned, which tasters strongly disliked). However tasters were not happy with purees made with the frozen lima beans, pointing out off, vegetal flavors, sulfurous aromas, and chalky textures. We then turned to a product found next to frozen lima beans in the grocer's freezer section: edamame (soy beans). Unfortunately the edamame tasted bland, and the texture never really smoothed out, no matter how long we whirled them in the food processor.

Next up were canned black-eyed peas, which made a terribly gritty puree with an unavoidable muddy flavor. We thought we might have some luck with chickpeas, but tasters complained that they tasted thin and tinny in the puree. Finally, we moved on to canned white bean varieties such as navy, great Northern, and cannellini. Navy beans had an unavoidable stale, canned taste, and great Northern beans tasted great but did not create purees as creamy as we wanted. Cannellini beans however, worked perfectly, as their tough skins disappeared when processed, and their mashed-up creamy centers made for silky, rich puree.

With cannellini beans as our favorite, we turned to flavoring them with Mediterranean flavors, such as garlic, rosemary, and roasted red peppers. We added a dash of red pepper flakes for background spice, and found a bit of fresh lemon juice stirred in at the end a welcome addition in our variation. We finished this puree with extra-virgin olive oil, a much fuller, more complex product than pure olive oil, and well suited to the flavors we had lined up. Now we had two distinct, flavorful purees that can accompany a variety of dishes—and that we think are a welcome departure from the usual.

MAKEOVER AT A GLANCE

—Classic—
Refried Beans
(per serving)

Calories: 310   Cholesterol: 0 mg
Fat: 12 g   Saturated Fat: 1.5 g

—Light—
Refried Beans
(per serving)

Calories: 230   Cholesterol: 0 mg
Fat: 3 g   Saturated Fat: 0 g

How We Did It

- Pureed beans with 1 cup of water to make them smooth and creamy without adding fat
- Used red kidney beans, which added a deeper, nuttier flavor than the traditional pinto beans
- Boosted flavor with onion, jalapeño, garlic, cumin, and fresh cilantro
- Sweated the onion and jalapeño in a covered saucepan using only 1 teaspoon of oil to draw out moisture and concentrate flavors
- Stirred in 1 tablespoon of olive oil at the end for flavor and richness

Refried Beans
SERVES 6

If you like your beans on the spicy side, don't bother removing the seeds and ribs from the chile. Refried beans can be served with a variety of garnishes, including warm tortillas, salsa, pickled jalapeño chiles (sold in cans in most supermarkets), sliced scallions, shredded low-fat Monterey Jack or cheddar cheese, and light sour cream. For a change of pace, try using canned black beans instead of the kidney beans.

3   (15.5-ounce) cans red kidney beans, drained and rinsed
1   cup water
1   medium onion, chopped fine
1   large jalapeño chile, seeds and ribs removed (see note), then minced

4 teaspoons olive oil
Salt
2 medium garlic cloves, minced or pressed
through a garlic press (about 2 teaspoons)
I teaspoon ground cumin
¼ cup minced fresh cilantro leaves (optional)
Hot pepper sauce

1. Process the beans and water in a food processor until smooth, about 2 minutes, scraping down the sides of the bowl as needed; set aside.

2. Combine the onion, jalapeño, 1 teaspoon of the oil, and ½ teaspoon salt in a medium saucepan. Cover and cook over medium-low heat, stirring occasionally, until the vegetables are softened, 8 to 10 minutes. Stir in the garlic and cumin and cook until fragrant, about 30 seconds. Stir in the pureed beans until thoroughly combined. Reduce the heat to low and cook, stirring frequently, until the beans have thickened and the flavors have blended, about 10 minutes. Stir in the remaining 1 tablespoon oil and cilantro (if using), and season with salt and hot sauce to taste.

PER SERVING: Cal 230; Fat 3 g; Sat fat 0 g; Chol 0 mg; Carb 38 g; Protein 14 g; Fiber 11 g; Sodium 780 mg

White Bean Puree with Rosemary

SERVES 6

The puree goes perfectly with grilled meats, poultry, vegetables, and fish. A good fruity extra-virgin olive oil elevates all the flavors in this dish.

3 (15.5-ounce) cans cannellini beans, drained and rinsed
I cup water
4 teaspoons extra-virgin olive oil
4 medium garlic cloves, minced or pressed
through a garlic press (about 4 teaspoons)
⅛ teaspoon red pepper flakes
I teaspoon minced fresh rosemary
Salt and ground black pepper

1. Process the beans and water in a food processor until smooth, about 2 minutes, scraping down the sides of the bowl as needed; set aside.

2. Heat 1 teaspoon of the oil in a medium saucepan over medium-low heat until shimmering. Add the garlic and red pepper flakes and cook until fragrant, about 30 seconds. Stir in the pureed beans and rosemary until thoroughly combined. Reduce the heat to low and cook, stirring frequently, until the beans have thickened and the flavors have blended, about 10 minutes. Stir in the remaining 1 tablespoon oil and season with salt and pepper to taste.

PER SERVING: Cal 200; Fat 4 g; Sat fat 0 g; Chol 0 mg; Carb 31 g; Protein 9 g; Fiber 9 g; Sodium 460 mg

➤ VARIATION

White Bean Puree with Roasted Red Peppers and Basil

Follow the recipe for White Bean Puree with Rosemary, reducing the water to ½ cup, and adding 5 ounces jarred, roasted red peppers, rinsed, patted dry, and chopped (about ¾ cup) to the food processor with the beans in step 1. Omit the rosemary and add ¼ cup minced fresh basil leaves and 1 teaspoon lemon juice with the salt and pepper in step 2.

PER SERVING: Cal 210; Fat 4 g; Sat fat 0 g; Chol 0 mg; Carb 33 g; Protein 9 g; Fiber 9 g; Sodium 540 mg

BEST CANNED WHITE BEANS

Cannellini beans are our top choice for purees. Navy beans tasted stale and canned, and great Northern beans—although they tasted great—did not give us the creamy texture we sought. Cannellini beans easily break down into a smooth, rich puree.

PROGRESSO
Cannellini Beans

LENTILS

COOKING LENTILS IS STRAIGHTFORWARD and fairly hands off. A one-pot side dish, lentils are usually added, along with liquid, to sautéed aromatics, and then simmered for 40 to 45 minutes. However, the type of lentils used and a keen eye toward the end of cooking usually determine the outcome. Our experiences with bad lentils have typically involved an unevenly cooked, underseasoned mess of legumes, swimming in a pallid liquid visually akin to dishwater. Who would want that on their dinner plate? We knew that, when done right, lentils have a slightly resistant bite that yields creamy centers with deep earthy flavor, and we were determined to achieve this ideal. Also, knowing that lentils have a hearty richness on their own, we knew we wouldn't need a lot of fat to elevate this simple side dish.

Right from the start, we knew that glossy green lentilles du Puy were our bean of choice. These French green lentils have a firm texture and retain their shape better than other varieties. Next, we looked for simple ways to boost and deepen the flavor of our side dish. We experimented with a variety of aromatics, including garlic, shallots, scallions, and onions. We settled on the onions for their sweetness and body. Much of the flavor in our lentil dish, however, was to come from an unexpected ingredient: chard stems. Chard is an unusual green in that its stems are as desirable as its leaves. Chard stems possess an earthy, beet-like flavor; in fact, chard is a relative of beets that is bred for its leaves instead of its roots. Chard stems are at their best sautéed, so we cooked the stems with the onion using just 1 teaspoon of oil.

As for the type of liquid in which to cook the lentils, tasters preferred the round fullness of chicken broth. Water worked OK, but didn't have the depth of flavor that the chicken broth did. And a small amount of fresh thyme, added with the liquid, was a welcome ingredient—its woodsy flavor boosted the heartiness of the broth and complemented the flavor of the lentils.

At this point, some felt that the lentils still needed a bit more richness and flavor, and a small amount of fruity extra-virgin olive oil was just the thing. Finally, to liven things up a bit, tasters found the addition of a little fresh lemon juice to be a nice contrast to the lentils' deep earthy flavor.

⤚⥲

Lentils with Chard

SERVES 6

Search the lentils carefully for small pebbles and other hidden grit. A white plate or bowl makes foreign objects easy to see. Puy lentils are prized for holding their shape; however, if overcooked they can disintegrate quickly. The best way to check for lentil doneness is to taste a small amount. Perfect doneness for these tiny legumes yields a tender texture with a bit of bite.

1	medium onion, chopped fine
1	medium bunch chard (10 to 12 ounces), stems and leaves separated, stems chopped fine, leaves chopped medium
4	teaspoons extra-virgin olive oil
	Salt
1¾	cups low-sodium chicken broth
1	cup Puy lentils, picked over and rinsed
1	teaspoon minced fresh thyme leaves
2	teaspoons juice from 1 lemon
	Ground black pepper

1. Combine the onion, chard stems, 1 teaspoon of the oil, and ½ teaspoon salt in a large saucepan. Cover and cook over medium-low heat, stirring occasionally, until the vegetables are softened, 8 to 10 minutes.

2. Add the broth, lentils, and thyme, and bring to a boil. Reduce the heat to low, cover, and continue to cook, stirring occasionally, until the lentils are mostly tender but still slightly crunchy, about 35 minutes.

3. Stir in the chard leaves and continue to cook, uncovered and stirring occasionally, until the lentils are completely tender, about 8 minutes. Stir in the lemon juice and remaining 1 tablespoon oil, and season with salt and pepper to taste.

PER SERVING: Cal 150; Fat 3.5 g; Sat fat 0 g; Chol 0 mg; Carb 23 g; Protein 9 g; Fiber 6 g; Sodium 490 mg

6

PASTA

FEW FOODS RIVAL PASTA IN TERMS OF EITHER speed or convenience. Pasta is almost always on hand, it cooks in minutes, and it can serve as the basis for literally hundreds of one-dish meals. But food trends being what they are, pasta dishes have earned a bad rap for being notoriously high in calories, packed with dreaded "carbs," and topped with sauces often loaded with fat, most of it saturated—think fettuccine Alfredo and macaroni and cheese.

While every recipe in this chapter presented unique challenges, we learned some fat-busting tricks worth mentioning. With many of our sauces, we found that when you take out significant amounts oil or butter (or eliminate them altogether), the flavors tend to get muted. To compensate for this, we simply bumped up all of the flavor contributors, beginning with the aromatics. When we added hefty amounts of onion, and especially garlic, to our recipes, not one taster felt their presence was overpowering—instead they were a welcome boost of flavor.

For recipes that traditionally depend upon heavy cream, like fettuccine Alfredo, we found that we could just replace heavy cream with half-and-half. Sometimes it wasn't so simple. In our Everyday Macaroni and Cheese (page 185), we used a mixture of half-and-half and 2 percent milk thickened with cornstarch. Our efforts were rewarded with a silky, creamy sauce and not one taster missed the superfluous fat.

With cheese, a defining element in many classic pasta recipes, we found that it's not how much you use, but rather how you use it. Most recipes simply don't need cheese by the cupful to be flavorful. You can also serve extra cheese on the side for those who feel the need to augment what is already in the recipe. Parmesan cheese, our favorite cheese for grating, is not only lower in fat than most cheeses—but its assertive, tangy flavor means just a little can go a long way. We offer recommendations on the best tasting Parmesan on page 176—the brand does make a difference. In recipes requiring soft, melting cheeses, we found low-fat versions to be perfectly acceptable. While you wouldn't want to serve them on a cheese board, they add just enough fat and body to be a perfect substitute for the real thing when grated into a

sauce or in a lasagna filling. There was only one instance where we turned to fat-free cheese, and that was in our lasagna filling. Here, we found that fat-free ricotta cheese was a fine stand-in for the full-fat version.

In addition to cheese, oil was an ingredient we watched closely. When sautéing aromatics or vegetables, we found that we could get away with using just 1 teaspoon of oil as long as we covered the pot or skillet and cooked over low heat. In addition, we worked hard to cut any additional oil out of the dish as we proceeded, preferring to finish it with a couple of teaspoons of good extra-virgin olive oil. Adding just a little at the end, as we did with Pasta with Garden Vegetable Sauce (page 166) and Pasta with Chicken and Broccoli (page 168), gave the dish richness and flavor, without excessive calories. And for all of our pasta dishes with vegetables, we made sure to emphasize the vegetables by bulking up on the quantity of them, which not only makes the dishes tastier but healthier as well.

Last, a word about portion sizes and pasta. If you look on most packages of dried pasta, 1 pound of pasta serves eight. This is actually pretty skimpy. In fact, chances are that most servings on package labels, whether it's pasta, cereal, or rice, are much smaller than what people actually serve themselves.

On the other end of the spectrum, some restaurant chains are famous for their stupefyingly large plates of pasta—and somewhere along the way, pasta portions everywhere seemed to grow. Eating such large portions may be fine for a carbo-loading marathoner, but not for regular folks. We needed to find some middle ground. While we didn't resort to child-sized portions in this chapter, we did take a hard look at what constitutes a reasonable serving. And no one wants to be shortchanged, so when developing these recipes we measured a serving, transferred the serving to a dinner plate, and asked the test kitchen staff to evaluate the serving's appearance. Too skimpy? Too much? And then of course, we dug in. Plates of pasta later, we heard no complaints. Where did we end up? Depending on the sauce and other ingredients in the dish, 1 pound of dried pasta generally serves six and 9 ounces of fresh pasta serves four.

TEST KITCHEN MAKEOVER

SPAGHETTI AND MEATBALLS

SPAGHETTI AND MEATBALLS IS THE QUINT-essential Italian-American supper. But with 42 grams of fat per serving, this dish can wreak havoc on a healthy lifestyle. Our goal was to create meatballs that were healthier in terms of both fat and cholesterol than traditional meatballs, but delivered the same great flavor. And while we were at it, we also wanted to make a quick tomato sauce with long-simmered flavor.

Traditional meatballs start with a mix of beef and pork, eggs, bread or bread crumbs, and a hefty amount of Parmesan cheese for flavor. Typically, meatballs are fried in about 1¼ cups of oil to get a nice crisp crust, then simmered in an olive oil–laden tomato sauce. This was certainly a dish ready for a healthier makeover.

To start, we focused on our choice of meat. Ground turkey, which is lower in fat and cholesterol than ground beef, was a healthier option for our meatballs. We gathered several varieties available in our local supermarkets: all white meat, all dark meat, and combinations thereof. Meatballs made with all dark meat were nearly as high in fat as ground beef so we deemed them an unacceptable substitute. Meatballs made with all white meat were tough and grainy. Tasters unanimously preferred the flavor and texture of the meatballs made with a combination of white and dark meat labeled 93 percent lean. They had a meaty flavor and cooked up to a soft moist texture.

With the kind of turkey settled, we moved on to the binders that were necessary to keep the meatballs tender and prevent them from falling apart during cooking. We started with the egg. Wondering if we could eliminate it, we made batches both with and without an egg and it was clear that the egg added much-needed moisture. We did, however, find the meatball mixture a tad sticky and hard to handle. We tried using just the egg white, but the meatballs didn't hold together

---

INGREDIENTS: Dried Pasta

In the not-so-distant past, American pasta had a poor reputation, and rightly so. It cooked up gummy and starchy, and experts usually touted the superiority of Italian brands. We wondered if this was still the case.

To find out, we tasted eight leading brands of spaghetti—four American and four Italian. The pastas were cooked in salted water until we judged them to be al dente (with a good bite), then drained and served unadorned so we could really taste them. Tasters evaluated the pastas on both flavor and texture.

The results of the taste test, conducted again with a panel of Italian cookbook authors and chefs, were shocking. In both cases, American brands took two of the three top spots, while two Italian brands landed at the bottom of the rankings. It seems that American companies have mastered the art of making pasta.

American-made Ronzoni was the top finisher, with tasters praising its "nutty, buttery" flavor and superb texture. Mueller's, another American brand, took third place. DeCecco was the highest-scoring Italian brand, finishing second in the tasting. It

cooked up "very al dente" and was almost chewy. Other Italian brands did not fare quite so well. Martelli, an artisanal pasta that costs three times as much as the winner, finished in next-to-last place, with comments like "gritty" and "mushy" predominating on tasters' score sheets. Another Italian brand, Delverde, sank to the bottom of the ratings.

Our conclusion: Save your money and don't bother with most imported pasta—American brands are just fine. If you want to serve Italian pasta in your home, stick with DeCecco.

THE BEST DRIED PASTA

RONZONI SPAGHETTI
This American brand won tasters over with its firm texture and its "nutty," "buttery," "classic" flavor.

very well and they tasted too lean. We then tried just the yolk, which contains all the fat and emulsifiers that contribute smoothness. These meatballs were a breeze to handle and tasted terrific.

As for binders, the possibilities included dried bread crumbs, fresh bread crumbs, ground crackers, and bread soaked in milk. We found that bread and cracker crumbs soaked up any available moisture, making the meatballs harder and drier

when cooked. By comparison, the meatballs made with bread soaked in milk were moist, creamy, and rich. Milk was clearly an important part of the equation. We liked the milk but wondered if we could do better. We tried adding yogurt (which works well in our favorite meat loaf recipe) but had to thin it with milk in order to mix it with the bread. Meatballs made with thinned yogurt were even creamier and more flavorful than those made

---

INGREDIENTS: Canned Diced Tomatoes

The conventional wisdom holds that canned tomatoes surpass fresh for much of the year because they are packaged at the height of ripeness. After holding side-by-side tests of fresh, off-season tomatoes and canned tomatoes while we were developing recipes for this book, we agree. But with so many brands of canned tomatoes available, there is an obvious question: Which brand tastes best? Having sampled eight brands of canned diced tomatoes, both plain and cooked into a simple sauce, we have the answer.

Depending on the season and the growing location, more than 50 varieties of tomato are used to make these products. Packers generally reserve the ripest, best-colored specimens for use as whole, crushed, and diced tomatoes, products in which consumers demand vibrant color and fresher flavor. Lower-grade tomatoes are generally used in cooked products, such as paste, puree, and sauce.

Before processing, the tomatoes are peeled by means of either steam—always the choice of Muir Glen, the only organic brand in our lineup—or a hot lye bath, which many processors currently favor. Because temperatures in lye peeling are not as high as those in steaming, many processors believe that lye leaves the layer of flesh just beneath the skin in better condition, giving the peeled tomato a superior appearance. Tasters, however, could not detect specific differences in the canned tomatoes based on this aspect of processing. Two of our three highly recommended products, Muir Glen and S&W, use steam, while the third, Redpack, uses lye.

After peeling, the tomatoes are sorted again for color and the presence of any obvious deficiencies, and then they're diced. After the dice are sorted, the cans are filled with the tomatoes and topped off with salt and filler ingredients (usually tomato juice, but sometimes puree, which our tasters downgraded). Finally, the lids are attached to the cans and the cans are cooked briefly for sterilization, then cooled and dried so they can be labeled.

The flavor of a ripe, fresh tomato balances elements of sweetness and tangy acidity. The texture should be somewhere

between firm and pliant, and certainly not mushy. Ideally, canned diced tomatoes should reflect the same combination of characteristics. Indeed, tasters indicated that excessive sweetness or saltiness (from the salt added during processing), along with undesirable texture qualities, could make or break a can of diced tomatoes. If the tasters thought that any one of these characteristics was out of whack, they downgraded that sample.

Oddly, no one flavor profile dominated. The three highly recommended brands, Muir Glen, S&W, and Redpack, displayed a range of flavor characteristics. Muir Glen led the ratings with a favorable balance of sweetness and saltiness and a notably "fresh" flavor in the sauce. Redpack also ranked high for its fresh flavor in the sauce. The same group of tasters, however, gave the thumbs up to S&W tomatoes, a brand noted for its bracing acidity and powerful, almost exaggerated tomato flavor.

THE BEST CANNED DICED TOMATOES

MUIR GLEN ORGANIC
DICED TOMATOES
"Sweet," "fresh tasting," and "most like fresh tomatoes" were some of the comments that explained why this brand of diced tomatoes received high marks.

S&W "READY-CUT" PREMIUM,
PEELED TOMATOES
This West Coast brand was liked for its "tangy," "vibrant" flavor.

REDPACK DICED TOMATOES
(known as Redgold on the
West Coast)
These tomatoes exhibited a "fresh tomato-y taste" and a texture that "did not break down at all."

with plain milk. Our results with buttermilk were just as good, and there was no need to thin the liquid. After trying various amounts, we settled on 3 tablespoons of buttermilk, mixed with the bread to form a panada, or paste. We also added the requisite Italian flavors of Parmesan cheese and garlic to our meatball mixture.

Now that we had our mixture figured out, we turned to our cooking method. Although meatballs are traditionally fried, we wanted to try other, lighter cooking methods. We started with roasting and broiling. Roasting yielded dry, crumbly meatballs, with little or no browning. Broiling was extremely messy and also tended to produce dry, unevenly cooked meatballs. We knew that pan-frying produces meatballs with a rich, dark crust and moist texture, but it's also the method that adds the most fat. And there was another issue to tackle: the meatballs tended to fall apart in the skillet, leaving us with meat sauce, instead of meatballs. We found that a brief stay in the refrigerator helped the mixture firm up, which made it much easier to brown the meatballs and keep them intact.

We still needed a way to cook the meatballs in less oil and wondered if we could simply par cook them by browning them (for flavor), and then finish cooking them in the sauce. After testing varying amounts of oil, we found that in a 12-inch nonstick skillet, we needed a mere tablespoon of oil. We "fried" the meatballs over medium heat, turning them occasionally to promote the crisp crust we were looking for. Once they were nicely browned, we removed them from the skillet. With the meatballs down, it was time to turn to the sauce.

We wondered if we could save clean-up time and build more flavor into the tomato sauce by making it in the same pan used to fry the meatballs. Not only did this method prove convenient, but it also gave the sauce depth, as the browned bits that had formed when the meatballs were fried loosened from the pan bottom and dissolved in the sauce. Also, because we had the browned bits, there was no need to use additional oil in the sauce.

Meatballs need a thick, smooth sauce, the kind produced by canned crushed tomatoes, but we found consistency problems from brand to brand. Some were like thinned tomato paste, while others were too watery. To solve the problem, we used diced tomatoes, but processed a good portion of them in the food processor to get the consistency we were looking for. The sauce was nice and thick, but with a texture that set it apart from canned puree. After we had browned the meatballs, we set them aside, built the sauce in the same skillet, and then returned the meatballs to the simmering sauce so they could finish cooking. This did push the skillet's capacity to the max, but simmering the meatballs in the sauce flavored both the sauce and the meatballs, and married their flavors. Our makeover complete, we now had guilt-free meatballs, with a quick tasty sauce to serve over pasta.

MAKEOVER AT A GLANCE

–Classic–
Spaghetti and Meatballs
(per serving)

Calories: 770	Cholesterol: 90 mg
Fat: 42 g	Saturated Fat: 10 g

–Light–
Spaghetti and Meatballs
(per serving)

Calories: 550	Cholesterol: 105 mg
Fat: 13 g	Saturated Fat: 3.5 g

How We Did It

- Replaced ground beef chuck and ground pork with ground turkey
- Browned the meatballs in 1 tablespoon oil instead of pan-frying them in 1¼ cups oil
- Eliminated oil in the tomato sauce and instead used the same skillet for the sauce as we used for the meatballs to impart a meaty flavor to the sauce

Spaghetti and Meatballs

SERVES 6

It is important to let the meatballs chill for at least 1 hour before cooking, which allows them to firm up and remain intact during cooking. Do not use ground turkey breast meat (sometimes also labeled as 99 percent fat free), or the meatballs will be dry and grainy. You will need a 12-inch nonstick skillet or sauté pan with at least 2-inch sides to accommodate both the meatballs and the sauce; the skillet will be quite full.

MEATBALLS

2	slices high-quality white sandwich bread, crusts discarded, cut into ¼-inch cubes (about 1½ cups)
3	tablespoons buttermilk or 1½ tablespoons plain yogurt mixed with 1½ tablespoons milk
1	large egg yolk
1½	pounds 93 percent lean ground turkey
1	ounce Parmesan cheese, grated (½ cup), plus extra for serving
¼	cup minced fresh parsley leaves
2	medium garlic cloves, minced or pressed through a garlic press (about 2 teaspoons)
	Salt and ground black pepper
1	tablespoon olive oil

TOMATO SAUCE

3	(14.5-ounce) cans diced tomatoes
1	medium onion, minced
4	medium garlic cloves, minced or pressed through a garlic press (about 4 teaspoons)
¼	teaspoon red pepper flakes
1	pound spaghetti
3	tablespoons minced fresh basil leaves

1. FOR THE MEATBALLS: Combine the bread, buttermilk, and egg yolk in a large bowl, cover, and set aside until the bread softens, about 5 minutes. When soft, mash the mixture to a smooth paste. Add the turkey, ½ cup Parmesan, parsley, garlic, ¾ teaspoon salt, and ¼ teaspoon pepper. Combine the mixture gently using your hands until uniform, then form into 18 meatballs (each about 1¼ inches in diameter). Spread the meatballs out on a large plate, cover, and refrigerate until firm, about 1 hour.

2. Heat the oil in a 12-inch nonstick skillet or sauté pan over medium heat until just smoking. Add the meatballs and cook, turning them gently, until well browned on all sides, about 10 minutes. Transfer the meatballs to a paper towel–lined plate and set aside (leave the residual fat in the skillet).

3. Meanwhile, bring 4 quarts water to a boil in a large pot for the pasta.

4. FOR THE SAUCE: Process 2 cans of the tomatoes with their juices in a food processor until almost smooth, about 5 seconds. Add the onion and ¼ teaspoon salt to the fat left in the skillet, cover, and cook over medium-low heat until the onion is softened, 8 to 10 minutes. Stir in the garlic and pepper flakes, and cook until fragrant, about 30 seconds. Stir in the pureed tomatoes and remaining 1 can of diced tomatoes with its juice, and simmer for 10 minutes. Return the meatballs to the skillet, cover, and cook until the meatballs are cooked through, about 10 minutes.

5. While the meatballs are cooking, add 1 tablespoon salt and the pasta to the boiling water, and cook, stirring often, until al dente. Drain, reserving ½ cup of the pasta cooking water, and return the pasta to the pot.

6. Gently stir several large spoonfuls of the tomato sauce (without the meatballs) and the basil into the pasta. Add the reserved pasta cooking water as needed to loosen the sauce. Season with salt and pepper to taste. Divide the pasta among six individual bowls. Top each bowl with the remaining tomato sauce and three meatballs. Serve, passing the extra Parmesan separately.

PER SERVING : Cal 550; Fat 13 g; Sat fat 3.5 g; Chol 105 mg; Carb 73 g; Protein 38 g; Fiber 3 g; Sodium 1270 mg

MINCING BASIL

Stack a few leaves of fresh basil, then roll the leaves tightly like a cigar and slice thinly.

Spaghetti with Classic Italian Meat Sauce

ITALIAN MEAT SAUCES ARE UNDENIABLY RICH and luxurious. But you pay a price for this luxury. Along with richness come excess fat, calories, and cholesterol—certainly not things you want in a workhorse dish that you might serve quite often. In addition to the fact that these recipes include ground beef, pork, and veal, they are often simmered with milk, or even finished with heavy cream, like the classic Bolognese. We wondered if we could take a traditional, flavor-packed meat sauce and lighten it up so it needn't be reserved for a special occasion.

To begin with, we knew that we would have to replace the ground beef, pork, and veal with ground turkey in order to cut out some of the saturated fat and cholesterol. Following the model for a traditional sauce, we sautéed the aromatics (onion and garlic) then added a pound of ground turkey in the hopes of browning it to add flavor to our sauce. Then we added diced tomato, red pepper flakes, and a bay leaf and simmered the sauce until it had thickened, which took about 30 minutes. We were disappointed with the results. The sauce had a watery texture and had no meaty flavor whatsoever. The turkey had turned an unappetizing gray color and had the texture of soggy Grape-Nuts.

We decided to tackle the tomato problem first, since that was the base of our sauce. Canned diced tomatoes alone could not produce the texture we were looking for. We tried a combination of diced tomatoes and pureed tomatoes, but found the sauce to be too ketchup-like in consistency. To find a happy medium, and control the consistency of the sauce, we decided that a combination of diced and crushed tomatoes would be ideal, but opted to make our own "crushed" tomatoes by processing some of the diced tomatoes in the food processor until almost smooth. Then, to deepen the tomato flavor, we browned tomato paste along with the aromatics. This did the trick; the sauce had the perfect blend of tomato pieces bound with a smooth tomato base.

Next we turned to the flavor, or lack thereof, in the sauce. While it may be lighter and more appealing to many, ground turkey just doesn't have the assertive, meaty flavor of other ground meat. Hoping to bring out the meatiness of the turkey, we added chicken broth to the sauce. We simmered sauces with chicken broth, increasing it in ½-cup increments to determine how much it would take to make an impact on the flavor of our sauce. Two cups, simmered in the sauce for 45 minutes, added the flavor boost we were hoping for. The broth brought out the flavor of the turkey, and we found that by simmering the sauce for that length of time we were able to concentrate the flavors even more. The one remaining problem was the texture of the turkey. When cooked for 45 minutes, the initial pound of turkey had broken down considerably into the sauce, which thickened the sauce nicely, but left us wanting a slightly chunkier meat texture. To that end, we added ½ pound of turkey at the beginning, reserving the remaining turkey to be added during the last 30 minutes of simmering. Several tasters commented (to our delight) that our sauce now had the richness and flavor of a Bolognese. To put the finishing touches on our sauce, we added minced fresh basil and 2 teaspoons of extra-virgin olive oil (see "Save the Best for Last" on page 164). With just 8 grams of fat and 440 calories per serving (including the pasta), we finally had a light meat sauce worth eating.

Spaghetti with Classic Italian Meat Sauce
SERVES 6

Do not use ground turkey breast meat (sometimes labeled 99 percent fat free), or the sauce will be dry and grainy. To make the meat sauce ahead, follow the recipe through step 4 and cool. Refrigerate the sauce in an airtight container for up to 3 days, or freeze for up to 1 month. Reheat over medium-low heat, adding water as needed to adjust the consistency. Any shape of pasta can be substituted for the spaghetti here.

2   (14.5-ounce) cans diced tomatoes
1   small onion, chopped fine
1   tablespoon olive oil
    Salt
4   medium garlic cloves, minced or pressed
    through a garlic press (about 4 teaspoons)
1   pound 93 percent lean ground turkey
2   tablespoons tomato paste
2   cups low-sodium chicken broth
1   bay leaf
1/8 teaspoon red pepper flakes
1   pound spaghetti
1/2 cup minced fresh basil leaves
    Ground black pepper

1. Process 1 can of the tomatoes in a food processor until almost smooth, about 5 seconds; set aside.

2. Combine the onion, 1 teaspoon of the oil, and ¼ teaspoon salt in a Dutch oven. Cover and cook over medium-low heat, stirring often, until softened, 8 to 10 minutes. Stir in the garlic and cook until fragrant, about 30 seconds.

3. Add half of the ground turkey and increase the heat to medium high. Cook, breaking the meat into small pieces with a wooden spoon, until the meat loses its raw color, about 5 minutes. Stir in the tomato paste and continue to cook until the tomato paste begins to brown, about 2 minutes. Stir in the pureed tomatoes, canned tomatoes with their juices, chicken broth, bay leaf, and pepper flakes. Reduce the heat to medium and simmer uncovered, stirring occasionally, for 45 minutes.

4. Stir the remaining turkey into the sauce and continue to simmer, stirring occasionally, until the turkey is no longer pink and the sauce is thickened, 25 to 30 minutes. Discard the bay leaf.

5. Meanwhile, bring 4 quarts water to a boil in a large pot. Stir in 1 tablespoon salt and the pasta and cook until al dente. Drain, reserving ½ cup of the cooking water, and return the pasta to the pot.

6. Stir the remaining 2 teaspoons olive oil and the basil into the sauce, and season with salt and pepper to taste. Toss 3 cups of the sauce with the cooked pasta, adding the reserved pasta cooking water as needed to loosen the sauce. Divide the pasta among six individual bowls, top each bowl with a portion of the remaining sauce, and serve.

PER SERVING: Cal 440; Fat 8 g; Sat fat 2 g; Chol 45 mg; Carb 66 g; Protein 27 g; Fiber 3 g; Sodium 820 mg

TEST KITCHEN MAKEOVER

PESTO

TRADITIONAL PESTO IS MADE WITH PUREED basil, garlic, nuts, cheese, and a generous amount of olive oil—it's definitely not low-fat fare. In fact, most pestos (both basil pesto and the myriad variations you see around today) have about 270 calories and 28 grams of fat per serving. We would have to reduce these numbers significantly if we wanted a truly light pesto.

In our quest to develop a flavorful pesto that would not be prohibitively fat-laden, we knew the one thing we'd need to tackle was the olive oil. Most pestos rely on at least ½ cup of oil to emulsify and blend the sauce. We knew that we would need to change the character of the pesto somewhat in order to drastically reduce the oil, but our hope was that we could still keep its trademark flavorful punch intact. Thinking that ricotta cheese, when pureed with the other ingredients, would make a creamy sauce, we tried multiple batches lowering the amount of olive oil each time. The combination of ¼ cup part-skim ricotta and 2 tablespoons olive oil gave us a creamy texture as well as a sweet and welcome dairy flavor.

Garlic is a hallmark ingredient in pesto and we planned on using generous amounts in our recipe. A classic recipe for pesto uses about 3 cloves to make ¾ cup pesto. We were in the same ballpark, yieldwise, but thought we'd up the amount. We tried four, six, and eight cloves. Although our test kitchen is full of garlic lovers, they balked after tasting these pestos. Oil does tame the harshness of garlic and since our lightened pesto contains far less oil than the standard pesto, it made sense that the garlic flavor was overpowering. We then tried toasting the garlic to tame the flavor, which worked wonders. We settled on four cloves, but our pesto still seemed a bit lackluster. A colleague suggested adding a minced shallot to give the garlic a boost without the harsh bite. The shallot did the trick.

Next, we eliminated the nuts from our recipe. Nuts add bulk as well as flavor, so we increased the amount of basil to compensate for both losses. We also bruised the basil with the back of a wooden spoon. Bruising the leaves helps release their oils and intensifies flavor.

While our lightened pesto doesn't look or taste like original pesto, it is a very tasty stand-in. And, with just 6 grams of fat and 80 calories per serving, it's a lighter choice for tossing with pasta, as well as using as an all-around condiment. Because basil isn't readily available year-round we experimented with other popular pesto flavors and found success with two. In one, we paired roasted red peppers with thyme and parsley; the other features earthy mushrooms.

Creamy Basil Pesto

MAKES ABOUT 1 CUP, ENOUGH TO
SAUCE 1 POUND COOKED PASTA

Do not substitute nonfat ricotta for the part-skim or the pesto will be dry and a bit gummy. Do not include the stems or buds of the basil because they taste bitter. Bruising the basil leaves helps to bring out their sweet flavor. This pesto and the others that follow can be served not only in pasta, but as a condiment—try a spoonful on a baked potato or spread onto pizza dough before baking.

4	medium garlic cloves, unpeeled
3	cups fresh basil, stems and buds discarded (2 to 3 bunches)
1	ounce Parmesan cheese, grated (about 1/2 cup)
1/4	cup part-skim ricotta cheese
1	shallot, minced (about 2 tablespoons)
2	tablespoons extra-virgin olive oil
	Salt and ground black pepper

1. Toast the garlic in a small skillet over medium heat, shaking the pan occasionally, until the color of the cloves deepens slightly, about 7 minutes. Transfer the garlic to a plate to cool, then peel the cloves and chop or press through a garlic press.

2. Place the basil in a heavy-duty gallon-sized zipper-lock bag. Pound the bag with the flat side of a meat pounder or rolling pin until all the leaves are lightly bruised.

3. Process the garlic, basil, Parmesan, ricotta, shallot, oil, and 1/2 teaspoon salt in a food processor until smooth, about 30 seconds, stopping to scrape down the sides of the bowl as needed. Transfer the mixture to a small bowl, and season with salt and pepper to taste. (The pesto can be covered with a sheet of plastic wrap pressed flush against its surface and refrigerated for up to 3 days.)

PER 2 1/2-TABLESPOON SERVING: Cal 80; Fat 6 g; Sat fat 1.5 g; Chol 5 mg; Carb 2 g; Protein 3 g; Fiber 1 g; Sodium 270 mg

---

MAKEOVER AT A GLANCE

—Classic—
Basil Pesto
(per serving)

Calories: 270	Cholesterol: 0 mg
Fat: 28 g	Saturated Fat: 4 g

—Light—
Creamy Basil Pesto
(per serving)

Calories: 80	Cholesterol: 5 mg
Fat: 6 g	Saturated Fat: 1.5 g

How We Did It

- Replaced 6 tablespoons olive oil with 1/4 cup part-skim ricotta cheese
- Toasted the garlic to tame its flavor
- Added a shallot for further allium flavor
- Eliminated the nuts
- Increased the amount of basil to compensate for loss in bulk and flavor and bruised the basil leaves to further intensify their flavor

Roasted Red Pepper Pesto

MAKES ABOUT 2 CUPS, ENOUGH TO SAUCE
I POUND COOKED PASTA

See page 7 for information on our testing of jarred roasted red peppers. You need lots of peppers to flavor this pesto, and correspondingly, a lot of pesto to flavor a pound of pasta.

4	medium garlic cloves, unpeeled
I	(17-ounce) jar roasted red peppers, drained, rinsed thoroughly, patted dry, and cut into 2-inch pieces (about I 1/2 cups)
I	ounce Parmesan cheese, grated (about 1/2 cup)
1/4	cup part-skim ricotta cheese
I	shallot, minced (2 tablespoons)
1/4	cup packed fresh parsley leaves
I	tablespoon fresh thyme leaves
2	tablespoons extra-virgin olive oil
	Salt and ground black pepper

1. Toast the garlic in a small skillet over medium heat, shaking the pan occasionally, until the color of the cloves deepens slightly, about 7 minutes. Transfer the garlic to a plate to cool, then peel the cloves and chop or press through a garlic press.

2. Process the garlic, peppers, Parmesan, ricotta, shallot, parsley, thyme, oil, and 1/2 teaspoon salt in a food processor until smooth, about 30 seconds, stopping to scrape down the sides of the bowl as needed. Transfer the mixture to a small bowl and season with salt and pepper to taste. (The pesto can be covered with a sheet of plastic wrap pressed flush against its surface and refrigerated for up to 3 days.)

PER 1/3-CUP SERVING: Cal 110; Fat 7 g; Sat fat 2 g; Chol 10 mg; Carb 6 g; Protein 4 g; Fiber 1 g; Sodium 590 mg

Mushroom Pesto

MAKES ABOUT I 1/3 CUPS, ENOUGH TO
SAUCE I POUND COOKED PASTA

Woodsy thyme pairs perfectly with mushrooms in this variation.

1/2	ounce dried porcini mushrooms
10	ounces white mushrooms, wiped clean and sliced thin
I	shallot, minced (2 tablespoons)
2	tablespoons extra-virgin olive oil
	Salt
4	medium garlic cloves, minced or pressed through a garlic press (about 4 teaspoons)
I	tablespoon fresh thyme leaves
I	ounce Parmesan cheese, grated (about 1/2 cup)
1/4	cup part-skim ricotta cheese
1/4	cup packed fresh parsley leaves
	Ground black pepper

1. Mix the dried porcini mushrooms with 1/2 cup hot tap water in a small microwave-safe bowl. Cover with plastic wrap, cut several steam vents in the plastic wrap with a paring knife, and microwave on high power for 30 seconds. Let stand until the mushrooms soften, about 5 minutes. Lift the mushrooms from the liquid with a fork and mince. Pour the liquid through a small strainer lined with a single sheet of paper towel into a measuring cup.

2. Meanwhile, combine the white mushrooms, shallot, 1 tablespoon of the oil, and 1/2 teaspoon salt together in a 12-inch nonstick skillet. Cover and cook over medium-low heat until the mushrooms release their juices, about 7 minutes. Stir in the garlic and thyme. Turn the heat to medium-high

---

CORE TECHNIQUE

SAVE THE BEST
FOR LAST

Many pasta recipes are off the fat charts because of their generous use of olive oil. To lighten up our recipes, we naturally took out a lot of the oil, but we missed the flavor it added. We found that drizzling the pasta with 2 teaspoons of good, extra-virgin olive oil just before serving gave our lighter dishes a fruity boost of flavor and a little added richness without adding significant fat or calories.

and continue to cook, uncovered, until the mushroom juices have evaporated and the mushrooms are golden brown, about 5 minutes. Off the heat, stir in the strained porcini water, scraping up any browned bits.

3. Process the sautéed mushroom mixture, minced porcini, Parmesan, ricotta, parsley, and remaining 1 tablespoon of oil in a food processor until smooth, about 30 seconds, stopping to scrape down the sides of the bowl as needed. Transfer the mixture to a small bowl and season with salt and pepper to taste. (The pesto can be covered with a sheet of plastic wrap pressed flush against its surface and refrigerated for up to 3 days.)

PER 3 1/2-TABLESPOON SERVING: Cal 100; Fat 7 g; Sat fat 2 g; Chol 10 mg; Carb 5 g; Protein 5 g; Fiber 1 g; Sodium 300 mg

Pasta with Pesto

SERVES 6

Pasta made with these creamy low-fat pestos should be served immediately.

Salt
| pound linguine or spaghetti
| recipe Creamy Basil Pesto (page 163),
Roasted Red Pepper Pesto (page 164), or
Mushroom Pesto (page 164)
Ground black pepper

Bring 4 quarts water to a boil in a large pot. Stir in 1 tablespoon salt and the pasta and cook, stirring often, until al dente. Reserving ¾ cup of the cooking water, drain the pasta and return it to the pot. Stir the pesto into the pasta, adding the reserved pasta cooking water as needed to loosen the sauce. Season with salt and pepper to taste, and serve immediately.

Pasta with Creamy Basil Pesto
PER SERVING: Cal 360; Fat 8 g; Sat fat 2 g; Chol 10 mg; Carb 59 g; Protein 14 g; Fiber 3 g; Sodium 390 mg

Pasta with Roasted Red Pepper Pesto
PER SERVING: Cal 380; Fat 8 g; Sat fat 2.5 g; Chol 10 mg; Carb 63 g; Protein 15 g; Fiber 3 g; Sodium 690 mg

Pasta with Mushroom Pesto
PER SERVING: Cal 370; Fat 8 g; Sat fat 2 g; Chol 10 mg; Carb 61 g; Protein 15 g; Fiber 3 g; Sodium 400 mg

PASTA WITH GARDEN VEGETABLE SAUCE

WHEN THE END OF SUMMER ROLLS AROUND, and backyard gardens and farmers markets are overflowing with bumper crops of ripe vegetables and fresh herbs, pasta with garden vegetable sauce is an ideal way to reap the benefits of this bounty, and what could be healthier? Tossing pasta with vegetables sounded like an easy task, but it turned out to be much more difficult than we had imagined. We were looking for a fresh and light-tasting dish that mimicked the brightness of a hearty tomato sauce, but where the vegetables were the star. The trick was to sort out how to cook the vegetables and how to bind the vegetables with the pasta without resorting to fatty ingredients like oil, meat, or cheese.

Many of the recipes we tried turned out soggy vegetables (especially true with summer squashes), with heavy tomato sauces that virtually obscured not only the flavor but also the brilliant colors of the vegetables. We wanted perfectly cooked pasta with a light, clean-tasting sauce. We wanted the vegetables to be crisp, not mushy, with vibrant colors and a toothsome texture.

We began by figuring out the most ideal vegetables, and the best method for cooking them. We gathered a mixture of our favorites: zucchini (a vegetable that seems to multiply with ferocity in the garden), carrots, cherry tomatoes, onion, bell peppers, and garlic. We quickly sautéed the lot until just softened, then transferred them to a large bowl and tossed them with pasta and fresh basil. The results were tasty, but the dish had the appearance and flavor of something more akin to a warm pasta salad than pasta with an abundant vegetable sauce. It just wasn't saucy enough and the flavors were too homogenous.

Next we decided to try adding the vegetables to the skillet in batches, rather than all at once, to allow them to retain their individual flavors. First, we sautéed the zucchini until browned, then we added the cherry tomatoes and cooked them until they were just softened. We then removed those vegetables from the skillet and added the firmer vegetables: onion, carrots, and bell peppers. We covered the skillet and cooked the vegetables until they softened.

Now that we had a flavorful base, we needed to extend it into a sauce. We turned to tomato paste, adding 3 tablespoons to the skillet with the vegetables, and cooked until the paste browned. Garlic and red pepper flakes were then added to the skillet and sautéed until fragrant. We needed to add a liquid to the mixture and tested both water and chicken broth. Tasters preferred the richness and consistency of the chicken broth.

At this point we returned the zucchini-tomato mixture back to the skillet and cooked it all to marry the flavors and warm the vegetables through. This sauce was delicious served with our pasta but tasters felt that it was lacking a little something. Chopped parsley added a nice burst of bright green color, but not much in the way of flavor. We then tried tossing in some arugula, which wilted perfectly when tossed with the hot pasta. Its peppery and slightly bitter taste elevated our pasta to a new level. To pull it all together, we finished the dish by adding 2 teaspoons of extra-virgin olive oil and salt and pepper and giving it a good toss. Now we had a summer pasta dish worth waiting all summer for.

Pasta with Garden Vegetable Sauce

SERVES 4 TO 6

We like this recipe made with low-sodium chicken broth, but if you'd like to make it vegetarian, substitute vegetable broth for the chicken broth. Yellow summer squash can be substituted for the zucchini. Small curly pasta shapes such as rotini work best in this dish. Substituting other pasta shapes (even if small and curly) for the rotini may affect both the dry measurement and final portion size. Serve with grated Parmesan cheese.

4	teaspoons extra-virgin olive oil
2	medium zucchini (about 6 ounces each), halved lengthwise and sliced 1/4 inch thick
1	pint cherry tomatoes, halved
3	medium carrots, peeled and sliced 1/2 inch thick
1	medium onion, sliced thin
1	medium red bell pepper, stemmed, seeded, and cut into 1/4-inch pieces
	Salt
3	tablespoons tomato paste
3	medium garlic cloves, minced or pressed through a garlic press (about 1 tablespoon)
1/8	teaspoon red pepper flakes
1 1/2	cups low-sodium chicken broth
1/2	pound rotini pasta (about 2 cups)
3	ounces baby arugula, washed and stemmed (about 3 cups)
1/4	cup minced fresh basil leaves
	Ground black pepper
	Parmesan cheese (for serving)

1. Bring 4 quarts water to a boil in a large pot for the pasta.

2. Meanwhile, heat 1 teaspoon of the oil in a 12-inch nonstick skillet over medium-high heat until just smoking. Add the zucchini and cook, stirring often, until well browned, about 3 minutes. Add the cherry tomatoes and toss to combine and wilt slightly, about 1 minute. Transfer to a large bowl and set aside.

3. Add 1 more teaspoon oil to the now-empty skillet and return to medium-high heat. Add the carrots, onion, bell pepper, and 1/4 teaspoon salt. Cover and cook until the onions and peppers have softened, about 5 minutes. Stir in the tomato paste and continue to cook until it begins to brown, about 1 minute. Stir in the garlic and pepper flakes and cook until fragrant, about 30 seconds. Stir in the broth, scraping up any browned bits. Bring to a simmer and cook until slightly thickened, about 1 minute; cover and set aside.

4. Stir 1 tablespoon salt and the pasta into the boiling water and cook, stirring often, until al dente. Reserving 1/2 cup of the pasta water, drain the pasta and return it to the pot. Gently stir the sautéed zucchini-tomato mixture, carrot-sauce

mixture, arugula, basil, and remaining 2 teaspoons olive oil into the pasta. Cover and let sit off the heat until the vegetables are hot, about 1 minute. Add the reserved pasta cooking water as needed to loosen the sauce. Season with salt and pepper to taste. Divide among six individual bowls and serve, passing the Parmesan cheese separately.

PER SERVING: Cal 230; Fat 4 g; Sat fat 5 g; Chol 0 mg; Carb 41 g; Protein 9 g; Fiber 5 g; Sodium 390 mg

PASTA WITH CHICKEN AND BROCCOLI

ITALIAN CHAIN RESTAURANTS KNOWN FOR cheap wine and doughy breadsticks almost always list pasta with chicken and broccoli on the menu. It sounds good—and even good for you—but this dish often falls short. The broccoli is usually mushy and sparse, the pasta is overcooked and has no flavor, and the chicken is dry and flavorless. Some recipes bind the dish together with a heavy cream sauce or go overboard with the olive oil. Our goal was obvious: We wanted to reclaim this dish with fresh, crisp broccoli, tender chicken, and a light, flavorful sauce. We also wanted a recipe that was easy and healthy enough to eat regularly at home.

In order to figure this dish out, we needed to break it down into its four components—the chicken, the broccoli, the sauce, and the pasta—and tackle each individually. Right off the bat, we decided that boneless, skinless chicken breasts were the best choice for this recipe and tested various cooking methods, including broiling, sautéing, and poaching. Broiling and sautéing both produced meat with the most flavor; however, we quickly ruled out broiling for the simple reason that turning on the oven seemed entirely unnecessary—this is a dish you should be able to make on the stovetop. The nicely browned sautéed chicken added great flavor to the dish and provided flavorful browned bits in our skillet, which would help us build our sauce. We cooked the chicken for about five minutes per side, and then let it rest while we were putting together the rest of the dish. We also noted that a nonstick skillet made cleanup

a breeze, and that a pound of chicken (along with the broccoli and pasta) was an ample amount for six people for dinner. With the chicken cooked properly, it was time to focus on the broccoli.

Many recipes use broccoli florets, or the "top of the tree." We thought this was a waste of the perfectly good broccoli stems, which pack loads of flavor as well as fiber. While the stems can be woody and tough when used as is, we found that by peeling and thinly slicing them we could eliminate this problem. We tried multiple ways to cook the broccoli, including simmering it in the sauce, steaming, blanching (a quick dunk in boiling water), and microwaving. Simmering it in the sauce was a disaster—the broccoli gave the sauce both an off flavor and a dirty color. Steaming on the stovetop and in the microwave both worked OK, but neither was as easy as blanching, especially since we already had a pot of water boiling for the pasta. Cooking the broccoli in the pasta water first, we simply scooped it from the water using a slotted spoon, then returned the water to a boil before adding the pasta. We ran into the problem of broccoli with an army green color and slightly mushy texture when we simply let it sit in a bowl after being blanched—it continued to steam as the pieces sat in a big pile. Dunking the broccoli pieces in a bowl of ice water prevented this, but then we had a hard time warming them up again before tossing them with the pasta and sauce (they always remained a bit chilled).

Finally, we tried spreading the blanched broccoli pieces out on a large plate as the pasta cooked. This allowed them to cool off enough so as not to turn an ugly color, yet they were easily warmed through by the hot pasta and sauce. The key, then, was to slightly undercook the broccoli in the boiling water and let it continue to cook a little as it waited for everything else to be done. As for how much broccoli to use, we tested 1 to 2 pounds of broccoli. Even though it was a headliner in this recipe, 2 pounds proved to overpower the dish, while 1 pound left us wanting more. One and a half pounds was the perfect amount, providing the right proportion of broccoli to pasta.

Finally, we turned our attention to the sauce. Many recipes we found relied on a classic base of cream thickened with a roux (a flour and butter combination). We wanted something lighter that wouldn't eclipse the flavor of the broccoli and chicken. What we needed was a vehicle to carry the flavors of the garlic, pepper flakes, and fresh herbs that we knew we wanted in the dish. We wondered how tasters would react to a broth-based sauce. We simmered chicken broth with the aromatics and were pleased with the results. The flavor of the aromatics now jumped out, and there was a significant boost in chicken flavor. The sauce still needed a final kick of flavor. We found we needed a hefty amount of garlic to flavor the otherwise bland pasta. Twelve garlic cloves (about ¼ cup minced) proved to be the ideal amount, lending a powerful presence without dominating the dish. Although not traditional to the dish, the addition of sun-dried tomatoes, simmered along with the broth, gave the sauce a deep tomato flavor that coated every bite of pasta. To boost the flavor even more, we added minced anchovy fillets—again not traditional, but even the most avid anchovy haters in the test kitchen agreed that they added a subtle dimension to the dish.

What we often miss when developing healthier pasta recipes is the addition of the cheese that is so often grated with abandon on top of your dinner in restaurants. We tried varying amounts of Parmesan and found that unless we used a full cup, we weren't getting the flavor we were looking for. Asiago, a firm Italian cow's milk cheese, has a stronger, more intense flavor than Parmesan and gave us more bang for the buck. A little went a long way. Just 1 ounce (½ cup) gave us the serious flavor we were looking for. Pecorino Romano, another Italian cow's milk cheese, can be substituted for the Asiago with good results.

We had discovered early on in testing that shaped pastas, such as rotini or radiatore, trapped sauces better than flat pastas. With these pastas, the flavor-packed sauce gets trapped in their ridges and doesn't end up in a puddle at the bottom of your plate.

When the sauce and pasta were tossed with ample amounts of perfectly cooked broccoli and tender chicken that we had sliced on the bias, we had a healthy, great-tasting dinner that was worth staying home for, any night of the week.

Pasta with Chicken and Broccoli

SERVES 6

We like to use broccoli florets and stalks for this recipe. Peeling the stalks ensures that they will be tender. We prefer to use a pasta with lots of nooks and crannies, such as rotini, to keep the flavors on the pasta, not at the bottom of your bowl.

1	pound boneless, skinless chicken breasts (about 2 large breasts)
	Salt and ground black pepper
4	teaspoons extra-virgin olive oil
1	medium onion, minced
1	(8 ½-ounce) jar oil-packed sun-dried tomatoes, rinsed, patted dry, and sliced into ¼-inch strips (about 1 cup)
12	medium garlic cloves, minced or pressed through a garlic press (about ¼ cup)
5	anchovy fillets, rinsed, patted dry, and minced to a paste (about 2 teaspoons)
¼	teaspoon red pepper flakes
¾	cup low-sodium chicken broth
1½	pounds broccoli (about 1 large bunch), florets cut into 1-inch pieces, stalks peeled, halved lengthwise, and sliced ¼ inch thick (see page 75)
1	pound rotini pasta
¼	cup minced fresh basil leaves
1	ounce Asiago or Pecorino Romano cheese, grated (about ½ cup)

1. Bring 4 quarts water to a boil in a large pot for the broccoli and the pasta.

2. Meanwhile, pat the chicken dry with paper towels and season with salt and pepper. Heat 1 teaspoon of the oil in a 12-inch nonstick skillet over medium-high heat until just smoking. Add the chicken and cook until browned on the first side, about 5 minutes. Using tongs, flip the chicken over. Reduce the heat to medium-low, add ½ cup water, and cover the pan. Continue to cook until the thickest part is no longer pink and registers about 160 degrees on an instant-read thermometer, about 5 minutes. Transfer the chicken to a plate, tent loosely with foil, and set aside. When

cool enough to handle, slice the chicken on the bias into ½-inch-thick pieces; keep covered and set aside.

3. Pour off any water left in the skillet and add the onion, sun-dried tomatoes, garlic, anchovies, pepper flakes, 1 more teaspoon of the oil, and ¼ teaspoon salt. Return the skillet to medium-low heat, cover, and cook until the onion begins to soften, about 5 minutes. Stir in the broth and continue to cook, covered, until the tomatoes have softened, about 2 minutes. Remove the lid and simmer until the mixture has thickened slightly, 3 to 5 minutes; cover and set aside off the heat.

4. Stir in 1 tablespoon of salt and the broccoli into the boiling water, and cook until the broccoli is bright green and tender but still crisp in the center, about 2 minutes. Using a slotted spoon, transfer the broccoli to a large paper towel–lined plate; set aside to cool. Return the water to a boil, stir in the pasta and cook until al dente. Reserving ½ cup of the cooking water, drain the pasta and return it to the pot.

5. Gently stir the chicken, broccoli, basil, Asiago, sauce, and remaining 2 teaspoons olive oil into the pasta. Cover and let sit off the heat until the sauce and chicken are hot, about 1 minute. Add the reserved pasta cooking water as needed to loosen the sauce. Season with salt and pepper to taste, divide among six individual bowls, and serve.

PER SERVING: Cal 510; Fat 10 g; Sat fat 2.5 g; Chol 50 mg; Carb 73 g; Protein 35 g; Fiber 7 g; Sodium 680 mg

➤ VARIATION

Pasta with Turkey Sausage and Broccoli

Follow the recipe for Pasta with Chicken and Broccoli, substituting 1 pound raw turkey sausage links for the chicken. Do not season the sausage with salt and pepper, and brown in the hot oil in step 2 until lightly browned on all sides, about 8 minutes, before adding the water. Continue to cook, cool, slice the sausage as described in step 2, and proceed as directed.

PER SERVING: Cal 540; Fat 15 g; Sat fat 3.5 g; Chol 65 mg; Carb 73 g; Protein 32 g; Fiber 7 g; Sodium 990 mg

PASTA WITH BEANS AND GREENS

ITALIANS HAVE A KNACK FOR TRANSFORMING simple, humble ingredients into remarkable meals, and the rustic trio of pasta, beans, and hearty greens is no exception. When carefully prepared, the combination is sublime. In many recipes we found, dried cannellini (white kidney) beans are gently simmered until tender, then pancetta, olive oil, aromatics, and garden-fresh greens are tossed together with al dente pasta and a sprinkling of Parmesan; the result is rich, earthy, and ultimately satisfying. This dish is tasty to be sure, but it tops out on the high end of our daily fat intake. We wanted not only to speed up the cooking time, but also to substantially cut back on the fat that the pancetta and olive oil pack into this rustic comfort food meal. As with all our lightened pasta dishes, our ultimate goal was to eliminate some of the fat without sacrificing the flavor and richness it provided.

We decided to start with the easiest elements of the dish first: the beans and the greens. We knew we'd need to forgo the dried cannellini beans that are traditional in this dish since they take at least an hour to cook and we were after a weeknight dinner. Canned beans performed admirably. As for the choice of hearty greens, Italians usually choose from among the following: turnip, dandelion, chicory, mustard, broccoli rabe, collards, and kale. And a five-step approach is the well-known cure for the bitterness that many of them possess: Blanch, shock (dunk in ice water), squeeze dry, chop, and sauté. When handled this way, the unpleasant bitterness is tamed and the resulting greens are robust, but not overpowering. The downside? The whole process commands precious time, not to mention multiple pieces of kitchen equipment. So we wanted to gauge the relative bitterness of each type of green and hopefully choose the mildest one available to avoid this cumbersome process. We conducted a tasting of plain greens, each cooked in a small amount of salted water. Two of the choices, kale and collard greens, were absolute standouts: tasters noted their appealing vegetal and mineral qualities but made no mention of bitterness. Kale, however, won out overall. Collard greens, although delicious, are not widely available and take longer to cook, not fitting into our goal of a quick-to-prepare weeknight pasta dish.

Now that we had canned beans and hearty kale to work with we still needed a way to marry them with the pasta. To begin with, we decided to use bacon for flavor, and we found that one slice, when diced and mixed with a small amount of extra-virgin olive oil, was enough. The fruitiness of the oil combined with the subtle smokiness of the bacon became the base of our sauce. We discovered that when we withheld fat from this recipe, we needed to bump up the quantities of aromatics that we used. We settled on two onions and twelve cloves of garlic, red pepper flakes for heat, and fresh thyme to bring it all together. To build the sauce, we added low-sodium chicken broth and the canned cannellini beans. This became not only the sauce for our pasta, but a medium in which to cook the large quantity of kale that tasters wanted in this dish. We added the kale to the Dutch oven, (it barely fit, but wilted down substantially when cooked) and steamed it until barely tender, then tossed it with the pasta. At this point the flavors were great, but tasters bemoaned the consistency of the sauce, saying it lacked cohesiveness. The pasta, beans, and greens remained separate entities, not the union of the three we had been hoping for, and the sauce failed to cling to the pasta. To solve the problem, we found that coarsely mashing some of the beans with the back of a spoon or a potato masher helped to thicken the sauce and bind everything together. The mashed beans acted as a fat replacer in terms of texture, and helped, as oil does, to carry the flavors of the aromatics throughout the dish.

The last challenge we faced lay in the practicality of our cooking technique. We needed a large pot to cook the pasta, but we also needed a large pot to accommodate the bulky kale. Knowing that most home cooks have only one large pot, we decided to cook the pasta first, then set it aside and use the same pot for our sauce and kale. Reheating the pasta in the pot with the kale and beans took no time at all, and gave the pasta time to absorb the deep flavors of the sauce. One final trick we learned is that the intense flavor of extra-virgin olive goes a long way when you're trying to cut down on fat (see "Save the Best for Last" on page 164). A mere 2 teaspoons drizzled over the pasta gave our dish the final burst of flavor we were looking for.

Pasta with Beans and Greens
SERVES 6
You will need a Dutch oven (or large pot) to accommodate the kale. The kale will fill the pot initially, but it will cook down considerably. We like this dish when made with small curly pasta shapes such as rotini. Substituting other pasta shapes for the rotini (even if small and curly) may affect both the dry measurement and final portion size. This dish is also tasty with whole-wheat pasta—see the results of our tasting on page 171 for our recommended brand.

	Salt
1	slice bacon (1 ounce), minced fine
2	medium onions, minced
12	medium garlic cloves, minced or pressed through a garlic press (about 1/4 cup)
1	tablespoon extra-virgin olive oil
1	teaspoon minced fresh thyme leaves
1/4	teaspoon red pepper flakes
2	cups low-sodium chicken broth
2	(15.5-ounce) cans cannellini beans, drained and rinsed
1 1/2	pounds kale, thick stems removed, washed, and chopped into 1-inch pieces
1	pound rotini pasta (see note)
1	ounce Parmesan cheese, grated (about 1/2 cup)
	Ground black pepper

1. Add the bacon to a large pot and cook over low heat. Cook until the fat is rendered and the bacon is crisp, about 8 minutes. Stir in the onions, garlic, 1 teaspoon of the olive oil, thyme, and pepper flakes. Turn the heat to medium-low, cover, and cook, stirring occasionally, until the onion has softened, 8 to 10 minutes.

2. Stir in the chicken broth, half of the beans,

and ¼ teaspoon salt. Bring to a simmer and cook, uncovered, until the sauce has thickened slightly, about 10 minutes. Add the kale, cover, and continue to cook over medium heat, tossing occasionally, until the kale is tender, about 10 minutes. Mash some of the beans using the back of a spoon or a potato masher and cover to keep warm.

3. Meanwhile, bring 4 quarts water to a boil in another large pot. Stir in 1 tablespoon salt and the pasta, and cook, stirring often, until al dente. Reserving ½ cup of the cooking water, drain the pasta.

INGREDIENTS: Whole-Wheat Pasta

We've never been big fans of whole-wheat pasta, thanks to the coarse, gummy texture and out-of-place "oatmeal" flavor that plagued too many of the varieties we've tried. In recent years, however, the options available in the pasta aisle have multiplied dramatically. With so many new products—and a hunch that a distinct, nutty flavor might be a good match for our hearty greens and beans—we decided to take another look. We tasted 10 brands plain and then tried several of the top and bottom finishers in our pasta recipe. Eight of the 10 contenders were made from whole durum wheat, the notably hard, dense wheat from which semolina, the primary ingredient in traditional pasta, is processed. Though texture has improved overall since our previous tastings, several of the pastas were almost as gritty and gluey as we remembered—and lacking in hearty whole grain flavor to boot. Our top finishers, Ronzoni Healthy Harvest Whole Wheat Blend Pasta and Eden Organic, blended whole durum wheat with regular semolina, so they're not 100 percent "whole" wheat. But the combination of a pleasantly chewy texture and a deep, wheaty flavor was worth the nutritional trade-off of just 1 gram less fiber per serving than the most fiber-laden whole-wheat brand in our lineup.

THE BEST WHOLE-WHEAT PASTA
RONZONI HEALTHY HARVEST
The only pasta that tasted "undeniably wheaty" without a gummy or grainy texture.

4. Stir the cooked pasta and remaining beans into the kale mixture and cook over medium heat, stirring occasionally, until the pasta absorbs most of the liquid and the mixture is warm, about 2 minutes. Stir in the Parmesan and remaining 2 teaspoons olive oil. Season with salt and pepper to taste. Divide among six individual bowls and serve.

PER SERVING: Cal 500; Fat 8 g; Sat fat 2 g; Chol 5 mg; Carb 87 g; Protein 21 g; Fiber 9 g; Sodium 740 mg

LINGUINE WITH SHELLFISH

PASTA AND SHELLFISH ARE A NATURAL combination, appearing in many guises—most often shrimp, scallops, clams, or mussels—on the menus of restaurants both humble and fancy. The seafood is the star of this dish, and the pasta serves as a vehicle for just about any kind of sauce that gets thrown its way. More often than not, though, the seafood is overcooked and rubbery, and the sauces are watery, greasy, and flavorless. To compensate for lack of body, they are often finished with copious amounts of butter, which masks the delicate brininess of the shellfish. We wanted a dish in which the shellfish was the star, but where the pasta could hold its own as a co-star, rather than a dispensable extra. We wanted a sauce packed with flavor, but not so much so that it brought the curtain down on the seafood. And it had to be easy on the waistline.

We started our testing with shrimp—one of the most universal favorites to pair with pasta—in part because it's easy to find either fresh or frozen. We knew we had to begin by exploring ways to cook the shrimp, our primary concern being the risk of overcooking it. Some in the test kitchen preferred the shrimp sautéed, while others felt poaching was the best way to go. Several tests showed that both methods worked, but in the end, sautéing proved to be a bit trickier in terms of timing, and the shrimp had to be browned in two batches. Poaching proved to be the best method for three reasons; we could poach the shrimp in the sauce we were making for the pasta, the shrimp could be cooked all at once, and the degree of doneness could be more easily controlled when the shrimp were cooked just before we sauced the pasta.

With the method of cooking the shrimp settled, we moved on to the sauce. Fish stock seemed like a natural choice for the base of our sauce, but we found it impractical to make our own. Bottled clam juice served as an adequate replacement, but tasters felt it was overpowering unless diluted with another liquid. We tried a combination of clam broth and chicken broth that gave us the balance we were looking for. Neither stood out on its own, but each complemented the other, and the shrimp. We decided early on in testing that this sauce needed lots of flavor, and most tasters wanted lots of garlic and lemon. To that end, we started building our sauce with aromatics: one onion and eight garlic cloves. For a subtle hit of heat we added red pepper flakes, while some fresh thyme and a bay leaf rounded things out. Then we added the broths, and simmered until the sauce had reduced and the flavors concentrated, which took about ten minutes.

At this point, the flavor of the sauce was perfect, and we were ready to poach our shrimp, but a unique problem arose. We knew that at some point, the sauce was going to have to be thickened by some means in order to coat the pasta. We weren't looking for pasta and seafood in brodo, or "in broth"—it had to be a clingy, cohesive sauce that wouldn't end up in a pool on our dinner plate. The time to thicken seemed to be before we added the shrimp, otherwise we would find ourselves having to fish the shrimp out of the broth, then thicken, then add them back in to reheat; too fussy for us. Adding butter, which would slightly thicken the sauce, was out of the question. We wondered if a bit of cornstarch would do the trick, if we whisked it into a paste, or slurry. We started with 3 tablespoons, mixed it with water, and stirred it into the sauce along with a good amount of fresh lemon juice. Tasters liked the fact that the sauce was thicker and clung to the pasta, but the cornstarch taste was too obvious, too starchy in a chalky kind of way. We cut the cornstarch back to 2 tablespoons with much better results. The texture was now just right, but the dish tasted too lean. It clearly needed some sort of fat to add an undertone of creaminess and richness to the sauce.

One of the tricks that had been successful in many of our sauces was the use of light cream cheese. Just a little (3 tablespoons) goes a long way. When melted in with the broth and clam juice, it gave the sauce the subtle richness we were looking for, without imparting a "cream sauce" quality, which we didn't care for with seafood. To brighten the sauce and give it a fresh look, we added minced fresh parsley (fresh basil or oregano would be great too). The shrimp were tender and perfectly cooked. The pasta (which tastes great with this sauce even without the shrimp) was packed with the lemon-garlic flavor we were hoping for.

Having now mastered linguine with shrimp we decided to give sea scallops a try. But when the scallops were poached, as the shrimp had been, not one taster liked their flavor, texture, or appearance. They looked anemic and added nothing to the flavor of our sauce. In addition, their shape and size made it hard to integrate them into the dish overall. They just weren't working. Wanting to find another type of shellfish but not willing to drag out another pan, we turned to clams, a natural combination with linguine.

We decided on littleneck clams (with a shell dimension of less than two inches) and opted for steaming them in our lemon garlic sauce (instead of the poaching technique we used for the shrimp). Determining that we needed about six clams per person (about 3 pounds), we steamed them, covered, in the sauce until they just popped open. Then we transferred them to a bowl, poured the sauce over the pasta and made sure it was seasoned correctly, and nestled the clams snugly into the pasta. Our second seafood and pasta dish was a cinch to prepare and tasters were impressed.

Linguine with Shrimp, Lemon, and Garlic

SERVES 6

It is best to buy shell-on shrimp and peel them yourself. Pre-peeled shrimp are often treated with a sodium solution, which affects their flavor and gives them a rubbery texture. Take care not to overcook the shrimp or they will be tough. Vary the amount of red pepper flakes according to your taste.

- 1 medium onion, minced
- 1 teaspoon olive oil
  Salt
- 8 medium garlic cloves, minced or pressed through a garlic press (about 2 tablespoons plus 2 teaspoons)
- 2 cups low-sodium chicken broth
- 2 (8-ounce) bottles clam juice
- 1/8 teaspoon red pepper flakes (see note)
- 2 teaspoons minced fresh thyme leaves
- 1 bay leaf
- 2 tablespoons cornstarch
- 2 tablespoons water
- 1/2 cup juice from 4 lemons
- 3 tablespoons light cream cheese
- 1 1/2 pounds extra-large shrimp (21 to 25 per pound), peeled and deveined
- 1 pound linguine or spaghetti
- 3 tablespoons minced fresh parsley leaves
  Ground black pepper

1. Bring 4 quarts water to a boil in a large pot for the pasta.

2. Meanwhile, combine the onion, oil, and 1/2 teaspoon salt in a 12-inch nonstick skillet. Cover and cook over medium-low heat, stirring often, until softened, 8 to 10 minutes. Stir in the garlic and cook until fragrant, about 30 seconds. Add the broth, clam juice, pepper flakes, thyme, and bay leaf to the skillet, scraping up any browned bits. Bring to a boil and cook until the sauce measures about 2 cups, 7 to 10 minutes.

3. Whisk the cornstarch and water together, then whisk it into the simmering sauce. Continue to simmer the sauce until it has thickened, about 2 minutes. Off the heat, whisk in the lemon juice and cream cheese until smooth. Add the shrimp, cover,

and let sit off the heat until the shrimp are firm and no longer translucent in the center, 7 to 10 minutes. Discard the bay leaf; cover and set aside.

4. While the shrimp are cooking, stir 1 tablespoon salt and the pasta into the boiling water and cook, stirring often, until al dente. Reserving 1/2 cup of the pasta water, drain the pasta and return it to the pot. Gently stir the shrimp-sauce mixture and parsley into the pasta. Cover and let sit off the heat until the shrimp are hot, about 1 minute. Add the reserved pasta cooking water as needed to loosen the sauce. Season with salt and pepper to taste. Divide among six individual bowls and serve.

PER SERVING: Cal 460; Fat 5 g; Sat fat 1.5 g; Chol 180 mg; Carb 66 g; Protein 36 g; Fiber 3 g; Sodium 860 mg

Linguine with Fresh Clam Sauce

SERVES 6

We prefer to use littleneck clams for this recipe. Ask your fishmonger for the smallest littlenecks, and figure on about 6 clams per person. Be sure to discard any open clams or clams with broken shells. Feel free to add more red pepper flakes for a spicier sauce.

- 1 medium onion, minced
- 1 teaspoon olive oil
- 8 medium garlic cloves, minced or pressed through a garlic press (about 2 tablespoons plus 2 teaspoons)
- 2 teaspoon minced fresh thyme leaves
- 1/8 teaspoon red pepper flakes (see note)
- 2 cups low-sodium chicken broth
- 2 (8-ounce) bottles clam juice
- 1 bay leaf
- 36 littleneck clams (about 3 pounds), scrubbed thoroughly (see page 174)
- 2 tablespoons cornstarch
- 2 tablespoons water
- 1/2 cup juice from 4 lemons
- 3 tablespoons light cream cheese
  Salt
- 1 pound linguine or spaghetti
- 1/4 cup minced fresh parsley leaves
  Ground black pepper

1. Bring 4 quarts water to a boil in a large pot for the pasta.

2. Combine the onion and oil in a 12-inch nonstick skillet. Cover and cook over medium-low heat, stirring often, until softened, 8 to 10 minutes. Stir in the garlic, thyme, and pepper flakes and cook until fragrant, about 30 seconds. Add the broth, clam juice, and bay leaf, scraping up any browned bits. Bring to a simmer and cook until the sauce measures about 2 cups, 7 to 10 minutes.

3. Add the clams and continue to simmer until the clams have opened, 4 to 8 minutes. Using tongs, transfer the clams to a large bowl, cover, and set aside. Whisk the cornstarch and water together, then whisk it into the simmering sauce. Continue to simmer the sauce until it has thickened, about 2 minutes. Off the heat, whisk the lemon juice and cream cheese into the sauce until smooth. Discard the bay leaf; cover and set aside.

4. While the clams are cooking, stir 1 tablespoon salt and the pasta into the boiling water and cook, stirring often, until al dente. Reserving ½ cup of the pasta water, drain the pasta and return it to the pot. Gently stir the sauce and parsley into the pasta. Cover and let sit off the heat until the sauce is hot, about 1 minute. Add the reserved pasta cooking water as needed to loosen the sauce. Season with salt and pepper to taste. Divide the pasta among six individual bowls and nestle the

SCRUBBING CLAMS

Use a soft brush, sometimes sold in kitchen shops as a vegetable brush, to scrub away any bits of sand trapped in the shell.

cooked clams into each serving, along with any accumulated juices.

PER SERVING: Cal 420; Fat 4.5 g; Sat fat 1.5 g; Chol 45 mg; Carb 68 g; Protein 27 g; Fiber 3 g; Sodium 580 mg

TEST KITCHEN MAKEOVER

FETTUCCINE ALFREDO

A TRADITIONAL FETTUCCINE ALFREDO IS made with aged Parmigiano-Reggiano cheese, sweet butter, heavy cream, and homemade fresh egg fettuccine. Boasting 580 calories and 43 grams of fat per serving, this dish is something we indulge in only once, maybe twice, a year. But we wondered if we could eat it more often if we lightened it up? Given its simplicity and the fact that it relies on a handful of high-fat ingredients, we were dubious about whether it was just better left alone. Nonetheless, we decided to give it a try.

A classic Alfredo sauce is made by simmering and reducing heavy cream until it thickens to a sauce-like consistency, then finishing it with butter and Parmesan. Setting the issue of the butter and Parmesan aside for now, we began looking for a way to replace the reduced heavy cream; if we could find an acceptable substitute, then the odds were good that we could make a decent low-fat Alfredo sauce.

Traditionally, when making an Alfredo sauce you must simmer about 1½ cups of heavy cream until it reduces down to roughly ¾ cup to coat half a pound of pasta (the amount of calories and fat do not reduce with the cream, of course). Our idea was to start with a smaller amount of cream—just ¾ cup—and then find another way to thicken it to a sauce-like consistency. Three alternative thickening options came to mind: a roux (a mixture of flour and butter), cornstarch, and light cream cheese. Giving all three of these ideas a go in a basic Alfredo sauce, we found that the roux, although it performed nicely, added nearly as much fat as we had removed, thanks to the butter.

The light cream cheese was also able to thicken the heavy cream into a nice sauce; however, tasters complained that it had a simple, generic "cheese" flavor that competed with the Parmesan; in short, it just didn't taste right. The cornstarch was the clear winner here, producing a clean, silky sauce that allowed the Parmesan flavor to shine. Using the cornstarch had helped trim about 17 grams of fat per serving from the original recipe, and although we still had a long way to go, we now believed we were on the right track.

We wondered whether we could reduce the fat even more, now that we had solved the basic technique for the sauce, by replacing the heavy cream with a lower fat alternative, such as half-and-half, milk, or evaporated milk. The milk-based sauce was disastrous—it curdled and turned a strange grey color. The evaporated milk made a nice creamy sauce, but tasters found that its sweet, milky flavor overwhelmed the Parmesan, and in the end, the sauce didn't taste like a classic Alfredo. The

half-and-half, on the other hand, produced a stellar sauce with good creamy body and a simple but rich flavor—the tasters unanimously approved.

The next ingredient we put to the test was the Parmesan, the key flavor in an Alfredo sauce. Parmesan amounts range from 1 to 4 ounces (½ cup to 2 cups) in other recipes we researched, so we started out with 4 ounces of authentic Parmigiano-Reggiano and made batches of Alfredo with incrementally less cheese. Tasters found that when this Alfredo sauce was made with less than 2 ounces of cheese (1 cup), it just wasn't worth eating. Luckily, Parmesan is relatively low in fat (2 ounces adds just under 4 grams of fat per

MAKEOVER AT A GLANCE

—Classic—
Fettuccine Alfredo
(per serving)

Calories: 580 Cholesterol: 185 mg
Fat: 43 g Saturated Fat: 27 g

—Light—
Fettuccine Alfredo
(per serving)

Calories: 300 Cholesterol: 70 mg
Fat: 11 g Saturated Fat: 6 g

How We Did It
- Substituted ¾ cup half-and-half thickened with cornstarch for 1½ cups heavy cream
- Omitted all the butter
- Used just 2 ounces of finely grated, authentic Parmesan for flavor

INGREDIENTS: Fresh Fettuccine

While developing our Fettuccine Alfredo recipe, we wondered how "fresh" fettuccine from the supermarket would compare with both fresh pasta from a local Italian market and fresh homemade pasta. We headed into the test kitchen to find out, testing dried fettuccine from the supermarket as well.

Tasters immediately recognized the bowl of dried fettuccine—it was swimming in the Alfredo sauce. Dried pasta is extruded through dies that leave a perfectly smooth, virtually impenetrable surface. By contrast, fresh pasta has a rough, porous surface that is better able to absorb sauce. All three fresh pastas, including Buitoni (from the supermarket refrigerator section), received high marks from tasters. All had an "eggy" flavor and firm but yielding texture. The pasta we purchased from a local Italian market had the "wheatiest" flavor and chewiest texture. It was made with a mixture of durum flour and semolina. Durum-only Buitoni and our homemade pasta (made with all-purpose flour) were more bland and soft but still very good.

Our advice? Buitoni is by far the most convenient option, and it can ably compete with homemade. But if you have access to locally made fresh pasta (especially one made with semolina), give it a try.

THE BEST SUPERMARKET FETTUCCINE
Contadina Buitoni Fettuccine is your best option at the supermarket when you can't get locally made fresh pasta.

INGREDIENTS: Parmesan Cheese

When it comes to grated Parmesan cheese, there's a wide range of options—everything from the whitish powder in plastic containers to imported cheese that costs up to $17 a pound. You can buy cheese that has been grated, or you can pick out a whole hunk and grate it yourself. We wondered if the "authentic" Parmigiano-Reggiano imported from Italy would be that much better when tasted side by side with a domestic Parmesan at half the price.

The samples in our tasting included five pregrated Parmesan cheeses (domestic and imported), three wedges of domestic Parmesan, a wedge of Grana Padano (an Italian grating cheese considered a Parmesan type), one of Reggianito (another Parmesan-type cheese from Argentina), and two of Parmigiano-Reggiano. All of the cheeses were tasted grated, at room temperature.

Most of the cheeses in the tasting—except the Parmigiano-Reggiano—were extremely salty. In fact, Parmigiano-Reggiano contains about two-thirds less sodium than other Parmesans. This is because the wheels of Parmigiano-Reggiano are so large that they do not become as saturated with salt during the brining process that is one of the final steps in making the cheese. (The average wheel is about 9 inches high and 16 to 18 inches in diameter and weighs 75 to 90 pounds; domestic Parmesan wheels average 24 pounds.)

One domestic Parmesan scored well enough to be recommended. This was Wisconsin-made DiGiorno. The other less expensive options paled in comparison with the real thing. The pregrated cheeses received especially low ratings and harsh comments from our panel. Most were much too salty and marred by odd off flavors. Most everyone agreed that these poor imitations could actually ruin a dish.

THE BEST PARMESANS
Nothing compares with real Parmigiano-Reggiano (left). If you can, buy a piece freshly cut from a large wheel. Expect to spend $12 to $17 per pound. Priced at just $8 per pound, domestically made DiGiorno Parmesan (right) is surprisingly good and it is our best buy.

serving) and packs a flavorful punch. We tried using domestic and other imported brands of Parmesan, but their flavors were subdued or off. Using the real cheese here makes a big difference.

As for the butter, we whisked various amounts of it into the finished sauce to see if we could cut the fat further. Some recipes call for up to 6 tablespoons, and we made sauce after sauce with less and less butter until we had eliminated it all together. Tasters actually preferred the flavor of this Alfredo without any butter—they thought it muted the Parmesan flavor and simply wasn't worth the extra fat. The butter did, however, play a key role in keeping the sauce from drying out while it was tossed with the cooked pasta. We simply replaced the butter with pasta cooking water (which is lightly starchy and seasoned) to help keep the sauce fluid as it is tossed with the cooked fettuccine. Finally, we discovered that whisking the water into the sauce, then adding the cooked fettuccine and tossing it all together over low heat just before serving, helped the pasta absorb some flavor and ensured that the sauce would be the right consistency. It was neither too thin and watery nor too thick and gloppy.

Last, we focused on the pasta. We put both dried and fresh fettuccine to the test with our new Alfredo sauce. Tasters chose the fresh pasta as their favorite because it tasted more delicate and clung to the sauce better. Fresh noodles have about 1 gram more fat per serving, but they were worth it. Because fresh pasta cooks in just a minute or so, we found it easiest to get the sauce started before cooking the pasta. Also, adding the cooked pasta to the sauce and cooking it for about a minute before serving helped the sauce to coat the pasta more evenly. Seasoned simply with salt, pepper, and a pinch of nutmeg, our low-fat fettuccine Alfredo boasts just 300 calories and 11 grams of fat per serving.

Fettuccine Alfredo
SERVES 4

Fresh pasta is the best choice for this dish; supermarkets sell 9-ounce containers of fresh pasta in the refrigerator section (see our tasting of brands on page 175). For optimum Parmesan flavor, it is essential that Parmigiano-Reggiano cheese be used in this recipe. Note that Fettuccine Alfredo must be served immediately and does not hold or reheat well. The texture of the sauce changes dramatically as the dish stands for even a few minutes; serving in warmed bowls helps to ensure that the dish retains its creamy texture while it's being eaten.

³/₄	cup half-and-half
¹/₈	teaspoon freshly grated nutmeg
	Salt
1	teaspoon cornstarch
9	ounces fresh fettuccine
2	ounces Parmigiano-Reggiano cheese, grated fine (about 1 cup)
	Ground black pepper

1. Bring 6 quarts water to a boil in a large pot. Using a ladle or heatproof measuring cup, fill four individual serving bowls with about ½ cup of the boiling water each; set the bowls aside to warm.

2. Meanwhile, bring ½ cup of the half-and-half, nutmeg, and ¼ teaspoon salt to a simmer in a 3- to 4-quart saucepan. Whisk the cornstarch and remaining ¼ cup half-and-half together, then whisk it into the simmering mixture. Continue to simmer the sauce, whisking constantly, until it has thickened, about 1 minute. Cover and set the pot off the heat.

3. Stir 1 tablespoon salt and the pasta into the boiling water and cook, stirring constantly, until al dente, 1 to 2 minutes. Reserving ¾ cup of the pasta cooking water, drain the pasta.

4. Return the half-and-half mixture to medium-low heat and whisk in ½ cup of the pasta cooking water. Slowly whisk in the Parmesan. Add the pasta and cook, coating the pasta evenly with the sauce, until the sauce has thickened slightly, about 1 minute. Season with pepper to taste. Working quickly, empty the serving bowls of water, divide the pasta among the bowls, and serve.

PER SERVING: Cal 300; Fat 11 g ; Sat Fat 6 g; Chol 70 mg; Carb 36 g; Protein 15 g; Fiber 2 g; Sodium 580 mg

EQUIPMENT: Cheese Graters

In the old days, you grated cheese on the fine teeth of a box grater. Now cheese graters come in several distinct designs. Unfortunately, many of them don't work all that well. With some designs, you need Herculean strength to move the cheese over the teeth with sufficient pressure for grating; with others, you eventually discover that a large portion of the grated cheese has remained jammed in the grater instead of going where it belongs, on your food.

Whether you are dusting a plate of pasta or grating a full cup of cheese to use in a recipe, a good grater should be efficient and easy to use. We rounded up 15 models and set about determining which was the best grater. We found five basic configurations. Four-sided box graters have different-size holes on each side to allow for both fine grating and coarse shredding. Flat graters consist of a flat sheet of metal that is punched through with fine teeth and attached to some type of handle. With rotary graters, you put a small chunk of cheese in a hopper and use a handle to press it down against a crank-operated grating wheel. Porcelain dish graters have raised teeth in the center and a well around the outside edge to collect the grated cheese. We also found a model that uses an electric motor to push and rotate small chunks of cheese against a grating disk. After grating more than 10 pounds of Parmesan, we concluded that success is dependent on a combination of sharp grating teeth, a comfortable handle or grip, and good leverage for pressing the cheese onto the grater.

Our favorite model was a flat grater based on a small, maneuverable woodworking tool called a rasp. Shaped like a ruler, but with lots and lots of tiny, sharp raised teeth, the Microplane Grater (as it is called) can grate large quantities of cheese smoothly and almost effortlessly. The black plastic handle, which we found more comfortable than any of the others, also earned high praise. Other flat graters also scored well. What about traditional box graters? Box graters can deliver good results and can do more than just grate hard cheese. However, if grating hard cheese is the task at hand, a box grater is not our first choice.

THE BEST GRATER
The Microplane Grater has very sharp teeth and a solid handle, which together make grating cheese a breeze. This grater also makes quick work of ginger and citrus zest.

TEST KITCHEN MAKEOVER

MEAT AND CHEESE LASAGNA

MEAT AND CHEESE LASAGNA CAN BE FOUND everywhere from school cafeterias and chain restaurants to the frozen food section of the grocery store. Whether homemade, ordered out, or frozen, its universal appeal is understandable, given the familiar ingredients. Tender noodles, layered with gooey cheese and a rich, tomato meat sauce—few can refuse its decadent allure. We made a typical recipe (to set a standard for our light recipe) and tasters commented on the rich and creamy filling, the great meat flavor, and the generous portion size. Granted, this lasagna was good, but with one portion weighing in at 540 calories and 30 grams of fat per serving, the lasagna wasn't the only thing tipping the scales after our tasting.

TESTING NOTES

Choosing a Creamy Ricotta

WHOLE MILK RICOTTA
32 fat grams per cup
Whole milk ricotta has a rich taste, but way too much fat for our lightened lasagna.

PART-SKIM RICOTTA
24 fat grams per cup
Sounds skinnier, but it didn't save us much fat.

THE WINNER

FAT-FREE RICOTTA
0 fat grams per cup
Fat-free ricotta gave us the flavor and moisture we needed for a rich and creamy lasagna filling without any added fat.

We cooked up some of the light recipes we had found in our research, and even pitted them against some of the more popular frozen "lean" lasagna entrées. It seems that people are willing to make quite a few sacrifices in order to eat what they perceive as a healthier lasagna. None of the recipes we tried were worth the trimmed down calories they contained, with the frozen entrées earning the harshest comments. They all may have cut calories and fat, but in the process they had also cut flavor, and cut it dramatically. Fillings were either bland or nonexistent, the meat in the sauce was sparse, and the pasta was either like cardboard or horrendously overcooked. Some contained cottage cheese (which was watery), or tofu (we didn't care for the soy flavor) to replace the ricotta cheese. We wanted a lasagna that would satisfy the need for gooey cheese and meaty flavor, but it had to earn better comments than "not awful, for low fat." There was not a test cook among us that wasn't hoping against all odds that we could come up with a light lasagna worth eating, and worth making more than once a year for special occasions. With our goals in mind, we began testing.

We started by figuring out what the biggest offenders were in the monstrous calorie and fat counts. Not surprisingly, the meat sauce and cheeses were the issue. We started with the meat sauce and turned to the meat sauce recipe that we had recently lightened (see Spaghetti with Classic Italian Meat Sauce on page 161). In that recipe, we had replaced red meat with ground turkey, and after tweaking flavor and texture we came up with a great sauce. For our meat sauce in the lasagna, we made a few modifications: we increased the tomatoes and garlic to accommodate the yield for the lasagna and we also reduced the chicken broth by half for a slightly thicker sauce. With one key component out of the way, we moved on to the most offending culprit, the cheeses.

A standard recipe can contain close to a pound of whole milk ricotta cheese, a pound of whole milk mozzarella, and 1¼ cups of Parmesan cheese. The three of these combined contributed 21 grams of fat and 294 calories . . . per serving! We could fix this. Our first inclination was to simply cut back on the amount of each cheese. We cut the ricotta back to ½ pound, the mozzarella by half, and the Parmesan by half. The results were disappointing. The proportion of filling to lasagna noodles and sauce was out of whack, and the assembled dish wasn't substantial enough to qualify as lasagna. We clearly needed the volume of the original filling recipe, but we needed to figure out how to get it without all the fat from the cheese.

There are many reduced-fat and no-fat versions of cheese on the market today, and many of them are acceptable, but we find that how or if they work is entirely recipe-specific. In our effort to figure out which versions would work in this recipe, we ran dozens of tests trying many combinations of nonfat and low-fat (or part-skim) ricotta and mozzarella. The fat-free mozzarella

added an unpleasant "chewing gum" texture to the lasagna, but the reduced-fat mozzarella was perfectly acceptable and melted surprisingly well. We tested varying amounts of mozzarella, curious as to how little we could get away with and still have the characteristic chew we wanted, and settled on 12 ounces: 8 for the filling, and the remainder to sprinkle on top for a nice brown crust. As for the ricotta, the nonfat version had all the moisture of the full fat and we felt it worked fine in our filling. To round out the filling, we added a small amount of Parmesan cheese—just enough to add flavor without tons of fat. A little freshly minced basil finished it, adding some much-needed bright flavor.

With the filling resolved, we worked on the assembly. We had settled on using no-boil lasagna noodles since we knew they'd cut the preparation time substantially. The filling (which yielded about three cups) was easily divided into ⅓-cup measurements to spread on each noodle, making assembly instructions easy. Once assembled in a 13 by 9-inch baking dish (you can use a lasagna pan if desired) we covered the dish with foil, baked it for 45 minutes, then scattered the remaining mozzarella cheese on top and continued cooking uncovered for another fifteen minutes. After a 15-minute respite (to allow the filling to set up a bit, and the pasta to firm up) we were ready for tasting. We cut the lasagna into 10 servings (each a generous 8-ounce portion), and waited for the response.

To begin with, the portion size was perfect; ample enough for even the heartiest of eaters, without being over the top. The filling, sauce, and pasta were perfectly married to create the gooey texture and chew of the original. More than one taster commented "I would definitely make this now, and not feel guilty," just the unsolicited response we were looking for. So how did the final numbers stack up? We had cut the calories significantly—from 540 calories to 340 calories and taken the fat from 30 to 10 grams. We had more than lightened this dish; we had breathed new life into an all-time favorite.

TESTING NOTES

Choosing Gooey and Good Mozzarella

WHOLE MILK MOZZARELLA

28 fat grams per cup of shredded cheese
Whole milk mozzarella is rich and creamy, but too high in fat for our lightened lasagna.

PART-SKIM MOZZARELLA

24 fat grams per cup of shredded cheese
Yes, it's lighter, but it didn't reduce the fat as much as we'd like.

FAT-FREE MOZZARELLA

0 fat grams per cup of shredded cheese
Great substitute for bubble gum, but not for cheese.

THE WINNER

REDUCED-FAT MOZZARELLA CHEESE

18 fat grams per cup of shredded cheese
Great melting qualities, good flavor, and even less fat than part-skim, reduced-fat mozzarella was the obvious choice.

MAKEOVER AT A GLANCE

—Classic—
Meat and Cheese Lasagna
(per serving)

Calories: 540	Cholesterol: 110 mg
Fat: 30 g	Saturated Fat: 15 g

—Light—
Meat and Cheese Lasagna
(per serving)

Calories: 340	Cholesterol: 70 mg
Fat: 10 g	Saturated Fat: 4 g

How We Did It

- Used ground turkey instead of ground beef and pork in the sauce
- Made the sauce even leaner by removing most of the oil
- Replaced whole milk ricotta with fat-free ricotta
- Replaced whole milk mozzarella with reduced-fat mozzarella
- Reduced the Parmesan to just 1 ounce, from 2½ ounces

Meat and Cheese Lasagna

SERVES 10

Do not use ground turkey breast meat (sometimes labeled as 99 percent fat free) for this recipe, or the sauce will be dry and grainy. Do not use fat-free mozzarella or the filling will be rubbery. See page 181 for our taste test of no-boil noodles.

SAUCE

2	(28-ounce) cans diced tomatoes
1	medium onion, minced
1	teaspoon olive oil
	Salt
6	medium garlic cloves, minced or pressed through a garlic press (about 2 tablespoons)
2	tablespoons tomato paste
¼	teaspoon red pepper flakes
1	pound 93 percent lean ground turkey
1	cup low-sodium chicken broth
2	bay leaves
½	cup minced fresh basil leaves
	Ground black pepper

FILLING AND PASTA LAYERS

1	pound fat-free ricotta cheese
12	ounces reduced-fat mozzarella cheese, shredded (about 3 cups)
1	ounce Parmesan cheese, grated (about ½ cup)
½	cup minced fresh basil leaves
1	large egg, lightly beaten
½	teaspoon salt
½	teaspoon ground black pepper
	Vegetable oil spray
12	no-boil lasagna noodles from one 8-ounce package

1. FOR THE SAUCE: Process 1 can of tomatoes with their juices in a food processor until almost smooth, about 5 seconds. Combine the onion, oil, and ½ teaspoon salt in a large nonstick skillet. Cover and cook over medium-low heat until softened, 8 to 10 minutes.

2. Stir in the garlic, tomato paste, and pepper flakes and cook until the garlic is fragrant, about 30 seconds. Stir in half of the ground turkey and cook, breaking the meat into small pieces with a wooden spoon, until the meat loses its raw color but has not browned, about 4 minutes. Add the pureed tomatoes, remaining can of diced tomatoes with their juices, broth, and bay leaves. Bring to a simmer and cook, stirring occasionally, until the flavors are blended and the sauce is thickened, about 45 minutes.

3. Stir the remaining turkey into the sauce and continue to simmer, stirring occasionally, until the sauce measures about 6 cups, 20 to 30 minutes. Remove the bay leaves and stir in the basil. Season with salt and pepper to taste.

4. FOR THE FILLING: Mix the ricotta, 2 cups of the mozzarella, Parmesan, basil, egg, salt, and pepper together in a large bowl until thoroughly combined (you should have about 3 cups of filling).

5. To ASSEMBLE AND BAKE: Adjust an oven rack to the middle position and heat the oven to 375 degrees. Spray a 13 by 9-inch baking dish with vegetable oil spray. Spread 1½ cups of the sauce evenly over the bottom of the baking dish.

6. Lay 3 lasagna noodles on top of the sauce, spaced evenly apart. Place ⅓ cup of the filling on top of each noodle and spread it out evenly over the entire noodle using a rubber spatula. Spread 1 cup of the sauce evenly over the filling. Repeat this layering twice more.

7. Lay the remaining 3 noodles over the top. Spread the remaining 1½ cups sauce evenly over the noodles, making sure to cover the edges. Spray a large piece of foil with vegetable oil spray and cover the lasagna tightly.

8. Place the lasagna on a rimmed baking sheet and bake for 45 minutes. Remove the foil and sprinkle the lasagna evenly with the remaining 1 cup mozzarella. Continue to bake, uncovered, until the cheese is bubbling and slightly brown, 10 to 15 minutes longer. Remove from the oven and cool on a wire rack for at least 15 minutes before serving.

PER SERVING: Cal 340; Fat 10 g; Sat fat 4 g; Chol 70 mg; Carb 31 g; Protein 29 g; Fiber 1 g; Sodium 1110 mg

VEGETABLE AND CHEESE LASAGNA

A BAD VEGETABLE LASAGNA CAN USUALLY BE attributed to one of three motives. Either it was a half-hearted attempt to use up the vegetable odds and ends in the crisper drawer, a thinly veiled trick to get your family to more vegetables, or an initial effort at vegetarian cooking. Regardless of the cook's intentions, the most common cause of a vegetable lasagna failure is the inclusion of too many vegetables. When the balance of cheese, pasta, and vegetables is tipped too far in favor of the vegetables, the dish simply tastes bland—a

INGREDIENTS: No-Boil Noodles

Over the past few years, no-boil (also called oven-ready) lasagna noodles have become a permanent fixture on supermarket shelves. Much like instant rice, no-boil noodles are precooked at the factory. The extruded noodles are run through a water bath and then dehydrated mechanically. During baking, the moisture from the sauce softens, or rehydrates, the noodles, especially when the pan is covered as the lasagna bakes. Most no-boil noodles are rippled, and the accordion-like pleats relax as the pasta rehydrates in the oven, allowing the noodles to elongate.

No-boil lasagna noodles come in two shapes. The most common is a rectangle measuring 7 inches long and 3½ inches wide. Three such noodles make a single layer in a conventional 13 by 9-inch lasagna pan when they swell in the oven. In local markets, we found three brands of this type of no-boil lasagna noodle: Ronzoni (made by New World Pasta, which sells the same product under the American Beauty, Skinner, and San Giorgio labels in certain parts of the country); DeFino (made in the United States); and Barilla (imported from Italy). Italian noodles made by Delverde came in 7-inch squares.

We made lasagnas with all four noodles to see how they would compare.

Ronzoni and DeFino are both thin and rippled, and although tasters preferred the Ronzoni for their flavor and DeFino for their sturdiness, both brands worked well. Barilla noodles tasted great but their texture was subpar. Two squares of Delverde noodles butted very closely together fit into a 13 by 9-inch pan, but when baked, the noodles expanded and the edges jumped out of the pan and became unpleasantly dry and tough. The only way to avoid this is to soak these noodles in hot water until tender. You can then cut them with scissors to fit the measurements of the pan. These noodles were no timesavers.

THE BEST NO-BOIL NOODLES

With their "lightly eggy" and "wheaty" flavor and "tender," "perfectly al dente" texture, Ronzoni Oven Ready Lasagne noodles were the tasters' favorite.

homogenous mixture of steamed vegetables tossed with pasta sauce.

Using too many vegetables between the layers of pasta and cheese can also ruin the construction of the dish so that it no longer holds together, but rather slides apart when serving so that you wind up simply slopping it into bowls with a spoon. Another common problem is that the vegetables never cook at the same rate so that, come serving time, some of the vegetables are overdone and mushy, while others taste raw and crunchy. Our mission was simple: We wanted to make a vegetable lasagna comprised of tender noodles enveloping evenly cooked vegetables, where the flavor of each vegetable could stand on its own. Creamy cheese and tangy tomato sauce would pull the dish together into a hearty crowd pleaser for vegetarians and carnivores alike.

Having already developed a great meat lasagna recipe, we knew a few things about lasagna: First, we like to use no-boil noodles because they successfully cut down on the amount of prep. Second, we like to make our own tomato sauce because not only does it taste better, but we can make its consistency a bit looser to accommodate the no-boil noodles, which soak up a lot of the sauce as the lasagna bakes. Third, when making a lasagna that is lighter in terms of fat and calories, we like to use reduced-fat mozzarella because it offers the best ratio of flavor to fat. Although many vegetable lasagnas omit the ricotta, we like the creamy richness that it adds to lower fat lasagna.

Cobbling together a decent working recipe, the biggest question was which vegetables to include, and how to prepare them before sprinkling them between the layers of pasta. Looking at other recipes for inspiration, we found no shortage of ideas. Concentrating on the most common vegetables, we made more than 10 lasagnas using eggplant, mushrooms, zucchini, bell peppers, broccoli, carrots, and spinach. We ruled out eggplant because it not only required lots of prep (cutting, salting, pressing, and sautéing), but its flavor seemed to get lost. Bell peppers and carrots also didn't make the cut because their sweetness and crunchy texture seemed out of place. Zucchini and mushrooms were both well liked and just needed to be sautéed in order to drive off some of their moisture so

the lasagna would not turn soggy. We thought we were going to like fresh spinach; however, we found it simply required too much work (cleaning, stemming, steaming, and squeezing) for this already prep-heavy dish. We then turned to frozen spinach, but found that we needed to use at least three packages to make this vegetable's presence felt in our dish. Some tasters, too, thought it added little flavor and texture alongside the other vegetables. Last, we tested broccoli, both fresh and frozen, and surprisingly, tasters preferred the mellower flavor and softer texture of frozen chopped broccoli florets. Another plus was the convenience of the frozen broccoli; the frozen florets simply need to be thawed, squeezed dry, and chopped.

Some recipes direct you to mix the vegetables together before assembling and baking the lasagna, but we think this takes away from each vegetable's individual flavor. We preferred to let each vegetable shine in its own layer. When cut into squares, the layers of vegetables look more attractive, too. Far from a dish made from crisper drawer rejects, this is a lasagna worth a trip to the supermarket.

Vegetable Lasagna
SERVES 10

Take care to defrost the broccoli just enough to bring it to room temperature, to allow the ice to melt. Be sure to squeeze as much moisture as possible out of the broccoli before you chop it. See page 181 for our recommendation for no-boil lasagna noodles. We like this recipe made with low-sodium chicken broth, but if you'd like to make this dish vegetarian, substitute vegetable broth for the chicken broth. Note that the baking dish will be quite full, and the lasagna may rise a bit above the rim of the dish when baking (due to the moisture in the vegetables), but as it rests, it will settle back into the dish.

SAUCE

2	(28-ounce) cans diced tomatoes
1	medium onion, minced
1	teaspoon olive oil
	Salt
6	medium garlic cloves, minced or pressed through a garlic press (about 2 tablespoons)
2	tablespoons tomato paste

⅛ teaspoon red pepper flakes

1 cup low-sodium chicken broth

2 bay leaves

½ cup minced fresh basil leaves

Ground black pepper

FILLING AND PASTA LAYERS

1 pound cremini or white mushrooms, wiped clean and sliced thin

2 teaspoons olive oil

¾ teaspoon salt

2 medium zucchini (about 6 ounces each), sliced ¼ inch thick

1 pound fat-free ricotta cheese

12 ounces reduced-fat mozzarella cheese, shredded (about 3 cups)

1 ounce Parmesan cheese, grated (about ½ cup)

½ cup minced fresh basil leaves

1 large egg, lightly beaten

½ teaspoon ground black pepper

Vegetable oil spray

12 no-boil lasagna noodles from one 8-ounce package

1 (10-ounce) package frozen broccoli florets, thawed to room temperature, pressed dry with paper towels, and chopped coarse

1. FOR THE SAUCE: Process 1 can of the tomatoes with their juices in a food processor until almost smooth, about 5 seconds. Combine the onion, oil, and ½ teaspoon salt in a 12-inch nonstick skillet. Cover and cook over medium-low heat until softened, 8 to 10 minutes. Stir in the garlic, tomato paste, and pepper flakes and cook until the garlic is fragrant, about 30 seconds.

2. Stir in the broth, pureed tomatoes, remaining can of diced tomatoes with their juices, and bay leaves. Bring to a simmer and cook, stirring occasionally, until the flavors are blended and the sauce is thickened, about 45 minutes. Remove the bay leaves and stir in the basil. Season with salt and pepper to taste.

3. FOR THE FILLING: Combine the mushrooms, 1 teaspoon of the oil, and ¼ teaspoon of the salt in a 12-inch nonstick skillet. Cook over medium-low heat until the mushrooms have released their

liquid, about 8 minutes. Remove the cover and continue to cook until all of the liquid evaporates, about 5 minutes. Transfer the mushrooms to a bowl; set aside.

4. Add the remaining teaspoon oil to the skillet and return to high heat until just smoking. Add the zucchini and cook, stirring often, until well browned, about 3 minutes. Transfer to a separate bowl and set aside.

5. Mix the ricotta, 2 cups of the mozzarella, Parmesan, basil, egg, pepper, and remaining ½ teaspoon salt together in a large bowl until thoroughly combined. (You should have about 3 cups of filling.)

6. TO ASSEMBLE AND BAKE: Adjust an oven rack to the middle position and heat the oven to 375 degrees. Spray a 13 by 9-inch baking dish with vegetable oil spray. Spread 1½ cups of the sauce evenly over the bottom of the baking dish.

7. Lay 3 lasagna noodles on top to the sauce, spaced evenly apart. Place ⅓ cup of the filling on top of each noodle and spread it out evenly over the entire noodle using a rubber spatula. Scatter the mushrooms evenly over the filling, then spread 1 cup of the sauce evenly over the mushrooms. Repeat this layering twice more, substituting the broccoli and zucchini for the mushrooms (each vegetable has its own layer).

8. Lay the remaining 3 noodles over the top. Spread the remaining 1½ cups sauce evenly over the noodles, making sure to cover the edges. Spray a large piece of foil with vegetable oil spray and cover the lasagna tightly.

9. Place the lasagna on a rimmed baking sheet and bake for 45 minutes. Remove the foil and sprinkle the lasagna evenly with the remaining 1 cup mozzarella. Continue to bake, uncovered, until the cheese is bubbling and slightly brown, 10 to 15 minutes longer. Remove from the oven and cool on a wire rack for at least 15 minutes before serving.

PER SERVING: Cal 310; Fat 9 g; Sat fat 3.5 g; Chol 45 mg; Carb 36 g; Protein 22 g; Fiber 3 g; Sodium 1150 mg

TEST KITCHEN MAKEOVER

EVERYDAY MACARONI AND CHEESE

WEIGHING IN AT ABOUT 650 CALORIES AND 40 grams of fat per serving, a bowl of homemade mac and cheese should really be a treat every once in awhile, like a slice of cheesecake. The truth, however, is that it winds up on the dinner table much more often because it's easy to prepare and kids will eat it without complaint. We wanted to develop a macaroni and cheese recipe that could be used as a weekly workhorse meal with reasonable amounts of calories and fat, but without losing too much of the cheesy flavor or creamy texture that make it such a perennial favorite.

Starting off in our cookbook library, we found dozens of recipes for low-fat mac and cheese. Making a few of these lightened recipes to get the lay of the land, we wondered if we had bitten off more than we could chew. Some of the recipes were downright awful, producing flavorless, rubbery mixtures due to large amounts of nonfat cheese, while other recipes turned out versions with a grainy texture because they included ricotta or cottage cheese. Obviously, we were on our own here. Heading into the kitchen with the motto "Make the fat count," our philosophy was that every calorie and gram of fat needed to work for us and that none would slip by unaccounted for.

With lots of ideas to test, we decided to focus on the cooking method first, then tweak the ingredients and flavors. The most common cooking method for mac and cheese is to make a béchamel (a milk sauce thickened with butter and flour) and then stir in the cheese and cooked macaroni. Another popular *Cook's Illustrated* method involves slowly cooking a mixture of milk, eggs, cheese, butter, and cooked macaroni over low heat until it thickens and becomes creamy. Yet a third, and somewhat unusual, method calls for boiling the pasta in a small amount of milk (the pasta starch thickens the milk to a sauce-like consistency)

then stirring in cheese to finish. Giving these three methods a whirl, we were able to eliminate two right off the bat. The popular method of cooking a mixture of milk, eggs, cheese, butter, and cooked macaroni over low heat yields great-tasting mac and cheese but it simply doesn't work without the eggs and lots of cheese, both of which are very fatty; this approach was out. Also, cooking the pasta right in the milk was an interesting and naturally low-fat technique; however, tasters found the resulting flavor to be one-dimensional and the texture of the pasta to be gummy. Making a béchamel was the winning approach so far, but we still had a lot of calories and fat to trim.

Using 2 percent, 1 percent, or skim milk instead of whole milk in the béchamel was an

---

MAKEOVER AT A GLANCE

–Classic–
Macaroni and Cheese
(per serving)

Calories: 650	Cholesterol: 200 mg
Fat: 40 g	Saturated Fat: 27 g

–Light–
Macaroni and Cheese
(per serving)

Calories: 360	Cholesterol: 40 mg
Fat: 10 g	Saturated Fat: 6 g

How We Did It

- Replaced 12 ounces of full-fat cheddar cheese with 8 ounces of low-fat cheddar cheese
- Replaced the whole milk with 2 percent milk
- Added a can of 2 percent evaporated milk for creaminess
- Replaced the buttery roux with cornstarch

obvious way to reduce more fat and calories. Testing them side by side in batches of mac and cheese, tasters didn't like the sauces made with 1 percent and skim milk because they tasted too thin and didn't coat the pasta well. The sauce made with 2 percent milk, however, was acceptable and helped to trim about 2 grams of fat per serving.

Wanting to reduce the fat in the sauce further, we took a closer look at the roux (butter and flour mixture) used to thicken the milk into a béchamel. Cutting back on the butter as far as we could from the original 3 tablespoons, we found we needed at least 1 tablespoon of butter to make a roux with the flour. But even 1 tablespoon of butter adds a fair amount of fat and we wondered if we could lose it all together. Making two sauces without any butter, we tried thickening the milk with either a flour slurry (flour dissolved in a liquid) or a cornstarch slurry (cornstarch dissolved in a liquid). Both slurries were able to thicken the milk to an appropriate sauce consistency, but tasters described the sauce thickened with flour as tasting grainy and pasty, while the sauce thickened with cornstarch had a smooth, silky texture. Using cornstarch instead of a traditional roux had saved us another 10 or so grams of fat per serving.

The cheese is obviously one of the heavier ingredients in the dish, and using low-fat cheese was an easy way to trim even more off the calorie and fat counts. Most mac and cheese recipes use about 12 ounces of cheddar per ½ pound pasta (serving 4 to 5 people), and we made batches of mac and cheese using incrementally less cheese until the tasters cried uncle. Eight ounces of cheese turned out to be the breaking point, beyond which tasters thought the mac and cheese tasted too bland. We then tested several batches of mac and cheese substituting other types of cheese (including Parmesan, Monterey Jack, and Gouda) for some of the cheddar, but tasters preferred the flavor of the cheddar alone. Finally, we made two more batches pitting nonfat cheddar against low-fat cheddar, and the tasters unanimously hated the rubbery texture and sweet flavor of the nonfat cheddar. Using 8 ounces of low-fat cheddar in place of the 12 ounces of regular cheddar, however, had already saved us a whopping 72 grams of fat in the overall recipe.

By now our recipe had been substantially reduced to just 422 calories and 13 grams of fat per serving, but we realized that somewhere along the line, we had lost the creamy, velvety texture of the original. Had we gone too far? Looking into how we could add back some of that silky texture, we landed on the idea of evaporated milk (an ingredient used in the popular *Cook's Illustrated* method which we had dismissed earlier). Substituting a can of evaporated milk for some of the milk in the sauce, we hit the jackpot. The evaporated milk rounded out the texture of the sauce and even fooled some of the tasters into thinking that they were eating the real deal—full-fat mac and cheese. Testing the difference between whole evaporated milk, 2 percent evaporated milk, and skim evaporated milk in the béchamel, we found that tasters preferred the texture, flavor, and fat content of the 2 percent evaporated milk. Using low-fat (2 percent) evaporated milk not only helped the mac and cheese's texture, but it actually reduced its fat and calorie count even further, to just 360 calories and 10 grams of fat per serving.

Everyday Macaroni and Cheese
SERVES 5

Don't be tempted to use either preshredded or nonfat cheddar cheese in this dish—the texture and flavor of the mac and cheese will suffer substantially. For best results, choose a low-fat cheddar cheese that is sold in block form and has roughly 50 percent of the fat and calories of regular cheese (we like Cabot brand).

	Salt
½	pound elbow macaroni (about 2 cups)
1	(12-ounce) can reduced-fat evaporated milk
¾	cup 2 percent milk
¼	teaspoon dry mustard
⅛	teaspoon garlic powder or celery salt (optional)
	Pinch cayenne
2	teaspoons cornstarch
8	ounces 50 percent light cheddar cheese, grated (about 2 cups)

1. Bring 2 ½ quarts water to boil in a large saucepan. Stir in 2 teaspoons salt and the macaroni; cook until the pasta is completely cooked and tender, about 5 minutes. Drain the pasta and leave it in the colander; set aside.

2. Add the evaporated milk, ½ cup of the 2 percent milk, mustard, garlic powder (if using), cayenne, and ½ teaspoon salt to the now-empty saucepan. Bring the mixture to a boil, then reduce to a simmer. Whisk the cornstarch and remaining ¼ cup milk together, then whisk it into the simmering mixture. Continue to simmer, whisking constantly, until the sauce has thickened and is smooth, about 2 minutes.

3. Off the heat, gradually whisk in the cheddar until melted and smooth. Stir in the macaroni, and let the macaroni and cheese sit off the heat until the sauce has thickened slightly, 2 to 5 minutes, before serving.

PER SERVING: Cal 360; Fat 10 g; Sat fat 6 g; Chol 40 mg; Carb 45 g; Protein 24 g; Fiber 1 g; Sodium 720 mg

➤ VARIATION

Everyday Macaroni and Cheese with Ham and Peas

Follow the recipe for Everyday Macaroni and Cheese, adding 2 ounces deli-style baked ham, cut into ⅓-inch pieces, and ¾ cup frozen peas with the macaroni in step 3.

PER SERVING: Cal 390; Fat 10 g; Sat fat 6 g; Chol 45 mg; Carb 49 g; Protein 28 g; Fiber 3 g; Sodium 880 mg

---

THE LOWDOWN ON LIGHT CHEDDAR CHEESE

Typically high in fat and calories, cheese is an ingredient we usually use with a very light hand when developing lower fat recipes. But cutting back on or omitting cheese entirely is simply not an option in recipes where cheese takes center stage. Take mac and cheese, for example. Sure, the roux, milk, and macaroni are important, but it would be nothing without the cheddar cheese. In the past we have simply avoided such dishes when trying to reduce our fat intake. With just 1 ounce (a mere 1 inch cube) of cheddar cheese boasting 9 grams of fat and 110 calories, the numbers add up fast. Was there any way to incorporate this dish into our healthier repertoire?

Here in the test kitchen, we normally turn our noses up at any cheese labeled fat-free, low-fat, reduced-fat, or light. But in developing recipes for this book, we realized we were going to have to give them an honest try. We rounded up all the products available to us to determine if there was a significant difference between them. Fat content ranged from fat-free to 75 percent light, 50 percent light, and 2 percent reduced-fat. In addition, the cheeses were available preshredded, presliced, and in blocks.

We tasted all of these options on their own with crackers and in batches of our Everyday Macaroni and Cheese. Tasters unanimously agreed that the preshredded and presliced cheeses were out, along with the fat-free cheese, which was rubbery and overly sweet. The 2 percent reduced-fat cheese gained high marks, but at 6 grams of fat per 1-ounce serving, it was unfortunately still a little high in fat for our purposes. The 75 percent light cheddar (only 2.5 grams of fat per serving) produced mac and cheese that was grainy with a bitter aftertaste. The 50 percent light cheddar, on the other hand, worked well.

With just 4.5 grams of fat and 70 calories per ounce (as well as no unpronounceable ingredients) we were happy. Though it doesn't quite stack up against fine aged cheddar when eaten on a cracker, tasters liked the creaminess and cheesy flavor that it lent to our mac and cheese.

7

POULTRY AND MEAT

WHEN THINKING ABOUT THIS BOOK, WE knew that we wanted to incorporate leaner cuts of meat into our repertoire of healthy recipes, but like most people, what came to our minds was the image of a Spartan serving of broiled chicken or pork with nary a sauce in sight. We wanted to create lighter recipes that worked within the context of a full meal and here that meant a reasonable portion of meat, prepared in a way that didn't break the calorie bank (allowing us room to enjoy some side dishes, too).

As a result, you'll find in this chapter many recipes for simple sautéed chicken breasts and cutlets, pork chops, and also a handful of roasts. Many people have trouble cooking these leaner cuts of meat at home. The meat can be bland and dry because these cuts don't have much fat, which provides flavor and moisture. Sauces and glazes help solve both of these problems, but you must also pay attention to how you cook lean cutlets, chops, and roasts. To build flavor in the meat itself, it must have a nicely browned exterior. Here are the key points we've discovered in the test kitchen over the years: (1) A large skillet minimizes crowding that can cause meat to steam. (2) A heavy skillet conducts heat without scorching and is essential for maximum browning. (3) The skillet should be preheated—the oil in the pan should almost smoke before you place meat in the pan. (4) Patting the meat dry before it goes into the pan removes excess moisture that might otherwise inhibit the formation of a browned crust on the meat. (5) The browned bits that remain on the pan will be essential for building your sauce.

As for the sauces, we found a couple of ways to create light versions that were as rich-tasting as their high-fat counterparts that rely on butter and cream. After much testing we learned that a couple of tablespoons of light cream cheese along with broth, wine, and aromatics gave some sauces a deceptive richness, while milk mixed with cornstarch thickened and finished others. Along with sauces such as Mushroom-Sherry Sauce (page 193) and Creamy Whole-Grain Mustard and Dill Sauce (page 193), we created relish-like "sauces" using vegetables or fresh or dried fruit and plenty of spices which added lots of flavor to simple sautéed meats but few calories and almost no fat. Glazes also saved the day when it came to dressing up roast pork loin or tenderloin. Here honey or fruit preserves, paired with interesting fresh fruits and spices, made a flavorful and light coating for the meats.

We also found that cooking boneless breasts en papillote—essentially steaming them in foil packets in the oven—was yet another way to take advantage of the virtues of chicken (see Chicken with Fennel, Carrots, and Orange en Papillote on page 195). The secret to making this technique successful (rather than bland and boring) is to toss the vegetables with a little oil, fresh herbs, and aromatics and to layer heartier vegetables below the chicken (so they cook through) and juicier fruits and vegetables on top (so they release their juices into the chicken and also form a sauce).

This chapter also highlights the test kitchen's success making over several high-fat chicken dishes, from Chicken Parmesan (where we toasted the crumbs before coating the chicken instead of pan-frying breaded chicken) and Chicken Pot Pie (where we used lighter biscuits as a topping and eliminated the butter-rich roux), to Chicken Enchiladas (where light cheese and vegetable oil spray came to the rescue). We also put lean ground turkey to work in our meatloaf and burger recipes and used a few tricks to keep them flavorful and moist (see pages 208–211).

Since grilling is the ultimate healthy cooking technique because it requires little fat while adding great depth of flavor, you'll find information about the best way to grill lean cuts of poultry and meat (like flank steak and beef tenderloin), plus a host of rubs and salsas to complement them.

SAUTÉED CHICKEN BREASTS

FOR ANYONE WHO WANTS TO EAT HEALTHIER, boneless, skinless chicken breasts are a requisite ingredient. Virtually fat free and packed with protein, boneless chicken breasts also have the added bonus of being exceptionally easy to prepare. And while you can certainly broil chicken or cook it en papillote, sautéing is the only way is to achieve that beautiful golden brown exterior. The major problem with sautéing, however, is that it tends to dry out the chicken. And when the chicken dries out, you might as well be eating cardboard in terms of flavor. We found many recipes for sautéed breasts that offer up flavorless chicken with a tough, pale exterior and we knew we could do better. We also wanted to develop a handful of pan sauces that would jazz up simple chicken breasts without relying on butter and heavy cream to add flavor.

To begin, we investigated different pan choices, knowing that the type of pan we used would be crucial to a successful sauté. We found that a large, 12-inch, traditional skillet was absolutely necessary to promote the best browning. In a smaller pan, the chicken was crowded. Crowding led to the creation of steam, which then led to a pale and unappetizing-looking crust. Also, we noted that a nonstick skillet did not work as well as a traditional skillet. While this may seem counterintuitive for healthier cooking (because nonstick pans allow you to cook with less fat), we found that regardless of skillet type, a certain amount of fat is necessary for a good sauté. Without enough fat the crust turns out spotty—burnt in some spots and completely pale in others. And using a traditional skillet is necessary when making pan sauces; those flavorful browned bits left in the skillet are essential for the flavor.

Although we knew we needed to use oil in order to achieve a golden, evenly sautéed crust, we had to determine which type of oil was best and exactly how much of it we needed. Many light recipes use olive oil because of its reputation for promoting good health; however, we prefer vegetable oil in this case. Not only does

it have a higher smoke point but, unlike olive oil, the flavor of vegetable oil is neutral and will pair with anything. Cooking our way through nearly 12 pounds of chicken, we found the optimum amount of vegetable oil for a sauté to be 4 teaspoons. Chicken sautéed with less (including vegetable oil sprays) resulted in chicken with unattractive, spotty crusts (as well as slightly scorched pans).

We also experimented with various heat levels. When we sautéed the chicken over the highest level of heat, it became too dark too quickly while remaining underdone on the inside. On the other hand, cooking the chicken very slowly over low heat made the chicken chewy and didn't produce that all-important golden crust. Working between these two ranges, we determined that the optimal heat level was a combination of medium and medium-low. First, we achieved a golden crust on one side over medium heat, then flipped the chicken over, turned the heat to medium-low and continued to cook the chicken through. This way, the chicken achieved a gorgeous, sautéed crust while its interior remained tender.

REMOVING THE TENDERLOIN

Sometimes a small strip of meat, called a tenderloin, is attached to the underside of a boneless, skinless breast. Tenderloins should be removed from the breast because they tend to fall off when cooking and dramatically affect the cooking times. They can either be reserved for another use, such as a stir-fry, or simply cooked off in a separate batch from the breasts (note that they will cook through more quickly).

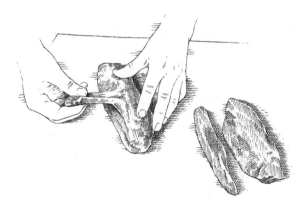

The tenderloin is easy to remove by simply pulling it off the breast.

Up to this point we had been using unfloured breasts. We were curious whether flouring the breasts would make a difference in the outcome. Indeed, it did prove to be beneficial. Flour promoted a more even browning on the exterior of the chicken. More important, however, it seemed to protect both the crust and the interior of the chicken. It prevented the crust from turning tough and stringy, while keeping the interior more moist. In a side-by-side test, we found that floured chicken seemed more moist when cooked the same amount of time as unfloured chicken.

Now that we felt we had mastered the techniques for sautéing chicken breasts, we wanted to see how they would transfer to cutlets (which are about half as thick as boneless, skinless chicken breasts; in other words, breasts that have been sliced in half horizontally to yield two pieces). Using the same skillet, we found we could cut out 1 teaspoon of the oil (per batch) without any ill effects. This is because cutlets are essentially half as thick as breasts and cook more than twice as fast. When cooking chicken breasts, the extra oil is necessary to prevent the pan from scorching during the longer cooking time, but it is unnecessary with the quick-cooking cutlets—the cutlets cook through before anything has a chance to burn. Also, we found we needed to increase the heat to medium-high for the entire cooking time so that the cutlets would brown. In fact, the cutlets cook so quickly that we found we only had time to brown one side. The second side of the cutlets are given just enough time to cook through, but will not brown. This method produced a nicely cooked chicken cutlet with sufficient flavor from the browning but without the rubbery texture of overcooked meat. That said, since the multiple cutlets took up too much room in the pan, we had to cook them in two batches (using 1 tablespoon of oil per batch).

Topping off our perfectly sautéed chicken with a pan sauce, we uncovered a few tricks to keep these sauces low in fat without losing any flavor. Pan sauces are typically finished with some sort of fat—cream or butter—to add richness and help emulsify the sauce. We tried many substitutes for the butter and cream including low-fat sour cream, buttermilk, yogurt, yogurt cheese, milk, and half-and-half. The winning substitutes turned out to be a whole milk–cornstarch slurry for the butter, and light cream cheese for the heavy cream. We also came across some relish-style sauces (using fruit or tomatoes) that are naturally low in fat, and make good use of those flavorful browned bits left in the pan.

Sautéed Chicken Breasts with a White Wine and Herb Pan Sauce

SERVES 4

We prefer the flavor of whole milk in the sauce; however, 2 percent milk or half-and-half will also work. Do not use 1 percent or skim milk. Any of the sauces on pages 192–194 can be substituted for the white wine sauce.

CHICKEN

- 1/2 cup unbleached all-purpose flour
- 4 boneless, skinless chicken breasts (about 6 ounces each), trimmed of excess fat and tenderloins removed
  Salt and ground black pepper
- 4 teaspoons vegetable oil

SAUCE

- 1 medium shallot, minced (about 3 tablespoons)
  Salt
- 2 medium garlic cloves, minced or pressed through a garlic press (about 2 teaspoons)
- 1/2 cup dry white wine or vermouth
- 1 1/2 cups low-sodium chicken broth
- 2 tablespoons whole milk
- 1 teaspoon cornstarch
- 2 teaspoons minced fresh parsley leaves
- 2 teaspoons minced fresh tarragon leaves
  Ground black pepper

1. FOR THE CHICKEN: Spread the flour in a shallow dish. Pat the chicken dry with paper towels, then season with salt and pepper. Lightly dredge the chicken in the flour and shake off the excess; set aside.

2. Heat the oil in a 12-inch skillet over medium heat until just smoking. Lay the chicken in the skillet and cook until golden brown, 6 to 8 minutes. Flip the chicken over, reduce the heat to medium-low, and continue to cook until the chicken is no longer pink in the center and the thickest part registers 160 degrees on an instant-read thermometer, 6 to 8 minutes longer. Transfer the chicken to a plate and cover with foil; set aside.

3. FOR THE SAUCE: Add the shallot and ¼ teaspoon salt to the oil left in the skillet, return to medium-low heat, and cook until softened, about 2 minutes. Stir in the garlic and cook until fragrant, about 30 seconds. Stir in the wine, scraping up the browned bits. Add the broth, bring to a simmer, and cook until the mixture measures ¾ cup, about 5 minutes.

SLICING CHICKEN BREASTS INTO CUTLETS

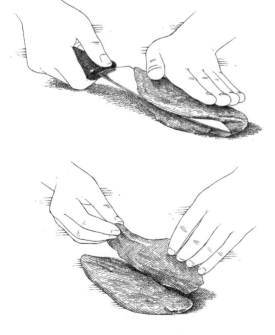

Lay the chicken breast flat on a cutting board, smooth side facing up. Rest one hand on top of the chicken, and using a sharp chef's knife, carefully slice the chicken in half horizontally to yield two thin cutlets between ⅜ and ½ inch thick.

4. Pour any accumulated chicken juices into the simmering sauce. Whisk the milk and cornstarch together in a small bowl, then whisk into the simmering sauce. Continue to simmer the sauce until it has thickened, about 1 minute. Off the heat, stir in the parsley and tarragon and season with salt and pepper to taste. Spoon the sauce over the chicken before serving.

PER SERVING: Cal 280; Fat 7 g; Sat fat 1 g; Chol 100 mg; Carb 6 g ; Protein 41 g; Fiber 0 g; Sodium 620 mg

PER SERVING WITHOUT SAUCE: Cal 240; Fat 7 g; Sat fat 1 g; Chol 100 mg; Carb 0 g; Protein 40 g; Fiber 0 g; Sodium 260 mg

Sautéed Chicken Cutlets with a White Wine and Herb Pan Sauce

SERVES 4

One cutlet per person makes a skimpy serving, so we call for a total of eight cutlets to serve four people. For additional pan sauces, see pages 192–194.

CUTLETS

½ cup unbleached all-purpose flour
4 boneless, skinless chicken breasts (about 6 ounces each), trimmed of excess fat, tenderloins removed, and sliced into cutlets (see the illustrations on page 189 and at left)
   Salt and ground black pepper
2 tablespoons vegetable oil

SAUCE

1 medium shallot, minced (about 3 tablespoons)
   Salt
2 medium garlic cloves, minced or pressed through a garlic press (about 2 teaspoons)
½ cup dry white wine or vermouth
1 ½ cups low-sodium chicken broth
2 tablespoons whole milk
1 teaspoon cornstarch
2 teaspoons minced fresh parsley leaves
2 teaspoons minced fresh tarragon leaves
   Ground black pepper

1. FOR THE CUTLETS: Spread the flour in a shallow dish. Pat the cutlets dry with paper towels, then

season with salt and pepper. Lightly dredge the cutlets in the flour and shake off the excess; set aside.

2. Heat 1 tablespoon of the oil in a 12-inch skillet over medium-high heat until just smoking. Lay half of the cutlets in the skillet and cook until lightly golden, about 3 minutes. Flip the cutlets over and continue to cook until the meat is no longer pink in the center and feels firm when pressed with a finger, about 2 minutes. Transfer the cutlets to a plate and cover with foil; set aside. Repeat with the remaining oil and cutlets.

3. FOR THE SAUCE: Add the shallot and ¼ teaspoon salt to the oil left in the skillet, return to medium-low heat, and cook until softened, about 2 minutes. Stir in the garlic and cook until fragrant, about 30 seconds. Stir in the wine, scraping up the browned bits. Add the broth, bring to a simmer, and cook until the mixture measures ¾ cup, about 5 minutes.

4. Pour any accumulated chicken juices into the simmering sauce. Whisk the milk and cornstarch together in a small bowl, then whisk into the simmering sauce. Continue to simmer the sauce until it has thickened, about 1 minute. Off the heat, stir in the parsley and tarragon and season with salt and pepper to taste. Spoon the sauce over the cutlets before serving.

PER SERVING: Cal 310; Fat 10 g; Sat fat 1.5 g; Chol 100 mg; Carb 9 g; Protein 41 g; Fiber 0 g; Sodium 620 mg

PER SERVING WITHOUT SAUCE: Cal 270; Fat 9 g; Sat fat 1.5 g; Chol 100 mg; Carb 5 g; Protein 40 g; Fiber 0 g; Sodium 260 mg

➤ VARIATION

Sautéed Turkey Cutlets with a White Wine and Herb Pan Sauce

Follow the recipe for Sautéed Chicken Cutlets with a White Wine and Herb Pan Sauce substituting 1½ pounds turkey cutlets for the chicken cutlets.

PER SERVING: Cal 300; Fat 9 g; Sat fat 1 g; Chol 100 mg; Carb 8 g; Protein 42 g; Fiber 0 g; Sodium 660 mg

PER SERVING WITHOUT SAUCE: Cal 260 Fat 8 g; Sat Fat 1 g; Chol 65 mg; Carb 5 g; Protein 41 g; Fiber 0 g; Sodium 300 mg

LOW-FAT PAN SAUCES AND RELISHES

WE COOKED UP LOTS OF LOW-FAT PAN SAUCES in the test kitchen, and here are a few of our favorites for chicken. Simply follow the master recipe for Sautéed Chicken Breasts or Cutlets with a White Wine and Herb Pan Sauce (pages 190 and 191), replacing the "Sauce" ingredients and cooking directions in steps 3 and 4 with any of the sauces below. Be sure not to wash out the pan after browning the chicken—those browned bits remaining on the bottom of the skillet add important flavor. All of the recipes that follow yield enough sauce for four chicken breasts or eight cutlets.

Piccata Sauce
MAKES ENOUGH FOR 4 SERVINGS

1	medium shallot, minced (about 3 tablespoons)
	Salt
2	medium garlic cloves, minced or pressed through a garlic press (about 2 teaspoons)
1½	cups low-sodium chicken broth
½	lemon, ends trimmed, sliced thin
2	tablespoons whole milk
1	teaspoon cornstarch
2	tablespoons juice from 1 lemon
2	tablespoons capers, rinsed and patted dry
1	tablespoon minced fresh parsley leaves
	Ground black pepper

1. Add the shallot and ¼ teaspoon salt to the oil left in the skillet, return to medium-low heat, and cook until softened, about 2 minutes. Stir in the garlic and cook until fragrant, about 30 seconds. Stir in the broth and lemon slices, scraping up the browned bits. Bring to a simmer and cook until the mixture measures 1 cup, about 5 minutes.

2. Pour any accumulated chicken juices into the simmering sauce. Whisk the milk and cornstarch together in a small bowl, then whisk into the simmering sauce. Continue to simmer the sauce until it has thickened, about 1 minute. Off the heat, stir

in the lemon juice, capers, and parsley, and season with salt and pepper to taste. Spoon the sauce over the chicken before serving.

PER SERVING: Cal 25; Fat .5 g; Sat fat 0 g; Chol 0 mg; Carb 4 g; Protein 1 g; Fiber 0 g; Sodium 490 mg

Mushroom-Sherry Sauce
MAKES ENOUGH FOR 4 SERVINGS

10   ounces white mushrooms, brushed clean, trimmed, and sliced thin
1   medium shallot, minced (about 3 tablespoons)
1   teaspoon sugar
2   medium garlic cloves, minced or pressed through a garlic press (about 2 teaspoons)
1   teaspoon minced fresh thyme leaves
1/4   cup plus 1 teaspoon dry sherry
1 1/2   cups low-sodium chicken broth
2   tablespoons whole milk
1   teaspoon cornstarch
1   tablespoon minced fresh parsley leaves
   Salt and ground black pepper

1. Add the mushrooms, shallot, and sugar to the oil left in the skillet. Return to medium-low heat, cover, and cook until the mushrooms have released their liquid, about 7 minutes. Stir in the garlic and thyme and continue to cook, uncovered, until the mushroom juices have evaporated and the mushrooms are golden brown, about 2 minutes. Stir in 1/4 cup of the sherry, scraping up any browned bits. Add the broth, bring to a simmer, and cook until the mixture measures 1 1/2 cups, about 5 minutes.

2. Pour any accumulated chicken juices into the simmering sauce. Whisk the milk and cornstarch together in a small bowl, then whisk into the simmering sauce. Continue to simmer the sauce until it has thickened, about 1 minute. Off the heat, stir in the remaining 1 teaspoon sherry and the parsley and season with salt and pepper to taste. Spoon the sauce over the chicken before serving.

PER SERVING: Cal 50; Fat .5 g; Sat fat 0 g; Chol 0 mg; Carb 7 g; Protein 2 g; Fiber 0 g; Sodium 230 mg

Creamy Whole-Grain Mustard and Dill Sauce
MAKES ENOUGH FOR 4 SERVINGS

1   medium shallot, minced (about 3 tablespoons)
   Salt
2   medium garlic cloves, minced or pressed through a garlic press (about 2 teaspoons)
1/4   cup dry white wine
1 1/2   cups low-sodium chicken broth
3   tablespoons light cream cheese
1/4   cup whole-grain mustard
1   tablespoon minced fresh dill
   Ground black pepper

1. Add the shallot and 1/4 teaspoon salt to the oil left in the skillet, return to medium-low heat, and cook until softened, about 2 minutes. Stir in the garlic and cook until fragrant, about 30 seconds. Stir in the wine, scraping up the browned bits. Add the broth, bring to a simmer, and cook until the mixture measures 3/4 cup, about 5 minutes.

2. Pour any accumulated chicken juices into the simmering sauce. Turn the heat to medium-low, whisk in the cream cheese, and continue to simmer until the sauce has thickened, about 1 minute. Off the heat, stir in the mustard and dill and season with salt and pepper to taste. Spoon the sauce over the chicken before serving.

PER SERVING: Cal 70; Fat 3 g; Sat fat 1.5 g; Chol 5 mg; Carb 5 g; Protein 3 g; Fiber 1 g; Sodium 720 mg

Roasted Red Pepper Relish
MAKES ENOUGH FOR 4 SERVINGS
Be sure to rinse the jarred red peppers thoroughly of their packing brine before adding them to the sauce.

1   medium shallot, minced (about 3 tablespoons)
   Salt
2   medium garlic cloves, minced or pressed through a garlic press (about 2 teaspoons)
2   cups jarred roasted red peppers, rinsed and patted dry, chopped medium
1/4   cup green olives, pitted and chopped fine

2   tablespoons sherry vinegar
2   tablespoons minced fresh basil or
    parsley leaves
    Ground black pepper

1. Add the shallot and ¼ teaspoon salt to the oil left in the skillet, return to medium-low heat, and cook until softened, about 2 minutes. Stir in the garlic and cook until fragrant, about 30 seconds. Stir in the peppers and olives, scraping up the browned bits, and cook until heated through, about 2 minutes.

2. Pour any accumulated chicken juices into the simmering sauce. Off the heat, stir in the vinegar and basil and season with salt and pepper to taste. Spoon the sauce over the chicken before serving.

PER SERVING: Cal 130; Fat 0 g; Sat fat 0 g; Chol 0 mg; Carb 19 g; Protein 4 g; Fiber 0 g; Sodium 1150 mg

Apricot-Orange Relish with Chipotle

MAKES ENOUGH FOR 4 SERVINGS

I   medium shallot, minced (about
    3 tablespoons)
    Salt
2   medium garlic cloves, minced or pressed
    through a garlic press (about 2 teaspoons)
½   chipotle chile in adobo sauce, minced
I   cup orange juice
½   cup dried apricots, chopped medium
I   orange, peeled, quartered, and cut crosswise
    into ¼-inch wedges
I   tablespoon minced fresh cilantro leaves
    Ground black pepper

1. Add the shallot and ¼ teaspoon salt to the oil left in the skillet, return to medium-low heat, and cook until softened, about 2 minutes. Stir in the garlic and chipotle chile and cook until fragrant, about 30 seconds. Stir in the orange juice and apricots, scraping up the browned bits. Bring to a simmer and cook until the apricots are plump and the juice has thickened, about 2 minutes.

2. Pour any accumulated chicken juices into

the simmering sauce. Off the heat, stir in the orange and cilantro and season with salt and pepper to taste. Spoon the sauce over the chicken before serving.

PER SERVING: Cal 130; Fat 0 g; Sat fat 0 g; Chol 0 mg; Carb 30 g; Protein 2 g; Fiber 3 g; Sodium 150 mg

CHICKEN AND VEGETABLES EN PAPILLOTE

DESPITE ITS REPUTATION FOR DELIVERING bland food, steaming is an excellent method for cooking chicken. Not only is it a low-fat method of cooking, but it is fast, convenient, and keeps food moist. There are a few problems inherent in this approach, though, namely difficulty infusing flavor and coordinating the timing so both the meat and vegetables are properly cooked. We solved these problems when we developed our recipe for Fish and Vegetables en Papillote (see page 234) and thought we could incorporate some of the same strategies as we developed our recipe for Chicken and Vegetables en Papillote.

First, we looked at how to select vegetables that were both suitable for steaming without becoming flavorless and mushy, and compatible with the cooking time of the chicken. After a lot of trial and error, we found that using two types of vegetables was best. Firmer vegetables like carrots, fennel, and squash provided a sturdy base for the chicken and protected it from the direct heat of the oven. In addition, these firm vegetables, when properly cut, matched the cooking time of the chicken perfectly. We also found it essential to use juicy vegetables (and fruit) like tomatoes and oranges. These vegetables, which we placed on top of the chicken, exuded a lot of moisture and created the steam needed for cooking; and as an added benefit their flavorful juices also seeped into the chicken.

But still, the overall flavor of this dish was rather bland. We needed to find a way to add more potent flavor. Simply by mixing a little olive oil with garlic, shallots, crushed red pepper flakes, and assertive herbs such as oregano to the vegetables before placing them in the foil packets, we were able to enliven the flavor of the dish overall. And while we were reluctant to add the fat and calories of oil, the oil was essential in creating a satisfying sauce around the chicken.

Chicken with Zucchini and Tomatoes en Papillote

SERVES 4

The packets can be assembled several hours ahead of time and refrigerated, but they should be baked just before serving. To prevent overcooking, open each pack promptly after baking. Serving this dish on warmed dinner plates is a nice touch. Stack the plates in the rear of your stovetop on an unlit burner before you start cooking. By the time dinner is ready, the plates should be warmed through.

2	tablespoons extra-virgin olive oil
2	medium garlic cloves, minced or pressed through a garlic press (about 2 teaspoons)
1	teaspoon minced fresh oregano leaves
1/4	teaspoon red pepper flakes Salt and ground black pepper
3	medium plum tomatoes (about 12 ounces), cored, seeded, and diced
2	medium zucchini (about 12 ounces), sliced 1/4 inch thick
4	boneless, skinless chicken breasts (6 ounces each), trimmed of excess fat
1/4	cup minced fresh basil leaves

1. Adjust an oven rack to the middle position and heat the oven to 450 degrees. Combine the oil, garlic, oregano, pepper flakes, 1/4 teaspoon salt, and 1/8 teaspoon pepper in a medium bowl. Measure half of the oil mixture into a separate medium bowl and gently toss with the tomatoes. Add the zucchini to the remaining olive oil mixture and toss to coat.

2. Cut four 12-inch squares of heavy-duty foil and lay them flat on a work surface. Following illustration 1 on page 235, shingle the zucchini in the center of each piece of foil. Season the

chicken with salt and pepper and place on top of the zucchini. Top the chicken with the tomatoes then tightly crimp the foil into packets following illustration 2.

3. Set the packets on a rimmed baking sheet and bake until the chicken is no longer pink in the center and the thickest part registers 160 degrees on an instant-read thermometer, about 25 minutes.

4. Carefully open the packets, allowing the steam to escape away from you, and let cool briefly. Following illustration 3 on page 235, smooth out the edges of the foil and, using a spatula, gently push the chicken, vegetables, and any accumulated juices out onto warmed dinner plates. Sprinkle with the basil before serving.

PER SERVING: Cal 280; Fat 9 g; Sat fat 1.5 g; Chol 100 mg; Carb 7 g; Protein 41 g; Fiber 2 g; Sodium 270 mg

Chicken with Fennel, Carrots, and Orange en Papillote

SERVES 4

The packets can be assembled several hours ahead of time and refrigerated, but they should be baked just before serving. To prevent overcooking, open each pack promptly after baking. Serving this dish on warmed dinner plates is a nice touch. Stack the plates in the rear of your stovetop on an unlit burner before you start cooking. By the time dinner is ready, the plates should be warmed through.

2	tablespoons extra-virgin olive oil
1	medium shallot, sliced thin
1	teaspoon minced fresh tarragon leaves Salt and ground black pepper
2	medium oranges, peeled, quartered, and cut crosswise into 1/4-inch wedges
2	carrots, peeled and cut into matchsticks (see the illustrations on page 235)
1	medium fennel bulb (about 1 pound), trimmed, halved, cored, and sliced into 1/4-inch-thick strips (see the illustrations on page 238)
4	boneless, skinless chicken breasts (6 ounces each), trimmed of excess fat
2	scallions, thinly sliced

1. Adjust an oven rack to the middle position and heat the oven to 450 degrees. Combine the oil, shallot, tarragon, ¼ teaspoon salt, and ¼ teaspoon pepper in a medium bowl. Measure half of the oil mixture into a separate medium bowl and gently toss with the oranges. Add the carrots and fennel to the remaining olive oil mixture and toss to coat.

2. Cut four 12-inch squares of heavy-duty foil and lay them flat on a work surface. Following illustration 1 on page 235, mound the fennel and carrots in the center of each piece of foil. Season the chicken with salt and pepper and place on top of the vegetables. Top the chicken with the oranges then tightly crimp the foil into packets following illustration 2.

3. Set the packets on a rimmed baking sheet and bake until the chicken is no longer pink in the center and the thickest part registers 160 degrees on an instant-read thermometer, about 25 minutes.

4. Carefully open the packets, allowing the steam to escape away from you, and let cool briefly. Following illustration 3 on page 235, smooth out the edges of the foil and, using a spatula, gently push the chicken, vegetables, and any accumulated juices out onto warmed dinner plates. Sprinkle with the scallions before serving.

PER SERVING: Cal 330; Fat 9 g; Sat fat 1.5 g; Chol 100 mg; Carb 18 g; Protein 41 g; Fiber 5 g; Sodium 310 mg

INGREDIENTS: Boneless, Skinless Chicken Breasts

In a world of low-fat fanaticism, it's not a surprise that boneless, skinless chicken breasts are a standard in many home kitchens. And while we've come up with countless recipes to add zip to the chicken, we never stopped to look at the chicken itself. Is there a difference in flavor among the popular brands? To find out, we gathered six brands of boneless, skinless chicken breasts, broiled them without seasoning, and had 20 tasters sample the chickens side by side. Among the contenders were one kosher bird, two "natural," and one "free-range." The remaining two were just "chicken."

The koshering process involves coating the chicken with salt to draw out any impurities; this process, similar to brining, results in moist, salty meat (for this reason, we do not recommend brining kosher birds). Natural—in the case of chicken—simply means there are no antibiotics or hormones, and the birds are fed a vegetarian diet. "Free-range" means exactly what it says: The birds are not confined to small cages but are allowed to roam freely.

Last place finishers (and lowest priced) Perdue and White Gem (our local store brand) were downgraded for poor texture and unnatural flavor. Tasters were also put off by the brash yellow color of the birds. Springer Farms All-Natural and Eberly's Free-Range chickens scored well, but the tie for first place went to Empire Kosher and the all-natural Bell & Evans. The only kosher bird, Empire won points with tasters for its superior flavor; namely, salt.

OVEN-FRIED CHICKEN

FRIED CHICKEN RANKS HIGH ON THE LIST of forbidden foods for those watching calories and fat, which is why there is no shortage of recipes for oven-fried chicken. But much to our dismay, a lot of the oven-fried chicken recipes we found were equally as fatty as the real thing. It looked like we had some work to do to find a recipe for light oven-fried chicken.

After gathering up the most promising low-fat oven-fried chicken recipes we could find, we headed into the test kitchen. Right away, we knew the crust would pose our major challenge. Most recipes turned out either greasy or dry chicken coated with a wide array of different "crusts," none of which even began to approximate that of real fried chicken.

Determined to investigate every possible crust alternative, we gathered together a host of possible ingredients and we tried them all (or what felt like all). We tested cereals such as cornflakes and Grape-Nuts, but the distinct flavor of these cereals (among others) overpowered the chicken. Cracker crumbs did not work, because they either had too much fat or produced bland and dry coatings. Flour or cornmeal failed to provide the crunch we sought and often flaked off the chicken while (or shortly after) cooking.

We finally tried some crackers from the specialty aisle in the grocery store: the humble Melba toast. Melba toast is super crunchy, has a good (but subtle) flavor, and has zero fat. Alone, the toasts were too dry and had a tendency to flake off the chicken. We needed to add something to their crumbs to form a cohesive coating. So we tried a bit of oil, which gave them a touch of "fried" flavor without adding a lot of fat. A light spray of vegetable oil also gave the chicken an appealing deep bronze color.

But we were still stuck on how to adhere this innovative coating to the chicken. Up to this point, we had been using eggs in all of our tests, but we knew they added too much fat. So we substituted several low-fat dairy products, such as buttermilk, low-fat milk, sour cream, and yogurt. All of these dairy bases made the coating too soggy; it lacked the crispness that is the hallmark of fried chicken. Additionally, low-fat mayonnaise and a variety of salad dressings were too greasy, causing the coating to just fall off the chicken before it reached our mouths. Eggs were really the best choice. And then it hit us: what if we just used egg whites? This turned out to be the answer. The tackiness of the egg whites helped the crumbs adhere, but it was a very thin coating that didn't become soggy and, best of all, it had no fat whatsoever.

Now that we had resolved the coating, we turned our attention to the best way to "oven-fry" the chicken. We found that a moderately hot oven (450 degrees) was helpful in browning the coating while also allowing the chicken to cook through perfectly in 40 minutes and remain moist and tender. Also, it's important to put the chicken on a rack set on a baking pan—this helps keep the coating uniformly crunchy (otherwise, the bottom of the pieces will be soft).

Some of us sought a spicy fried chicken while others wanted it gently seasoned, so for flavoring we added a bit of Dijon, plus some garlic, thyme, and cayenne. This balance of seasonings satisfied those of us who wanted a richer-tasting fried chicken and those of us who wanted some heat. The spiced, extra-crunchy coating was a wonderful complement to the juicy, sweet chicken fresh out of the oven. With less mess and a lot less fat than fried chicken, we'll take this satisfying alternative any day of the week.

TESTING NOTES

Finding the Right Coating

Because there's an oven-fried chicken recipe on the back of many cereal and cracker boxes, we had plenty of coating options when it came to testing our oven-fried chicken. We started with over a dozen types of coatings—here is a summary of what we found:

CORNFLAKES
Too Sweet
Cornflakes gave the coating a good crunch and color but too much corn flavor. In general, we found that most cereals, with their distinct flavor, overpowered the dish.

RITZ CRACKERS
Too Soft
Many of the crackers failed to make a crisp crunchy coating and were too sweet. In addition, many crackers were very high in fat and calories.

FRESH BREAD CRUMBS
Too Chewy
A coating made with fresh bread crumbs had a beautiful color and tasted great, but the finished product came out of the oven slightly soggy and chewy.

WINNER

MELBA TOAST
To our surprise, Melba toast scored the highest in texture, flavor, and color. The coating made with Melba toast was crisp, crunchy, flavorful, and baked up to a rich copper-brown color. As an added bonus, Melba is completely fat free.

NUTRITION 101
Fats Demystified

Most health experts recommend that people eat no more than 30 percent of their calories from fats, preferably from mono- and polyunsaturated fats. Because most people don't use a calculator to tally fat calories when planning their menus, nor can they easily tell one type of fat from another, following the experts' advice can be tough. To make matters more confusing, when you pick up a variety of foods at the supermarket—say, a box of crackers, a bag of chips, a bottle of salad dressing—you'll find one labeled "no trans fats," another "low-fat," another "reduced-fat," and so on, making grocery shopping seem more like a game of Russian roulette. Here's what you need to know:

All fats are made up of building blocks known as "fatty acids," which come in three forms: saturated, polyunsaturated, and monounsaturated. You've probably seen these words many times on food labels in your kitchen. Every fat is a mixture of all three types and each contains a different proportion of these fatty acids. For example, butter is made up of 68 percent saturated, 4 percent polyunsaturated, and 28 percent monounsaturated fat. Because the highest percentage of fat in butter is saturated, it's regarded as a saturated fat.

Saturated fats are often referred to as "bad" fats because they may stimulate the body to produce more LDL ("bad") cholesterol, and they contribute to the plaque that clogs arteries. Dairy foods such as butter and cream, as well as fats from animal sources, like meat, are saturated fats. Many processed and fast foods also contain saturated fat but the amount varies depending on the food. Fats from animal sources aren't the only fats that are saturated. Palm and coconut oils are vegetable sources of saturated fat, which are used in commercial baking and cooking. These oils are liquid at room temperature and may be broken down quicker than saturated fats from animal sources. That's not to say that saturated fats from vegetable sources are any healthier; the jury is still out, and research is ongoing.

Polyunsaturated fats are found in a variety of foods and contain omega-3 fatty acids, found in fish, flax, and walnuts, and omega-6 fatty acids, found in corn, safflower, soybean, sunflower, and sesame oils. These fats may lower total and LDL cholesterol levels, but some of them may also lower HDL ("good") cholesterol levels as well. Polyunsaturated fats, especially omega-3s, promote joint, skin, immune, neurological, cardiovascular, and nervous system health.

Monounsaturated fats can be found in high amounts in olive, peanut, and canola oils, as well as avocados. These fats lower total cholesterol and LDL cholesterol but don't affect HDL cholesterol.

What about trans fat? Although small amounts of trans fats occur naturally in butter, milk, and other animal foods, trans fats are also manufactured. Hydrogenated fats, such as vegetable shortening and margarine, were first developed over a century ago as an alternative to butter and lard. Why? They are less costly to develop and they don't become rancid as quickly—therefore they will extend a product's shelf life. The downside is that trans fats are a by-product of hydrogenation. Like saturated fats, trans fats contribute to the plaque that collects on the walls of arteries. That's bad enough, but here's why trans fats have become so controversial: trans fats may not only increase your LDL ("bad") cholesterol levels, but some of them may also lower HDL "good" cholesterol. In essence, this double liability makes them the most unhealthy of all fats, which is why most experts agree that trans fats should be eliminated (or at least greatly minimized) from a healthy diet.

GETTING THE FATS STRAIGHT

SOURCE	% SATURATED FAT	% MONO-UNSATURATED FAT	% POLY-UNSATURATED FAT
CANOLA OIL	7%	62%	31%
OLIVE OIL	14%	75%	11%
PEANUT OIL	18%	49%	34%
SOYBEAN OIL	15%	24%	61%
CORN OIL	14%	29%	57%
SUNFLOWER OIL	11%	20%	69%
SAFFLOWER OIL	7%	15%	78%
COTTONSEED OIL	27%	19%	54%
BUTTER	68%	28%	4%
LARD	41%	47%	12%
MARGARINE (HARD STICK MADE FROM SOYBEAN OIL) *	17%	49%	34%
MARGARINE (SOFT STICK MADE FROM CORN AND SOYBEAN OILS) *	20%	50%	31%
VEGETABLE SHORTENING *	26%	47%	27%

Values derived from 2005 USDA National Nutrient Database for Standard Reference, Release 18.

* Note that the type and percentage of fats used in the manufacturing of margarine can vary. These foods may also contain trans fat, which increases the level of harmful cholesterol in the body and which may increase the risk of heart disease. Food companies are working to eliminate trans fats from these food products as the result of a new law that requires them to add the amount of trans fat in a food to the Nutrition Facts panel. This will allow you to see for the first time, how much of all three—saturated fat, trans fat, and cholesterol—are in the foods you choose.

Oven-Fried Chicken Breasts

SERVES 4

Although we like to use bone-in chicken for this recipe, you can substitute 4 boneless, skinless chicken breasts, and reduce the cooking time to 25 minutes.

I	(5-ounce) box plain Melba toast, broken into 1-inch pieces
2	tablespoons vegetable oil
3	large egg whites
I	tablespoon Dijon mustard
2	teaspoons minced fresh thyme leaves
1/4	teaspoon garlic powder
1/8	teaspoon cayenne
4	bone-in, split chicken breasts (about 10 ounces each), trimmed following the illustration at right and skin removed
	Salt and ground black pepper
	Vegetable oil spray

1. Adjust an oven rack to the upper-middle position and heat the oven to 450 degrees. Cover a baking sheet with foil and place a wire rack on top. Process the Melba toast into coarse crumbs in a food processor, about twelve 1-second pulses. Spread the crumbs in a shallow dish and toss with the oil.

2. In a separate shallow dish, whisk the egg whites, mustard, thyme, garlic powder, and cayenne together.

3. Pat the chicken dry with paper towels, then season with salt and pepper. Working with one piece of chicken at time, dip it into the egg white mixture, then coat with the Melba crumbs. Press on the Melba crumbs to make sure they adhere to the chicken. Lay the chicken on the wire rack and spray the tops with vegetable oil spray.

4. Bake until the coating is golden, the chicken is no longer pink in the center, and the thickest part registers 160 degrees on an instant-read thermometer, about 40 minutes. Serve immediately.

PER SERVING: Cal 460; Fat 11 g; Sat fat 1.5 g; Chol 130 mg; Carb 28 g; Protein 59 g; Fiber 2 g; Sodium 720 mg

TRIMMING SPLIT CHICKEN BREASTS

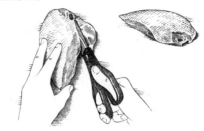

Using kitchen shears, trim off the rib sections from each breast following the vertical line of fat from the tapered end of the breast up to the socket where the wing was attached.

TEST KITCHEN MAKEOVER

CHICKEN PARMESAN

THE BEST PART OF CHICKEN PARMESAN— composed of breaded, fried chicken cutlets topped with tomato sauce, Parmesan cheese, and melted mozzarella—is the crisp, golden coating on the cutlets. Unfortunately, this terrific breaded coating is the result of frying the cutlets in a good amount of oil. Sure there are lots of recipes for low-fat or "un-fried" chicken Parmesan that bake the breaded cutlets rather than frying them, but none that we tried even came close to the flavor, color, or crispness of a traditional fried recipe. They literally paled by comparison, with their flavorless, washed-out-looking crusts. We wondered if we couldn't develop a better low-fat version, one actually worth eating.

Setting the issue of the sauce and cheese aside, we started with how to cook the breaded cutlets. Obviously deep-frying and pan-frying the cutlets were both out—these methods simply used too much oil to be healthy. That left us with just the oven, but simply breading the cutlets (using the classic breading of flour, then egg—in this case egg whites—then bread crumbs) and baking them on a cookie sheet didn't work. The breading never turned brown or crisp, the bottoms turned soggy, the breading tasted stale, and the chicken was rubbery and dry—a real loser on all counts. We had our work cut out for us.

Homing in on the issue of oven temperature first, we found that baking the cutlets for 15 minutes at 475 degrees produced the most tender and juicy chicken. We tried coating the baking sheet with a thin film of oil and heating it in the oven before adding the breaded chicken to encourage browning, but the bread crumbs merely soaked up the oil and turned greasy. Baking the chicken on a wire rack set over a baking sheet quickly solved the soggy bottom issue, and spraying the tops with vegetable oil spray helped the breading on top of the cutlets crisp up nicely. We still, however, had issues with their bland flavor and pale color.

Then it hit us—why don't we toast the bread crumbs to a golden color before breading the cutlets? We toasted the bread crumbs in a skillet over medium heat until golden, then breaded the cutlets, sprayed the tops with vegetable oil, and baked them on the rack. These cutlets were a big improvement, with an even golden color and crisp fried texture. The flavor of the breading, however, still needed help. Adding a tablespoon of olive oil to the crumbs as they toasted gave them a nice "fried" flavor without turning them greasy or adding too many calories, and tossing them with some grated Parmesan cheese helped boost their flavor dramatically. The cutlets now actually tasted like a traditional chicken Parmesan—we were getting somewhere.

Testing the difference between store-bought dried bread crumbs, fresh bread crumbs, and panko (Japanese-style bread crumbs), the test kitchen universally disliked the "old," "ground

BREADING CUTLETS

1. Lightly dredge the cutlets thoroughly in flour, shaking off the excess.

2. Using tongs, dip both sides of the cutlets in the egg mixture taking care to coat them thoroughly and allowing the excess to drip back into the dish to ensure a very thin coating. Tongs keep the egg from coating your fingers.

3. Dip both sides of the cutlets in the bread crumbs, pressing the crumbs on with your fingers to form an even, cohesive coat.

4. Place the breaded cutlets in a single layer on a wire rack set over a baking sheet—this prevents the bottom of the cutlets from becoming soggy.

cardboard" flavor of the store-bought dried bread crumbs. Both the fresh bread crumbs and the panko were well liked, however, tasters preferred the neutral flavor and ultra-crisp texture of panko over that of the fresh bread crumbs, which had a sweeter flavor and sandy texture (fresh bread crumbs can be used if panko is unavailable).

Now that we had flavorful, crisp, golden, "oven-fried" cutlets, we tried layering them into a casserole dish with some tomato sauce and low-fat shredded mozzarella. Returning the casserole dish to the oven so that the mozzarella could melt, we were disappointed at how quickly the crisp breading turned soggy. Any area of breading that touched the sauce, cheese, or other cutlets lost its crispness. Looking for a better method, we

decided to leave the cutlets right on the rack and spoon just a small portion of the sauce and mozzarella onto the center of each piece of chicken, leaving the edges clean. Returning the rack to the oven, the clean edges and bottoms of the breaded cutlets remained crisp while the mozzarella cheese melted. Bingo! Served with extra sauce and grated Parmesan on the side, these oven-baked chicken Parmesan cutlets not only knock 14 grams of fat and 100 calories per serving off the traditional recipe, but they really do taste just as good.

Chicken Parmesan
SERVES 6

If you are tight on time, you can substitute 2 cups of your favorite plain tomato sauce for the Simple Tomato Sauce. Two cups of fresh bread crumbs can be substituted for the panko (they will shrink as they toast). Because these cutlets are breaded, we found that one cutlet per person was plenty—but try to buy the largest chicken breasts you can to ensure good-sized portions.

1½	cups panko (Japanese-style bread crumbs)
1	tablespoon olive oil
1	ounce Parmesan, grated (about ½ cup), plus extra for serving
½	cup unbleached all-purpose flour
1½	teaspoons garlic powder
	Salt and ground black pepper
3	large egg whites
1	tablespoon water
	Vegetable oil spray
3	large boneless, skinless chicken breasts (about 8 ounces each), trimmed of excess fat and sliced into cutlets (see the illustrations on page 191)
1	recipe Simple Tomato Sauce for Chicken Parmesan (page 202), warmed
3	ounces low-fat mozzarella, shredded (about ¾ cup)
1	tablespoon minced fresh basil leaves

1. Adjust an oven rack to the middle position and heat the oven to 475 degrees. Combine the bread crumbs and oil in a 12-inch skillet and toast over medium heat, stirring often, until golden, about 10

MAKEOVER AT A GLANCE

–Classic–
Chicken Parmesan
(per serving)

Calories: 410   Cholesterol: 125 mg
Fat: 22 g   Saturated Fat: 6 g

–Light–
Chicken Parmesan
(per serving)

Calories: 310   Cholesterol: 75 mg
Fat: 8 g   Saturated Fat: 2.5 g

How We Did It

- Toasted the bread crumbs with a little oil before coating the chicken to give them flavor and color
- Baked the breaded cutlets on a rack in a 475-degree oven instead of frying them
- Replaced full-fat mozzarella with low-fat mozzarella
- Topped the individual cooked cutlets with sauce and mozzarella and heated them through on the rack rather than in a casserole dish so they remained crisp

minutes. Spread the bread crumbs in a shallow dish and cool slightly; when cool, stir in the Parmesan.

2. In a second shallow dish, combine the flour, garlic powder, 1 tablespoon salt, and ½ teaspoon pepper together. In a third shallow dish, whisk the egg whites and water together.

3. Line a rimmed baking sheet with foil, place a wire rack on top, and spray the rack with vegetable oil spray. Pat the chicken dry with paper towels, then season with salt and pepper. Lightly dredge the cutlets in the flour, shaking off the excess, then dip into the egg whites, and finally coat with the bread crumbs, following the illustrations on page 200. Press on the bread crumbs to make sure they adhere. Lay the chicken on the wire rack.

4. Spray the tops of the chicken with vegetable oil spray. Bake until the meat is no longer pink in the center and feels firm when pressed with a finger, about 15 minutes.

5. Remove the chicken from the oven. Spoon 2 tablespoons of the sauce onto the center of each cutlet and top the sauce with 2 tablespoons of the mozzarella. Return the chicken to the oven and continue to bake until the cheese has melted, about 5 minutes. Sprinkle with the basil and serve, passing the remaining sauce and Parmesan separately.

PER SERVING: Cal 310; Fat 8 g; Sat fat 2.5 g; Chol 75 mg; Carb 20 g; Protein 38 g; Fiber 1 g; Sodium 790 mg

CORE TECHNIQUE

CREATING THAT DEEP-FRIED CRUST WITHOUT FRYING

Oven-frying breaded foods, rather than frying them in oil, is an obvious way to cut lots of calories and fat. And after oven-frying numerous batches of chicken, we learned a few tricks that can be used anytime you want to oven-fry something breaded. First, mix the bread crumbs with a little oil before you bread the food. Second, always bake the breaded food on a wire rack (set over a baking sheet to catch crumbs) so that the hot air of the oven can circulate all around the food and make the breading crisp—this eliminates soggy bottoms. And finally, spray the tops of the breaded food with vegetable oil spray to make the top crumbs extra-crisp (this adds negligible fat). This small amount of oil adds that "fried" flavor to the crumbs, giving your food the illusion of being truly fried without making it greasy or adding too much fat, and ensures that it will emerge from the oven gorgeously golden.

Simple Tomato Sauce for Chicken Parmesan

MAKES ABOUT 2 CUPS

This easy sauce also works well with pasta.

1	(28-ounce) can diced tomatoes
4	garlic cloves, minced or pressed through a garlic press (about 4 teaspoons)
1	tablespoon tomato paste
1	teaspoon olive oil
⅛	teaspoon red pepper flakes
1	tablespoon minced fresh basil leaves
	Salt and ground black pepper

Pulse the tomatoes with their juices in a food processor until mostly smooth, about ten 1-second pulses; set aside. Cook the garlic, tomato paste, oil, and pepper flakes in a medium saucepan over medium heat until the tomato paste begins to brown, about 2 minutes. Stir in the pureed tomatoes and cook until the sauce is thickened and measures 2 cups, about 20 minutes. Off the heat, stir in the basil and season with salt and pepper to taste. Cover and set aside until needed.

PER ⅓-CUP SERVING: Cal 35; Fat 1 g; Sat fat 0 g; Chol 0 mg; Carb 7 g; Protein 1 g; Fiber 0 g; Sodium 360 mg

CHICKEN POT PIE

POT PIES ARE KNOWN FOR THEIR RICHNESS; IN particular, their thick, creamy filling and buttery, flaky crust. This richness comes with a price, however. Pot pies are typically very high in fat and calories. Could we develop a low-fat version that would be as hearty and taste as rich as the classic full-fat versions? We knew that altering this American classic would be a daunting task.

We gathered as many low-fat chicken pot pie recipes as we could find and tried them out. The results, not surprisingly, were disappointing. The fillings were watery and bland and the low-fat crusts (both pastry and biscuit) were chewy and tough. At the end of the day, these pot pie experiments were like eating Styrofoam on top of runny chicken stew. We knew we'd need to get creative if we were to succeed in doing better than this, so we set out to attack each component one by one.

In our experience, pot pie fillings typically rely on chicken thighs to deliver good flavor to what might otherwise be a bland filling. But we wanted to cut down on fat so we turned to the lower fat option of boneless chicken breasts. However, switching to breasts had a couple of drawbacks: they had less flavor than thighs and they made the filling slightly drier.

To compensate for this, we knew we'd need to experiment with the way we cooked the chicken. At first, we were cubing and poaching the chicken breasts in the broth. This created knobs of dry, tough chicken that did not meld well with the other ingredients. We experimented instead with poaching the whole breasts in a flavorful broth, letting them soak up the liquid, and later shredding the chicken into the filling. This method gave us a filling that was well balanced and also produced moist chicken that, in conjunction with the vegetables, formed a homogenous filling.

For the vegetables, we knew we wanted lots of them. Not just because so many recipes seem to skimp on them, but because we thought their heft would increase the heartiness of our dish without adding any extra fat. After testing various amounts of the usual pot pie suspects, carrots and peas, tasters approved 6 carrots and 1 cup peas. We also added the traditional aromatics like garlic, onion, and celery for further flavor.

Traditional pot pies thicken the sauce with a roux, a combination of butter (or chicken fat) and flour. Obviously, we couldn't follow this route without adding an unacceptable amount of fat and calories to the dish. So we left the traditional roux behind and we experimented instead with cornstarch and a small amount of half-and-half. We were pleased to find that this combination of

---

MAKEOVER AT A GLANCE

–Classic–
Chicken Pot Pie
(per serving)

Calories: 510	Cholesterol: 110 mg
Fat: 28 g	Saturated Fat: 15 g

–Light–
Chicken Pot Pie
(per serving)

Calories: 380	Cholesterol: 85 mg
Fat: 9 g	Saturated Fat: 5 g

How We Did It

- Used lean boneless, skinless chicken breasts instead of fattier chicken thighs
- Thickened the filling with cornstarch instead of a butter-laden roux
- Increased the amount of vegetables in order to make the pot pie heartier without adding extra fat
- Instead of topping the pot pie with a high-fat pastry dough, we used low-fat buttermilk and only 4 tablespoons of butter to make a flavorful and flaky biscuit without a lot of fat

ingredients gave us the thick, rich consistency we were aiming for without sacrificing any flavor.

With the filling thickened and ready to go, we focused on the crust. The dreamy pie dough that envelopes our favorite pot pies contains way too much fat—we needed an alternative. But our experience in the test kitchen (see page 352 for details) taught us that there was no such thing as a tasty low-calorie pie dough. So we decided to follow a different route: a biscuit topping. Testing various proportions of butter and liquid to flour, we were surprised by how much fat we could omit from our biscuit dough without compromising its richness. We found we could use a minimal amount of butter—only 4 tablespoons—and still produce flaky biscuits by melting the butter instead of cutting it into the flour. This method distributed the butter more evenly and allowed us to use less of it. And instead of cream or milk, we used buttermilk. Gently formed by hand and placed on top of the filling, the biscuits baked up tender and golden—the perfect topping for our healthier version of chicken pot pie. And in the end, all of our work was worth it—we now had a delicious pot pie with 19 fewer grams of fat and 130 less calories per serving.

⤙⤚

Chicken Pot Pie

SERVES 8

It is best to mix and shape the biscuits after making the filling and just before baking the casserole. The filling must be warm when you top it or the biscuits will be gummy. For individual pot pies, pour the filling into heatproof bowls or ramekins and top each with a single portion of biscuit dough (the cooking time will be about 5 minutes shorter).

FILLING

6   medium carrots, peeled and sliced ¼ inch thick
2   small celery ribs, sliced ¼ inch thick
1   medium onion, chopped fine
2   medium garlic cloves, minced or pressed
     through a garlic press (about 2 teaspoons)
2   teaspoons minced fresh thyme (or
     ½ teaspoon dried thyme)
1   teaspoon vegetable oil
     Salt

¼   cup dry sherry
3   cups low-sodium chicken broth
2   bay leaves
2   pounds boneless, skinless chicken breasts
     (about 5 medium breasts), trimmed of
     excess fat
¼   cup cornstarch
¼   cup half-and-half
1   cup frozen green peas
2   tablespoons minced fresh parsley leaves
     Ground black pepper

BISCUITS

2   cups (10 ounces) unbleached all-purpose flour
2   teaspoons baking powder
½   teaspoon baking soda
½   teaspoon salt
4   tablespoons (½ stick) unsalted butter, melted
⅔   cup buttermilk

1. Adjust an oven rack to the lower-middle position and heat the oven to 425 degrees.

2. FOR THE FILLING: Combine the carrots, celery, onion, garlic, thyme, oil, and ½ teaspoon salt in a large Dutch oven. Cover and cook over medium-low heat, stirring often, until the vegetables have softened, 8 to 10 minutes. Stir in the sherry, broth, and bay leaves, and bring to a simmer. Nestle the chicken breasts into the sauce. Reduce the heat to low, cover, and cook until the chicken is no longer pink in the center and the thickest part registers 160 degrees on an instant-read thermometer, 10 to 12 minutes. Transfer the chicken to a plate; set aside to cool.

3. Return the sauce to a simmer. Whisk the cornstarch and half-and-half together, then whisk into the simmering sauce. Continue to simmer the sauce until thickened, about 1 minute. Off the heat, discard the bay leaves, stir in the peas and parsley, and season with salt and pepper to taste.

4. Once the chicken is cool enough to handle, shred it into bite-sized pieces. Stir the shredded chicken into the sauce and then pour the mixture into a 13 by 9-inch baking dish.

5. FOR THE BISCUITS: Whisk the flour, baking powder, baking soda, and salt together in a large bowl. In a separate bowl, whisk the melted

butter and buttermilk together. Gently stir the buttermilk mixture into the flour mixture with a rubber spatula until just combined and no pockets of flour remain.

6. To ASSEMBLE AND BAKE: Pinch off 8 equal pieces of the biscuit dough and arrange them on top of the hot filling, spaced ½ inch apart. Bake until the biscuits are golden and the filling is bubbly, about 20 minutes. Cool for 5 to 10 minutes before serving.

PER SERVING: Cal 380; Fat 9 g; Sat fat 5 g; Chol 85 mg; Carb 38 g; Protein 33 g; Fiber 4 g; Sodium 820 mg

TEST KITCHEN MAKEOVER

CHICKEN ENCHILADAS

WE LOVE ENCHILADAS FOR ALL THE THINGS that make them a calorie- and fat-laden nightmare: the gooey cheese, the juicy chicken, and the heavy, rich sauce. This recipe was in definite need of some overhauling to be considered even remotely healthy.

We started with the chicken filling, determining right off the bat that dark meat chicken would have to go; it was too fatty. When we tried simply substituting roasted or sautéed boneless breasts, we found that they made the filling dry, chewy, and flavorless.

Now that we knew that boneless breasts couldn't just be substituted for chicken thighs, we turned to cooking technique as a possible solution. Instead of sautéing or roasting the chicken and then adding shredded chicken to the filling, we decided to make a flavorful sauce and then poach the chicken in it. This approach had several benefits: It moistened the chicken, it flavored the chicken, and it flavored the sauce. The chicken retained much of the sweet and spicy taste of the sauce and the sauce developed a deeper, richer flavor from the stewing chicken.

To capitalize on this process, we developed a sauce that was well spiced and would impart its flavors efficiently to the meat. We settled on chili powder and cumin to flavor the tomatoey sauce and reduced the amount of oil to half a teaspoon.

Now that we had solved the issue of the filling, we turned our attention to the tortillas, which are traditionally heated quickly in oil prior to being rolled so that they will not crack or break. Because tortillas soak up a lot of oil, this step adds significant fat to the dish. So we had to come up with an alternative that avoided the calories but accomplished the same goal. We tried simply microwaving the tortillas to make them soft and pliable. This worked to an extent. Once the heat wore off, the tortillas were again stiff and somewhat brittle. Even if we got the tortilla rolled in time, it would then dry out once in the oven. So

MAKEOVER AT A GLANCE

—Classic—
Enchiladas
(per serving)

Calories: 580	Cholesterol: 110 mg
Fat: 34 g	Saturated Fat: 18 g

—Light—
Enchiladas
(per serving)

Calories: 350	Cholesterol: 65 mg
Fat: 10 g	Saturated Fat: 4.5 g

How We Did It

- Used lean boneless, skinless chicken breasts instead of fattier chicken thighs
- Poached the chicken in the sauce instead of sautéing or roasting it, which would add fat to the dish
- Warmed the tortillas in the microwave and then sprayed them lightly with vegetable oil spray to keep them pliable (rather than heating them in oil)
- Used low-fat cheddar cheese and used less than traditional recipes

we combined a short stint in the microwave with a touch of vegetable oil spray—just enough to grease the tortilla and keep it from drying out. This combination worked well, resulting in a pliable tortilla that remained chewy once cooked through.

Dealing with the cheese was our last hurdle. Surprisingly, it turned out to be the easiest to surmount. Full-fat enchiladas call for upwards of a pound of cheese. Obviously, we couldn't use this much cheese. We tried many different amounts and found that if we used less than a half a pound, the enchiladas lacked the quintessential cheesiness that we all desired. But a half pound of cheese still added too much fat to the dish. So we turned to low-fat cheddar cheese and were pleased by the satisfying flavor and texture. We found that with half in the filling and half sprinkled on top, we were satisfied with the rich, cheesy flavor of the dish, and in the process we had reduced the overall fat content per serving by 24 grams.

In the end, the chicken combined with the piquant sauce and the melted cheese required little else to make this a delicious dish. We added only pickled jalapeños and ½ cup cilantro (admittedly a lot of cilantro!) to give this lightened Mexican dish brightness and punch.

Chicken Enchiladas

SERVES 6

Make sure that the cooked chicken is finely shredded, or the edges of large pieces will tear through the tortillas. In addition to the lime wedges, serve these enchiladas with low-fat sour cream, diced avocado, shredded lettuce, and hot sauce.

1	medium onion, chopped fine
½	teaspoon vegetable oil
	Salt
3	medium garlic cloves, minced or pressed through a garlic press (about 1 tablespoon)
3	tablespoons chili powder
2	teaspoons ground cumin
2	teaspoons sugar
2	(8-ounce) cans tomato sauce
1	cup water
1	pound boneless, skinless chicken breasts (about 2 large breasts), trimmed of excess fat
	Ground black pepper
8	ounces 50 percent light cheddar cheese, shredded (2 cups)
1	(4-ounce) can pickled jalapeño chiles, drained and chopped
½	cup minced fresh cilantro leaves
12	(6-inch) soft corn tortillas
	Vegetable oil spray
1	lime, cut into wedges (for serving)

1. Adjust an oven rack to the middle position and heat the oven to 400 degrees. Combine the onion, oil, and ½ teaspoon salt in a large saucepan. Cover and cook over medium-low heat, stirring often, until the onion has softened, 8 to 10 minutes. Stir in the garlic, chili powder, cumin, and sugar and cook until fragrant, about 30 seconds. Stir in the tomato sauce and water, bring to a simmer, and cook until slightly thickened, about 5 minutes.

2. Nestle the chicken into the sauce. Reduce the heat to low, cover, and cook until the chicken is no longer pink in the center and the thickest part registers 160 degrees on an instant-read thermometer, 10 to 12 minutes. Transfer the chicken to a plate; set aside to cool. Strain the sauce through a medium-mesh strainer into a medium bowl, pressing on the onions to extract as much liquid as possible; discard the onion. Season the sauce with salt and pepper to taste.

3. Once the chicken is cool enough to handle, shred into bite-sized pieces. Toss together the shredded chicken, ½ cup of the enchilada sauce, 1 cup of the cheddar, jalapeños, and cilantro and season with salt and pepper to taste.

4. Stack the tortillas on a microwave-safe plate, cover with plastic wrap, and microwave on high until warm and pliable, 40 to 60 seconds. Spread the warm tortillas out over a clean work surface. Place ⅓ cup of the chicken mixture evenly down the center of each tortilla. Tightly roll each tortilla around the filling and lay them seam-side down in a 13 by 9-inch baking dish.

5. Lightly spray the tops of the enchiladas with vegetable oil spray. Pour 1 cup of the remaining

sauce over the enchiladas to coat them thoroughly. Sprinkle the remaining 1 cup cheddar down the center of the enchiladas. Cover the baking dish with foil and bake until the enchiladas are heated through, 20 to 25 minutes.

6. Remove the foil and continue to bake until the cheese browns, about 5 minutes longer. Serve, passing the remaining 1 cup sauce and the lime wedges separately.

PER SERVING: Cal 350; Fat 10 g; Sat fat 4.5 g Chol 65 mg; Carb 37 g; Protein 33 g; Fiber 7 g; Sodium 980 mg

ONE-POT CHICKEN AND RICE

GETTING A FULL MEAL ON THE TABLE FOR A family is not an easy task. Getting a nutritious healthy meal on the table can be even tougher. When cooking for a family, casseroles and one-dish meals are perfect. They require a minimum of fuss and everything is on the table in one fell swoop. But most of these dishes are filled with fatty, calorie-dense ingredients, making them a poor choice for anyone watching their diet. In search of healthier one-dish meals, we experimented with dishes that were inherently healthy or could be reconfigured to be healthy. One dish came to mind immediately: chicken and rice.

We thought the combination of juicy chicken and tender grains of rice was a sure winner, and if we selected our ingredients carefully, and perfected our cooking techniques, this dish had the potential to be a perfect low-fat, one-dish meal. This feat, however, was not as easy as we had hoped. After several tests, we found that consistently cooked chicken and rice was hard to achieve. Add a vegetable to the mix, and things got even trickier. Somewhat taken aback by our difficulties, we were even more determined to develop a healthy and streamlined one-pot chicken and rice dish.

Instead of trying to figure out the three variables (chicken, rice, and vegetables) all at once, we started by focusing on the chicken and rice components, hoping that the vegetables would fall in line later. The type of chicken to use was our first concern. Normally, we would use chicken thighs because of their moistness and because their cooking time closely matches that of the rice. But in this particular case, we knew that they would add too much fat. With thighs out of the question, we felt bone-in breasts were an attractive alternative because the rib bones would provide some protection and keep the meat from drying out. But the flavor of bone-in breasts was not much better than that of boneless, skinless breasts, which are virtually fat free. The challenge with boneless breasts, however, was that they would cook so quickly—likely before the rice was done. We knew it would be tricky to work out the timing.

Cooking the chicken and the rice together from the start did not work. The rice cooked unevenly and the chicken was inevitably overcooked. We hit on the idea of staggering the cooking of the two ingredients, but using the same pot. We first seared the chicken, then removed it from the heat. Next we sautéed the aromatics (onion and garlic) and added the broth and rice. Once the mixture came to a simmer, we cooked the rice for 10 minutes. Without the chicken, the rice had room to cook and wasn't weighed down by the meat. Once the rice had absorbed the broth, we could add the chicken back to the pot so that it would both flavor the rice and finish cooking.

Last, we focused on the vegetables. Now that we had an established cooking routine for the rice, we identified several stages during which we could add vegetables. We tried to add the vegetables to the pot in the first 10 minutes, but we found that, like the chicken, the vegetables inhibited the rice from absorbing water and the result was unevenly cooked rice. So next we tried adding the vegetables to the pot with the chicken, but found that there was too much food in the pan, which again led to uneven cooking. Last, we tried adding frozen vegetables at the very end of the cooking time, after we removed the chicken from the pot, to allow the rice to sit off the heat. This turned out to be the perfect solution and, much to our surprise, frozen vegetables tasted great and retained their vibrant color and crisp texture after just a few minutes in the pot.

To finish the dish, we wanted to elevate the flavor and richness with a little cheese; since we had used so little oil or other fat in the cooking, we had room to indulge without ruining the healthy aspects of our finished dish. We found that low-fat cheddar contributed both flavor and creaminess to a version that included frozen broccoli, while Parmesan, which is a low-fat cheese, added a nice depth of flavor to a variation with carrots and peas.

One-Pot Chicken and Rice with Broccoli and Cheddar

SERVES 6

When adding the chicken to the pot, lay it gently on top of the rice without pressing down. If the chicken is pressed too deeply into the rice, the rice will cook unevenly.

6	boneless, skinless chicken breasts (6 ounces each), trimmed of excess fat
	Salt and ground black pepper
4	teaspoons vegetable oil
1	medium onion, chopped fine
4	medium garlic cloves, minced or pressed through a garlic press (about 4 teaspoons)
1	teaspoon minced fresh thyme leaves
1/8	teaspoon red pepper flakes
1 1/2	cups long-grain white rice, rinsed (see page 131)
1/2	cup white wine
3 1/4	cups low-sodium chicken broth
3/4	pound frozen broccoli florets, thawed
4	ounces 50 percent light cheddar cheese, shredded (about 1 cup)

1. Pat the chicken dry with paper towels, then season with salt and pepper. Heat 1½ teaspoons of the oil in a large Dutch oven over medium-high heat until just smoking. Lay half of the chicken in the pan and cook until browned on both sides, 5 to 8 minutes. Transfer the chicken to a plate; set aside. Return the pan to medium-high heat and repeat with 1½ teaspoons more oil and the remaining chicken breasts.

2. Add the remaining teaspoon oil, onion, garlic, thyme, pepper flakes, and ½ teaspoon salt to the pot. Cover and cook over medium-low heat, stirring often, until the onion has softened, 8 to 10 minutes. Stir in the rice, increase the heat to medium, and cook, uncovered, until the edges turn translucent, about 3 minutes. Stir in the wine and broth and bring to a simmer. Cover, reduce the heat to low, and cook for 10 minutes.

3. Gently lay the chicken on top of the rice and continue to cook, covered, until the chicken is no longer pink in the center and the thickest part registers 160 degrees on an instant-read thermometer, 10 to 15 minutes.

4. Transfer the chicken to a plate and cover with foil. Stir the broccoli thoroughly into the rice, cover, and let the pot stand off the heat until the rice is tender and the broccoli has warmed through, about 10 minutes. Stir in the cheese and season with salt and pepper to taste. Portion the rice and broccoli onto individual plates, add the chicken, and serve immediately.

PER SERVING: Cal 460; Fat 9 g; Sat fat 3 g; Chol 110 mg; Carb 42 g; Protein 50 g; Fiber 2 g; Sodium 840 mg

VARIATION

One-Pot Chicken and Rice with Carrots, Peas, and Parmesan

Follow the recipe for One-Pot Chicken and Rice with Broccoli and Cheddar, omitting the red pepper flakes. Substitute ¾ pound frozen pea and carrot medley, thawed, for the broccoli, and replace the cheddar with ½ cup grated Parmesan.

PER SERVING: Cal 450; Fat 8 g; Sat fat 2 g; Chol 105 mg; Carb 41 g; Protein 48 g; Fiber 1 g; Sodium 890 mg

TURKEY MEATLOAF

THERE ARE FEW DISHES MORE HOMEY AND satisfying than meatloaf, with its deep meaty flavor and hearty but light texture. Like most comfort meals, however, meatloaf is packed with fat and calories. Enter turkey meatloaf. We wondered if it was possible to use naturally low-fat ground turkey in place of beef to make a meatloaf just as good.

We found a number of turkey meatloaf recipes, but most contained ingredients like spinach and dried cranberries, which we felt were too strange; we were looking for an all-American meatloaf. We began our testing with the ground turkey itself. There were three kinds of ground turkey meat to choose from (see page 211 for more information): ground dark meat, ground white meat, and a combination of the two. Meatloaf made with all dark turkey was sufficiently moist and flavorful but it was still so high in fat and calories that we may as well have made it with ground beef. The meatloaf made with all white turkey was a total disaster; it was so dry and stiff that it resembled a foam block in both taste and texture. This left the combination of ground white and dark meat. This turkey produced a moist loaf that would satisfy even the most avid beef lover. Now that we had settled on the kind of ground turkey for our meatloaf, we began experimenting with binders.

Most meatloaf has some sort of binder. When experimenting with various recipes, we learned that those prepared without a binder were coarse-textured and dense, like a big hamburger. We tried a wide range of binders, from cereal and oatmeal to crackers and bread crumbs. After trying them all, we found that bread crumbs provided the best texture without adding an off flavor or superfluous fat. We also found that a little bit of whole milk and several eggs helped to bind the meatloaf together and provided some added richness.

In addition to bread crumbs, milk, and eggs, the tasters unanimously approved of sautéed onion and several cloves of garlic to flavor the mixture. Although these aromatics added time to the preparation, their contribution to the overall flavor was undeniable. We found it was important to sweat these ingredients in a sauté pan before adding them to the meat mixture, otherwise they would become too overpowering in the dish. In addition to onion and garlic, a healthy dose of chopped thyme and parsley gave our low-fat meatloaf a fuller, more complex flavor.

Now that we were satisfied with the flavor of our meatloaf, all that was left was to determine the best cooking method. We tried baking the meatloaf in a traditional loaf pan, but this produced an unappealing meatloaf since the sides of the loaf steamed rather than baked. We therefore made a free-form loaf and baked it on a wire rack set on a baking sheet that was covered in foil. This method allowed the top as well as the sides to get brown, creating a delicious caramelized exterior. As for oven temperatures, we tried a wide range of heat levels (and times) and learned that it was optimal to cook the loaf at a low temperature for a longer time since this helped ensure a juicy meatloaf.

We thought we were done at this point, but tasters asked for more in the form of a sauce or a glaze to complement the meat. So we returned to the kitchen and experimented with a number of sweet and sticky ingredients, such as honey, syrup, jams, and preserves. Good old ketchup mixed with a little bit of brown sugar turned out to be the winner. Brushed on the loaf before baking and then again halfway through the cooking time, this glaze hugged the loaf and reminded us of the best home-cooked full-fat meatloaf we had tasted.

Turkey Meatloaf with Brown Sugar–Ketchup Glaze
SERVES 8

Do not use ground turkey breast meat (sometimes also labeled as 99 percent fat free) or the meatloaf will be very dry and grainy.

1	medium onion, chopped fine
2	medium garlic cloves, minced or pressed through a garlic press (about 2 teaspoons)
1	teaspoon vegetable oil
	Salt
1/2	cup milk or plain yogurt
2	large eggs
2	teaspoons minced fresh thyme leaves
2	teaspoons Dijon mustard
2	teaspoons Worcestershire sauce
1/4	teaspoon hot pepper sauce
1/2	teaspoon ground black pepper
2	pounds 93 percent lean ground turkey
1 1/3	cups fresh bread crumbs (see page 11)
1/4	cup minced fresh parsley leaves
1/2	cup ketchup
1/4	cup packed light brown sugar
4	teaspoons cider or white vinegar

1. Adjust an oven rack to the middle position and heat the oven to 350 degrees. Line a rimmed baking sheet with foil and place a wire rack on top; set aside. Fold a piece of heavy-duty foil into a 10 by 6-inch rectangle; set aside.

2. Combine the onion, garlic, oil, and ⅛ teaspoon salt in a medium skillet. Cover and cook over medium-low heat, stirring often, until the onion has softened, 8 to 10 minutes; set aside to cool. In a medium bowl, whisk the milk, eggs, thyme, mustard, Worcestershire, hot sauce, pepper, and ¼ teaspoon salt together.

3. In a large bowl, mix the turkey, bread crumbs, parsley, cooked onion mixture, and egg mixture together with your hands until uniformly combined. Press the mixture together into a compact mass, then turn it out onto the foil rectangle. Using your hands, press the meat into an evenly thick loaf about 2 inches tall and 1 inch smaller than the foil on all sides.

4. Transfer the foil and meatloaf to the center of the prepared wire rack. Stir the ketchup, sugar, and vinegar together, then brush half of the mixture evenly over the meatloaf. Bake the meatloaf for 45 minutes.

5. Brush the meatloaf with the remaining ketchup glaze, and continue to bake until the center of the loaf registers 160 degrees on an instant-read thermometer, about 15 to 20 minutes longer. Cool at least 20 minutes before slicing into 1-inch-thick pieces.

PER SERVING: Cal 260; Fat 10 g; Sat fat 3 g; Chol 120 mg; Carb 18 g; Protein 26 g; Fiber 1 g; Sodium 480 mg

TURKEY BURGERS

WHETHER GRILLED, FRIED, OR BROILED, burgers are one of America's favorite foods. Unfortunately, a good hamburger is usually made with the fattiest meat you can find (about 34 grams of fat for a 5-ounce burger). To satisfy a burger craving, you can try a low-fat turkey burger. But in our experience, these burger substitutes are pretty bad—dry, tasteless, and colorless. We set out to develop a turkey burger that would satisfy us whenever the craving for a burger struck.

We first struggled with the type of ground turkey to use. The turkey burgers we made from ground dark meat cooked up juicy and flavorful, but did not save us much on fat or calories, considering that, like typical all-beef burgers, they were between 15 and 20 percent fat. The burgers made with white turkey meat were as dry as could be. There was so little fat in them that they tended to burn when cooking and boy, were they bland. The burgers made with 93 percent lean ground turkey were promising. They had a decent, meaty flavor and were relatively juicy. We figured this was a good start and, with a little help, we knew this meat would make a flavorful burger.

We noticed first that our patties lacked heft and moistness. We began to correct this by adding a combination of milk and bread (also called a panada) to the turkey meat—the same mixture we used to lend moisture to meatballs. The resulting burgers tasted, well, like meatballs, and the patties had an unattractive pale color. We tried a whole host of other ingredients (mashed beans, rehydrated mushrooms, and minced tempeh among them), but they were no better. All of these ingredients either gave the burgers a strong flavor that overshadowed the turkey or failed to add any moistness to the patties. Then we stumbled onto fat-free ricotta. It was exactly what we were looking for. The ricotta gave the burgers a moist, chewy texture and its mild flavor allowed the turkey flavor to stand out.

Flavoring the turkey patties was tricky, though. We tried every ingredient in the test kitchen we thought would add a meaty flavor to the burgers, from teriyaki sauce and fermented black beans to olive paste. After eating a lot of bad (and some good) burgers, we found two ingredients that gave our turkey burgers the optimal beef flavor: Worcestershire sauce and Dijon mustard. Whether by association (because these are condiments that typically complement beef) or pure chemistry, these sharp and tangy flavors made our turkey burger taste like a real beef burger (or at least close enough to satisfy our craving).

Because turkey must be cooked to well done for safety reasons, figuring out how to maintain a juicy burger was difficult. Too high a heat and the burgers burn before they're done; too low and they are pale and virtually steam-cooked (and very unappealing). We experimented with several different cooking methods, including broiling and roasting, but nothing beat the simplicity of browning in a heavy-bottomed skillet. We found the best way to cook the turkey burgers without drying them out was to sear them over medium heat, then cook them partially covered over low heat until they reached an internal temperature of 160 degrees. This resulted in a burger that had a rich crust and remained moist inside (and

THE LOWDOWN ON GROUND TURKEY

Greasy ground beef was not an option for our light recipes, and extra-lean ground beef (95 percent lean, 5 percent fat) was dry and sandy when cooked, but we still wanted to include the likes of chili, meatloaf, burgers, and stuffed bell peppers in our chapters, so we turned to ground turkey. When buying ground turkey, you will often find three different options. The variation depends on the type of turkey meat that is ground and the corresponding percentage of fat it contains.

Ground white meat has 1 to 2 percent fat (also labeled 98 to 99 percent lean). In most applications, we found ground white meat turkey to be exceedingly dry and almost void of flavor. On the other end of the spectrum is ground dark meat, which has 15 to 20 percent fat (80 to 85 percent lean). Dark meat turkey was the most flavorful and juiciest of all the turkey we tried, but because it was so high in fat it wasn't a good choice when it came to light cooking.

A blend of the two (simply labeled ground turkey) contains about 7 percent fat (93 percent lean). This variety of ground turkey proved to be the most popular style at the supermarket and was the best option for our light recipes. With a mild, meaty flavor and moderate juiciness, this meat worked in all of our recipes that called for ground meat without adding a surplus of fat.

required a minimal amount of fat to cook). This burger was now so good that if we closed our eyes we would swear we were eating a real full-fat hamburger.

Turkey Burgers
SERVES 4

The ricotta cheese can burn easily, so keep a close watch on the burgers as they cook.

1¼	pounds 93 percent lean ground turkey
½	cup fat-free ricotta cheese
2	teaspoons Worcestershire sauce
2	teaspoons Dijon mustard
½	teaspoon salt
½	teaspoon ground black pepper
1	tablespoon vegetable oil

1. Combine the turkey, ricotta, Worcestershire, mustard, salt, and pepper together in a large bowl with your hands until uniformly combined. Divide the mixture into 4 portions. Lightly toss one portion from hand to hand to form a ball, then lightly flatten the ball with your fingertips into a 1-inch-thick patty. Repeat the process with the remaining portions.

2. Heat the oil in a 12-inch nonstick skillet over medium heat until smoking. Lay the burgers in the skillet and cook until light brown and crusted, 3 to 4 minutes. Flip the burgers over and continue to cook until the second side is light brown, 3 to 4 minutes longer.

3. Reduce the heat to low, partially cover, and continue to cook until the burgers are no longer pink in the center and the thickest part registers 160 degrees on an instant-read thermometer, 8 to 10 minutes longer, flipping once more if necessary for even browning.

PER SERVING: Cal 250; Fat 12 g; Sat fat 3 g; Chol 85 mg; Carb 3 g; Protein 30 g; Fiber 0 g; Sodium 520 mg

ROAST BEEF TENDERLOIN

WHEN PEOPLE THINK OF HEALTHY EATING, beef is just about the last thing that comes to mind. But not all beef is unhealthy and we wanted to come up with a recipe for one of the leaner cuts of beef that are available. Given the richness (and fat content) of even the leanest cuts of beef, we knew that we'd want portion sizes of about 5 ounces per person (uncooked). This size ruled out steaks since we knew it would be difficult, if not impossible, to prepare individual steaks of this size that were well browned on the outside yet medium-rare on the inside. Steaks this size are just too small to cook properly with sufficient ease, and cooking a larger steak and then cutting them in half into 2 servings wasn't an appealing option. It then occurred to us: why not make a beef roast? This solved several problems: it was simpler handling one piece of meat, we could easily produce a caramelized exterior and a medium-rare interior, and we could cut each 4-ounce portion into thin slices, which would look and feel more plentiful.

So we turned to all the various roasts available, looking for the leanest choice that would deliver big, satisfying flavor both alone and paired with a simple sauce (see the sauces on page 213). We did some reading and some research at the supermarket and identified cuts that were on the leaner side. Top sirloin roast, round roast, and tenderloin were all lean roasts but we settled on tenderloin because it was the most tender and the most widely available. Because it starts out very tender, this elegant roast can be cooked very quickly at a high oven temperature, delivering buttery, fork-tender slices. The other roasts we tried all had a decent beefy flavor but they were either too tough or too difficult to find.

Our choice of roast settled, we moved on to the roasting method. Roasting the beef in the oven for the entire time left us with a pale exterior and no flavor. We tried broiling, but it was difficult to achieve a well-browned exterior and a properly cooked interior. After a few more tests, we finally settled on a hybrid cooking method. We started by searing the roast in a large skillet, which provided us with an evenly browned and flavorful exterior. We then transferred the roast to the oven and let it come up to the desired temperature. This technique provided us with exactly what we wanted—a flavorful, well-developed crust and a perfectly cooked interior. An added benefit to our approach was that we used less oil cooking one large piece of meat than we would have used cooking individual steaks, thus saving ourselves precious fat and calories.

Roast Beef Tenderloin

SERVES 6

If you don't have an ovenproof skillet, transfer the tenderloin to a baking dish in step 3.

- I   (2-pound) center-cut beef tenderloin roast, silver skin removed (see page 218) and tied at even intervals (see below)
  Salt and ground black pepper
- I   tablespoon vegetable oil

1. Let the tenderloin sit at room temperature, covered, for 1 hour before roasting.

2. Adjust an oven rack to the upper-middle position and heat the oven to 425 degrees. Pat the tenderloin dry with paper towels, then season with salt and pepper.

3. Heat the oil in an ovenproof 12-inch skillet over medium-high heat until smoking. Brown the tenderloin on all sides, reducing the heat if the fat

HOW TO TIE A ROAST

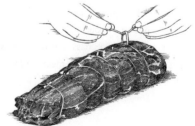

Wrap a piece of butcher's twine around the roast and fasten with a double knot. Snip off the excess and repeat down the length of the roast, spacing each tie about 1½ inches apart. The knots should be snug but not tight.

LOW-FAT PAN SAUCES FOR BEEF TENDERLOIN

WHILE OUR RECIPE FOR ROAST BEEF TENDERLOIN IS GREAT ON ITS OWN, YOU CAN add either of the following light sauces to complement it. To do so, after browning the tenderloin, instead of putting the skillet in the oven, transfer the tenderloin to a 13 by 9-inch baking dish. After the tenderloin has finished roasting and is resting, use the skillet to prepare the sauce. (Don't wash out the pan after browning the roast—those remaining browned bits add important flavor.) In addition to these sauces try the Mushroom-Sherry Sauce on page 193 or the Brandy and Prune Cream Sauce on page 216.

Red Wine Sauce
MAKES ABOUT 1 1/4 CUPS

1	medium shallot, minced (about 3 tablespoons)
	Salt
1/2	cup dry red wine
1 1/2	cups low-sodium chicken broth
1	tablespoon light brown sugar
2	tablespoons whole milk
1	teaspoon cornstarch
1	teaspoon minced fresh thyme
	Ground black pepper

1. Add the shallot and ¼ teaspoon salt to the oil left in the skillet, return to medium-low heat, and cook until softened, about 4 minutes. Stir in the wine, scraping up the browned bits. Add the broth and sugar, bring to a simmer, and cook until the mixture measures 1 cup, about 8 minutes.

2. Pour any accumulated beef juices into the simmering sauce. Whisk the milk and cornstarch together in a small bowl, then whisk into the simmering sauce. Continue to simmer the sauce until it has thickened, about 1 minute. Off the heat, stir in the thyme and season with salt and pepper to taste. Spoon the sauce over the sliced beef before serving.

PER 3 1/2-TABLESPOON SERVING: Cal 35; Fat 0 g; Sat fat 0 g; Chol 0 mg; Carb 4 g; Protein 1 g; Fiber 0 g; Sodium 240 mg

Cognac and Mustard Sauce
MAKES ABOUT 1 1/2 CUPS

2	medium shallots, minced (about 6 tablespoons)
	Salt
1/2	cup cognac or brandy
1 1/2	cups low-sodium chicken broth
2	tablespoons whole milk
1	teaspoon cornstarch
2	tablespoons whole-grain mustard
1	tablespoon juice from 1 lemon
2	teaspoons minced fresh tarragon
	Ground black pepper

1. Add the shallots and ¼ teaspoon salt to the oil left in the skillet, return to medium-low heat, and cook until softened, about 4 minutes. Stir in the cognac, scraping up the browned bits. Add the broth, bring to a simmer, and cook until the mixture measures 1 cup, about 8 minutes.

2. Pour any accumulated beef juices into the simmering sauce. Whisk the milk and cornstarch together in a small bowl, then whisk into the simmering sauce. Continue to simmer the sauce until it has thickened, about 1 minute. Off the heat, stir in the mustard, lemon juice, and tarragon and season with salt and pepper to taste. Spoon the sauce over the sliced beef before serving.

PER 1/4-CUP SERVING: Cal 70; Fat .5 g; Sat fat 0 g; Chol 0 mg; Carb 4 g; Protein 1 g; Fiber 0 g; Sodium 350 mg begins to smoke, about 10 minutes. Transfer the skillet to the oven and roast the tenderloin until the center registers 125 degrees on an instant-read thermometer, 20 to 25 minutes, flipping it over halfway through the roasting time.

4. Remove the tenderloin from the oven (the skillet handle will be very hot) and transfer to a carving board. Cover with foil and let rest for 15 to 20 minutes before slicing into ¼-inch-thick pieces.

PER SERVING: Cal 180; Fat 8 g; Sat fat 2 g; Chol 80 mg; Carb 0 g; Protein 29 g; Fiber 0 g; Sodium 270 mg

SIMPLE SAUTÉED PORK CHOPS

AFTER CHICKEN, PORK IS PROBABLY THE MOST popular meat in the repertoire of anyone looking to cook healthier. Through years of selective breeding, pork producers have created a lean meat that is low in fat and full of protein. But we wanted to go beyond a plain pork chop. Our goal was to create a juicy pan-seared chop with a rich-tasting pan sauce, that wouldn't be so full of fat and calories that you couldn't have some mashed potatoes on the side as well.

In researching an optimal pork chop recipe, we first had to determine what kind of chop to use. In the past, we've been partial to bone-in chops because the bone protects the meat from drying out. In this case, however, the bone-in pork contributed too much fat to the dish—fat that keeps the meat moist and couldn't be trimmed away with a knife. This left us with pork loin chops as the best option. Extra thick, boneless chops (over an inch thick) were less apt to dry out and had less fat, but they required both the stovetop and the oven for proper preparation, which felt like too much work. In the other direction, thin chops (under ¼ inch) were impossible to cook and keep juicy. After many experiments, a ¾-inch pork chop turned out to be the perfect thickness. These pork chops were thick enough to stay moist during sautéing, but thin enough that we could cook them entirely on the stovetop.

While testing various types of chops, we also experimented with cooking methods. The first technique we tried was to brown the chops and then cover them to finish cooking. Doing this yielded a fairly moist piece of meat, but we created steam by covering the chops and ruined their attractive and tasty golden brown exterior. A more traditional approach was ultimately the most successful. This called for searing the chops on one side over medium-high heat. Once they developed a deep brown crust, we flipped the chops and reduced the heat to medium, allowing the chops to slowly come up to a temperature of 135 degrees (see below). This technique yielded a well-browned exterior and a juicy interior, exactly what we were looking for.

It took us a while to decide upon the optimum temperature at which to remove the chops from the heat. We tried a number of chops cooked at various temperatures and found that pork chops cooked to 145 to 150 degrees were the best tasting. This meant that if we removed them from the pan at around 135 degrees, they would continue to cook as they rested and the juices would

EQUIPMENT:
Instant-Read Thermometers

There are two types of commonly sold handheld thermometers: digital and dial face. While they both take accurate readings, we prefer digital thermometers because they register temperatures faster and are easier to read. After testing a variety of digital thermometers, we preferred the Thermapen ($80) for its well-thought-out design—a long, folding probe and comfortable handle—and speed (just 10 seconds for a reading). If you don't want to spend so much money on a thermometer, at the very least purchase an inexpensive dial-face model. There's no sense ruining your dinner because you don't own even a $10 thermometer.

THE BEST INSTANT-READ THERMOMETER
The Thermapen ($80) is our top choice for its pinpoint accuracy and quick response time.

redistribute throughout the meat. After a 5- to 10-minute rest, the chops were perfectly juicy and ready to eat.

When searing the pork, we found that the large surface area of a 12-inch skillet was necessary to build the exterior crust we desired. Chops were simply too crowded in a smaller pan. We were surprised that both traditional and nonstick skillets performed similarly well in the various tests. We opted to use a traditional skillet, however, so that we could take advantage of the leftover fond to build a pan sauce. This required us to use some oil, which added fat to the dish. Just 1 tablespoon was necessary, however. Any less than a tablespoon and the pan would scorch and the pork would brown unevenly.

We finished our testing by experimenting with pan sauces. Because we had learned a lot from developing pan sauces for chicken (we thickened them with a cornstarch-milk mixture or with light cream cheese), we could focus on the sauce flavors that best complemented pork. After trying a number of combinations, we settled on sauces with a sweet component as our favorites. In addition to a little sweetness, potent ingredients like shallots, garlic, rosemary, and sage, and other flavorful components like port and brandy helped to deepen the flavors of the sauces. With these bold ingredients, we didn't miss the more typical (and higher fat) ingredients, such as cream, that usually bump up the flavor. With very little fat or calories, these sauces were the perfect way to finish our pork chops.

Sautéed Pork Loin Chops with Port Wine and Cherry Sauce
SERVES 4

If you have time and can plan ahead, we recommend brining the pork—as long as you are buying unenhanced pork—as it will further enhance its flavor and texture. For information on enhanced pork, see Pork 101 on page 218. Any of the sauces on pages 216–217 can be substituted for the Port Wine and Cherry Sauce.

PORK
4   boneless loin chops, ¾ inch thick (6 to 7 ounces each), brined if desired (see at left)
    Salt and ground black pepper
1   tablespoon vegetable oil

SAUCE
1   medium shallot, minced (about 3 tablespoons)
    Salt
½   cup dry port
1 ½ cups low-sodium chicken broth
½   cup dried cherries
2   tablespoons whole milk
1   teaspoon cornstarch
2   teaspoons minced fresh rosemary
    Ground black pepper

1. FOR THE PORK: Pat the pork chops dry with paper towels, then season with salt and pepper. Heat the oil in a 12-inch skillet over medium-high heat until just smoking. Lay the chops in the skillet and cook until light brown, about 3 minutes. Flip the chops over, reduce the heat to medium, and continue to cook until the centers of the chops register 135 degrees on an instant-read thermometer, 5 to 10 minutes.

2. Transfer the chops to a plate, cover with foil, and let them rest until the centers reach an internal temperature of 145 to 150 degrees, 5 to 10 minutes.

CORE TECHNIQUE
BRINING=JUICIER PORK

Brining pork chops and loin roasts (no need to brine pork tenderloins or enhanced pork) will ensure juicy, tender, and flavorful meat time after time. To brine pork, dissolve 3 tablespoons table salt and 3 tablespoons sugar in 2 quarts of water in a container or bowl large enough to hold the brine and meat. Submerge the meat completely in the brine. Cover and refrigerate for 1 hour (30 minutes for pork chops). Remove the meat from the brine, rinse, and pat dry with paper towels. The meat is now ready to cook.

3. FOR THE SAUCE: While the chops rest, add the shallot and ¼ teaspoon salt to the oil left in the skillet, return it to medium-low heat, and cook until the shallot is softened, about 2 minutes. Stir in the port, scraping up the browned bits. Stir in the broth and cherries, bring to a simmer, and cook until the mixture measures ¾ cup, about 5 minutes.

4. Pour any accumulated pork juices into the simmering sauce. Whisk the milk and cornstarch together in a small bowl, then whisk into the simmering sauce. Continue to simmer the sauce until it has thickened, about 1 minute. Off the heat, stir in the rosemary and season with salt and pepper to taste. Spoon the sauce over the pork before serving.

PER SERVING: Cal 450; Fat 16 g; Sat fat 4.5 g; Chol 110 mg; Carb 20 g; Protein 46 g; Fiber 2 g; Sodium 600 mg

PER SERVING WITHOUT SAUCE: Cal 330; Fat 15 g; Sat fat 4.5 g; Chol 110 mg; Carb 0 g; Protein 44 g; Fiber 0 g; Sodium 230 mg

LOW-FAT PAN SAUCES FOR PORK

HERE ARE A FEW OF OUR FAVORITE LOW-FAT pan sauces for pork chops or pork tenderloin. If making pork chops, simply follow the recipe for Sautéed Pork Loin Chops with Port Wine and Cherry Sauce, replacing the sauce ingredients and cooking directions in steps 3 and 4 with any of the sauces below. If roasting pork tenderloins, prepare the sauce while the tenderloins are either roasting in the oven, or resting after being roasted. Be sure not to wash out the skillet after cooking or browning the pork; those browned bits remaining on the bottom of the skillet add important flavor. In addition to these sauces, feel free to try Creamy Whole-Grain Mustard and Dill Sauce (page 193) or Mushroom-Sherry Sauce (page 193). All of the recipes that follow yield enough sauce for four pork chops or two pork tenderloins.

Apple and Sage Cream Sauce

MAKES ENOUGH FOR 4 PORK CHOPS OR 2 PORK TENDERLOINS

1	medium Granny Smith apple, peeled, cored, and sliced into 12 wedges
½	medium onion, sliced thin (about ½ cup)
	Salt
⅓	cup apple cider
3	tablespoons applejack or brandy
½	cup low-sodium chicken broth
2	tablespoons minced fresh sage leaves
3	tablespoons light cream cheese
2	teaspoons cider vinegar
	Ground black pepper

1. Add the apple, onion, and ¼ teaspoon salt to the oil left in the skillet, return to medium-low heat, and cook, covered, until the onion has softened, 8 to 10 minutes. Stir in the cider and applejack, scraping up the browned bits. Stir in the broth and sage, bring to a simmer, and cook until the mixture measures ¾ cup, about 5 minutes.

2. Pour any accumulated pork juices into the simmering sauce. Turn the heat to medium-low, whisk in the cream cheese, and continue to cook until the sauce has thickened, about 1 minute. Off the heat, stir in the vinegar and season with salt and pepper to taste. Spoon the sauce over the pork before serving.

PER SERVING: Cal 90; Fat 2 g; Sat fat 1.5 g; Chol 5 mg; Carb 10 g; Protein 2 g; Fiber 1 g; Sodium 280 mg

Brandy and Prune Cream Sauce

MAKES ENOUGH FOR 4 PORK CHOPS OR 2 PORK TENDERLOINS

1	medium shallot, minced (about 3 tablespoons)
	Salt
¼	cup brandy
1 ½	cups low-sodium chicken broth
⅓	cup quartered pitted prunes
3	tablespoons light cream cheese

2   teaspoons minced fresh thyme leaves
I   teaspoon juice from I lemon
     Ground black pepper

1. Add the shallot and ¼ teaspoon salt to the oil left in the skillet, return to medium-low heat, and cook until softened, about 2 minutes. Stir in the brandy, scraping up the browned bits. Add the broth and prunes, bring to a simmer, and cook until the mixture measures ¾ cup, about 5 minutes.

2. Pour any accumulated pork juices into the simmering sauce. Turn the heat to medium-low, whisk in the cream cheese, and continue to cook until the sauce has thickened, about 1 minute. Off the heat, stir in the thyme and lemon juice and season with salt and pepper to taste. Spoon the sauce over the pork before serving.

PER SERVING: Cal 100; Fat 2 g; Sat Fat 1.5 g; Chol 5 mg; Carb 11 g; Protein 2 g; Fiber 1 g; Sodium 420 mg

Quick Ginger-Apple Chutney

MAKES ENOUGH FOR 4 PORK CHOPS
OR 2 PORK TENDERLOINS

2   medium Granny Smith apples, peeled, cored, and cut into $1/2$-inch dice
I   small onion, chopped fine
     Salt
I   tablespoon grated fresh ginger
$1/4$ teaspoon ground allspice
$1/8$ teaspoon cayenne
I   cup apple cider
$1/4$ cup packed light brown sugar
     Ground black pepper

1. Add the apples, onion, and ¼ teaspoon salt to the oil left in the skillet, return to medium-low heat, and cook, covered, until the onion has softened, 8 to 10 minutes. Stir in the ginger, allspice, and cayenne and cook until fragrant, about 1 minute. Stir in the cider and sugar, scraping up the browned bits. Bring to a simmer and cook until the cider is reduced and slightly thickened, about 4 minutes.

2. Pour any accumulated pork juices into the simmering sauce. Season with salt and pepper to taste. Spoon the sauce over the pork before serving.

PER SERVING: Cal 120; Fat 0 g; Sat Fat 0 g; Chol 0 mg; Carb 32 mg; Protein 0 g; Fiber 2 g; Sodium 160 mg

Cranberry-Orange Sauce

MAKES ENOUGH FOR 4 PORK CHOPS
OR 2 PORK TENDERLOINS

I   medium shallot, minced (about 3 tablespoons)
     Salt
$1\frac{1}{2}$ cups orange juice
I   cup fresh or frozen thawed cranberries
$1/2$ cup low-sodium chicken broth
$1/4$ cup sugar
I   teaspoon minced fresh thyme leaves
I   teaspoon juice from I lemon
     Ground black pepper

1. Add the shallot and ¼ teaspoon salt to the oil left in the skillet, return to medium-low heat, and cook until softened, about 2 minutes. Stir in the orange juice, scraping up the browned bits. Stir in the cranberries, broth, and sugar, bring to a simmer, and cook until the mixture measures 1 cup, about 8 minutes.

2. Pour any accumulated pork juices into the simmering sauce. Off the heat, stir in the thyme and lemon juice and season with salt and pepper to taste. Spoon the sauce over the pork before serving.

PER SERVING: Cal 110; Fat 0 g; Sat fat 0 g; Chol 0 mg; Carb 26 g; Protein 1 g; Fiber 1 g; Sodium 220 mg

PORK 101

BECAUSE MODERN PORK HAS BEEN BRED to be so lean, it is now a popular staple in the repertoire of light cooking, but this leanness comes at a price; namely, dryness. To counter this problem, many pork producers are now selling what is called enhanced pork, which is pork injected with a solution of water, salt, and other additives that help flavor the meat and keep it moist during cooking. After tasting both unenhanced and enhanced pork side by side, we found that the enhanced pork was juicier and more tender, while the unenhanced pork had a more genuine flavor. We also found that enhanced pork can leach juices that inhibit browning and make for salty pan sauces. To tell if the pork you are buying is enhanced, check the label; pork containing additives must be labeled as such, with a list of ingredients. Our recommendation is to look for unenhanced pork and brine it at home (see page 215 for information on brining). If you cannot find unenhanced pork, then use the enhanced product—just be sure to hold back on seasoning, and definitely don't brine.

Another way to ensure moist and tender pork is not to overcook it. The old belief that pork must be cooked until completely gray is no longer true. (Although the U.S. Department of Agriculture recommends cooking all meat to an internal temperature of 160 to kill bacteria such as salmonella. If safety is your primary concern, follow the USDA's guidelines.) Our approach is to cook the pork to medium doneness, then take it off the heat and let the residual heat continue to cook it through for 5 to 10 minutes before slicing and eating. So how do you know when to take it off the heat? Cook the pork until the very center registers 135 degrees on an instant-read thermometer (see page 214 for our testing of instant-read thermometers). As the pork sits, the temperature will continue to increase 10 to 15 degrees. When you're ready to eat, the pork will have a rosy center and be very juicy.

ROAST PORK LOIN AND TENDERLOIN

NOTHING IS SIMPLER (OR TASTIER) THAN A juicy pork loin or tenderloin, roasted to perfection and dressed up with a flavorful glaze. And because today's pork is as lean as chicken and turkey in terms of fat and calories, there was little we would need to do except perfect our cooking technique and develop glazes that wouldn't tip the calorie scale.

We set out to develop a recipe for roast pork that would accommodate both pork loin and pork tenderloin. We started our testing by trying a number of different cooking techniques. The winning approach required both the stovetop and the oven. Searing the roast first on the stovetop aids the development of a rich, sweet coating and seals in the juices. Then putting the roast in the oven for just a short time allows it to cook through without drying out. We found also that the pork loin needed a lower heat over a longer time than the smaller tenderloins to cook through without drying the exterior. To ensure the moistness of the tenderloins we needed to cook them at 450 degrees (as opposed to 375 for the pork loin) for only 10 to 15 minutes (as opposed to 50 to 70 minutes for the pork loin).

We found that only a tablespoon of oil was necessary to coat either one loin or two tenderloins and facilitate an evenly browned exterior in the sauté pan while keeping fat and calories to a minimum. The subtle flavors of the pork were drawn out with

REMOVING THE SILVER SKIN FROM A PORK TENDERLOIN

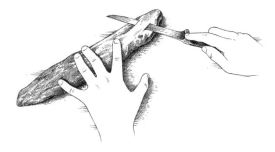

Slip a knife under the silver skin, angle it slightly upward, and use a gentle back and forth motion to remove the silver skin. Discard the skin. You can also use this method to remove the silver skin from beef tenderloin.

just salt and pepper before sautéing. Over medium high heat, we browned all sides of the pork, paying careful attention to the heat to avoid burning. Once the pork had browned, we transferred it to a baking dish and finished it in the oven.

The tricky part of this process came when we had to determine when to remove the roast from the oven. We found that the ideal temperature at which the roast should be removed from the oven was 135 degrees. While out of the oven and resting, the meat keeps cooking. This is called "carry over cooking" because of the meat's retention of heat. After resting, the pork will reach a temperature of between 145 and 150 degrees and will be juicy and ready to serve.

Now that we had determined how best to cook the roast, we turned our attention to developing some flavorful glazes. After deglazing the pan with a mixture of the desired ingredients (see page 220) and scraping up the fond, the glaze simmers until the flavors are melded. We found that the glaze should only be added to the loin during the last 15 minutes of cooking or it will burn. But because the tenderloin is so much smaller, the glaze can be added when you first put it in the oven. Concerned that these glazes were adding a surplus of calories to the dish, we limited the amount to a cup. This amount was just enough to coat the pork and provide a little extra to serve at the table while adding a minimal amount of calories. And in conjunction with the lean pork roast it was hard to pass up.

Roast Pork Loin
SERVES 8

If you have time and can plan ahead, we recommend brining the pork to enhance its flavor and texture. This roast can be prepared using any of the glazes on page 220. If using a glaze, brush it over the pork during the final 15 to 20 minutes of roasting (when the center of the roast registers about 110 degrees). If the glaze begins to dry up or burn in the oven, stir about ¼ cup warm water into the baking dish.

I (3-pound) boneless pork loin roast, brined if desired (see page 215) and tied at even intervals (see page 212)
   Salt and ground black pepper
I tablespoon vegetable oil

1. Let the pork loin sit at room temperature, covered, for 30 minutes or up to 1 hour before roasting.

2. Adjust an oven rack to the lower-middle position and heat the oven to 375 degrees. Pat the pork dry with paper towels, then season with salt and pepper. Heat the oil in a 12-inch skillet over medium-high heat until just smoking. Brown the pork on all sides, reducing the heat if the fat begins to smoke, about 10 minutes. Transfer the pork to a 13 by 9-inch baking dish.

3. Roast the pork until the center registers 135 degrees on an instant-read thermometer, 50 to 70 minutes, flipping it over once halfway through the roasting time.

4. Transfer the pork to a carving board, cover with foil, and let rest until the center reaches an internal temperature of 145 to 150 degrees, 5 to 10 minutes. Remove the twine and slice into ¼-inch-thick pieces.

PER SERVING: Cal 250; Fat 10 g; Sat fat 3 g; Chol 105 mg; Carb 0 g; Protein 37 g; Fiber 0 g; Sodium 260 mg

Roast Pork Tenderloin
SERVES 4

For a more flavorful roast, pour a half recipe of one of the glazes on page 220 over the pork before you place it in the oven. If the glaze begins to dry up or burn in the oven, stir about ¼ cup warm water into the baking dish or make a pan sauce (pages 216–217). Pork tenderloins are often sold two to a package. Unlike pork chops and pork loin roasts, pork tenderloins do not need to be brined to enhance their flavor and texture.

2 (12-ounce) pork tenderloins, silver skin removed (see page 218)
   Salt and ground black pepper
I tablespoon vegetable oil

1. Adjust an oven rack to the lower-middle position and heat the oven to 450 degrees.

2. Pat the tenderloins dry with paper towels,

then season with salt and pepper. Heat the oil in a 12-inch skillet over medium-high heat until just smoking. Brown the tenderloins on all sides, reducing the heat if the fat begins to smoke, about 10 minutes. Transfer the tenderloins to a 13 by 9-inch baking dish.

3. Roast the tenderloins until the thickest part registers 135 degrees on an instant-read thermometer, 10 to 15 minutes, flipping the tenderloins over halfway through the roasting time.

4. Transfer the tenderloins to a carving board, cover with foil, and let rest until the pork reaches an internal temperature of 145 to 150 degrees, 5 to 10 minutes, before slicing into ¼-inch-thick pieces.

PER SERVING: Cal 230; Fat 9 g; Sat fat 2.5 g; Chol 110 mg; Carb 0 g; Protein 36 g; Fiber 0 g; Sodium 380 mg

---

LOW-FAT GLAZES FOR PORK ROASTS

USE THESE GLAZES TO BOOST THE FLAVOR OF ROAST PORK, BOTH PORK TENDERLOIN AND boneless pork loin roasts. **(For 2 tenderloins, you only need half the amount of glaze and you can easily cut these recipes accordingly; the glaze should be brushed over the pork tenderloins before roasting.)** For a boneless pork loin roast, an entire recipe of the glaze should be brushed over the roast during the final 15 or 20 minutes of cooking (when the roast registers about 110 degrees). If the glaze begins to dry up or burn in the oven, stir about ¼ cup warm water into the baking dish.

Maple Glaze
MAKES ENOUGH FOR I PORK LOIN
OR 4 PORK TENDERLOINS

1 ¼	cups maple syrup
½	teaspoon cinnamon
¼	teaspoon cloves
⅛	teaspoon cayenne

After browning the pork, pour off the fat left in the skillet. Add all of the glaze ingredients to the skillet, stirring and scraping up any browned bits, and simmer until slightly thickened and fragrant, about 30 seconds.

PER SERVING: Cal 130; Fat 0 g; Sat Fat 0 g; Chol 0 mg; Carb 34 g; Protein 0 g; Fiber 0 g; Sodium 10 mg

Spicy Honey Glaze
MAKES ENOUGH FOR I PORK LOIN
OR 4 PORK TENDERLOINS

1	cup honey
½	cup juice from 4 limes
2	chipotle chiles in adobo sauce, minced
1 ½	teaspoons cumin

After browning the pork, pour off the fat left in the skillet. Add all of the glaze ingredients to the skillet, stirring and scraping up any browned bits, and simmer until slightly thickened and fragrant, about 2 minutes.

PER SERVING: Cal 140; Fat 0 g; Sat fat 0 g; Chol 0 mg; Carb 36 g; Protein 1 g; Fiber 1 g; Sodium 0 mg

Apricot-Orange Glaze
MAKES ENOUGH FOR I PORK LOIN
OR 4 PORK TENDERLOINS

1	cup apricot preserves
½	cup orange juice
3	tablespoons juice from I lemon
¼	cup dried apricots, quartered

After browning the pork, pour off the fat left in the skillet. Add all the glaze ingredients to the skillet, stirring and scraping up any browned bits, and simmer until slightly thickened and fragrant, about 3 minutes.

PER SERVING: Cal 120; Fat 0 g; Sat fat 0 g; Chol 0 mg; Carb 32 g; Protein 1 g; Fiber 1 g; Sodium 20 mg

GRILLING

GRILLING IS AN IDEAL HEALTHY COOKING method because it adds flavor while requiring little fat. Grilling involves cooking food directly over heat, whether generated by charcoal or gas. The goal is to cook the food quickly over a lot of heat. We prefer the flavor that charcoal adds to grilled food; however, there is no disputing that a gas grill is easier to set up. We leave the choice of grill up to you, and we provide directions in the following pages for both charcoal and gas grills. In addition, we provide recipes for rubs (both wet and dry), glazes, and salsas that deliver lots of flavor with very little fat.

LIGHTING THE GRILL

FOR CHARCOAL: The easiest way we've found to light a charcoal fire is using a chimney starter (also called a flue starter). To use this simple device, fill the bottom section with crumpled newspaper, set the starter on the bottom grill grate, and fill the chimney with charcoal (a large starter holds about six quarts of charcoal). When the newspaper is lit, the flames ignite the charcoal. Once the coals are coated with even layer of fine gray ash, they are ready to be turned out into the grill.

FOR GAS: To preheat a gas grill, turn all the burners on high with the lid down for 15 minutes.

ADJUSTING THE HEAT OF THE GRILL TO MEET YOUR NEEDS

IT IS NECESSARY TO ARRANGE THE LIT COALS IN A CHARCOAL GRILL, OR ADJUST THE GAS burners, to suit the type of food you are cooking. Once the coals have been arranged in the bottom of the grill, put the cooking grate in place and put the cover on for five minutes to heat up the grate.

SINGLE-LEVEL FIRE

A single-level fire is great for foods that cook fairly quickly, such as fish, shellfish, vegetables, and boneless, skinless chicken breasts. This fire delivers even, moderate heat.

CHARCOAL: Arrange all of the lit charcoal in an even layer across the bottom of the grill.

GAS: Adjust all the burners to the same level.

TWO-LEVEL FIRE

This fire creates two cooking zones—a hotter area for searing and a medium area to finish the cooking process. We use this fire for steaks and pork chops.

CHARCOAL: Arrange one-third of the lit coals in a single layer over half of the grill and pile the remaining coals over the other half.

GAS: Leave one burner on high or medium-high and turn the other(s) to medium or medium-low.

MODIFIED TWO-LEVEL

This fire allows searing over the coals and then slow cooking over indirect heat. We use this fire to grill-roast beef tenderloin, pork loin, and pork tenderloin.

CHARCOAL: Arrange all of the coals over half of the grill and leave the other half of the grill empty.

GAS: Leave one burner on high and turn the other burner(s) off.

Tips for Grilling

GRILLING LEAN CUTS OF MEAT

Lean cuts of meat are prone to drying out on the grill. And because lean meat contains less fat, it's also more likely to stick to the grill. Taking a few precautions will help you avoid these problems. Follow the steps below for successful results.

1. Set up and preheat the grill as described on page 221. Once the grill is heated, check the grill temperature (see below right), then scrape it clean. Once it's clean, oil the cooking grate (see the illustration below).
2. Pat the meat dry with paper towels, then spray with vegetable oil and season with salt and pepper.
3. Grill as directed in the chart, checking the doneness temperature in the center of the meat using an instant-read thermometer (see illustration at right). Transfer the grilled meat to a platter or carving board, tent with foil, and let sit until the rested doneness temperature has been reached, 5 to 15 minutes, before serving.

CLEANING A GRILL GRATE

Oiling your cooking grate is a must for preventing fish, burgers, and other foods from sticking to the grill. But the cooking grate should be cleaned before it is oiled. Use a grill brush or this improvised method:

Once your cooking grate is hot, fashion your own grill brush with a crumpled wad of aluminum foil and long-handled tongs.

OILING THE GRILL GRATE

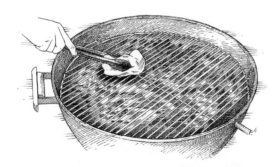

Once your cooking grate is clean, a slick of oil over the grate will further prevent food from sticking. Simply dip a wad of paper towels in vegetable oil, grasp the oiled towels with a pair of long-handled tongs, and rub the oil over the hot cooking grate.

GETTING AN ACCURATE READ FROM YOUR INSTANT-READ THERMOMETER

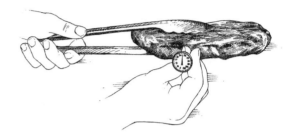

An instant-read thermometer is your best bet for checking the doneness of meat and poultry. The sensor on most thermometers is located an inch or two up from the tip of the shaft, which isn't a problem when you're inserting it through the top of a whole chicken, beef tenderloin, or other thick pieces of meat. But if you poke the thermometer straight down into a thinner piece of meat, such as a steak, burger, or even some chicken breasts, you aren't going to get an accurate reading. Instead, insert the tip of the thermometer through the side of the meat until most of the shaft is embedded. Make sure the shaft is not touching any bone, which will throw off the reading. And make sure to check each piece of meat—based on their thickness and location on the grill, some will cook faster than others.

GAUGING THE TEMPERATURE OF YOUR GRILL

Use the chart below to determine the intensity of the fire. We use the terms "hot fire," "medium-hot fire," and so forth in our grilling recipes. To take the temperature of the fire, hold your hand 5 inches above the cooking grate and count how many seconds you can comfortably leave it in place.

INTENSITY OF FIRE	TIME YOU CAN HOLD YOUR HAND 5 INCHES ABOVE GRATE
Hot	2 seconds
Medium-hot	3 to 4 seconds
Medium	5 to 6 seconds
Medium-low	7 seconds

WET RUBS FOR GRILLED MEAT AND FISH

WET RUBS CAN BE USED IN PLACE OF SALT AND PEPPER ON QUICK-COOKING ITEMS AND are best reserved for cuts that don't necessarily need a seared crust to taste good, such as pork chops and tenderloins, chicken pieces, fish, and shellfish. (You can use wet rubs on beef steaks, but we prefer ours with a crust.) Wet rubs typically consist of fresh herbs, spices, and aromatic vegetables bound by a liquid (most often oil). Making and applying a wet rub is done in the same manner as a dry rub. Simply mix the ingredients together and rub into the meat. You'll need a little over 1 tablespoon of rub per portion. Don't make these rubs more than a few hours ahead or they will lose their flavor.

Orange, Sage, and Garlic Wet Rub

MAKES ABOUT 1/4 CUP

This rub is a winner on chicken and pork.

- 1   tablespoon orange marmalade or honey
- 1   tablespoon grated orange zest
- 1   tablespoon vegetable oil
- 1   tablespoon chopped fresh sage or 1 teaspoon dried sage
- 3   medium garlic cloves, minced or pressed through a garlic press (about 1 tablespoon)
- 1/2   teaspoon ground black pepper
- 1/4   teaspoon salt

PER 1 TABLESPOON: Cal 40; Fat 3 g; Sat fat 0 g; Chol 0 mg; Carb 4 g; Protein 0 g; Fiber 0 g; Sodium 120 mg

Jamaican Jerk Wet Rub

MAKES ABOUT 3/4 CUP

Jerk is classic with chicken or pork. The habanero chile is extremely hot, so you may want to use rubber gloves when handling it. Two jalapeño chiles can be substituted for the habanero.

- 2   tablespoons vegetable oil
- 4   scallions, minced
- 2   tablespoons light molasses
- 1   tablespoon dried thyme
- 3   garlic cloves, minced or pressed through a garlic press (about 1 tablespoon)
- 2   teaspoons allspice
- 1/2   teaspoon salt
- 1   habanero chile, stemmed, seeded, and minced (see note)

PER 1 TABLESPOON: Cal 45; Fat 2.5 g; Sat fat 0 g; Chol 0 mg; Carb 5 g; Protein 0 g; Fiber 1 g; Sodium 110 mg

Asian-Spiced Wet Rub

MAKES ABOUT 1/2 CUP

This combination of flavors is particularly well suited to pork and poultry.

- 2   tablespoons vegetable oil
- 1/4   cup minced fresh cilantro leaves
- 2   tablespoons soy sauce
- 1   tablespoon grated ginger
- 1   jalapeño chile, stemmed, seeded, and minced
- 1   medium garlic clove, minced or pressed through a garlic press (about 1 teaspoon)

PER 1 TABLESPOON: Cal 25; Fat 3 g; Sat fat 0 g; Chol 0 mg; Carb 1 g; Protein 0 g; Fiber 0 g; Sodium 105 mg

Honey, Mustard, and Garlic Wet Rub

MAKES ABOUT 1/4 CUP

Use this rub on chicken, pork, or even salmon.

- 1   tablespoon vegetable oil
- 3   garlic cloves, minced or pressed through a garlic press (about 1 tablespoon)
- 2   teaspoons honey
- 2   teaspoons Dijon mustard
- 2   teaspoons chopped fresh rosemary or 1 teaspoon dried rosemary
- 1   teaspoon grated lemon zest
- 1/2   teaspoon ground black pepper
- 1/4   teaspoon salt

PER 1 TABLESPOON: Cal 40; Fat 3 g; Sat fat 0 g; Chol 0 mg; Carb 3 g; Protein 0 g; Fiber 0 g; Sodium 170 mg

Grilling Lean Cuts of Meat 101

This chart pertains to grilling on both charcoal and gas grills. Refer to pages 221–222 for information on setting up a charcoal fire, gauging heat level, and for preheating a gas grill. Also, see the key points for grilling lean cuts of meat on page 222. Because gas grills put out a lot less heat than a charcoal fire, the lids should always be kept down so that food browns properly. This step isn't necessary with charcoal fires. When covering a charcoal grill, we prefer to use a disposable aluminum roasting pan because a charcoal grill's lid builds up soot over time, which imparts off flavors to grilled foods. The yields in the chart are based on recipes in this chapter—you can, of course, grill more or less, depending on your needs. When you want to add even more flavor to grilled meat, use a rub or glaze, or serve with a salsa. (See the recipes on pages 223 and 225–226.)

PREP AND YIELD	TYPE OF FIRE	GRILLING INSTRUCTION	DONENESS TEMPERATURE*
BONELESS, SKINLESS CHICKEN BREASTS (6 to 7 ounces each), trimmed of excess fat 4 Breasts Serves 4	Medium-hot, single-level fire	Cook, uncovered, flipping once, 10 to 12 minutes	160 degrees
BONELESS PORK LOIN CHOPS (¾ to 1 inch thick and 6 to 7 ounces each), trimmed of excess fat 4 Chops Serves 4	Medium-hot, two-level fire	Grill, on the hot side, uncovered, flipping once, until nicely browned, 10 to 12 minutes. Move to the cool side and continue to grill (uncovered if using charcoal), flipping once, 2 to 4 minutes.	135 degrees
BONELESS PORK LOIN ROAST (3 pounds), trimmed of excess fat, tied at even intervals (see page 212) 1 Roast Serves 8	Medium-hot, modified two-level fire	Grill on the hot side, uncovered, turning several times, until nicely browned all over, 10 to 12 minutes. Move to the cool side, cover, and continue to grill, flipping and rotating once, 30 to 45 minutes.	135 degrees
BONELESS PORK TENDERLOINS (¾ pound), trimmed of silver skin (see page 218) 2 Tenderloins Serves 4	Medium-hot, modified two-level fire	Grill on the hot side, uncovered, turning several times, until nicely browned all over, 10 to 12 minutes. Move to the cool side, cover, and continue to grill, 3 to 5 minutes.	135 degrees
FLANK STEAK Trimmed of excess fat and silver skin (see page 218) 2 Pounds Serves 8	Hot, modified two-level fire	Grill on the hot side, uncovered, until well seared on one side, 5 to 7 minutes. Flip over, move to the cool side, and continue to grill, uncovered, to desired doneness, 2 to 7 minutes.	120 degrees for rare, 125 degrees for medium-rare, 130 to 135 degrees for medium
BEEF TENDERLOIN (2-pound center-cut tenderloin roast), silver skin removed (see page 218), tied at even intervals (see page 212) 1 Roast Serves 6	Medium-hot, modified two-level fire	Grill on the hot side, uncovered, until well seared on all sides, 8 minutes. Move to the cool side, cover, and continue to grill to desired doneness, 10 to 20 minutes.	120 degrees for rare, 125 degrees for medium-rare, 130 to 135 degrees for medium

*The temperature at which to remove the food from the grill. The temperature of the meat will continue to rise as it's resting.

LOW-FAT GLAZES FOR GRILLED MEAT AND FISH

GLAZES, UNLIKE RUBS, ARE USED TO FLAVOR FOODS THAT ARE ALREADY ON THE GRILL. To make a glaze, simply whisk the ingredients together in a small bowl. Begin basting grilled foods liberally about 5 minutes before they finish cooking, so that the glaze has enough time to adhere to the food, but does not burn. We use glazes most often on pork, poultry, and seafood. The recipes that follow each yield enough for one of our pork, chicken, turkey, or seafood recipes that serve 8. To make enough glaze to serve 4, simply cut the recipes in half.

Lime Glaze with Jalapeño and Coriander

MAKES ABOUT 1 1/4 CUPS

This glaze is a natural with pork.

- 1 cup juice from 8 limes
- 2 tablespoons olive oil
- 2 tablespoons minced fresh cilantro leaves
- 4 medium garlic cloves, minced or pressed through a garlic press (about 4 teaspoons)
- 1 jalapeño chile, stemmed, seeded, and minced
- 2 teaspoons ground coriander

PER SERVING: Cal 45; Fat 4 g; Sat fat 1 g; Chol 0 mg; Carb 3 g; Protein 0 g; Fiber 0 g; Sodium 0 mg

Hoisin, Honey, and Ginger Glaze

MAKES ABOUT 1 1/2 CUPS

This glaze is superb on chicken and fish.

- 1/2 cup low-sodium soy sauce
- 6 tablespoons honey
- 1/4 cup ketchup
- 2 tablespoons juice from 1 lemon
- 1 1/2 tablespoons hoisin sauce
- 2 garlic cloves, minced or pressed through a garlic press (about 2 teaspoons)
- 1 teaspoon grated ginger

PER SERVING: Cal 70; Fat 4 g; Sat fat 1 g; Chol 0 mg; Carb 18 g; Protein 18 g; Fiber 0 g; Sodium 720 mg

Smoky Orange-Chili Glaze

MAKES ABOUT 1 CUP

Go easy when applying this glaze; you need only a little for a lot of flavor.

- 1/4 cup orange juice
- 1/4 cup minced fresh cilantro leaves
- 4 chipotle chiles in adobo sauce, minced
- 2 tablespoons vegetable oil
- 2 teaspoons light molasses
- 1 teaspoon grated orange zest

PER SERVING: Cal 45; Fat 3.5 g; Sat fat 0 g; Chol 0 mg; Carb 3 g; Protein 0 g; Fiber 0 g; Sodium 0 mg

Maple-Mustard Glaze

MAKES ABOUT 1 1/4 CUPS

Soy sauce can be substituted for the balsamic vinegar.

- 2/3 cup whole-grain mustard
- 1/2 cup maple syrup
- 1 tablespoon balsamic vinegar

PER SERVING: Cal 80; Fat 1.5 g; Sat fat 0 g; Chol 0 mg; Carb 17 g; Protein 1 g; Fiber 1 g; Sodium 410 mg

Sesame-Soy Glaze

MAKES ABOUT 1/2 CUP

This glaze does wonders for grilled vegetables. Mirin is a rice wine used in Japanese cooking; look for it in Asian markets or the international aisle of any well-stocked supermarket.

- 1/4 cup low-sodium soy sauce
- 2 tablespoons mirin
- 1 tablespoon rice vinegar
- 1 tablespoon sesame seeds, toasted
- 1 tablespoon honey
- 2 teaspoons grated ginger
- 1 teaspoon toasted sesame oil

PER SERVING: Cal 35; Fat 1 g; Sat fat 0 g; Chol 0 mg; Carb 4 g; Protein 1 g; Fiber 0 g; Sodium 270 mg

SALSAS FOR GRILLED MEAT AND FISH

THE FOLLOWING SALSAS ARE A SIMPLE, HEALTHY WAY TO SPICE UP ANY GRILLED FOOD. FOR the best flavor, allow the mixed ingredients to sit for an hour in order for their flavors to meld. Any of these salsas can be doubled if you're serving a crowd.

Spicy Yellow Pepper and Tomato Salsa

MAKES ABOUT 2 CUPS

Most of a chile's heat resides in the ribs. If you prefer more heat, we suggest mincing the ribs along with the seeds and adding them to the recipe to taste; if you prefer less heat, discard the seeds and ribs. This salsa is perfect with grilled fish.

2	small tomatoes (about $1/2$ pound), cored and cut into $1/4$-inch dice
$1/2$	medium yellow bell pepper, stemmed, seeded, and cut into $1/4$-inch dice (about $1/2$ cup)
$1/4$	cup finely chopped red onion
1	jalapeño chile, seeds and ribs removed and set aside (see note), then minced
1	tablespoon juice from 1 lime
1	tablespoon chopped fresh cilantro leaves
1	medium garlic clove, minced or pressed through a garlic press (about 1 teaspoon)
$1/2$	teaspoon hot pepper sauce (optional)
$1/2$	teaspoon salt
$1/4$	teaspoon sugar

Mix all of the ingredients together in a medium bowl. Refrigerate the salsa in an airtight container to blend the flavors at least 1 hour or up to 2 days.

PER $1/4$ CUP: Cal 10; Fat 0 g; Sat fat 0 g; Chol 0 mg; Carb 3 g; Protein 0 g; Fiber 1 g; Sodium 150 mg

Mango Salsa

MAKES ABOUT 2 CUPS

This salsa goes especially well with chicken and fish.

2	medium mangos, peeled, pitted, and cut into $1/4$-inch dice
$1/2$	medium red onion, minced
2	scallions, sliced thin

$1/2$	medium jalapeño chile, seeds and ribs removed, then minced
2	tablespoons minced fresh cilantro leaves
1	tablespoon juice from 1 lime
	Salt and ground black pepper

Mix all of the ingredients, including salt and pepper to taste, together in a medium bowl. Refrigerate the salsa in an airtight container to blend the flavors at least 1 hour or up to 2 days.

PER $1/4$ CUP: Cal 40; Fat 0 g; Sat fat 0 g; Chol 0 mg; Carb 10 g; Protein 0 g; Fiber 1 g; Sodium 0 mg

Pineapple Salsa

MAKES ABOUT 3 CUPS

This sweet and spicy salsa works well with pork.

$1/2$	small pineapple, peeled, cored, and cut into $1/2$-inch dice (about 2 cups)
1	small barely ripe banana, peeled and cut into $1/2$-inch dice
$1/2$	cup seedless green grapes, halved or quartered
$1/2$	firm avocado, peeled, pitted, and cut into $1/2$-inch dice
1	jalapeño chile, seeds and ribs removed, then minced
4	teaspoons juice from 1 to 2 limes
1	teaspoon minced fresh oregano leaves
	Salt

Mix all of the ingredients, including salt to taste, together in a medium bowl. Let the salsa stand at room temperature for 30 minutes to blend the flavors. (The banana will darken if the salsa is prepared much further in advance.)

PER $1/4$ CUP: Cal 40; Fat 1.5 g; Sat fat 0 g; Chol 0 mg; Carb 8 g; Protein 0 g; Fiber 1 g; Sodium 0 mg

8

FISH AND SHELLFISH

IT'S NO SECRET THAT FISH AND SHELLFISH ARE naturally healthy fare. Generally low in fat and calories, fish and shellfish are an excellent way to incorporate high-quality protein into your diet. The best thing about fish and shellfish is that they are diverse in species (salmon, cod, red snapper, haddock, halibut, swordfish, tuna, sole, mussels, shrimp, and crab, to name just a few) and means of preparation (poached, steamed, sautéed, oven-fried,

broiled, grilled, and the list goes on), allowing you lots of choices when contemplating dinner.

Thumbing through some of the light cookbooks on the market, we noticed that poaching and steaming (the plainly obvious low-fat and low-calorie cooking methods) were the predominant cooking techniques for fish and shellfish. Poaching and steaming are simple methods of preparation that can showcase the delicate texture of salmon or sweet, briny flavor of mussels. And in fact, some of our testing focused on improving the flavor, texture, and technique of fish or shellfish prepared by these methods. In the pages that follow, you'll see how we succeeded in improving upon naturally lean recipes like Poached Salmon and Vegetables with an Herb Broth (page 230) and Mussels Steamed in White Wine (page 259).

But we must admit, sometimes we just want a crunchy, perfectly fried piece of fish accompanied by a cool, creamy dipping sauce. Lightening fried classics without losing all the flavor in the process is not without its obstacles, but we accepted the challenge and made over well-known fried-seafood-platter fare, creating Oven-Fried Fish (page 249) and developing a new approach to Crab Cakes (page 257). We even went as far as developing lighter—but still full-flavored—versions of the accompaniments to these dishes, including Tartar Sauce (page 250) and Creamy Chipotle Chile Sauce (page 258).

In the test kitchen, we also explored sautéing, roasting, and baking fish with excellent results. Many of the recipes in this chapter are entire meals in themselves. Soy-Glazed Salmon and Rice Bake with Mushrooms and Bok Choy (page 244), for instance, consists of a protein with a sauce, a starch, and vegetables, all baked together. And our Oven-Baked Shrimp and Orzo (page 246) combines plump, sweet shrimp and pilaf-style orzo with the bold flavors of the Mediterranean for a simple one-dish meal.

In the pages that follow we have also included some general information on cooking fish. Steaming Fish 101 (page 236), Sautéed White Fish Fillets (page 240), Grilling Fish and Shellfish 101 (page 260), and Tips for Broiling Fish (page 247) will point you in the right direction when

BUYING FISH AND SHELLFISH

BUYING TOP-QUALITY FISH AND SHELLFISH is just as important as employing the proper cooking technique. Here are a few general points to keep in mind when purchasing fish.

- Always buy from a trusted source, preferably one with a high volume, to help ensure freshness. The store, and the fish in it, should smell like the sea, not fishy or sour.

- All the fish should be on ice or be properly refrigerated.

- The flesh of the fish should look bright, shiny, and firm, not dull or mushy. Whole fish should have moist, taut skin, clear eyes, and bright red gills.

- When possible, have your fishmonger slice steaks and fillets to order rather than buying precut pieces that may have been sitting around for some time.

- As an extra precaution, especially if you have a long ride home, ask your fishmonger for a plastic bag of ice to lay the fish on. At home, store fish in the coldest part of your refrigerator (in a sealed bag over a bowl of ice is best).

- Cook the fish on the same day you buy it.

it's time to head into the kitchen, offering tips for quick, uncomplicated, and healthy fish dishes. So go ahead and eat your fish, it's good for you.

FROZEN FISH: THE BASICS

WE HAVE DEVELOPED OUR FISH RECIPES with fresh fish in mind, but we know that not everybody has access to fresh fish all the time. Therefore, we also tested our recipes using a variety of frozen fish and learned that, with some attentive shopping and a little care, it works well.

• When buying frozen fish, make sure the fish is frozen solid, with no signs of freezer burn or excessive crystallization around the edges, and no blood inside the packaging.

• Read the ingredients on the side of the package, which should list nothing but the name of the fish you are buying.

• The best way to defrost fish is to let it thaw overnight in the refrigerator, out of its packaging but covered with plastic wrap; keep it in a single layer on a rimmed plate or dish (to catch the released water). While it is possible to defrost fish in the sink under cold running water (in the original wrapper if it's leakproof, or sealed in a zipper-lock bag with the air squeezed out), it's difficult to evenly defrost more than two pieces at a time. We do not recommend using a microwave to defrost fish, since it is impossible to do so without altering the texture of the fish, or worse, partially cooking it.

• Fish will throw off a fair amount of water as it thaws, so be sure to dry the fish thoroughly with paper towels before seasoning and cooking.

POACHED SALMON AND VEGETABLES WITH AN HERB BROTH

UNLIKE PAN-SEARING OR BAKING, POACHING is a moist, gentle cooking method that produces a softer and more supple texture in the finished fish. It is a classically light means of cooking, which, unfortunately, has gained it a reputation as "diet food." Our goal was to create a quick, easy, and elegant dish of perfectly poached fish and vegetables, with a poaching liquid tasty enough to serve as a broth. Sure, we wanted our recipe to be healthy enough to serve at a spa, but it also had to be tasty enough to serve company.

Looking to classic poached fish recipes for inspiration, we decided that salmon would be our choice. Salmon is a richly flavored fish, high in fat (the good kind—omega-3 fatty acids) and hearty enough to be served simply. We set out to find not only the best poaching liquid and the easiest method for poaching the fish, but also the best way to incorporate vegetables into the finished dish. Most of all, we wanted a poached salmon dish that was really delicious—not just healthy.

We began by testing the poaching liquid. Referred to as court-bouillon, this mixture typically consists of water, an acid (vinegar, wine, or lemon), aromatics (carrots, onions, and celery), and herbs and spices.

First, we needed to determine which acid, if any, should be included. To keep things simple, we left out the aromatics, herbs, and spices during this test. We simply poached the fish in plain salted water as well as water spiked with three different acids: cider vinegar, dry vermouth, and lemon juice. The plain salted water produced a fish that paradoxically tasted both overly rich and flat at the same time. By contrast, the cider vinegar produced a clean-flavored fish that was bright and fresh, but the broth itself was slightly too harsh and acidic to accompany the fish.

The bright, clean flavors of the fish were also apparent in the salmon poached with the dry vermouth, but the flavor of the broth was more balanced than that made with the vinegar. (Acid, it seems, provides a nice counterpoint to the richness of the salmon and heightens the overall flavor, but not all acids are suited to a flavorful, well-rounded broth.) The flavors of the fish were less pronounced with lemon juice, but the broth benefited from its inclusion. We tried poaching the fish in a broth with both dry vermouth and lemon juice. For a more floral lemon flavor, we threw the juiced lemons into the mix. This combination struck a perfect balance.

Having settled on a combination of dry vermouth and lemon, we started to put the aromatics, herbs, and spices into the equation. We tried various flavor combinations using carrots, leeks, celery, garlic cloves, parsley, dill, thyme, bay leaf, and peppercorns. Carrots and leeks lent a welcome, complementary sweetness, but celery overpowered some of the other flavors, so we chose to leave it out. Putting the vegetables on double duty, we cut them into matchsticks and simmered them in the broth (as aromatics), and then served them alongside the poached salmon (as a side dish). The garlic cloves, herbs, and peppercorns gave the fish a subtle flavor boost, and by tying them in a cheesecloth sack we were able to easily remove them from the broth. The addition of salt proved essential to heightening the flavor of the fish and making it taste more like the sea.

We now wondered how long the poaching liquid needed to be simmered before cooking the fish. We found 15 to 20 minutes adequate time for the vermouth to mellow and the vegetables to soften and infuse their flavor into the liquid. Any less and the liquid tasted harsh and unseasoned.

Up to this point, we had been cooking the fish at a gentle simmer with just a tiny bit of bubbling of the poaching liquid, but we wondered if there might not be a better approach. We decided to test two other methods: boiling the poaching liquid with the fish in it, and bringing the liquid to a boil, adding the fish, then turning off the heat. Not surprisingly, the boiled version tasted watery, as if the flavors of the fish had been boiled away. The fish also cooked unevenly, with a 30-degree difference between the center and the outside of the fish. Turning off the heat after submerging the fish was not that much better. It took longer to cook (16 minutes versus 10) and the cooking was also uneven. It was clear that our original method of poaching the fish at a gentle simmer for about 10 minutes was ideal.

We were finally happy with our recipe: a well-rounded meal of perfectly poached fish, tender vegetables, and a flavorful broth all cooked in one pot. This recipe can easily be altered to serve more than six people. Simply increase the amount of salmon and vegetables as needed, then add a cup or so more water to ensure that the fish will be completely submerged as it cooks. Any leftover poaching liquid can be strained and refrigerated for up to one week, or frozen for up to one month. Either use it again for poaching, or substitute it in recipes that call for fish stock or bottled clam broth.

Poached Salmon and Vegetables with an Herb Broth
SERVES 6

Skin-on or skinless salmon can be used here; however, you may want to peel off the skin before serving. If you don't have cheesecloth, tie the aromatics together in a paper coffee filter.

3	sprigs fresh dill, tarragon, or parsley
2	medium garlic cloves, peeled
2	teaspoons black peppercorns
6	cups water
1	cup dry vermouth
4	medium leeks, washed well, white and light green parts cut into matchsticks
4	carrots, peeled and cut into 2-inch-long matchsticks (see the illustrations on page 235)
	Salt
1	lemon, halved
6	center-cut salmon fillets, 1 to 1 1/4 inches thick (about 6 ounces each)
	Ground black pepper
1	tablespoon minced fresh dill, tarragon, or parsley leaves

1. Tie the dill sprigs, garlic, and peppercorns together in a loose cheesecloth sack. Combine the water, vermouth, leeks, carrots, cheesecloth sack,

and 1 teaspoon salt in a large Dutch oven. Squeeze all the juice from the lemon into the pot and add the spent lemon halves. Bring to a simmer and cook, partially covered, until the broth is flavorful, about 20 minutes.

2. Pat the salmon dry with paper towels and season it with salt and pepper. Gently slip the salmon into the broth and return to a gentle simmer. Cover and cook until the fish just flakes apart, 6 to 10 minutes.

3. Using a slotted spoon, gently transfer the fish to individual shallow bowls. Discard the cheesecloth sack. Stir the minced dill into the broth and season with salt and pepper to taste. Using a slotted spoon, remove the vegetables from the broth and arrange them around the fish. Ladle some of the hot broth over the fish and vegetables and serve immediately.

PER SERVING: Cal 330; Fat 11 g; Sat fat 1.5 g; Chol 95 mg; Carb 14 g; Protein 35 g; Fiber 2 g; Sodium 610 mg

OVEN-POACHED SIDE OF SALMON

POACHED SALMON IS THE ULTIMATE SUMMER brunch dish, especially when you are serving a crowd. Light and cool, with a hint of fresh lemon and herbs, it is a versatile dish, excellent over a simple salad, with a bagel or a piece of crusty bread, or on its own, perhaps with a dollop of creamy horseradish sauce. Moreover, a whole side of salmon displayed elegantly on a platter is a sure-fire way to impress your guests, who will invariably be surprised that you actually poached the salmon yourself.

Here in the test kitchen, we thought that poaching a side of salmon was a fairly straightforward task until we tried to get it right. Since almost all of the recipes we found required the use of a fish poacher (a piece of equipment we didn't own) we had to ask ourselves: Were we ready to spend $80 for a fish poacher used almost exclusively for this recipe that we might only make once or twice a year? OK, perhaps we're a little stingy, but we also

thought there might be another way to poach our fish without the aid of this equipment, and we were determined to figure it out.

In fact when pressed, most of the test-kitchen staff readily admitted that in the past they have cheated when poaching salmon. One test cook confessed to cutting a beautiful 4-pound side of salmon into several large sections—whatever was necessary to get the fish to fit into his largest pot. He'd then filled the pot with water and seasonings, added the fish, brought it to a boil, covered, and turned off the heat. About 30 minutes later, the fish was done.

We liked this method, but it only works if your style of entertaining is like that of the above-mentioned test cook: You don't really care how things look, only how they taste. Hacking the side of salmon up into two or three pieces simply won't do if presentation is any concern. How, then, to fit a whole side of salmon into a pot that's clearly too small? The answer seemed simple enough: Make the fish fit the pot. If you fill a large pot with water

PREPARING THE SALMON

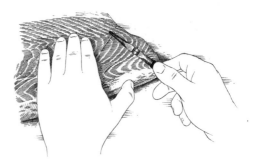

1. Run your fingers over the surface to feel for pinbones, then remove them with tweezers or needle-nosed pliers.

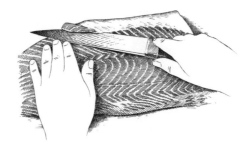

2. Hold a sharp chef's knife at a slight downward angle to the flesh and cut off and discard the whitish, fatty portion of the belly.

WRAPPING THE SALMON FOR OVEN-POACHING

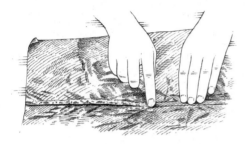

1. Cut two pieces of heavy-duty foil about a foot longer than the fish. Overlap their edges by one inch, and fold to secure the seam.

2. Lay a third sheet of foil over the seam and coat the sheets with vegetable oil spray.

3. Lay the salmon down the center of the foil and arrange the herbs and lemon slices on top. Fold the edges up over the salmon.

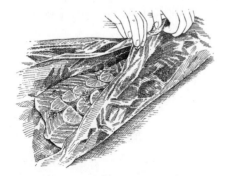

4. Fold the foil up at the ends to secure the seam, but do not crimp too tightly.

and seasonings and gently bend the side of salmon to fit inside, the fish obediently curves along the pot's sides, cooks evenly, and tastes great. But the problem of presentation remains: The curved fish looks incredibly odd and the flesh flakes apart at the bend.

Try as we might, we could not figure out a way to poach a whole side of salmon without a fish poacher (the companies manufacturing and selling these fairly pricey pieces of equipment were onto something), unless we altered its shape. So we did what we should have done in the first place: borrowed a fish poacher. And the results were good, especially when the fish was poached in a mildly acidic mixture containing aromatic vegetables (see Poached Salmon and Vegetables with an Herb Broth, page 230).

But we still wanted to figure out a way to moist-cook a whole side of salmon without a poacher. It was then that we decided to get rid of the water altogether and steam the salmon in its own moisture. No one cares, we reasoned, how we get the salmon on the platter—just make it look and taste like poached salmon and no one will know that it wasn't really poached.

We piled three long sheets of heavy-duty foil on the counter, plopped the side of salmon down the middle of them, seasoned it, and wrapped it up. We baked the fish on a baking sheet at 300 degrees, poking a trusty instant-read thermometer right through the foil every 20 minutes or so. Our first couple of tries were near-disastrous failures— it seemed to take about two hours to go from 33 degrees to 110 degrees, and then about two minutes to go from 110 degrees to 140 degrees. The salmon we cooked at this temperature had three problems: It was overcooked, with a chalky, throat-clogging texture; the skin stuck to the foil; and the flavor was bland.

In an attempt to gain more control over the cooking process, we lowered the oven temperature to 250 degrees. This meant a relatively long cooking time, but we knew it would be largely unattended. Still, we had problems with overcooking; the internal temperature of the fish, like that of a roast, continued to rise after we removed it from the oven. And, like many roasts that are an odd shape—think of leg of lamb—the thinner side became overcooked before the thicker side was done. We could compensate for the overcooking of the thinner end by removing the fish from the oven before it was done (that was easy enough) but then wouldn't the thicker portion be undercooked?

We gained more control by cooking the foil packet directly on the oven rack; this kept the bottom from cooking more rapidly than the top. But in the end, all we could really do was undercook the thickest part slightly in hopes of keeping the tail end palatable. And, indeed, that was a fine solution; because fully cooked salmon is somewhat chalky, some people like it when it's slightly translucent, anyway. Serve from the thick end of the fish and if there are any leftovers, they'll be from the overcooked tail (use them to make salmon salad, cakes, or croquettes).

Solving the sticky skin was easy: We just coated the aluminum foil with vegetable oil spray. All we needed to do to spark the fish's flavor was give it a dose of vinegar and lemon juice. At that point, it was so close to "real" poached salmon that we returned the fish poacher, never to borrow it again. When we served it with lemon wedges and a zesty horseradish or cool dill sauce (see the recipes on page 234), we had everyone fooled into thinking our oven-poached salmon was the real thing.

Oven-Poached Side of Salmon
SERVES 8

If serving a big crowd, you can oven-poach two individually wrapped sides of salmon in the same oven (on the upper- and lower-middle racks) without altering the cooking time. White wine vinegar can be substituted for the cider vinegar. Be sure to follow our directions for wrapping the salmon in foil (see page 232)—otherwise the fish's juices may leak onto the bottom of your oven, creating a pesky mess. To test the fish for doneness, simply poke an instant-read thermometer right through the foil. Serve with one of the sauces that follow.

Vegetable oil spray
1   side of salmon (about 4 pounds)
    Salt
2   tablespoons cider vinegar
6   sprigs fresh tarragon or dill
2   lemons, sliced thin
2   tablespoons minced fresh tarragon or dill leaves (for serving)
1   lemon, cut into wedges (for serving)

1. Adjust an oven rack to the middle position and heat the oven to 250 degrees. Following illustrations 1 and 2 on page 232, assemble three sheets of foil and coat them with vegetable oil spray.

2. Remove any pinbones and trim the belly from the salmon following the illustrations on page 231. Pat the salmon dry with paper towels then season both sides with salt. Lay the salmon, skin-side down, on top of the foil. Sprinkle with the vinegar and lay the herb sprigs on top. Arrange the lemon slices on top of the herbs. Crimp the foil down over the fish into a tight packet.

3. Lay the foil-wrapped fish directly on the oven rack (without a baking sheet) and cook until the color of the flesh has turned from pink to orange, and the thickest part measures 135 to 140 degrees on an instant-read thermometer, 45 to 60 minutes.

4. Remove the fish from the oven, open the foil packet, and discard the lemon slices and herbs. Let the salmon cool at room temperature, on the foil, for 30 minutes.

5. Pour off any accumulated liquid, reseal the salmon in the foil, and refrigerate until cold, about 1 hour. (The poached salmon can be refrigerated for up to 2 days. Let the salmon sit at room temperature for 30 minutes before serving.)

6. To serve, unwrap the salmon and brush away any gelled poaching liquid. Slide your hands under both ends of the salmon and carefully transfer the fish to a serving platter. Sprinkle the salmon with the minced tarragon. Serve with the lemon wedges.

PER SERVING: Cal 320; Fat 14 g; Sat fat 2 g; Chol 125 mg; Carb 1 g; Protein 45 g; Fiber 0 g; Sodium 320 mg

Horseradish Sauce

MAKES ABOUT 1 CUP

This sauce complements poached salmon beautifully, but it is also excellent on Roast Beef Tenderloin (page 212).

1/2	cup reduced-fat mayonnaise
1/4	cup low-fat sour cream
3	tablespoons prepared horseradish
2	tablespoons juice from 1 lemon
1/2	teaspoon garlic powder
1/2	teaspoon salt
1/4	teaspoon ground black pepper
	Water

Mix all the ingredients together, adding the water as needed to thin the sauce out. Cover and refrigerate until the flavors blend, about 30 minutes. (The sauce can be refrigerated for several days.)

PER 2-TABLESPOON SERVING: Cal 40; Fat 2.5 g; Sat fat 1 g; Chol 5 mg; Carb 4 g; Protein 1 g; Fiber 0 g; Sodium 300 mg

Creamy Dill Sauce

MAKES ABOUT 1 CUP

If serving this sauce, use dill as the herb of choice in the salmon poaching liquid.

1/2	cup reduced-fat mayonnaise
1/4	cup low-fat sour cream
2	tablespoons juice from 1 lemon
2	tablespoons minced fresh dill
2	medium shallots, minced (about 6 tablespoons)
1/2	teaspoon salt
1/4	teaspoon ground black pepper
	Water

Mix all the ingredients together, adding the water as needed to thin the sauce out. Cover and refrigerate until the flavors blend, about 30 minutes. (The sauce can be refrigerated for several days.)

PER 2-TABLESPOON SERVING: Cal 40; Fat 2.5 g; Sat fat 1 g; Chol 5 mg; Carb 4 g; Protein 1 g; Fiber 0 g; Sodium 280 mg

FISH AND VEGETABLES EN PAPILLOTE

COOKING FISH EN PAPILLOTE IS A CLASSIC French method that involves baking fish in a tightly sealed parchment paper packet. In effect, the fish steams in its own juices, developing a flaky, delicate texture and an intense, clean flavor. Unlike many other classic French cooking methods, which usually feature butter and cream, cooking en papillote is naturally light and healthy. Some might even call it spa cuisine: Since there is so much moisture and concentrated flavors sealed in the packet, little added fat is needed. With the addition of vegetables, the fish becomes a well-rounded main course. Best of all, this dish takes little work outside of assembly; there's no stovetop cooking and little mess. Our goal in the test kitchen was to develop an easy, more contemporary version of this French classic, with perfectly moist and tender pieces of fish, well-seasoned vegetables, and flavorful juices.

Traditional French methods for cooking en papillote are somewhat arcane. Pieces of thick parchment must be trimmed to an exact size, and folding patterns reminiscent of origami are employed to ensure a tight seal. Admittedly, the results make for a dramatic presentation—the paper balloons and browns in the oven and is slit open at the table by the diner. Because many home kitchens do not have parchment paper on hand, however, we opted to use aluminum foil as a more convenient, modern upgrade. While it lacks the dramatic presentation of the parchment, aluminum foil works just as effectively and doesn't require labor-intensive folding. The seams can simply be crimped together.

Our first step would be to decide what type of fish works best in this dish and how long it would take to cook. After trying a variety of fish fillets, we quickly determined that we favored flaky, mild fish over more assertive, oilier fish like salmon or tuna, which can overpower the delicate flavor of the vegetables. Haddock and cod became our first choices for flavor and texture, although red snapper and halibut were a close second.

Determining when the fish was done proved

more challenging: It was hard to nick and peek when the fish was sealed tightly in foil. The old rule of thumb for fish—10 minutes of cooking time per inch of thickness—failed in this case, as the fish was barely opaque within that period. After experimenting with oven temperatures, we found that 1-inch-thick fillets cooked best at 450 degrees for 20 minutes. While this seemed like an excessive length of time at such high heat, the fish was well insulated within the sealed packets and became flaky without drying out. Cooking the packets for this amount of time at a relatively high temperature also helped concentrate the exuded liquid so neither the fish nor the vegetables became waterlogged.

Having determined the length of time it would take to cook the fish, we could now turn our attention to selecting the vegetables. Since it was obvious that the fish and vegetables would have to cook at the same rate (because they are all contained in one packet), we knew there would be some limitations. Dense vegetables like potatoes were immediately out of the running because they took far too long to cook through, and we knew that any other vegetables we did choose would have to be thinly cut. Light, clean-tasting zucchini was a crowd-pleaser, and it took little work

MAKING FOIL PACKETS

This method for preparing foil packets to cook the fish and vegetables en papillote also applies to our recipes for chicken and vegetables en papillote on page 195.

1. Arrange the vegetables and seasoned fish in the center of a 12-inch sheet of heavy-duty aluminum foil.

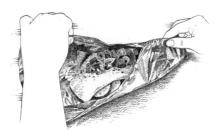

2. Bring the sides of the foil up to meet over the fish. Crimp the edges together in a ¼-inch fold, and then fold over three more times. Fold the open edges at either end of the packets together in ¼-inch fold, and then fold over twice again to seal.

3. When opening the packets after baking, take care to keep steam away from your hands and face. Uncrimp and smooth out the edges of the foil. Using a spatula, gently slide the fish, vegetables, and any accumulated juices out onto warmed dinner plates.

CUTTING CARROTS INTO MATCHSTICKS

1. Start by slicing the carrot on the bias into rounds.

2. Fan the rounds and cut them into strips that measure about 2 inches long and ¼ inch thick.

to slice the squash into thin rounds. For sweetness and body, we added diced tomatoes. But tasters also liked the combination of fennel, carrots, and oranges, so we decided to create two recipes.

For flavorings with the zucchini and tomatoes, we turned to garlic, crushed red pepper flakes, and oregano for an assertive kick and to intensify the mild flavor of the fish. Shallot and tarragon proved to be the perfect complements to the anise-flavored fennel, sweet carrots, and oranges.

While tasters liked these fish and vegetable combinations, they felt that they tasted a little too lean, so we searched for a way to add a bit more flavor and fullness to the dish. Tasters thought that butter was "too rich" for the delicate en papillote method. Olive oil, however, was welcomed for its clean flavor, and extra-virgin olive oil in particular was praised for the "light and summery flavor" it lent to the dish. Additionally, the oil mixed with the juices in the packet to create a delicious broth to be sopped up with bread. For a finishing touch of flavor and color, we added chopped basil to the fish with zucchini and tomatoes, and some thinly sliced scallion to the version with fennel, carrots, and oranges. We had achieved our goal not once, but twice, with two recipes for fish cooked en papillote, featuring perfectly moist and tender pieces of fish, well-seasoned vegetables, and a flavorful broth.

STEAMING FISH 101

A PERFECTLY STEAMED PIECE OF FRESH FISH IS SO PURE AND DELICIOUS THAT IT WILL MAKE you forget you are eating healthy. Serve simply with lemon wedges, or turn up the heat with a fruit salsa (see page 226) or Creamy Chipotle Chile Sauce (page 258).

Although we have found the steaming times listed below to be very reliable, the temperature, thickness, and quality of the fish will all influence the cooking time. Use these times, therefore, as a guideline, but start checking the fish for doneness before the suggested time to avoid overcooked fish. If you are going to be steaming a fish that is not listed on the chart below, compare it to a fish on the chart that has similar texture and thickness.

SIMPLE STEAMED FISH: Fit a large Dutch oven with a lightly oiled steamer basket. Fill the pot with water until it just touches the bottom of the basket. Bring the water to a boil. Gently lay the fish in the steamer basket, cover, and cook, following the times in the chart below. Remove the fish from the steamer and let sit for 5 minutes before serving.

FISH	CUT	STEAMING TIME
ARCTIC CHAR	Fillet (1 inch thick)	5 to 7 minutes
BLUEFISH	Fillet (¾ to 1 inch thick)	6 to 8 minutes
COD	Fillet (1 inch thick)	6 to 8 minutes
FLOUNDER AND SOLE	Fillet (¼ to ½ inch thick, thin ends tucked under)	4 to 6 minutes
GROUPER	Fillet (1 to 1 ½ inches thick)	10 to 12 minutes
HADDOCK	Fillet (½ to 1 inch thick)	5 to 7 minutes
HALIBUT	Fillet (1 inch thick); Steak (1 inch thick)	6 to 8 minutes
MONKFISH	Fillet (1 inch thick)	10 to 12 minutes
SALMON	Fillet (1 ¼ inches thick); Steak (1 ¼ to 1 ½ inches thick)	6 to 8 minutes for medium-rare; 7 to 9 minutes for medium
SEA BASS	Fillet (1 to 1 ¼ inches thick)	8 to 10 minutes
RED SNAPPER	Fillet (1 ¼ inches thick)	8 to 10 minutes
TILEFISH	Fillet (¾ to 1 inch thick)	6 to 8 minutes

Haddock with Zucchini and Tomatoes en Papillote

SERVES 4

Serving this dish on warmed dinner plates is a nice touch. But use caution and don't warm the plates in the oven—the heat will be too intense. Instead, stack them in the rear of your stovetop on an unlit burner before you start cooking. By the time dinner is ready, the plates should be warmed through. Cod, red snapper, thick sole fillets, halibut, and tilapia also work well in this recipe. Ask your fishmonger to remove the skin from the fillets. The packets may be assembled several hours ahead of time and refrigerated, but they should be baked just before serving. Because the fish is sealed tightly in the packet, it will continue to cook out of the oven. To prevent overcooking, open each packet promptly after baking.

2	tablespoons extra-virgin olive oil
2	medium garlic cloves, minced or pressed through a garlic press (about 2 teaspoons)
1	teaspoon minced fresh oregano leaves
1/8	teaspoon red pepper flakes
	Salt and ground black pepper
3	medium plum tomatoes (about 12 ounces), cored, seeded, and chopped into 1/2-inch pieces
2	medium zucchini (about 6 ounces each), sliced 1/4 inch thick
4	haddock fillets, 1 inch thick (about 6 ounces each)
1/4	cup minced fresh basil leaves

1. Adjust an oven rack to the middle position and heat the oven to 450 degrees. Combine the oil, garlic, oregano, pepper flakes, ¼ teaspoon salt, and ⅛ teaspoon pepper in a medium bowl. Measure half of the oil mixture into a separate medium bowl and toss gently with the tomatoes. Add the zucchini to the remaining olive oil mixture and toss to coat.

2. Cut four 12-inch squares of heavy-duty foil and lay them flat on a work surface. Shingle the zucchini in the center of each piece of foil. Season the fillets with salt and pepper and place on top of the zucchini. Top the fish with the tomatoes (see illustration 1 on page 235) then tightly crimp the foil into packets following illustration 2.

3. Set the packets on a rimmed baking sheet and bake until the fish just flakes apart, about 20 minutes. Carefully open the packets, allowing the steam to escape away from you, and let cool briefly. Following illustration 3, smooth out the edges of the foil and, using a spatula, gently push the fish, vegetables, and any accumulated juices out onto warmed dinner plates. Sprinkle with the basil before serving.

PER SERVING: Cal 240; Fat 9 g; Sat fat 1.5 g; Chol 95 mg; Carb 5 g; Protein 35 g; Fiber 2 g; Sodium 410 mg

Cod with Fennel, Carrots, and Orange en Papillote

SERVES 4

Serving this dish on warmed dinner plates is a nice touch. But use caution and don't warm the plates in the oven—the heat will be too intense. Instead, stack them in the rear of your stovetop on an unlit burner before you start cooking. By the time dinner is ready, the plates should be warmed through. Haddock, red snapper, thick sole fillets, halibut, and tilapia also work well in this recipe. The packets may be assembled several hours ahead of time and refrigerated, but they should be baked just before serving. To prevent overcooking, open each packet promptly after baking. To test the doneness of the fish, you will need to open one of the packets and test with a fork.

2	tablespoons extra-virgin olive oil
1	medium shallot, sliced thin
1	teaspoon minced fresh tarragon leaves
	Salt and ground black pepper
2	medium oranges, peeled, quartered, and cut crosswise into 1/4-inch wedges
2	carrots, peeled and cut into matchsticks (see the illustrations on page 235)
1	medium fennel bulb (about 1 pound), trimmed, halved, cored, and sliced into 1/4-inch-thick strips (see the illustrations on page 238)
4	cod fillets, 1 inch thick (about 6 ounces each)
2	scallions, thinly sliced

1. Adjust an oven rack to the middle position and heat the oven to 450 degrees. Combine the oil, shallot, tarragon, ¼ teaspoon salt, and ⅛ teaspoon pepper in a medium bowl. Measure half of the oil mixture into a separate medium bowl and toss gently with the oranges. Add the carrots and

PREPARING FENNEL

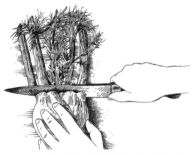

1. Cut off the stems and feathery fronds. (The fronds can be minced and used for a garnish.)

2. Trim a very thin slice from the base and remove any tough or blemished outer layers from the bulb.

3. Cut the bulb in half through the base. Use a small, sharp knife to remove the pyramid-shaped core.

4. Lay the cored fennel on a work surface and, with the knife parallel to the cutting board, cut the fennel in half crosswise. With the knife perpendicular to the cutting board, cut the fennel pieces lengthwise into ¼-inch-thick strips.

fennel to the remaining olive oil mixture and toss to coat.

2. Cut four 12-inch squares of heavy-duty foil and lay them flat on a work surface. Mound the fennel and carrots in the center of each piece of foil. Season the fish with salt and pepper and place on top of the vegetables. Top the fish with the oranges (see illustration 1 on page 235) then tightly crimp the foil into packets following illustration 2.

3. Set the packets on a rimmed baking sheet and bake until the fish just flakes apart, about 20 minutes. Carefully open the packets, allowing the steam to escape away from you, and let cool briefly. Following illustration 3, smooth out the edges of the foil and, using a spatula, gently push the fish, vegetables, and any accumulated juices out onto warmed dinner plates. Sprinkle with the scallions before serving.

PER SERVING: Cal 270; Fat 8 g; Sat fat 1 g; Chol 75 mg; Carbs 18 g; Protein 32 g; Fiber 5 g; Sodium 440 mg

SAUTÉED FISH FILLETS

WE HAVE ALWAYS THOUGHT OF SAUTÉED FISH as a slam-dunk supper. A hot skillet, a squeeze of lemon, and a healthy dinner is served. After further examination, we realized there is a lot to consider. First of all, there's the daunting task of fish selection. With the myriad choices of fillets versus steaks, thick versus thin, and endless species, fish shopping is akin to choosing an insurance policy (see page 228 for information on buying fish). Next—let's face it—sautéed fish without a pan sauce can be boring. Unfortunately, most of the classic pan sauces for fish are based on butter, not an option for a light recipe. On top of that, getting a hot pan sauce and hot fish on the table at the same time isn't always so easy because fish (especially thin fillets) cools down quickly. This was beginning to sound like a case of swimming upstream, but, in typical test-kitchen style, we decided to start at square one.

We began working on the sauté with four 5-ounce haddock fillets of an even ½-inch thickness.

We knew that we wanted to use a heavy, large nonstick skillet—it's perfect for cooking delicate fish because the fillets won't stick and break apart. (For information on nonstick skillets, see page 286.) Additionally, with a nonstick skillet, we would be able to achieve a browned crust using less oil than in a traditional skillet. With a browned crust in mind, we tried sautéing the fish both with a coating of flour (a technique we used for sautéed chicken breasts) and without. The flour added just the right amount of crust (not too tough) and color, but it didn't always adhere properly. We discovered that by seasoning the fish with salt and pepper and then letting it sit for a few moments before flouring, moisture in the fish would bead on the surface, helping the flour adhere without having to add any fat.

We then tested other white fish fillets using this technique. As for size, we found that anything thinner than ¼ inch would fall apart and should not be sautéed. Very thick fillets—more than 1 inch—required a different cooking method, including some oven time, so we also excluded them from further testing. Fillets between ¼ and 1 inch thick could be cooked in the same way (a bit longer on the first side, less on the second side) and are our first choice.

Most recipes for sautéed fish with a pan sauce call for slightly undercooking the fish, removing it from the pan, making the sauce, and then tossing the fish back into the sauce to finish cooking. This method showed some promise at first, but the tender fish began to flake apart around the edges by the time it was reheated, and the crisp outer layer was history. Next we followed a similar procedure but finished the fillets and sauce in a hot oven. Once again, the fish fell apart as soon as it was served, and the whole dish was a mess.

It then occurred to us that the solution might be the simplest method: What if we had the pan sauce waiting for the fish instead of the other way around? Unlike a steak, for example, the fish was not creating a fond (browned bits on the bottom of the pan) that was going to contribute a lot of flavor. (Because we were using a nonstick skillet, the fond formation would be minimal even with beef or pork.) We made the sauce in a separate saucepan and kept it warm while we cooked the fish. As soon as the second side was sautéed, we placed the fish on a plate and then spooned the sauce over it.

EQUIPMENT: Fish Spatulas

While they may be called fish spatulas, these flexible, thin spatulas are equally good at flipping chicken cutlets and steaks. Priced around $7, the Matfer High Heat Slotted Pelton Spatula is our favorite, outperforming spatulas costing eight times as much. The Matfer received raves for its comfortable handle, long blade, and exceptional performance. Because of its smooth, slippery plastic surface, the spatula nimbly flipped fish without scarring the delicate flesh, and it is completely safe for nonstick skillets. We recommend this fish spatula with one caveat: It is designed for right-handed cooks. Some companies make left-handed versions as well, but Matfer does not.

FLIPPING FISH FILLETS

To turn fish fillets without breaking them, use two spatulas—a regular model and an extra-wide version especially designed for fish. (In the test kitchen, we use a spatula that is 8 inches wide by 3 inches deep for this job.) Using the regular spatula, gently lift the long side of the fillet. Then, supporting the fillet with the extra-wide spatula, flip it so that the browned side faces up.

THE BEST FISH SPATULA

The Matfer High Heat Slotted Pelton Spatula, priced at just $7, outperformed spatulas costing eight times as much.

Indeed, this fish was tender and moist, with a good crust. And because we didn't have to worry about the fish cooling off, we could give the sauces a bit more attention.

An added benefit of making the sauce first was that we could take a bit more time (up to five minutes or so) to reduce the liquids (such as wine) and concentrate the flavors. This proved to be crucial to the flavor development of our sauce, since without the significant amounts of butter that most pan sauces contain, we had to find another way to build flavor. We were able to create a healthier, but equally tasty, version of a classic white wine sauce by replacing butter with chicken stock and light cream cheese. Brightness was added via lemon juice and capers, and shallots and parsley added some bite and a welcome depth. In addition to the traditional white wine–shallot sauce, we developed a warm tomato relish, punctuated by toasty garlic and sweet basil, as well as a simple grapefruit vinaigrette, which

TUCKING THE TAIL

This trick can be used with any piece of fish that has a thin tapered end, in any type of recipe including sautéed, oven-fried, steamed, or baked.

1. With a sharp knife, cut halfway through the flesh crosswise 2 to 3 inches from the tail end. This will create a seam to fold the tail under.

2. Fold the tail end under to create a fillet of relatively even thickness.

is perhaps the easiest sauce of all, as it requires no cooking.

Sautéed White Fish Fillets
SERVES 4

For the purpose of this recipe, we are putting the fish into two categories: thick and thin fillets. Fish fillets that are ½ to 1 inch thick fall into the thick category, while the thin category includes fillets that are ¼ to ½ inch thick. Note that the sauce recipes that follow are meant to be prepared before the fish fillets are cooked. The sauce is then held until serving.

4   boneless, skinless thick fish fillets,
    ½ to 1 inch thick (about 6 ounces each)
    or 8 boneless, skinless thin fish fillets, ¼ to ½
    inch thick (about 3 ounces each)
    Salt and ground black pepper
½   cup unbleached all-purpose flour
2   tablespoons vegetable oil
1   lemon, cut into wedges (for serving)

1. Pat the fish fillets dry with paper towels and season them with salt and pepper. Let the fish stand until glistening with moisture, about 5 minutes. If using tail-end fillets, score and tuck the end under following the illustrations at left. Spread the flour in a shallow dish. Lightly dredge the fillets in the flour and shake off the excess (keeping any tail ends tucked).

2. Heat 1 tablespoon of the oil in a 12-inch nonstick skillet over high heat until shimmering but not smoking. Place half of the fillets in the pan in a single layer and immediately reduce the heat to medium-high. Cook, without moving the fish, until the edges of the fillets are opaque and the bottoms are golden brown, 3 to 4 minutes for thick fillets or 2 to 3 minutes for thin fillets.

3. Using a spatula, gently flip the fillets over. Continue to cook on the second side until the thickest part of the fillets is firm to the touch and the fish just flakes apart, 2 to 3 minutes for thick fillets, or 30 to 60 seconds for thin fillets.

4. Transfer the fillets to a serving platter and tent with foil. Add the remaining 1 tablespoon oil to the skillet and return to high heat until the oil is

shimmering but not smoking; cook the remaining fillets in the same manner as the first ones. Place the second batch of fillets on the platter with the first batch; tilt the platter to discard any accumulated liquid. Serve the fish immediately with the lemon wedges or one of the following sauces, if desired.

PER SERVING: Cal 260; Fat 9 g; Sat fat 1 g; Chol 80 mg; Carb 10 g; Protein 34 g; Fiber 0 g; Sodium 280 mg

White Wine–Shallot Sauce with Lemon and Capers

MAKES ABOUT 3/4 CUP

This sauce is a healthier version of the classic sauce for sautéed fish, which is usually based on butter.

1	teaspoon vegetable oil
3	medium shallots, minced (about 1/2 cup)
1/4	cup dry white wine
1/2	cup low-sodium chicken broth
3	tablespoons light cream cheese
1	tablespoon capers, rinsed and drained
1	tablespoon minced fresh parsley leaves
1	tablespoon juice from 1 lemon
	Salt and ground black pepper

1. Combine the oil and shallots in a small saucepan over medium-low heat. Cover and cook, stirring occasionally, until softened, about 4 minutes. Add the wine, increase the heat to medium-high, and simmer until the pan is almost dry, about 2 minutes. Add the chicken broth and continue to simmer until the mixture has reduced slightly, 3 to 5 minutes.

2. Off the heat, whisk in the cream cheese, capers, parsley, and lemon juice. Season with salt and pepper to taste. Cover to keep warm and set aside while cooking the fish. Spoon 1/2 cup of the sauce over the fish and serve, passing the remaining sauce separately.

PER 3-TABLESPOON SERVING: Cal 60; Fat 3 g; Sat fat 1.5 g; Chol 5 mg; Carb 5 g; Protein 2 g; Fiber 0 g; Sodium 200 mg

Warm Tomato Relish

MAKES ABOUT 2 CUPS

This sauce is also great served on broiled or grilled fish.

2	medium garlic cloves, minced or pressed through a garlic press (about 2 teaspoons)
1	tablespoon extra-virgin olive oil
1/4	cup dry white wine
3	cups cherry tomatoes (about 12 ounces), quartered
1/4	cup minced fresh basil leaves
	Salt and ground black pepper

1. Combine the garlic and oil in a 12-inch nonstick skillet over medium-low heat. Cook until the garlic softens and begins to turn light brown, about 6 minutes. Add the wine and increase the heat to medium-high. Simmer until the pan is almost dry, about 2 minutes.

2. Stir in the tomatoes and cook until warmed through and beginning to soften, about 2 minutes. Transfer the relish to a bowl, cover to keep warm, and set aside while cooking the fish. (Clean and dry the skillet before cooking the fish.)

3. Before serving, stir the basil into the relish and season with salt and pepper to taste. Spoon 1 cup of the relish over the fish and serve, passing the remaining relish separately.

PER 1/2-CUP SERVING: Cal 60; Fat 3.5 g; Sat fat .5 g; Chol 0 mg; Carb 4 g; Protein 1 g; Fiber 1 g; Sodium 5 mg

Grapefruit-Lime Vinaigrette with Mint and Chives

MAKES ABOUT 1 1/4 CUPS

Make sure to remove all the white pith and membranes from the grapefruit sections or the sauce will taste very bitter.

1	medium pink grapefruit, halved
2	tablespoons juice from 2 limes
1	medium shallot, minced (about 3 tablespoons)
1	tablespoon extra-virgin olive oil
1	tablespoon minced fresh mint leaves
1	tablespoon minced fresh chives

I   teaspoon honey
I   teaspoon Dijon mustard
    Salt and ground black pepper

1. Cut away the peel, pith, and membrane from one of the grapefruit halves, and dice the flesh into ¼-inch pieces; set aside. Juice the remaining grapefruit half for 2 tablespoons juice (discard any excess juice).

2. Whisk the grapefruit juice, lime juice, shallot, oil, mint, chives, honey, and mustard together in a medium bowl. Season with salt and pepper to taste. Set aside while cooking the fish.

3. Before serving, whisk the vinaigrette briefly to recombine and stir in the diced grapefruit. Spoon ¾ cup of the sauce over the fish, passing the remaining sauce separately.

PER 5-TABLESPOON SERVING: Cal 60; Fat 3.5 g; Sat fat .5 g; Chol 0 mg; Carb 8 g; Protein 1 g; Fiber 1 g; Sodium 35 mg

BAKED COD FILLETS WITH ROASTED POTATOES

SINCE COD AND POTATOES ARE A CLASSIC pairing, it made sense for us to try to turn them into an oven-to-table-style casserole. It's an inherently healthy dish because cod is so lean, but more often than not, it can be bland from underseasoning or too little fat, or greasy from too much butter or oil. And once the seasonings are nailed down, there is the problem of getting the potatoes and fish to finish cooking at the same time; rockhard or mushy potatoes and rubbery fish were at the forefront of our minds.

We knew that the potatoes would need a significant amount of time in the oven to become tender and spotty-brown before the fish fillets were added, but we thought that by slicing them thin we could speed up this process. Well, we did in fact speed up the cooking time, but in a 400-degree oven the thinly sliced potatoes quickly overcooked and fell apart before they even had a chance to brown.

For the next batch we tried cutting the potatoes in chunks. Though they took longer to cook, they held their shape and tasters preferred their more substantial presence to the delicate slices. We were able to speed up the cooking process significantly by increasing the oven temperature to 425 degrees and covering the potatoes tightly with aluminum foil for the first 15 minutes in the oven so they steamed and began to soften. We then removed the foil and allowed the potatoes to brown and the flavors to concentrate.

Now that our method was set for cooking the potatoes, we had to focus on flavor. We began by seasoning the potatoes simply, with a little extra-virgin olive oil, salt, and pepper. Tasters complained that the potatoes were "boring," and quickly put in their requests for more vibrant flavors. Thinly sliced garlic cloves and minced fresh thyme provided a backbone of flavor, while slices of red onion added a welcome bite. Still, the mixture was missing something—it was a little dry. Adding broth only diluted the flavors of the vegetables and prevented the potatoes from browning, but drained canned diced tomatoes did the trick. They became sweet as they roasted in the oven, and they provided moisture without watering down the other flavors.

For the fish, we began by nestling six cod fillets on top of the almost-tender potatoes. After testing a variety of oven temperatures and times, we were happy to discover that at 425 degrees (the same temperature at which we cooked the potatoes), for 10 to 15 minutes, the fish cooked through evenly with no ill effects on texture or flavor. Because cod is a relatively wet fish, it stands up well to high heat.

As the fish baked it released its flavorful juices into the potatoes, while at the same time, the essence of garlic, onion, and tomatoes wafted up from below to season the fish. Quite a mutually beneficial situation, if you ask us. We finished things off by drizzling the fish with sherry vinegar for brightness and sprinkling it with fresh basil for an herbal note and some color. Served with lemon wedges, this simple recipe is great, with richly flavored, browned and creamy chunks of potato, and sweet, tender pieces of lightly seasoned cod.

☙
Baked Cod Fillets with Roasted Potatoes

SERVES 6

You can substitute Arctic char, catfish, trout, red snapper, grouper, or tilefish fillets for the cod. For the results of our tasting of canned diced tomatoes, see page 158.

2	tablespoons extra-virgin olive oil
6	medium garlic cloves, sliced thin
I	teaspoon minced fresh thyme leaves
	Salt and ground black pepper
2	pounds red potatoes (about 6 medium potatoes), scrubbed and cut into 1-inch chunks
I	medium red onion, halved and sliced 1/4 inch thick
I	(28-ounce) can diced tomatoes, drained
6	cod fillets, I inch thick (about 6 ounces each)
I 1/2	tablespoons sherry vinegar
I	tablespoon minced fresh basil leaves
I	lemon, cut into wedges (for serving)

1. Adjust an oven rack to the middle position and heat the oven to 425 degrees. Whisk the oil, garlic, thyme, ½ teaspoon salt, and ⅛ teaspoon pepper together in a large bowl. Add the potatoes, onion, and tomatoes and toss to coat evenly.

2. Spread the vegetables in a 13 by 9-inch baking dish. Cover tightly with foil and roast until the potatoes have begun to soften, about 15 minutes. Remove the foil and continue to cook, stirring occasionally, until the potatoes are tender and brown in spots, about 45 minutes.

3. Pat the cod fillets dry with paper towels and season them with salt and pepper. Nestle the fish into the roasted vegetables. Continue to bake, uncovered, until the fish just flakes apart, 10 to 15 minutes. Sprinkle with the vinegar and basil and serve with the lemon wedges.

PER SERVING: Cal 320; Fat 6 g; Sat fat 1 g; Chol 75 mg; Carb 29 g; Protein 34 g; Fiber 4 g; Sodium 580 mg

SOY-GLAZED SALMON AND RICE BAKE WITH VEGETABLES

IT'S A SAFE BET THAT THE PROMISE OF SPRING played a role in the conception of this recipe. Our craving for fresh fish, crisp vibrant vegetables, and clean flavors led us to develop an Asian-inspired recipe that would combine salmon, white rice, and vegetables in a light and satisfying one-dish meal suitable for the oven (and a casserole dish).

Glazing salmon with soy sauce is often done on the grill or in a skillet, with great success. The soy sauce forms a lacquered exterior that is both tasty and attractive. We wondered if we could achieve this same effect on salmon that was baked in the oven along with rice and vegetables. And since we knew that a dish with all these components would need a sauce to unify them, we decided to devise a soy-based sauce that would withstand the time it took to cook both the salmon and the vegetables.

Thinking that the sauce might be the trickiest part of this recipe, we decided to tackle it first, starting with a combination of dry sherry, chicken broth, soy sauce (low-sodium, of course), rice vinegar, and chili sauce. The rice vinegar balanced the saltiness of the soy sauce, and the chili sauce added spiciness and heat. To tame the harsh bite of the chili sauce, we sweetened the mix with sugar. We knew that ginger and garlic were the key flavoring components that we wanted in this dish. So we tried adding them raw to the sauce mixture and found their flavors harsh, almost medicinal. Seeking to mellow their flavors, we decided to sweat them in just 1 teaspoon oil (a technique we developed for our soups) along with shiitake mushrooms, which we had chosen over white mushrooms for their meaty flavor and texture. Then we deglazed the skillet with the sauce mixture. The sauce now had the flavor we were seeking, but it lacked the viscosity needed to coat the salmon. A small amount of cornstarch dissolved in the glaze did the trick and provided just enough thickening to coat the salmon without reminding us of bad Chinese takeout.

The choice of additional vegetables for the casserole revolved around those that were fairly firm and could withstand the heat of the oven while still retaining their integrity. We wanted crisp vegetables, when all was said and done, and there were many good options from which to choose. We narrowed the field down to red peppers, for their sweetness and color, and bok choy. This green leafy vegetable that resembles Swiss chard is full of vitamins and nutrients, and its tender leaves and firm stalks make it ideal for this dish. Blanching the vegetables briefly brought up their flavor and diminished their raw vegetable taste, but that meant another dirty pot, and we had yet to deal with the rice. We discovered that instead of draining the water that we used to blanch the vegetables, we could simply recycle it and use it to cook the rice.

We boiled long-grain white rice until just tender in the blanching water, then drained it and combined it with the vegetables. This light mixture of rice and vegetables went into our baking dish, and we laid the salmon on top of the rice. Instead of mixing the sauce with the rice to moisten it, we found that if we poured the soy mixture over the salmon, the fish became glazed with the sauce, which protected it from the drying heat of the oven. Leaving a bit of space between the pieces of salmon ensured that the sauce would make its way down to the rice and vegetables below to perfume the rice and impart its Asian flavors, without drowning the rice and vegetables in liquid.

The salmon, baked at 450 degrees, turned the caramelized color that we wanted, due to the sugar and the soy in the sauce mixture. The oiliness of the salmon was tempered by the clean flavors of ginger, garlic, and rice vinegar. The bright bell peppers, along with a sprinkle of scallions just before serving, lend the dish a hit of color and burst of freshness. Here was a wholesome casserole where the salmon was the star but the vegetables remained crisp and vibrant, and the rice tender, flavorful, and moist.

Soy-Glazed Salmon and Rice Bake with Mushrooms and Bok Choy
SERVES 6

Asian chili sauce can be found in the international section of most supermarkets. If it is not available, 1 to 2 teaspoons of Tabasco can be substituted. You can substitute 1½ pounds of napa cabbage, cored and shredded into ½-inch-thick pieces, for the bok choy. Ask your fishmonger to remove the salmon skin for you, or see the illustration on page 245 to remove it yourself.

1	medium red bell pepper, stemmed, seeded, and sliced into ¼-inch-thick strips
1	small head bok choy (about 1¼ pounds), cored and sliced crosswise into ½-inch-thick shreds
	Salt
1½	cups long-grain white rice
1	cup low-sodium chicken broth
½	cup low-sodium soy sauce
½	cup dry sherry
¼	cup rice vinegar
¼	cup sugar
1	tablespoon Asian chili sauce (see note)
1	tablespoon cornstarch
12	ounces shiitake mushrooms, wiped clean, stems discarded, sliced into ¼-inch-thick strips
1	teaspoon vegetable oil
2	tablespoons grated fresh ginger
6	medium garlic cloves, minced or pressed through a garlic press (about 2 tablespoons)
6	skinless, center-cut salmon fillets, 1 to 1¼ inches thick (about 6 ounces each)
4	scallions, sliced thin

1. Adjust an oven rack to the middle position and heat the oven to 450 degrees. Bring 4 quarts water to a boil in a large pot (with a perforated pasta insert, if available) over high heat. Stir in the bell pepper, bok choy, and 1 tablespoon salt and cook for 10 seconds. Transfer the vegetables to a colander using a slotted spoon (or by lifting them out with the pasta insert if using). Pat dry with paper towels and transfer to a large bowl.

2. Return the water to a simmer (without the insert) and stir in the rice. Simmer until the rice is almost tender but still slightly firm to the bite, about 12 minutes. Drain through a fine-mesh strainer, shaking to remove any excess water. Toss with the red pepper and bok choy; set aside.

3. Whisk the chicken broth, soy sauce, sherry, rice vinegar, sugar, chili sauce, and cornstarch together in a medium bowl; set aside.

4. Combine the mushrooms and oil in a 12-inch nonstick skillet. Cover and cook over medium-low heat, stirring occasionally, until the mushrooms release their juices, about 7 minutes. Turn the heat to medium-high and continue to cook, uncovered, until the mushroom juices have evaporated and the mushrooms are golden brown, about 5 minutes. Stir in the ginger and garlic and cook until fragrant, about 30 seconds. Briefly re-whisk the sauce, then add it to the pan. Bring to a simmer and cook, stirring often, until the sauce has thickened, about 2 minutes. Remove the sauce from the heat.

5. Spread the rice and vegetable mixture into a 13 by 9-inch baking dish. Lay the salmon fillets, skinned-side down, about ½ inch apart on top of the rice. Pour the shiitake sauce evenly over the salmon. Bake until the fish just flakes apart and the rice is steaming, about 20 minutes. Sprinkle with the scallions before serving.

PER SERVING: Cal 530; Fat 12 g; Sat fat 2 g; Chol 95 mg; Carb 61 g; Protein 41 g; Fiber 3 g; Sodium 1120 mg

SKINNING A FISH FILLET

Starting at the end of the fillet, slide a knife between the skin and flesh until you can grab hold of the skin with a paper towel. Use this "handle" to help steady the skin as you continue to cut the flesh away from it.

Oven-Baked Shrimp and Orzo

WHEN IT COMES TO COOKING FOR COMPANY, most people avoid casserole-style dishes believing they lack panache. Not true. Take the classic Greek-style baked shrimp with orzo: We can't think of many guests who'd turn up their nose at shrimp paired with creamy orzo pasta in a garlicky broth. Unfortunately, rubbery overcooked shrimp, or orzo that is either undercooked or mushy, often ruins this light dish. Our challenge, then, would be to find a way to get flavorful and perfectly cooked shrimp and orzo on the table in one dish.

Orzo, the tiny rice-shaped pasta, is usually added to Italian-style soups or made into pasta salad. In our research, we came across recipes that called for simmering the orzo until tender, as you would with other pasta, and then transferring it to a baking dish with the other ingredients to bake. We made several of these recipes and they resulted in casseroles that were watery and bland in flavor. And by the time they baked in the oven, the individual grains of orzo were no longer distinct, but mushy and porridge-like.

There is a more novel way to prepare orzo that we thought we would explore for our casserole. Orzo can be cooked "pilaf style," or sautéed briefly in oil with flavorings before liquid is added, deepening the pasta's flavor and color. And, if diligently stirred as it simmers, the orzo will release starches into the cooking liquid and turn it creamy—not quite as creamy as risotto, perhaps, but rich and velvety nevertheless. The method for the orzo pilaf was all set; choosing appropriate vegetables, broth, and a method in which to prepare the shrimp was a different matter.

We wanted to limit the vegetables to a select few to keep preparation brief—nothing adds to prep time like cleaning and cutting a long list of vegetables. Red onion seemed like a natural for depth and body, as did the crisp, sweet crunch of red bell peppers. Sautéed until just beginning to brown, the vegetables added solid flavor and a bit of bite to the otherwise tender-textured pilaf. For flavor, color, and acidity, we also decided to add tomatoes. Canned diced tomatoes kept things easy and flavorful. In order for the orzo to toast properly, we added the tomatoes after the orzo, instead of sautéing them with the other vegetables.

As for flavoring the pilaf, a healthy dose of garlic seemed essential, in keeping with the Mediterranean spirit of things. A handful of coarsely chopped fresh herbs seemed apropos as well, and after testing a slew of options, tasters favored a simple combination of oregano and scallions. The oregano lent the casserole a decidedly Greek edge while the scallions, sprinkled raw over the top, added a sharp bite to accent things.

After we had prepared a few batches of the pilaf, we realized that the straw-yellow color of the toasted orzo seemed pale against the deep red of the bell pepper and tomato. Though it isn't classically Greek, we took a cue from other Mediterranean cuisines and added a pinch of saffron to intensify the orzo's color. Toasted with the orzo, the saffron suffused the pasta with a sunny orange hue and its characteristic warm flavor.

Finally ready to tackle the shrimp, we knew that we had a variety of things to test. First off, we preferred larger shrimp, left whole, because they stayed moist longer than smaller shrimp, an important factor considering that they were to be baked. As for the cooking method, searing the shrimp in a smoking skillet gave the shrimp a sweet, caramelized flavor that, surprisingly, tasters thought clashed with the light, bright flavors of the pilaf. Baking the shrimp on top of the pilaf, however, only dried them out and turned them rubbery.

Embedding the raw shrimp in the pilaf and then baking it, however, was a whole different story. The orzo shielded the shrimp from the oven's direct heat, effectively preventing them from drying out and toughening. A relatively hot oven, 400 degrees, cooked the shrimp evenly in about 20 minutes—just enough time for the flavors of the pilaf and the shrimp to combine.

While we liked the overall concept and flavor of the casserole, we thought it was a little bland. It needed a splash of acid, something sharp and pungent to provide an accent. Lemon wedges

squeezed over the finished dish certainly helped. Capers and anchovies were both interesting additions, but tasters had mixed feelings in each case. We then decided to try feta cheese, which as cheeses go is fairly low in fat but high in flavor. The cheese's salty, briny bite perfectly pointed up the sweetness of the shrimp and the fruitiness of the tomato and bell pepper. We normally shy away from combining cheese and fish, but in this instance, it was a perfect pairing. At first, we crumbled the cheese and scattered it over the finished dish, but found it actually tasted better if baked on top of the casserole, where it browned slightly and intensified in flavor. Authentically Greek, feta cheese was the perfect ingredient to finish our dish.

⤙⤚

Oven-Baked Shrimp and Orzo
SERVES 6

Make sure that the orzo is al dente, or slightly firm to the bite; otherwise it may overcook in the oven. If you don't have saffron, ¼ teaspoon ground turmeric can add a similar orange hue, but different flavor. Be careful not to add too much turmeric because its flavor is bitter when used in excessive amounts.

1 ½	pounds large shrimp (31 to 40 per pound), peeled and deveined (see page 48)
	Salt and ground black pepper
1	medium red onion, minced
1	large red bell pepper, stemmed, seeded, and cut into ½-inch pieces
1	teaspoon extra-virgin olive oil
6	medium garlic cloves, minced or pressed through a garlic press (about 2 tablespoons)
1	pound orzo
	Pinch saffron
4	cups low-sodium chicken broth
1	cup water
1	(28-ounce) can diced tomatoes, drained
1	cup frozen peas (optional)
4	teaspoons minced fresh oregano leaves
4	ounces feta cheese, crumbled (about 1 cup)
4	scallions, sliced thin
1	lemon, cut into wedges (for serving)

1. Adjust an oven rack to the middle position and heat the oven to 400 degrees. Pat the shrimp dry with paper towels and season them with salt and pepper; set aside.

2. Combine the onion, bell pepper, oil, and ½ teaspoon salt together in a large stockpot or Dutch oven. Cover and cook over medium-low heat until the vegetables have softened, 8 to 10 minutes. Stir in the garlic and cook until fragrant, about 30 seconds. Stir in the orzo and saffron and cook, stirring frequently, until the orzo is coated with oil and lightly browned, about 4 minutes.

3. Stir in the broth and water and continue to cook, stirring occasionally, until the grains of orzo are mostly tender yet still slightly firm at the center, about 12 minutes. Stir in the tomatoes, peas (if using), oregano, and shrimp.

4. Pour into a 13 by 9-inch baking dish and sprinkle the feta evenly over the top. Bake until the shrimp are cooked through and the cheese is lightly browned, about 20 minutes. Sprinkle with the scallions and serve with the lemon wedges.

PER SERVING: Cal 520; Fat 7 g; Sat fat 3 g; Chol 180 mg; Carb 71 g; Protein 40 g; Fiber 6 g; Sodium 1230 mg

TIPS FOR BROILING FISH

Broiling is a great technique for cooking fish because the intense heat can actually brown and caramelize the exterior of the fish without overcooking the interior. And much like grilling, broiling doesn't require significant amounts of fat or oil in order to develop great flavor. Another nice thing about broiled fish is how easily and quickly it can be made ready for a healthy dinner.

Unfortunately, broilers vary dramatically and we found it nearly impossible to develop a universally accurate recipe for broiled fish. We did, however, discover a few helpful broiling tricks and techniques, and came up with some simple glazes that punch up the flavor of plain broiled fish without adding significant fat and calories.

- Choose thicker, sturdier fish such as salmon, swordfish, tuna, halibut, catfish, or trout.
- Do not broil thin or flaky fish such as sole, tilapia, cod, or haddock, because they break or flake apart too easily.
- Broil the fish on a slotted broiler pan top (set over a broiler pan bottom) or a wire rack (set over a baking sheet) so that the fish doesn't sit in its liquid as it cooks.
- Spray the rack with vegetable oil spray to help to keep the fish from sticking. If possible, leave the skin on the fish to help keep it from sticking to the rack.
- Line the broiler pan bottom or baking sheet with foil for easy cleanup.
- Season the fish simply with salt, pepper, and a pinch of sugar to encourage browning. You could also use a spice rub, or brush the fish with a glaze (see page 248).

- Place the oven rack anywhere from 4 to 8 inches from the broiler element, depending on the type and strength of your broiler.
- If the fish is browning too fast, move the fish farther away from the broiler element. Alternatively, if the fish is not browning at all, move it closer to the broiler element.
- Broil the fish until the edges flake apart easily when prodded with a fork and the very center is just slightly translucent, 4 to 10 minutes, depending on the thickness of the fish and the broiler strength. Be careful not to overcook.
- Let the fish rest for 5 minutes or so before serving. During this resting time, the fish will finish cooking through so that it flakes apart easily when prodded with a fork, without being overdone or dried out.

LOW-FAT GLAZES FOR BROILED FISH

TO USE THESE GLAZES, SIMPLY WHISK ALL THE INGREDIENTS TOGETHER THEN BRUSH evenly over the tops and sides of the fish before broiling and several times throughout the broiling time. Each glaze makes about ½ cup, or enough to glaze 8 pieces of fish. If you have extra glaze, pass it separately at the table or drizzle it over plain rice or steamed vegetables.

Hoisin and Ginger Glaze
MAKES ENOUGH FOR 8 PIECES OF FISH
If desired, sprinkle the glazed fish with thinly sliced scallions or toasted sesame seeds before serving.

- ¼ cup hoisin sauce
- 3 tablespoons rice vinegar
- 3 tablespoons light brown sugar
- 2 teaspoons grated fresh ginger (see page 285)
- 1 teaspoon toasted sesame oil
- ½ teaspoon salt
- ⅛ teaspoon red pepper flakes

PER SERVING: Cal 40; Fat .5 g; Sat fat 0 g; Chol 0 mg; Carb 10 g; Protein 0 g; Fiber 0 g; Sodium 420 mg

Mustard and Brown Sugar Glaze
MAKES ENOUGH FOR 8 PIECES OF FISH
If desired, sprinkle the glazed fish with minced fresh dill before serving.

- ¼ cup packed light brown sugar
- 3 tablespoons cider vinegar
- 3 tablespoons whole-grain mustard
- 2 garlic cloves, minced or pressed through a garlic press (about 2 teaspoons)
- 1 teaspoon vegetable oil
- ½ teaspoon salt
- ¼ teaspoon ground black pepper

PER SERVING: Cal 40; Fat 1 g; Sat fat 0 g; Chol 0 mg; Carb 8 g; Protein 0 g; Fiber 0 g; Sodium 260 mg

Honey and Chipotle Glaze
MAKES ENOUGH FOR 8 PIECES OF FISH
If desired, sprinkle the glazed fish with minced fresh cilantro leaves before serving.

- ¼ cup honey
- 3 tablespoons lime juice from 2 to 3 limes
- 2 garlic cloves, minced or pressed through a garlic press (about 2 teaspoons)
- 1 teaspoon vegetable oil
- 1 teaspoon minced canned chipotle chile in adobo, plus 2 teaspoons adobo sauce
- ½ teaspoon salt
- ¼ teaspoon ground black pepper

PER SERVING: Cal 40; Fat .5 g; Sat fat 0 g; Chol 0 mg; Carb 9 g; Protein 0 g; Fiber 0 g; Sodium 150 mg

Sesame-Soy Glaze
MAKES ENOUGH FOR 8 PIECES OF FISH
If desired, sprinkle the fish with minced scallions before serving.

- ¼ cup low-sodium soy sauce
- 2 tablespoons mirin
- 1 tablespoon rice vinegar
- 1 tablespoon honey
- 1 tablespoon toasted sesame seeds
- 2 teaspoons grated fresh ginger (see page 285)
- 1 teaspoon toasted sesame oil

PER SERVING: Cal 35; Fat 1 g; Sat fat 0 g; Chol 0 mg; Carb 5 g; Protein 1 g; Fiber 0 g; Sodium 270 mg

TEST KITCHEN MAKEOVER

OVEN-FRIED FISH

WHAT'S THE ALLURE OF FRIED FISH? FOR STARTERS, it tastes great. Like all fried foods, the crunchy coating is a textural delight. And who doesn't enjoy dipping a fried clam or fish stick into rich tangy tartar sauce? But truth be told, fried fish often makes a bacon cheeseburger look like diet fare. A typical fast-food fish sandwich can contain as much as 500 calories and 31 grams of fat, and a fried fish platter can be as high as 1200 calories and 50 grams of fat! Typical methods of frying fish turn a naturally healthy food into an extremely

MAKEOVER AT A GLANCE

–Classic–
Deep-Fried Fish
(per serving)

Calories: 500   Cholesterol: 135 mg

Fat: 31 g   Saturated Fat: 7 g

–Light–
Oven-Fried Fish
(per serving)

Calories: 300   Cholesterol: 75 mg

Fat: 7 g   Saturated Fat: 1 g

How We Did It

- Replaced the oil-absorbent batter with egg whites seasoned with mustard, thyme, garlic powder, and cayenne
- Used crushed Melba toast, tossed with a little oil, for a crunchy coating
- Sprayed the fish with vegetable oil spray to promote a golden brown exterior
- Baked the fish on a wire rack in the oven, allowing air to circulate and crisp the crumb coating

unhealthy meal, so it was obvious that a serious makeover was in order.

Following the method we used for oven-fried chicken (see page 196), we were able to create a recipe for crunchy and delicious oven-fried fish; one which allows you to still reap the nutritious benefits of the fish itself. We seasoned the fish with salt and pepper, dipped it in a mixture of egg whites seasoned with mustard, fresh thyme, garlic powder, and cayenne, and coated it in crunchy Melba-toast crumbs that were moistened with a little vegetable oil. We then placed the fish on a wire rack set over a foil-lined baking sheet, sprayed it liberally with vegetable cooking spray, and baked it in a 450-degree oven until golden brown and crunchy. Since cod is widely available and commonly used to make fried fish, we ironed out the recipe using cod, but then tested several other types of fish. We were pleased to find out that many fish, including haddock, catfish, trout, tilapia, and even thick sole fillets worked well in this application; simply ask your fishmonger what is fresh. It is important, however, to avoid using very thin and delicate fish fillets, as they have a tendency to break apart.

For our dipping sauce, we looked toward our Light and Creamy Dip Base (page 6) as a starting point. The combination of reduced-fat mayonnaise and low-fat sour cream was the perfect foil for piquant cornichons, capers, and red onion. At just 300 calories and 7 grams of fat per serving for oven-fried fish, our days of ordering fried fish in a restaurant are over.

Oven-Fried Fish
SERVES 4

Catfish, trout, haddock, thick sole fillets, or tilapia can be substituted for the cod. Stay away from very delicate fillets or thick, meaty fish such as swordfish or tuna. If some of the pieces have thin, tapered ends, tuck them under before breading (see page 240) to prevent them from overcooking and drying out. Generously coat the fish with the Melba crumbs, but do not pile them on or they will not adhere to the fish; there will be crumbs left over. Serve with Tartar Sauce (page 250).

1   (5-ounce) box plain Melba toast, broken into
     1-inch pieces
2   tablespoons vegetable oil
3   large egg whites
1   tablespoon Dijon mustard
2   teaspoons minced fresh thyme leaves
1/4 teaspoon garlic powder
1/8 teaspoon cayenne
4   cod fillets, 1 inch thick (about 6 ounces each)
     Salt and ground black pepper
     Vegetable oil spray
1   lemon, cut into wedges (for serving)
     Tartar Sauce, optional (recipe follows)

1. Adjust an oven rack to the upper-middle position and heat the oven to 450 degrees. Cover a baking sheet with foil and place a wire rack on top. Process the Melba toast into coarse crumbs in a food processor, about twelve 1-second pulses. Spread the crumbs in a shallow dish and toss with the oil.

2. In a separate shallow dish, whisk the egg whites, mustard, thyme, garlic powder, and cayenne together.

3. Pat the cod dry with paper towels then season with salt and pepper. Working with one piece of fish at a time, dip it into the egg white mixture, then coat with the Melba crumbs. Press on the Melba crumbs to make sure they adhere to the fish. Lay the coated fish onto the prepared wire rack and spray the tops with vegetable oil spray.

4. Bake until the coating is golden and the fish just flakes apart, 12 to 15 minutes. Serve with the lemon wedges and Tartar Sauce, if desired.

PER SERVING: Cal 300; Fat 7 g; Sat fat 1 g ; Chol 75 mg; Carb 21 g; Protein 35 g; Fiber 2 g; Sodium 530 mg
PER SERVING WITH TARTAR SAUCE: Cal 345; Fat 9.5 g; Sat fat 2 g ; Chol 80 mg; Carb 26 g; Protein 36 g; Fiber 2 g; Sodium 920 mg

Tartar Sauce

MAKES ABOUT 1/2 CUP

This is our lighter version of the classic sauce.

1/4 cup reduced-fat mayonnaise
2   tablespoons low-fat sour cream
3   large cornichons, minced (about
     1 1/2 tablespoons)
2   teaspoons cornichon pickling juice
2   tablespoons minced red onion
1   tablespoon capers, rinsed and minced
     Salt and ground black pepper
     Water

Mix all the ingredients together, adding water as needed to thin the sauce out. Cover and refrigerate until the flavors blend, about 30 minutes. (The sauce can be refrigerated for several days.)

PER 2-TABLESPOON SERVING: Cal 45; Fat 2.5 g; Sat fat 1 g; Chol 5 mg; Carb 5 g; Protein 1 g; Fiber 0 g; Sodium 390 mg

PAN-SEARED SCALLOPS

SCALLOPS ARE NOT ONLY INCREDIBLY RICH and sweet, but surprisingly low in fat. Sautéing is our favorite method for preparing scallops. Cooking them over high heat caramelizes the exterior to a crisp, nutty flavored crust, which enhances the natural sweetness of the scallop and provides a crisp contrast to the tender interior.

The most common problem a cook runs into with scallops is getting a good crust before the scallops overcook and toughen. And to make matters more difficult, we were looking to use only a minimal amount of fat to cook them. In the test kitchen we have pan-seared everything from chicken to pork to salmon, so we have learned from experience that moisture is the enemy of a crusty brown exterior. Since scallops by nature are wet even when they are "dry" (see page 251), we knew something had to be done to ensure that they were perfectly parched going into the hot pan. We laid the scallops out in a single layer over a towel-lined plate, seasoned them with salt and pepper, and placed paper towels over the top. The towel and paper towels absorbed any moisture that the scallops released and, as an extra precaution just before they went into the pan, we pressed the paper towel flush to surface of the scallops. No drop of moisture was going to prevent our crust from forming. Or was it?

Even though they were bone-dry going into the pan, we still had trouble getting the scallops to brown. It seemed that an overcrowded pan was the culprit; the scallops were so close together that they released moisture and steamed rather than sautéed. We decided to try cooking the scallops in two batches. Once the first batch was browned on one side, but still rare, we transferred them to a plate (browned side up) while the second batch seared. We then lowered the heat and returned the first batch to the pan to cook through.

It's critical for the formation of a good crust to leave the scallop alone once it hits the pan. Place the scallops carefully in the pan, one at a time, with one flat side down for maximum contact with the hot pan. The best tool for transferring and turning scallops is a pair of tongs, although a spatula can be used in a pinch.

Typically, scallops are sautéed in a traditional skillet with, at the very least, 2 tablespoons of fat. We were determined to get the fat grams down, so right away we knew we'd be using a nonstick skillet. But we'd still have to use some fat to promote even browning, and since scallops cook quickly and the amount of fat we used was a concern, we knew it would be important to choose a fat that browned efficiently. We tried butter, olive oil, vegetable oil, and a combination of butter and oil.

In order to achieve a golden exterior without overcooking the scallops, we had to crank the heat to high. At this intense temperature the butter began to burn before the scallops had a chance to form a crust. The scallops browned best in the olive and vegetable oils. Since tasters didn't detect a flavor difference between the two, we went with

INGREDIENTS: Scallops

When it comes to scallops, your local fish market or the fish counter at your grocery store offers several choices. There are three main varieties of scallops—sea, bay, and calico. Sea scallops are available year-round throughout the country and are the best choice in most instances. Like all scallops, the product sold at the market is the dense, disk-shaped muscle that propels the live scallop in its shell through the water. The guts and roe are usually jettisoned at sea because they are so perishable. Ivory-colored sea scallops are usually at least an inch in diameter (and often much bigger) and look like squat marshmallows. Sometimes they are sold cut up, but we found that they can lose moisture when handled this way and are best purchased whole.

Small, cork-shaped bay scallops (about half an inch in diameter) are harvested in a small area from Cape Cod to Long Island. Bay scallops are seasonal—available from late fall through midwinter—and are very expensive, up to $20 a pound. They are delicious but nearly impossible to find outside of top restaurants.

Calico scallops are a small species (less than half an inch across and taller than they are wide) harvested in the southern United States and around the world. They are inexpensive (often priced at just a few dollars a pound) but generally not terribly good. Unlike sea and bay scallops, which are harvested by hand, calicos are shucked by machine steaming. This steaming partially cooks the scallops and gives them an opaque look.

Calicos are often sold as "bays" but they are not the same thing. In our test kitchen, we found that calicos are easy to overcook and often end up with a rubbery, eraser-like texture. Our recommendation is to stick with sea scallops, unless you have access to real bay scallops.

In addition to choosing the right species, you should inquire about processing when purchasing scallops. Most scallops (by some estimates up to 90 percent of the retail supply) are dipped in a phosphate and water mixture that may also contain citric and ascorbic acids. Processing extends shelf life but harms the flavor and texture of scallops. Their naturally delicate, sweet flavor can be masked by the bitter-tasting chemicals. Besides the obvious objections (why pay for water weight or processing that detracts from their natural flavor?), processed scallops are more difficult to cook. During processing scallops absorb water, which is thrown off when they are cooked. You can't brown processed scallops in a skillet—they shed so much liquid that they steam.

By law, processed scallops must be identified at the wholesale level, so ask your fishmonger. Also, look at the scallops. Scallops are naturally ivory or pinkish tan; processing turns them bright white. Processed scallops are slippery and swollen and usually sitting in milky white liquid at the store. Unprocessed scallops (also called dry scallops) are sticky and flabby. If they are surrounded by any liquid (and often they are not), the juices are clear, not white.

vegetable oil, which is known to have a slightly higher smoke point.

To preserve the creamy texture of the flesh, we cooked the scallops to medium-rare, which means the scallop is hot all the way through but the center still retains some translucence. As a scallop cooks, the soft flesh firms and you can see an opaqueness that starts at the bottom of the scallop, where it sits in the pan, and slowly creeps up toward the center. The scallop is medium-rare when the sides have firmed up and all but about the middle third of the scallop has turned opaque.

As for accompaniments, tasters agreed that they wanted some sort of sauce to drizzle over the scallops. Rich and creamy-style sauces were quickly nudged aside for the overpowering effect they had on the scallops. And while some tasters liked the pairing of scallops with fruit salsas, others disliked the salsas' chunky nature and preferred a smoother sauce. Using a core technique borrowed from our fruit juice vinaigrettes (see page 32) that involves simmering fruit juice (we used tangerine and pomegranate juices) until it has reduced to a syrup, we were able to create bold, fruit-flavored sauces. The syrups, which we found achieved the perfect silky-smooth drizzling viscosity when thickened with a little cornstarch, just needed a little honey to temper their acidity, as well as some shallots and thyme to round out their rich fruit flavors. These sauces can be made

ahead of time and kept warm until the scallops are ready to be served. The acidity of the fruit juice reductions is the perfect contrast to the sweet, rich scallops. Who knew eating healthy could taste so decadent?

Pan-Seared Scallops

SERVES 4

In order to achieve a beautiful brown exterior on the scallops, they must be completely dry before they go into the hot skillet. If desired, make one of the sauces that follow ahead of time to serve with the scallops, or serve simply with lemon wedges.

1 ½	pounds large sea scallops (20 to 24 scallops), tendons removed
	Salt and ground black pepper
2	tablespoons vegetable oil
1	lemon, cut into wedges (for serving)

1. Lay the scallops out on a dish towel–lined plate and season them with salt and pepper. Lay a single layer of paper towels over the scallops; set aside. Heat 1 tablespoon of the oil in a 12-inch nonstick skillet over high heat until just smoking.

2. Meanwhile, press the paper towels onto the scallops to dry them. Add half of the scallops to the skillet, dry side facing down, and cook until evenly golden, 1 to 2 minutes. Using tongs, transfer the scallops to large plate, seared side facing up; set aside.

3. Wipe out the skillet with a wad of paper towels, add the remaining 1 tablespoon oil, and return to high heat until just smoking. Add the remaining scallops, dry side facing down, and cook until evenly golden, 1 to 2 minutes. Turn the heat to medium, flip the scallops over, and return the first batch to the pan, seared side facing up. Cook until the sides have firmed up and all but the middle third of the scallop is opaque, 30 to 60 seconds longer. Transfer the scallops to a large plate and serve immediately with the lemon wedges (or one of the following sauces).

REMOVING TENDONS FROM SCALLOPS

The small, rough-textured, crescent-shaped muscle that attaches the scallop to the shell will toughen when cooked. Use your fingers to peel the tendon away from the side of each scallop before cooking.

PER SERVING: Cal 210; Fat 8 g; Sat fat 1 g; Chol 55 mg; Carb 4 g; Protein 29 g; Fiber 0 g; Sodium 420 mg

Tangerine Juice Reduction

MAKES ABOUT ½ CUP

If tangerines aren't available, oranges can be used instead. If desired, add more honey to taste. This sauce can be held in the refrigerator for up to 2 days and reheated over low heat.

2	cups fresh tangerine juice from 4 to 5 tangerines
3	sprigs fresh thyme
I	medium shallot, minced (about 3 tablespoons)
½	teaspoon cornstarch
½	teaspoon grated tangerine zest
½	teaspoon honey

1. Simmer all but 1 tablespoon of the tangerine juice with the thyme and shallot in a small saucepan until the mixture measures about ½ cup, 40 to 45 minutes.

2. Strain the sauce into a clean saucepan, discarding the solids, and return to a simmer. Whisk the remaining 1 tablespoon juice with the cornstarch, then whisk into the simmering sauce and cook until thickened, about 1 minute. Stir in the zest and honey. Drizzle over the scallops and serve immediately.

PER 2-TABLESPOON SERVING: Cal 60; Fat 0 g; Sat fat 0 g; Chol 0 mg; Carb 15 g; Protein 1 g; Fiber 0 g; Sodium 0 mg

Pomegranate Juice Reduction

MAKES ABOUT ½ CUP

Pomegranate juice is available at most supermarkets and natural food stores. Be sure to purchase straight pomegranate juice, which is sweet and slightly tart, not a flavored variety. If desired, add more honey to taste. This sauce can be held in the refrigerator for up to 2 days and reheated over low heat.

2	cups pomegranate juice
3	sprigs fresh thyme
I	medium shallot, minced (about 3 tablespoons)
½	teaspoon cornstarch
½	teaspoon honey

1. Simmer all but 1 tablespoon of the pomegranate juice with the thyme and shallot in a small saucepan until the mixture measures about ½ cup, 40 to 45 minutes.

2. Strain the sauce into a clean saucepan, discarding the solids, and return to a simmer. Whisk the remaining 1 tablespoon juice with the cornstarch, then whisk into the simmering sauce and cook until thickened, about 1 minute. Stir in the honey. Drizzle over the scallops and serve immediately.

PER 2-TABLESPOON SERVING: Cal 80; Fat 0 g; Sat fat 0 g; Chol 0 mg; Carb 20 g; Protein 1 g; Fiber 0 g; Sodium 15 mg

PAN-SEARED SHRIMP

SHRIMP AREN'T THE LUXURIOUS, ONCE-IN-A-while indulgence they once were and are welcome on the healthy table anytime. Having prepared tons of shrimp in the test kitchen and in our own home kitchens, we have found that pan-searing produces the ultimate combination of a well-caramelized exterior and a moist, tender interior. If executed properly, this cooking method also preserves the shrimp's plumpness and trademark briny sweetness. Pan-searing is ideal because shrimp don't need to be cooked in a lot of fat, since they are so rich and flavorful on their own.

That said, a good recipe for pan-seared shrimp is hard to find, and certainly not published in any of the healthy cookbooks in our libraries. Of the handful of recipes we uncovered, the majority resulted in shrimp that were variously dry, flavorless, pale, tough, or gummy—hardly appetizing. It was time to start some serious testing.

We quickly uncovered a few basic rules (the latter two rules we borrowed from pan-searing scallops). First, tasters unanimously favored shrimp that were peeled before being cooked. Peeled shrimp are easier to eat, and unpeeled shrimp fail to pick up the delicious caramelized flavor that pan-searing provides. Second, the shrimp were best cooked in a 12-inch skillet; its large surface area keeps the shrimp from overcrowding the pan and steaming—a surefire way to prevent

253

caramelization. Third, oil was the ideal cooking medium, favored over both a dry pan (which made the shrimp leathery and metallic-tasting) and butter (which tended to burn). Fortunately, we discovered that we only needed 2 tablespoons for the entire batch of shrimp.

However, we found that in the time it took to get the shrimp to brown, they turned out tough and overcooked. Looking for another way to promote browning in a shorter time frame, we thought to add a pinch of sugar to the shrimp. Not only did the sugar caramelize into a nice brown crust, it also accentuated the shrimp's natural sweetness, nicely setting off their inherent sea-saltiness.

Even in a 12-inch skillet, 1½ pounds of shrimp must be cooked in two batches, or they will steam instead of sear. The trick was to develop a technique that neither overcooked the shrimp nor let half of them turn cold while the other half finished cooking. To prevent overcooking, we tried searing the shrimp on one side, removing the pan from the flame, and then allowing the residual heat to finish cooking the other side of the shrimp. This worked like a charm. Better yet, the residual heat from the pan also solved the cold shrimp problem. As soon as the second batch finished cooking (the first batch was now near room temperature), we tossed the first batch back into the pan, covered it, and let the residual heat work its magic once again. After about a minute, all of the shrimp were both perfectly cooked and piping hot. Now all we needed were a few ideas for some quick sauces.

We tested sauces made from assertive ingredients such as garlic, ginger, and chipotle chile mixed with plenty of acidity as a foil for the shrimp's richness. The most successful of these sauces were those that clung to the shrimp like a glaze. All of these low-fat and low-calorie sauces could easily be made ahead of time and quickly tossed with the shrimp during the last stage of cooking, once the pan was removed from the heat. Served over rice or polenta, pan-seared shrimp makes a quick and satisfying meal.

INGREDIENTS: Frozen Shrimp

Even the most basic market now sells several kinds of shrimp. We cooked more than 100 pounds to find out just what to look for (and avoid) at the supermarket.

Fresh or Frozen?

Because nearly all shrimp are frozen at sea, you have no way of knowing when those "fresh" shrimp in the fish case were thawed (unless you are on very personal terms with your fishmonger). We found that the flavor and texture of thawed shrimp deteriorate after a few days, so you're better off buying frozen.

Peeled or Unpeeled?

If you think you can dodge some work by buying frozen shrimp that have been peeled, think again. Someone had to thaw those shrimp in order to remove their shells, and they can get pretty banged up when they are refrozen (compare the left and center photos below).

Check the Ingredients

Finally, check the ingredient list. Frozen shrimp are often treated or enhanced with additives such as sodium bisulfate, STP (sodium tripolyphosphate), or salt to prevent darkening (which occurs as the shrimp ages) or to counter "drip loss," the industry term referring to the amount of water in the shrimp that is lost as it thaws. We have found that treated shrimp have a strange translucency and an unpleasant texture and suggest that you avoid them (see the photo at right). Look for the bags of frozen shrimp that list shrimp as the only ingredient.

| UNPEELED & UNTREATED | PEELED & UNTREATED | PEELED & TREATED |

Pan-Seared Shrimp

SERVES 4

The cooking times that follow are for extra-large shrimp (21 to 25 shrimp in a pound). If this size is not available in your market, buy large shrimp (31 to 40 per pound) and reduce the cooking time slightly. Either a nonstick or traditional skillet will work for this recipe, but a nonstick skillet simplifies cleanup. Serve with a simple green salad or on a bed of sautéed spinach.

2	tablespoons vegetable oil
1 ½	pounds extra-large shrimp (21 to 25 per pound), peeled and deveined (see page 48)
¼	teaspoon salt
¼	teaspoon ground black pepper
⅛	teaspoon sugar

1. Heat 1 tablespoon of the oil in a 12-inch skillet over high heat until just smoking. Meanwhile, toss the shrimp with the salt, pepper, and sugar in a medium bowl.

2. Add half of the shrimp to the pan in a single layer and cook until spotty brown and the edges turn pink, about 1 minute. Remove the pan from the heat. Using tongs, flip each shrimp over and let stand until all but the very center is opaque, about 30 seconds. Transfer the shrimp to a large plate. Repeat with the remaining oil and shrimp.

3. After the second batch has stood off the heat, return the first batch to the skillet and toss to combine. Cover the skillet and let stand until the shrimp are cooked through, 1 to 2 minutes. Serve immediately.

PER SERVING: Cal 240; Fat 10 g; Sat fat 1.5 g; Chol 260 mg; Carb 2 g; Protein 35 g; Fiber 0 g; Sodium 400 mg

➤ VARIATIONS

Pan-Seared Shrimp with Garlic-Lemon Sauce

Serve over pasta, rice, or mashed potatoes.

Whisk 2 tablespoons light cream cheese, 2 tablespoons low-sodium chicken broth, 2 tablespoons juice from 1 lemon, 1 tablespoon minced fresh parsley leaves, and 2 medium garlic cloves, minced (about 2 teaspoons) together in a small bowl. Follow the recipe for Pan-Seared Shrimp, adding the sauce when returning the first batch of shrimp to the skillet in step 3. Serve with lemon wedges, if desired.

PER SERVING: Cal 260; Fat 11 g; Sat fat 2 g; Chol 260 mg; Carb 4 g; Protein 35 g; Fiber 0 g; Sodium 450 mg

Pan-Seared Shrimp with Ginger-Hoisin Glaze

We like to serve these shrimp with steamed white or brown rice.

Stir 2 tablespoons hoisin sauce, 1 tablespoon rice vinegar, 1½ teaspoons low-sodium soy sauce, 2 teaspoons grated fresh ginger, 2 teaspoons water, and 2 scallions, sliced thin, together in a small bowl. Follow the recipe for Pan-Seared Shrimp, substituting an equal amount of red pepper flakes for the black pepper and adding the sauce when returning the first batch of shrimp to the skillet in step 3.

PER SERVING: Cal 260; Fat 10 g; Sat fat 1.5 g; Chol 260 mg; Carb 8 g; Protein 35 g; Fiber 0 g; Sodium 740 mg

Pan-Seared Shrimp with Chipotle-Lime Glaze

Try serving these shrimp with quinoa as an alternative to the usual grain dish.

Stir 2 tablespoons juice from 2 limes, 2 tablespoons minced fresh cilantro leaves, 1 minced canned chipotle chile in adobo sauce, 2 teaspoons adobo sauce, and 4 teaspoons brown sugar together in a small bowl. Follow the recipe for Pan-Seared Shrimp, adding the chipotle mixture when returning the first batch of shrimp to the skillet in step 3. Serve with lime wedges, if desired.

PER SERVING: Cal 260; Fat 10 g; Sat fat 1.5 g; Chol 260 mg; Carb 7 g; Protein 35 g; Fiber 0 g; Sodium 400 mg

TEST KITCHEN MAKEOVER

CRAB CAKES

HERE IN THE TEST KITCHEN WE LOVE CRAB cakes, but we also know that a good crab cake should taste first and foremost of sweet crabmeat, not greasy filler ingredients. And while a cool and creamy dipping sauce is certainly complementary to a piping hot and golden brown crab cake, it doesn't have to put you off the charts in terms of caloric intake. Our goal, then, was to make crab cakes (and dipping sauces to go along with them) that preserve the integrity of the crabmeat in terms of flavor, texture, and, of course, calories and fat. In other words, we wanted these crab cakes to taste really good.

Great crab cakes begin with top-quality crabmeat. We tested all the various options, and the differences are stark. Canned crabmeat is horrible; like canned tuna, it bears little resemblance to the fresh product. Fresh pasteurized crabmeat is watery and bland. Frozen crabmeat is stringy and wet. There is no substitute for fresh blue crabmeat, preferably "jumbo lump," which indicates the largest pieces and highest grade. This variety costs a couple of dollars a pound more than other types of fresh crabmeat, but, since a 1-pound container is enough to make crab cakes for four, in our opinion, it's money well spent.

Fresh lump blue crab is available year-round but tends to be most expensive from December to March. The meat should never be rinsed, but it does need to be picked over to remove any shells or cartilage the processors may have missed.

Once we figured out what type of crab to use, our next task was to find the right binder. None of the usual suspects worked quite right. Crushed saltines were a pain to smash into small-enough crumbs and fresh bread crumbs blended into the crabmeat a little too well, giving our crabcakes a somewhat pasty texture. We finally settled on fine dry bread crumbs. They have no overwhelming flavor, are easy to mix in, and didn't mask the texture of the crabmeat. The trickiest part is knowing when to stop; crab cakes need just enough binder to hold them together but not so much that the filler overwhelms the seafood. Cooks who economize by padding their pricey seafood with bread crumbs will end up with dough balls, not crab cakes. We started out with 1 cup of crumbs but gradually worked our way down to just 2 to 4 tablespoons for our final recipe.

We knew that we would need some moisture to keep our crab cakes from drying out, so we tried the obvious low-fat options. Low-fat yogurt and buttermilk offered too much moisture, while light sour cream and cream cheese had too much tang and dairy flavor. Traditional crab cake recipes call for full-fat mayonnaise, so it only made sense to try the reduced-fat version. The reduced-fat mayonnaise provided the right amount of moisture, but it was somewhat sweet (a problem we have run into before). Some Dijon mustard provided just the right sharpness to cut through any sweetness. We found that we only needed to use ¼ cup of mayonnaise to bind all the ingredients, so the crab remained the star. Instead of the whole egg that most recipes call for, we used an egg white to make the crab, crumbs, and seasonings meld together both before and during cooking.

Classic recipes call for spiking crab cakes with everything from Tabasco to Worcestershire sauce, and those are both fine. But we'd decided to go with Old Bay Seasoning combined with freshly ground black pepper, minced scallion, and minced fresh

---

MAKEOVER AT A GLANCE

–Classic–
Crab Cakes
(per serving)

Calories: 340	Cholesterol: 140 mg
Fat: 24 g	Saturated Fat: 3 g

–Light–
Crab Cakes
(per serving)

Calories: 250	Cholesterol: 85 mg
Fat: 11 g	Saturated Fat: 1.5 g

How We Did It

- Replaced full-fat mayonnaise with reduced-fat mayonnaise and mustard to provide moisture and flavor without adding a lot of fat
- Used an egg white to replace a whole egg
- Pumped up the flavor with fresh herbs and spices
- Sautéed the crab cakes in a nonstick skillet, rather than pan-frying them

herbs, which tasters overwhelmingly approved.

Just as essential as careful seasoning is careful mixing. We found a rubber spatula works best, and should be used in a folding motion rather than stirring. This was important because we wanted to end up with a chunky consistency—those lumps aren't cheap and we had no intention of reducing them to mush.

We were pleased with our light recipe on most fronts, but we still had trouble keeping the somewhat lean cakes together as they cooked. Not wanting to add more binder, our last breakthrough came when we tried chilling the shaped cakes before cooking. As little as half an hour in the refrigerator made an ocean of difference: The cold firmed up the cakes so that they cooked up into perfect, plump rounds without falling apart. We found that formed cakes can be kept, refrigerated and tightly wrapped in plastic wrap, for up to 24 hours.

We also tried different cooking methods—there would be no deep-frying of our pristine cakes. After baking, pan-frying, and broiling, we settled on sautéing in a nonstick skillet over medium-high heat. This method is fast and also gives the cook complete control over how brown and crisp the cakes get. As we had with our sautéed chicken breasts and white fish fillets, we dredged the crab cakes very lightly in flour. This facilitated the formation of a deeply golden and crisp crust on the exterior of the cakes. As for the cooking medium, we first tried sautéing in butter, but it burned as it saturated the crab cakes and turned the flour coating gummy. Cut with vegetable oil, it was still too heavy and made a mess of the pan. Vegetable oil alone turned out to be ideal. It can be heated without burning (as it has a high smoke point), it creates a crisp crust, and it doesn't overpower the delicate flavor of the crab.

And last but certainly not least was the dipping sauce. Taking a cue from the creamy dips in our Appetizers chapter, we made a creamy sauce base using reduced-fat mayonnaise and sour cream. We jazzed this base up with fresh lemon juice, thyme, and parsley to create Creamy Lemon-Herb Sauce (page 258), and for a sauce with a kick, we added chipotle chiles in adobo sauce, lime juice, and cilantro to create Creamy Chipotle Chile Sauce (page 258).

Crab Cakes
SERVES 4

The amount of bread crumbs you add will depend on the crabmeat's juiciness. Start with the smallest amount, adjust the seasonings, and then add the egg white. If the cakes won't hold together at this point, add more bread crumbs as needed, 1 tablespoon at a time. Serve with one of the sauces that follow.

- 1 pound jumbo lump crabmeat, picked over to remove cartilage or shells
- 4 scallions, green parts only, minced (about 1/2 cup)
- 4 teaspoons minced fresh herbs, such as cilantro, dill, basil, or parsley leaves
- 1 teaspoon Old Bay Seasoning
- 2–4 tablespoons plain dry bread crumbs (see note)
- 1/4 cup reduced-fat mayonnaise
- 2 tablespoons Dijon mustard
  Salt and ground black pepper
- 1 large egg white
- 1/4 cup unbleached all-purpose flour
- 2 tablespoons vegetable oil
- 1 lemon, cut into wedges (for serving)

1. Gently fold the crabmeat, scallions, herbs, Old Bay, 2 tablespoons of the bread crumbs, mayonnaise, and mustard together in a medium bowl, being careful not to break up the lumps of crab. Season to taste with salt and pepper. Carefully fold in the egg white with a rubber spatula until the mixture just holds together, adding the remaining bread crumbs as needed.

2. Divide the crab mixture into 4 portions and shape each into a round cake, about 3 inches across and 1½ inches high. Arrange on a baking sheet lined with waxed or parchment paper. Cover with plastic wrap and chill at least 30 minutes. (The crab cakes can be refrigerated for up to 24 hours.)

3. Spread the flour in a shallow dish. Lightly dredge the crab cakes in the flour and shake off the excess. Heat the oil in a 12-inch nonstick skillet over medium-high heat until shimmering. Gently lay the chilled crab cakes in the skillet and cook until the outsides are crisp and browned, 4 to 5 minutes per side. Drain the crab cakes

briefly on paper towels, and serve with the lemon wedges.

PER SERVING: Cal 250; Fat 11 g; Sat fat 1.5 g; Chol 85 mg; Carb 12 g; Protein 27 g; Fiber 1 g; Sodium 800 mg
PER SERVING WITH CREAMY LEMON-HERB SAUCE: Cal 290; Fat 13.5 g; Sat fat 2.5 g; Chol 90 mg; Carb 15 g; Protein 28 g; Fiber 1 g; Sodium 1080 mg
PER SERVING WITH CREAMY CHIPOTLE CHILE SAUCE: Cal 290; Fat 13.5 g; Sat fat 2.5 g; Chol 90 mg; Carb 15 g; Protein 28 g; Fiber 1 g; Sodium 935 mg

Creamy Lemon-Herb Sauce

MAKES ABOUT ½ CUP

¼	cup reduced-fat mayonnaise
2	tablespoons low-fat sour cream
1	tablespoon juice from 1 lemon
2	teaspoons minced fresh parsley leaves
2	teaspoons minced fresh thyme leaves
1	scallion, minced
¼	teaspoon salt
⅛	teaspoon ground black pepper
	Water

Mix all the ingredients together, adding the water as needed to thin the sauce out. Cover and refrigerate until the flavors blend, about 30 minutes. (The sauce can be refrigerated for several days.)

PER 2-TABLESPOON SERVING: Cal 40; Fat 2.5 g; Sat fat 1 g; Chol 5 mg; Carb 3 g; Protein 1 g; Fiber 0 g; Sodium 280 mg

Creamy Chipotle Chile Sauce

MAKES ABOUT ½ CUP

¼	cup reduced-fat mayonnaise
2	tablespoons low-fat sour cream
1	teaspoon minced canned chipotle chile in adobo sauce
1	medium garlic clove, minced or pressed through a garlic press (about 1 teaspoon)
2	teaspoons minced fresh cilantro leaves
1	tablespoon juice from 1 lime
	Water
	Salt and ground black pepper

Mix all the ingredients together, adding the water as needed to thin the sauce out. Season with salt and pepper to taste. Cover and refrigerate until the flavors blend, about 30 minutes. (The sauce can be refrigerated for several days.)

PER 2-TABLESPOON SERVING: Cal 40; Fat 2.5 g; Sat fat 1 g; Chol 5 mg; Carb 3 g; Protein 1 g; Fiber 0 g; Sodium 135 mg

STEAMED MUSSELS

MUSSELS ARE HEALTHFUL AND DELICIOUS, but unfortunately, most of the recipes for mussels that we're accustomed to eating call for large quantities of oil, bacon, butter, and/or cream. We wanted to focus our attention on alternative ways of infusing mussels with serious flavor, but first we had to address the more basic problem of getting the mussels really clean and grit-free.

Mussels are easy to cook: When they open, they are done. However, perfectly cooked mussels can be made inedible by lingering sand.

After much trial and error, we concluded that it is impossible to remove all the sand from dirty mussels before cooking. We tried various soaking regimens—such as soaking in cold water for two hours, soaking in water with flour, soaking in water with cornmeal, and scrubbing and rinsing in five changes of water. None of these techniques worked. Dirty mussels must be rinsed and scrubbed before cooking, and any cooking liquid must be strained through cheesecloth or a fine-mesh strainer after cooking.

During the course of our testing, we noticed that some varieties of mussels were extremely clean and free of grit. A quick scrub of the shell exterior and these bivalves were ready for the pot. Best of all, the cooking liquid could be served without straining. After talking to seafood experts around the country, we finally came to the conclusion that if you want to minimize your kitchen work and ensure that your mussels are free of grit, you must shop carefully.

Most mussels are now farmed either on ropes or along seabeds. (You may also see "wild" mussels at the market. These mussels are caught the old-fashioned way—by dredging along the sea floor.

In our tests, we found them extremely muddy and basically inedible.) Rope-cultured mussels can be as much as twice the cost of wild or bottom-cultured mussels, but we found them to be free of grit in our testing. Since mussels are generally inexpensive (no more than a few dollars a pound), we think clean mussels are worth the extra money.

When shopping, look for tightly closed mussels (avoid any that are gaping, which may be dying or dead). Mussels may need scrubbing as well as debearding. Simply grab onto the weedy protrusion, pull it out from between the shells, and discard. Don't debeard mussels until you are ready to cook them, as debearding can cause the mussels to die. Mussels kept in sealed plastic bags or underwater will also die. Keep them in a bowl in the refrigerator and use them within a day or two for best results.

Now that we had our grit-free mussels, it was time to start cooking. With steaming in broth as our preferred all-purpose cooking method for mussels, we started to test various amounts and types of liquids, including fish stock, water, wine, and beer. Tasters liked white wine with the mussels the best—the bright acidity of white wine balanced the briny flavor of the mussels. While it is possible to steam 4 pounds of bivalves in just half a cup of liquid (naturally, the pot must be tightly sealed), we like to have extra broth for dunking bread or for saucing rice. We settled on using 2 cups of white wine to cook 4 pounds of mussels.

This was typically the point at which we would finish the steamed mussels with generous amounts of butter and/or cream. Was there a lower fat, but equally flavorful, alternative? We began making batches of steamed mussels with a whole slew of finishing ingredients. We tried finishing with only 1 tablespoon butter (as opposed to the typical 4 tablespoons), replacing the butter with light cream cheese, replacing the cream with half-and-half, and even thickening the broth with a cornstarch slurry. Interestingly, tasters preferred the flavor of the mussels and the broth straight from the pot, without any finishing ingredients, which they claimed masked the subtlety of the shellfish's sweet, briny flavor. Sometimes simpler is just better.

Since we weren't going to finish our broth with butter or cream, we decided to make some refinements to the cooking broth. Garlic, shallots, thyme sprigs, and a bay leaf enriched the flavor of the shellfish. Simmering the broth for three minutes before adding the shellfish is sufficient time for these seasonings to flavor the broth. These steamed mussels are great on their own, with a crusty loaf of bread to dunk into their light and flavorful broth, or served over steamed rice.

Mussels Steamed in White Wine
SERVES 4

To debeard a mussel, simply grab onto the weedy protrusion, pull it out from between the shells, and discard. The basic flavorings in this recipe work with all kinds of mussels, and also with either littlenecks or cherrystone clams. Serve with warm bread or rice.

I	teaspoon olive oil
3	medium shallots, minced (about $1/2$ cup)
4	medium garlic cloves, minced or pressed through a garlic press (about 4 teaspoons)
2	cups dry white wine
3	sprigs fresh thyme
I	bay leaf
4	pounds mussels, scrubbed and debearded (see note)
$1/2$	cup minced fresh parsley leaves

1. Combine the oil and shallots in a Dutch oven over medium-low heat. Cover and cook, stirring occasionally, until softened, about 4 minutes. Stir in the garlic and cook until fragrant, about 30 seconds. Increase the heat to high, add the wine, thyme, and bay leaf, and simmer, uncovered, to blend the flavors, about 3 minutes.

2. Add the mussels, cover, and cook until the mussels open, 4 to 8 minutes, stirring occasionally. Use a slotted spoon to transfer the mussels to a large serving bowl, discarding any that have not opened. Stir the parsley into the broth and pour the broth over the mussels. Serve immediately.

PER SERVING: Cal 500; Fat 12 g; Sat fat 2 g; Chol 125 mg; Carb 23 g; Protein 55 g; Fiber 0 g; Sodium 1310 mg

Grilling Fish and Shellfish 101

This chart pertains to grilling on both charcoal and gas grills. Refer to pages 221–222 for information on setting up a charcoal fire, gauging heat level, and for preheating a gas grill. Only sturdy, medium-firm to firm-fleshed fish should be grilled. (Thin, flaky fish, such as flounder, are better cooked indoors.) Fish and shellfish should be always be cooked over a medium-hot single level fire. Before grilling, spray the fish lightly with vegetable oil spray and sprinkle with salt and pepper. Cook until browned, about 3 minutes (if the fish has skin, start the fillet skin-side up). Then flip and finish cooking the fish until the flesh flakes apart when gently prodded with a paring knife. For shrimp and scallops, thread them onto metal skewers (see the illustrations below) and then spray lightly with vegetable oil spray before grilling. To prevent the fish and shellfish from sticking to the grill, coat the cooking grate with vegetable oil (see page 222). For added flavor, sprinkle the fish or shellfish with a wet rub (page 223) or brush with a glaze (page 225) while grilling. Grilled fish and shellfish can also be served with a fruit salsa (see page 226).

PREP AND YIELD	GRILLING INSTRUCTION
BLUEFISH (¾ to 1 inch thick and 6½ ounces each), 4 fillets serves 4	6 to 8 minutes, turning once
HALIBUT (1 inch thick and about 1 pound each), 2 steaks serves 4	6 to 8 minutes, turning once
SWORDFISH (1 to 1½ inches thick and about 1 pound each) 2 steaks serves 4	8 to 10 minutes, turning once
SALMON (1½ inches thick and 6 ounces each), 4 fillets serves 4	5 to 7 minutes, turning once
TUNA (1 to 1½ inches thick and about 1 pound each), 2 steaks serves 4	4 to 6 minutes for rare or 6 to 8 minutes for medium-rare, turning once
SCALLOPS (large scallops, tendons removed), 1½ pounds serves 4	5 to 7 minutes, turning once
SHRIMP (large shrimp, deveined and if desired shelled, and skewered) 1½ pounds serves 4	5 to 7 minutes, turning once

PREPARING SHRIMP FOR GRILLING

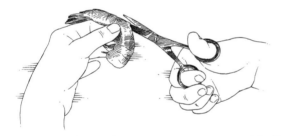

1. When grilling shrimp, we find it best to keep them in their shells. The shells hold in moisture as well as flavor while the shrimp cook. However, eating shrimp cooked in the shell can be a challenge. As a compromise, we found it helpful to slit the back of the shell with a pair of manicure or other small scissors with a fine point. When ready to eat, each person can quickly and easily peel away the shell.

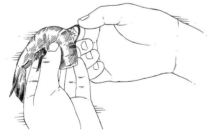

2. Slitting the back of the shell makes it easy to devein the shrimp as well. In our testing, we found that deveining is beneficial only in cases where the vein is especially dark and thick. If you choose to devein shrimp, slit open the back of the shell as in step 1. Invariably, you will cut a little into the meat and expose the vein as you do this. Use the tip of the scissors to lift up the vein and then grab it with your fingers and discard.

SKEWERING SHRIMP

Thread shrimp on skewers by passing the skewer through the body near the tail, folding the shrimp over, and passing the skewer through the body again near the head. Threading each shrimp twice keeps it in place and makes it easier to cook the shrimp on both sides by turning the skewer just once.

PREPARING SCALLOPS FOR THE GRILL

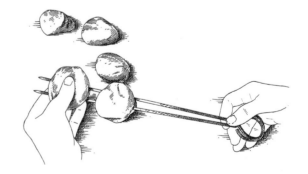

Thread the scallops onto doubled skewers so that the flat sides of each scallop will directly touch the cooking grate. This promotes better browning on each scallop. To turn the skewers, gently grasp one scallop with a pair of tongs and flip.

GUACAMOLE **PAGE 18**

261

SHRIMP SALAD WITH AVOCADO AND GRAPEFRUIT **PAGE 48**

CREAM OF ROASTED BUTTERNUT SQUASH SOUP **PAGE 78** WITH SPICED CROUTONS **PAGE 42**

SCALLOPED POTATOES **PAGE 116**

QUINOA PILAF WITH CORN AND JALAPEÑOS **PAGE 149**

265

MEAT AND CHEESE LASAGNA **PAGE 180**

FETTUCCINE ALFREDO **PAGE 176**

CHIPOTLE CHICKEN SKEWERS WITH CREAMY CILANTRO DIPPING SAUCE **PAGE 26**

CHICKEN PARMESAN **PAGE 201**

269

ROAST BEEF TENDERLOIN **PAGE 212** WITH MUSHROOM-SHERRY SAUCE **PAGE 193**

HADDOCK WITH ZUCCHINI AND TOMATOES EN PAPILLOTE **PAGE 237**

STIR-FRIED TOFU AND BOK CHOY IN GINGER SAUCE **PAGE 290**

LEMON BUNDT CAKE **PAGE 345**

QUICK CINNAMON ROLLS WITH BUTTERMILK ICING **PAGE 317**

SUGAR COOKIES **PAGE 330**, CHOCOLATE CHIP COOKIES **PAGE 323**, AND OATMEAL COOKIES **PAGE 325**

BROWNIES **PAGE 333**

276

9

STIR-FRIES

AMERICANS LOVE MEAT, OFTEN MAKING IT THE centerpiece of the meal—a rack of barbecued ribs, a pan-seared steak, a braised veal shank—you get the picture. Many other cultures incorporate meat into their diets in a less expensive and decidedly more healthful manner, by using meat (and other proteins such as fish and tofu) as a team player alongside vegetables. Take stir-fries, for example. A good stir-fry for four people generally calls for only ¾ pound protein to 1½ pounds prepared vegetables. This ratio keeps the stir-fry from becoming too heavy, providing a little bit of protein and lots of healthy vegetables.

Most stir-fries start with the protein—lean cuts of beef or pork, chicken breasts, shrimp, or tofu. All the protein is cut into bite-sized pieces, which not only gives the illusion of more meat in the stir-fry, but also provides more surface area for absorbing flavors and for browning. The protein is marinated in a simple mixture of flavorful ingredients (we use low-sodium soy sauce and dry sherry, which don't add much in the way of fat and calories). The marinated protein is then cooked quickly over very high heat to maximize caramelization.

After the protein has been cooked, it is removed from the pan and bite-sized vegetables are added in batches. By adding just a small volume of food at a time, the intense heat in the pan is maintained. Slow-cooking vegetables such as onions and mushrooms go into the pan first, followed by quicker-cooking items such as celery and snow peas. Leafy greens and herbs go in last.

For vegetables that won't soften even after several minutes of stir-frying, we add a bit of water to the pan and cover it to trap some steam. This method works especially well with broccoli and green beans. Once the vegetables are crisp-tender, the cover comes off so the excess water can evaporate.

We found that cooking times are affected by how the vegetables are prepared. For instance, sliced mushrooms cook more quickly than whole mushrooms. In many cases, we've found it necessary to remove cooked vegetables from the pan before adding the next batch. This is especially important if you are cooking a large volume of vegetables.

For maximum flavor without a lot of fat, we found that you need a generous amount of aromatics—minced garlic, ginger, and scallions. However, most recipes add these aromatics at the outset of the cooking process, when the pan is empty, or saturate them with as much as ¼ cup of oil, adding unnecessary fat and calories. Both approaches are big mistakes. By the time the stir-fry is done, the aromatics that have been added to the empty pan have burned and become harsh-tasting, and the oil-sodden aromatics make for a greasy stir-fry.

In our testing, we found it best to cook the aromatics after the vegetables. When the vegetables are done, we push them to the sides of the pan, add the aromatics mixed with just a little oil to the center, and cook until the aromatics are fragrant but not colored, about 45 seconds. The small amount of oil is important here because it keeps the aromatics from burning and becoming harsh-tasting. We then stir the fragrant aromatics

RESCUING STIR-FRIES FROM BURNT GARLIC

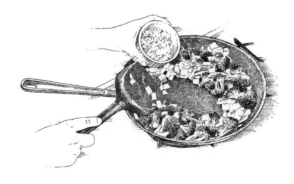

Many recipes add the garlic as well as other aromatics like ginger and scallions at the beginning of the stir-frying process. This is a recipe for burnt garlic. We prefer to stir-fry the vegetables until they are crisp-tender, clear the center of the pan, and then add the garlic and other aromatics mixed with just a little oil to the center of the pan. Once the aromatics are fragrant, they should be stirred back into the vegetables and the sauce should be added to keep them from burning.

into the vegetables. At this point, the seared beef, chicken, seafood, or tofu is returned to the pan along with the sauce.

To stir-fry properly, you need plenty of intense heat. The pan must be hot enough to caramelize sugars, deepen flavors, and evaporate unnecessary juices. All this must happen in minutes. The problem for most American cooks is that the Chinese wok and the American stovetop are a lousy match that generates moderate heat at best.

Woks are round-bottomed because in China they traditionally rest in conical pits that contain the fire. Food is cut into small pieces to shorten cooking time, thus conserving fuel. Only one vessel is required for many cooking methods, including sautéing (stir-frying), steaming, boiling, and deep-frying.

Unfortunately, what is practical in China makes no sense in the United States. A wok was not designed for stovetop cooking, where heat comes from the bottom only. On an American stove, the bottom of the wok gets hot, but the sides are only warm. A flat heat source requires a flat pan. Therefore, for stir-frying at home, we recommend a large skillet, 12 to 14 inches in diameter, with a nonstick coating. If you insist on using a wok for stir-frying, choose a flat-bottomed model. It won't have as much flat

surface area as a skillet, but it will work better on an American stove than a conventional round-bottomed wok.

In this chapter, we have featured some of our favorite stir-fry combinations, utilizing lean cuts of beef and pork, chicken breasts, shrimp, and tofu, and a wide range of nutritious vegetables, from classics like carrots, broccoli, and red bell peppers to Asian vegetables such as shiitake mushrooms, napa cabbage, and bok choy. Also included in this chapter are a variety of light and healthy stir-fry sauces, which you can mix and match with your favorite protein and vegetables. Using low-sodium chicken broth, low-sodium soy sauce, fresh fruit juices, and other flavorful ingredients like Asian chili sauce, oyster sauce, rice vinegar, hoisin sauce, and sesame oil, we have created a variety of strongly flavored sauces that won't weigh you down.

Also, many stir-fry recipes use quite a bit of oil, typically calling for anywhere from 2 to 4 tablespoons, but we use much less. The combination of intense heat, a large nonstick skillet pan, and cooking in batches allows us to use just 3 to 5 teaspoons of oil, depending on the vegetables in each recipe. The recipes in this chapter are designed to serve four as a main course with rice (see the rice recipes on page 280).

SLICING FLANK STEAK FOR STIR-FRIES

In stir-fries, it is important that the meat be cut into uniform pieces so that they all cook at the same rate. Partially freezing the meat makes slicing easier. Simply freeze the steak for 10 to 15 minutes before slicing.

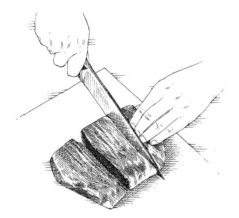

1. Slice partially frozen flank steak lengthwise into 2-inch-wide pieces.

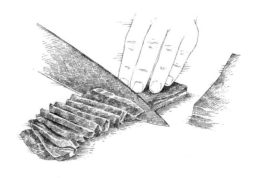

2. Cut each piece of flank steak against the grain into very thin slices.

Beef, Pork, and Chicken Stir-Fries

BEEF STIR-FRIES ARE BEST MADE WITH FLANK steak, which is relatively lean, slices thin, and stays tender when cooked over high heat. We tried other cuts, such as top round, and found that they toughen when stir-fried. Flank steak is easier to slice thin when slightly frozen than when at room temperature. The same is true of chicken and pork. Ten or 15 minutes in the freezer firms the texture nicely. Another option is to defrost meat in the refrigerator and slice it before defrosting is complete.

Although some stir-fry recipes call for ground pork, we find that strips of lean meat from the tenderloin are the best option because sometimes ground pork can be quite fatty. (We tested boneless chops, but the meat was not as tender and flavorful.)

The chicken recipes in this chapter call for boneless, skinless breasts cut into ½-inch-wide strips. In the world of stir-frying, chicken requires a fairly long time to cook through and brown slightly—at least 3 or 4 minutes.

Stir-Fried Beef and Broccoli in Garlic Sauce
SERVES 4

See the illustrations on page 75 for tips on peeling broccoli stalks. Let the beef marinate as you make the sauce and prepare the vegetables.

¾	pound flank steak, sliced thin against the grain (see the illustrations on page 279)
2	teaspoons low-sodium soy sauce
2	teaspoons dry sherry

Sticky White Rice
SERVES 4

This traditional Chinese cooking method yields sticky rice that works well as an accompaniment to a stir-fry, especially if you are eating with chopsticks. The rice is first boiled hard to release its starches and then covered and steamed over very low heat until tender.

1 ½	cups water
1	cup long-grain white rice
¼	teaspoon salt

1. Bring the water, rice, and salt to a boil in a medium saucepan over medium-high heat. Cook, uncovered, until the water level drops below the top surface of the rice and small holes appear in the surface of the rice, about 10 minutes.

2. Reduce the heat to very low, cover, and cook until the rice is tender, about 15 minutes longer.

PER SERVING: Cal 150; Fat 0 g; Sat fat 0 g; Chol 0 mg; Carb 35 g; Protein 3 g; Fiber 0 g; Sodium 150 mg

Sticky Brown Rice
SERVES 4

While not quite as sticky as our Sticky White Rice, this is a nice hearty alternative.

2	cups water
1	cup long-grain brown rice
¼	teaspoon salt

1. Bring the water, rice, and salt to a boil in a medium saucepan over medium-high heat. Cook, uncovered, until the water level drops below the top surface of the rice and small holes appear in the surface of the rice, about 15 minutes.

2. Reduce the heat to very low, cover, and cook until the rice is tender, 15 to 20 minutes longer.

PER SERVING: Cal 170; Fat 1.5 g; Sat fat 0 g; Chol 0 mg; Carb 36 g; Protein 4 g; Fiber 2 g; Sodium 150 mg

3   medium garlic cloves, minced or pressed
    through a garlic press (about I tablespoon)

I   tablespoon grated fresh ginger (see page 285)

3   scallions, white parts only, minced

4   teaspoons peanut or vegetable oil

8   ounces shiitake mushrooms, wiped clean,
    tough stems removed, and sliced 1/2 inch thick
    (about 3 cups)

I 1/2   pounds broccoli (I bunch), florets cut into
        1-inch pieces, stalks trimmed and sliced thin
        (see the illustrations on page 75)

1/2   cup water

I   recipe Garlic Sauce (page 291)

1. Toss the beef with the soy sauce and sherry in a medium bowl. In a small bowl, combine the garlic, ginger, scallion whites, and 2 teaspoons of the oil.

2. Heat 1 more teaspoon oil in a 12-inch non-stick skillet over high heat until just smoking. Add the beef and cook, stirring occasionally and breaking up clumps, until lightly browned, 2 to 3 minutes. Transfer the beef to a clean bowl.

3. Add the remaining teaspoon oil to the pan and return to high heat until shimmering. Add the shiitakes and cook, stirring frequently, until browned, about 3 minutes. Transfer the shiitakes to a clean bowl.

4. Add the broccoli and water to the pan, cover, and cook until the broccoli begins to turn bright green, 1 to 2 minutes. Uncover and cook, stirring frequently, until the liquid evaporates and the broccoli is crisp-tender, 2 to 4 minutes longer. Return the shiitakes to the pan.

5. Clear the center of the pan and add the garlic mixture. Cook, mashing the garlic mixture into the pan with the back of a spatula, until fragrant, about 45 seconds. Stir the garlic mixture into the broccoli. Add the beef and toss to combine. Whisk the sauce to recombine, then add it to the pan, and bring to a simmer. Off the heat, toss until the beef and vegetables are well coated with sauce and sizzling hot. Serve immediately.

PER SERVING: Cal 320; Fat 11 g; Sat fat 2.5 g; Chol 30 mg; Carb 34 g; Protein 25 g; Fiber 6 g; Sodium 810 mg

Stir-Fried Beef and Eggplant in Oyster Sauce
SERVES 4

If you like, add 1 teaspoon minced fresh hot chile pepper to the garlic mixture in step 1. Let the beef marinate as you make the sauce and prepare the vegetables. We find it unnecessary to peel the eggplant here; however, you may peel it if desired.

3/4   pound flank steak, sliced thin against the grain
      (see the illustrations on page 279)

2   teaspoons low-sodium soy sauce

2   teaspoons dry sherry

3   medium garlic cloves, minced or pressed
    through a garlic press (about I tablespoon)

I   tablespoon grated fresh ginger (see page 285)

3   scallions, white parts minced and green parts
    cut into 1/4-inch lengths

5   teaspoons peanut or vegetable oil

I   globe eggplant (about I pound), cut into
    1/2-inch cubes

I   medium red bell pepper, stemmed, seeded,
    and cut into 1/2-inch-wide strips

I   recipe Oyster Sauce (page 291)

1. Toss the beef with the soy sauce and sherry in a medium bowl. In a small bowl, combine the garlic, ginger, scallion whites, and 2 teaspoons of the oil.

2. Heat 1 more teaspoon oil in a 12-inch non-stick skillet over high heat until just smoking. Add the beef and cook, stirring occasionally and breaking up clumps, until lightly browned, 2 to 3 minutes. Transfer the beef to a clean bowl.

3. Add 1 more teaspoon oil to the pan and return to high heat until shimmering. Add the eggplant and cook, stirring frequently, until browned and no longer spongy, about 5 minutes. Transfer the eggplant to a clean bowl.

4. Add the remaining teaspoon oil and the bell pepper and cook until crisp-tender, 1 to 2 minutes. Return the eggplant to the pan.

5. Clear the center of the pan and add the garlic mixture. Cook, mashing the garlic mixture into the pan with the back of a spatula, until fragrant, about 45 seconds. Stir the garlic mixture into the

vegetables. Add the scallion greens and beef and toss to combine. Whisk the sauce to recombine, then add it to the pan and bring to a simmer. Off the heat, toss until the beef and vegetables are well coated with sauce and sizzling hot. Serve immediately.

PER SERVING: Cal 260; Fat 12 g; Sat fat 2.5 g; Chol 30 mg; Carb 15 g; Protein 22 g; Fiber 5 g; Sodium 940 mg

≫━

Stir-Fried Pork and Napa Cabbage in Hot-and-Sour Sauce

SERVES 4

Let the pork marinate as you make the sauce and prepare the vegetables. Due to the high moisture content of the cabbage, this stir-fry is a bit saucier than most of the other recipes in this chapter.

¾	pound pork tenderloin, cut into thin strips (see the illustrations at right)
2	teaspoons low-sodium soy sauce
2	teaspoons dry sherry
3	medium garlic cloves, minced or pressed through a garlic press (about 1 tablespoon)
1	tablespoon grated fresh ginger (see page 285)
3	scallions, white parts only, minced
5	teaspoons peanut or vegetable oil
1	medium red bell pepper, stemmed, seeded, and cut into ¼-inch-wide strips
1	small napa cabbage (about 1 pound), cut into 1-inch strips (about 8 cups)
1	recipe Hot-and-Sour Sauce (page 291)

1. Toss the pork with the soy sauce and sherry in a medium bowl. In a small bowl, combine the garlic, ginger, scallion whites, and 2 teaspoons of the oil.

2. Heat 1 more teaspoon oil in a 12-inch non-stick skillet over high heat until just smoking. Add the pork and cook, stirring occasionally and breaking up clumps, until lightly browned, about 2 minutes. Transfer the pork to a clean bowl.

3. Add 1 more teaspoon oil to the pan and return to high heat until shimmering. Add the bell pepper and cook, stirring occasionally, until crisp-tender, about 1 minute. Add half of the cabbage and cook until crisp-tender, about 1 minute.

Transfer the peppers and cabbage to a clean bowl. Add the remaining teaspoon oil and the remaining cabbage and cook until crisp-tender, about 1 minute. Return the first batch of cabbage and the bell peppers to the pan.

4. Clear the center of the pan and add the garlic mixture. Cook, mashing the garlic mixture into the pan with the back of a spatula, until fragrant, about 45 seconds. Stir the garlic mixture into the vegetables. Add the pork and toss to combine. Whisk the sauce to recombine, then add it to the pan and bring to a simmer. Off the heat, toss until the pork and vegetables are well coated with sauce and sizzling hot. Serve immediately.

PER SERVING: Cal 230; Fat 10 g; Sat fat 2 g; Chol 55 mg; Carb 10 g; Protein 20 g; Fiber 2 g; Sodium 570 mg

SLICING PORK FOR STIR-FRIES

Partially freeze the pork tenderloin for 10 to 15 minutes before slicing it into uniform pieces.

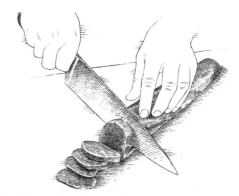

1. Cut the partially frozen tenderloin crosswise into ¼-inch-thick medallions.

2. Slice each medallion into ¼-inch-wide strips.

Stir-Fried Pork, Scallions, and Peppers in Garlic Sauce

SERVES 4

Sliced scallion whites and greens are used as a vegetable in this recipe. You will need four or five bunches of scallions (about ¾ pound). Let the pork marinate as you make the sauce and prepare the vegetables.

¾	pound pork tenderloin, cut into thin strips (see the illustrations on page 282)
2	teaspoons low-sodium soy sauce
2	teaspoons dry sherry
3	medium garlic cloves, minced or pressed through a garlic press (about I tablespoon)
I	tablespoon grated fresh ginger (see page 285)
5	teaspoons peanut or vegetable oil
I	cup scallion whites, sliced on the bias into I-inch pieces
2	medium red bell peppers, stemmed, seeded, and cut into ¼-inch-wide strips
I ½	cups scallion greens, sliced on the bias into ½-inch pieces
I	recipe Garlic Sauce (page 291)

1. Toss the pork with the soy sauce and sherry in a medium bowl. In a small bowl, combine the garlic, ginger, and 2 teaspoons of the oil.

2. Heat 1 more teaspoon oil in a 12-inch non-stick skillet over high heat until just smoking. Add the pork and cook, stirring occasionally and breaking up clumps, until lightly browned, about 2 minutes. Transfer the pork to a clean bowl.

3. Add 1 more teaspoon oil to the pan and return to high heat until shimmering. Add the scallion whites and cook, stirring occasionally, until tender, about 1 minute. Add the remaining teaspoon oil and the bell peppers and cook, stirring occasionally, until crisp-tender, 1 to 2 minutes.

4. Clear the center of the pan and add the garlic mixture. Cook, mashing the garlic mixture into the pan with the back of a spatula, until fragrant, about 45 seconds. Stir the garlic mixture into the vegetables. Add the pork and scallion greens and toss to combine. Whisk the sauce to recombine, then add it to the pan and bring to a simmer. Off the heat, toss until the pork and vegetables are well coated with sauce and sizzling hot. Serve immediately.

PER SERVING: Cal 250; Fat 10 g; Sat fat 2 g; Chol 55 mg; Carb 19 g; Protein 21 g; Fiber 3 g; Sodium 760 mg

Stir-Fried Chicken, Pineapple, and Red Onion in Sweet-and-Sour Sauce

SERVES 4

Let the chicken marinate as you make the sauce and prepare the vegetables. Most markets sell fresh pineapple chunks in the produce section that can be used in this recipe; however, drained canned pineapple can be substituted.

¾	pound boneless, skinless chicken breasts, cut into uniform pieces (see the illustrations on page 284)
2	teaspoons low-sodium soy sauce
2	teaspoons dry sherry
3	medium garlic cloves, minced or pressed through a garlic press (about I tablespoon)
I	tablespoon grated fresh ginger (see page 285)
3	scallions, white parts minced and green parts cut into ¼-inch lengths
4	teaspoons peanut or vegetable oil
2	small red onions, halved and cut into ½-inch-thick wedges
2	cups fresh pineapple, cut into I-inch pieces
I	recipe Sweet-and-Sour Sauce (page 291)

1. Toss the chicken with the soy sauce and sherry in a medium bowl. In a small bowl, combine the garlic, ginger, scallion whites, and 2 teaspoons of the oil.

2. Heat 1 more teaspoon oil in a 12-inch non-stick skillet over high heat until just smoking. Add the chicken and cook, stirring occasionally and breaking up clumps, until lightly browned and cooked through, 3 to 4 minutes. Transfer the chicken to a clean bowl.

3. Add the remaining teaspoon oil to the pan and return to high heat until shimmering. Add the onions and cook, stirring occasionally, until lightly browned, about 2 minutes. Add the pineapple and

cook until heated through, about 1 minute.

4. Clear the center of the pan and add the garlic mixture. Cook, mashing the garlic mixture into the pan with the back of a spatula, until fragrant, about 45 seconds. Stir the garlic mixture into the vegetables. Add the scallion greens and chicken and toss to combine. Whisk the sauce to recombine, then add it to the pan and bring to a simmer. Remove the pan from the heat and toss until all the ingredients are well coated with sauce and sizzling hot. Serve immediately.

PER SERVING: Cal 290; Fat 7 g; Sat fat 1 g; Chol 50 mg; Carb 40 g; Protein 21 g; Fiber 2 g; Sodium 550 mg

Stir-Fried Chicken and Green Beans in Spicy Orange Sauce
SERVES 4

Let the chicken marinate as you make the sauce and prepare the vegetables.

¾	pound boneless, skinless chicken breasts, cut into uniform pieces (see the illustrations at right)
2	teaspoons low-sodium soy sauce
2	teaspoons dry sherry
3	medium garlic cloves, minced or pressed through a garlic press (about 1 tablespoon)
1	tablespoon grated fresh ginger (see page 285)
3	scallions, white parts only, minced
3	teaspoons peanut or vegetable oil
1	tablespoon sesame seeds
1 ½	pounds green beans, cut on the bias into 2-inch lengths
½	cup water
1	recipe Spicy Orange Sauce (page 292)

1. Toss the chicken with the soy sauce and sherry in a medium bowl. In a small bowl, combine the garlic, ginger, scallion whites, and 2 teaspoons of the oil.

2. Toast the sesame seeds in a 12-inch nonstick skillet over medium heat until golden, 2 to 3 minutes. Transfer the seeds to a clean bowl.

3. Heat the remaining teaspoon oil in the pan over high heat until just smoking. Add the chicken and cook, stirring occasionally and breaking up clumps, until lightly browned and cooked through, 3 to 4 minutes. Transfer the chicken to a clean bowl.

4. Add the green beans and water to the pan, cover, and cook until the beans begin to turn bright green, 1 to 2 minutes. Uncover and cook, stirring frequently, until the liquid evaporates and the beans are crisp-tender, 2 to 4 minutes longer.

5. Clear the center of the pan and add the garlic mixture. Cook, mashing the garlic mixture into the pan with the back of a spatula, until fragrant, about 45 seconds. Stir the garlic mixture into the green beans. Add the chicken and toss to combine. Whisk the sauce to recombine, then add it to the pan and bring to a simmer. Remove the pan from the heat and toss until all the ingredients are well

SLICING CHICKEN FOR STIR-FRIES

When stir-frying, it's best to cut your meat into uniform slices. To make this task as easy as possible, freeze the chicken for 10 to 15 minutes before slicing.

1. To produce uniform pieces of chicken, separate the tenderloins from the partially frozen skinless, boneless breasts. Slice the breasts across the grain into ½-inch-wide strips that are 1½ to 2 inches long. Center pieces need to be cut in half so they are approximately the same length as the end pieces.

2. Cut the tenderloins on the diagonal to produce pieces about the same size as the strips of breast meat.

coated with sauce and sizzling hot. Sprinkle with the sesame seeds and serve immediately.

PER SERVING: Cal 250; Fat 8 g; Sat fat 1 g; Chol 50 mg; Carb 21 g; Protein 24 g; Fiber 6 g; Sodium 490 mg

SHRIMP STIR-FRIES

SHRIMP WORKS WELL WITH A VARIETY OF flavors and is well suited to stir-fries because it cooks quickly. Shrimp may be stir-fried in the shell, but they are easier to eat when shelled (and deveined) before cooking. Buy extra-large shrimp, which can be peeled more quickly than smaller shrimp. We bought 1 pound of shrimp in order to have ¾ pound shelled shrimp ready to stir-fry. Shrimp should be stir-fried until bright pink, about 1½ minutes. See page 254 for more information on buying shrimp.

Stir-Fried Shrimp and Asparagus in Lemon Sauce

SERVES 4

Let the shrimp marinate as you make the sauce and prepare the vegetables.

I	pound extra-large shrimp (21 to 25 per pound), peeled and deveined (see page 48)
2	teaspoons low-sodium soy sauce
2	teaspoons dry sherry
3	medium garlic cloves, minced or pressed through a garlic press (about I tablespoon)
I	tablespoon grated fresh ginger (see right)
3	scallions, white parts minced and green parts cut into ¼-inch lengths
5	teaspoons peanut or vegetable oil
I	pound asparagus, tough ends removed, sliced on the bias into 2-inch lengths (see page 97)
2	carrots, peeled and cut into 2-inch matchsticks (see the illustrations on page 235)
I	recipe Lemon Sauce (page 292)
	Salt and ground black pepper

1. Toss the shrimp with the soy sauce and sherry in a medium bowl. In a small bowl, combine the garlic, ginger, scallion whites, and 2 teaspoons of the oil.

2. Heat 1 more teaspoon oil in a 12-inch non-stick skillet over high heat until just smoking. Add the shrimp and cook, stirring occasionally, until curled and bright pink, about 1½ minutes. Transfer the shrimp to a clean bowl.

3. Add 1 more teaspoon oil to the pan and return to high heat until shimmering. Add the asparagus and cook, stirring occasionally, until crisp-tender, 2 to 3 minutes. Transfer the asparagus to a clean bowl. Add the remaining teaspoon oil and carrots to the pan and cook, stirring occasionally, until crisp-tender, about 2 minutes. Return the asparagus to the pan.

4. Clear the center of the pan and add the garlic mixture. Cook, mashing the garlic mixture into the pan with the back of a spatula, until fragrant, about 45 seconds. Stir the garlic mixture into the vegetables. Add the scallion greens and shrimp and toss to combine. Whisk the sauce to recombine, then add it to the pan and bring to a simmer. Remove the pan from the heat and toss until all the ingredients are well coated with sauce and sizzling hot. Season with salt and pepper to taste and serve immediately.

PER SERVING: Cal 260; Fat 8 g; Sat fat 1 g; Chol 170 mg; Carb 17 g; Protein 27 g; Fiber 4 g; Sodium 610 mg

GRATING GINGER

Most cooks who use fresh ginger have scraped their fingers on the grater when the piece of ginger gets down to a tiny nub. Instead of cutting a small chunk of ginger off a larger piece and then grating it, try this method. Peel a small section of the large piece of ginger. Grate the peeled portion, using the rest of the ginger as a handle to keep your fingers safely away from the grater.

Stir-Fried Shrimp and Snow Peas in Coconut Curry Sauce

SERVES 4

Let the shrimp marinate as you make the sauce and pre-pare the vegetables.

1	pound extra-large shrimp (21 to 25 per pound), peeled and deveined (see page 48)
2	teaspoons low-sodium soy sauce
2	teaspoons dry sherry
3	medium garlic cloves, minced or pressed through a garlic press (about 1 tablespoon)

1	tablespoon grated fresh ginger (see page 285)
3	scallions, white parts minced and green parts cut into 1/4-inch lengths
5	teaspoons peanut or vegetable oil
1	medium red bell pepper, stemmed, seeded, and cut into 1/4-inch-wide strips
3/4	pound snow peas, strings removed
1/4	cup minced fresh basil leaves
1	recipe Coconut Curry Sauce (page 292)

1. Toss the shrimp with the soy sauce and sherry in a medium bowl. In a small bowl, combine the garlic, ginger, scallion whites, and 2 teaspoons of the oil.

EQUIPMENT: Inexpensive Nonstick Skillets

We prefer a 12- or 14-inch nonstick skillet for stir-frying. This pan requires a minimum of oil and prevents foods from burning onto the surface as they stir-fry. You can use a regular skillet, but without the nonstick coating you will need to use more oil. Do not use a smaller skillet; the ingredients will steam and stew rather than stir-fry.

Most cooks would rather purchase a relatively inexpensive pan for stir-frying. (It makes more sense to spend the big bucks on a conventional skillet for searing steaks and browning chicken breasts.) We assembled eight inexpensive skillets (all priced under $50) to see if we could find one we liked.

In their new, off-the-shelf condition, all of our pans turned in a reasonable to good performance cooking the foods best suited to nonstick cooking: eggs and fish. In fact, every pan but the Revere produced evenly cooked omelets and released them with ease. The omelet made in the Farberware pan was especially impressive. The Farberware also did a particularly nice job searing salmon fillets to an even, crusty medium brown. Overall, however, our tests indicate that any of these pans can easily handle such light-duty tasks as cooking eggs. Low cost does not mean a big trade-off in this instance.

Sauté speed is also an important measure of a pan's performance. We tested this by sautéing 1½ cups chopped onions over medium heat for 10 minutes in the hope of ending up with pale gold onions that bore no trace of burning. And you know what? For the most part, we did. The Wearever, T-Fal, Innova, and Revere pans, which were all on the light side in terms of weight, turned out the darkest onions, but they were still well within an acceptable color range. Onions sautéed in the Farberware, Meyer, Calphalon, and Bialetti pans were a shade lighter, indicating a slightly slower sauté speed. The Farberware–sautéed onions, however, took top honors based on how evenly all the pieces colored.

So which pan do we recommend? Although the Farberware's rubber handle is only heat safe to 400 degrees, it is our top choice since we use nonstick skillets more for egg scrambling and stir-frying than for high-heat pan-roasting. And testers actually grew fond of the heat protection offered by the rubber grip while sautéing over high heat. Just don't stick it underneath the broiler.

THE BEST INEXPENSIVE NONSTICK SKILLET

Of the pans we tested, the $40 Farberware Millennium Soft Touch Stainless 12-Inch Nonstick Skillet offered the best combination of good nonstick performance (in suitable applications), pleasing heft, and solid construction.

---

2. Heat 1 more teaspoon oil in a 12-inch non-stick skillet over high heat until just smoking. Add the shrimp and cook, stirring occasionally, until curled and bright pink, about 1½ minutes. Transfer the shrimp to a clean bowl.

3. Add 1 more teaspoon oil to the pan and return to high heat until shimmering. Add the bell pepper and cook, stirring occasionally, until crisp-tender, 1 to 2 minutes. Transfer the bell pepper to a clean bowl. Add the remaining teaspoon oil to the pan, add the snow peas, and cook, stirring occasionally, until crisp-tender, about 1 minute. Return the bell pepper to the pan.

4. Clear the center of the pan and add the garlic mixture. Cook, mashing the garlic mixture into the pan with the back of a spatula, until fragrant, about 45 seconds. Stir the garlic mixture into the vegetables. Add the scallion greens, basil, and shrimp and toss to combine. Whisk the sauce to recombine, then add it to the pan and bring to a simmer. Remove the pan from the heat and toss until all the ingredients are well coated with sauce and sizzling hot. Serve immediately.

PER SERVING: Cal 260; Fat 10 g; Sat fat 2.5 g; Chol 170 mg; Carb 15 g; Protein 27 g; Fiber 4 g; Sodium 480 mg

PROTECTING NONSTICK SURFACES

If you stack your cookware (as we do), you run the risk of scratching the nonstick surface. Some cooks slip each pan into a large zipper-lock bag before stacking it, while others place plastic lids (from sour cream, coffee, or yogurt containers) between pans to keep them from scratching each other. Our favorite way to protect nonstick cookware is to slide a doubled piece of paper towel between the pans.

INGREDIENTS: Soy Sauce

Soy sauce is made from fermented soybeans with roasted wheat or barley added. We prefer low-sodium, naturally brewed soy sauces to synthetic sauces, which are very salty (and include hydrolyzed vegetable protein in their ingredient lists). Tamari is a Japanese soy sauce that by definition contains no wheat, although many products that call themselves "tamari" do in fact contain some wheat. Tamari is typically richer and stronger in flavor than other soy sauces and is best used for cooking. Soy sauce will keep indefinitely without refrigeration. We like San-J Reduced Sodium Tamari Natural Soy Sauce. Although it contains 25 percent less sodium than most tamaris, tasters ranked it as the saltiest of the sauces when tasted plain; however, the salty edge subsided significantly when used in a stir-fry.

THE BEST SOY SAUCE
SAN-J Reduced Sodium Tamari Natural Soy Sauce is our top choice for stir-fries.

TOFU STIR-FRIES

TOFU IS A STAPLE OF ASIAN CUISINES THAT IS becoming increasingly popular in the United States. Made from the curds of soymilk, tofu is a great source of low-calorie protein for individuals looking to cut meat out of their diet.

Tofu works well in stir-fries for several reasons. It absorbs the flavors of the sauce well and in the process of browning acquires a pleasantly crisp exterior. Firm or extra-firm tofu (rather than soft or silken varieties) holds its shape best and is the best choice for stir-fries.

Tofu is most commonly sold in 14-ounce blocks, which is why our tofu stir-fry recipes have slightly more protein than our recipes containing beef, pork, chicken, and shrimp. Like dairy products, tofu is perishable and should be kept well chilled to maximize its shelf life. We prefer to use it within a few days of opening (which is why we tailored our recipes to use a whole block). If you want to keep an open package of tofu fresh for several days, cover the tofu with fresh water and store it in the refrigerator in an airtight container.

Change the water daily to keep the tofu fresh. Any hint of sourness and the tofu is past its prime.

When you're ready to stir-fry, drain the tofu and place it in a pie plate. Set a heavy plate on top of it and weight the plate with two heavy cans (such as 28-ounce cans of tomatoes). Let the tofu drain for 15 to 25 minutes. Pressing the tofu will expel moisture and help to promote a golden brown exterior.

Cutting the tofu into ½-inch cubes speeds up cooking. Exterior caramelization is promoted by turning the tofu as little as possible, no more than two or three times, as it sears. Because it is hard to overcook, you can let it brown for 4 to 6 minutes.

Because tofu is fairly bland on its own, it works best in stir-fries when paired with highly flavorful sauces, such as those made with lots of ginger, chili sauce, and vinegar.

Stir-Fried Tofu, Shiitakes, and Napa Cabbage in Hot-and-Sour Sauce

SERVES 4

Pressing the tofu expels moisture, which helps the tofu to achieve a golden brown exterior. It is important to use firm or extra-firm tofu in this recipe. To drain the tofu, place the block of tofu in a pie plate and set a heavy dinner plate on top of it. Weight the plate with 2 heavy cans, such as 28-ounce cans of tomatoes, and let the tofu drain for 15 to 25 minutes (the tofu should release about ½ cup of liquid).

1	(14-ounce) package firm or extra-firm tofu
2	teaspoons low-sodium soy sauce
2	teaspoons dry sherry
3	medium garlic cloves, minced or pressed through a garlic press (about 1 tablespoon)
1	tablespoon grated fresh ginger (see page 285)
3	scallions, white parts minced and green parts cut into ¼-inch lengths
5	teaspoons peanut or vegetable oil
8	ounces shiitake mushrooms, wiped clean, tough stems removed, and caps sliced ½ inch thick (about 3 cups)
1	small napa cabbage (about 1 pound), cut into 1-inch strips (about 8 cups)
1	recipe Hot-and-Sour Sauce (page 291)

1. Place the tofu in a pie plate and set a heavy plate on top of it. Weight the plate with 2 heavy cans (such as 28-ounce cans of tomatoes) and let drain for 15 to 25 minutes. Cut the drained tofu into ½-inch cubes and pat dry.

2. Toss the tofu with the soy sauce and sherry in a medium bowl. In a small bowl, combine the garlic, ginger, scallion whites, and 2 teaspoons of the oil.

3. Heat 1 more teaspoon oil in a 12-inch non-stick skillet over high heat until just smoking. Add the tofu and cook, stirring occasionally, until lightly browned, 4 to 6 minutes. Transfer the tofu to a clean bowl.

4. Add 1 more teaspoon oil to the pan and return to high heat until shimmering. Add the shiitakes and cook until browned, about 3 minutes. Add half of the cabbage and cook until crisp-tender, about 1 minute. Transfer the shiitakes and cabbage to a clean bowl. Add the remaining teaspoon oil and the remaining cabbage to the pan and cook until crisp-tender, about 1 minute. Return the first batch of cabbage and the shiitakes to the pan.

5. Clear the center of the pan and add the garlic mixture. Cook, mashing the garlic mixture into the pan with the back of a spatula, until fragrant, about 45 seconds. Stir the garlic mixture into the vegetables. Add the scallion greens and tofu and toss to combine. Whisk the sauce to recombine, then add it to the pan and bring to a simmer. Remove the pan from the heat and toss until all the ingredients are well coated with sauce and sizzling hot. Serve immediately.

PER SERVING: Cal 260 ; Fat 14 g ; Sat fat 2 g; Chol 0 mg; Carb 19 g; Protein 14 g; Fiber 4 g; Sodium 540 mg

CREATE-YOUR-OWN STIR-FRY

THIS IS MORE A FORMULA THAN A RECIPE, WITH a ratio of 1 part protein to 2 parts vegetables. Plug in your favorite vegetables and a sauce from the end of this chapter. Use oil as needed to cook the vegetables and make sure the harder, longer-cooking vegetables go into the pan before the softer, quicker-cooking vegetables. Increase the garlic or ginger to taste.

Basic Stir-Fry
SERVES 4

¾ pound protein (such as flank steak, pork tenderloin, boneless, skinless chicken breasts, shrimp, or extra-firm tofu), cut into small, even pieces

2 teaspoons low-sodium soy sauce

2 teaspoons dry sherry

3 medium garlic cloves, minced or pressed through a garlic press (about 1 tablespoon)

1 tablespoon grated fresh ginger (see page 285)

3 scallions, white parts only, minced

5 teaspoons peanut or vegetable oil

1 ½ pounds prepared vegetables, cut into small pieces and divided into batches based on cooking times

1 recipe stir-fry sauce (pages 291–292)

1. Toss the protein with the soy sauce and sherry in a medium bowl. In a small bowl, combine the garlic, ginger, scallion whites, and 2 teaspoons of the oil.

2. Heat 1 more teaspoon oil in a 12-inch non-stick skillet over high heat until just smoking. Add the protein and cook, stirring occasionally and breaking up clumps, until lightly browned, 1 to 4 minutes. Transfer the protein to a clean bowl.

3. Add 1 more teaspoon oil to the pan and return to high heat until shimmering. Add the first batch of longer-cooking vegetables and cook, stirring occasionally, until crisp-tender, 1 to 5 minutes. (For very tough vegetables such as broccoli and green beans, add ½ cup water to the pan with the vegetables, cover, and steam for about 2 minutes. Remove the lid and cook off the water, about 3 minutes, before continuing).

4. Add the remaining teaspoon oil and the faster-cooking vegetables, and cook until the vegetables are crisp-tender, 30 seconds to 1 minute.

5. Clear the center of the pan and add the garlic mixture. Cook, mashing the garlic mixture into the pan with the back of a spatula, until fragrant, about 45 seconds. Stir the garlic mixture into the vegetables. Add the protein and toss to combine. Whisk the sauce to recombine, then add it to the pan and bring to a simmer. Off the heat, toss until the protein and vegetables are well coated with the sauce and sizzling hot. Serve immediately.

LONG-COOKING VEGETABLES 1 TO 5 MINUTES	Carrots, Onions, Bell peppers, Mushrooms, Asparagus, Bok choy, Eggplant
SHORT-COOKING VEGETABLES 30 SECONDS TO 1 MINUTE	Cabbage, Celery, Chard, Fennel, Tender greens, Scallions, Tomatoes, Snow peas
VERY TOUGH VEGETABLES (REQUIRE WATER DURING COOKING) 3 TO 6 MINUTES	Broccoli, Green beans, Cauliflower

Stir-Fried Tofu and Bok Choy in Ginger Sauce

SERVES 4

One pound of baby bok choy may be used in place of regular bok choy if available; simply quarter it lengthwise. Pressing the tofu expels moisture, which helps the tofu to achieve a golden brown exterior. It is important to use firm or extra-firm tofu in this recipe.

1	(14-ounce) package firm or extra-firm tofu
2	teaspoons low-sodium soy sauce
2	teaspoons dry sherry
3	medium garlic cloves, minced or pressed through a garlic press (about 1 tablespoon)
1	tablespoon grated fresh ginger (see page 285)
3	scallions, white parts minced and green parts cut into 1/4-inch lengths
5	teaspoons peanut or vegetable oil
1	pound bok choy (1 small head), stems and leaves separated, stems trimmed and cut crosswise 1 inch thick, leaves torn in large pieces
2	carrots, peeled and cut into 2-inch matchsticks (see the illustrations on page 235)
1	recipe Ginger Sauce (page 292)

1. Place the tofu in a pie plate and set a heavy plate on top of it. Weight the plate with 2 heavy cans (such as 28-ounce cans of tomatoes) and let drain for 15 to 25 minutes. Cut the drained tofu into 1/2-inch cubes.

2. Toss the tofu with the soy sauce and sherry in a medium bowl. In a small bowl, combine the garlic, ginger, scallion whites, and 2 teaspoons of the oil.

3. Heat 1 more teaspoon oil in a 12-inch nonstick skillet over high heat until just smoking. Add the tofu and cook, stirring occasionally, until lightly browned, 4 to 6 minutes. Transfer the tofu to a clean bowl.

4. Add 1 more teaspoon oil to the pan and return to high heat until shimmering. Add the bok choy stems and cook until crisp-tender, about 3 minutes. Transfer the stems to a clean bowl. Add the remaining teaspoon oil and the carrots to the pan and cook until crisp-tender, about 2 minutes. Return the bok choy stems and the leaves to the pan and toss until the leaves begin to wilt, about 30 seconds.

5. Clear the center of the pan and add the garlic mixture. Cook, mashing the garlic mixture into the pan with the back of a spatula, until fragrant, about 45 seconds. Stir the garlic mixture into the vegetables. Add the scallion greens and tofu and toss to combine. Whisk the sauce to recombine, then add it to the pan and bring to a simmer. Remove the pan from the heat and toss until all the ingredients are well coated with sauce and sizzling hot. Serve immediately.

PER SERVING: Cal 240; Fat 14 g; Sat fat 2 g; Chol 0 mg; Carb 16 g; Protein 15 g; Fiber 4 g; Sodium 1070 mg

LOW-FAT STIR-FRY SAUCES

STRONGLY FLAVORED SAUCES ARE THE KEY TO vibrant stir-fries. In our testing, we found that too much cornstarch (many recipes call for 1 tablespoon or more) makes sauces thick and gloppy. We prefer the cleaner flavor and texture of sauces made with a minimum of cornstarch—no more than 2 teaspoons for a typical stir-fry. With so little cornstarch, it is necessary to limit the amount of liquid ingredients in the sauce—about 1 cup in the recipes that follow. One cup of sauce will nicely coat the ingredients in our standard stir-fry without being too liquid. We have made a specific sauce suggestion for each stir-fry, but feel free to create your own combinations of sauce, vegetables, and protein (see page 289).

A caution about the use of sugar: Even sweet sauces, such as sweet-and-sour, should contain only a minimum of sugar. Too much Chinese food prepared in the United States is overly sweet. A little sugar is authentic (and delicious) in many recipes; a lot of sugar is not. These sauces can be made in advance and stored in the refrigerator for up to two days.

Hot-and-Sour Sauce

MAKES ENOUGH FOR 1 STIR-FRY RECIPE

For a spicier sauce, increase the chili sauce. This sauce works well with chicken, pork, or tofu.

6	tablespoons rice vinegar
1/4	cup low-sodium chicken broth
1/4	cup dry sherry
2	tablespoons low-sodium soy sauce
1	tablespoon Asian chili sauce
2	teaspoons sugar
2	teaspoons cornstarch
1	teaspoon toasted sesame oil

Combine all the ingredients in a small bowl.

PER SERVING: Cal 40; Fat 1 g; Sat fat 0 g; Chol 0 mg; Carb 5 g; Protein 1 g; Fiber 0 g; Sodium 420 mg

Garlic Sauce

MAKES ENOUGH FOR 1 STIR-FRY RECIPE

This sauce adds a rich garlic flavor to beef and seafood but does not overpower other ingredients. Adjust the heat as desired by adding more red pepper flakes to the stir-fry.

1/2	cup low-sodium chicken broth
1/4	cup dry sherry
3	tablespoons hoisin sauce
1	tablespoon low-sodium soy sauce
2	teaspoons cornstarch
1	teaspoon toasted sesame oil
3	medium garlic cloves, minced or pressed through a garlic press (about 1 tablespoon)
1/8	teaspoon red pepper flakes

1. Combine all the ingredients except the garlic and pepper flakes in a small bowl and set aside.

2. Add the garlic and pepper flakes to the garlic mixture in step 1 of the stir-fry recipe.

PER SERVING: Cal 60; Fat 1 g; Sat fat 0 g; Chol 0 mg; Carb 9 g; Protein 1 g; Fiber 0 g; Sodium 620 mg

Sweet-and-Sour Sauce

MAKES ENOUGH FOR 1 STIR-FRY RECIPE

Pineapple juice or store-bought orange juice can be used in this recipe instead of freshly squeezed orange juice. Pineapple juice is especially appropriate when pineapple is in the stir-fry. The flavors in this sauce are good with chicken, pork, and shrimp. Due to the thick consistency of the ketchup, less cornstarch than usual is needed in this sauce.

6	tablespoons red wine vinegar
6	tablespoons juice from 1 to 2 oranges
6	tablespoons sugar
3	tablespoons ketchup
1	teaspoon cornstarch
1/2	teaspoon salt

Combine all the ingredients in a small bowl.

PER SERVING: Cal 100; Fat 0 g; Sat fat 0 g; Chol 0 mg; Carb 25 g; Protein 0 g; Fiber 0 g; Sodium 420 mg

Oyster Sauce

MAKES ENOUGH FOR 1 STIR-FRY RECIPE

As its name suggests, jarred oyster sauce is made with fermented oysters, along with salt and spices. The flavor is not overly fishy, but it is quite salty, so a little goes a long way. This sauce works well with beef and shrimp. Due to the thick consistency of the oyster sauce, less cornstarch than usual is needed in this sauce.

6	tablespoons dry sherry
3	tablespoons low-sodium chicken broth
3	tablespoons jarred oyster sauce
2	tablespoons low-sodium soy sauce
1	teaspoon toasted sesame oil
1	teaspoon sugar
1	teaspoon cornstarch
1/4	teaspoon ground black pepper

Combine all the ingredients in a small bowl.

PER SERVING: Cal 50; Fat 1 g; Sat fat 0 g; Chol 0 mg; Carb 5 g; Protein 3 g; Fiber 0 g; Sodium 800 mg

Coconut Curry Sauce

MAKES ENOUGH FOR I STIR-FRY RECIPE

Use canned unsweetened light coconut milk in this recipe, not sweetened coconut cream. The flavors in this sauce are great with chicken, shrimp, and tofu.

2/3	cup unsweetened light coconut milk
6	tablespoons low-sodium chicken broth
I	teaspoon sugar
I	teaspoon cornstarch
1/4	teaspoon salt
2	teaspoons curry powder
1/8	teaspoon red pepper flakes

1. Combine all the ingredients except the curry powder and pepper flakes in a small bowl and set aside.

2. Add the curry powder and pepper flakes to the garlic mixture in step 1 of the stir-fry recipe.

PER SERVING: Cal 35; Fat 2 g; Sat fat 1.5 g; Chol 0 mg; Carb 4 g; Protein 0 g; Fiber 0 g; Sodium 210 mg

Lemon Sauce

MAKES ENOUGH FOR I STIR-FRY RECIPE

The flavors in this sauce are mild and work especially well with shrimp.

6	tablespoons low-sodium chicken broth
1/4	cup juice from 2 lemons
1/4	cup dry sherry
2	tablespoons low-sodium soy sauce
2	teaspoons sugar
2	teaspoons cornstarch
1/4	teaspoon ground black pepper

Combine all the ingredients in a small bowl.

PER SERVING: Cal 35; Fat 0 g; Sat fat 0 g; Chol 0 mg; Carb 6 g; Protein 1 g; Fiber 0 g; Sodium 320 mg

Spicy Orange Sauce

MAKES ENOUGH FOR I STIR-FRY RECIPE

The citrus flavors in this sauce are especially good with chicken and shrimp. If a spicier sauce is desired, add up to 2 teaspoons more chili sauce.

1/2	teaspoon grated zest and 1/2 cup juice from 2 oranges
1/4	cup dry sherry
2	tablespoons low-sodium soy sauce
2	teaspoons Asian chili sauce
2	teaspoons sugar
2	teaspoons cornstarch
I	teaspoon toasted sesame oil

Combine all the ingredients in a small bowl.

PER SERVING: Cal 50; Fat 1 g; Sat fat 0 g; Chol 0 mg; Carb 7 g; Protein 1 g; Fiber 0 g; Sodium 340 mg

Ginger Sauce

MAKES ENOUGH FOR I STIR-FRY RECIPE

This classic sauce has a clean, bright ginger flavor that complements any meat, seafood, or tofu.

6	tablespoons low-sodium soy sauce
6	tablespoons low-sodium chicken broth
2	tablespoons dry sherry
I	tablespoon sugar
2	teaspoons cornstarch
I	teaspoon toasted sesame oil
I	tablespoon grated fresh ginger (see page 285)

1. Combine all the ingredients except the ginger in a bowl and set aside.

2. Add the ginger to the garlic mixture in step 1 of the stir-fry recipe.

PER SERVING: Cal 50; Fat 1 g; Sat fat 0 g; Chol 0 mg; Carb 7 g; Protein 1 g; Fiber 0 g; Sodium 850 mg

10

QUICK BREADS

QUICK BREADS CAN TAKE MANY SIZES AND shapes—loaves, muffins, biscuits, and even cinnamon rolls—but they all share a few key characteristics. All of these baked goods can be quickly prepared (the batter or dough can usually be assembled in the time it takes to preheat the oven) and quickly baked. This sets them far apart from yeast breads, which must rise for hours on the counter. All quick breads contain chemical leaveners (baking soda and baking powder) that are speedy and reliable. Unfortunately, most quick breads also rely on an abundance of fat to give them a tender, flavorful crumb.

For that reason, most people watching their fat intake ban these easy-to-prepare baked goods from their diet. This means no muffins, no coffeecake, and certainly no cinnamon rolls—all typically loaded with fat. But we cringe at the alternatives. Packaged low-fat banana bread with artificial flavoring? Low-fat recipes that yield bland, dense muffins? Dry, crumbly biscuits that bear little resemblance to the real thing? These weak imposters inspired us to roll up our sleeves and head into the test kitchen. We were determined to develop lighter, everyday recipes for quick breads, muffins, and biscuits that actually tasted good.

After extensive testing, we came away with some firm conclusions. It was, indeed, possible to use less fat in these baked goods. During our development of Banana Bread (page 298), we found that by using the right mix of flours (all-purpose and cake) and the correct mixing method, we were successful in getting lower amounts of fat to work in all of our recipes.

The most common method for mixing quick breads—appropriately referred to as the quick-bread method—relies on a good amount of fat for both flavor and texture. However, when we tried using this method in our lightened quick breads (which include less fat), the end result was dense, heavy muffins and breads with bland flavor—not acceptable.

We therefore turned to a technique more commonly found in mixing cake batters: the creaming method (see "Creaming a Quick Bread?" on page 299). This method not only gave us the tender crumb we desired, but it also dispersed the butter

more evenly throughout the batter, ensuring great buttery flavor in every bite. This technique worked perfectly for everything from Blueberry Muffins (page 306) to Zucchini Bread (page 300).

We also looked at a couple of savory quick breads, such as Southern Cornbread (page 302) and Fluffy Buttermilk Biscuits (page 312). We were determined to create a Southern-style cornbread with bold corn flavor and a moist crumb, instead of the traditionally dry and crumbly version. We found that using the right type of cornmeal and a generous amount of buttermilk was essential. Buttermilk was also key in our biscuit recipe because it gave us the lift and tender, fluffy texture we were after. Combining the buttermilk with the right amount of baking powder and baking soda, we achieved our goal without having to add too much fat and or too many calories.

Saving the best for last, we turned to a favorite breakfast treat—cinnamon rolls. With a few key ingredients such as light cream cheese and buttermilk, we were able to cut the fat by almost two-thirds in our Quick Cinnamon Rolls with Buttermilk Icing (page 317).

Go ahead, then, have a muffin or slice of banana bread—there's now very little to stand in your way.

TEST KITCHEN MAKEOVER

QUICK BREADS

WHEN MOST PEOPLE THINK OF QUICK BREADS, loaves of sweet banana or zucchini bread come to mind. Easy to prepare, using ingredients that are almost always on hand, they make a nice treat any time of the day, and a freshly made loaf is always appropriate for welcoming a newcomer to the neighborhood. These humble breads, however, can often be high in fat—usually butter or vegetable oil. Was there a way to make over the quick bread loaf with less fat? We were determined to find out.

We started our testing with one of our

favorites, banana bread. Good banana bread is soft and tender with plenty of banana flavor, and often, depending on personal preference, it is studded with toasty walnuts. But when we ran the numbers, we realized a slice of typical banana bread is not the best way to start the day. Packed with 16 grams of fat and 350 calories per serving, traditional banana bread recipes call for almost an entire stick of butter and more than a cup of walnuts. But low-fat recipes for banana bread are invariably disappointing, yielding dense, flavorless brick-like loaves that could easily double as building material. We wanted to make over this classic recipe, reducing the fat and calories, but keeping it light and moist with great banana flavor.

Starting with the bananas, we found it very important to pay close attention to their condition. Sweet, older, darkly speckled bananas infused the bread with both moisture and flavor. We also experimented with the way we prepared the bananas for the batter: slightly mashed, mashed well, and pureed. Loaves with slightly mashed bananas left chunks of fruit. We preferred a smoother texture, but pureeing the bananas turned out to be a bad idea because the batter did not rise as well. Bananas well mashed by hand were best.

We next decided to address the fat. Most banana bread recipes call for almost a stick of butter. We tried going as low as we could with the butter, thinking that bananas, with their moisture, would help us achieve a more delicate crumb without having to add more fat. We tested three different banana breads with low amounts of butter—2 tablespoons, 3 tablespoons, and 4 tablespoons —and tasted them side by side. The loaf made with 2 tablespoons of butter had little merit, as it was bland with a resistant crumb and unacceptable denseness. Tasters were surprised by what a difference an extra tablespoon of butter made in the banana bread. The loaf made with 3 tablespoons of butter had a decent, tender crumb, good flavor, and moderate lightness. Four tablespoons of butter, however, was the winning amount, producing a flavorful, delicate crumb, and well-balanced density in the bread.

We had our winner, but after running the recipe through a nutritional analysis, we found that 4 tablespoons of butter was a bit higher in fat and calories than we wanted for our lightened bread. Therefore, we were determined to see if we could make 3 tablespoons of butter work. Perhaps we could look to technique for creating a less dense banana bread with a tender crumb.

We began with the mixing method. Up until this point we had been using a common mixing method often referred to as the "quick-bread" method. The technique entails measuring wet ingredients (including melted butter) and dry ingredients separately, pouring wet into dry, and then mixing them together as quickly as possible,

THE LOWDOWN ON NONSTICK SPRAYS

There's nothing worse than flipping a bread tin over and seeing a partial loaf of banana bread drop out. A coating of butter and flour does the trick, but we aren't wild about the crusty white "frost" it sometimes leaves behind on baked goods. We wondered if nonstick baking spray could be a suitable replacement. From a healthy standpoint, the savings in fat and calories is negligible but the convenience of a nonstick spray is appealing.

We tested two nonstick cooking sprays (vegetable or canola oil under aerosol pressure) and two nonstick baking sprays (nonstick cooking sprays with an additional flour component) in our recipes for quick breads and cakes. The nonstick cooking sprays—one called Everbake, sold by a baking supply company, and the ubiquitous Pam—both worked well. (We also found them useful for spraying over breading to promote browning; however, if flavor is your primary concern, we recommend an olive oil mister.) The two nonstick baking sprays, Pam for Baking No-Stick Cooking Spray ($2.99) and Baker's Joy ($2.69), worked very well in applications where greasing and flouring is important. How? The uniformly blended flour-oil mixture made it easy to achieve an even coating. Also, the more solid texture of the baking sprays kept grease from pooling in the corners of the pan.

NO MORE STICKING

Pam ensures an easy release for muffins and other baked goods and Pam for Baking—with added flour—keeps quick breads and cakes from sticking without the "frosted" look of traditional butter and flour.

usually with a wooden spoon or spatula. We typically prefer this method for our quick breads because it is easy and makes for a hearty final product that also has a delicate crumb. However when it comes to making quick breads with less fat, we discovered that this technique doesn't work very well, mostly due to the fact that its success relies largely on a copious amount of melted butter. And because we were using such a small amount of fat, the loaves mixed using this quick-bread method had trace amounts of unwanted springiness and did not rise as much as we had desired. This led us to believe that we would need to find an alternative mixing method if we were to keep the butter to a minimum.

We then turned to another technique, called the creaming method, which is sometimes used to make quick breads but is more common to cake batters. This method starts with creaming butter and sugar until light and fluffy, usually with an electric mixer. Eggs and flavorings are beaten in, then the dry and liquid ingredients are added alternately.

Eager to try the creaming method, we noticed that we had a minor issue. We knew that we couldn't cream the amount of sugar (¾ cup) with the amount of butter we had decided upon (3 tablespoons). There was too much sugar to butter in the ratio and we would wind up with a pale slush, rather than the light and fluffy mixture we

STORING OVERRIPE BANANAS
FOR BANANA BREAD

Place overripe unpeeled bananas in a zipper-lock plastic bag and freeze them. As available, add more bananas to the bag. When you are ready to make bread, thaw the bananas on the counter until softened.

were after. To rectify this, we simply reduced the amount of sugar mixed into the butter and mixed the remaining sugar in with the dry ingredients. This worked great, as did the creaming method. Whipping the butter and sugar until airy created flavorful loaves with a softer texture and good volume.

Now that we had great flavor and the right denseness, we examined a problem we were still having with the crumb: a subtle, yet distracting springiness. Although the bread had a decent, soft crumb, it still wasn't delicate enough for some tasters. We suspected the culprit might be the type of flour we were using.

We knew that flour contains protein, and when the protein mixes with liquid, gluten develops. Therefore, the more you stir or work the mixture, the more the gluten proteins form into long, orderly bundles. These bundles create, at worst, an elastic batter that resists changing shape, which makes for dense, squat bread. Our problem, however, was minor and we deduced that we might have been using a flour type with too much protein.

Most quick bread recipes call for unbleached all-purpose flour, which is relatively high in protein and—up to this point—was the type of flour we had been using in our tests. Researching further, we came across some recipes that mix unbleached all-purpose flour with cake flour, a low-protein flour that doesn't produce as much tough gluten when mixed with liquid. Cake flour is known for giving baked goods crumb that is delicate and fine, albeit sometimes too fine. We experimented with the right balance of the two flours. We knew that all-purpose would add basic structure, and cake flour would lend the delicate refinement to the crumb we were looking for—and hopefully rid our bread of that unwanted springiness. After many tests, we determined that loaves made with 1½ cups of all-purpose flour and ½ cup of cake flour were best. This particular ratio of flours gave us banana bread with the best rise and the delicate crumb we were after. Tasters, however, commented that the bread was still a little on the dry side.

Wanting to get more moisture in our bread, we tried different loaves mixing in milk, buttermilk, low-fat sour cream, and low-fat yogurt. The low-fat sour cream added a bit of richness to our bread, but it also made for a heavy texture and an unattractive, pebbly crust. Milk produced banana bread with little flavor and created a slick, shiny top crust on the loaf. Buttermilk added a delightful tang, but low-fat yogurt let the banana flavor stand out best. And because low-fat yogurt has more solids than buttermilk, it made for a somewhat more solid loaf, which we preferred.

Adding walnuts to the banana bread proved to be a controversial topic. Our tasting panel was split right down the middle regarding those who preferred nuts in the bread and those who didn't. In the end, we decided to make them optional. Overall, we subtracted a cup of the walnuts from the classic recipes, leaving only ¼ cup in our low-fat version. And, in an effort to stretch the flavor and crunch of the nuts, we found that sprinkling the nuts on top of the batter before baking was more effective than mixing them in. Because they were on top of the bread, the nuts became toasted and more flavorful. At last, with 240 calories and 6 grams of fat per slice, our banana bread had shaped up to become a tasty, lighter way to start the day.

It didn't take us long to realize we could apply the basics of what we had learned from our banana bread to almost any other quick bread, then simply address the problems specific to that bread. Take zucchini bread for example. Typical recipes may call for up to 1 cup of vegetable oil, but after some preliminary testing, tasters determined that oil offered little in terms of flavor, making the bread taste flat and bland. Butter, on the other hand, boosted the subtle flavor of the zucchini and contributed a pleasant richness that tasters favored. With butter as our fat of choice we were able to use the creaming method that worked so well with the banana bread. We used the same ratio of all-purpose to cake flour, added a touch of lemon juice to the plain low-fat yogurt for a little acidity and pleasant citrus note, and increased the sugar slightly.

The main issue with zucchini bread was the zucchini itself. To this point, we had been adding only 6½ ounces zucchini, the size of a small zucchini, which produced about 1½ lightly packed cups when shredded. The zucchini flavor and texture were subtle, almost too subtle. We wondered if the bread shouldn't have a more pronounced zucchini flavor. We tried increasing the zucchini to 3 cups and found ourselves with a bread that looked and tasted virtually like mashed zucchini.

We wanted more zucchini flavor without the excess zucchini moisture. We decided to drain the zucchini to extract as much water as possible so that we could add more than 6 ounces of the squash and still retain a texture that was more like a moist quick bread than squashed squash. We shredded 1 pound of zucchini, tossed it with 2 tablespoons of the sugar, and placed it in a fine-mesh strainer set

EQUIPMENT: Loaf Pans

A good loaf pan should evenly brown banana bread and other quick breads (as well as yeast breads, such as sandwich bread, and cakes like pound cake). In addition, loaves should release cleanly and pans should be easy to get in and out of the oven, with little chance of sticking an oven mitt into the batter or baked bread.

We tested 10 loaf pans made from a variety of materials, including metal, glass, and stoneware. We found that dark-colored metal loaf pans browned breads more evenly than light-colored metal pans. Most of the dark metal pans were lined with a nonstick coating that also made the release of baked breads especially easy. We found that sweet breads, such as banana bread, were especially prone to burning in glass loaf pans. Sticking was also a problem in these pans. Stoneware loaf pans did a decent job of browning, but we had trouble removing loaves from these pans, too. Our testers found that pans with handles at either end were easier to work with and kept us from sticking an oven mitt into the edge of a baked loaf.

In the end, we recommend that you buy metal loaf pans with a nonstick coating. Although there's no harm in spending more money on heavier pans, we were pleased to find that the cheapest, lightest pan in our testing (Baker's Secret, $4) was our favorite.

THE BEST LOAF PAN

Our top choice is the Baker's Secret Nonstick Loaf Pan. It browns and releases baked goods flawlessly, and the handles make it easy to maneuver.

about 2 inches above the bottom of a bowl. After 30 minutes, the sugar had drawn nearly half a cup of liquid from the zucchini. Draining the zucchini turned out to be a very important step. Thirty minutes passed quickly as we prepared the pan and the remaining ingredients for the bread. The resulting bread, dotted with green flecks of the squash, had a notably increased zucchini flavor as well as a moist, but not gummy, texture.

We tried our finished loaf with other flavorings found in various recipes: ground cinnamon, grated nutmeg, ground allspice, ground ginger, vanilla, nuts, and raisins. Tasters liked a loaf made with a combination of cinnamon, allspice, and the nutty sweetness of pecans (sprinkled over the top, as with our banana bread). The small amount of cinnamon (½ teaspoon) and allspice (¼ teaspoon) added a great depth to the bread and brought out the zucchini's subtle flavor even more.

Banana Bread

MAKES ONE 9-INCH LOAF; SERVES 10

If you don't have very ripe bananas on hand, try this trick for coaxing out the prized natural sugars in nearly ripe bananas. Before peeling and mashing the bananas, lay them on a baking sheet and pop them into the heated oven for 15 minutes. If you don't have nonstick baking spray with flour, butter the pan and dust with flour.

	Nonstick baking spray with flour (see note)
1½	cups (7½ ounces) unbleached all-purpose flour
½	cup (2 ounces) cake flour
1	teaspoon baking powder
1	teaspoon baking soda
½	teaspoon salt
¾	cup (5¼ ounces) sugar
3	very ripe, darkly speckled large bananas (about 1¼ pounds), mashed well (about 1½ cups)
¼	cup plain low-fat yogurt
1	teaspoon vanilla extract
3	tablespoons unsalted butter, softened
2	large eggs
¼	cup walnuts, chopped (optional)

1. Adjust an oven rack to the middle position and heat the oven to 350 degrees. Spray the bottom and sides of a 9 by 5-inch loaf pan with the nonstick baking spray. Mix the all-purpose flour, cake flour, baking powder, baking soda, salt, and ¼ cup of the sugar together in a medium bowl; set aside. In a separate bowl, mix the mashed bananas, yogurt, and vanilla together; set aside.

2. Beat the remaining ½ cup sugar and butter together with an electric mixer on medium-high speed until light and fluffy, 3 to 5 minutes, scraping down the sides of the bowl with a rubber spatula as needed. Add the eggs, one at a time, beating well after each addition.

3. Reduce the mixer speed to low. Beat in half of the flour mixture until just incorporated, followed by one-third of the banana mixture,

---

MAKEOVER AT A GLANCE

–Classic–
Banana Bread
(per serving)

Calories: 350   Cholesterol: 60 mg
Fat: 16 g   Saturated Fat: 6 g

–Light–
Banana Bread
(per serving)

Calories: 240   Cholesterol: 50 mg
Fat: 4.5 g   Saturated Fat: 3 g

How We Did It

- Lowered the amount of butter to only 3 tablespoons
- Creamed the butter and sugar to achieve a lighter, airy texture
- Substituted cake flour for some of the all-purpose flour to create a more delicate crumb
- Used low-fat yogurt to add moisture, richness, and a subtle, complex tang
- Reduced the nuts (if using) to ¼ cup and sprinkled them on top of the bread

scraping down the bowl as needed. Add half of the remaining flour, followed by another one-third of the banana mixture. Repeat this process once more, being careful not to overmix the batter, which should look thick and chunky.

4. Scrape the batter into the prepared loaf pan and sprinkle the top evenly with the walnuts (if using). Bake until the loaf is golden brown and a toothpick inserted in the center comes out with just a few crumbs attached, about 55 minutes, rotating the pan halfway through baking. Cool the bread in the pan for 10 minutes, then transfer the loaf to a wire rack. Serve warm or at room temperature. (The bread can be wrapped with plastic wrap and stored at room temperature for up to 3 days.)

PER SLICE: Cal 240; Fat 4.5 g; Sat fat 3 g; Chol 50 mg; Carb 46 g; Protein 4 g; Fiber 2 g; Sodium 190 mg

PER SLICE WITH NUTS: Cal 260; Fat 6 g; Sat fat 3 g; Chol 50 mg; Carb 46 g; Protein 5 g; Fiber 3 g; Sodium 190 mg

➤ VARIATION

Orange-Spice Banana Bread

Follow the recipe for Banana Bread, adding 1 teaspoon ground cinnamon, ¼ teaspoon freshly grated nutmeg, and 1 tablespoon grated orange zest to the flour mixture in step 1.

PER SLICE: Cal 240; Fat 4.5 g; Sat fat 3 g; Chol 50 mg; Carb 46 g; Protein 4 g; Fiber 2 g; Sodium 190 mg

PER SLICE WITH NUTS: Cal 260; Fat 6 g; Sat fat 3 g; Chol 50 mg; Carb 47 g; Protein 5 g; Fiber 3 g; Sodium 190 mg

CORE TECHNIQUE

CREAMING A QUICK BREAD?

Typically, we prefer the quick-bread mixing method for making quick breads and muffins. In a rapid assembly of ingredients, wet ingredients (including melted butter) and dry ingredients are measured out separately and then the wet is simply stirred into the dry. But we found that this method requires quite a bit of fat to effectively yield well-risen, light, and moist breads and muffins. When we tried the quick-bread method with our lower fat batters, the results produced dense, tough baked goods.

Frustrated, we looked to an alternate mixing method sometimes used for quick breads: the creaming method. More often used for cake batters, this method starts with creaming butter and sugar until light and fluffy, usually with an electric mixer. Eggs and flavorings are beaten in, and then the dry and liquid ingredients are added alternately. We had great success with this technique in a number of lighter quick bread and muffin recipes. Creaming the butter and sugar created a light and tender crumb, which tasters preferred. Happy with our success, we were still curious as to why one method would work better than the other.

It turns out that the creaming method guards against overmixing, or the over-development of glutens in the flour. When flour is mixed with liquid it develops gluten, which provides structure to baked goods. Too much gluten development and muffins and breads turn out tough and elastic. Too little and baked goods have an overly soft, gummy crumb.

We looked at the science of the creaming method to see if we could better understand exactly what was happening. Adding some of the flour mixture to the creamed butter mixture before the wet ingredients is key. The fat from the butter and egg coats most of the flour, protecting it from any gluten formation. The remaining flour and wet ingredients are added alternately at this point, stimulating only a part of the flour's gluten. (Some of the flour's gluten must be activated; otherwise the baked good would have no structure at all.) In the quick-bread method, all the wet ingredients and fats are added at once, denying the flour an opportunity to be coated with fat. Thus, there is more gluten developed during the mixing.

Zucchini Bread

MAKES ONE 9-INCH LOAF; SERVES 10

If you don't have nonstick baking spray with flour, butter the pan and dust it with flour.

	Nonstick baking spray with flour (see note)
1	pound zucchini (about 3 small or 2 medium), ends trimmed
1	cup (7 ounces) plus 2 tablespoons sugar
1½	cups (7½ ounces) unbleached all-purpose flour
½	cup (2 ounces) cake flour
1	teaspoon baking powder
1	teaspoon baking soda
½	teaspoon salt
½	teaspoon ground cinnamon
¼	teaspoon ground allspice
¼	cup plain low-fat yogurt
1	tablespoon juice from 1 lemon
3	tablespoons unsalted butter, softened
2	large eggs
¼	cup pecans, chopped

1. Adjust an oven rack to the middle position and heat the oven to 375 degrees. Spray the bottom and sides of a 9 by 5-inch loaf pan with the nonstick baking spray. Shred the zucchini on the large holes of a box grater (see right) and toss with the 2 tablespoons sugar. Transfer the mixture to a fine-mesh strainer set over a bowl and let drain for 30 minutes.

2. Meanwhile, whisk the all-purpose flour, cake flour, baking powder, baking soda, salt, cinnamon, allspice, and ½ cup of the sugar together in a medium bowl; set aside. After the zucchini has drained, squeeze it dry between several layers of paper towels. Mix the dried zucchini with the yogurt and lemon juice in a small bowl; set aside.

3. Beat the remaining ½ cup sugar and butter together with an electric mixer on medium-high speed until light and fluffy, 3 to 5 minutes, scraping down the sides of the bowl with a rubber spatula as needed. Add the eggs, one at a time, beating well after each addition.

4. Reduce the mixer speed to low. Beat in half of the flour mixture until just incorporated, followed by one-third of the zucchini mixture, scraping down the bowl as needed. Add half of the remaining flour, followed by another one-third of the zucchini mixture. Repeat this process once more, being careful not to overmix the batter.

5. Scrape the batter into the prepared loaf pan and sprinkle the top evenly with the pecans. Bake until the loaf is golden brown and a toothpick inserted in the center comes out with just a few crumbs attached, about 55 minutes, rotating the pan halfway through baking. Cool the bread in the pan for 10 minutes, then transfer the loaf to a wire rack. Serve warm or at room temperature. (The bread can be wrapped with plastic wrap and stored at room temperature for up to 3 days.)

PER SLICE: Cal 250; Fat 7 g; Sat fat 3 g; Chol 50 mg; Carb 43 g; Protein 5 g; Fiber 2 g; Sodium 190 mg

SHREDDING ZUCCHINI

1. Shred trimmed zucchini on the large holes of a box grater or in a food processor fitted with the shredding disk.

2. After sugaring and draining the zucchini, wrap it in paper towels and squeeze out excess liquid. Proceed immediately with the recipe.

SOUTHERN CORNBREAD

WHILE ALL CORNBREADS ARE QUICK TO make and bake, there are two very distinct types: Northern and Southern. Southern cornbread uses 100 percent white cornmeal and is usually a bit crumbly, lean, and flat—about one inch thick. Northern cornbread is typically sweeter, lighter, and higher—almost cakey—a result achieved by adding sugar and combining white flour and yellow cornmeal. Both types sport a brown crust, although Southern cornbread crusts have a certain lacey-crispness.

There is also a third, more general, category, which we designate all-purpose cornbread. This category comprises those recipes that don't fall in line with either of the other two styles, but fit somewhere in between. Most all-purpose cornbreads rise moderately high and have a somewhat cakey crumb that teeters on the edge of not-moist-enough.

Since both Northern and all-purpose cornbread are typically high in fat, we decided to focus our attention on Southern-style cornbread. Naturally the leanest of the three types, at its best this bread is moist and tender, with the warm fragrance of the cornfield and the subtle flavor of dairy in every bite.

We began by testing 11 different cornmeals in one simple Southern cornbread recipe. Before the cornmeal tests, we would have bet that the color of cornmeal was an idiosyncrasy that had little to do with flavor. But tasting proved otherwise. Cornbreads made with yellow cornmeal consistently had a more potent corn flavor than those made with white cornmeal.

Although we didn't want Southern cornbread to taste like dessert, we wondered whether a little sugar might enhance the corn flavor. So we made three batches—one with no sugar, one with 2 teaspoons, and one with a heaping tablespoon. The higher-sugar bread was really too sweet for Southern cornbread, but 2 teaspoons of sugar seemed to enhance the natural sweetness of the corn without calling attention to itself.

Most Southern-style cornbread batters are made with just buttermilk, but we found recipes calling for the full range of heavy and acidic dairy products—buttermilk, sour cream, yogurt, milk, and cream. With the exception of cream, we made batches of cornbread with each type of dairy. We still loved the pure, straightforward flavor of the buttermilk-based cornbread, but the batch made with sour cream was actually more tasty and baked into a more attractive shape. And we weren't worried about the fat and calories of the sour cream in our recipe, as the amount was still within our range for a lighter cornbread.

At this point we began to feel a little uneasy about where we were taking this regional bread. A couple of teaspoons of sugar might be overlooked, but using yellow cornmeal was heresy. And sour cream was really crossing the (Mason-Dixon) line.

So far all of our testing had been done with a composite recipe under which most Southern cornbread recipes seemed to fall. There were two recipes, however, that didn't quite fit the mold—one very rich and one very lean—and now seemed like the right time to give them a try.

Right off the bat we rejected the rich version, as it was closer to spoonbread, a soufflé-like dish, than cornbread. In addition, it was just too high in fat. We went to the other extreme. In the lean version, boiling water is stirred into the cornmeal, then modest amounts of milk, egg, butter, salt, and baking powder are stirred into the resulting cornmeal mush, and the whole thing is baked. So simple, so lean, so humble, this recipe would have been easy to pass over. But given our options at this point, we decided to give it a quick test. Just one bite completely changed the direction of our pursuit. Unlike anything we had tasted so far, the crumb of this cornbread was incredibly moist and fine and bursting with corn flavor.

We were pleased, but since the foundation of this bread was cornmeal mush, the crumb was actually more mushy than moist. In addition, the baking powder got stirred into the wet batter at the end. This just didn't feel right.

After a few unsuccessful attempts to make the cornbread less mushy, we started thinking that this great idea was a bust. In a last attempt to salvage it, we decided to make mush out of only half the cornmeal and mix the remaining cornmeal with

301

the leavener. To our relief, the bread made this way was much improved. Decreasing the mush even further—from half to a third of the cornmeal—gave us exactly what we were looking for. We made the new, improved cornbread with buttermilk and mixed a bit of baking soda with the baking powder, and it tasted even better. Finally, our recipe was starting to feel Southern again. Although we still preferred yellow cornmeal and a touch of sugar, we had achieved a bread that was moist, tender, and rather fine-crumbed without flour, and nicely shaped without sour cream, thus avoiding two ingredients that would have interfered with the strong corn flavor we wanted.

With this new recipe in hand, we performed a few final tests. Our recipe called for 1 tablespoon of butter, but many Southern cornbreads call for no more fat than is needed to grease the pan. We tried vegetable oil, peanut oil, shortening, butter, and bacon drippings—which we found, much to our surprise, are lower in saturated fat than butter—as well as a batch with no fat at all. To our delight, the cornbread with no added fat was as moist and delicious as the other breads. Butter and bacon drippings, however, each added a nice flavor, so we kept a little fat in our recipe.

Classically, Southern cornbread batter is poured into a scorching-hot, greased cast-iron skillet, which causes it to develop a thin, crisp crust as the bread bakes. How crucial is the cast-iron skillet? The cornbread we made in a pre-heated skillet worked great; however, it occurred to us that many people might not own a well-seasoned 8-inch cast-iron skillet. To boot, we discovered that if your skillet is not perfectly seasoned, the bread sticks to the bottom of the pan, ruining that beautiful crust. In the end, we found that simply pouring the batter into an unheated cake pan worked well and gave us the crust we were looking for.

Southern Cornbread

SERVES 8

Though some styles of Southern cornbread are dry and crumbly, we favor this dense, moist, tender version. Cornmeal mush of just the right texture is essential to this bread, so make sure that the water is at a rapid boil when it is added to the cornmeal. Also, we recommend using Quaker yellow cornmeal for this recipe, as stone-ground whole-grain cornmeal yields a drier and less tender cornbread. To accurately measure the water, bring a kettle of water to a boil, then measure out the ⅓ cup needed for this recipe. Bacon fat works well in this recipe and may be substituted for the butter.

	Vegetable oil spray
1	cup (5½ ounces) yellow cornmeal (see note)
2	teaspoons sugar
½	teaspoon salt
1	teaspoon baking powder
¼	teaspoon baking soda
⅓	cup boiling water (see note)
¾	cup buttermilk
1	large egg, beaten lightly
1	tablespoon unsalted butter, melted and cooled (see note)

1. Adjust an oven rack to the lower-middle position and heat the oven to 450 degrees. Spray a 9-inch round cake pan or 8-inch square baking pan with the vegetable oil spray.

2. Measure ⅓ cup of the cornmeal into a medium bowl. Whisk the remaining ⅔ cup cornmeal, sugar, salt, baking powder, and baking soda together in a small bowl; set aside.

3. Pour the boiling water all at once into the ⅓ cup cornmeal and stir to make a stiff mush. Whisk in the buttermilk gradually, breaking up lumps, until smooth, then whisk in the egg and melted butter. Stir the dry ingredients into the mush mixture until just moistened and pour the batter into the prepared pan.

4. Bake until the bread is golden brown, about 20 minutes. Remove from the oven and flip the cornbread onto a wire rack. Turn the bread right-side up, and cool for 5 minutes before slicing into wedges.

PER SERVING: Cal 100; Fat 2.5 g; Sat fat 1.5 g; Chol 30 mg; Carb 18 g; Protein 3 g; Fiber 1 g; Sodium 250 mg

TEST KITCHEN MAKEOVER

MUFFINS

COMPARED TO POPULAR BREAKFAST TREATS such as doughnuts and coffeecake, muffins seem to be a more healthful option. Maybe it's because muffins often contain fruit, bran, and other ingredients known to have nutritional value. The truth, however, is that a typical homemade muffin has 11 grams of fat and 300 calories And commercially prepared muffins are even worse. Those super-size breakfast treats at your local coffee shop can contain up to 590 calories and 24 grams of fat! It's true, too, that many of these coffee shops carry low-fat muffins; tastewise, these muffins fall short, but worse, they're not much better for you than their full-fat counterparts.

We wanted to created a recipe for great-tasting muffins that was not only lighter but simple too, one that we could reach for on a weekday morning and not be weighed down. We decided to start by focusing our attention on a classic—the blueberry muffin.

In our research, we came up with a number of existing low-fat blueberry muffin recipes to test. We baked muffins with a variety of results—from bland and airy to dense and pasty—but they were all lackluster and missing serious blueberry flavor. In addition, because low-fat muffins are found in almost every coffee shop in our neighborhood, we included them in our tasting. No one liked these muffins. They found them to be overly sweet, gluey specimens, shamelessly low on fresh blueberry flavor. And much to our dismay, we also discovered that the commercial versions are loaded with hydrogenated fats and preservatives.

We tossed the low-fat muffin recipes aside and, instead, decided to start with a full-fat muffin recipe and work toward our lower fat goals from there. To start, we wondered how much fat we could omit from a traditional muffin recipe. Working with some basic muffin proportions—3 cups of flour, 1 cup of sugar, 2 eggs, and 1¼ cups of milk—we aimed to take the amount of butter in

the recipe as low as we could go without compromising the muffins' textural and flavor integrity. We knew that traditional muffin recipes usually call for 8 to 10 tablespoons of butter, and we were hoping to reduce that to 3 to 5 tablespoons. Thus, for our first run of testing, we had tasters sample three separate batches of muffins made with 3 tablespoons, 4 tablespoons, and 5 tablespoons, respectively.

All agreed that the muffins made with 3 tablespoons of butter were a bit tough and a tad bland. However, there was a toss-up between muffins made with 4 tablespoons of butter versus those made with 5. Tasters liked the delicate crumb

CORE TECHNIQUE

HAVING YOUR CAKE FLOUR AND EATING IT TOO

When we minimized the amount of butter in our quick breads and muffins, we found that we needed to adjust the type of flour we used in the recipe. Most quick bread recipes call for unbleached all-purpose flour, a medium-protein flour that develops a lot of gluten, which creates a springy elasticity when the flour is mixed with liquid. Typically, in a full-fat recipe, an abundant amount of butter is used to quell the springy effect of developed gluten. Enter cake flour. A low-protein flour, cake flour does not develop much gluten when mixed into a batter or dough, meaning that it produces a tender, delicate crumb in baked goods. This appealed to us because it meant we didn't need to use as much fat to counter the gluten. During our testing of lighter quick bread and muffin recipes, we discovered that too much cake flour caused an overly cakey and gummy crumb; however, too little cake flour produced baked goods with a tough, dense crumb. In the end, we figured out that a small portion of cake flour mixed with a larger amount of all-purpose flour worked to give us the tender crumb we were after without having to add extra fat.

Choosing Dairy for Tender Muffins

During the development of our Blueberry Muffins, we wondered what effects different types of low-fat dairy would have on the finished muffins. We tried some common, and not-so-common, dairy products. Here are the details:

LOW-FAT SOUR CREAM
Too Gummy
This yielded a muffin with a tough exterior and an interior that had a "decent-looking crumb" but was "too gummy" for tasters.

BUTTERMILK
Off Flavor and Spongy
Tasters found muffins made with buttermilk just too dry and pasty, with "a stale-textured exterior." The crumb was tight and spongy, "like cotton."

CLABBERED MILK
Bland and Dry
Tasters had high hopes for clabbered milk; however, the muffins turned out "flavorless," with a dry interior and "crumbly exterior."

CLABBERED LOW-FAT EVAPORATED MILK
Too Bready
Although the texture of these muffins was too dry, tasters considered the flavor "pretty decent." Most complained that the muffins had a "bread-like texture, not quite cakey enough."

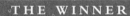

LOW-FAT YOGURT
We found that low-fat yogurt worked perfectly, producing "light, moist, and tender" muffins with a delicate crumb. One taster commented: "This is a good-looking muffin with the best flavor."

and depth of flavor of muffins made with 5 tablespoons of butter. The flavor of muffins made with 4 tablespoons of butter tasted just as good as those made with more butter, but the crumb left a little to be desired. We decided to work with 4 tablespoons of butter, reasoning that the extra tablespoon of butter was not worth the fat and calories, and then focused our attention on improving the crumb quality by other means.

Taking a cue from our quick breads, we knew we could probably achieve a more delicate crumb by altering our mixing method. For muffins we typically use the "quick-bread" method, but for the purposes of a lower fat recipe we decided to use the creaming method we had used with great results for our banana and zucchini breads. Again, we were able to maximize the dispersal of the butter throughout the batter, giving every muffin a more pronounced butter flavor. Taking another cue from our banana and zucchini breads, we cut the all-purpose flour with some lower-protein cake flour to get the delicate texture we wanted without adding more fat. A ratio of 2 cups all-purpose flour to 1 cup cake flour was just right.

As for dairy, we looked again at our quick breads and chose what worked well there—low-fat yogurt, which gave our muffins a nice tang and moist crumb. Since lemon is a natural partner with blueberries, a bit of lemon juice and lemon zest next went into the batter. We found that 2 teaspoons of lemon juice, coupled with 1 teaspoon of zest, added great brightness to the muffins; however, some tasters didn't care for the perfume of the lemon zest. We agreed to make the zest optional, and to balance the tanginess of the yogurt-lemon combination we added a bit of vanilla, which contributed a subtle sweetness that tasters appreciated.

With a basic batter down, we next addressed the blueberries and found that fresh is best—and that the size of the berry really matters. If possible, choose small, fresh, wild blueberries; they are much sweeter than their bigger cultivated cousins. And if you can't find good blueberries in the produce section, try frozen. One particular brand of frozen blueberries, Wyman's, tasted nearly as good as the fresh berries.

When it came to incorporating the berries into the finished batter, we found that it works best to toss them with a little bit of flour. This helps the berries stay evenly suspended in the batter. In addition, we discovered that berries must be folded into the batter with a gentle hand; otherwise, the blueberries bleed, giving the muffins an unappetizing blue-gray color.

Through additional testing, we discovered that this rather heavy batter required a full tablespoon of baking powder for enough lift; this seemed like a lot, but tasters noted no off chemical flavor. (If too much chemical leavener is added, some of it will fail to react and will give baked goods a bitter, soapy flavor.) We also included another leavener—baking soda—in our batter. When baking soda is mixed with an acid, such as lemon juice and yogurt, it releases carbon dioxide, the gas that causes baked goods to rise.

From this basic blueberry muffin recipe we created a couple of flavor variations (using raspberries and almonds in one and cranberries with orange juice and zest in another), then we turned to adapting the recipe to other popular muffins. We started with bran muffins—long considered a healthy way to start the day. But again, although loaded with bran, these muffins can also be loaded with sugar and fat, and many low-fat muffins we tasted were too dense and heavy. We rebuilt our blueberry muffin recipe to include the ingredients integral to bran muffins—wheat bran, dark brown sugar, raisins, and light (or mild) molasses. The main issue here was to determine just the right amount of wheat bran to use. By adding too much bran, we would run the risk of creating dense, brick-like muffins. Too little, and the hearty, nutty richness of the wheat bran would be totally lost. Tasters agreed that 1 cup of bran was just the right amount and we used it to replace the cake flour. With this amount, we had the right balance of lightness and bran flavor. And rather than adding lemon juice, we thinned out our yogurt with some milk (either whole or 2 percent was best) for further insurance that these muffins wouldn't be too dense.

With the major elements of our bran muffin recipe nailed down, we addressed complaints that the muffins still had a bit of a gritty texture. To this point, we had been mixing the bran with the dry ingredients; however, we realized after further research that this was a mistake. We discovered that we should have been hydrating the bran in the liquid ingredients before adding it to the batter. A quick 10-minute soak solved the problem. And by hydrating the wheat bran in the mixture of yogurt, milk, molasses, and vanilla extract, we found that the bran became infused with great flavor, which really came through in our muffins.

Corn muffins were up next. We wanted a corn muffin with a full corn flavor that wasn't

PORTIONING BATTER AND REMOVING MUFFINS FROM A TIN

1. Using a large serving spoon sprayed with nonstick baking spray with flour to spoon even amounts of batter into each cup of the muffin tin. The batter will slide easily from the spoon into the muffin cups.

2. The thin, slightly curved blade of a grapefruit knife is particularly well suited to getting under a stubborn muffin with little risk of tearing the muffin apart.

too dry—the shortcoming of most low-fat corn muffin recipes we tried. Our development process followed a similar track as that of the blueberry and bran muffins—halving the fat and using the creaming method for mixing. The big focus for these muffins was on the cornmeal itself: how much and what type to use. We quickly came to the conclusion that our recipe would have to call for a national brand of cornmeal to avoid these huge textural swings. The obvious option was Quaker yellow cornmeal, which is available in every supermarket from Miami to Seattle. Reliable though it is, Quaker cornmeal is degerminated, which means the germ (the heart of the kernel) is removed during processing. Its flavor is thus not as complex as whole-grain cornmeal, which has the germ left intact. However, in our tests, tasters did not feel that the flavor difference between degerminated and whole-grain cornmeal was an issue. In fact, they found that Quaker cornmeal

added plenty of solid corn flavor to our muffins, and more importantly, gave them a moist, consistently textured crumb, without grittiness. One cup did the trick and, as we had with the bran in our bran muffins, we used it in place of the cake flour. Also like our bran muffins, we thinned the yogurt out with a little milk to keep the muffins from being too dense and used a combination of ½ teaspoon baking soda and 1 tablespoon baking powder to give them the ideal height.

Finally we had several lightened muffin recipes—all based on the same basic techniques—that produced perfect low-fat muffins, every time.

MAKEOVER AT A GLANCE

–Classic–
Blueberry Muffins
(per muffin)

Calories: 300	Cholesterol: 60 mg
Fat: 11 g	Saturated Fat: 7 g

–Light–
Blueberry Muffins
(per muffin)

Calories: 250	Cholesterol: 45 mg
Fat: 5 g	Saturated Fat: 3 g

How We Did It

- Reduced butter to only 4 tablespoons
- Creamed the butter and sugar to achieve a lighter, airy texture
- Used low-fat yogurt to add moisture, richness, and a subtle, complex tang
- Substituted cake flour for some of the all-purpose flour for a more delicate crumb

---

Blueberry Muffins
MAKES I DOZEN MUFFINS

When fresh blueberries are not in season, frozen blueberries are a good alternative. To make sure that frozen berries do not bleed into the muffin batter (making the muffins an unappealing blue-gray color), rinse them under cool water in a mesh strainer until the water runs clear, then spread them on a paper towel–lined plate to dry.

	Vegetable oil spray
2	cups (10 ounces), plus 1 tablespoon unbleached all-purpose flour
1	cup (4 ounces) cake flour
1	tablespoon baking powder
½	teaspoon baking soda
½	teaspoon salt
1	cup (7 ounces) plus 1 tablespoon sugar
4	tablespoons (½ stick) unsalted butter, softened
2	large eggs
2	teaspoons juice from 1 lemon
1	teaspoon grated zest from 1 lemon (optional)
1	teaspoon vanilla extract
1½	cups plain low-fat yogurt
2	cups fresh blueberries

1. Adjust an oven rack to the middle position and heat the oven to 375 degrees. Spray a 12-cup muffin tin with the vegetable oil spray. Whisk 2 cups of the all-purpose flour, cake flour, baking powder, baking soda, salt, and ¼ cup of the sugar together in a medium bowl; set aside.

2. Beat an additional ¾ cup sugar and the butter together with an electric mixer on medium-high speed until light and fluffy, 3 to 5 minutes, scraping down the sides of the bowl with a rubber spatula as needed. Add the eggs, one at a time, beating well after each addition. Beat in the lemon juice, lemon zest (if using), and vanilla until incorporated.

3. Reduce the mixer speed to low. Beat in one-third of the flour mixture until just incorporated, followed by one-third of the yogurt, scraping down the bowl as needed. Repeat this process twice more, alternating between the remaining flour mixture and the yogurt until the ingredients are just incorporated. Do not overmix.

4. Toss the blueberries with the remaining tablespoon all-purpose flour, then gently fold them into the batter with a rubber spatula. Using a large ice-cream scoop or measuring cup, divide the batter evenly among the muffin cups, and sprinkle the tops with the remaining tablespoon sugar. Bake until golden and a toothpick inserted into the center of a muffin comes out with just a few crumbs attached, 25 to 30 minutes, rotating the pan halfway through baking. Cool the muffins in the pan for 5 minutes, then flip them out onto a wire rack and cool for 10 minutes before serving.

PER MUFFIN: Cal 250; Fat 5 g; Sat fat 3 g; Chol 45 mg; Carb 46 g; Protein 6 g; Fiber 1 g; Sodium 270 mg

APPLYING COOKING SPRAY WITHOUT THE MESS

Open the dishwasher door, place the muffin tin on the door, and spray away. Any excess or overspray will be cleaned off the door the next time you run the dishwasher.

> VARIATIONS

Raspberry and Almond Muffins

It's important that you use fresh raspberries here, as frozen ones are too fragile and bleed too much even when rinsed.

Follow the recipe for Blueberry Muffins, substituting 2 cups fresh raspberries for the blueberries, substituting ½ teaspoon almond extract for the vanilla, and omitting the lemon juice and zest.

PER MUFFIN: Cal 250; Fat 5 g; Sat fat 3 g; Chol 45 mg; Carb 45 g; Protein 5 g; Fiber 2 g; Sodium 270 mg

Cranberry and Orange Muffins

Combine 1½ cups dried cranberries, chopped fine, and ⅔ cup orange juice in a microwave-safe bowl. Cover tightly with plastic wrap and microwave on high until the juice is bubbling, about 1 minute. Let the cranberries stand, covered, until softened and plump, about 5 minutes. Strain the cranberries, discarding the juice. Meanwhile, process 1 cup plus 1 tablespoon sugar with 2 teaspoons grated orange zest until pale orange, about 10 seconds. Follow the recipe for Blueberry Muffins, substituting the rehydrated cranberries for the blueberries, substituting the processed orange sugar for the sugar and omitting the lemon juice and zest.

PER MUFFIN: Cal 290; Fat 5 g; Sat fat 3 g; Chol 45 mg; Carb 56 g; Protein 5 g; Fiber 2 g; Sodium 270 mg

Bran Muffins

MAKES 1 DOZEN MUFFINS

If you don't have whole milk on hand, 2 percent works fine here—the muffins just won't be as rich. Do not substitute skim milk; it produces inferior muffins.

	Vegetable oil spray
1	cup (2 ounces) unprocessed wheat bran
¾	cup plain low-fat yogurt
½	cup whole milk
6	tablespoons light molasses
1	teaspoon vanilla extract
2	cups (10 ounces) unbleached all-purpose flour
1	tablespoon baking powder

¹/₂	teaspoon baking soda
¹/₂	teaspoon salt
4	tablespoons (¹/₂ stick) unsalted butter, softened
³/₄	cup packed (5¹/₄ ounces) dark brown sugar
2	large eggs
1	cup raisins

1. Adjust an oven rack to the middle position and heat the oven to 375 degrees. Spray a 12-cup muffin tin with the vegetable oil spray. Stir the wheat bran, yogurt, milk, molasses, and vanilla together in a medium bowl until combined; let the mixture sit for at least 10 minutes. In a separate bowl, whisk the flour, baking powder, baking soda, and salt together; set aside.

2. Beat the butter and brown sugar together with an electric mixer on medium-high speed until light and fluffy, 3 to 5 minutes, scraping down the sides of the bowl with a rubber spatula as needed. Add the eggs, one at a time, beating well after each addition.

3. Reduce the mixer speed to low. Beat in one-third of the flour mixture until just incorporated, followed by one-third of the bran mixture, scraping down the bowl as needed. Repeat this process twice more, alternating between the remaining flour and bran mixtures until the ingredients are just incorporated. Do not overmix.

4. Gently fold the raisins into the batter with a rubber spatula. Using a large ice-cream scoop or measuring cup, divide the batter evenly among the muffin cups. Bake until golden and a toothpick inserted into the center of a muffin comes out with just a few crumbs attached, 25 to 30 minutes, rotating the pan halfway through baking. Cool the muffins in the pan for 5 minutes, then flip them out onto a wire rack and cool for 10 minutes before serving.

PER MUFFIN: Cal 270; Fat 5 g; Sat fat 3.5 g; Chol 50 mg; Carb 50 g; Protein 6 g; Fiber 3 g; Sodium 270 mg

Corn Muffins

MAKES 1 DOZEN MUFFINS

We recommend using Quaker yellow cornmeal for this recipe, as stone-ground whole-grain cornmeal yields drier and less tender muffins. And if you don't have whole milk on hand, 2 percent works fine here—the muffins just won't be as rich. Do not substitute skim milk; it produces inferior muffins.

	Vegetable oil spray
2	cups (10 ounces) unbleached all-purpose flour
1	cup (5¹/₂ ounces) yellow cornmeal (see note)
1	tablespoon baking powder
¹/₂	teaspoon baking soda
¹/₂	teaspoon salt
1	cup (7 ounces) sugar
³/₄	cup plain low-fat yogurt
¹/₂	cup whole milk
1	teaspoon vanilla extract
4	tablespoons (¹/₂ stick) unsalted butter, softened
2	large eggs

1. Adjust an oven rack to the middle position and heat the oven to 375 degrees. Spray a 12-cup muffin tin with the vegetable oil spray. Whisk the flour, cornmeal, baking powder, baking soda, salt, and ¼ cup of the sugar together in a medium bowl; set aside. In a separate bowl, stir the yogurt, milk, and vanilla together; set aside.

2. Beat the remaining ¾ cup sugar and butter together with an electric mixer on medium-high speed until light and fluffy, 3 to 5 minutes, scraping down the sides of the bowl with a rubber spatula as needed. Add the eggs, one at a time, beating well after each addition.

3. Reduce the mixer speed to low. Beat in one-third of the flour mixture until just incorporated, followed by one-third of the yogurt mixture, scraping down the bowl as needed. Repeat this process twice more, alternating between the remaining flour and yogurt mixtures until the ingredients are just incorporated. Do not overmix.

4. Using a large ice-cream scoop or measuring cup, divide the batter evenly among the muffin cups. Bake until golden and a toothpick inserted into the center of a muffin comes out with just a few crumbs attached, 18 to 20 minutes, rotating the pan halfway through baking. Cool the muffins in the pan for 5 minutes, then flip them out onto a wire rack and cool for 10 minutes before serving.

PER MUFFIN: Cal 240; Fat 5 g; Sat fat 3.5 g; Chol 50 mg; Carb 42 g; Protein 5 g; Fiber 1 g ; Sodium 260 mg

➤ VARIATIONS
Corn and Blueberry Muffins
When fresh blueberries are not in season, use frozen. To make sure that frozen berries do not bleed, rinse them under cool water in a strainer until the water runs clear, then spread them on a paper towel–lined plate to dry.

Follow the recipe for Corn Muffins, gently folding in 2 cups fresh or frozen blueberries, preferably wild, tossed with 1 tablespoon flour, into the finished batter. Sprinkle each muffin with ¼ teaspoon sugar before baking.

PER MUFFIN: Cal 260; Fat 5 g; Sat fat 3.5 g; Chol 50 mg; Carb 47 g; Protein 5 g; Fiber 2 g; Sodium 260 mg

Corn and Apricot Muffins with Orange Essence

1. Combine 1½ cups dried apricots, chopped fine, and ⅔ cup orange juice together in a microwave-safe bowl. Cover tightly with plastic wrap and microwave on high until the juice is bubbling, about 1 minute. Let the apricots stand, covered, until softened and plump, about 5 minutes. Strain the apricots, discarding the juice.

2. Meanwhile, process 1 cup plus 1 tablespoon sugar with 2 teaspoons grated orange zest until pale orange, about 10 seconds. Follow the recipe for Corn Muffins, substituting 1 cup of the processed orange sugar for the sugar. Stir the strained apricots into the finished batter and sprinkle the top of each muffin with ¼ teaspoon of the remaining orange sugar before baking.

PER MUFFIN: Cal 300; Fat 5 g; Sat fat 3.5 g; Chol 50 mg; Carb 58 g; Protein 6 g; Fiber 2 g; Sodium 270 mg

---

EQUIPMENT: Muffin Tins

The majority of muffin tins on the market are made of coated aluminum and are lightweight. We purchased two tins of this type, as well as two heavy-gauge "professional" aluminum tins and one "air-cushioned" aluminum tin. Three had a nonstick coating.

We baked two different varieties of muffins to test the two things that really matter—browning and sticking. We wanted the muffins to brown uniformly and to be easily plucked from the tin. Corn muffins were ideal for the browning test, blueberry for the sticking test—no one wants a sweet, sticky berry left in the tin rather than in the muffin.

Browning ended up being the deciding factor in these tests. Sticking was not an issue as long as the tins were coated with nonstick spray. The best tins browned the muffins evenly, the worst browned them on the top but left them pallid and underbaked on the bottom. As we had observed in other bakeware tests, darker coated metals, which absorb heat, do the best job of browning baked goods. The air-cushioned tin produced pale muffins that were also small (the cushioning made for a smaller cup capacity, about ⅓ cup rather than the standard ½ cup).

We found the heavier-gauge aluminum tins to have no advantage—they are much more expensive than other tins, weigh twice as much, and do not produce superior muffins. Their heft may make them durable, but unless you bake commercially, the lightweight models will last a lifetime. The supermarket staple Baker's Secret ($5.69) performed well and finished in a respectable second place. But Wilton Ultra-Bake ($7.99) was the clear winner, in part because of its generous 2-inch lip that provides a convenient handle.

THE BEST MUFFIN TIN

Wilton Ultra-Bake turns out ideal muffins and boasts the thoughtful (and rare) addition of handles.

MIXING BUTTERMILK BISCUIT DOUGH

Despite a short ingredient list and seemingly simply mixing method, biscuits are a challenge for many cooks. For fluffy biscuits there are a few key points to keep in mind: The butter must be well chilled and the dough only minimally handled. Although we recommend using a food processor to cut the butter into the flour, you can also do so by hand using a box grater and two butter knives.

USING A FOOD PROCESSOR:
Cut the chilled butter into ¼-inch cubes and with a spatula add the butter cubes to the food processor with the dry ingredients and pulse until the butter is evenly mixed into the dry ingredients.

BY HAND:
1. If you don't have a food processor, do not cut the butter into cubes. Instead place the butter into the freezer until frozen. Meanwhile, combine the dry ingredients in a bowl. Rub the frozen butter against the large holes of a box grater over the bowl with the dry ingredients.

2. With two butter knives, work the grated butter into the dry ingredients. By not using your fingertips, you reduce the chance that the butter will melt.

FLUFFY BUTTERMILK BISCUITS

AT FIRST, MAKING OVER BISCUITS TO BE LIGHTER seemed like an impossible task. Most biscuits, by their very nature, are full of fat; it's an essential component. Partially responsible for giving biscuits their rise, fat—whether it is butter, shortening, or lard—is wholly accountable for giving them a tender, tasty crumb.

Knowing that there are a number of biscuit styles out there, we hit the books, intending to find a leaner type of biscuit, and also to see if there were any decent low-fat recipes. After collecting a thick folder of research, we prepared a dozen or so recipes for our initial testing. Right off the bat, we ruled out "roll and cut" biscuits, as they require an abundance of fat (up to 10 tablespoons) in order to keep the crumb tender and flaky. And cream biscuits were out of the question as well, based on the fact that their success hinges on a large amount (often 1½ cups) of heavy cream.

We thought that buttermilk biscuits might be a leaner style of biscuit because buttermilk is a low-calorie, low-fat ingredient. The buttermilk biscuit recipes we came across, however, called for a stick of butter—an amount of fat that was way out of the ballpark for a lower fat biscuit. But these biscuits were made by the drop method, rather than the roll and cut method, which meant that they didn't necessarily need to contain a lot fat. Spurred on by the promise of a buttermilk drop biscuit, we became particularly intrigued by one recipe that used an unusual amount of buttermilk: twice as much as other drop-biscuit recipes called for. The dough turns out wet and is hand-shaped into round balls that are coated with flour and dropped into a cake pan. Once all of the biscuits have been fitted snugly in the pan, they are brushed with a bit of butter and into the oven they go.

We tried this recipe and the end result was a different-looking biscuit, one that looked like a rustic roll with a crisp, golden brown top that sat high above an extra-fluffy, moist, and tender crumb. Tasters approved of its rich and tangy flavor. The recipe contained 6 tablespoons of butter, which was less (but not much less) fat than a regular biscuit, which typically contains 8 tablespoons. We then focused on reducing the fat in this unconventional biscuit. We began by baking biscuits made with 5, 4, and 3 tablespoons of butter, and we decided to skip brushing butter over the tops of the biscuits. Tasters found that biscuits made with 3 tablespoons of butter were tougher, less fluffy, and blander than those made with 4 and 5 tablespoons of butter. And even though the biscuits made with 5 tablespoons of butter were flavorful, 4 tablespoons of butter proved to be the best and most balanced amount of fat. The biscuits made with this small amount turned out fluffy and tender, and had a nice, rich flavor. To incorporate the fat, we used the traditional method of cutting the butter into the flour before adding the liquid. You can do this with a food processor or by using a box grater and 2 butter knives (see page 310).

As for the liquid, we stuck with buttermilk, which was key. We found that the generous amount of buttermilk in our recipe ensured a moist biscuit that had a rich character and great tangy flavor—much more so than other dairy ingredients we tested. Also, biscuits made with other types of dairy did not have the great structure and rise of those made with buttermilk. After we stirred the buttermilk into the fat-flour mixture, the dough appeared airy, with a texture akin to that of whipped cottage cheese. The resulting biscuits were fluffy and moist, but they were still not quite as high as we wanted them to be.

To this point we had been using the traditional mix of baking soda and baking powder to give our biscuits lift; however, we suspected our amounts were off. We started our testing with a common ratio: ⅛ teaspoon baking soda to 1½ teaspoons baking powder. We then methodically increased the amount of one of the leaveners, holding the other steady. We ended up with hefty amounts of both baking soda (½ teaspoon) and baking powder (1 tablespoon), but we knew that these chemical leaveners were not solely responsible for getting good lift. Steam is also responsible for lift; as moisture in the dough converts to steam in the oven, it causes the biscuits to swell. We found that a very hot oven (500 degrees) was necessary for producing a good amount of rise. However, we only kept the temperature this high for the first five minutes of baking, after which we reduced the oven temperature to avoid burning the tops. Finally, our biscuits had the lift we were after—they rose over the top of the cake pan, some measuring more than 2 inches high!

Most biscuits are best hot from the oven, but ours were a bit gluey and damp in the middle. We learned that waiting a few minutes—as hard as that was—solved the problem by allowing some of the steam to escape from these high-moisture biscuits. With the waiting game over, we tucked into our low-fat buttermilk biscuits. We savored our accomplishment, proud of our success in creating a worthy low-fat biscuit.

SHAPING THE BISCUITS

1. Using a greased ¼-cup measuring cup, scoop 12 level portions of the dough onto a floured baking sheet. Lightly dust the top of each biscuit with flour.

2. With floured hands, gently pick up each piece of dough, coating the outside with flour, shaping it into a ball, and shaking off excess flour.

3. Place 9 biscuits snugly around the perimeter of a greased cake pan, then arrange the last 3 in the center.

Fluffy Buttermilk Biscuits

MAKES 12 BISCUITS

For the highest rise, use a double-acting baking powder, such as Calumet, Clabber Girl, or Davis. Store leftover biscuits in a zipper-lock bag. Reheat by placing them on a baking sheet in a 475-degree oven for 5 to 7 minutes.

	Vegetable oil spray
3	cups (15 ounces) unbleached all-purpose flour
1	tablespoon baking powder
1	tablespoon sugar
1	teaspoon salt
1/2	teaspoon baking soda
4	tablespoons (1/2 stick) cold unsalted butter, cut into 1/4-inch cubes
1 1/2	cups cold buttermilk

1. Adjust an oven rack to the middle position and heat the oven to 500 degrees. Spray a 9-inch round cake pan with the vegetable oil spray. Generously spray the inside and outside of a 1/4-cup dry measure with the same spray; set aside. Spread 1 cup of the flour out onto a rimmed baking sheet; set aside.

2. Process the remaining 2 cups of flour, baking powder, sugar, salt, and baking soda in a food processor to combine, about six 1-second pulses. Scatter the butter cubes evenly over the dry ingredients and pulse until the mixture resembles pebbly, coarse cornmeal, eight to ten 1-second pulses. Transfer the mixture to a medium bowl. Add the buttermilk and stir with a rubber spatula until just incorporated (the dough will be very wet and slightly lumpy).

3. Working quickly, use the prepared 1/4-cup measure to scoop a level amount of dough and drop it from the measuring cup into the flour on the baking sheet (if the dough sticks to the cup, use a small spoon to pull it free). Repeat with the remaining dough, forming 12 evenly sized mounds. Following the illustrations on page 311, dust the tops of each piece of dough with flour from the baking sheet. With floured hands, gently pick up a piece of dough and coat it with flour; gently shape the dough into a rough ball, shake off the excess flour, and place it in the prepared cake pan. Repeat with the remaining dough, arranging 9 rounds around the perimeter of the cake pan and 3 in the center.

4. Bake the biscuits for 5 minutes, then reduce the oven temperature to 450 degrees and continue to bake until the biscuits are a deep golden brown, about 15 minutes longer. Cool the biscuits in the pan for 2 minutes, then flip them out onto a clean kitchen towel. Turn the biscuits right-side up, break them apart, and cool for 5 more minutes before serving.

PER BISCUIT: Cal 150; Fat 4 g; Sat fat 3 g; Chol 10 g; Carb 23 g; Protein 4 g; Fiber 1 g; Sodium 370 mg

TESTING BAKING POWDER FOR FRESHNESS

Baking powder will lose its leavening ability with time. We suggest writing the date the can was opened on a piece of tape affixed to the can. After 6 months, the baking powder should be tested to see if it's still good. Mix 2 teaspoons baking powder with 1 cup hot tap water. If there's an immediate reaction of fizzing and foaming (right), the baking powder is fine. If the reaction is delayed or weak (left), throw the baking powder away and buy a fresh can. A can of baking powder that has been open for a year or more should be replaced.

TEST KITCHEN MAKEOVER

CRUMB COFFEECAKE

IN TRADITIONAL RECIPES FOR CRUMB coffeecake—in all its full-fat glory—the brown sugar topping perfectly complements the rich, buttery yellow cake. And although the cake is lightly flavored with cinnamon and vanilla, it gets most of its appeal from the two main ingredients: butter and sugar. Or, fat and calories. Maybe that's why it's so hard to say no to seconds. "No," however, would be easier to say knowing that a modest serving of a traditional crumb coffeecake contains nearly 320 calories and 14 grams of fat—a bit too rich for our morning breakfast table. In creating a lower fat crumb coffeecake we had our work cut out for us.

Our initial research on low-fat coffeecakes turned up a number of recipes that simply did not work. Most were bland, dry, and tough, while a few others were overly spiced, wet, and gummy. It was frustrating that there seemed to be no middle ground. We decided to really get serious in the test kitchen and develop a lower fat crumb coffeecake that had all the great flavor of the original without all the fat and calories.

We started our tests by removing most of the fat from a basic full-fat crumb coffeecake recipe. Most recipes call for 10 tablespoons of butter and our intent was to see how low we could go without compromising taste and texture. Our tasting panel sampled three cakes, one made with 2 tablespoons of butter, one with 3 tablespoons, and one with 4 tablespoons. Tasters found that the cake made with 2 tablespoons was a tad on the tough side and had minimal butter flavor; however, the cakes made with 3 and 4 tablespoons both did the job. They had great butter flavor and a decently delicate crumb. The difference between the two cakes was slight and we agreed that in an effort to save on fat and calories we would make our recipe with only 3 tablespoons of butter. This meant that with 1 tablespoon of butter in the topping, our coffeecake only called for 4 tablespoons of butter total.

Having only reduced the amount of butter, this cake was good but it was not perfect. Tasters complained that the cake was not as delicate as they wanted it to be. Stepping back, we took a good look at the mixing method and the type of flour we were using. While developing our quick breads, we had figured out that these two things have a profound effect on a recipe's outcome. Using what we learned in our quick breads and muffins, we

made a round of coffeecakes, mixing them with the creaming method and replacing a portion of the all-purpose flour with cake flour. By whipping the sugar and butter together until airy (creaming) and using a little bit of cake flour—a low-protein flour which bakes up more tender than all-purpose—we were successful at fulfilling tasters' requests for a more delicate crumb.

With the texture problem solved, we turned to the next issue: our cake was a little too sweet. Thus far our recipe called for granulated sugar in the cake and a mix of granulated and brown sugar in the topping. Our first step was to reduce the total amount of crumb topping, which worked well. But when we tried to reduce the sugar in the cake, we weren't so lucky. Tasters found that the

MAKEOVER AT A GLANCE

–Classic–
Crumb Coffeecake
(per serving)

Calories: 320	Cholesterol: 45 mg
Fat: 14 g	Saturated Fat: 7 g

–Light–
Crumb Coffeecake
(per serving)

Calories: 210	Cholesterol: 45 mg
Fat: 5 g	Saturated Fat: 3 g

How We Did It

- Lowered the amount of butter to only 4 tablespoons
- Creamed butter and sugar to achieve a lighter, airy texture
- Substituted cake flour for part of the all-purpose flour to create a more delicate crumb
- Used low-fat yogurt to add moisture, richness, and a subtle, complex tang
- Used brown sugar in the cake to add moisture to the crumb

cake was now horribly dry. The simple solution—an idea borrowed from the topping recipe—was to use a combination of brown and granulated sugars. Brown sugar added a fair amount of moisture, which was welcome, and in the end, our cake was no longer overly sweet because we were able to trim ½ cup of sugar. Tasters, however, still complained that the cake was a bit on the dry side. We suspected the culprit might be the type of dairy we were using, which to this point had been whole milk.

We tried the usual selection of low-fat dairy: buttermilk, low-fat sour cream, and low-fat yogurt. All produced lackluster results, with the exception of the low-fat yogurt, which added the extra moisture we were after as well as a pleasant richness and subtle tang. To round out the flavor of the yogurt we added a bit of vanilla to the batter. The vanilla worked double duty, complementing the modest amount of ground cinnamon in the topping (1 teaspoon), as well as adding a great depth of background flavor to the cake.

Finally, we found that tasters preferred the cake after it had cooled completely. When still warm, the cake had a cottony character, which gave the perception that it was dry. We discovered that cooling the cake completely helped to evenly distribute moisture, so that the texture had a balanced density and rich crumb. And with only 200 calories and 5 grams of fat per serving, our cake had an appeal that came from more than just a glut of butter and sugar.

Crumb Coffeecake

MAKES 12 SERVINGS

If you don't have nonstick baking spray with flour, butter the pan and dust with flour.

	Nonstick baking spray with flour
1½	cups (7½ ounces) unbleached all-purpose flour
½	cup (2 ounces) cake flour
¾	cup packed (5¼ ounces) light brown sugar
½	teaspoon salt
½	teaspoon baking powder
¼	teaspoon baking soda
1	teaspoon ground cinnamon
3	tablespoons unsalted butter, softened, plus 1 tablespoon melted and cooled
½	cup granulated sugar
2	large eggs
1	teaspoon vanilla extract
¾	cup plain low-fat yogurt

1. Adjust an oven rack to the middle position and heat the oven to 350 degrees. Spray an 8-inch-square baking pan with the nonstick baking spray. Whisk the all-purpose flour, cake flour, ½ cup of the brown sugar, salt, baking powder, and baking soda together in a medium bowl. Remove ¼ cup of the flour mixture and mix it with the remaining ¼ cup of brown sugar and the cinnamon in a small bowl; set aside.

2. Beat the 3 tablespoons of softened butter and the granulated sugar together with an electric mixer on medium-high speed until light and fluffy, 3 to 5 minutes, scraping down the sides of the bowl with a rubber spatula as needed. Add the eggs, one at a time, beating well after each addition.

3. Reduce the mixer speed to low. Beat in one-third of the flour mixture until just incorporated, followed by the vanilla and one-third of the yogurt, scraping down the bowl as needed. Repeat this process twice more, alternating between the remaining flour mixture and yogurt until the ingredients are just incorporated. Do not overmix.

4. Scrape the cake batter into the prepared baking pan. Stir the 1 tablespoon melted butter into the reserved cinnamon mixture and toss gently with a fork until the butter is evenly distributed, creating some large pea-sized crumbs. Sprinkle the crumb mixture evenly over the batter.

5. Bake until the crumb topping is golden brown and a toothpick inserted in the center of the cake comes out with a few crumbs attached, 35 to 40 minutes, rotating the pan halfway through baking. Transfer the baking pan to a wire rack and let the cake cool completely before cutting into squares.

PER SERVING: Cal 210; Fat 5 g; Sat fat 3 g; Chol 45 mg; Carb 38 g; Protein 4 g; Fiber 1 g; Sodium 150 mg

QUICK CINNAMON ROLLS

TRUTHFULLY, WE FIND IT NEAR IMPOSSIBLE TO pass up good cinnamon rolls. Their hypnotic brown-sugar swirl, thinly draped with a creamy-sweet glaze, radiates a soft cinnamon scent too hard to resist. It's no surprise that cinnamon rolls are quick to please as well as quick to tip the scales.

The roll is tender and fluffy, the filling is sweet and spicy, and the glaze is addictive, encouraging even the well-bred to lick the gooey remnants from their fingers. But with each roll bearing 11 grams of fat and 380 calories, we thought we might have to curb our impulses. Rather than give

them up entirely, we decided it would be better to make over the traditional cinnamon roll recipe.

We didn't want a yeasted roll—yeasted breads are great, but for our purposes we wanted a quick-bread type of roll that could be made quickly and easily. Our first step, logically, was to round up some decent low-fat cinnamon roll recipes. The recipes ranged in technique from replacing fat with jarred baby food to simply using canned biscuit dough. These low-fat versions were pretty grim, yielding rolls that were either cloying and dense or dry and bland.

We decided, then, to start with a traditional quick bread cinnamon roll and see if we could cut the fat from this basic recipe. Typically the dough is made using a biscuit method, whereby the fat is cut into the dry ingredients and then the liquid portion is stirred in to form the dough. The dough is rolled out to a rectangle, topped with the filling, rolled up, sliced, and baked. A typical recipe we found called for a couple cups of flour, a cup or

MAKING CINNAMON ROLLS

1. Pat the dough into a 12 by 9-inch rectangle and brush it with melted butter. Sprinkle the filling evenly over the dough, leaving a ½-inch border. Press the filling firmly into the dough.

2. Using a bench scraper or metal spatula, loosen the dough from the work surface. Starting at a long side, roll the dough, pressing lightly, to form a tight log. Pinch the seam to seal.

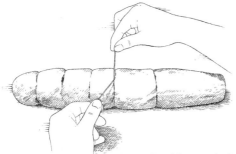

3. Roll the log seam-side down and, using dental floss, cut the formed roll into 3 even segments. Then cut each segment into 3 rolls, for a total of 9.

4. With your hand, slightly flatten each piece of dough to seal the open edges and keep the filling in place.

so of milk, baking powder, baking soda, a hefty amount of sugar, and a stick of butter. Undeterred by all the sugar and butter, we were confident that we could reduce these amounts without compromising the cinnamon rolls' allure.

Our first step was to eliminate some of the butter in the recipe. The dough itself only called for 2 tablespoons of butter, a surprisingly low amount. The rest of the butter was used to grease the pan, bind the sugary filling, and brush the dough—6 extra tablespoons of butter altogether—and we figured that at least some of this butter might be unnecessary. Our hunch was right, and we discovered that in addition to the 2 tablespoons of butter in the dough, we only needed 1 extra tablespoon of butter in the remainder of the recipe. We used this tablespoon to brush the dough before adding the sugar filling. The butter was essential for flavoring the interior of the rolls, as well as keeping them moist.

We found that we could use nonstick baking spray in place of the butter for greasing the pan. In addition, we discovered that the filling didn't really need extra butter to help with binding, as the moisture in brown sugar actually helped keep the filling intact. Also, we figured that we didn't need to brush the tops of the rolls with so much butter, because they would eventually be covered with a creamy glaze. Tasters agreed that the extra brushing of butter was not worth the fat and calories because the glaze obscured its richness.

When it comes to the liquid element of the roll dough, many recipes call for heavy cream. Obviously, this was not an option for us, due to cream's significant amount of fat and calories. We looked to other dairy products to make the dough more tender and light. We thought to test whole or skim milk in place of heavy cream, but whole milk made the rolls too heavy, and skim milk made them tough and bland. We increased the amount of baking powder to achieve lightness but ended up with metallic-tasting rolls. We then tested buttermilk—a common ingredient in biscuit dough—and had some success. We also added ½ teaspoon of baking soda to balance the acidity of the buttermilk. Baking soda reacts with the acid in buttermilk to produce carbon dioxide

gas, which causes lift. The acid in the buttermilk gave the buns a more complex flavor and tenderized the gluten in the dough, making the interior airy and light.

The next step was to determine the best method for incorporating the ingredients. First we tried the classic mixing method of cutting cold butter into dry ingredients. Unfortunately, this method turned out cinnamon rolls that were dense, flaky, and craggy rather than tender, light, and fluffy. We eventually realized that combining the ingredients was as simple as measuring the dry and wet ingredients (the butter is melted and mixed in with the buttermilk) separately and stirring the wet into the dry until a rough ball of dough formed. Next, we looked to the best way to assemble our cinnamon rolls.

Whereas most recipes instruct bakers to roll out the dough, we found it easier to pat the dough into a rough-shaped rectangle, thus making the recipe even simpler. For the cinnamon-sugar filling we decided on a union of brown sugar, granulated sugar, cinnamon, cloves, and salt. Before sprinkling the filling on the dough, we brushed the dough with that extra 1 tablespoon of melted butter we had decided on. The butter added great flavor and moisture, as well as helped the filling cling to the dough better. In the end, tasters felt that there was too much filling, and that the rolls were overly sweet. We corrected this by removing ⅓ cup of the sugar from the filling. We agreed that the new amount of filling was just right, and that we would save a bit on calories from the omission.

Next we addressed the look of our rolls. Instead of rising to the occasion in the oven, they were slouching in their seats. We reviewed some of the recipes we had researched for this style of cinnamon roll to see if we might find the source of the problem there. Sure enough, one of the recipes stated that if the dough wasn't kneaded before being shaped, it didn't rise nicely in the oven. We made two batches of dough, kneading one and not the other, and were surprised to find that just a quick 30-second knead solved the problem. Contrary to what one might think, the short knead didn't toughen the rolls; it just provided the dough with enough strength to take in a big breath and hold it.

To finish the rolls, we tried a very simple glaze using only confectioners' sugar and water, but tasters found it to be pasty and grainy; they voiced their preference for a creamy glaze. After a few trials, we found a way to sufficiently mask the graininess and pasty flavor by combining buttermilk and cream cheese, then sifting the confectioners' sugar over the mixture. (If the sugar is not sifted, the glaze will be lumpy.) Naturally we substituted light cream cheese for regular in order to cut some calories and fat. Tasters liked the light cream cheese and praised it for helping to make our glaze smooth, thick, and pleasantly tangy.

As for what to bake the rolls in, we chose an 8-inch-square baking pan. With its straight sides and square shape, a baking dish was perfect for our rolls. They were nestled together, three across and three down—anything larger caused the sides to dry out and become too crusty. We started baking at 425 degrees and got lucky the first time out. The rolls baked in about 25 minutes, rose and browned nicely, and were cooked all the way through. However, we still had one last minute refinement to make.

Some complained that the top crust on the rolls was a bit on the tough side—possibly an effect from omitting so much of the brushed butter from the recipe. Traditionally, the tops of the rolls are brushed with a generous amount of butter before going into the oven. The butter acts to keep the tops of the rolls tender during baking. Not wanting to add more fat and calories to our recipe, we took the suggestion of one taster who recommended we cover the baking pan with aluminum foil for the first half of baking. Covering the pan seemed like an odd technique; however, it worked beautifully to keep the crusty crunch on our rolls to a minimum. The cover promotes steam, keeping the rolls soft for the first half of baking, after which the foil is removed and the rolls are allowed to gently brown.

Our low-fat cinnamon rolls now had all of the appeal of their seductive full-fat cousins. And because they had only 4.5 grams of fat and 280 calories per roll, we enjoy them more often.

MAKEOVER AT A GLANCE

–Classic–
Quick Cinnamon Rolls with Buttermilk Icing
(per roll)

Calories: 380	Cholesterol: 35 mg
Fat: 11 g	Saturated Fat: 8 g

–Light–
Quick Cinnamon Rolls with Buttermilk Icing
(per roll)

Calories: 280	Cholesterol: 15 mg
Fat: 4.5 g	Saturated Fat: 3.5 g

How We Did It

- Used nonstick cooking spray instead of butter to grease the pan
- Removed ⅓ cup of sugar from the filling
- Left unnecessary butter out of the filling mix
- Omitted brushing the top of the rolls with extra butter
- Covered the rolls with foil for the first half of baking to ensure a tender top crust
- Used light cream cheese in the glaze

Quick Cinnamon Rolls with Buttermilk Icing

MAKES 9 ROLLS

Make sure that you knead the dough for a full 30 seconds here. We were surprised to find that kneading made the dough not only easier to work with, but it also gave the finished rolls a better rise and a great texture. Also, don't be afraid to use a little extra flour on the counter when shaping the buns, if the dough seems a little sticky. The rolls are best eaten as soon as they are iced, but they hold up well at room temperature for up to 2 hours.

Vegetable oil spray

FILLING

⅓ cup packed (2 ⅓ ounces) dark brown sugar

⅓ cup (2 ⅓ ounces) granulated sugar

2 teaspoons ground cinnamon

⅛ teaspoon ground cloves

⅛ teaspoon salt

DOUGH

2 ½ cups (12 ½ ounces) unbleached all-purpose flour, plus more for dusting the work surface

2 tablespoons granulated sugar

1 ¼ teaspoons baking powder

½ teaspoon baking soda

½ teaspoon salt

1 ¼ cups buttermilk

3 tablespoons unsalted butter, melted and cooled

ICING

2 tablespoons light cream cheese, softened

2 tablespoons buttermilk

¾ cup (3 ounces) confectioners' sugar

1. Adjust an oven rack to the upper-middle position and heat the oven to 425 degrees. Spray an 8-inch-square baking pan and a wire rack with the vegetable oil spray; set aside.

2. FOR THE FILLING: Mix all the ingredients together; set aside.

3. FOR THE DOUGH: Whisk the flour, granulated sugar, baking powder, baking soda, and salt together in a large bowl. In a separate bowl, whisk the buttermilk and 2 tablespoons of the melted butter together. Stir the buttermilk mixture into the flour mixture with a wooden spoon until the liquid is absorbed (the dough will look very shaggy), about 30 seconds. Transfer the dough to a floured work surface and knead until just smooth and no longer shaggy, about 30 seconds.

4. Pat the dough with your hands into a 12 by 9-inch rectangle. Brush the dough with the remaining tablespoon of melted butter. Sprinkle evenly with the filling, leaving a ½-inch border of plain dough around the edges. Following the illustrations on page 315, press the filling firmly into the dough. Using a bench scraper or metal spatula, loosen the dough from the work surface. Starting at the long side, roll the dough, pressing lightly, to form a tight log. Pinch the seam to seal. Roll the log seam-side down and cut it evenly into 9 pieces with dental floss. With your hand, slightly flatten each piece of dough to seal the open edges and keep the filling in place.

5. Arrange the rolls in the prepared baking dish (3 rows of 3 rolls). Cover the baking dish with foil and bake for about 12 minutes. Remove the foil and bake until the edges of the rolls are golden brown, 12 to 14 minutes longer.

6. Use an offset metal spatula to loosen the rolls from the pan. Wearing oven mitts, place a large plate over the pan and invert the rolls onto the plate. Place a greased wire rack over the plate and flip the rolls onto the rack. Let the rolls cool for 5 minutes before icing.

7. To ICE THE ROLLS: While the rolls are cooling, line a rimmed baking sheet with parchment paper (for easy cleanup). Set the rack of cooling rolls over the baking sheet. Whisk the cream cheese and buttermilk together in a large nonreactive bowl until thick and smooth (the mixture will look like cottage cheese at first). Sift the confectioners' sugar over the mixture; whisk until a smooth glaze forms, about 30 seconds. Spoon the glaze evenly over the rolls.

PER ROLL: Cal 280; Fat 4.5 g; Sat fat 3.5 g; Chol 15 mg; Carb 55 g; Protein 6 g; Fiber 1 g; Sodium 340 mg

11

DESSERTS

AT SOME POINT IN OUR LIVES, MOST OF US have tried to cut back on dessert for one reason or another—if not for a diet, perhaps just for better health. Even if you're not watching your weight, it would be tough to argue that the 43 grams of fat in a typical serving of New York–style cheesecake is good for anyone. Sure you can always have an apple, pear, or bowl of mixed berries, but on occasion, a proper dessert—cobbler, cake, cookie, and the like—just can't be beat. In which case, low-fat desserts seem like a good alternative. But the reality is that most of them are utterly disappointing: bland, dry cookies and spongy, artificial-tasting cakes are the norm. Most recipes attempt to replace the fat and calories with bizarre ingredients that have no place in a dessert (and perhaps not in anything else). Baby food and applesauce may be fine for people at certain stages of life, but they do not belong in an oatmeal cookie. So we wondered: Could we really develop a recipe for a low-fat cheesecake that had the richness and texture of a classic New York deli–style cheesecake? Would it be possible to make a reduced fat chocolate chip cookie that even kids would love? We were skeptical, but one thing we knew for sure: We weren't willing to compromise. If we couldn't create a low-fat alternative as satisfying as its full-fat counterpart, it wouldn't make our list.

We cautiously headed into the kitchen for some serious testing. Dessert is a particularly difficult category to lighten. While it might work fine to use less of an ingredient or make a substitution elsewhere, the same cannot always be said of baked goods, where altering the ingredients may change the entire structure of the resulting product. Harder still, some desserts—such as sugar cookies or the cream cheese frosting on a carrot cake—contain so few ingredients that there simply isn't much to alter. Many light cookbooks skirt these challenges by simply keeping the ingredients the same and then reducing the portions to an absurdly tiny size. While moderate portion size is an essential component of a healthy diet (and one we do incorporate into this chapter), a serving still has to satisfy. We'd rather have no cookie than one so small it disappears in one bite.

Knowing what we didn't want—oddball ingredients and minuscule portions—we set out to find other ways to achieve our goal of developing recipes for low-fat desserts that taste just as good as the real thing. Or at least good enough that we could serve them to company or children without raising any eyebrows. What we found surprised us. For the most part it wasn't necessary to make substitutions for high-fat ingredients. We were surprised, for example, to discover that in most cases we could simply reduce the amount of butter in a recipe without replacing it with another ingredient. True, we only saved a few calories and fat grams overall. But that's an important savings when it comes to baked goods such as cookies, since most people usually eat a handful (or more). We also found that brown sugar can often be used instead of granulated sugar to compensate for any moisture loss—it's a key ingredient in our Oatmeal Cookies (page 325) and Peanut Butter Cookies (page 327). To emphasize chocolate flavor in recipes like our Chocolate Bundt Cake (page 341)—without adding loads of fat—we replaced some of the chocolate with cocoa and added a little espresso powder.

That is not to say we had success lightening every recipe we tried. Apple crisp was just insufficiently, well, crispy. Yellow layer cake quickly fell by the wayside, as did pudding, and we struggled for weeks to create a low-fat pie dough before we finally gave up. These were a few cases where butter was such an essential ingredient (and in such enormous quantities) that we could not create a satisfactory low-fat alternative. Rather than compromise our high standards for taste and texture, we simply struck them from the list.

In this chapter you'll also find a handful of naturally low-fat recipes such as Angel Food Cake (page 347) and Cider-Baked Apples with Dried Cranberries (page 353). Our goal with these recipes was to give them a serious flavor boost by creating multiple variations on the standard.

In the end, our hard work paid off. How do we know? In a side-by-side comparison of our regular cheesecake and chocolate Bundt cake with our new reduced-fat versions, the test kitchen staff (including several senior editors) were hard pressed to tell the difference, and many of them preferred the low-fat versions. We think you'll be pleased with the results of our work, too. We can honestly say that there's no comparison between the recipes in this chapter and those found in a typical "light" cookbook.

TEST KITCHEN MAKEOVER

CHOCOLATE CHIP COOKIES

RICH AND BUTTERY, WITH SOFT, TENDER centers and crisp edges, chocolate chip cookies are the standard by which all cookies are judged. Given the popularity of chocolate chip cookies in America, and considering how much fat and calories they contain, it's no wonder there are hundreds of light recipes. However, most of these recipes miss the mark entirely, yielding cookies that are cakey, artificial tasting, and completely lacking in chocolate flavor. We set out to develop a recipe for light chocolate chip cookies that had the same chocolatey taste and buttery crispness of the full-fat version.

Before we attempted to develop a recipe for lower fat chocolate chip cookies, we found it helpful to try a handful of published recipes. We found all manner of fat-reducing tricks in these recipes, from whipping egg whites and grinding chocolate chips to using light cream cheese and applesauce, but none produced a cookie that met our criteria. Discouraged by these cumbersome techniques and unorthodox ingredients, we forged ahead with our own specific tests.

To start, we noticed that many low-fat cookie recipes simply made the cookies smaller, rather than reducing the fat. This isn't so off the mark—your typical cookie today can be gargantuan in size (much like muffins and other baked goods have become). The problem with most of the low-fat recipes we tried is that the size has been reduced so much, you couldn't possibly be satisfied by a serving (see page 323). We wanted a

cookie that would not only satisfy but also taste good—with less fat and fewer calories.

Testing cookies made with varying amounts of dough, from a skimpy 1 teaspoon to a generous 3 tablespoons, we found that 1 tablespoon made a perfect 2½-inch diameter cookie—we'd found our middle ground in the size department. Given that we wanted our recipe to yield 2 dozen cookies, we scaled back our working recipe, starting with 1¼ cups flour, 1 cup chocolate chips, 1 cup sugar, 8 tablespoons butter, and one egg.

A far tougher challenge than making the chocolate chip cookies smaller was finding a way to reduce the fat—namely the chocolate chips, butter, and egg. Starting with the chocolate chips, we looked for a way to take out some of the chips while allowing them to maintain their presence in the cookie. We first tried grinding up the chocolate chips. This did allow a smaller amount of chocolate to go further, but tasters did not like such small pieces and missed the pockets of chocolate that chips create. We also tried using mini chocolate chips, thinking we could use less of them, but tasters thought they looked silly and, again, didn't create those chocolatey pockets. Returning to regular chips, we then made batches of cookies with ¼, ½, and ¾ cups of chips and compared them to an original batch made with 1 cup. The cookies made with just ¼ cup of chips were dismal and didn't have much chocolate flavor. Obviously the more chips in the batter the better the cookie; however, tasters thought that a generous ½ cup of chips provided a good amount of flavor and chocolate chip presence while still reducing the fat content significantly. The one problem with using only ½ cup of chips, however, was that the chips often got lost in the dough and some of the cookies wound up looking naked or "chip-less." Our solution was to set some of the chips aside and then sprinkle two or three over each cookie before we baked them. These cookies tasted great and had the emblematic melted chips visible right on top.

With the amount of fat from the chips tamed, we could turn our focus to reducing some of the fat from the butter. In our initial testing we had tried some low-fat cookies made with fruit purees (apple, prune, and banana); however, these cookies came out more like muffins than cookies. They were cakey, dry, and had unwelcome fruity flavors. We also tried replace the butter with ingredients like low-fat sour cream, light cream cheese, light butter, and vegetable oil, but these cookies had odd textures and artificial flavors. Since it was obvious that there would be no acceptable substitute for the butter, we set out to determine the smallest amount of butter we could get away with. Our working recipe called for 8 tablespoons of butter, and we made batch after batch, each with one less tablespoon. The magic number turned out to be 4 tablespoons—any less and the cookies turned out too dry and cakey. Just 4 tablespoons of butter made a surprisingly good cookie with a proper spread and just enough richness, while cutting 52 more grams of fat from the dough.

With the fat from the chocolate and butter curbed, we looked at the last fat-contributing ingredient—the egg. We tried cookies with just egg whites, but they had a cakey texture and an unmistakable "diet" cookie flavor. Hoping to make our cookies less cakey, we tried making them with just one yolk. These had a better flavor, but without the protein-laden egg white, the cookies lacked structure. We determined that one whole egg was our best option and provided the proper structure and flavor.

We now directed our attention to the sugar. After several tests, we found that 1 cup of sugar was necessary to provide the right amount of sweetness and crisp texture. Many chocolate chip cookie recipes use a mix of granulated and light or dark brown sugar and we tried using them each on their own, or in combination with one another in several different batches of cookies. Cookies made with granulated sugar alone looked seriously pale and were a bit drier than the cookies made with either dark or light brown sugar. Dark brown sugar tasted good, but made the cookies look much too dark and taste too cloying. In the end, tasters preferred the appearance, flavor, and moist texture of the cookies made with all light brown sugar.

Up until now, we had been creaming the butter and sugar together with an electric mixer (a common cookie mixing method), but the cookies were cakier than we liked. With a full-fat cookie, this method is essential (otherwise the cookies would be tough), but with so little butter, the method whipped too much air into the cookies. Our other option was to melt the butter and simply mix the ingredients together in a large bowl by hand. These cookies were the best yet. They had a great chewy interior texture with crisp edges.

Our final hurdle was to determine the best baking method for the cookies. A 350-degree oven proved best since the modest heat allowed the cookies to spread properly. More important, we found that it was absolutely necessary to bake the

MAKEOVER AT A GLANCE

–Classic–
Chocolate Chip Cookies
(per cookie)

Calories: 110	Cholesterol: 15 mg
Fat: 6 g	Saturated Fat: 3.5 g

–Light–
Chocolate Chip Cookies
(per cookie)

Calories: 100	Cholesterol: 15 mg
Fat: 3.5 g	Saturated Fat: 2 g

How We Did It

- Lowered the amount of chocolate chips from 1 cup to ½ cup, reserving some of the chips to sprinkle over the top of the cookies before baking for visual appeal
- Reduced the amount of butter from 8 to 4 tablespoons
- Melted the butter and mixed the dough by hand for a tender cookie
- Used all light brown sugar to maintain moistness
- Baked the cookies one tray at a time to ensure they spread and browned correctly

cookies one tray at a time. This ensured that the cookies would receive even heat, caramelize properly, and spread nicely. (If we baked two trays of cookies at once, those on the top rack did not spread evenly even if they were rotated while baking.) At last we had a low-fat cookie worth eating.

Chocolate Chip Cookies

MAKES 24 COOKIES

In order for the cookies to spread and brown properly, it is important to bake them one tray at a time. Because the size of chocolate chips varies slightly between brands, you should weigh them for the most accurate measurement. Note that the chips are added in two steps. The cookies are best eaten within 2 days of baking because they tend to dry out more quickly than full-fat cookies. Be sure to store them in an airtight container.

1 ¼   cups (6 ¼ ounces) unbleached all-purpose flour
 ¼   teaspoon baking soda
 ¼   teaspoon salt
 4   tablespoons (½ stick) unsalted butter, melted and cooled
 1   large egg
 2   teaspoons vanilla extract
 1   cup packed (7 ounces) light brown sugar
 4   ounces semisweet chocolate chips (a generous ½ cup)

1. Adjust an oven rack to the middle position and heat the oven to 350 degrees. Line 2 baking sheets with parchment paper.

2. Whisk the flour, baking soda, and salt together in a medium bowl; set aside. In a large bowl, whisk the butter, egg, and vanilla together. Stir in the brown sugar until smooth, smearing any remaining clumps of sugar against the side of the bowl with a rubber spatula. Stir in the flour mixture and 3 ounces (a generous ⅓ cup) of the chocolate chips until thoroughly combined.

3. Working with a level tablespoon of dough each time, roll the dough into 1-inch balls. (If the dough is too soft to roll, refrigerate it until firm.) Place the balls on the prepared baking sheets, spacing them about 2½ inches apart (you will fit 12

Does Size Matter?

One of the keys to healthy eating is controlling the portion size of the food you eat. And while this is sound advice, when it comes to cookies a reduced portion can leave one feeling unsatisfied. As we developed our light cookie recipes we searched for the perfect balance—a cookie that was low in fat and calories yet big enough to satisfy.

TOO BIG

Some traditional full-fat cookies use 3 or sometimes 4 tablespoons of dough to make one cookie. For those counting, that's about 280 calories and 13 grams of fat.

TOO SMALL

Many of the light cookies recipes we tried simply took full-fat cookie dough and baked it in tiny portions—several recipes used a measly teaspoon of dough per cookie. In addition to being hopelessly small these cookies were always dry and overcooked. In our opinion they're not worth the effort.

JUST RIGHT

While we were able to reduce fat and calories in our cookies by altering the ingredients, we also found reducing the amount of dough per cookie a valuable technique. But how much dough makes a satisfying cookie that isn't ridiculously small? After a number of batches the answer was 1 tablespoon. One tablespoon of dough yielded a 2½-inch cookie that was moist and chewy. And one cookie was enough to satiate our sweet tooth.

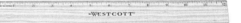

cookies on each baking sheet). Press the remaining chips into the top of the dough (2 or 3 chips per cookie).

4. Bake the cookies, one tray at a time, until the edges are light golden and the centers are just set, 11 to 13 minutes, rotating the tray halfway through baking (do not overbake). Cool the cookies on the baking sheets for 5 minutes, then serve warm, or transfer to a wire rack and cool completely. Bake the second tray while the first tray cools.

PER COOKIE: Cal 100; Fat 3.5 g; Sat fat 2 g; Chol 15 mg; Carb 16 g; Protein 1 g; Fiber 0 g; Sodium 30 mg

EQUIPMENT: Parchment Paper

How do you keep baked goods from sticking to cake pans, baking sheets, and the like without adding extra calories? Parchment paper is the answer. Simply line your baking sheet or cake pan—anything that requires being greased—with parchment paper. Cookies come away easily and, with a gentle tug, parchment will peel away from cakes. Are all brands created equal? We tested four brands—Fox Run Craftsmen (flat sheets), Beyond Gourmet (unbleached roll), Reynolds (bleached roll), and SuperParchment (a washable and reusable product). In the end, all were acceptable. Reynolds is the most widely available brand and, at 14 inches, is the widest of the lot. It's sold nationwide in 30-square-foot rolls for approximately $2.50.

OATMEAL COOKIES

IN THE COOKIE WORLD, OATMEAL COOKIES always play second fiddle to chocolate chip cookies. Perhaps due to their inclusion of oats and dried fruit in lieu of chocolate, they do have a somewhat "healthy" reputation, so we set out to develop an oatmeal cookie that had a full oat flavor and chewy moist texture—and was low-fat to boot.

In looking over myriad light oatmeal cookie recipes, we noticed that they all tried to do away with fat completely, usually by replacing it with unorthodox ingredients such as fruit purees or baby food. But most of these oatmeal cookies seemed dry and cakey to us. We too wanted to cut the fat in our cookies, but we wanted to keep the texture and flavor of a full-fat cookie. Before diving into some serious cookie testing, however, we scaled down a traditional oatmeal cookie recipe to make 2 dozen 2½-inch cookies (using just 1 tablespoon of dough per cookie). Unlike those gargantuan-sized cookies you can buy at the mall, these slightly smaller cookies are a more appropriate size when trying to eat light without being skimpy. Using this scaled down recipe as a base, we then began to tinker with the ingredients.

Looking for ways to trim the fat, we started our testing following what others have done: substitute fruit purees such as prune puree, applesauce, and mashed bananas for some of the butter. The flavor of these cookies was passable, but the texture was dry and crumbly—more like a fruit and oat muffin than an oatmeal cookie. In addition to fruit purees, we also looked at dairy substitutions, such as light cream cheese, sour cream, and light butter. Again these cookies were dry and cakey, and now they had an odd, artificial aftertaste as well. Out of curiosity, we tried using oil in place of the butter. These cookies seemed to be a little moister, but they tasted dull and lifeless. Put off by these tests, we decided that butter was clearly the best choice and set out to find a way to just use less of it. After multiple tests using varying amounts of butter, we reached the conclusion that 4 tablespoons melted butter (as opposed to 8 tablespoons creamed butter in our base recipe) provided the cookies with the proper texture and flavor.

Conventional oatmeal cookie recipes normally call for equal parts brown and granulated sugar. This usually gives the best balance of crispness to chewiness. However, it made our reduced-fat cookies taste a tad too dry. To rectify the dryness, we switched to all brown sugar because it actually helps the cookies hold onto water during the baking process. Testing the difference between light and dark brown sugar, tasters preferred the color and more intense flavor of the dark brown sugar. We tried cutting the amount of sugar back from the 1 cup used in our base recipe; however, this had a huge impact on the texture and spread of the cookie—more so than the butter. Leaving the sugar at 1 cup was necessary.

Lastly, we experimented with various amounts

Replacing the Fat in Oatmeal Cookies

Of all the varieties of light cookie recipes we unearthed, oatmeal cookies seemed to have the widest range of unconventional ingredients and techniques added in an attempt to reduce fat and calories. We tried some of these ploys and here are the results of a few botched tests.

FRUIT PUREE

Too Dry

We found fruit purees like applesauce, prune puree, and mashed bananas as a fat substitute in a number of recipes, but despite their popularity we couldn't justify their use. Oatmeal cookies made with prune puree had a "dry, muffin-like texture" and didn't spread.

EGG WHITES

No Flavor

Replacing whole eggs with egg whites is a sure way to reduce fat, but not a good choice when it comes to oatmeal cookies. Cookies baked with just egg whites had "virtually no flavor" and a "dry, cakey" crumb.

LIGHT CREAM CHEESE

Too Thin and Crisp

On your morning toast, light cream cheese might be a good alternative to butter, but in an oatmeal cookie it wasn't a good match. Light cream cheese made the cookies "too thin and crispy." It also gave the cookies an artificial aftertaste.

BUTTER

After trying a number of fat substitutes, we found that there was no beating butter. The secret was simply to use less of it. Cookies made with a reduced portion of butter were still "thick and chewy" with a "balanced oat flavor," but had a fraction of the fat of traditional cookies.

of oats and found that in order to produce a real oat flavor, we needed at least 1 cup of oats. We also found that old-fashioned rolled oats had a heartier flavor and better texture than quick oats, which were deemed slightly mealy with a wimpy flavor. A generous amount of vanilla and a dash of cinnamon did wonders at adding a depth of flavor without overwhelming the oats. And as a finishing touch we added a handful of raisins to the dough—their chewy sweetness was a naturally healthy complement to our oatmeal cookies.

Oatmeal Cookies

MAKES 24 COOKIES

While we prefer the texture and flavor of old-fashioned rolled oats, quick oats can be used in a pinch. Dried cranberries or dried cherries can be substituted for the raisins. In order for the cookies to spread and brown properly it is important to bake them one tray at a time.

I	cup old-fashioned rolled oats
3/4	cup (3 3/4 ounces) unbleached all-purpose flour
1/4	teaspoon ground cinnamon
1/4	teaspoon baking soda
1/4	teaspoon salt
4	tablespoons (1/2 stick) unsalted butter, melted and cooled
I	large egg
I	tablespoon vanilla extract
I	cup packed (7 ounces) dark brown sugar
1/2	cup raisins

1. Adjust an oven rack to the middle position and heat the oven to 350 degrees. Line 2 baking sheets with parchment paper.

2. Whisk the oats, flour, cinnamon, baking soda, and salt together in a medium bowl; set aside. In a large bowl, whisk the butter, egg, and vanilla together. Stir in the brown sugar until smooth, smearing any remaining clumps of sugar against the side of the bowl with a rubber spatula. Stir in the oat mixture and raisins until thoroughly combined.

3. Working with a level tablespoon of dough each time, roll the dough into 1-inch balls. (If the

dough is too soft to roll, refrigerate it until firm.) Place the balls on the prepared baking sheets, spacing them about 2½ inches apart (you will fit 12 cookies on each baking sheet).

4. Bake the cookies, one tray at a time, until the edges are light golden and the centers are just set, 11 to 13 minutes, rotating the tray halfway through baking (do not overbake). Cool the cookies on the baking sheets for 5 minutes, then serve warm, or transfer to a wire rack and cool completely. Bake the second tray while the first tray cools.

PER COOKIE: Cal 90; Fat 2.5 g; Sat fat 1.5 g; Chol 15 mg; Carb 16 g; Protein 1 g; Fiber 1 g; Sodium 30 mg

TEST KITCHEN MAKEOVER

PEANUT BUTTER COOKIES

IS IT FOOLISH TO THINK WE COULD LIGHTEN a peanut butter cookie? Of all the classic American cookies, there are few that have more fat and calories than a peanut butter cookie. With some recipes containing about a cup of peanut butter (136 grams of fat) and two sticks of butter (176 grams of fat), peanut butter cookies could use a serious makeover. But no matter how we reached our goal, we still wanted to retain the quintessential characteristics of a really good peanut butter cookie—crisp edges, a chewy center, and strong peanut flavor.

We started our tests by focusing on the type of fat we would use. We quickly determined that butter accentuated the peanut flavor, while other fats like oil and shortening diminished it. In addition butter was crucial for lightness and a chewy texture. As with all our cookies, we wanted a reasonably sized cookie about 2½-inches in diameter (about 1 tablespoon of dough per cookie).

The real challenge, however, would be to determine the best ratio of peanut butter to butter. We first tried making cookies with a scant ¼ cup of each (only a quarter of what most regular peanut butter cookie recipes use). We were surprised to find that these cookies were actually quite good—moist and chewy with a mild peanut flavor. But the amount of fat was still too high. We needed to cut a couple more tablespoons to reach our desired amount. Not wanting to exceed 6 tablespoons between the two ingredients, we tried every ratio we could think of. The ratio of 2 tablespoons peanut butter to 4 tablespoons butter struck the perfect balance. More peanut butter led to cookies that were too dry and cakey, and more butter created cookies with very little peanut flavor. We now had a cookie with the desired combination of chew on the inside and crispness on the outside.

In our testing, we noticed that the type of peanut butter we used really mattered. Natural peanut butters (which have a layer of oil on top) contain no emulsifiers and they made the cookies sandy. Commercial brands, which contain partially hydrogenated vegetable oils that are similar to shortening, helped the cookies rise and achieve a crisper edge and chewier center. And as for chunky versus smooth-style peanut butter, we tested them both and, not surprisingly, we felt that the chunky style contributed more peanut flavor.

In addition to traditional peanut butters, we also wanted to try our recipe with some of the available reduced-fat and reduced-calorie peanut butters. As we expected these peanut butters didn't perform that well. The cookies made with them tasted stale, with off flavors and a dry, cakey texture. And after reading the nutritional analysis of these peanut butters, we were surprised to find that the savings in fat and calories were minimal, especially since we were already using such a small amount of peanut butter.

But we still didn't have quite the level of peanut flavor we were after. Clearly, for real peanut flavor we would need peanuts as well as peanut butter. We found that whole peanuts tended to slip out of the dough, so we tried chopping them and mixing them directly into the dough—this was a big improvement. And since the chopped peanuts really pack a lot of flavor, ¼ cup was all we needed.

At this point, we focused our attention on the sweetener. We had been using a cup of granulated sugar and now began to wonder if a different sweetener might make the cookies chewier and moister (especially since we had removed so much fat). We tried a couple of liquid sweeteners, molasses and corn syrup, but they produced an overly chewy texture that was more confection than cookie. We tried dark brown sugar and found that it both accentuated the peanut flavor, making the cookies taste nuttier, and added some much needed moisture. To shave off more calories

we tried cutting the sugar back to ¾ cup, but the resulting cookies were too dry and did not spread properly during baking. It looked like a cup of sugar was the right amount. Considering that we had trimmed a good amount of the fat (from 6 grams to 3½ grams) without losing much in the way of flavor, we happily celebrated with our healthier cookies and a glass of milk (skim, of course).

Peanut Butter Cookies
MAKES 24 COOKIES

For the best flavor use dry-roasted salted peanuts. If you are concerned about the amount of sodium, you can substitute reduced-salt or unsalted peanuts. In order for the cookies to spread and brown properly it is important to bake them one tray at a time.

1 ¼	cups (6 ¼ ounces) unbleached all-purpose flour
¼	teaspoon baking soda
¼	teaspoon salt
4	tablespoons (½ stick) unsalted butter, melted and cooled
1	large egg
2	teaspoons vanilla extract
1	cup packed (7 ounces) dark brown sugar
2	tablespoons chunky peanut butter
¼	cup dry-roasted salted peanuts, chopped coarse

1. Adjust an oven rack to the middle position and heat the oven to 350 degrees. Line 2 baking sheets with parchment paper.

2. Whisk the flour, baking soda, and salt together in a medium bowl; set aside. In a large bowl, whisk the butter, egg, and vanilla together. Stir in the brown sugar and peanut butter until smooth, smearing any remaining clumps against the side of the bowl with a rubber spatula. Stir in the flour mixture and peanuts until thoroughly combined.

3. Working with a level tablespoon of dough each time, roll the dough into 1-inch balls. (If the dough is too soft to roll, refrigerate it until firm.) Place the balls on the prepared baking sheets,

---

MAKEOVER AT A GLANCE

–Classic–
Peanut Butter Cookies
(per cookie)

Calories: 110	Cholesterol: 15 mg
Fat: 6 g	Saturated Fat: 2.5 g

–Light–
Peanut Butter Cookies
(per cookie)

Calories: 90	Cholesterol: 15 mg
Fat: 3.5 g	Saturated Fat: 1.5 g

How We Did It

- Reduced the amount of peanut butter from ½ cup to 2 tablespoons and replaced the loss in flavor with ¼ cup dry-roasted peanuts, chopped coarse, which also added texture
- Reduced the amount of butter from 8 to 4 tablespoons
- Melted the butter and mixed the dough by hand for a tender cookie
- Used all brown sugar to maintain moistness
- Baked the cookies one tray at a time to ensure they spread and browned evenly

spacing them about 2½ inches apart (you will fit 12 cookies on each baking sheet).

4. Bake the cookies, one tray at a time, until the edges are light golden and the centers are just set, 11 to 13 minutes, rotating the tray halfway through baking (do not overbake). Let the cookies cool on the baking sheets for 5 minutes, then serve warm, or transfer to a wire rack and let cool completely. Bake the second tray while the first tray cools.

PER COOKIE: Cal 90; Fat 3.5 g; Sat fat 1.5 g; Chol 15 mg; Carb 14 g; Protein 2 g; Fiber 0 g; Sodium 45 mg

THE LOWDOWN ON REDUCED-FAT PEANUT BUTTER

In response to the trend of healthier eating, peanut butter manufacturers have introduced a wide range of low-carb, low-sugar, and reduced-fat varieties of peanut butter. Thinking that these versions of peanut butter might allow us to further shave fat and calories from our peanut butter cookies, we headed off to the test kitchen to give them a try in our lightened peanut butter cookie recipe. On average, these products contain 6 fat grams per tablespoon, compared to 8 fat grams per tablespoon of full-fat peanut butter. (Not an incredibly significant reduction.)

After tasting all the cookies side by side, we found that the peanut butters performed adequately but they weren't worth the 4 grams of fat and 20 calories on average we would trim from the entire batch of cookies. Overall, the cookies made with the low-fat, low-sugar varieties of peanut butter were cakier and drier than the cookies made with traditional peanut butter. Tasters also complained that the cookies lacked a sufficient peanut butter punch. The bottom line: If you want the best flavor and texture from your light peanut butter cookies stick with our favorite peanut butter—regular Skippy.

TEST KITCHEN MAKEOVER

SUGAR COOKIES

SUGAR COOKIES ARE THE MOST BASIC OF ALL American cookies. But as anyone who has ever eaten a good one can attest, they are addictively rich and delicate with a big vanilla flavor—not to mention their trademark crackling sugary exterior. We wondered whether it would even be possible to develop an acceptable lower fat version since this cookie relies on only a few basic ingredients —butter, sugar, eggs, flour, and vanilla. As we had with our other cookies, we built a base recipe with which we could begin testing by scaling down a traditional sugar cookie recipe to yield 2 dozen 2½-inch cookies (using about 1 tablespoon of dough per cookie).

Working with our scaled down sugar cookie recipe, which used roughly 1¼ cups flour, 10 tablespoons butter, and 1 cup sugar, we decided to tackle the fat first. Wondering if all that fat was necessary, we began to make batches of cookies removing a tablespoon of butter at a time. We were pleased to find that we could reduce the amount of fat by half, all the way down to 5 tablespoons, before the texture became too dry and the taste too floury.

The next ingredient we looked at was the sugar. We tried a batch of cookies using less than the 1 cup of sugar in our base recipe, but met with horrible results. These cookies were dry and crumbly—not at all the right texture for a sugar cookie. Previous cookie tests had led us to believe that sugar is the cookie's main source of moisture (especially with so much fat removed), and without a full cup of sugar the balance was spoiled. We had assumed that granulated sugar was the best choice for this cookie; however, when developing our other low-fat cookies we had found that brown sugar could sometimes be beneficial for flavor and texture. We wondered if that would be the case here. We made another batch of sugar cookies substituting brown sugar for some of the granulated sugar, but the cookies turned out too dark and had an uncharacteristic candy-like texture. It was obvious to us that all granulated sugar was the way to go with sugar cookies.

We usually use unbleached all-purpose flour in our cookies for the best texture, but in this case all-purpose flour made our cookies heartier and less delicate. Thinking that cake flour, which is lower in protein than all-purpose flour, would lend a more appropriately delicate crumb to the sugar cookies, we made another batch replacing the all-purpose flour with cake flour. These cookies definitely had a lighter texture, but they were too delicate and crumbly. We found it better to use a combination of all-purpose and cake flour. This yielded cookies that were much more tender and crisp, yet still held their shape.

As for the leavener, we found that sugar cookies made with baking powder were superior to those made with baking soda (which we use in our other cookie recipes). Baking powder produced delicate, light-colored cookies with an airier texture. One-half teaspoon baking powder did the trick, giving our sugar cookies just the right amount of lift

THE LOWDOWN ON SPLENDA BAKING BLENDS

Artificial sweeteners, like Sweet 'N Low, have been around for decades, and while these sugar substitutes are fine in coffee they are not particularly suited for baking cakes and cookies. Recently, however, Splenda (a brand name of sucralose) has introduced a new sweetener that is designed especially for baking. Splenda's Sugar Blend for Baking is supposed to let a baker "reduce the sugar in baked goods while maintaining the great sugar taste." Intrigued by this claim, we tried using this baking blend in three of our existing light recipes—sugar cookies, brownies, and angel food cake.

The first thing we noticed is that when substituting Splenda for sugar you are instructed to use half the amount, the idea being that a half cup of Splenda has the same sweetening ability as one cup of sugar, with half the calories. The sugar cookies made with Splenda were noticeably different than the cookies made with all sugar. The Splenda cookies were "puffy" with no browned edges. They were also a lot drier than the real sugar cookies because they contained only half the amount of sweetener. As for flavor, some tasters felt they were "sweeter" (despite the fact they were made with less sweetener) and artificial tasting. The difference between the brownies made with sugar and the Splenda brownies was similar, but more pronounced. The brownies made with Splenda had lost the requisite chewiness and had a "desert-like dryness." The flavor of the brownies, like that of the cookies, was markedly sweeter with an artificial finish.

The problems with using less sweetener in a recipe were most dramatic when we tried using Splenda in angel food cake. Because the ingredient list is relatively short and the ratios so carefully balanced in this cake, we met with disaster when we used only half the amount of sweetener. Even before we put the cake in the oven, we noticed that it had significantly less volume than an angel food cake made with regular sugar. After it was baked, the cake had a "funky," "bread-like" texture with a "sour" flavor. In the end, we were disappointed with the performance of Splenda's Baking Blend, especially as a substitute for sugar. We'd much rather enjoy the pure, clean flavor of real sugar, even if it means a few more calories.

Splenda also makes a brown sugar alternative, Brown Sugar Blend. Using half the amount as we would have of regular brown sugar, we tested the brown sugar blend in three applications—chocolate chip cookies, blondies, and a streusel topping (sprinkled over a yellow cake)—tasting them side by side with versions prepared with regular brown sugar. Tasters detected a "bitter" and "soapy" aftertaste in the cookies and blondies made with Brown Sugar Blend and also found them somewhat dry.

The cause of the texture problem was clear. Real sugar has hygroscopic (moisture-retaining) properties; because the Splenda blend contains less real sugar, it retains less moisture. Where Brown Sugar Blend really failed as a substitute, though, was in the streusel topping: Because the ratio of brown sugar to butter had to be drastically reduced (package instructions suggest cutting the quantity in half because the product is twice as sweet), the "topping" simply sank into the batter instead of crunching up into a recognizable streusel. Not much of a replacement in our book—even if you do save a few calories.

SPLENDA BAKING BLEND
This sugar alternative gave our angel food cake a bread-like texture and sour flavor. It also lent an unpleasant dryness to our cookies and brownies. As for flavor, "artificial-tasting," came up again and again.

SPLENDA BROWN SUGAR BLEND
A dry texture and "bitter" and "soapy" aftertastes plagued baked goods made with this brown sugar substitute.

without adding any chemical flavors.

What about the egg? We tried one egg, all whites, and various yolk-and-white combinations. Using just one whole egg provided the cookies with the right structure while adding a minimal amount of fat. Vanilla extract was the final piece of this puzzle. We tried varying amounts and settled on a whopping tablespoon of extract. This seemed like a lot (especially compared to our base recipe, which used just 1 teaspoon) but with less fat to flavor the cookie it was a welcome (and essential) addition.

MAKEOVER AT A GLANCE

–Classic–
Sugar Cookies
(per cookie)

Calories: 110	Cholesterol: 20 mg
Fat: 6 g	Saturated Fat: 4 g

–Light–
Sugar Cookies
(per cookie)

Calories: 90	Cholesterol: 15 mg
Fat: 2.5 g	Saturated Fat: 1.5 g

How We Did It

- Reduced the butter from 10 to just 5 tablespoons
- Used all granulated sugar for the best balance of moistness and crispness
- Used a combination of all-purpose and cake flour for tenderness
- Mixed the cookies by creaming the butter and sugar together for a tender texture
- Increased the vanilla extract from 1 teaspoon to 1 tablespoon for a more pronounced flavor
- Baked the cookies one tray at a time to ensure that they spread and browned correctly

---

Last, we addressed the traditional sugary outer crust. Initially we thought we'd skip this step in order to cut calories, but after tasting the cookies, we all missed the crackly crisp exterior that the sugar coating provided. We found we could limit the sugar for the coating to a scant ⅓ cup if we used a light hand when rolling the dough in the sugar before baking.

With the ingredients perfected we turned to the mixing method, especially important for a cookie whose hallmarks include an ethereally light texture. Most baking recipes call for butter and sugar to be creamed together until fluffy. Looking for shortcuts, we tried using melted butter, thinking that we would be better able to distribute the small amount of fat more evenly throughout the cookie, but this mixing method left us with chewy, super-flat cookies. In this case creaming was the best mixing method, and although this was a little unusual to do with such a small amount of butter, the resulting cookies were meltingly tender.

Now the dough was ready for the oven, and we quickly discovered that proper baking times and temperatures can really make or break these cookies. Normally, we bake cookies at 350 degrees; however, these sugar cookies didn't spread enough at this temperature. Testing batches of cookies baked at 375 and 400 degrees, we found that 400 degrees was more than the cookies could handle— they were pasty and underdone on the inside and over-browned on the outside. A 375-degree oven, however, was just right. The cookies spread to a perfect 2½-inch diameter and became just lightly browned at the very edges. At last we had a sugar cookie that we could be proud of, with just 2½ grams of fat and 90 calories.

Sugar Cookies
MAKES 24 COOKIES
In order for the cookies to spread and brown properly it is important to bake them one tray at a time.

¾	cup (3 ¾ ounces) unbleached all-purpose flour
½	cup (2 ounces) cake flour
½	teaspoon baking powder

¼   teaspoon salt

5   tablespoons unsalted butter, softened

1 ⅓   cups (9 ⅓ ounces) sugar

1   large egg, lightly beaten

1   tablespoon vanilla extract

1. Adjust an oven rack to the middle position and heat the oven to 375 degrees. Line 2 baking sheets with parchment paper.

2. Whisk the flours, baking powder, and salt together in a medium bowl; set aside. Using an electric mixer, cream the butter and 1 cup of the sugar together at medium speed until light and fluffy, 3 to 5 minutes, scraping down the sides of the bowl with a rubber spatula as needed. Add the egg and vanilla and continue to beat at medium speed until combined, 30 to 60 seconds. Add the flour mixture and continue to beat at low speed until just combined, 30 to 60 seconds, scraping down the bowl as needed.

3. Place the remaining ⅓ cup sugar in a shallow bowl. Working with a level tablespoon of dough each time, roll the dough into 1-inch balls. (If the dough is too soft to roll, refrigerate it until firm.) Carefully roll the balls in the sugar and place them on the prepared baking sheets, spacing them about 2½ inches apart (you will fit 12 cookies on each baking sheet).

4. Bake the cookies, one tray at a time, until the edges are light golden and the centers are just set, 9 to 11 minutes, rotating the tray halfway through baking (do not overbake). Cool the cookies on the baking sheets for 5 minutes, then serve warm, or transfer to a wire rack and cool completely. Bake the second tray while the first tray cools.

PER COOKIE: Cal 90; Fat 2.5 g; Sat fat 1.5 g; Chol 15 mg; Carb 16 g; Protein 1 g; Fiber 0 g; Sodium 40 mg

➤ VARIATIONS
Lemon Sugar Cookies
Lime or orange zest can be substituted for the lemon zest.

Follow the recipe for Sugar Cookies, adding 2 teaspoons grated lemon zest with the egg in step 2. Before coating the cookies in sugar, process the remaining ⅓ cup sugar with 1 teaspoon grated lemon zest in a food processor until fragrant, about 10 seconds. Coat, bake, and cool the cookies as directed.

PER COOKIE: Cal 90; Fat 2.5 g; Sat fat 1.5 g; Chol 15 mg; Carb 16 g; Protein 1 g; Fiber 0 g; Sodium 40 mg

Almond Sugar Cookies
Follow the recipe for Sugar Cookies, reducing the vanilla extract to 1 teaspoon and adding ½ teaspoon almond extract along with the vanilla. Before coating the cookies, process the remaining ⅓ cup sugar with ¼ cup sliced almonds in a food processor until finely ground, 10 to 15 seconds. Coat, bake, and cool the cookies as directed.

PER COOKIE: Cal 90; Fat 3 g; Sat fat 2 g; Chol 15 mg; Carb 16 g; Protein 1 g; Fiber 0 g; Sodium 40 mg

TEST KITCHEN MAKEOVER

BROWNIES

BROWNIES CONTAIN SO MUCH CHOCOLATE, butter, and sugar that just thinking about them seems to put on the pounds. We wondered if it were at all possible to develop a recipe for a lighter brownie—one you could eat without feeling like you need to hit the gym afterward. But we weren't willing to sacrifice great texture and taste in the process. We wanted a low-fat brownie with a moist, dark interior, crisp edges, and serious chocolate flavor.

Our initial testing of low-fat recipes was not encouraging. Results ranged from dry and cakey squares to pale, fudge-like slabs with no substantial chocolate flavor. Since chocolate contributes the major portion of fat (and flavor) to brownies, we began our investigation here.

Brownies are made with one or a combination of unsweetened, bittersweet, and semisweet chocolate. Unsweetened chocolate contains more fat than bittersweet and semisweet, so we focused on the latter. Sometimes cocoa powder, which contains only a minuscule amount of fat, is added to deepen and round out the chocolate flavor. This was something we were definitely going to try in our light brownies, in an effort to knock the fat grams down and keep the chocolate flavor up. In past tests, we'd had success with bittersweet chocolate because its somewhat bitter flavor also meant a more intense chocolate flavor, but in this application paired with cocoa powder, the flavor was too overpowering. Instead, tasters preferred semisweet chocolate for its pleasant full round flavor.

For the most intense chocolate flavor, most brownie recipes use anywhere from 2 to 6 ounces of chocolate. (Note that brownies containing lesser amounts of chocolate usually pad their brownies with anywhere from 8 to 12 tablespoons of butter, and from ¾ to 1¾ cups of sugar, depending on the type of chocolate used.) After testing various ratios of semisweet chocolate to cocoa powder, we found that by using 2 tablespoons of cocoa powder we were able to use just 3 ounces chocolate, yet still retain an intense chocolate flavor. This was about half the amount of chocolate (and much less fat) that most traditional brownies contain.

Butter, another fat contributor to brownies, was up next. Traditional recipes for brownies contain between 8 and 12 tablespoons of butter (that's about 10 grams of fat per brownie). Many low-fat recipes replace this fat with all sorts of ingredients. Applesauce, prune puree, yogurt,

even pureed black beans—you name it, we tried it. None of these brownies was worth a second bite. They were all dry and cakey with an unpleasant, muted chocolate flavor. We also tried substituting oil for the butter (a trick that works with our chocolate cakes); however, the texture of the brownies turned overly sticky and moist. Sticking with straight butter, we tested batch after batch of brownies using less butter each time. When we hit two tablespoons, much to our surprise, the brownies still had potent chocolate flavor and a tender crumb.

Sugar was the next ingredient subject to scrutiny. The combination of both granulated and brown sugar created a moister, slightly wetter brownie than one made with all granulated sugar, but it overshadowed the chocolate flavor. Clearly granulated sugar was the best choice. Wanting to reduce some of the calories, we slowly decreased the amount of sugar. We were happy to find that with just ½ cup of sugar the brownies had a subtle sweetness and toothsome chew. We also found that a generous amount of vanilla and a dash of espresso powder were needed to enhance the chocolate flavor and give the brownies added depth.

Our brownies now had good flavor, but they were a tad dry. Adding a little lean dairy to the batter seemed like an obvious starting point. We added a couple tablespoons of fat-free cream cheese (an ingredient used in several low-fat

LINING A BROWNIE PAN FOR EASY REMOVAL

1. Place two 16-inch sheets of parchment paper or aluminum foil perpendicular to each other in the pan, pushing the paper or foil into the corners. If using foil, lightly spray the foil with vegetable oil spray.

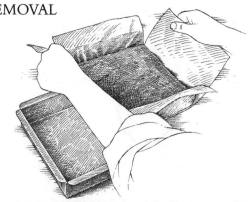

2. After the brownies have baked and cooled, use the paper or foil to transfer them to a cutting board, then slice into individual portions.

recipes we had found), but this made the brownies gummy. Milk and buttermilk gave us moisture, but clouded the chocolate flavor. It then hit us—why not use a little water? From prior testing, we already knew that when we mixed cocoa powder with warm, or hot, water, the cocoa flavor bloomed. Maybe it would also add moisture without dulling the brownie's chocolate intensity. Just 1 tablespoon did the trick.

Many recipes call for creaming the butter, but with so little fat in our recipe this was out of the question. We tried whipping the eggs and sugar together until the mixture was pale and fluffy, but these brownies rose in the oven and then collapsed. Much to our delight, the easiest method worked best: Melt the chocolate and butter, add the sugar, eggs, and vanilla, and then fold in the flour.

As simple as their ingredients are to combine, these brownies need to be baked just right to guarantee the perfect texture. We found that a moderate oven temperature of 350 degrees gave us the brownies we wanted—any higher and the edges dried out. Also, it is important to start checking the brownies a few minutes before the end of the baking time. Insert a toothpick into the center of a brownie and if a few moist crumbs remain attached, the brownies are ready to come out of the oven.

MAKEOVER AT A GLANCE

–Classic–
Brownies
(per brownie)

Calories: 200	Cholesterol: 50 mg
Fat: 10 g	Saturated Fat: 7 g

–Light–
Brownies
(per brownie)

Calories: 130	Cholesterol: 25 mg
Fat: 5 g	Saturated Fat: 2.5 g

How We Did It

- Used a combination of semisweet chocolate and cocoa powder instead of all unsweetened chocolate, which is higher in fat and must be used in combination with more sugar and butter
- Used a little espresso powder to accentuate the chocolate flavor
- Used just 2 tablespoons butter, instead of the usual 8 to 12 tablespoons
- Added 1 tablespoon warm water to the batter to help bloom the cocoa flavor and keep the brownies moist

Brownies
MAKES 12 BROWNIES

Be sure to use semisweet chocolate and not semisweet chips—the additives in chips will result in a drier, squat brownie. To ensure moist, fudgy brownies it is important not to overbake them. Be sure to check the brownies for doneness several minutes before the specified baking time has elapsed.

1/2	cup (2 1/2 ounces) unbleached all-purpose flour
1/2	teaspoon baking powder
2	tablespoons Dutch-processed cocoa powder
1	tablespoon warm water
1	tablespoon vanilla extract
1/2	teaspoon instant espresso powder
2	tablespoons unsalted butter
3	ounces semisweet chocolate, chopped fine
1/2	cup (3 1/2 ounces) sugar
1/8	teaspoon salt
1	large egg, lightly beaten

1. Adjust an oven rack to the middle position and heat the oven to 350 degrees. Following the illustrations on page 332, line an 8-inch square metal baking pan with parchment paper or foil then lightly coat with vegetable oil spray.

2. Whisk the flour and baking powder together in a small bowl; set aside. In a separate bowl, whisk the cocoa, water, vanilla, and espresso powder together; set aside. Microwave the butter and chocolate together in a medium microwave-safe bowl on 50 percent power until melted, about 1

minute; whisk until the mixture is smooth. Whisk in the sugar and salt until completely incorporated. Whisk in the cocoa mixture, then whisk in the egg. Stir in the flour mixture until just incorporated (do not overmix).

3. Pour the batter into the prepared pan and smooth the top. Bake until a toothpick inserted into the center comes out with a few moist crumbs attached, 20 to 25 minutes, rotating the pan halfway through baking (do not overbake). Cool completely on a wire rack, about 1 hour, lift the brownies out of the pan by grasping onto the parchment paper, and cut into 12 brownies.

PER BROWNIE: Cal 130; Fat 5 g; Sat fat 2.5 g; Chol 25 mg; Carb 19 g; Protein 2 g; Fiber 1 g; Sodium 55 mg

THE LOWDOWN ON FRUIT PUREES

Many recipes for baked goods in low-fat and light cookbooks use applesauce, pureed bananas, and even baby food (in the form of pureed prunes) to replace the fat. Because fruit purees are fat-free, low in calories, and have a natural sweetness (which we hoped would allow us to reduce the amount of sugar), it only made sense for us to give them a try.

We tried all three of the above-mentioned fruit purees in some of our baked goods recipes, including chocolate chip cookies and brownies. Overall, the baked goods made with fruit purees were cakey, dry, and had unwelcome fruity flavors; not worth the savings in fat, in our opinion.

TEST KITCHEN MAKEOVER

CHOCOLATE SHEET CAKE

IN OUR EXPERIENCE, MOST LOW-FAT CHOCOLATE cakes are dry, spongy slabs without any discernable chocolate flavor and definitely not worth eating. Better to just skip dessert. Undaunted by these substandard cakes, we were determined to make a lighter version of a traditional chocolate

sheet cake, one that would be moist and tender, with undeniable chocolate flavor. We wanted the kind of cake you might serve your children after school or to a crowd of friends after a casual dinner—the easy kind.

Because we weren't the first to want it all—a great chocolate cake that's also low in fat—we began by examining existing recipes for low-fat chocolate cake. But none of the recipes we tried were even remotely worth the reduced calories, and it seemed the more desperate recipe writers got, the goofier the ingredients became. Although canned beets provided moistness and a dark chocolatey color to one cake, they also added a metallic-vegetal flavor as well. Marshmallow fluff and egg whites used as a fat substitute produced a sickly sweet cake with the texture of sticky, compressed cotton candy.

Tossing these oddball low-fat chocolate cake recipes aside, we turned to a basic, chocolate "bowl cake" (a cake in which the ingredients are simply mixed together in a bowl). Our goal was to have as much deep chocolate flavor as possible while keeping the mixing method easy. We began by replacing some of the flour with cocoa powder, which contains a lot of flavor but not much fat. With cocoa powder in the recipe, we were able to use just 3 ounces of bittersweet chocolate, rather than the 6 to 8 ounces common in most regular chocolate cake recipes. Choosing bittersweet over unsweetened chocolate decreased the fat significantly. (Bittersweet chocolate is leaner than unsweetened since the added sugar reduces the cocoa butter content by half.) To intensify the chocolate flavor, we borrowed a professional baker's trick and added a bit of instant espresso powder. As a flavor enhancer rather than flavoring agent, the coffee boosted the chocolate flavor but stayed quietly in the background.

Trying to replace the butter entirely with common low-fat substitutes like applesauce, sour cream, or yogurt was unsuccessful. The cakes made with these replacements were unappealingly dense, gummy, and odd tasting. Instead of cutting the butter out entirely, we simply used less—6 tablespoons instead of the two sticks found in most recipes. Out of curiosity we tried substituting oil for the butter. To our surprise, we found the cake with oil had a moister texture and a more intense chocolate flavor. Obviously the flavor of the butter, which is usually a welcome addition in cakes, was masking the reduced amount of chocolate in our cake. To further reduce the amount of fat in the cake we reduced the number of eggs to two (most cakes have four) without affecting the texture or flavor of the cake.

Up until now, we were using 1½ cups granulated sugar in the cake. We tried lowering this amount, but the texture of the cake turned awfully dry. We tried substituting brown sugar for the granulated sugar (a trick we had had success with in some of our other low-fat baking recipes), but this made the texture too dense—good for a heartier-textured Bundt cake, for example, but

not delicate enough for a sheet cake. We also tried substituting corn syrup for some of the granulated sugar to add some moistness, but tasters found the texture of these cakes to be dense and leaden. Although 1½ cups of granulated sugar was more than we had envisioned, we found the resulting moist and tender texture of this super-chocolatey cake to be worth the extra calories.

The last adjustment we made to our chocolate sheet cake was the serving size. Many recipes claim that a 13 by 9-inch cake will serve 12 people; however, we found that when we cut this size cake into 16 pieces, they were perfect—neither too large, nor too skimpy.

MAKEOVER AT A GLANCE

–Classic–
Chocolate Sheet Cake
(per serving)

Calories: 360 — Cholesterol: 75 mg
Fat: 16 g — Saturated Fat: 9 g

–Light–
Chocolate Sheet Cake
(per serving)

Calories: 270 — Cholesterol: 25 mg
Fat: 9 g — Saturated Fat: 1.5 g

How We Did It

- Replaced a portion of the bittersweet chocolate with cocoa powder, which has far less fat per ounce
- Replaced 12 tablespoons of butter with 6 tablespoons vegetable oil, which not only reduced fat grams but allowed more of the chocolate flavor to come through
- Used a little espresso powder to accentuate the chocolate flavor

Chocolate Sheet Cake
SERVES 16

Dutch-processed cocoa will give the cake a richer taste and darker appearance than non-alkalized cocoa. To accurately measure the boiling water needed for this recipe, bring the water to a boil first, then measure out the correct amount. Serve this dark chocolate cake dusted with confectioners' sugar if desired.

	Vegetable oil spray
3	ounces bittersweet chocolate, chopped fine
¾	cup (2¼ ounces) Dutch-processed cocoa
1	teaspoon espresso powder
1¼	cups boiling water
1½	cups (7½ ounces) unbleached all-purpose flour
1½	teaspoons baking soda
½	teaspoon salt
1½	cups (10½ ounces) sugar
2	large eggs, lightly beaten
1	tablespoon vanilla extract
6	tablespoons vegetable oil

1. Adjust an oven rack to the middle position and heat the oven to 350 degrees. Lightly coat a 13 by 9-inch metal baking pan with vegetable oil spray, then line the bottom with parchment paper.

2. Combine the chocolate, cocoa, and espresso powder in a large bowl. Pour the boiling water over the chocolate mixture, cover, and let sit for 5 minutes to melt the chocolate. Whisk the

chocolate mixture until smooth, then set aside to cool slightly, about 2 minutes. In a separate bowl, whisk the flour, baking soda, and salt together.

3. Whisk the sugar, eggs, and vanilla into the cooled chocolate mixture. Slowly whisk in the oil. Sift half of the flour mixture over the batter and whisk in. Repeat with the remaining flour mixture and continue to whisk the batter gently until most of the lumps are gone (do not overmix).

4. Pour the batter into the prepared pan and smooth the top. Bake until a toothpick inserted into the center comes out with few moist crumbs attached, 35 to 40 minutes, rotating the pan halfway through baking (do not overbake). Cool the cake in the pan for 10 minutes, then invert onto a wire rack and remove the parchment paper. Flip the cake right-side up, and cool completely on the wire rack before serving, about 2 hours.

PER SERVING: Cal 270; Fat 9 g; Sat fat 1.5 g; Chol 25 mg; Carb 41 g; Protein 6 g; Fiber 5 g; Sodium 80 mg

TEST KITCHEN MAKEOVER

CARROT CAKE

A RELIC OF THE HEALTH FOOD CRAZE, CARROT cake was once heralded for its use of vegetable oil in place of butter and use of carrots as a natural sweetener. But was it ever a healthy cake? With most tipping the scales at 500 calories and 31 grams of fat per slice, carrot cake seemed ripe for a test kitchen makeover. We wanted to create a truly great carrot cake, one where the natural sweetness of the carrots takes center stage. Most important, it had to be moist and rich without being soggy and greasy from an overabundance of fat.

Working with a basic carrot cake recipe, our first mission was to find a way to reduce the amount of fat. After some initial testing, it was obvious that tasters preferred oil rather than butter for its

---

CORE TECHNIQUE

INCREASING THE CHOCOLATE FLAVOR IN LOW-FAT CAKES

Most brands of bittersweet chocolate contain about 130 calories and 9 grams of fat per ounce. Because of this, many low-fat chocolate cake recipes slash the amount of chocolate, but as one would imagine this leads to bland, dull cakes. After numerous tests, we uncovered several secrets to making a light cake with plenty of chocolate flavor.

Our first tactic was to replace the majority of the chocolate with cocoa powder. Cocoa powder, which is essentially chocolate without the sugar or most of the fat, has far fewer calories and less fat than chocolate while providing the same, if not more, flavor. While cocoa powder is not without fat, we found that because of its concentrated flavor we could use far less of it and still impart an intense chocolate flavor. We also found that we could coax more chocolate flavor from the cocoa powder if it were "bloomed" in a hot or warm liquid. This technique helped to disperse the cocoa particles more evenly through the cake, and the heat helped to bring out the cocoa's nuances.

In addition to cocoa powder, we found a couple of other ingredients that helped boost chocolate flavor. In chocolate cakes, we found it better to use vegetable oil as opposed to butter. Because we were using a reduced amount of chocolate, we had to be sure every bit counted. The rich flavor of butter tended to mask the flavor of the reduced amount of chocolate, whereas the neutral-flavored oil let the chocolate flavor come through. Another ingredient that brought out the cake's chocolate flavor was espresso powder. The earthy overtones of the coffee helped to draw out similar characteristics in the chocolate. The coffee, in addition to our other finds, resulted in cakes with a big chocolate flavor without excessive fat and calories.

cleaner, subtler presence in the cake. But most typical versions of carrot cake contain around 1½ cups oil—not our idea of low fat. To find out how much oil we could remove without compromising the flavor or structure of the cake, we gradually reduced the oil ¼ cup at a time. Surprisingly, we found that the cake made with only ½ cup of oil was as moist, tender, and flavorful as some of the full-fat versions containing three times as much oil. Most carrot cake recipes also called for four to five eggs per cake, but we found that three eggs gave the cake a slight spring and a tender crumb without adding unnecessary fat.

Next we focused on the sugar. The cake clearly benefited from both granulated and light brown sugar, the former giving the cake clean sweetness and the latter bringing out the warmth of the spices. After trying different ratios of the two sugars, we settled on 1 cup of granulated sugar and 1 cup of brown sugar. This 50/50 ratio is very different from traditional carrot cake recipes, which use, at most, a third as much brown sugar as granulated. We found, however, that the additional brown sugar guaranteed that the cake would stay moist, even with the drastic reduction in oil.

Now that we had significantly reduced the amount of fat and calories, we could turn our attention to the other key ingredients. We knew we wanted our cake to contain enough carrots to confirm at first glance that it was indeed carrot cake. We flatly rejected any idea of first boiling, steaming, or pureeing the carrots, as was called for in some recipes. It was just too much work, and we thought that this should be a simple recipe. Grating the carrots was clearly the way to go—the carrots steam and soften in the cake as it bakes so that no annoying, stringy bits mar the cake's finished texture. It took a few failed efforts before we realized that just the right amount of carrots was paramount, because their high moisture content could determine whether the cake was perfectly moist or downright soggy. After baking cakes with as few as 1 cup grated carrots (no carrot presence) and as many as 5 cups (soaking wet cake), we found that 3 cups (1 pound of carrots) was the perfect amount to give the cake a pleasantly moist

texture and just enough carrot flavor.

For the dry ingredients, all-purpose flour worked better than cake flour (the latter proved too delicate for this sturdy American classic), and we used 2½ cups as the base for our tests. We quickly found that this cake would need healthy amounts of baking soda and baking powder, 1 teaspoon and 1¼ teaspoons, respectively (nearly twice the amount found in many recipes), to give it sufficient lift and a beautiful brown color. While many recipes use handfuls of every baking spice in the pantry, we found that a conservative touch with cinnamon, along with a little help from nutmeg and cloves, won the approval of tasters.

It was time to perfect our mixing technique. Just as we would with a butter-based cake, we tried creaming the oil into the sugar and then beat in the eggs with an electric mixer before adding the dry ingredients and carrots. The cake tasted good, but the bottom of the cake was much too dense and wet. We then wondered if we could use a food processor to mix the cake, and tried processing the eggs and oil together with the sugar, before stirring in the flour and carrots. This was better; however, the texture of the cake was still a bit too heavy and leaden. Moving to an electric mixer, we wondered if beating some air into the eggs before adding the oil, flour, and carrots would have any impact on the cake. You bet it did—no more soggy bottom, no more heavy texture. Because we had whipped air into the batter by way of the eggs, the cake now had a moist, delicate crumb and a very nice rise.

Our cake was now good enough to eat on its own, but there was no way we were going to pass up the frosting. Traditional cream cheese frostings consist of cream cheese, butter, and confectioners' sugar—extremely tasty, but hardly healthy. We were able to reduce some fat by replacing the full-fat cream cheese with Neufchâtel reduced-fat cream cheese (other lower fat substitutions such as nonfat and light cream cheese made the frosting runny and gummy). We added the requisite butter and confectioners' sugar and whirred the mixture together in a food processor. We wanted to lower the fat further, so we tried removing the butter from the frosting, but its absence made the frosting too loose. The solution turned out to be the mixing method. Instead of mixing the cream cheese and sugar in the food processor, which overworked the mixture into a soupy mess, we mixed it by hand, This decidedly low-tech method allowed us to control the consistency and end up with a frosting that was spreadable. The result? Even with the addition of our cream cheese frosting, this carrot cake has significantly less fat and calories than the original cake alone. Add to that a healthy dose of carrots, and this is one dessert we can feel good about.

MAKEOVER AT A GLANCE

–Classic–
Carrot Cake with Cream Cheese Frosting
(per serving)

Calories: 500	Cholesterol: 80 mg
Fat: 31 g	Saturated Fat: 7 g

–Light–
Carrot Cake with Cream Cheese Frosting
(per serving)

Calories: 350	Cholesterol: 55 mg
Fat: 13 g	Saturated Fat: 4 g

How We Did It

- Reduced the amount of oil from 1½ cups to ½ cup
- Reduced the number of eggs from 5 to 3
- Whipped air into the eggs to keep the cake from being too dense and leaden
- Replaced the cream cheese and butter in the frosting with Neufchâtel reduced-fat cream cheese and mixed it by hand to prevent it from becoming runny

---

Carrot Cake with Cream Cheese Frosting
SERVES 16

You can either use the large holes of a box grater or the large-holed shredding disk in a food processor for grating the carrots. Use a metal cake pan, not a glass or Pyrex pan, for best results. This cake is terrific with a dusting of confectioners' sugar, or for a special treat, try it with our Cream Cheese Frosting (recipe follows).

	Vegetable oil spray
2½	cups (12½ ounces) unbleached all-purpose flour
1¼	teaspoons baking powder
1	teaspoon baking soda
1¼	teaspoons ground cinnamon
½	teaspoon ground nutmeg
⅛	teaspoon ground cloves
½	teaspoon salt
3	large eggs
1	cup packed (7 ounces) light brown sugar
1	cup (7 ounces) granulated sugar
½	cup vegetable oil
1	pound carrots (about 6 medium), peeled and grated (about 3 cups)
	Cream Cheese Frosting (recipe follows)

1. Adjust an oven rack to the middle position and heat the oven to 350 degrees. Lightly coat a 13 by 9-inch metal baking pan with vegetable oil spray, then line the bottom with parchment paper.

2. Whisk the flour, baking powder, baking soda, spices, and salt together in a medium bowl; set aside. Using an electric mixer, beat the eggs and sugars together in a medium bowl until they turn thick and creamy, 1 to 3 minutes. Turn the mixer to low and slowly whip in the oil until thoroughly combined and emulsified, 30 to 60 seconds. Sift half the flour mixture over the batter and gently mix in. Repeat once more with the remaining flour mixture and continue to whisk the batter gently until most of the lumps are gone (do not overmix). Using a rubber spatula, gently stir in the carrots.

3. Pour the batter into the prepared pan and

smooth the top. Bake until a toothpick inserted into the center of the cake comes out with a few moist crumbs attached, 35 to 40 minutes, rotating the pan halfway through baking (do not over-bake). Cool the cake in the pan for 10 minutes, then invert the cake onto a wire rack and remove the parchment paper. Flip the cake right-side up, and cool completely on a wire rack, about 2 hours, before frosting (if desired) and serving.

PER SERVING: Cal 350; Fat 12.5 g; Sat fat 4 g; Chol 55 mg; Carb 54 g; Protein 5 g; Fiber 1 g; Sodium 240 mg
PER SERVING WITHOUT FROSTING: Cal 250; Fat 8 g; Sat fat 1 g; Chol 40 mg; Carb 42 g; Protein 3 g; Fiber 1 g; Sodium 150 mg

Cream Cheese Frosting
MAKES ABOUT 2 CUPS
Be sure to mix the frosting by hand—an electric mixer or food processor will turn the frosting soupy.

12	ounces Neufchâtel (⅓ less fat) cream cheese, softened but still cool
1	teaspoon vanilla extract
1½	cups (6 ounces) confectioners' sugar

Mix the cream cheese and vanilla together in a large bowl with a rubber spatula. Add the confectioners' sugar and stir until thoroughly combined and smooth.

PER 2 TABLESPOONS: Cal 100; Fat 4.5 g; Sat fat 3 g; Chol 15 mg; Carb 12 g; Protein 2 g; Fiber 0 g; Sodium 90 mg

THE LOWDOWN ON LIGHT CREAM CHEESE
Cream cheese is soft, unripened cheese made from milk and milkfat that often contains stabilizers such as xanthan, carob bean, or guar gums to increase firmness and shelf life. Its creamy texture and tangy flavor is welcome on bagels and in many baked goods, but at 5 grams of fat and 50 calories per tablespoon, we needed to explore the possibility of using its low-fat cousins. Here's what we found:

Fat-free cream cheese, at 15 calories per tablespoon, was awful across the board. With its long list of ingredients, including stabilizers, emulsifiers, and artificial flavors and colors, it produced a rubbery, tacky cheesecake with a vinyl-like top, and a gummy frosting with "objectionable flavor."

Light cream cheese is usually sold in plastic tubs and contains about 2 grams of fat and 30 calories per tablespoon. It produced a soupy frosting that slid down the side of the cake, but was excellent for finishing pan sauces, giving pasta sauces and scalloped potatoes a creamy richness, and roasted artichoke dip the taste and mouthfeel of the full-fat version. The cheesecake made with light cream cheese (in combination with yogurt cheese and low-fat cottage cheese) rivaled a traditional cheesecake, with its smooth and creamy texture and characteristically tangy flavor.

Traditional Neufchâtel, which is soft, white, creamy, unripened cheese that originated in the French town of Neufchâtel in the region of Normandy, is worlds apart from the product packaged and sold in your local supermarket dairy case. **American Neufchâtel cheese,** available in plastic tubs or in square blocks, is marketed as reduced-fat cream cheese, having one third less fat than cream cheese. It contains 3 grams of fat and 35 calories per tablespoon. Tasters praised Neufchâtel  for its likeness to regular cream cheese, but unfortunately, it boosted the fat level too high for many of our recipes. Neufchâtel did, however, provide us with the "perfect" cream cheese frosting. Mixed by hand (the food processor made it runny) the frosting had the consistency and flavor of its full-fat counterpart.

CHOCOLATE BUNDT CAKE

A BUNDT CAKE IS BAKING AT ITS SIMPLEST. With their decorative shape, Bundt cakes don't require frosting or fussy finishing techniques. In fact, we think they are just great served plain. This is especially true of a chocolate Bundt cake, which should taste every bit as good as it looks, with a fine crumb, moist texture, and rich chocolate flavor. Unfortunately when it comes to low-fat chocolate Bundt cakes, this is usually not the case. Despite their tantalizing looks, most of these cakes deliver a minimum of chocolate flavor, and many are dry, rubbery, and devoid of any flavor whatsoever. We were determined to improve upon these low-fat disasters and create a chocolate Bundt cake that tastes as good as it looks.

A traditional chocolate Bundt cake calls for 6 to 8 ounces of bittersweet chocolate (plus cocoa powder), but this amount of chocolate was far too much for a cake we were trying to lighten. Our first thought was to remove the melted chocolate altogether and replace it with cocoa powder, which is much lower in fat. The resulting cake tasted bitter and its texture was chalky—reminiscent of third-rate brownies. We then tried adding the melted chocolate back an ounce at a time. With 3 ounces of chocolate and ¾ cup of cocoa, we found a good balance. The cake had a more robust chocolate flavor and a lot less fat. We then came upon a trick to develop the chocolate flavor even more. Several recipes we had seen called for mixing hot water with the cocoa powder before adding it to the cake batter. So we poured boiling water over the cocoa and chocolate to dissolve them, and found that this step not only dispersed the cocoa particles throughout the batter but also helped to bloom the flavor. In addition, we dissolved a small amount of espresso powder along with the chocolate and cocoa and added a healthy tablespoon of vanilla extract. Both flavors

complemented the floral nuances of the chocolate. We now had the best chocolate flavor possible.

The next fat-laden culprit we turned our attention to was the butter, since most cakes have 12 tablespoons or more. With other low-fat chocolate cakes (such as our Chocolate Sheet Cake, page 335) we had discovered that using oil in place of butter yielded a cake that had a much more intense chocolate flavor (the butter masked the chocolate flavor). We were curious if that would be the case with this cake as well, and indeed it was. The cake made with ½ cup of oil had a rich, intense chocolate flavor. Another source of fat in the cake was the eggs. In order to achieve a solid, dense structure that will hold it shape, most Bundt cakes use four or five eggs. After some tinkering, we found that we could reduce the eggs to two and increase the leavener slightly and still achieve a statuesque cake with a fine, tender crumb (and save ourselves 15 grams of fat).

Now that we had a great, complex chocolate flavor and had reduced a significant portion of the fat, we could focus on the texture. Although our cake had great flavor and a nice crumb, it still lacked moisture. We tried decreasing the flour but this compromised the structure of the cake. We considered increasing the oil or adding an egg, but these alternatives seemed counterproductive to our core mission of developing a lower fat cake. Finally, we switched from granulated to light brown sugar, which not only added moistness but also improved the flavor.

But even after making this change to the recipe we were still falling short of our goal of a really moist cake. In our initial tests we used buttermilk as the liquid base for the cake. We liked the tangy flavor the buttermilk added to the cake, but we began to wonder if the thickness of the buttermilk was causing the cake to seem dry. We tried making the cake using low-fat milk. This cake was an improvement, but we were now curious about whether the dairy was masking the chocolate flavor (just as the butter did). So we made the cake again but this time we omitted the dairy and used water. It gave us the results we wanted: The batter was looser, the finished cake was significantly more moist, and the chocolate flavor intensified.

Up until now, we had simply been whisking everything together by hand, but it wasn't easy. The batter is heavy, there are a lot of ingredients to incorporate, and it takes a lot of batter to fill a Bundt pan—stirring the ingredients turned out to be more like arm wrestling. Looking for an easier solution, we tried both an electric mixer and a food processor. The electric mixer didn't work as well as we had hoped because the batter became overworked before all the ingredients had been incorporated—the result was a tougher, denser cake. We then turned to the food processor. We pureed all the liquid ingredients and melted chocolate together to a uniform, emulsified consistency

(which also helped ensure that the chocolate was thoroughly melted and dispersed throughout the batter). But when we added the dry ingredients, we hit the same problem that we had with the electric mixer—overworked batter. We found an easy fix—a dual mixing method. After pureeing all the liquid ingredients together, we poured the liquid into a large bowl and gently whisked in the dry ingredients by hand.

Sprinkled with confectioners' sugar, our cake was almost perfect. But some of us felt that it needed something else to finish it, especially if we were going to serve it to company. Frostings and whipped cream concoctions were out of the question, but an intensely flavored glaze was just the ticket. While a glaze added calories, we found that if it was strongly flavored, we didn't have to use a lot of it. And considering we had cut out 100 calories per serving and significantly reduced the fat, we think this small splurge is worth it.

MAKEOVER AT A GLANCE

–Classic–
Chocolate Bundt Cake
(per serving)

Calories: 420   Cholesterol: 100 mg
Fat: 18 g   Saturated Fat: 10 g

–Light–
Chocolate Bundt Cake
(per serving)

Calories: 320   Cholesterol: 25 mg
Fat: 11 g   Saturated Fat: 2 g

How We Did It

- Replaced some of the chocolate with cocoa powder, which has less fat per ounce
- Mixed the cocoa with hot water to bloom its flavor
- Used a little espresso powder to accentuate the chocolate flavor
- Replaced the butter with vegetable oil in order to bring out the chocolate flavor
- Used water in place of milk to bring out the chocolate flavor
- Used all brown sugar to retain moisture

Chocolate Bundt Cake
SERVES 16

Although you can substitute natural cocoa for Dutch-processed, the cake won't rise as high. If you don't have baking spray with flour, mix 1 tablespoon butter with 1 tablespoon cocoa powder into a paste and brush inside the pan.

	Nonstick baking spray with flour
3	ounces bittersweet chocolate, chopped fine
¾	cup (2 ¼ ounces) Dutch-processed cocoa powder
1	teaspoon espresso powder
1	cup boiling water
1 ¾	cups (8 ¾ ounces) unbleached all-purpose flour
1	teaspoon salt
1	teaspoon baking soda
2	cups packed (14 ounces) light brown sugar
½	cup vegetable oil
2	large eggs
1	tablespoon vanilla extract
	Confectioners' sugar, for dusting (optional), or a glaze (optional), recipes follow

1. Adjust an oven rack to the lower-middle position and heat the oven to 350 degrees. Lightly spray the inside of a standard 12-cup bundt pan with the nonstick baking spray.

2. Combine the chocolate, cocoa, and espresso powder in a large bowl. Pour the boiling water over the chocolate mixture, cover, and let sit for 5 minutes to melt the chocolate. Whisk the chocolate mixture until smooth, then set aside to cool slightly, about 2 minutes. In a separate bowl, whisk together the flour, salt, and baking soda.

3. Process the melted chocolate mixture, sugar, oil, eggs, and vanilla together in a food processor until smooth, about 1 minute. Transfer the batter to a large bowl. Sift half of the flour mixture over the batter and gently whisk in. Repeat with the remaining flour mixture and continue to whisk the batter gently until most of the lumps are gone (do not overmix).

4. Pour the batter into the prepared Bundt pan and smooth the top. Wipe any drops of batter off the sides of the pan. Bake until a toothpick inserted into the center comes out with a few moist crumbs attached, about 50 to 55 minutes, rotating the pan halfway through baking (do not overbake).

5. Transfer the cake to a wire rack and cool in the pan for 10 minutes. Invert the cake onto the rack and cool completely, 1 to 2 hours. When cool, dust with confectioners' sugar (if using), or drizzle with one of the glazes below and let the glaze set before serving, about 15 minutes.

PER SERVING: Cal 320; Fat 11 g; Sat fat 2 g; Chol 25 mg; Carb 51 g; Protein 6 g; Fiber 5 g; Sodium 170 mg

PER SERVING WITH GLAZE: Cal 350; Fat 11 g; Sat fat 2 g; Chol 25 mg; Carb 58 g; Protein 6 g; Fiber 5 g; Sodium 180 mg

---

EQUIPMENT: Bundt Pans

Bundt pans were introduced by Nordic Ware (which is still in possession of the registered trademark) in the 1950s, based on the traditional cast-iron kugelhopf molds of Eastern Europe. (A kugel is a baked pudding, but a kugelhopf is a yeasted bread common to much of Europe, especially Austria, Germany and Poland.) These fluted, turban-shaped baking pans eventually gained widespread popularity, largely thanks to a slew of Bundt cake mixes marketed by Pillsbury.

To assess quality and performance, we tested eight so-called nonstick pans. Ranging in price from $9.99 to $27.99, each had a simple ridged design and a minimum capacity of 12 cups. In addition to preparing our chocolate Bundt cake in each pan, we baked vanilla cakes to test for evenness and depth of browning.

Ease of release was our top concern. All of the chocolate cakes released easily, but some of the vanilla cakes did stick, most notably in the Kaiser, Calphalon, and Nordic Ware Bubble pans. All of the vanilla cakes baked properly, varying in cooking time from 5 to 10 minutes, although some were not as evenly browned in the center (the only cake with no color at all was baked in the Silicone Zone pan). Some pans (the KitchenAid, Exeter, Silicone Zone, and Kaiser) lost points for design flaws—specifically, an unsightly crease where the center tube and the ring were joined. The best performer overall was the Nordic Ware Platinum (also the most expensive.) It had the best shape (with the most clearly defined ridges), it browned the cake evenly and deeply, and released it easily. The runner-up was the Baker's Secret, picked up at our local supermarket for a mere $11.99. Although it was made of lightweight material, it passed all of our tests with above-average results.

THE BEST BUNDT CAKE PANS

The Nordic Ware Platinum Series 12-Cup Bundt Pan ($27.99), top, is made from thick, durable, cast aluminum, which produced caked with even browning and a clean, well-defined shape. As a less expensive alternative at $11.99, the Baker's Secret Nonstick Fluted Tube Pan, bottom, also performed well in our tests.

Vanilla Glaze

MAKES ENOUGH TO GLAZE ONE CAKE

I   cup (4 ounces) confectioners' sugar
I   tablespoon low-fat milk
I   tablespoon vanilla extract
     Pinch salt

Whisk all the ingredients together in a medium bowl. Drizzle the cake with the glaze and let set for 15 minutes before serving.

PER SERVING: Cal 30; Fat 0 g; Sat fat 0 g; Chol 0 mg; Carb 7 g; Protein 0 g; Fiber 0 g; Sodium 10 mg

➤ VARIATIONS

Nutty Glaze

Follow the recipe for Vanilla Glaze, increasing the milk to 5 teaspoons and substituting 1 teaspoon almond or coconut extract for the tablespoon of vanilla extract.

PER SERVING: Cal 30; Fat 0 g; Sat fat 0 g; Chol 0 mg; Carb 7 g; Protein 0 g; Fiber 0 g; Sodium 10 mg

Coffee Glaze

Follow the recipe for Vanilla Glaze, substituting 5 teaspoons brewed coffee for the milk and ¾ teaspoon instant espresso powder or instant coffee powder for the vanilla extract.

PER SERVING: Cal 30; Fat 0 g; Sat fat 0 g; Chol 0 mg; Carb 7 g; Protein 0 g; Fiber 0 g; Sodium 10 mg

Orange Glaze

Follow the recipe for Vanilla Glaze, substituting 5 teaspoons orange juice for the milk and 1 teaspoon grated orange zest for the vanilla extract.

PER SERVING: Cal 30; Fat 0 g; Sat fat 0 g; Chol 0 mg; Carb 7 g; Protein 0 g; Fiber 0 g; Sodium 10 mg

TEST KITCHEN MAKEOVER

LEMON BUNDT CAKE

NOW THAT WE HAD A LOWER FAT CHOCOLATE Bundt cake under our belts, we wanted to turn our attention to lemon Bundt cake. We wanted a foolproof lemon Bundt cake with a zippy lemon flavor and rich, tender texture, but without all the calories and fat.

Most lemon Bundt cake recipes we found were similar to pound cake batters that have been doubled in volume and baked in a Bundt pan. But we didn't want the fat and calories that come from the large amounts of butter, sugar, and eggs in pound cake.

We found that in most pound cake recipes, a pound of butter and 8 eggs was the norm. Admittedly we needed a lot of these two ingredients to fill a large Bundt pan, but this amount seemed excessive. We started with the butter. We first reduced the amount of butter to ½ pound (16 tablespoons). We were surprised to find that tasters liked both the flavor and the texture of the cake. Encouraged by our good fortune, we tried reducing the butter to 8 tablespoons. Once again we found the cake to still be moist and flavorful. We halved again, but this time we met with disaster. The cake was so dry, it was all we could to choke a bite down. It looked like 8 tablespoons of butter was as low as we could go. In addition to cutting the amount of butter drastically, we also tried replacing it with oil (as we had done with our low-fat chocolate cakes). The resulting cake seemed to be moister, but it lacked flavor. The answer was to split the difference. A cake with 4 tablespoons butter and ¼ cup oil was both moist and flavorful.

The eight eggs in most recipes were also a major source of fat. We first cut the amount of eggs to six, and found virtually no difference. Confident we could go further, we tried four eggs. We now noticed that the cake was losing its cake-like structure and becoming too dense and more along the lines of bread. We thought we could bulk up the structure of the cake by adding a little more leavener. This was a good choice. With a slight increase in the baking soda the cake had the moist cakey texture we were looking for. In fact this technique worked so well, we were able to remove one more egg, leaving us with three. In addition, the use of cake flour rather than all-purpose provided an even more tender (and less bread-like) crumb which tasters appreciated.

With the major fat contributors addressed, we focused on the cake's other ingredients. Because we had reduced the fat components so substantially, we found that the cake was a little dry. In past experiences when we've encountered dry low-fat baked goods we've added a little bit more sugar to combat this dryness. But in this case adding any more than 2 cups of sugar made the cake needlessly sweet. We tried adding some yogurt, buttermilk, and milk to three separate cakes thinking they would add moisture and also a little richness. All three did the job of adding moisture and flavor, but only the milk tasted right. Both the yogurt and buttermilk added a tang that clashed with the acidity of the lemon. In the end, we used a cup of whole milk (skim and low-fat milk tasted too lean) to lend the cake a subtle richness and enough moistness without becoming heavy or soggy.

We now felt like we had a well-balanced formula of ingredients, but one thing still plagued us—a slightly rubbery texture. It occurred to us that this might not be an ingredient issue, but rather a mixing issue. Up to this point we had been using a food processor to mix the cake, as we had done with our chocolate Bundt cake, but we wondered if this might be the problem. We tried a more conventional creaming method, and while this method led to better results it was hard to cream the sugar and such a small amount of butter. It then struck us—why don't we whip the egg whites for added volume and a lighter texture, as is done with cakes such as angel food? We whisked together the dry ingredients in one bowl and the wet ingredients in a second bowl. After whipping the egg whites to stiff peaks, we stirred together the wet and dry ingredients. After folding in the whites, we transferred the batter to a Bundt pan and baked the cake. Forks in hand, we gathered

in the test kitchen to taste the cake—everyone approved of the extremely light tender texture and there was no rubberiness at all.

The last thing for us to do was figure out the final flavorings of the cake. With a large volume of batter we figured it would take a fair amount of lemon to flavor the cake. We started with a tablespoon each of lemon juice and lemon zest, but we could hardly taste it. We increased the juice and zest by a tablespoon each and tried again. This cake was better, but we wanted more punch. Another tablespoon of each yielded a cake with great flavor, but we noticed the lemon juice was making the cake a little soggy. We backed off on the juice a little and further increased the zest. After all this, a ratio of 2 tablespoons juice and a

MAKEOVER AT A GLANCE

—Classic—
Lemon Bundt Cake
(per serving)

Calories: 300	Cholesterol: 85 mg
Fat: 13 g	Saturated Fat: 9 g

—Light—
Lemon Bundt Cake
(per serving)

Calories: 250	Cholesterol: 50 mg
Fat: 8 g	Saturated Fat: 3 g

How We Did It

- Used cake flour to provide a tender crumb
- Used a combination of oil and butter to provide the best flavor and moisture
- Decreased the number of eggs from 8 to 3
- Folded in whipped egg whites to give the cake a more delicate and tender crumb
- Added milk for moisture and richness without adding a lot of fat

whopping ¼ cup zest provided us with a Bundt cake with a resounding lemon flavor.

Although we were happy with our slimmed-down lemon Bundt cake, we felt that it could be further improved with a glaze. Not wanting to add too much fat or too many calories, we started with a cup of confectioners' sugar and added enough lemon juice to make a thick but flowing glaze. Drizzled over the cake and allowed to set for 15 minutes, the glaze heightened the cake's lemony flavor and made us forget we were eating a low-fat cake.

Lemon Bundt Cake

SERVES 16

This cake tastes best when made with whole milk. When separating the eggs for this cake, be sure not to get any yolk into the white, or the whites will not whip properly. The cake can be served plain, dusted with confectioners' sugar, or served with the lemon glaze. If you don't have nonstick baking spray with flour, mix 1 tablespoon butter with 1 tablespoon flour into a paste and brush inside the pan.

	Nonstick baking spray with flour
3	cups (12 ounces) cake flour
2	cups (14 ounces) sugar
¼	cup finely grated zest from 4 lemons
1	teaspoon salt
1	teaspoon baking powder
½	teaspoon baking soda
1	cup whole milk, at room temperature
3	large eggs, yolks and whites separated
¼	cup vegetable oil
4	tablespoons (½ stick) unsalted butter, melted and cooled
1	tablespoon vanilla extract
	Pinch cream of tartar
2	tablespoons juice from 1 lemon
	Confectioners' sugar for dusting (optional) or Lemon Glaze (optional), recipe follows

1. Adjust an oven rack to the lower-middle position and heat the oven to 350 degrees. Lightly spray the inside of a standard 12-cup bundt pan with the nonstick baking spray.

2. Whisk the flour, 1½ cups of the sugar, the zest, salt, baking powder, and baking soda together in a large bowl; set aside. In a separate bowl, whisk the milk, egg yolks, oil, butter, and vanilla together.

3. In a medium bowl, beat the egg whites with an electric mixer on low speed until just broken up and foamy. Add the cream of tartar and increase the speed to medium-high. Continue to beat, adding the remaining ½ cup sugar, 1 tablespoon at a time, until all the sugar is added and the whites are shiny and form stiff peaks.

4. Slowly whisk the milk mixture and lemon juice into the flour mixture until smooth. Fold one-third of the beaten egg whites into the batter until combined, smearing any stubborn pockets of egg white against the side of the bowl. Gently fold the remaining egg whites into the batter.

5. Pour the batter into the prepared Bundt pan and smooth the top. Wipe any drops of batter off the sides of the pan. Bake until deep golden brown and a toothpick inserted into the center of the cake comes out with a few moist crumbs attached, 40 to 45 minutes, rotating the pan halfway through baking (do not overbake).

6. Transfer the cake to a wire rack and cool in the pan for 10 minutes. Invert the cake onto the rack and cool completely, 1 to 2 hours. When cool, dust with confectioners' sugar (if using), or drizzle with the glaze (recipe follows) and let the glaze set before serving, about 15 minutes.

PER SERVING: Cal 250; Fat 8 g; Sat fat 3 g; Chol 50 mg; Carb 44 g; Protein 3 g; Fiber 1 g; Sodium 200 mg
PER SERVING WITH GLAZE: Cal 280; Fat 8 g; Sat fat 3 g; Chol 50 mg; Carb 52 g; Protein 3 g; Fiber 1 g; Sodium 210 mg

Lemon Glaze

MAKES 1 GENEROUS CUP

1	cup (4 ounces) confectioners' sugar
5	teaspoons juice from 1 lemon
1	tablespoon grated zest from 1 lemon
	Pinch salt

Whisk all the ingredients together in a medium bowl. Drizzle the cake with the glaze and let set for 15 minutes before serving.

PER SERVING: Cal 30; Fat 0 g; Sat fat 0 g; Chol 0 mg; Carb 8 g; Protein 0 g; Fiber 0 g; Sodium 10 mg

ANGEL FOOD CAKE

ANGEL FOOD CAKE IS A DIETER'S DREAM. With no butter, oil, dairy, or egg yolks, it is a fat-free dessert. But angel food cake can be fickle. At its best, an angel food cake is tall and perfectly shaped with a tender, snow-white crumb encased in a delicate, golden crust. At its worst, the cake is dense, chewy, and devoid of flavor (think Styrofoam). We wanted an angel food cake that would appeal to the masses, not just to those counting calories. In addition to perfecting the basics, we hoped to create some variations that would provide a serious flavor boost.

All angel food cakes contain six ingredients: egg whites, sugar, flour, cream of tartar, salt, and flavorings. But they are also distinguished by what they lack: egg yolks, chemical leaveners, and fat. Beyond that, there are literally hundreds of variations on this basic theme. The type of flour used, the baking temperature, the type of sugar, and even the use of baking powder (a serious transgression, according to most experts) are all controversial. What is not in dispute is that angel food cake requires a delicate balance of ingredients and proper technique.

Because there is no fat in angel food cake, sugar is critical to its taste and texture. In developing other low-fat cake recipes, we've had success with brown sugar, which adds much needed moisture to a cake when the fat has been reduced. But we found that its flavor overwhelmed the delicate character of this cake. We then tried confectioners' sugar but the cornstarch in it makes the cake too dense. Superfine sugar is simply too fine, making a soft cake with little substance—while we wanted a tender crumb, the cake should still have some structure. We finally determined that the clean sweetness of granulated sugar is best in this recipe.

Flour sets the cake batter, but because it also adds weight, the flour should be as light and airy as possible. We found that cake flour, which is finer than all-purpose flour, is easier to incorporate into beaten egg whites without the whites deflating—and since the egg whites serve as the leavener in angel food cake, it is particularly important that this doesn't happen. The lower protein content of

UNMOLDING ANGEL FOOD CAKE

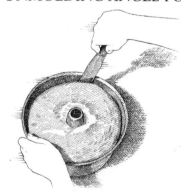 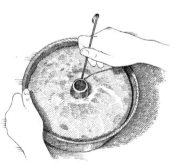 

1. After the cake has cooled, flip the pan upright and insert a thin knife between the cake and the side of the pan. Pressing against the pan, run a knife around the edge of the cake, being careful not to separate the golden crust from the cake.

2. Loosen the cake from the center tube using a wire cake tester or skewer. Slide the cake with the removable cake pan bottom out of the pan.

3. Run a knife between the cake and the pan bottom to loosen, then gently flip the cake out onto a platter, bottom side (presentation side) facing up.

cake flour also results in a more delicate, tender crumb, which we preferred. We found sifting to be essential; it makes the flour lighter in texture and easier to incorporate into the whites. We determined that sifting the flour once, just before adding it to the beaten whites, was sufficient for maximum lightness.

We tried adding some baking powder for extra leavening and stability but found that the resulting cake was not as white and had a coarser crumb. Adding baking powder also felt like cheating. If you separate and beat the egg whites properly, there should be no need to add baking powder.

Now that we had the essentials down, it was time to focus on flavor. Salt is added for flavor and also helps stabilize the beaten whites. Other common additions are vanilla and almond extracts (we like to use both), which add flavor without changing the basic chemistry of the batter. We like to add a little citrus juice and for variations we also add some citrus zest to get the fullest flavor without altering the cake's delicate balance of ingredients. In addition to citrus, we found that small amounts of other intensely flavored ingredients can be added to really take this cake to the next level. Cinnamon, ginger, nutmeg, allspice, and cloves add their fragrant notes to one cake for a spiced variation. And finely grated bittersweet chocolate is an easy way to infuse the entire cake with serious chocolate flavor without adding a significant amount of fat. Add to that a little Grand Marnier and orange zest, and we had an elegant cake we could serve to guests without feeling like we were depriving them.

One last note: We baked the same recipe in the same pan at 300, 325, 350, and 375 degrees, baking each cake until it tested done with a skewer and the top bounced back when pressed lightly. Surprisingly, all the cakes cooked evenly, but those baked at 350 and 375 degrees had a thicker, darker crust, while the cakes baked at 300 and 325 degrees had a more desirable, delicate, evenly pale golden crust. After many taste tests, we decided that 325 degrees was the ideal temperature.

Angel Food Cake
SERVES 12

The best tool to remove an angel food cake from the pan is a thin, flexible, non-serrated knife that is at least 5 inches long. Present the cake sitting on its wide, crustier top, with the delicate and more easily sliced bottom crust facing up. To cut the cake, use a long, serrated knife, and pull it back and forth with a gentle sawing motion.

1	cup (4 ounces) cake flour
1½	cups (10½ ounces) sugar
12	large egg whites, at room temperature
1	teaspoon cream of tartar
¼	teaspoon salt
1½	teaspoons juice from 1 lemon
1½	teaspoons vanilla extract
½	teaspoon almond extract

1. Adjust an oven rack to the lower-middle position and heat the oven to 325 degrees. Have ready an ungreased large tube pan (9-inch diameter, 16-cup capacity), preferably with a removable bottom. (If the pan bottom is not removable, line it with parchment paper or waxed paper.)

2. Whisk the flour and ¾ cup of the sugar in a small bowl; set aside. Beat the egg whites with an electric mixer on low speed until just broken up and foamy. Add the cream of tartar and salt and increase the speed to medium-high. Continue to beat, adding the remaining ¾ cup sugar, 1 tablespoon at a time, until all the sugar is added and the whites are shiny and form soft peaks. Beat in the lemon juice, vanilla extract, and almond extract until just blended.

3. Sift the flour mixture over the whites, about ¼ cup at a time, and gently fold it in using a large rubber spatula. Gently scrape the batter into the pan and smooth the top with a spatula. Give the pan a couple of raps on the counter to release any large air bubbles. Bake until the cake is golden brown and the top springs back when pressed firmly, 55 to 60 minutes.

4. If the cake pan has prongs around the rim for elevating the cake, invert the pan onto them. If the pan does not have prongs, invert the pan onto

the neck of a bottle or funnel. Let the cake cool completely upside-down, 2 to 3 hours.

5. To unmold, following the illustrations on page 346, run a knife around the edge of the cake pan, being careful not to separate the golden crust from the cake. Loosen the cake from the center tube using a wire cake tester or skewer. Slide the cake with the removable cake bottom out of the pan. Run a knife between the cake and the pan bottom to loosen, then gently flip the cake out onto a platter, bottom side facing up (the bottom is the presentation side). (If the pan bottom is not removable, loosen the cake from the edges and center tube as described, then flip out onto a platter and remove the parchment paper.) Cut slices by sawing gently with a large, serrated knife. This cake tastes best when served the same day it is made.

PER SERVING: Cal 150; Fat 0 g; Sat fat 0 g; Chol 0 mg; Carb 33 g; Protein 4 g; Fiber 0 g; Sodium 105 mg

➤ VARIATIONS

Citrus Angel Food Cake

Any citrus flavor, lemon, lime, orange, or grapefruit, works well in this cake.

Follow the recipe for Angel Food Cake, decreasing the vanilla extract to ½ teaspoon and omitting the almond extract. Increase the lemon juice to 2 tablespoons (or substitute 2 tablespoons lime juice, orange juice, or grapefruit juice) and add 2 tablespoons grated lemon, lime, orange, or grapefruit zest with the vanilla in step 2.

PER SERVING: Cal 150; Fat 0 g; Sat fat 0 g; Chol 0 mg; Carb 33 g; Protein 4 g; Fiber 0 g; Sodium 105 mg

Chocolate-Orange Angel Food Cake

Be sure to grate the peel of the orange, not the white pith underneath—it will give the cake an unpleasantly bitter flavor.

Follow the recipe for Angel Food Cake, omitting the lemon juice and almond extract and decreasing the vanilla extract to ½ teaspoon. Add 2 teaspoons grated orange zest and 1 tablespoon Grand Marnier with the vanilla in step 2. Gently fold 2 ounces finely grated bittersweet chocolate into the batter after folding in the flour mixture in step 3.

PER SERVING: Cal 170; Fat 1.5 g; Sat fat 1 g; Chol 0 mg; Carb 36 g; Protein 5 g; Fiber 1 g; Sodium 105 mg

Spiced Angel Food Cake

Freshly grated nutmeg works best here.

Follow the recipe for Angel Food Cake, omitting the lemon juice and almond extract. Whisk ½ teaspoon cinnamon, ½ teaspoon ginger, ¼ teaspoon nutmeg, ¼ teaspoon allspice, and ⅛ teaspoon cloves into the flour with the sugar in step 2.

PER SERVING: Cal 150; Fat 0 g; Sat fat 0 g; Chol 0 mg; Carb 33 g; Protein 4 g; Fiber 0 g; Sodium 105 mg

Coconut-Lime Angel Food Cake

A spoonful of fresh blueberries makes a nice accompaniment to this variation.

Follow the recipe for Angel Food Cake, omitting the lemon juice, vanilla extract, and almond extract. Beat ½ teaspoon coconut extract, 1 tablespoon juice from 1 lime, and 1 tablespoon grated zest from 1 lime into the whipped egg whites at the end of step 2 until just blended.

PER SERVING: Cal 150; Fat 0 g; Sat fat 0 g; Chol 0 mg; Carb 33 g; Protein 4 g; Fiber 0 g; Sodium 105 mg

Mocha Angel Food Cake

If you cannot find espresso powder, substitute an equal amount of instant coffee powder.

Follow the recipe for Angel Food Cake, omitting the lemon juice and almond extract. Stir 1 tablespoon espresso powder and 1 tablespoon Kahlùa together in a small bowl. Add the espresso-Kahlùa mixture to the beaten egg whites with the vanilla in step 2. Gently fold 2 ounces finely grated bittersweet chocolate into the batter after folding in the flour mixture in step 3.

PER SERVING: Cal 180; Fat 1.5 g; Sat fat 1 g; Chol 0 mg; Carb 37 g; Protein 5 g; Fiber 1 g; Sodium 105 mg

New York Cheesecake

OF ALL THE DESSERTS THAT PEOPLE LONG FOR in a low-fat form, cheesecake is probably the most popular—but it's also the most difficult to lighten. Since just one modest slice has more fat than most people should consume in a day, never mind in one dessert, cheesecake would require a serious makeover, and we had our doubts that it would be a successful one. Truthfully, we'd rather eat cheesecake once a year and really enjoy it than settle for something that didn't deliver its trademark tang and creamy texture. But we were determined to give it a shot. Low-fat recipes in hand, we headed into the kitchen to get a handle on the landscape of low-fat alternatives.

Just about every low-fat cookbook has tried to create some version of a reduced-fat cheesecake. The result is usually a rubbery, gummy mess, chock full of artificial and off flavors. And it's no wonder: Cheesecake is pretty much 100 percent fat in a graham cracker crust. Removing the fat would take away everything we love about the ideal New York cheesecake: its thick, smooth, satiny, creamy core, a velvety exterior, and sweet and tangy richness throughout. Or would it?

A standard New York cheesecake contains 580 calories and 43 grams of fat per slice. These jaw dropping numbers mostly come from the whopping 2½ pounds of cream cheese that make up the base. In order to trim some fat it was obvious we were going to have to find an alternative to the cream cheese. We had hoped that we could simply substitute nonfat cream cheese for the full-fat cheese, but we quickly realized this was not the case. Cheesecakes made this way had an unsettling gummy mouthfeel and a dry, chalky texture. Using all Neufchâtel reduced-fat cream cheese still gave us a cheesecake with a high amount of fat. Light cream cheese was a better alternative but the flavor was still off. Instead, we knew we'd need to cut one of these lower fat cream cheeses with something else. We tried tofu, ricotta, and low-fat mayonnaise. In each case the cakes were beyond disappointing. Either they tasted terrible or they had a texture that bore a striking resemblance to linoleum. That was until we tried cottage cheese. We had seen several recipes with cottage cheese,

Putting the Cheese in Cheesecake

The big culprit behind cheesecake's 43 grams of fat and 580 calories per slice is the 2½ pounds of cream cheese found in the recipe. To get around this high level of fat and calories many recipes substitute either nonfat dairy or other low-fat ingredients. In search of the best light cheesecake, we tried a lot of different ingredients. Here are some highlights (and lowlights) from our tests:

FAT-FREE CREAM CHEESE *Too Dense*
The cheesecake made with fat-free cream cheese had a "tough," "dense" texture and was "tasteless."

RICOTTA CHEESE *Too Grainy*
Ricotta's subtle sweetness was perfect in a light cheesecake. However, when baked the ricotta gave the cake a curdled, grainy texture that was dismissed by tasters.

YOGURT *Too Soft*
Tasters liked the tanginess that yogurt lent the cheesecake, but because the yogurt had such a high proportion of water the cheesecake had a soft, runny texture.

THE WINNERS

LIGHT CREAM CHEESE, LOW-FAT COTTAGE CHEESE, AND LOW-FAT YOGURT CHEESE
We found that a combination of ingredients was the right choice for our light cheesecake. The cottage cheese provided a low-fat, neutral-flavored base for the cheesecake. Light cream cheese provided the requisite rich silkiness. And the yogurt cheese (also called labne) provided the cheesecake with tanginess, but didn't make a soggy mess like the plain yogurt did. Using these three ingredients we were able to remove 30 grams of fat and 240 calories from a slice of cake and still have a great taste.

but had dismissed this ingredient because we were concerned it would make the filling grainy. But then we wondered, what would happen if we processed the cottage cheese? We put a pound of 1 percent milkfat cottage cheese in the food processor and let it run until it was perfectly smooth. The processed cottage cheese with a pound of light cream cheese was a great combination. The filling was smooth and rich with just the right density. There was one drawback, however. It was a little loose from the liquid in the cottage cheese. We simply spooned the cottage cheese into a bowl lined with paper towels and allowed them to draw off some of the moisture while we prepared the other ingredients in the cheesecake. This worked perfectly, wicking away the majority of the moisture.

With the cottage cheese–light cream cheese combo we had an ideal base and knew we were on a roll, but we also knew it was missing that trademark tang that is essential to any great New York cheesecake. Most cheesecakes use sour cream to provide this tang, but when we tried to substitute no-fat and low-fat sour cream we found that the cakes had a tacky texture and odd aftertaste. We then tried yogurt, and while it certainly provided the tang we sought, the yogurt was too watery and made a cake that was too runny. Someone in the test kitchen then suggested yogurt cheese, also called labne, which is essentially plain yogurt drained of its whey (see page 8 for more information). It was the perfect solution. It offered a touch of tartness and helped give the cheesecake a smoother, creamier texture without making it too wet. We decided to make our own yogurt cheese using low-fat plain yogurt (see page 8).

Eggs help bind a cheesecake, giving it structure and a creamy texture; they also contribute a fair amount of fat. While some cheesecakes use a combination of whole egg and yolks, we decided to stick with just whole eggs in order to get the most structure with the least fat. We tried as few as one and as many as six whole eggs, and found that three eggs were the right number. Three eggs helped build a firm, rigid structure and gave our cheesecake the requisite dense, velvety texture without adding an excessive amount of fat. Our

cheesecake was now on its way and suddenly there was renewed interest among the once-doubtful test kitchen staff: Volunteer tasters were beginning to crawl out of the woodwork.

Perfecting the flavor of the cheesecake was easy. Lemon juice is an ingredient commonly found in New York cheesecake and we liked the way it brightened the other flavors in our cheesecake, but found it clashed slightly with the already tangy filling. For us, lemon zest was a better route. It provided a floral note and subtle tang without being too aggressive. Just a bit of salt (cream cheese already contains a good dose of sodium) and a couple teaspoons of vanilla extract rounded out the flavors. Simple was decidedly better—everyone in the test kitchen appreciated this minimalist approach.

With the filling behind us we could now turn our attention to the all-important graham cracker

---

MAKEOVER AT A GLANCE

–Classic–
New York Cheesecake
(per serving)

Calories: 580	Cholesterol: 265 mg
Fat: 43 g	Saturated Fat: 26 g

–Light–
New York Cheesecake
(per serving)

Calories: 340	Cholesterol: 85 mg
Fat: 13 g	Saturated Fat: 8 g

How We Did It

- Replaced full-fat cream cheese and sour cream with a combination of light cream cheese, low-fat cottage cheese, and low-fat yogurt cheese
- Used just whole eggs instead of whole eggs and yolks
- Pureed the filling in a food processor for an ultrasmooth texture

crust. In order to keep fat and calories to a minimum we considered a simple dusting of crumbs on the bottom of the cheesecake, but tasters were unanimous in their protest. They wanted a crust with more presence. We tried making a thicker crust with low-fat graham crackers, a tablespoon of butter, and no sugar. But this crust was very wet. We tried brushing the crust with egg whites in order to form a protective barrier, but this gave the crust an odd, spongy texture. It was obvious we needed the butter to provide a moisture barrier, and we would have to use more of it. We increased the butter a tablespoon at a time, and settled on 4 tablespoons of butter. This amount gave the crust a rich, toasty flavor and crisp texture. Although this was more fat than we ideally wanted in the crust, we would rather have a little bit more fat than a soggy bottom.

When it came to baking the cheesecake we preferred the standard New York method—500 degrees for about 10 minutes, then 200 degrees for about an hour and a half. This method yielded the nut-brown surface that is a distinguishing mark of an exemplary New York cheesecake. It also produced a lovely graded texture, soft and creamy at the center and firm and dry at the periphery. To ensure a properly baked cheesecake, we found it best to bake cake to an internal temperature of 150 degrees. Although it may seem unnecessary, an instant-read thermometer inserted into the cake is the most reliable means of judging the doneness of the cheesecake.

After the cheesecake had chilled, we knew we had achieved perfection. It sliced into a neat slab with a cleanly set center texture—not a wet, sloppy one. Each slice kept its shape, and each bite felt satiny on the tongue—cheesecake heaven.

New York Cheesecake

SERVES 12

Be sure to use light cream cheese in this recipe—it is most commonly sold in tubs, not blocks (see page 339). You can buy low-fat yogurt cheese (also called labne) or make your own with low-fat yogurt—allow at least 12 hours for the yogurt to drain (see page 9 for instructions). For a more lemony flavor, use the higher amount of lemon zest.

CRUST

9   whole graham crackers (5 ounces), broken into rough pieces and processed in a food processor to fine even crumbs (about 1¼ cups)

4   tablespoons (½ stick) unsalted butter, melted

1   tablespoon sugar

FILLING

1   pound 1 percent cottage cheese

1   pound light cream cheese, at room temperature

8   ounces (1 cup) low-fat yogurt cheese (see note)

1½   cups (10½ ounces) sugar

¼   teaspoon salt

½–1   teaspoon grated zest from 1 lemon

1   tablespoon vanilla extract

3   large eggs, at room temperature

     Vegetable oil spray

     Fresh Strawberry Topping (optional), recipe follows

1. FOR THE CRUST: Adjust an oven rack to the middle position and heat the oven to 325 degrees. In a medium bowl, stir together the graham cracker crumbs, melted butter, and sugar until combined. Transfer the mixture to a 9-inch springform pan and press evenly into the pan bottom. Bake the crust until fragrant and beginning to brown, 10 to 15 minutes. Cool on a wire rack. Increase the temperature to 500 degrees.

2. FOR THE FILLING: Meanwhile, line a medium bowl with a clean dish towel or several layers of paper towels. Spoon the cottage cheese into the bowl and let drain for 30 minutes.

3. Process the drained cottage cheese in a food processor until smooth and no visible lumps remain, about 1 minute, scraping down the work bowl as needed. Add the cream cheese and yogurt cheese and continue to process until smooth, 1 to 2 minutes, scraping down the sides of the bowl as needed. Add the sugar, salt, lemon zest, and vanilla and continue to process until smooth, about 1 minute, scraping down the sides of the bowl as needed. With the processor running, add the eggs one at a time and continue to process until smooth.

4. Being careful not to disturb the baked crust,

spray the insides of the springform pan with vegetable oil spray. Set the springform pan on a rimmed baking sheet. Pour the processed cheese mixture into the cooled crust.

5. Bake for 10 minutes. Without opening the oven door, reduce the oven temperature to 200 degrees and continue to bake until an instant-read thermometer inserted into the center of the cheesecake reads 150 degrees, about 1½ hours.

6. Transfer the cake to a wire rack and run a paring knife around the edge of the cake to loosen. Cool the cake at room temperature until barely warm, 2½ to 3 hours, running a paring knife around the edge of the cake every hour or so. Wrap the pan tightly in plastic wrap and refrigerate until cold, at least 3 hours.

7. To unmold the cheesecake, wrap a hot kitchen towel around the springform pan and let stand for 10 minutes. Remove the sides of the pan and blot any excess moisture from the top of the cheesecake with paper towels. Let the cheesecake stand at room temperature about 30 minutes before slicing.

PER SERVING: Cal 340; Fat 13 g; Sat fat 8 g; Chol 85 mg; Carb 41 g; Protein 11 g; Fiber 0 g; Sodium 530 mg

PER SERVING WITH TOPPING: Cal 400; Fat 13 g; Sat fat 8 g; Chol 85 mg; Carb 57 g; Protein 11 g; Fiber 1 g; Sodium 540 mg

Fresh Strawberry Topping
MAKES ABOUT 3 CUPS

A ruby-colored, glazed strawberry topping is the classic accompaniment to New York cheesecake. This topping is best served the same day it is made.

I	pound strawberries, hulled and cut lengthwise into ¼- to ⅜-inch wedges
¼	cup sugar
	Pinch salt
½	cup strawberry jam
I	tablespoon juice from I lemon

1. Toss the berries, sugar, and salt in a medium bowl and let stand until the berries have released some juice and the sugar has dissolved, about 30 minutes, tossing occasionally to combine.

2. Process the jam in a food processor until smooth, about 8 seconds. Transfer the jam to a small saucepan and bring to a simmer over medium-high heat. Simmer, stirring frequently, until dark and no longer frothy, about 3 minutes. Stir in the lemon juice, then gently stir the warm jam into the strawberries. Cover with plastic wrap and refrigerate until cold, at least 2 hours or up to 12. To serve, spoon a portion of sauce over individual slices of cheesecake.

PER ¼-CUP SERVING: Cal 60; Fat 0 g; Sat Fat 0 g; Chol 0 mg; Carb 16 g; Protein 0 g; Fiber 1 g; Sodium 10 mg

BAKED APPLES

HOMEY AND COMFORTING, BAKED APPLES have been forgotten over the years. But this naturally light dessert is so simple that it was hard to pass up an opportunity to perfect a recipe for making them. We soon found, however, that despite their simplicity there were some pitfalls to overcome before finding the best recipe.

The most common problem during testing was that the apples split or became too mushy when baked. We think the ideal baked apple holds its shape during baking and softens and remains moist without becoming mushy. We tested nine apple varieties to see how they would hold up and taste when baked. Among common varieties, only Golden Delicious apples rated well. McIntosh were mushy and Red Delicious and Granny Smith were too dry. Several lesser-known varieties also baked up nicely, including Baldwin, Cortland, Ida Red, and Northern Spy.

After further testing we surmised that steam was causing the apple skin to split open. To allow the steam to escape and to keep the apples from bursting in the oven, we found it helpful to remove a strip of skin around the stem with a vegetable peeler. To fill the apples we hollowed out the core without puncturing the blossom end of the apple. The easiest way to core a whole apple thoroughly is with a melon baller. Start at the stem end and use the melon baller to scoop out and remove the core.

When it came to baking, we found that the apples required a moderate oven heat of 350 degrees; higher temperatures caused the apples to split. To keep the apples moist, we found it best to bake them surrounded by a pool of cider, which reinforced the apple's flavor without adding too many calories. However, there was one drawback from this baking method: the sauce was always too watery. Many recipes we found rectify this problem by finishing the sauce with cream or butter, but in our case that wasn't possible. Our solution was to take the liquid remaining in the pan after the apples had finished cooking and reduce it on the stovetop. After a brief simmer, we had a super-concentrated sauce that clung to the apples, and this was all done naturally without any extra fat or calories.

Now that we had perfected the technique for baking the apples, we directed our attention to the flavorings. A quarter cup of sugar sprinkled over the apples before they went in the oven helped to tame their inherent tartness and a dash of cinnamon helped bring forth the apples' flavor. Dried fruit provided a contrasting tang to the apples while adding no fat and just a few calories. Finally, we scattered some toasted walnuts over the apples right before serving—although optional, their good texture and flavor really made this dish stand out. After tinkering with the recipe, each serving contained a grand total of 5 grams of fat and 250 calories (with the walnuts). Considering how low

these numbers are and how great the apples taste we think this healthy dish deserves a revival.

Cider-Baked Apples with Dried Cranberries
SERVES 4

Golden Delicious, Cortland, and Baldwin are the best apples for baking. A melon baller is the best tool to use to core the apples. Take care not to puncture the blossom end (opposite the stem end) of the apples when coring them. The walnuts add great flavor and texture to the finished apples; however, they do add calories and fat to the dish. Feel free to substitute dried cherries for the cranberries. For a special treat, serve the baked apples with a dollop of low-fat ice cream or frozen yogurt.

4	large apples (about 8 ounces each)
1/2	cup dried cranberries
1/4	cup (1 3/4 ounces) sugar
1/4	teaspoon ground cinnamon
1 1/2	cups apple cider
2	cinnamon sticks
1/4	cup walnuts, toasted and chopped fine (optional)

1. Adjust an oven rack to the middle position and heat the oven to 375 degrees. Using a vegetable peeler, remove a strip of apple peel from the top of each apple. Following the illustration at left, use a melon baller to remove the stem and core of the apple, being careful not to cut all the way through the blossom end.

2. Place the apples in an 8-inch square baking dish. Sprinkle 1/4 cup of the dried cranberries evenly among the apple cavities. Mix the sugar and cinnamon together in a small bowl, then sprinkle in and around the apples. Pour the cider into the dish, then add the cinnamon sticks and the remaining 1/4 cup dried cranberries.

3. Bake the apples until they are tender when pierced with a paring knife or skewer, 45 to 55 minutes, brushing the apples with the cider several times during baking. (Be careful not to overbake, or the skins will split.) Transfer the apples to a serving platter and tent with foil while making the sauce.

PREPARING APPLES FOR BAKING

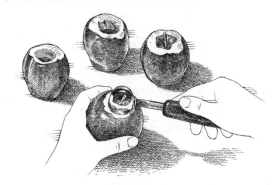

Using a vegetable peeler, remove a strip of peel from the stem end of the apple. Using a melon baller, scoop out the core, being careful not to puncture the blossom end.

LOW-FAT PIE CRUST:
IS IT POSSIBLE?

IN DEVELOPING THE RECIPES FOR THIS BOOK, WE STARTED WITH DESSERT, OUR FAVORITE course. But before we mixed a cake or baked even a single cookie, we grabbed our rolling pins and decided to tackle what we knew would be the ultimate challenge: a low-fat pie crust that met our test kitchen standards. If we could find a winning formula for constructing one, then we'd have lots of ways to develop healthy desserts using seasonal or frozen fruit. And, after all, we thought, many low-fat cookbooks contain recipes for low-fat pie crust. Why not us?

Traditional recipes for single crust pie dough contain, at the very least, 10 tablespoons of fat in the form of butter or shortening, or a combination of the two. And these crusts contain upwards of 14 grams of fat and 200 calories per serving. Keep in mind too that this is a single crust, without a filling; don't even get us started on a double crust pie.

Along with being high in fat and calories, traditional pie crusts can be finicky—even an accomplished baker can often go astray. We have found that perfect pie dough relies on many things, from the right balance of fat to flour to the temperature of the fat and the way it is incorporated into the flour. We've written volumes on how to get it right. And now, with much trepidation, we were heading into the kitchen to challenge our findings in the quest for a lighter pie dough.

In order to reduce or eliminate the fat, we tried substituting the following ingredients in every conceivable combination and amount in our search for a way to reduce the fat in a traditional pie crust. And rest assured, we left no possibility on the table—we tried other ingredients not listed here such as buttermilk, skim milk, and even apple juice. And when all these ingredients failed us, we turned to technique for solutions, from grating the butter (so a lesser amount would be more evenly distributed) to pressing softer doughs into the pie plate (instead of attempting to roll them out). But after weeks of tasting sub-par pie crusts, we threw in the towel. Low-fat pie crust, simply put, isn't worth it. If you want healthy ways to enjoy a baked fruit, we recommend Baked Apples (page 352) or Fruit Cobbler (page 355).

LIGHT BUTTER
A wet sticky mess of a dough and a thin, tough crust with little butter flavor.

LIGHT BUTTER AND VEGETABLE OIL
A greasy, thin crust with little butter flavor.

REDUCED-FAT MAYONNAISE
A dough that was impossible to roll out and a cracker-like crust with no butter flavor whatsoever.

LOW-FAT SOUR CREAM
A dough that was tough to work with and an unevenly browned crust with a cracker-like bottom and chewy sides.

REDUCED-FAT CREAM CHEESE
A dough too soft to work with and a chewy crust.

EGG WHITES
A wet and sticky dough and a rubbery, flavorless crust.

PART-SKIM RICOTTA CHEESE
A crust with chewy layers that stuck to the pie plate.

BAKING SODA AND LOW-FAT SOUR CREAM
A doughy crust with an off flavor.

4. Pour the cooking liquid into a small saucepan. Bring to a simmer and cook until the liquid has reduced to about 1 cup, 7 to 10 minutes. Remove and discard the cinnamon sticks. Spoon some of the sauce over each apple and sprinkle with the walnuts (if using). Serve, passing the remaining sauce separately.

PER SERVING: Cal 200; Fat 0 g; Sat fat 0 g; Chol 0 mg; Carb 53 g; Protein 0 g; Fiber 3 g; Sodium 10 mg

PER SERVING WITH WALNUTS: Cal 250; Fat 5 g; Sat fat 0 g; Chol 0 mg; Carb 54 g; Protein 2 g; Fiber 4 g; Sodium 10 mg

➤ VARIATIONS

Cider-Baked Apples with Rum and Golden Raisins

Follow the recipe for Cider-Baked Apples with Dried Cranberries, substituting ½ cup golden raisins for the dried cranberries. Add ¼ cup golden or dark rum to the dish with the cider in step 2. Just before serving, stir 2 more tablespoons rum into the sauce.

PER SERVING: Cal 260; Fat 0 g; Sat fat 0 g; Chol 0 mg; Carb 56 g; Protein 1 g; Fiber 4 g; Sodium 15 mg

PER SERVING WITH WALNUTS: Cal 310; Fat 5 g; Sat fat 0 g; Chol 0 mg; Carb 57 g; Protein 2 g; Fiber 4 g; Sodium 15 mg

Cider-Baked Apples with Fresh Ginger and Orange

Follow the recipe for Cider-Baked Apples with Dried Cranberries, substituting a 3-inch-long strip of peel from one orange, and a 1-inch piece of fresh ginger, peeled and cut into coins, for the cinnamon sticks in step 2. Remove and discard the peel and ginger coins from the sauce before serving.

PER SERVING: Cal 200; Fat 0 g; Sat fat 0 g; Chol 0 mg; Carb 53 g; Protein 0 g; Fiber 3 g; Sodium 10 mg

PER SERVING WITH WALNUTS: Cal 250; Fat 5 g; Sat fat 0 g; Chol 0 mg; Carb 54 g; Protein 2 g; Fiber 4 g; Sodium 10 mg

FRUIT COBBLERS

IN THE PANTHEON OF AMERICAN FRUIT desserts, fruit cobbler sits at the top. The combination of sweet, juicy fruit and a patchwork of crisp tender biscuits is irresistible. Add simplicity to the list of its virtues and you'll know why we like to make fruit cobbler again and again—especially in the summer months. But this recipe could use some refinement from a health standpoint. Excess amounts of sugar can be a calorie culprit in the fruit filling and the biscuit topping can contain high amounts of fat.

We started with the filling. We found that most fruits do benefit from the addition of a small amount of sugar, since they often are too tart when baked without. We found that ¼ to ½ cup of sugar (depending on the type and ripeness of the fruit) provided a hint of sweetness and thickened the fruit juices into a light syrup, while keeping the calories to a minimum.

Some recipes swear by one thickener and warn that other choices will ruin the filling. We found this to be partly true. Tasters were all in agreement that flour—the most common choice in recipes—gave the fruit filling an unappealing starchy texture and turned the juices cloudy. Ground tapioca can actually thicken fruit too much and gave our filling a jammy consistency. Neither is recommended in cobblers. For a natural, thin, silky syrup, we prefer cornstarch, arrowroot, or potato starch. Used in small quantities, we found it difficult to tell much difference between the three. Though they all worked equally well at thickening the fruit juices, we recommend cornstarch because it is the most widely available.

In terms of the biscuit topping, we had two choices: rolled and dropped. Rolled biscuits call for cold butter to be cut into dry ingredients, after which the dough is rolled out and cut. Drop biscuits have an easier mixing method—mix the dry ingredients, mix the wet ingredients, mix the two together and drop over the fruit. After trying the two side by side, we chose drop-style biscuits not only because they are simple to prepare, but also because the mixing method allowed us to use significantly less butter and still have tender, flavorful biscuits. Their light and rustic appearance only added to the appeal.

As for the biscuit ingredients, we quickly eliminated eggs because the biscuits we made with them were much too heavy. When it comes to dairy, most cobbler biscuits use half-and-half or heavy cream, but we found these to be too rich and too high in fat. We tried milk and low-fat milk, but found the biscuits too bland. We then tried buttermilk. Buttermilk is low in fat and also solved our blandness issue by adding a distinct creamy tang to the biscuits. Lastly, we added a few tablespoons of cornmeal (a common ingredient in cobbler biscuits) for both texture and flavor and tasters unanimously approved.

The one problem we encountered with these drop biscuits was getting them to cook all the way through. Unlike rolled biscuit dough, which has a drier texture, these wetter drop biscuits have a tendency to remain doughy. For example, no matter how long we left the biscuits on a berry filling in a 400-degree oven, they simply turned more and more brown on top while the bottoms remained doughy and raw. We realized that what the biscuits needed was a blast of heat from below—that is, from a hot filling. We then tried baking the filling alone for 25 minutes until hot and bubbling. Then we dropped the portions of the biscuit dough on top of the hot filling. Bingo! The heat from the bubbling fruit helped to cook the biscuits from underneath, while the dry heat of the oven cooked them from above.

We now had the crisp, well-browned, evenly cooked biscuits we desired. Couple these low-fat biscuits with our calorie-trimmed fruit, and you have a homey, satisfying dessert.

MAKING A COBBLER WITH FROZEN FRUIT

WHILE SUMMER'S SUN-RIPENED FRUITS make the best cobblers, there is an alternative: individually quick frozen (IQF) fruits. Most of the frozen fruits on the market today are picked and frozen when perfectly ripe, making them the fruit of choice in the dead of winter (and much better than using out-of-season fresh fruits in the market that are flown in from South America). When you're buying frozen fruit, we recommend that you look for bags of frozen fruit as opposed to boxes, because the boxed fruits are not individually quick frozen and are apt to be encased in a block of ice, making them sodden when thawed.

We've had good results using frozen strawberries, blueberries, blackberries, raspberries, peaches, and sour cherries in our cobblers. Simply substitute 2 pounds of frozen fruit for the fresh (regardless of fruit type), use the smaller amount of sugar, and double the amount of cornstarch. There is no need to thaw the frozen fruit; just toss it with the filling ingredients, and increase the baking time in step 1 of the Fresh Fruit Cobbler recipe to 50 to 60 minutes.

~

Blueberry Cobbler
SERVES 8

The recipe can be doubled and baked in a 13 by 9-inch dish—you may need to increase the baking time by five to ten minutes. Be sure not to combine the wet and dry biscuit ingredients until the filling is ready. Before you assemble the filling, first taste the berries. Add the smaller amount of sugar if the berries are on the sweet side, and more sugar if the fruit is tart.

FILLING

30	ounces (6 cups) blueberries, rinsed and picked over
¼–⅓	cup sugar (see note)
2	tablespoons juice from I lemon
I	tablespoon cornstarch
½	teaspoon ground cinnamon

BISCUIT TOPPING

I	cup (5 ounces) unbleached all-purpose flour
3	tablespoons yellow cornmeal
¼	cup plus 2 teaspoons sugar
I	teaspoon baking powder
¼	teaspoon baking soda
¼	teaspoon salt
⅓	cup buttermilk

3	tablespoons unsalted butter, melted
1/2	teaspoon vanilla extract
1/8	teaspoon ground cinnamon

1. FOR THE FILLING: Adjust an oven rack to the middle position and heat the oven to 400 degrees. Toss the fruit filling ingredients together in a 9-inch deep-dish pie plate. Place the pie plate on a rimmed baking sheet and bake until the fruit releases its liquid and is hot and bubbling around the edges, 20 to 30 minutes.

2. FOR THE BISCUIT TOPPING: Meanwhile, whisk the flour, cornmeal, 1/4 cup of the sugar, the baking powder, baking soda, and salt together in a large bowl; set aside. In a separate bowl, whisk the buttermilk, butter, and vanilla together; set aside. In a third small bowl, mix the remaining 2 teaspoons sugar with the cinnamon; set aside.

3. When the filling is ready, stir the buttermilk mixture into the flour mixture with a rubber spatula until just combined and no pockets of flour remain. Remove the cobbler filling from the oven and stir. Pinch off 8 equal pieces of the biscuit dough and arrange them on top of the hot filling, spaced 1/2 inch apart. Sprinkle the tops of the biscuits with the cinnamon sugar.

4. Continue to bake the cobbler until the biscuits are golden brown on top and cooked through and the filling is again hot and bubbling, 15 to 20 minutes. Cool the cobbler on a wire rack for 15 minutes before serving.

PER SERVING: Cal 230; Fat 4.5 g; Sat fat 3 g; Chol 10 mg; Carb 46 g; Protein 3 g; Fiber 3 g; Sodium 150 mg

➤ VARIATIONS

Sour Cherry Cobbler
Follow the recipe for Blueberry Cobbler, making the following changes: Substitute two 24-ounce jars sour cherries for the blueberries; increase the cornstarch to 1½ tablespoons; omit the cinnamon; and substitute 2 teaspoons almond extract and substitute 1 tablespoon kirsch (cherry brandy) for lemon juice.

PER SERVING: Cal 230; Fat 4.5 g; Sat fat 3 g; Chol 10 mg; Carb 43 g; Protein 3 g; Fiber 2 g; Sodium 160 mg

Strawberry Cobbler
Follow the recipe for Blueberry Cobbler, making the following changes: Substitute 2 quarts strawberries, rinsed and hulled for the blueberries; omit the cinnamon; and substitute 1 teaspoon vanilla extract for the lemon juice.

PER SERVING: Cal 220; Fat 5 g; Sat fat 3 g; Chol 10 mg; Carb 42 g; Protein 3 g; Fiber 3 g; Sodium 150 mg

Strawberry-Rhubarb Cobbler
Follow the recipe for Blueberry Cobbler, making the following changes: Substitute 1 quart strawberries, rinsed and hulled, and 10 ounces rhubarb but into 1/2-inch chunks for the blueberries; use 1/3 cup of sugar, omit the cinnamon; and substitute 1 teaspoon vanilla extract for the lemon juice.

PER SERVING: Cal 210; Fat 4.5 g; Sat fat 3 g; Chol 10 mg; Carb 39 g; Protein 3 g; Fiber 3 g; Sodium 160 mg

Apricot Cobbler
Follow the recipe for Blueberry Cobbler, making the following changes: Substitute 1¾ pounds (about 9 or 10) apricots, halved and pitted for the blueberries; reduce the cornstarch to 2 teaspoons; use 1/4 to 1/2 cup sugar; omit the cinnamon; and substitute 1 teaspoon vanilla extract and 1/2 teaspoon almond extract for the lemon juice.

PER SERVING: Cal 240; Fat 5 g; Sat fat 3 g; Chol 10 mg; Carb 44 g; Protein 2 g; Fiber 1 g; Sodium 150 mg

HULLING STRAWBERRIES

Early-season strawberries can have tough, white cores that are best removed. If you don't own a strawberry huller (and almost no one does), you can improvise with a plastic drinking straw. Push the straw through the bottom of the berry and up through the leafy stem end. The straw will remove the core as well as the leafy top.

Peach Cobbler

Substitute an equal amount of nectarines for the peaches if you like.

Follow the recipe for Blueberry Cobbler, making the following changes: Substitute 1¾ pounds peaches (3 to 4), pitted, peeled, and sliced for the blueberries; reduce the cornstarch to 2 teaspoons; substitute a pinch of cloves for the cinnamon; and substitute 1 tablespoon brandy and 1 teaspoon vanilla extract for the lemon juice.

PER SERVING: Cal 220; Fat 4.5 g; Sat fat 3 g; Chol 10 mg; Carb 39 g; Protein 3 g; Fiber 2 g; Sodium 150 mg

Plum Cobbler

Follow the recipe for Blueberry Cobbler, making the following changes: Substitute 1¾ pounds (6 to 8) plums, pitted and quartered for the blueberries; reduce the cornstarch to 2 teaspoons; and substitute 1 teaspoon vanilla extract for the lemon juice.

PER SERVING: Cal 230; Fat 5 g; Sat fat 3 g; Chol 10 mg; Carb 44 g; Protein 3 g; Fiber 2 g; Sodium 150 mg

Raspberry or Blackberry Cobbler

Follow the recipe for Blueberry Cobbler, making the following changes: Substitute 30 ounces (about 6 cups) raspberries or blackberries, rinsed, for the blueberries; omit the cinnamon; and substitute 1 teaspoon vanilla extract for the lemon juice.

PER SERVING: Cal 230; Fat 5 g; Sat fat 3 g; Chol 10 mg; Carb 43 g; Protein 3 g; Fiber 7 g; Sodium 150 mg

PEELING RHUBARB

Rhubarb stalks, especially thick ones, can be covered with a stringy outside layer that should be removed before cooking. Make sure to cut away and discard any leaves, which are inedible.

1. Trim both ends of the stalk and then partially slice a thin disk from the bottom of the stalk, being careful not to cut all the way through. Gently pull the partially attached disk away from the stalk, pull back the outer peel, and discard.

2. Make a second cut partway through the bottom of the stalk in the reverse direction. Pull back the peel on the other side of the stalk and discard. The rhubarb is now ready to be sliced or chopped as needed.

PEELING PEACHES

A vegetable peeler will mash the fruit on most peaches, especially ripe ones. Instead, we prefer to dip the peaches into a pot of simmering water to loosen their skins.

1. With a paring knife, score a small x at the base of each peach.

2. Lower the peaches into a pan of boiling water. Turn the peaches occasionally and simmer 30 seconds to 1 minute, depending on the ripeness of the peaches.

3. Transfer the peaches to a bowl of ice water. Let stand to stop the cooking process, about 1 minute, and cool.

4. Starting from the scored x, peel each peach. Use a paring knife to lift the skin from the flesh and pull the skin off in strips.

Resources for Further Reading

THE CONSUMER MARKET OVERFLOWS WITH PUBLICATIONS ON NUTRITION. THE PUBLICATIONS and Web sites listed here represent resources covering a broad range of nutrition topics and identifies and describes books, newsletters, and Web sites that provide timely science-based nutrition information you can trust.

AMERICAN DIETETIC ASSOCIATION

The nation's largest organization of food and nutrition professionals. Its Web site provides tips, resources, and guidelines on weight control and nutrition. Consumers seeking the services of a registered dietitian can use the site's "Find a Nutrition Professional" feature.

WWW.EATRIGHT.ORG

AMERICAN DIETETIC ASSOCIATION COMPLETE FOOD AND NUTRITION GUIDE, 2ND EDITION

by Roberta Larson Duyff, MS, RD, FADA. Wiley, 2002

Offers quick access to timely advice on a multitude of food and nutrition topics. Includes chapters on eating for fitness, maintaining a healthy weight, and getting the appropriate nutrition for every stage of life.

BOWES AND CHURCH'S FOOD VALUES OF PORTIONS COMMONLY USED, 18TH EDITION

by Jean A. T. Pennington, PhD, RD, and Judith Spungen Douglass, MS, RD. Lippincott Williams & Wilkins, 2004

Often used as a professional resource, this spiral-bound collection provides quick and easy access to the nutritional values of more than 8,000 foods, including brand-name foods and popular fast-food restaurant items.

DIETARY GUIDELINES FOR AMERICANS

This set of guidelines is jointly published every five years by the U.S. Department of Health and Human Services and the U.S. Department of Agriculture. It includes government recommendations on the type and amount of foods Americans should eat to maintain good health and prevent chronic diseases such as diabetes.

WWW.HEALTHIERUS.GOV/DIETARYGUIDELINES

NUTRITION ACTION HEALTHLETTER

Contains reliable information on current research in nutrition and health. This newsletter is published by the Center for Science in the Public Interest (CSPI), an advocacy group concerned with nutrition, food safety, alcohol policy, and other consumer health issues.

WWW.CSPINET.ORG/NAH

TUFTS UNIVERSITY HEALTH & NUTRITION LETTER

Provides health and nutrition advice through content based on the research and expertise of the Friedman School of Nutrition Science and Policy at Tufts University.

WWW.HEALTHLETTER.TUFTS.EDU

USDA NATIONAL NUTRIENT DATABASE FOR STANDARD REFERENCE

This database sponsored by the U.S. Department of Agriculture provides information on the nutrient content of almost every food.

WWW.NAL.USDA.GOV/FNIC/FOODCOMP/SEARCH

INDEX